Reading Christian Theology in the Protestant Tradition

Reading Christian Theology in the Protestant Tradition

Edited by

Kelly M. Kapic & Hans Madueme

Bloomsbury T&T Clark
An imprint of Bloomsbury Publishing Plc

B L O O M S B U R Y
LONDON · OXFORD · NEW YORK · NEW DELHI · SYDNEY

Bloomsbury T&T Clark

An imprint of Bloomsbury Publishing Plc

Imprint previously known as T&T Clark

50 Bedford Square   1385 Broadway
London   New York
WC1B 3DP   NY 10018
UK   USA

www.bloomsbury.com

BLOOMSBURY, T&T CLARK and the Diana logo are trademarks of Bloomsbury Publishing Plc

First published 2018

© Kelly Kapic and Hans Madueme, 2018

Kelly Kapic and Hans Madueme have asserted their right under the Copyright, Designs and Patents Act, 1988, to be identified as the Editors of this work.

British Library Cataloguing-in-Publication Data
A catalogue record for this book is available from the British Library.

ISBN: HB: 978-0-5675-6676-8
          PB: 978-0-5672-6614-9
        ePDF: 978-0-5676-5563-9
        ePub: 978-0-5676-5564-6

Library of Congress Cataloging-in-Publication Data
A catalog record for this book is available from the Library of Congress.

Typeset by RefineCatch Limited, Bungay, Suffolk
Printed and bound in Great Britain

To Our Sisters and Brothers Around the World:
Our Shared Traditions will be stronger and
more prophetic as your voices grow louder

Brief Contents

Part I The Early Church Period

Part II The Medieval Period

Part III The Reformation Period

Part IV The Seventeenth and Eighteenth Centuries

Part V The Nineteenth and Twentieth Centuries

Full Contents

Part II The Medieval Period (500–1500)
Gerald Bray

List of Figures

Acknowledgments

Thankful! That is how I feel now that this project is complete. It was back around 2010 that Thomas Kraft, a T&T Clark editor some years ago, graciously approached me with the idea for this volume. Between then and now it has been a significant journey. Eventually Tom moved back to Germany and Anna Turton stepped in, consistently offering timely cheer and needed encouragement. More challenges were faced than normal (e.g., after a heart attack, one of our contributors obviously needed to withdraw from the project). Yet, through the years I have had the help of many people who not only made this undertaking possible, but also enjoyable.

Melanie Gibson Murray Webb, a former student of mine who went on to get a Ph.D. from Princeton, offered invaluable help and guidance in the early years. This project owes a great deal to Melanie, as she was faithful beyond expectation with all her untiring assistance. Thank you so much, friend!

A few years ago I approached my colleague and friend Hans Madueme, asking him to join me as a co-editor for this large project. I caught him at a moment of weakness and he agreed! He has offered not only his careful editing skills, but more than that, his humor and perseverance. Working with Hans has been one of the great joys for me doing this book. I have no doubt that Hans not only helped this tome get completed, but was also instrumental in making it a much better volume than it would have been without his excellent work. Furthermore, the contributors for this volume were notable scholars who were nevertheless willing to receive feedback as we sought to bring our readers the best and most accessible book possible. In the abstract the idea of writing twelve short (4,000 word) essays sounds like no big deal, but in truth crafting something short is often much more difficult than composing something long. In the end when the work was complete almost every contributor had essentially written a short book! Thank you each for pushing through, offering your labors for the sake of students learning to discover some classic works for the first time. You all have been a delight as co-laborers and I can only hope that you will experience genuine satisfaction as readers benefit from the fruit of your labors. Thank you.

A few others deserve special mention. Josh Fikkert graciously read through all the essays and caught any number of things we missed. Jimmy Myers read through much of the manuscript and offered helpful feedback and Brian Hecker ably provided the index for this large volume. John Yates, as usual, provided extremely helpful editorial feedback to me, especially regarding my introductions.

Personally, I would like to thank my family. Quickly approaching twenty-five years of marriage I am so happy to say that it has been a profound gift to walk this journey with you, Tabitha. You always offer wisdom, reassurance, and grace when I need to hear it, including during the extended work on this project. Jonathan and Margot, you always dependably make me laugh, calling me in your own ways to rest in the goodness that we have been allowed to have together. I am so thankful for you all.

Kelly
~Lent 2017

"I caught him at a moment of weakness"—Kelly says. Hardly! It is always an honor to collaborate with my good friend and colleague, the one and only Kelly Kapic, a man for whom I have the deepest respect. As fellow theologians at Covenant College we labor daily, prayerfully, through the many joys (and occasional frustrations!) of teaching, inviting our students into the blessedness of good theology—indeed the blessedness of God. So I'm grateful that Kelly invited me to participate in co-editing this worthy volume. Editorial work at the best of times is mentally draining and often quite unpredictable, but it has been a delight to bring together this rich collection of essays.

My thanks to our publisher T&T Clark, especially Anna Turton. Her patience and flexibility made our work that much easier. Three of my students—Dustin Hayes, Hunter Rasmussen, and Drew Lattner—were a tremendous help at various stages of the project. My good friend, Jonathan "J.K." King, was always steadfast in providing keen feedback as well as ridicule—in equal doses.

If not for the lovely family You gave me, O Lord, where would I be? Destitute and lonely, for sure. I have been blessed beyond measure by my wife Shelley without whom my soul would be a smaller, paltry thing. Her love and affection make me a better person. And every day my children Caleb and Zoë remind me that I have so much for which to be grateful. Life together with them has been a balm as I completed this project. The Lord is good; His love endures forever.

Hans
~March 2017

List of Contributors

David P. Barshinger (Ph.D., Trinity Evangelical Divinity School) is the author of various scholarly articles and of the volume *Jonathan Edwards and the Psalms: A Redemptive-Historical Vision of Scripture* (Oxford University Press, 2014). He is currently an editor in the book division at Crossway, having also taught courses at numerous schools, including Trinity Christian College, Trinity International University, and Wheaton College.

Gerald Bray (D. Litt., University of Paris-Sorbonne) is Research Professor of Divinity at Beeson Divinity School, Samford University and editor of *Churchman*. A prolific scholar specializing in the areas of historical and systematic theology, his books include the award-winning *Biblical Interpretation: Past and Present* (2000), as well as the more recent volumes *God has Spoken: A History of Christian Theology* (2014) and *The Church* (2016).

W. Stephen Gunter, Associate Dean for Methodist Studies at Duke Divinity School, earned his Ph.D. in historical theology at The University of Leiden (The Netherlands). He concentrates his historical research on the ecclesial traditions that have grown out of the theology of Jacobus Arminius and John Wesley. His publications include *Wesley and The Quadrilateral* (co-author, 1997), *The Quotable Mr. Wesley* (1999 and 2002), *John Wesley and The Netherlands* (co-author, 2002), and *Arminius and His "Declaration of Sentiments"* (2012). His current project is a set of articles and a book with the working title, *The Missionary Imagination in Mainline Protestant Christianity*.

Amy Brown Hughes is an Assistant Professor of Theology at Gordon College in Wenham, Massachusetts. She received her Ph.D. in historical theology with an emphasis on early Christianity from Wheaton College in 2013. Her dissertation explores how early Christian virgins contributed substantively to the development of Christology. She is also the co-author of *Christian Women in the Patristic World: Influence, Authority and Legacy* (Baker Academic, 2017) with Professor Lynn H. Cohick.

George Kalantzis (Ph.D. Northwestern University) is Professor of Theology at Wheaton College and the Director of The Wheaton Center for Early Christian Studies. His research and writing focus on the dynamic relationship between the written documents of sacred Scripture and their interpretation in early Christianity, paying particular attention to the development of Christological and Trinitarian thought, as well as on the interplay of classical Greco-Roman society and early Christianity. He has written and edited several books and numerous articles, including *Caesar and the Lamb: Early Christian Attitudes on War and Military Service*, *Evangelicals and the Early Church: Recovery • Reform • Renewal*, *Christian Political Witness*, *The Sovereignty of God Debate*, and *Life in the Spirit: Spiritual Formation in Theological Perspective*. Professor Kalantzis also serves as the series editor for *Ad Fontes: Early Christian Sources* (Fortress Press).

Kelly M. Kapic (Ph.D., King's College, University of London) is professor of theological studies at Covenant College in Lookout Mountain, Georgia. He is the author or editor of over ten books including *A Little Book for New Theologians*, *Mapping Modern Theology*, *God So Loved He Gave*, *Communion with God*, *Sanctification*, and *Pocket Dictionary of the Reformed Tradition*.

Hans Madueme (Ph.D., Trinity Evangelical Divinity School) is Associate Professor of Theological Studies at Covenant College in Lookout Mountain, Georgia. His recent work examines the doctrine of sin in light of modern biological questions; he was awarded a two-year grant by Oxford University to participate in the Bridging the Two Cultures of Science and Humanities project, sponsored by the Templeton Religion Trust. He is on the Advisory Council for The Creation Project funded by a grant from the Templeton Religion Trust. He co-edited the book, *Adam, the Fall, and Original Sin* (Baker Academic, 2014), and he has a forthcoming book—*The Evolution of Sin? Sin, Theistic Evolution, and the Biological Question*.

Kirsi I. Stjerna (Ph.D., Boston University) is the First Lutheran Los Angeles, Southwest Synod Professor of Lutheran History and Theology, Chair, at the Pacific Lutheran Theological Seminary of California Lutheran University, and also serves in the Core Doctoral Faculty, Graduate Theological Union, Berkeley, CA. A native of Finland, she is a Docent at the Theological Faculty in Helsinki University. She has authored and edited broadly in the field of Luther and Reformation studies, e.g., *Women and the Reformations* (2009), and *Martin Luther, the Bible and the Jewish People* (2012) and *Encounters* *with Luther: New Directions for Critical Studies* (2016) with Rev. Dr Brooks Schramm. She is a co-general editor, a volume editor, and a contributor with the six-volume *Annotated Luther* from Fortress Press (2015–2017).

Douglas A. Sweeney (Ph.D., Vanderbilt) is Professor of Church History and the History of Christian Thought at Trinity Evangelical Divinity School. He has published widely on Jonathan Edwards, early modern Protestant thought, and the history of evangelicalism. His books include two volumes in the Yale Edition of *The Works of Jonathan Edwards* (Yale, 1999, 2004), *Nathaniel Taylor, New Haven Theology, and the Legacy of Jonathan Edwards* (Oxford, 2003), and *Edwards the Exegete: Biblical Interpretation and Anglo-Protestant Culture on the Edge of the Enlightenment* (Oxford, 2016).

Wesley Vander Lugt (Ph.D. University of St Andrews) is the lead pastor of Warehouse 242 in Charlotte and has taught courses at St Andrews, Gordon-Conwell Theological Seminary and Covenant Seminary. His publications include *Living Theodrama: Reimagining Theological Ethics* (2014), *Pocket Dictionary of the Reformed Tradition* (2013), co-authored with Kelly Kapic, and *Theatrical Theology: Explorations in Performing the Faith* (2014), edited with Trevor Hart.

Introduction to *Reading Christian Theology in the Protestant Tradition*

Kelly M. Kapic

An invitation to a feast

Are you hungry? Come, sit at the table prepared for you. Be ready to linger over this meal, since it will include almost sixty small samples of distinct dishes—some are, admittedly, healthier than others, but each has a discrete flavor and value.

But, you protest, you have no experience with "fancy" foods and your palate is not refined. Thankfully the dishes for this meal are prepared by people trained in the culinary arts, because these specialty chefs want you to understand and appreciate what you are about to savor. Each chef promises to explain patiently a little bit about each course, providing you a small sample of a classic dish. No dish alone is intended to fill you up, but rather to excite your senses and make you ask for more.

By the end of this banquet, a strange paradox will occur: you will be both satisfied and hungry for more. You will have a sense of the options, and will be prepared in the future to move from tastings to a full meal. Having sampled from this vast menu, you will be able to order wisely the next time hunger pains strike. Do come sit at the table and eat.

Entering a conversation

Reading this book is meant to function not simply like a tasting, but also like a summons to a vibrant conversation. This is a discussion that has been occurring for a long time, millennia in fact. In order to help readers enter into a vast and complex exchange of ideas, eight excellent masters have been recruited to serve as guides: each is considered an expert in his or her particular field:

Early church period: Amy Hughes and George Kalantzis
Medieval period: Gerald Bray
Reformation period: Kirsi I. Stjerna
Seventeenth–eighteenth century: David Barshinger, Stephen Gunter, and
   Doug Sweeney
Nineteenth–twentieth century: Wesley Vander Lugt.

These authors represent a variety of Protestant traditions, including Lutheran, Anglican, Presbyterian, Wesleyan, and Baptist. They also come from different backgrounds, born not only in America and Britain, but also Finland and Greece. These experienced guides will bring the readers into a conversation about the God of Abraham, Isaac, Mary and Paul. Here is a distinctly Christian discussion about a Jewish man named Jesus and his abiding significance.

Readers are invited to hear how past theological leaders understood what it means to be a Christian, about how salvation occurs and what it might look like to follow Jesus as King, not merely in the first century, but in the twenty-first century. Topics range from how to organize ecclesial life, to how to prepare for death; from how to defend the faith against non-Christian objections, to how to make sense of the claim that Jesus is both truly divine and truly human—without compromising the integrity of either assertion.

Our survey will include writers who stressed pastoral implications while others sought doctrinal clarity. While one leader might focus on making sense of the Trinity, another might carefully unpack a vision of imitating Jesus. One stresses Christian "freedom," while another wrestles through the Lord's Supper. We view some through poems or sermons, and others who produced monumental scholarly dogmatic tomes. Although some authors tried to accommodate this Faith so that it might be more easily accessible to readers of their day, others purposefully rejected adaptation, believing they should set forth historic orthodox convictions without modification. Some affirm that reason is a trustworthy guide, while others question the purported neutrality of rational reflection. Instead of concentrating on the power of the mind, these authors look to embodied cultural reflection on theology, hoping to escape the white male-dominated Western heritage and become a local, contemporary, people of active—even activist—devotion.

Composed of various traditions, Protestantism is a living Faith. No matter where one ends up, the student should at least become familiar with key classic works, while not expecting to agree with everything said. Nevertheless, to react to a tradition or an idea authentically, one must at a minimum learn about the significant players and their contributions.

This book calls its readers into a dialog. Not only are they invited to hear the concerns of past recognized leaders, but also called to begin to ask their own questions. Why have these authors and their books been so valued through the centuries? What might these writers have missed? What is helpful in each, and what is hurtful? What contributions of these "classics" should be retained and what elements should be strongly opposed?

The goal of our guides is not to tell you—the reader—what to believe, but to help you fairly understand key volumes from the history of the Church. These are books that have been consistently taught, reflected upon, and passed down through Christian history.

Catholicity and Protestant tradition(s)

When I was asked to edit a volume on *Reading Christian Theology in the Protestant Tradition*, a few challenges immediately emerged. Obviously the most difficult is picking which books to include, or, to put it more negatively, which genuinely important volumes to leave out. There is no way to make everyone happy (including me!), especially when you can only pick twelve samples from each period.[1] Put a well-trained group of scholars in a room and it doesn't take long to come up with hundreds of "classics." The task required a great deal of consultation with our experts in each field; it was never easy. We did our best. Because about 1,500 years of Christian tradition occur before the Protestant Reformation, the writings from the previous centuries are absolutely essential to Protestant identity. A few brief reflections on our selections and this history is thus in order.

First, early Protestant leaders self-consciously saw themselves as "catholic." Martin Luther and John Calvin, for example, had no interest in starting new religions. And even with their impassioned calls to "get back to the scriptures," they and other sixteenth-century leaders spent considerable time and energy making the case that their theology was not actually novel, but well supported in the Church's history. The indexes of their writings are full of references to the Cappadocian Fathers, Augustine, Anselm, Bernard of Clairvaux among countless others.

Second, because the Protestant Reformation grew out of the *Roman Catholic Church*, and since this young movement was nurtured in the soil of Europe, early Protestantism has a strongly Western feel to it. Protestant leaders did draw from a fair number of early Church authors who represented the East, but early Protestant formation happened without strong knowledge and influence from later non-Western quarters. Whether we like it or not, that was the case. Therefore, since this book is not meant primarily to say what *should* have been the case, but rather what *was* the case, the sampled "classics" in this book—especially from the first 1,500 years—are ones that Protestant authors knew about and often constructively drew upon. That means the selections represent a mostly Western perspective, and sometimes a dominant cultural one as well.

Third, until the last one hundred years or so, few female and minority voices were given significant status, and thus their work was not often preserved, taught, or valued as it should have been. Would it have benefited early Protestant leaders in their theology and practice to have a greater knowledge of female as well as non-western authors? Certainly! Without question. And we strongly encourage readers of this book to supplement what is here with readings from the "margins." For example, Miguel A. De La Torre and Stacey M. Floyd-Thomas have edited the valuable book *Beyond the Pale: Reading Theology from the Margins*, in which classic Christian works are critiqued in light of postcolonial theory. That can be a valuable exercise, but it is not the task of this volume. We would also recommend the reader become familiar with such helpful resources as *A World History of Christianity* (2000), *Theology in a Global Context* (2005), *Theology in the Context of World Christianity* (2007), *Disciples of All Nations* (2007), and the *Global Dictionary of Theology* (2008). Consulting such volumes can help place various ideas and histories within a larger global context.

Our commission here was to make sure students of Christian theology gain an understanding of what have often been considered classics, choosing works that were—until the later Modern period—usually treated as foundational for shaping Western Christian conceptions in general, and Protestant instincts in particular. We believe that one cannot properly critique until one has begun to understand, and this is the first step in that process. Students should not try to deconstruct *Moby Dick* without first reading it. Similarly, one should not dismiss Irenaeus without first reading this second-century Bishop who has profoundly influenced the shape of later Christian belief, including Protestant traditions. If his voice, for example, has been valued for almost two millennia, then we should seek to understand his contributions and how they have provided guidance for those who followed. Once someone like Irenaeus has been studied, then the thoughtful reader can raise legitimate concerns and questions.

Finally, Protestantism has been changing, and it is now more global and culturally diverse than ever. Twentieth-century authors in particular (e.g., Cone, Bonino, Koyama, McFague) provide our readers with a taste of potential dissatisfaction with earlier Protestant classics as they raise consciousness about the local, the particular, and the other, wondering about potential blind spots that have been ignored. With these contrasts, *Reading Christian Theology in the Protestant Tradition* exposes readers to influential works that shaped early Protestant identity, and then engages several contemporary criticisms of this tradition and its common assumptions. We deeply wish we could have expanded our selections to include many more voices, including introducing some for each period that few readers would have heard of—we do a little of that (e.g., Women Writers of the Sixteenth Century, Madame Goyon), but not a lot. Unfortunately, such an expansion would have made an already large book overwhelming for new students. Maybe one day in the near future we can have a companion volume on *Reading Christian Theology with Forgotten Voices*. In the meantime, we invite the reader to begin here with these samples, desiring that they will eventually take the time to sit down for a proper meal.

How to use this book

We know that most people don't have the time to read thousands and thousands of pages, and yet a student of Protestant theology must become familiar with key authors and their works. Without such study they simply cannot begin to understand the dynamics of this tradition—or, more accurately, tradition*s*.[2] Therefore, in this volume we have chosen fifty-eight works that represent a reasonable set of selections from the past 2,000 years. Our gathered scholars provide brief introductions to these authors and their volume under consideration. Each essay begins with a brief overview of the author's life. Turning to the "classic" under review, each article then offers a *descriptive* rather than *prescriptive* focus: we were not aiming to dictate theological conclusions, but to guide our readers through the long arc of theological reflection found in each text. Our guides discuss the distinctive theological flavor or contribution of the original document by drawing attention to two to five distinctive themes or contributions that arise from each book. At the end of each essay, readers are provided a brief bibliographical list of relevant primary and secondary literature related to the book reviewed, highlighting reliable translations and accessible scholarly discussions.

Finally, we have listed additional primary source books at the beginning of each of the five sections. Curious students are thus enabled to pursue further reading on their own, or, a faculty member might assign students to pick a book from the list for a class report, thus exposing all the students to even more significant works from each period. We have also tried to include some less well-known names and works as well, hopefully allowing students to at least begin to discover some voices that have too often been undervalued. Again, while these section lists could have been far more extensive, we aimed to keep them to around forty significant books each. This way professors and students can easily discuss other "classics" that are not reviewed in *Reading Christian Theology in the Protestant Tradition.*

We hope that our book is not an end, but a beginning, a beginning to a much longer conversation, or maybe better, to a much grander banquet. We aim to whet the reader's appetite and provoke fruitful conversations. With that said, pull up a seat and begin to savor what is laid before you. Taste and see . . .

Notes

1. Since this is a Protestant volume, however, we decided to treat the sixteenth century as its own period, but restricted it to ten representative volumes from that century.
2. For a helpful introduction to the variety, see W. David Buschart, *Exploring Protestant Traditions: An Invitation to Theological Hospitality* (Downers Grove: IVP Academic, 2006).

Part I

The Early Church Period

Introduction to the Early Church Period (100–500)

Kelly M. Kapic

First century Israel was filled with expectation and turbulence, as exemplified by the emergence of a Nazarene named Jesus and the devastating destruction of the Temple. Moving out from Jerusalem to Judea and Samaria, eventually going to the uttermost parts of the known world, a small but persistent group began to spread their distinct faith and practices (cf. Acts 1: 8). They became known as "Christians," followers of Jesus the Messiah (Acts 11:26). Rather than seeing themselves as a new religion, they believed Jesus fulfilled and embodied the promises of the ancient Hebrew scriptures as the divinely sent Messiah who had come for the good of the world (Jn. 3:16). Early Christians included Jews and Gentiles, slaves and free, women and men (cf. Gal. 3:28). Their mission was to spread the "good news" (Gospel) of Jesus wherever they could.

During the first two centuries of the Church, the missional drive of these Christians took them not only to distant lands, but also to their local non-Christian neighbors. Their message was relatively simple at first: tell people about Jesus the Messiah, and call them to repentance and faith. This evangelistic impulse created two challenges for early Christians: (1) learning to articulate this faith to those unfamiliar with the Christian story; and (2) figure out what ways of articulating the faith and worshiping were faithful to their Messiah. For this Faith to be preserved and even flourish, followers of Jesus needed to solidify their basic group identity even amid their genuine diversity.

The years from 100 to 800 AD have often been called "the Patristic era" (Lat. *patres*), pointing to the significance of early Church "Fathers" or "Holy

Fathers." Thankfully, there is now a greater appreciation of women, such as the "Desert Mothers," although sadly we have far fewer samples of their writings preserved. These leaders, many of whom were early Bishops, helped give voice and direction to the emerging Christian movement.

The first two centuries of the Church included significant debates with a group that become known as "Gnostics." Their tendencies included rejecting the Hebrew Bible and condemning the material world as inherently evil rather than valuing it as the good creation of a good God. Irenaeus of Lyons was a leading example of early Christian voices responding to Gnosticism. He affirmed the goodness of the material world and held together the story of Israel and the Church as united in Christ through whom God is making all things new. Christianity was not a secret left to a few with special knowledge, but rather a religion based upon public revelation, both discovered throughout the entire biblical witness and most clearly seen in the person of Jesus the Nazarene.

As the number of Christians grew, they also gained more public notice, and that attention was not always positive. Was this a *new* religion? Did it take away from the importance of the state? Was it a threat to society? Christians responded with a defense of their faith, also known as "Apologetics," in which they attempted (1) to show that their faith was reasonable; and (2) to demonstrate that Christianity was a positive force for social good. Through these efforts they sought to convince others that Jesus was the true Messianic King and Savior of the world. Believers thus tried to articulate the Christian faith in a way that would make sense to those unfamiliar with its teaching and practices. Efforts of this kind including reaching out to Jews as well as Hellenistic Greeks, among others.

Yet as the Church grew in different regions and among different peoples, so also grew the challenges of maintaining agreement in their affirmations of what must be believed. Defining what was "orthodoxy" (literally, "straight opinion") and what was heterodoxy ("opinion of a different kind") required much work to attain general agreement. To our contemporary ears, "heresy" is a harsh and unkind word. Yet this word "heresy" (Gk. *hairesis*, "choice") goes back to the idea of a person going in the wrong direction, persistently making a "choice" or forming a "system of principles" that takes one away from the received biblical tradition, handed down from the Prophets and Apostles. Before Nicaea (325), what were the properly "received" truths that could not be rejected? What were merely debatable opinions? Many people said things about Jesus, but what identified people as within the "true Church"?

Amid frequent threats and problematic teaching, the Church sought to settle its foundation and agree on what constituted the center of the Faith. What emerged was a series of strong statements that called for worshiping the One God who was eternally Father, Son, and Spirit (cf. the councils of Nicaea, Constantinople, etc.). And to worship this God rightly, one recognized Jesus the Messiah as truly man and truly God, two natures in one person (cf. Chalcedon). Jesus was thus deemed properly worshiped since he was uniquely identified with God, and yet also fully human, ably representing his people as their great and final high priest. Through Jesus's life, death, and resurrection, he achieved salvation for others; those who received and enjoyed this divinely given grace were then enabled by the Spirit to live in fellowship with other children of God, even as they also sought the good of the world.

This section, covering the early centuries of the church, will expose readers to the writings of those who helped shape early Christianity, writers whom Protestants later extensively drew upon. From the practical document known as the *Didache*—which provides a sample of early Church organization—to the passionate letters of Ignatius, we hear the voices of the past. These early Christian leaders tell us about dangers of dividing the Church (Cyprian) or devaluing creation (Irenaeus), as well as the need to be mindful of the surprising challenges of wealth and poverty (Chrysostom). They display the need to explain the Christian faith (Justin and Tertullian) and the struggle to figure out how best to approach interpreting the whole Bible (Origen). We are also invited into a profound conversation about the uniqueness of Jesus (Athanasius) and the wonder of the Triune God (Gregory of Nyssa and Gregory of Nazianzus). Each voice calls for our attention, and from each we are welcomed into ancient conversations that are relevant to the twenty-first century as well.

Protestants of the Reformation era often employed the work of early Church leaders to strengthen their own arguments, believing that their "reforms" were a legitimate attempt to reflect greater biblical fidelity. Leading Protestants like Luther and Calvin hoped to show that their doctrines more accurately reflected early Christian beliefs than the "corruptions" that had slowly moved into the Church through the centuries. Thus, Protestants wanted to go "back to the Bible," but along the way they wanted to go back to Irenaeus and Augustine, not merely Moses and Paul.

There is a legitimate debate about who is more faithfully representing these early Church authors. Many have argued, for example, that the Protestant Reformers adopted a version of Augustine's soteriology, while

Roman Catholic theologians emphasized Augustine's ecclesiology. Put simply, neither side could simply claim Augustine as their own, though each did believe they had the father of western orthodoxy on their side. For our purposes, what matters is to discover afresh these early Christian voices, allowing them to speak on their own terms. When we have done that, we will also find that they speak into our present.

List of Classic Works of the Early Church Period

Justin Martyr, *First Apology*, early first century

Ignatius, *The Letters of Ignatius*, early first century

Polycarp, *The Epistle of Polycarp to the Philippians*, 110–140

Aristides, *The Apology of Aristides the Philosopher*, 125

Anonymous, *The Shepherd of Hermas*, 140

Melito of Sardis, *On the Passover*, 150

Athenagoras, *Plea Regarding the Christians*, 177

Minucius Felix, *Octavius*, 197

Tertullian, *The Apology*, 197

Anonymous, first–second century

Clement of Rome, *The First Letter to Corinth [First Clement]*, 80–early second century

Tertullian, *On The Flesh of Jesus Christ*, c. 200

Perpetua, *The Martyrdom of Perpetua and Felicitas*, 202–203

Hippolytus, *The Apostolic Tradition*, 215

Dionysius of Alexandria, *On the Promises*, 230–265

Novatian, *On the Trinity*, c. 240

Gregory Thaumaturgus, *Declaration of Faith*, 240–270

Origen, *Against Celsus*, 250

Cyprian, *On the Unity of the Catholic Church*, c. 251

Lactantius Firmianus, *The Divine Institutes*, 304–313

Commodianus, *Instructions in Favor of Christian Discipline*, c. third century

Eusebius of Caesarea, *Ecclesiastical History*, 324

Cyril of Jerusalem, *The Catechetical Lectures*, c. 350

Faltonia Betitia Proba, *Cento Probae*, 350–360

Athanasius, *The Life of Antony*, 356–362

Basil, *The Longer Rules* and *The Shorter Rules*, 358–364

Athanasius, *Discourses against the Arians*, 360

Macrina the Younger (via Gregory of Nyssa), *On the Soul and Resurrection*, 380

St. Jerome, *Account of His Conversion*, late third century

Egeria (also known as Etheroiua or Aetheria), *Diary of a Pilgrimage*, late third century

Empress Aelia Eudocia, *Homeric Centos* and *The Martyrdom of St. Cyprian*, late third to early fourth century

Augustine, *On the Trinity XV*, 400

Ephraim the Syrian, *The Pearl*, c. 400

John Chrysostom, *On Vainglory and the Upbringing of Children 64–90*, c. 400

Theodore of Mopsuestia, *On the Incarnation VII*, c. 400

Rufinus of Aquileia, *A Commentary on the Apostles' Creed*, 404

Augustine, *City of God*, 413–426

John Cassian, *Conferences of the Desert Fathers*, 420

Various, *The Sayings of the Desert Mothers*, compiled over the fourth–fifth centuries

Anonymous, *Passion of Saint Alban*, fifth–sixth centuries

The *Didache*[1] (c. 50–90)

Διδαχὴ τῶν δώδεκα ἀποστόλων.
Διδαχὴ κυρίου διὰ τῶν δώδεκα ἀποστόλων τοῖς ἔθνεσιν. ὁδοὶ δύο
εἰσί, μία τῆς ζωῆς καὶ μία τοῦ θανάτου· διαφορὰ δὲ πολλὴ μετα-
ξὺ τῶν δύο ὁδῶν. ἡ μὲν οὖν ὁδός τῆς ζωῆς ἐστιν αὕτη· πρῶτον, ἀγαπή—

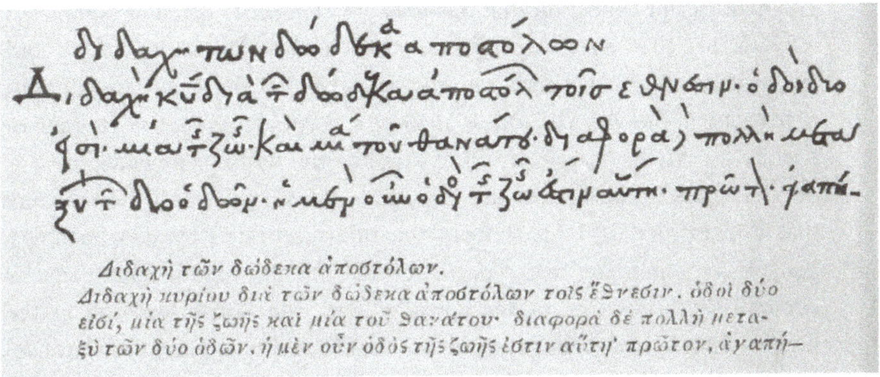

Figure 1.1 Two titles of the *Didache*

Introduction

Long considered lost and virtually forgotten in the West, the *Didache* caused quite a stir when a parchment manuscript of the Greek text was recovered, by chance, in 1873. The Orthodox archbishop Philotheos Bryennios discovered it while he was working in the library of the Greek Convent of the Holy Sepulchre in Istanbul. A short text (about the same length as the book of Galatians), the *Didache* is refreshing in its practical and straightforward approach to piety for Gentile converts. It is an invaluable document from a period in which we know little about the day-to-day functions of church life. As Kurt Niederwimmer observes, it is a document with pastoral immediacy: "The whole composition is unpretentious as literature, nourished by praxis and intended for immediate application."[2] The *Didache* is the earliest evidence for a method of baptism other than immersion, and it contains some of the oldest eucharistic prayers, both of which make it of great interest in understanding the development of Christian worship. Considerable attention has been given to the *Didache* since its recovery and this is indicative not only of its importance but also of the questions it raises with regard to the situation of the earliest church.

What is the *Didache*?

The manuscript collection that includes the *Didache* is dated as completed on June 11, 1056 by the scribe who calls himself "Leon the notary and sinner." The vocabulary and grammar are typical of the *koinē* Greek of the first century. But the *Didache* is neither a gospel (there is no attempt to narrate the life of Jesus), nor an epistle like the writings of Paul (there is no awareness in the text of the mission to the Gentiles and the theology that undergirded it).[3] Apart from the title—indicated by two headings, *didachē tōn apostolōn* and *didachē kyriou dia tōn dōdeka apostolōn tois ethnesin* ("the teaching of the apostles" and "the Lord's teaching to the nations through the twelve apostles")—the *Didache* never mentions "twelve" apostles. When it mentions "apostles" at all, the title is applied to itinerant charismatics.[4]

For the early Christians, the *Didache* was not a "precious" document because it was not directly associated with any of the apostles, but it was widely considered "useful." Long before it was recovered, a number of ancient witnesses attest to the existence of the *Didache* and its usefulness.[5] The original occasion for its composition is lost, but for its original recipients the *Didache* answered the question what it means to be a Christian. Fundamental to the Didachist's project was the assumption that Jesus came to form a new people, uniting different peoples into a new family. Navigating this precarious new union would be the early church's central project. Practically, this meant that each Christian needed to know how one is identified as part of this new family and what life changes result from it. This initiation took time and required personalized guidance. Thus, instead of a top-down oriented manual for church leaders, the *Didache* represents a process that was much more personalized, like that of a mentor–apprentice relationship.

Questions of dating, origin, and relationship to other ancient documents

The original composing of the *Didache* has proved to be notoriously difficult to locate geographically and controversial to date historically. Indeed, we really have no idea where the anonymous Didachist wrote this document. Some have suggested either Egypt or Syria, but neither option recommends itself with any certainty. The reception of the document in the nineteenth and twentieth centuries is also complicated by both Roman Catholic and Protestant "allergic reactions" to the *Didache*, especially to its accounting of sacramental practice.[6] This discomfiture often resulted in a later dating and treating the *Didache* as a peripheral document—thereby distancing the early church from this questionable document. Catholic scholars have written extensively on how the meal in the *Didache* was decidedly not a Eucharist, concluding instead that there were two types of meals—the Eucharist and agape feasts—and thus tending to date the *Didache* to the second century. For extreme Protestants, the proscribed days for fasting demonstrated in their minds the document's corruption and need for reforming. As a result, these Protestants designated the *Didache* as very late (third or fourth century), with some going so far as to say it might be a forgery.

The *Didache* is now widely recognized as a first-century document. Broad consensus locates the *Didache* as early as 50 CE or as late as 80 or 90.[7] Scholarship on the *Didache* has been reoriented, now viewing the *Didache* not as a disparate, loosely connected patchwork on guidance for early converts, but as an invaluable early witness to the most formative years of local church growth. As part of this shift, questions about the dependence of the *Didache* on other early writings have become central.

The Didachist includes two direct citations from the Old Testament: Malachi 1:11, 14 in *Did.* 14:3 ("In every place and time, offer to me a pure sacrifice. Because I am a great king, says the Lord, and my name is wondrous among the Gentiles") and Zechariah 14:5 in *Did.* 16:6–7 ("The Lord will come and all the holy ones with him"). As for the New Testament, although there are no clear references to the writings of Paul, Peter, or John, there does appear to be a fondness for the Matthean text, especially the Sermon on the Mount and the Olivet Discourse.[8] The question of dating comes into play here; if one hypothesizes a late date for the *Didache* then it makes sense to draw a direct line of dependence from Matthew and possibly Luke. There are parallels between Matthew and the *Didache* that have been variously explained as direct dependence of the *Didache* on Matthew, dependence of both documents on shared traditions (written or oral), dependence of Matthew on the *Didache*, or complete independence of the *Didache* from any gospel source.[9] The early dating of the *Didache* makes it most likely that it evolved along with the Jesus tradition. It is possible that the *Didache* was composed independent of the received gospels and it is also possible that there was a sharing of sources between them.

Another debated question is the extent to which the *Didache* is a work that evolved over time and took on a composite nature. As Michael Holmes notes, some scholars consider it to be the work of a single individual who combined traditional material (written and oral) with original contributions, while others consider the document to be a community production that evolved in stages.[10] According to Niederwimmer's analysis, the *Didache* is a compilation of sources that were gathered together into a community rule at the beginning of the second century. He cites a superficially Christianized Jewish Two Ways treatise, an archaic liturgical tradition of baptism and the Eucharist, an ancient tradition on the reception of itinerant charismatics, and a short apocalypse.[11] Other scholars, however, make the case for the *Didache*'s compositional unity.[12]

A crash course in the Way of Life (1:1–6:2)[13]

The *Didache* opens with a straightforward and familiar echo of Deuteronomy 30:14–18—"There are two ways: one of life and one of death! And there is a great difference between the two ways"—then immediately launches into an overview of what the preferred route entails. The familiar construction of first loving God and loving one's neighbor as oneself, along with a version of what is popularly called the "Golden Rule," comprise the guiding principle of the Way of Life. Everything that follows is an attempt to set both the individual and the local Christian community on the path to success in this endeavor. Practically, the outworking of this first principle looks like blessing one's enemies (1:3) and abstaining from desires that only serve to gratify the flesh, such as retaliation for an offense or the reflexive desire for self-preservation (1:4–5).

The second guiding rule for training in the Way of Life involves an adaptation of the Jewish Decalogue that reflects the concerns of Gentile converts who denied paganism.[14] Thus, alongside familiar commands that address enmity between people, such as "do not murder," we find prohibitions against sorcery and idolatrous practices specific to the current cultic context (2:1–3:6). In the beautifully constructed passage of *Did.* 3:2–6, the Didachist offers guidance for the young in faith, warning them that their becoming angry, lustful, etc., can lead to a way of being ruled by things like envy and thievery, which, in turn, will lead to the eventual birth of a variety of evils. Instead, a convert's growth should be oriented toward becoming gentle, merciful, good, and living in the constant awareness of God's sustaining power. At this point the Didachist turns the discussion outward, instructing converts on how to view those who lead and the new family to which they now belong. Guidance is also given on how to position oneself within that community as a giver, partner, good parent, good master, and faithful guardian of the truth as it was received (4.1–14).

The Way of Death, on the other hand, is associated with evil and those who hawk its wares (5:1–2). The Didachist gives an extensive list of the manifestations of evil that ends with a plea that young converts seek salvation from such destructive practices. This section is brief in comparison to the description of the Way of Life. The lack of expansion is perhaps intentional, reflecting the mind that regularly discerns between the authentic and the counterfeit: intimate knowledge of and experience with the authentic is the way to discern a counterfeit, not the other way around. The Didachist is well aware of the precarious situation facing Gentile converts and of how challenging it is to make radical life changes. To navigate the inevitable awkward and socially isolating steps that Christianity required, it was vital to choose the right teacher (6:1–2).

Regulations for eating, baptizing, fasting, and praying (6:3–11:2)

The *Didache* offers Gentile converts a modest and achievable way to make the necessary changes, such as doing the best they can to avoid food sacrificed to idols (6:3). What converts lose in abandoning their cultural mores they more than gain back, at least from the Didachist's perspective, through initiation into a new family and new set of cultural habits. The section outlining the rite of baptism (7:1–3) is monumental in its simplicity and accommodation:

> And concerning baptism, baptize thus: Having said all these things beforehand, immerse in the name of the Father and of the Son and of the holy Spirit in flowing water—if, on the one hand, you should not have flowing water, immerse in other water that is available; and if you are not able in cold, immerse in warm water; and if you should not have either, pour out water onto the head three times in the name of the Father and the Son and the holy Spirit.

This section is certainly fodder for ecumenical discussion, not just between Catholics and Protestants, but also within Protestantism itself. That one needs to be baptized and that it is a communal rite is paramount over the integrity of specific ritual details. Thomas O'Loughlin hones in on the core of the directive: "We should think of the ritual as a great drama where every person who attends a performance can take away a new meaning from it. The drama is the thing, and the many interpretations are a tribute to its depth and richness."[15] Aside from joining in with the one about to be baptized and the fast that customarily accompanied the rite, the fact that Christians deliberately fast on different days than their pagan neighbors (8:1) is another example of the Didachist's emphasis on the formation of a new family with its own set of traditions.

Continuing with this communal sentiment, the *Didache* offers examples of the earliest Christian prayers: one that bears similarity to what is commonly called the "Lord's Prayer" (8:2), a eucharistic prayer before the meal (9:2–4), and a prayer of thanksgiving after the meal (10:2–6). These communal activities are bonding agents for those new to the family and offer an entry point that indicates full initiation. The community formation aspect is clearly present in the post-meal prayer where the community is directed to "give thanks in this way (*eucharistisate*)" in 10:5: "Remember, Lord, your church, to save her from every evil and to perfect her in your love and to gather her together from the four winds as the sanctified into your kingdom which you have prepared for her, because yours is the power and the glory forever." These prayers are given as examples and not as prescriptions, since the Didachist concludes the section by directing the community to allow their prophets to give thanks (*eucharistein*) as much as they want (10:7). The *Didache* presents us with a community that seeks to learn and disciplines itself to discern. Those teachers who pass through are thus to be welcomed and carefully vetted with regard to their message (11:1–2).

Regulations for hospitality/testing various classes of visitors (11:3–13:2)

Itinerant apostles and prophets were apparently common in local *Didache* communities. The general rule seems to have been that if they stay more than two days or demonstrate parasitic tendencies, then the visitors have shifted from welcome representatives of the Lord to opportunistic salespeople (11:3–13:2). The *Didache* calls such a person a Christ-peddler (*christemporos*), literally one who sells Christ for personal gain. The provisions that limit itinerancy and require a skill from those who would settle in the community seem to be about protecting the integrity and generosity of local bodies and their mentorship arrangements.

Regulations for first fruits and for offering a pure sacrifice (13:3–15:4)

The *Didache* frequently offers occasion for meditation on how the fledgling Christian communities received the Jewish narrative and cultural traditions. We are reminded that Jewish and Christian traditions present a God who is consistent and comfortable with material demonstrations of worship. Our distance from the early, more agrarian versions of these traditions might mask the importance of oil or livestock or bread. The early Christians were to set aside the best of what they produced for others, whether it would go to the prophet who was just passing through or to the beggar on the street (13:3–7). The translation and folding of Jewish tradition into Christianity included retaining space in the developing rituals for those who functioned in some senses like a "high-priest," albeit reoriented to fit the budding and diffuse structures of local authority. Pagans were likely used to offering their first fruits. Since Christians had no shrines, temples, or priests, the *Didache* makes what Milavec calls a "bold and innovative" step when it designates the prophets as honorary "priests": "Now there was not a place but a person to whom the faithful could be directed when it came time for them to express their gratitude to the Lord."[16] This setting aside of the first fruits included having an established practice of meeting, giving thanks, and eating—together. Predicated upon the requisite confession and reconciliation, the communal bond would be strengthened and facilitate a pure offering (14:1–3). The language of the

Didache here is focused on "sacrifice" (*thysia*), not only on holocaust or burnt offering (*enagismos*).[17]

In order to help facilitate communal worship, the Didachist directs each local church to appoint bishops and deacons who are gentle, generous, and truthful, and who have had their character tested. These men are unpaid servants similar to the traveling prophets and teachers and should not be regarded as inferior.[18] One should note that *episkopos* (bishop) here should not be burdened with later ecclesiastical freight. Their job is that of oversight; there is no hint of teaching or consecrating. The community at large, however, is charged with living together in peace (15:3), giving (15:4), and generally living a life worthy of that community (16:1). This life should be characterized by watchfulness and readiness for the Lord's coming. While the apocalyptic section at the end of the *Didache* is often viewed as an addendum of sorts, the eschatological orientation of the Way of Life is present throughout the text. The Christian life is meant to be living into another reality that is yet to come. That reality is tapped in the communal bond of the saints in the various ways they come together in love and service for one another and the gospel. Anticipation colors all Christian activity with the shade of the trials and resurrection to come. For the Didachist, this living into the eschatological reality to come is part of a continuous narrative that began with Jewish tradition and continues in the form of early Christian communities until an undesignated time when "the world will see the Lord coming atop the clouds of heaven" (16:8).

Closing apocalyptic forewarnings and hope (16:1–8)

In *Did.* 16:1, the Didachist moves from the "already" of communal bonding toward the "not yet" of the Christian "last days." The *Didache*, however, presupposes that the Christian community prioritizes its familial bonds and Christian growth because of some connection to what is to come: "And frequently be gathered together, seeking the things pertaining to your souls; for the whole time of your faith will not be of use to you if in the end time you should have been perfected" (16:2). The forewarnings that follow give ample evidence for why gathering together to learn and discern will continue to be important. In addition to false prophets and those who are lawless, betrayers, and persecutors, there will be a deceiver who will test humanity (16:3–5). According to the *Didache*, this is when humanity itself will be the sacrifice and those who endure in their faith will be saved and resurrected (16:5–7). The ending is abrupt and likely unfinished, but it points toward the certainty of the hope in a triumphant God after the greatest evil is unleashed and the most intense trial has come. Strikingly, it is such things as reconciling a conflict, not being greedy, and frequently gathering together, that form the undercurrent of preparation for the last days.

Conclusion

Reading a document like the *Didache* is about more than attempting to fit together what the earliest expressions of Christianity looked like. It is an opportunity to engage in dialogue with early worshippers and enjoy community across two millennia. The *Didache* is invaluable for helping us to better understand from an inside perspective the context of the New Testament and how the gospel was received. It opens a small window into the concerns, issues, and priorities of the earliest Christians who gathered together.

Notes

1. Translated as *"The Teaching of the Lord to the Gentiles by the Twelve Apostles"* or *"The Teaching of the (Twelve) Apostles."*
2. Kurt Niederwimmer, *The* Didache: *A Commentary*, Hermeneia, trans., Linda M. Maloney, ed. Harold W. Attridge (Minneapolis: Fortress, 1998), 3.
3. Aaron Milavec, *The* Didache: *Text, Translation, Analysis, and Commentary* (Collegeville, MN: Liturgical, 2003), ix. Hereafter, all further references to this work shall be noted by employing in-text parenthetical citations.
4. It is possible that the association with the "Twelve Apostles" was introduced when it became important for works to claim apostolic authorship for validation (Milavec, *Didache*, 41).
5. For example, the *Didache* is listed in the canonical list of Eusebius, for whom the *Didache* was among the "spurious" books (also in this list: *Acts of Paul, Shepherd of Hermas, Apocalypse of Peter*, the *Epistle of Barnabas*, and *John's Apocalypse*) (Niederwimmer, *Didache*, 4). *The Teaching of the Apostles* also appears in the *Thirty-Ninth Easter Letter* of Athanasius of Alexandria (367) as not canonical but approved and useful.
6. Thomas O'Loughlin, *The* Didache: *A Window on the Earliest Christians* (Grand Rapids: Baker, 2010), 8.
7. Holmes posits the most probable date of the *Didache* as late first century. He bases that decision on the very early nature of the material in the

Didache, the simplicity of the prayers, the concern to differentiate Christian practices from Jewish rituals, and in particular the church structure that included the continued existence of itinerant ministers alongside a resident twofold structure of bishops and deacons, which point to a time closer to that of Paul and James (died in the 60s) than Ignatius (died after 110). See Michael W. Holmes, trans. and ed., *The Didache* in *The Apostolic Fathers: Greek Texts and English Translations*, 3rd ed (Grand Rapids: Baker, 2007), 337–38.

8. Earliest commentators assumed at least the use of Matthew, especially since the *Didache* refers four times to "the gospel," *The* Didache *in Modern Research*. Arbeiten zur Geschichte des antiken Judentums und des Urchristentums XXXVII, ed. Jonathan A. Draper (Leiden: Brill, 1996), 16. For a comparison of Matthew and the *Didache*, see William Varner, *The Way of the* Didache: *The First Christian Handbook* (Lanham, MD: University Press of America, 2007), 44–51.

9. Holmes, *Didache*, 338–39.

10. Ibid., 336.

11. One of the central debates surrounds the origin of the Two Ways tractate that comprises the first third of the *Didache*. Material similar to the Two Ways section is found in a number of other Christian writings from the first through the fifth centuries, including the *Epistle of Barnabas* and *The Didascalia*. Niederwimmer argues for an independent Two Ways tractate that was of Jewish origin and is now lost, making it impossible to reconstruct the original wording or oral tradition. The original form no longer exists (some would argue that it never did).

12. Milavec and Varner in particular make this argument. While acknowledging that the *Didache* might have utilized a number of Jewish sources and been edited at least once, they note that all of these versions are considered the provenance of the first century. It has also been noted, however, that these and other studies claiming compositional unity do not adequately explain the contradictions and overall lack of homogeneity in the *Didache*, see Nancy Pardee, *The Genre and Development of the* Didache, Wissenschaftliche Untersuchungen zum Neuen Testament 2, Reihe 339 (Tübingen: Mohr Siebeck, 2012).

13. I use Milavec's translation (with some adjustments) and structural divisions so as to retain the oral nature and inclusivity of the language of the *Didache* (Milavec, *Didache*, xviii).

14. The commandments against graven images and for the Sabbath would be unlivable in a Gentile world where every building was decorated with such images and the Roman lunar calendar did not grant a provision for cessation of work every seventh day. The commandment for children to honor their parents would be virtually impossible in this situation—except in rare

occasions of the conversion of a whole household—since the Christians were requiring of their converts a complete desertion of ancestral gods and abandonment of parental upbringing. Instead, the Didachist offers new "commandments," such as the prohibition of pedophilia and illicit sex (*porneia*), which were virtually unknown in Judaism but socially acceptable in the Greco-Roman world. Milavec concludes that the Didachist purposefully pursued a moderate but "countercultural" approach that was realistic (51–55).

15. O'Loughlin, *Didache*, 65.
16. Milavec, *Didache*, 74.
17. According to Milavec, "The absence of the term 'holocaust' (*enagismos*) . . . signals that neither Jews nor gentiles would have regarded the confession of failings or the discipline of reconciliation as required for the forgiveness of sins or the atonement of guilt. Atonement, in the *Didache*, was associated with almsgiving (4:6), and divine forgiveness was principally an eschatological event (8:2; 16:2, 5)" (75).
18. The language is specifically male in this instance. The itinerant prophets, teachers, and apostles are not designated to be specifically of one gender or the other.

Select Bibliography

Primary source

Milavec, Aaron. *The* Didache: *Text, Translation, Analysis, and Commentary.* Collegeville, MN: Liturgical, 2003.

Secondary sources

Draper, Jonathan A. ed. *The* Didache *in Modern Research*. Arbeiten zur Geschichte des antiken Judentums und des Urchristentums XXXVII. Leiden: Brill, 1996.

Holmes, Michael W., trans. and ed. *The* Didache in *The Apostolic Fathers: Greek Texts and English Translations*, 3rd ed. Grand Rapids: Baker, 2007.

Milavec, Aaron. *The* Didache: *Faith, Hope, and Life of the Earliest Christian Communities, 50–70 CE*. New York: Newman, 2003.

Niederwimmer, Kurt. *The* Didache: *A Commentary*. Hermeneia, trans., Linda M. Maloney, ed. Harold W. Attridge. Minneapolis: Fortress, 1998.

O'Loughlin, Thomas. *The* Didache: *A Window on the Earliest Christians*. Grand Rapids: Baker, 2010.

Varner, William. *The Way of the* Didache: *The First Christian Handbook*. Lanham, MD: University Press of America, 2007.

1.2

Select Epistles
Ignatius of Antioch
(d. c. 110–150 CE)

Figure 1.2 Rendering of Ignatius' martyrdom

Introduction

We first meet Ignatius on the road to his own execution. Bound between ten "leopards" (i.e., Roman soldiers), the bishop of Antioch writes a series of letters to various churches in which he gives greetings and instruction, encourages faithfulness and vigilance, and reflects on his impending martyrdom.[1] The circumstances that led up to and the reason for Ignatius's arrest are unknown, but it is clear that the Antiochene church was in a state of crisis.[2] The question of the authenticity and number of letters in the Ignatian corpus has been a matter of much debate, especially during and after the Protestant Reformation.[3] There is a general consensus now, however, that only seven of the letters attributed to Ignatius of Antioch are authentic.[4] His seven authentic letters are addressed to various groups and people in familiar biblical locations, including Ephesus, Rome, Philadelphia and Smyrna, as well as a letter to Bishop Polycarp. These short letters are a travel log of sorts, a series of snapshots for Ignatius's extended Christian family who later wrote (unreliable) accounts of his martyrdom, built upon his proto-creedal and early Christological formulations, and shared his passion for the unity of the church under the auspices of the bishop.

Letters from Smyrna, Part 1: *Ephesians, Magnesians, and Trallians*

One of the major themes in Ignatius's letters is unity.[5] The Antiochene bishop calls on the Ephesians to join in a harmonious chorus under the leadership of the bishop, presbyters, and deacons "so that by being harmonious in unanimity and taking your pitch from God you may sing in unison with one voice through Jesus Christ to the Father, in order that he may both hear you and, on the basis of what you do well, acknowledge that you are members of his Son (*Eph.* 4.2)." In order for the chorus to sing ably, maintaining harmony is important. Being out of tune or actively opposing the song of the bishop is equivalent to opposing the song of Jesus Christ, because all must "regard the bishop as the Lord himself" (*Eph.* 6.1). His repeated emphasis on the three-fold ecclesial leadership model of one bishop surrounded by a council of presbyters and supported by deacons has prompted scholars to offer various proposals about the Antiochene bishop's role in the model's invention and propagation.[6] Ignatius's famous three-fold schema is grounded in an ecclesiology that is undeniably Christological. The Antiochene bishop is known for a Christology that, while nascent compared to later formulations, is acutely articulated and displays a warmth of connection to Jesus Christ.

Who is Jesus Christ according to Ignatius? He is unequivocally God and human: "There is only one physician, who is both flesh and spirit, born and unborn, God in man, true life in death, both from Mary and from God, first subject to suffering and then beyond it, Jesus Christ our Lord" (*Eph.* 7.2). The true divinity and the true humanity of Jesus heralds a new reality for

Christians as he is the "perfect human" (cf. *Smry.* 4.2). Ignatius's Christology, then, is also his anthropology. Thus, Christianity is a new way to be human because "even those things that you do according to the flesh are in fact spiritual, for you do everything in Jesus Christ" (*Eph.* 6.2). Being "in Jesus Christ" and harmonizing with one another as "God-bearers and temple-bearers, Christ-bearers, bearers of holy things, adorned in every respect with the commandments of Jesus Christ" with the bishop, presbyters, and deacons fuels the life of the body of Christ, the church (*Eph.* 9.2).[7] This harmonious unity creates a melody that is not only the life of the body itself but is devastating to the powers of Satan and brings peace to raging wars among those in heaven and on earth (*Eph.* 13.1–2). Therefore, all humans gathered together in Christ, "who is Son of Man and Son of God," are to be of one mind with the bishop and the presbyters as they partake of life as one body, breaking the bread of the Eucharist, the "medicine of immortality," that connects Christians to the life of Jesus Christ (*Eph.* 20.2).

In his letter to the Magnesians, Ignatius reiterates his desire for unity for the sake of enduring together and thus reaching God (*Magn.* 1.2). For Ignatius, it is not enough merely to *be called* a Christian, one must actually *be* one. The Christian bears the stamp of God the Father through Jesus Christ and chooses "to die into his suffering" in order to live, as opposed to the one who embraces the label alone and still bears the impress of the world (*Magn.* 5.2). For Ignatius, well-ordered love (cf. *Magn.* 1.1) facilitates a unity in Jesus Christ with the bishop; and love drives harmony:

> Therefore as the Lord did nothing without the Father, either by himself or through the apostles (for he was united with him), so you must not do anything without the bishop and the presbyters. Do not attempt to convince yourselves that anything done apart from the others is right, but, gathering together, let there be one prayer, one petition, one mind, one hope, with love and blameless joy, which is Jesus Christ, than whom nothing is better. Let all of you run together as to one temple of God, as to one altar, to one Jesus Christ, who came forth from one Father and remained with the One and returned to the One (*Magn.* 7.1–2).

While Ignatius does not ground the bishop's authority in apostolic succession per se, he does root the loving harmony of the Christian community in the teachings of Jesus and the apostles.[8] In modern times, Ignatius's undeniable focus on the hierarchy of ecclesial leadership has been the focus of much debate among various Christian communities (especially between Protestants and Roman Catholics) on how the church ought to be structured. However, it is important to note that Ignatius does not see the bishop as a lone leader but as the head of a body that only has life because it is in Jesus Christ and who leads with the support of the "beautifully woven spiritual crown" that comprises the council of presbyters and deacons (*Magn.* 13.1).

In his letter to the Trallians, Ignatius states that, without the bishop and the presbyters, the church ceases to be a church. The connection to Jesus Christ and the apostles therefore would not exist and the church would be lifeless (*Tral.* 2.1–3; 3.1). A church is only alive if the bond of unity functions and the body of believers remains healthy. Ignatius explains how the health of the church depends on their staying away from "every strange plant, which is heresy" and subsisting only on "Christian food," that is, the continual nourishment that the Eucharist (the "medicine of immortality") provides (*Tral.* 6.1). For Ignatius, the Eucharist enforced the embodied reality of the current and the future human condition and was thus an important aspect of Ignatius's fight against the docetists.[9] As he will reiterate in *Smyrnaeans*, if Jesus "suffered in appearance only," then why in the world would the bishop submit to arrest, wild beasts, and death (*Smry.* 4.2; *Tral.* 9.1–2)? Ignatius is quite clear: if these events have no human reality, then humans can have no true life. Denial of the reality of Jesus's humanity only brings death (*Tral.* 11.1).

Letters from Smyrna, Part 2: *Romans* and the journey to martyrdom

Ignatius was under the impression that the Roman church had the power to prevent his martyrdom and he argues for them not to intervene. According to Ignatius, his martyrdom was pleasing to God and interfering would halt his not-to-be-missed opportunity to reach God and to be an offering to God for the sake of the church (*Rom.* 2.1–2).[10] As in *Magnesians*, Ignatius emphasizes in *Romans* the importance of not merely calling oneself a Christian but actually being one (*Rom.* 3.2). He views his impending tangle with wild beasts as his opportunity to *be* and not merely *be called*. Choosing to see his journey through to its end is important to Ignatius because in submitting to his martyrdom, he preserves agency (cf. *Rom.* 4.1). According to Gregory Vall, Ignatius is following Christ who, "in making himself an offering for others . . . acts in perfect freedom. No one takes his life from him; he lays it down of his own accord" (Jn 10:18). In suffering love, action and passion coincide. Jesus is fixed to the cross, handing over his life in the perfect freedom of love. This is the passion of his God that Ignatius wishes to imitate."[11] From Ignatius's perspective, the Roman church's interference would strip him of the power that comes with seeing his discipleship through in sacrifice (*Rom.* 4.2). Ignatius employs Eucharistic language in his plea: "I implore you: do not be unseasonably kind to me. Let me be food for the wild beasts, through whom I can reach God. I am God's wheat, and I am being ground by the teeth of the wild beasts, so that I may prove to be pure bread" (*Rom.* 4.1). He comes back to the Eucharistic imagery later:

> For though I am still alive, I am passionately in love with death (*erōn tou apothanein*) as I write to you. My passionate love has been crucified (*erōs estaupōtai*) and there is no fire of material longing within me, but only water living and speaking in me, saying within me, 'Come to the Father.' I take no pleasure in corruptible food or the pleasures of this life. I want the bread of God, which is the flesh of Christ who is of the seed of David; and for drink I want his blood, which is incorruptible love (*Rom.* 7.2–3).

In Ignatius's view, any move that would stay the hand of the executioner robbed him of his opportunity to be human (i.e., a human able to suffer like Christ) and sentenced him to a fate far worse than the beasts (*Rom.* 6.2–3).

How do we read Ignatius's "vivid, almost macabre eagerness" for martyrdom?[12] If Ignatius's strong sentiments are read as a zealous death wish or a bishop playing out a "martyr complex" in a wild effort to guilt the Antiochene church into a resolution of their crisis, then his witness (*martyrion*)—as he seems to have understood it—loses its coherence. While Ignatius's eagerness could be read as contradicting his affirmation of embodied Christianity, William R. Schoedel observes that, for Ignatius, "the reality of Christ's death confirms the value of Christian suffering, and the reality of his incarnation confirms the value of what Christians do in the flesh. In a curious way, then, martyrdom proves not to be a denial of this world but a final affirmation of the significance of what is done in the flesh."[13] Ignatius processes his martyrdom Christologically; he shares in the sufferings of Christ and suffers on behalf of Christ's body, the church. Thus, his martyrdom was a participation in a kind of spectacle that was efficacious for the sake of the church as Christ's unified body. Consequently, his arrest and impending death accorded Ignatius the opportunity to embrace the reality of the extent of what it meant to *be* Christian (suffering, death, and resurrection) and a bishop.

There were other routes the entourage could have taken, but, based on the consensus that identifies the seven letters of the middle recension as authentic, we are able to travel with Ignatius for a significant portion of his journey.[14] After his arrest, the Roman soldiers took Ignatius by ship from

Antioch and at some point disembarked at a port on the southern coast of Asia Minor and then traveled by land. Instead of going to Rome by ship from Ephesus, at some point the group turned north, passed through Philadelphia, and reached Smyrna sometime in August where they were delayed for a time. The delay gave Ignatius the opportunity to gain and nurture the support of his fellow Christians by receiving visitors from the various church communities that he had bypassed in his journey by turning north (probably at Laodicea) and to whom he wrote letters (Ephesus, Magnesia, and Tralles).[15] The entourage then traveled to Troas where Ignatius penned his letters to the churches at Philadelphia, Smyrna, and to Polycarp. He also received the very welcome news that "peace" had been restored at the church in Antioch. Their stay in Troas was apparently cut short and they departed for the port of Philippi, Neopolis. Our window into Ignatius's journey closes at this point. Presumably Ignatius was taken to Rome as planned and executed. We have no reason to question that he was indeed martyred. Generally, it is thought that Ignatius was martyred sometime during the reign of Trajan (98–117 CE) but some enlarge the time frame in the direction of Hadrian's reign (117–138 CE).[16]

Letters from Troas: *Philadelphians, Smyrnaeans, and Polycarp*

Scholars have debated the number of heresies Ignatius confronts in his letters but most land on two, the Judaizers and the docetists.[17] In *Philadelphians*, Ignatius warns against division and false teaching. Following the shepherd and remaining unified are key to eluding the attempts of "seemingly trustworthy wolves" to "take captive the runners in God's race" (*Phil.* 2.1–2). Ignatius returns to the botanical imagery he used in *Trallians* and warns the Philadelphians to avoid "evil plants" (*Phil.* 3.1). In order that the Philadelphians would never have to worry about their botanical discernment, Ignatius makes it clear: "all those who belong to God and Jesus Christ are with the bishop" (*Phil.* 3.2). Their love for each other will aid them in not being deceived. It seems that the Philadelphian church was dealing with Judaizers who were resisting Jesus Christ because they were not finding what they heard in the gospel in the "archives," i.e., the Old Testament (*Phil.* 8.2).[18] For Ignatius, the prophets "preached in anticipation" of Jesus Christ and the distinctly "unalterable archives" of his birth, suffering, and resurrection; the gospel is the "imperishably finished work" (*Phil.* 8.2; 9.2).

In his letter to the Smyrnaeans, Ignatius addresses the docetist heresy, which undermined the full humanity of Jesus by denying that he actually had a true human body during the Incarnation. Ignatius reinforced his unshakeable confidence on the fact that in the Incarnation Jesus was truly human by drawing out the implications of that fact: Jesus is "truly of the family of David with respect to human descent, Son of God with respect to the divine will and power, truly born of a virgin, baptized by John in order that all righteousness might be fulfilled by him, truly nailed in the flesh for us under Pontius Pilate and Herod the tetrarch (from its fruit we derive our existence, that is, from his divinely blessed sufferings)" and all of this for the sake of opening up all of humanity to the promise of their true *telos* (i.e., the ultimate end), the resurrection (*Smyr.* 1.1–2).

In his letter to the churches in Smyrna, Ignatius goes into greater detail about the problems with the idea that Jesus Christ "suffered in appearance only" (as the Docetists taught), equating the belief in a disembodied savior with a demonic, disembodied fate for humanity (*Smyr.* 2). Ignatius knew full well that if the actual physical, fleshly, embodied reality of our being is not affirmed and if it was not the reality which the Logos took upon himself in the Incarnation, then the perfection of humanity in Christ was nullified and the present Christian community is damaged:

> They have no concern for love, none for the widow, none for the orphan, none for the oppressed, none for the prisoner or the one released, none for the hungry or thirsty. They abstain from the Eucharist and prayer because they refuse to acknowledge that the Eucharist is the flesh of our savior Jesus Christ, which suffered for our sins and which the Father by his goodness raised up (*Smyr.* 6.2).

On behalf of this present Christian community, in his last letter Ignatius exhorts Polycarp, the bishop of Smyrna, to "bear with all people," continue to "endure all in love," pray without ceasing, ask for wisdom, and "keep alert with an unresting spirit" (*Pol.* 1.2–3). The Antiochene bishop's advice is practical: "Speak to the people individually," love the difficult ones even though it is more difficult to bring them into submission, administer your care accordingly since each person and situation is different, hold more meetings, and do not treat male or female slaves with contempt (*Pol.* 1.3; 2.1; 4.2–3).

Ignatius's bishop-to-bishop advising reads like a stern pep talk given to an athlete in order to push them to challenge their limits. Polycarp is "God's athlete" and, as such, Ignatius reminds him that he lacks nothing and abounds in "every spiritual gift" (*Pol.* 2.2). Ignatius even gives him a couple of motivational slogans that could adorn the walls of any gym: "where there is more work, there is much gain" (*Pol.* 1.3) and "it is the mark of a great athlete to be bruised, yet still conquer" (*Pol.* 3.1). He calls for Polycarp to increase his diligence and be patient as he waits expectantly for the God who is "the Eternal, the Invisible, who for our sake became visible; the Intangible, the Unsuffering, who for our sake suffered, who for our sake endured in every way" (*Pol.* 3.2). Ignatius then draws the congregation in, calling on them all to become of one purpose and one mind; to become a team: "Train together with one another: compete together, run together, suffer together, rest together, get up together, as God's managers, assistants, and servants" (*Pol.* 6.1).

Conclusion

In his letters, Ignatius of Antioch offers brisk instruction for young churches and their leaders. Quivering with the energy of a man who was determined to make the most of his impending death, the Antiochene bishop paints a picture of church unity in Jesus Christ that he fully expects to be reflective of reality and not merely utopian fantasy. In letters that display significant familiarity with at least one of the Gospels and portions of the Pauline corpus,[19] Ignatius speaks of Jesus Christ as God and as the suffering, crucified, and resurrected God-Man who heralded true humanity for all. With his death nearing, Ignatius displays verve and perhaps the kind of clarity that comes from staring down one's mortality, and so he speaks with urgency to the church to *be* and not merely *be called* Christian. Throughout the centuries, many Christians—Catholic, Orthodox, and Protestant—have found in Ignatius's letters a vision of Christ in their own suffering, a call to martyrdom, and a faithful response to divisions in the church.

Notes

1.   We know little about the Antiochene bishop outside of his letters. In his *Ecclesiastical History*, because Eusebius attempts to demonstrate apostolic succession he gives a somewhat problematic account of Ignatius (*H.E.* 3.36). For an examination of Eusebius's account, see Allen Brent, *Ignatius of Antioch: Martyr Bishop and the Origin of the Episcopacy* (New York:

Continuum/T&T Clark, 2007), 5–9, and Paul Foster, "The Epistles of Ignatius of Antioch" in *The Writings of the Apostolic Fathers*, ed. Paul Foster (London: T&T Clark, 2007), 85.

2. In each letter he wrote in Smyrna, Ignatius asks for prayers for the church in Syria (*Eph.* 21.2; *Magn.* 14; *Tral.* 13.1; *Rom.* 9.1). Once he reaches Troas he receives good news: that the church at Antioch is "at peace." He deems it appropriate for the churches to send ambassadors to Antioch to congratulate them (*Phil.* 10.1–2; *Smry.* 11.1–2; *Pol.* 7.1–2). For a discussion on these "ambassadors," see Brent, *Ignatius of Antioch*, 11–12, 51–68.

3. William R. Schoedel, *A Commentary on the Letters of Ignatius of Antioch*, ed. Helmut Koester (Philadelphia: Fortress, 1985), 2; Paul Foster, "The Epistles of Ignatius of Antioch" in *The Writings of the Apostolic Fathers*, ed. Paul Foster (London: T&T Clark, 2007), 82–83.

4. The work of the Anglican Bishop John Ussher helped to solidify the authenticity of the seven letters, known as the "middle recension," by discovering that the seven letters had earlier acceptance than the thirteen letters of the "long recension." The middle recension also opened the Ignatian corpus beyond the three letters (*Ephesians, Romans,* and *Polycarp*) that comprised the Syriac "short recension."

5. Gregory Vall notes that variations on "unity" (*henotēs*) or "union" (*henōsis*) or the verbal form occur twenty-four times in the seven short letters compared to just two times in the New Testament (*Learning Christ: Ignatius of Antioch and the Mystery of Redemption* [Washington DC: Catholic University of America Press, 2013], 89–90).

6. Vall, *Learning Christ*, 80–82; Brent, *Ignatius of Antioch*, 22–42; John D. Zizioulas, *Eucharist, Bishop, Church: The Unity of the Church in the Divine Eucharist and the Bishop During the First Three Centuries*, trans. Elizabeth Theokritoff (Brookline, MA: Holy Cross Orthodox Press, 2001), 107–28, 159.

7. Each of the seven letters opens with a salutation from "Ignatius the image-bearer (*theophorus*)." Michael W. Holmes points out that it is possible that Ignatius is using *theophorus* as a name but, if so, it would be the first example of such usage instead of describing someone who carries divine images or shrines in religious processions (*The Apostolic Fathers: Greek Texts and English Translations* [Grand Rapids: Baker, 2007], 183). According to Schoedel, there is a particular debate among Protestants regarding Ignatius's concept of imitation even though the distinctions made mirror the "problems of a later age." The question rests on whether he understands it in New Testament terms "as a matter of following after Christ (*Nachfolge*) or in non-biblical terms as a matter of replicating Christ-like qualities (*Nachahmung*). The former is seen as a species of faith

or obedience (conceived of as receptivity to divine grace and participation in the sufferings of Christ), the latter as an achievement of the saint" (*Commentary on the Letters of Ignatius*, 30).

8. Holmes notes that "it is interesting that Ignatius provides a theological rationale for the authority and place of the bishop and does not base it, as does his near contemporary Clement of Rome, upon the concept of apostolic succession" (*The Apostolic Fathers*, 168).

9. See Schoedel, *Commentary on the Letters of Ignatius*, 21.

10. Did Rome indeed have the power to intervene and stop his execution? According to Brent, Ignatius would have known of the Roman church's wealth (and the possibility of bribery that went with it) as well as the practice of popular petition for releasing a condemned person. While Ignatius might not have had a completely accurate perception of what the Roman church could feasibly do, he was certainly not paranoid (*Ignatius of Antioch*, 16–19).

11. Vall, *Learning Christ*, 145.

12. Holmes, *The Apostolic Fathers*, 169. Ignatius calls his chains his "spiritual pearls" (*Eph.* 11.2), speaks of coaxing the beasts to devour him quickly (*Rom.* 5.2), and exclaims (*Rom.* 5.3): "Fire and cross and battles with wild beasts, mutilation, mangling, wrenching of bones, the hacking of limbs, the crushing of my whole body, cruel tortures of the devil—let these come upon me, only let me reach Jesus Christ!"

13. Schoedel, *Commentary on the Letters of Ignatius*, 14.

14. Schoedel, *Commentary on the Letters of Ignatius*, 11.

15. Holmes notes that when the choice was made to take the northern road, messengers were likely sent to the Ephesian, Magnesian, and Trallian churches to inform them of Ignatius's itinerary so that they could dispatch delegations to meet him in Smyrna (*The Apostolic Fathers*, 167).

16. Holmes, *The Apostolic Fathers*, 170; Foster, "Epistles of Ignatius of Antioch," 86–89.

17. According to Vall, "*Trallians* and *Smyrnaeans* contain an antidocetic polemic (with no hint of anti-Judaizing polemic), *Magnesians* and *Philadelphians* contain an anti-Judaizing polemic (with no antidocetic polemic), and *Ephesians* contains a general warning against heteroorthodox teaching and the sexual immorality that accompanies it" (*Learning Christ*, 75).

18. In *Magnesians*, Ignatius also addresses those "still living in accordance with Judaism," which he notes undercuts the reception of grace (*Magn.* 8.1).

19. Holmes observes that though Ignatius does not turn to the Old Testament, he makes heavy use of the letters of Paul (at least 1 Corinthians and

probably Ephesians and 1 and 2 Timothy) as well as the Gospels (especially Matthew, but also Luke) (*The Apostolic Fathers*, 174). For discussion on Ignatius's use of "Paulinisms," see David M. Reis, "Following in Paul's Footsteps: *Mimēsis* and Power in Ignatius of Antioch" in *Trajectories Through the New Testament and the Apostolic Fathers*, eds Andrew F. Gregory and Christopher M. Tuckett (Oxford: Oxford University Press, 2005), 287–305.

Select Bibliography

Primary source

Holmes, Michael W. *The Apostolic Fathers: Greek Texts and English Translations*. Grand Rapids: Baker, 2007.

Secondary sources

Brent, Allen. *Ignatius of Antioch: Martyr Bishop and the Origin of the Episcopacy*. New York: Continuum/T&T Clark, 2007.
Schoedel, William A. *A Commentary on the Letters of Ignatius of Antioch*, ed. Helmut Koester. Philadelphia: Fortress, 1985.
Vall, Gregory. *Learning Christ: Ignatius of Antioch and the Mystery of Redemption*. Washington DC: Catholic University of America Press, 2013.
Zizioulas, John D. *Eucharist, Bishop, Church: The Unity of the Church in the Divine Eucharist and the Bishop During the First Three Centuries*, trans. Elizabeth Theokritoff. Brookline, MA: Holy Cross Orthodox Press, 2001.

1.3

Dialogue with Trypho[1] (c. 151–161 CE)

Justin, the Martyr (c. 100–165/6 CE)

Introduction

Like the writers of the New Testament, the primary object of the second-century Christian Apologists[2] was to demonstrate to both Jews and pagans that the divine *Logos* (the Word) was realized in the Person of the historic Jesus of Nazareth.

Justin's *Dialogue with Trypho* is one of the most significant and groundbreaking works in Christian apologetics.[3] It presents a sustained engagement with both Greek philosophy and second-century Jewish thought, delving into the relationship between the Old and New Testaments, Jesus and the Law, the role and place of Greek philosophy, and the very nature of God. As such, the *Dialogue* also preserves a contemporary witness to the final stages of the parting of the ways between Jewish religion and practices and the Christianity that emerged in the late-first and early-second centuries.

The importance of the *Dialogue*, however, is not limited to its historical value. The questions Justin engages in the *Dialogue* infuse our experiences and thought even in our day: Do Christians have to obey the ritual Law? Is philosophical inquiry and search for truth profitable, or even valid, outside Christianity? What about those among the pagans who searched for God before the coming of Christ? How many Gods do Christians have? Is the Church the new Israel?

Figure 1.3 Justin Martyr

Justin Martyr

Justin represents the generation of Christian Apologists right after the Apostles and the period of the New Testament, and, as a convert to Christianity, he was uniquely qualified for this role. Justin also represents the inquiring pagans who are looking for truth in various eclectic approaches to philosophy. For all ancient peoples, *philosophia*, the love of and enquiry into wisdom, was never separated from religion, as it is in our time. On the contrary, up to the advent of modernity and the rise of the universities, philosophy was understood to be part of what today we call *theology*. Its chief pursuit was the knowledge of what is good, true, and beautiful; of God and the moral life. Philosophical systems were judged to be good and profitable, therefore, by the moral character of those who claimed to be followers of this or that "philosophical school."

Justin was born in Flavia Neapolis (biblical Shechem or modern Nablus) in Samaria (*Dial.* 120), in Palestine, to a Greek-speaking pagan family that held Roman citizenship. Receiving a Greek philosophical education, he journeyed through a number of philosophical schools in his quest for true knowledge. He came to Christianity through the witness of an old man who walked with him along the sea shore in Ephesus and explained to him the Old Testament and the Gospel.

Justin left Asia Minor for Rome (c. 140), where he taught Christianity in the manner of a philosopher during the reign of Antoninus Pius (138–161). He moved back to Palestine in 151–155, and then returned to Rome a second time (155/56–65/66), where he continued to teach, presenting Christianity as "the only sure and beneficial philosophy" (*Dial.* 8.1). This approach to philosophy brought Justin in direct conflict with a number of the other philosophical schools active in Rome, including the Cynic philosopher Crescens who denounced him for being a Christian. Eventually, Justin and six of his companions were arrested and charged for holding Christian meetings (c. 165/66). Brought before the Prefect of Rome, Q. Junius Rusticus, to be interrogated, Justin and his companions were ordered to sacrifice to the gods but they refused, confessing to be Christian and sealing their fate. They were all condemned to be beaten with rods and beheaded. At the end, other Christians carried off their bodies in secret and buried them with honor. Because of his execution, Justin is best known by the sobriquet "Justin Martyr."[4]

Dialogue with Trypho

In the opening lines of the *Dialogue*, Justin tells us how he met Trypho early one morning as he was walking along the colonnades of the gymnasium in the city of Ephesus.[5] Trypho and his companions identified themselves as Hebrew refugees who were escaping the aftermath of the Jewish rebellion against Rome, known as the Bar Kochba revolt (132–135 CE). They were Hellenistic Jews with philosophical training who had first settled in Corinth.

Now in Ephesus, they recognized Justin's distinctive clothing as that of a philosopher and came to ask him questions, as they had done back in Corinth with the Greek philosophers of that city: "Do not the philosophers speak always about God?" asked Trypho, "Do they not constantly propose questions about [God's] unity and providence? Is this not the task of philosophy, to inquire about the Divine?" (*Dial.* 1.3). Justin and Trypho will spend the next two days asking each other questions and coming to conclusions about faith—their own and that of the other.

In telling the story of his meeting with Trypho and his friends, Justin adopted the Platonic model of a dialogue, which has a distinct format and approach to the questions it engages.[6] When we read the *Dialogue with Trypho*, we have to keep in mind that the work is not a memoir, narrating an encounter, but rather it is an *apology* presented in the form of a dialogue, that is, a defense against charges leveled against Christians by both Jews and pagans alike.

Among the most serious charges was the accusation that Christianity was a *novel religion*, barely a couple of generations old. In the ancient world, religious novelty was neither good nor desirable. Society was based on the understanding that the gods who had made the sky give rain and the earth its fruit for countless generations—the gods who had protected cities and peoples from war and disease—ought to be the ones to whom people turned in worship, not to new gods whose power and character had not been tested. Worse yet, Christians were accused both of having abandoned the philosophy (and, therefore, religion) of the Greeks and of having misinterpreted the religion of the Jews: they had dismissed the one and had supplanted the other. And so, Trypho asks of Justin: "Explain to us just what is your opinion on these matters, and what is your idea of God, and what is your philosophy" (*Dial.* 1.6).

A dialogue, a true discussion, is not a harried affair; it takes time. Justin, Trypho, and his companions were willing to spend two days thinking through things, searching for truth, engaging each other, and learning where they truly disagreed and why. At the end all we have are Justin's words, but his reasoned account of the Christian faith is much richer because of Trypho and his friends.

The simplest division of the *Dialogue* falls into two parts, the discussions held on the first day of their encounter, chapters 1–74, and those of the second day, chapters 75–142. On the other hand, a more detailed look at the dialogue reveals the sequence and structure of the arguments. The first part of the *Dialogue*, chapters 1–6, set up an introduction to Justin's life and philosophical inquiry. This section stands apart from the rest of the *Dialogue* and serves as an intellectual autobiography and is the basis for Justin's understanding of the relationship between Greek philosophy and the Christian faith. In chapters 7–8 Justin establishes the antiquity of the Christian faith as dependent on the Hebrew prophets. The prophets belong to the realm of *revealed truth* and *proof by miracle*, not simply reason. Beloved by God, the prophets were deemed more ancient than the Greek philosophers.

In chapters 9–47, Justin addresses one of the most basic Jewish objections to Christianity, namely, the need for the observance of the ritual aspects of the Mosaic Law. Responding to Trypho's assertion that Torah is binding for all and the true way of serving God, Justin argues that it is the moral decrees, rather than the ceremonial and ritual aspects of the Law, that are binding. "The law given on Horeb is already obsolete, and was intended for you Jews only," countered Justin, "whereas the law of which I speak is simply for all men...[It is] an everlasting and final law, Christ himself, and a trustworthy covenant has been given to us, after which there shall be no law, no ordinance, no commandment" (*Dial.* 11.2). The ritual laws were a temporary measure, instituted by God to curtail Israel's persistent disposition to sin and idolatry. Christians, on the other hand, have learned true righteousness from Christ who has the power to deliver them from evil.

Trypho had read the Christian Gospels (*Dial.* 10) and in the middle of this discussion (*Dial.* 45) he pondered whether those who lived according to the Law of Moses would rise in the resurrection of the dead (*Dial.* 45.2). Justin took this opening to launch into an extended section on Christology, arguing that Christians view eschatology in light of the person of Christ. This section, chapters 48–108, comprises the longest section of the *Dialogue* and argues that Christ is the Messiah, and that the unity of God is not threatened by recognizing the Son as divine. In the midst of this rich section, Justin and Trypho spar over issues of biblical interpretation, the canon of Scripture, and the problem of the crucifixion of Jesus (cf. Deut 21:23; Gal 3:13).

In chapters 109–141, Justin addresses the election of Jews and Gentiles and presents Christians as God's new chosen people and true heirs of the divine promises. In our own time, most people have heard of the Bible and many take it seriously, even if they don't identify themselves as Christians; many would even assent to the claim that Jesus is the Messiah. But during the early years of the Church almost no one outside the small Christian communities that dotted the Mediterranean basin did. For Greeks, Jews were barbarians; and the Bible was a barbarian text. For Jews, Christians were Gentiles, usurping sacred Scriptures and traditions that did not belong to them; for they were the preserve of the people of God.

Justin turned to the Bible he shared with Trypho to prove his claim. Launching into an extended exegesis of the Greek version of the Hebrew Scriptures (also called the *Septuagint*, or LXX), which is the version both Jews and Christians were using at this time, Justin gives us one of the earliest and most thorough scriptural arguments that the historic Jesus of Nazareth is the fulfillment of the Old Testament prophecies. Justin weaves a narrative that moves from the very nature of God and the Second Person to the Incarnation, the virgin birth, Jesus's divine and human natures, and concludes with the necessity for the crucifixion *and* resurrection of Christ. Convinced of the truthfulness of his argument, Justin leaves no quarter for his interlocutors: they either have to come to the same conclusion about the person of Jesus or be seen as rebels against the Christ of God. Throughout, Justin's claims are breathtaking. He insists that it is the Christians who are "the *true Israel* of the Spirit and the race of Judah" (*Dial.* 11.4) and that, as a result of their unwillingness to recognize the Messiah, Jews have lost a claim even to the Hebrew Scriptures, for they, too, "now belong to us" (*Dial.* 29.2).

Justin finds justification for this supersessionism in what he sees as the *correct* interpretation of the Old Testament. And it is here where Justin and the early Church differ from how many modern Christians (especially Protestants) read the Bible. For him, as for the rest of the early church, Christ *is* the interpretive lens for all Scripture (even for the Old Testament), the *fulcrum* on which everything turns. In our time, we have a tendency to read the Bible starting with Genesis and reading through to Revelation as if we read a straight historic narrative that leads sequentially from the beginning to the end. As for the Old Testament, though Christians recognize that it points to the Messiah, many Protestants tend to read it simply as background to the Messiah and as a setup for his coming. Such a reading of Scripture ignores the fact that once the Christ is revealed in the person of Jesus, all of the Old Testament needs to be *reinterpreted* in his light. Throughout history, Christians did not read the Old Testament only *Christotelically* (meaning that Christ is the end [Greek, *telos*] or fulfillment), but also *Christocentrically*, meaning that Jesus Christ is the center or lens by which we interpret both New and Old Testament. That is also Justin's approach.

Chapter 142 brings the *Dialogue* to the end of the second day, as Justin and Trypho exchange greetings and depart each other's company.

Can there be a relationship between philosophy and the Gospel?

As we have already seen, in his search for truth Justin followed the eclectic spirit of his time that fused together teachings from various sources and moved from teacher to teacher and from one philosophical school to another in search of the most fulfilling way of life, for philosophy leads to the knowledge of God (*Dial.* 2.1).

Justin tells us that he first sought to be instructed by a Stoic philosopher, who refused to teach him about the nature of God (*Dial.* 2.3), then by a Peripatetic (a follower of Aristotle) "who considered himself an astute teacher" (*Dial.* 2.3)—Justin left his tutelage when his new teacher was more concerned about the tuition than about Justin's welfare. Next, Justin attached himself to a Pythagorean, renowned for his emphasis on the natural sciences, but since Justin lacked the prerequisite training in music, astronomy, and geometry, they parted ways. Finally, Justin found a Platonist "whose fame was great" and whose teaching "added wings to my mind" (*Dial.* 2.4–5). Justin had arrived; or so he thought.

In telling his own story, Justin emphasizes that he was willing to listen, to be instructed, to follow, but through it all, he found an emptiness that was filled only when he met an old man at the seashore of Ephesus. During a day of solitary contemplation, a stranger approached Justin and walked along with him, engaging in philosophical conversation. This unnamed stranger took Justin through the Hebrew Scriptures and explained the Gospel to him, showing him how far superior the knowledge and experience of God gained through Christ was to any of the philosophers (*Dial.* 3.1–8.2): "My spirit was immediately set on fire, and a love for the prophets and of those who are friends of Christ, took hold of me" (*Dial.* 8.1).

Throughout the *Dialogue,* we see that when he became a Christian, Justin did not feel a need to abandon reason, philosophy, or intellection. On the contrary, Justin recognized the truth that was present in those who had searched deeply after the question of God *as* truth, and was willing to grant that "all truth is God's truth," wherever it may be found. Philosophy was not an enemy of faith. Justin claimed that true and good philosophy was a *preparatio evangelica,* a "preparation for the Gospel," and a *logos spermatikos* (Greek, "seminal word"), the seed of truth that God had sown in the hearts of all people as the formative principle of right knowledge and right living.

For Justin, educated pagans did not have to deny the insights of their philosophical backgrounds; rather, they had to recognize their fulfillment in Christ. In a more controversial statement made elsewhere with Greeks in mind, Justin insisted that those among the philosophers who sought after the good, the true, and the beautiful, who had spoken with reason and who lived their lives accordingly, manifested a connection with the divine *Reason*, the *Logos* (or *Word*), and could be considered Christians, even if they lived before Christ (*I Apol.* 46).

Some introductory treatments of the earliest Church have argued that the second-century Apologists like Justin gave too much weight to Greek philosophy and may have introduced elements into the Christian faith that are foreign to the Bible. This is what is often called the *hellenization of Christianity* (*hellenization* means "becoming Greek"). This claim has been argued at length among historians and theologians, but it has been shown to be inaccurate. We have to remember that for the first few centuries the Christians were a small minority in most of the cities in which they lived. They shared in a culture that did not accept their presuppositions and worldview.

Justin is among the group of Christian Apologists who had to provide an intellectual explanation of the relationship between Father and Son, as well as of the Incarnation of God without being able to assume their audience accepted this as a fact. They found in Greek philosophical language and thought the ability to give expression to some of the most basic Christian concepts, such as the deity of the Son and the Holy Spirit, and the relationships between the Persons of the Trinity. As ardent monotheists who tried to use language (both concepts *and* words) that is both biblical and can be understood by the long-standing tradition of philosophical thought, the Apologists ended up *developing*, *adopting*, and *adapting* the language and concepts they had inherited. Therefore, instead of thinking of this pivotal time as the period of the *hellenization* of Christianity, we ought to think of it as the beginning of the Christianization of Hellenism.

How many Gods?

Both Jews and Greeks constantly challenged the monotheistic claims of Justin and his fellow Christians because Christians worshiped not only God the Father, but also Jesus as another "God" (as well as the Holy Spirit). They claimed to be monotheist, like the Jews, but they betrayed themselves to be at least ditheists, if not tritheists. Though they are not to be judged with the light of later theological developments, the Apologists turned to the language and thought of Greek philosophy to explain the Christian faith.

Justin turned to the eclectic mixture of Aristotelianism and Platonism that is indicative of the middle-Platonism of his time (*Dial.* 127.2; 5.4). From Aristotle, Justin inherited the idea of God as the transcendent unmoved mover and from Plato the concept of God as creative *mind* (*demiourgos, nous*) that is moved by "the One," God, to create all that is. Middle Platonism affored Justin the intellectual freedom and gave him the linguistic tools to address the accusation of polytheism head on.

Since we are the inheritors of 2,000 years of Christian thinking and worship, we often forget how complex and difficult it is for us to articulate how we can confess both the unity and the plurality of God as triune. Justin was able to express the relationship between Father and Son as one of two numerically distinct (*heteros arithmō*) Persons (*Dial.* 61, 62, 128, 129) in a language that could be understood by the majority culture around him. Therefore, insisted Justin, Jesus is a *different* person than the Father. As such, *Logos* and Father are two distinct *names* of two distinct *persons*, just as the sun is different from the light (*Dial.* 128.3). This is a concept early Christian writers believed was clearly expressed in the Greek version of the Old Testament, the *Septuagint*, where the *logos* of God is not abstract but active communication. Earlier than Justin, Ignatius of Antioch (†*c.* 117) spoke of the *logos* as God made manifest.[7]

On the other hand, Justin also had to address Jewish concepts of monotheism, especially the otherness of the *Logos*. Justin turned to three sources for support. He argues that the otherness of the *Logos* is evident in the divine theophanies of the Old Testament (*Dial.* 56–59), the Old Testament passages that present God conversing with another, rational person (e.g. Gen 1:26, *Dial.* 62), and the great texts in the Wisdom literature that imply personification of Wisdom such as Proverbs 8:22ff (*Dial.* 62.4; 129).[8]

At the same time, in order to avoid the charge of ditheism or polytheism, Justin emphasizes the *unity* of the *Logos* and the Father anterior to creation. The *Logos* was begotten by the will and power of God, the Father. As a result, for Justin, the *Logos* was "begotten both *as* a beginning before all [God's] works, and as his offspring" (*Dial.* 62.4).[9] Justin's favorite title for the *Logos* is "first begotten" (*prototokos*) (cf. Col 1:15, 18; Rm 8:29, etc.).

But if the Father and the *Logos* are a unity before creation, how are they different? Justin found the solution in a subtle but very important distinction in the very language Scripture shares with philosophy. In

Greek, there is a difference between *agennētos* (ἀγέννητος), which means "unbegotten," or "uncaused," and which is applied properly to a self-caused being, and *agenētos* (ἀγένητος), which is applied only to something or someone who has *never had a beginning of any kind*, namely, the eternal nature of God. The Father is unbegotten, uncaused (*agennētos*), while the *Logos* is *begotten*, albeit eternally. Both Father and *Logos*, however, share in the *agenētos* nature of God. This distinction is the very basis of the language of the Nicene Creed that all Christians—whether Protestant, Catholic, or Orthodox—accept as the confession of our faith.

One with the Father, and yet a different Person, the *Logos* is both an "offspring," eternally with the Father (cf. Jn 1:1–3), always communing with the God and Father and, at the very same time, the mediator through whom the Father conceived and made all of creation (Jn 1:2–3). The *Logos* is the Father's messenger (ἄγγελος *angelos*, ἀπόστολος *apostolos*) and minister (ὑπηρέτης *hustēretēs*) (*Dial.* 56, 57, 60, 113, 125, 126). For Justin, then, *Logos* is subordinate to the Father both as to his person (because he was begotten at some point anterior to creation) and as to his office (as a Son).

Conclusion

It is said of the famous modern theologian and political theorist Jean Bethke Elshtain (1941–2013) that she "refused to change anything she thought or to attempt to change anything you thought simply in order to reach an agreeable reconciliation. Believing instead that falsehood is the opposite of dialogue, and that real disagreement is a hard-won victory accessible only through an honest meeting of minds, she gave it to you straight and demonstrated the refreshing value of frankness-with-charity and invective-against-twaddle."[10] And so did Justin. Following the advent of the Enlightenment, the rise of the natural sciences, and the forced separation of theology from other forms of intellectual inquiry sequestered in their appointed academic silos, many Christians have found ourselves struggling with the false dilemma between heart and mind. Justin knew all too well that to be on the journey of faith one has to be willing to engage in rigorous questioning of one's presuppositions, allowing others to disagree honestly, truthfully, honorably— and in doing so, to show us where our own claims and thinking need to be refined. Sometimes, because we lack the rootedness of a long ecclesial tradition that has withstood the test of time, Protestants can feel threatened by inquiring interlocutors.

Justin understood Philosophy to be a *preparatio evangelica*, but he also understood that Scripture is the *fons et origo* ("the fountain and origin") of the Christian faith. And though he spent substantial time and effort throughout his work to articulate a coherent understanding of the *Logos*, for Justin, the *Logos* was first and foremost a person, Jesus Christ—the historical event—the "whole Word" (*II Apol.* 8). Creation proceeded through him; redemption flowed from his Incarnation, death, and resurrection: because he is "the power of the ineffable Father, and not the mere instrument of human reason" (*II Apol.* 10).

Notes

1. Translated title of *Dialogus cum Tryphone*; references to the work (*Justin Martyr: Dialogue with Trypho* [trans. Thomas B. Falls; Washington, DC: The Catholic University of America Press, 2003]), employing in-text parenthetical citations.
2. By the terms "apologetics" and "Apologists" we describe those early Christian writers who presented an *apologia*, a defense for the truthfulness of the Christian faith and life to the world around them.
3. Justin also wrote two other works, called *First* and *Second Apology*, which address primarily pagan concerns about Christians.
4. For details of Justin's arrest, trial, and execution, see *The Acts of the Christian Martyrs*, ed. and trans. Herbert Musurillo (Oxford: Clarendon Press, 1972), 42–61. See also, Tatian, *Address to the Greeks* 19, and Eusebius *HE* 4.16.7–8.
5. Even though Justin does not identify Ephesus by name, the fourth-century historian Eusebius places the *Dialogue* in the city (Eusebius, *HE* 4.18).
6. Justin's *Dialogue with Trypho* has strong echoes of three of Plato's dialogues: the *Phaedrus*, the *Timaeus*, and (above all) *Protagoras*.
7. Ignatius of Antioch, *Epistle to the Ephesians* 19.
8. We need to note here that ancient people understood that one's words are a manifestation of one's wisdom, and, therefore, God's Wisdom, or *Sophia*, is a personification of God's Word, the *Logos*.
9. In the Greek version of the Old Testament, Proverbs 8:22 (LXX) Wisdom—and by extension the *Logos* in John 1:1—is understood to *be the* beginning (ἀρχή *archē*), not simply to "*be in* the beginning." This understanding of the beginning of the *Logos* before all created things as God's first act of creation was condemned later in the fourth century. Justin, however, did not have the benefit of the nuance of those discussions.

10. This tribute to Jean Bethke Elshtain comes from Mark LiVecce, her former student and now able scholar.

Select Bibliography

Primary source

Justin Martyr: Dialogue with Trypho, trans. Thomas B. Falls. Washington, DC: The Catholic University of America Press, 2003.

Secondary sources

Barnard, L.W. *Justin Martyr: His Life and Thought*. Cambridge: Cambridge University Press, 1967.

Chadwick, Henry. *Early Christian Thought and the Classical Tradition: Studies on Justin, Clement, and Origen*. New York: Oxford University Press, 1966.

Rajak, Tessa. "Talking at Trypho: Christian Apologetic as Anti-Judaism in Justin's 'Dialogue With Trypho the Jews'," in M. Edwards, M. Goodman and S. Price, eds., *Apologetics in the Roman Empire* (Oxford: Oxford University Press, 1999)" 511–533.

Wilken, Robert. *The Spirit of Early Christian Thought: Seeking the Face of God*. New Haven: Yale University Press, 2003.

1.4

Against the Heresies (c. 185 CE)

Irenaeus of Lyons (c. 130–202 CE[1])

Introduction: a man of peace

Irenaeus of Lyons is the last early Christian writer we know of who learned from someone who had a direct connection with the apostles.[2] As a young man, Irenaeus heard Polycarp speak in Smyrna (d. 155/156 CE) and was greatly influenced by the bishop who would become a famous martyr (3.3.4). Having traveled west to Gaul (modern-day France) by way of Rome from his eastern birthplace (probably somewhere in Asia Minor), Irenaeus became a bishop in the late 170s or early 180s in Lyons, a "Greek-speaking community in a Latin-speaking city nestled in the midst of a Celtic-speaking countryside."[3] Lyons and its neighboring city Vienne had vibrant Christian communities that had experienced brutal persecution around 177 CE, and those stories of martyrological strength traveled to Rome in the form of a letter (*Martyrs of Vienne and Lyons*) in the trusted hands of the bishop of Lyons (*H.E.* 5.4.1–2). Irenaeus wrote his expansive refutation *Against the Heresies* (*Refutation of Knowledge Falsely So Called*) at the request of an unnamed friend.[4] Intended for an intra-church audience, *Against the Heresies* is a polemic that provided information on heresies, exegetical and doctrinal instruction for how to refute them, and confidence in the hope that Christ would make all things right.

Figure 1.4 Statue of Irenaeus

It may seem odd for a polemicist to be remembered as such, but Eusebius of Caesarea remembers the bishop of Lyons as one who lived up to his name as a "man of peace" (*H.E.* 5.24.18). The church historian observes an irenic quality in Irenaeus's approach to heresies and was impressed with how the bishop of Lyons navigated the Quartodeciman Controversy, a debate over ancient traditions regarding the celebration of Easter. Irenaeus held to one faith among all churches and thus prioritized that "peace should prevail rather than uniformity of practice."[5] He thus gained a reputation as a peacemaker. What better person to call upon for an informed approach to handling pervasive heresies?

Against the Heresies aka Refutation of Knowledge Falsely So Called

Irenaeus opens *Against the Heresies* with the warrant for addressing those who claim to have the truth but who instead speak what is false (1.Pr. 1; cf. 1 Tim 1:4).[6] He has read the commentaries of disciples of the Valentinian "Gnostic" school and explains them as plainly as possible in order to show that "their statements are absurd, inconsistent, and discordant with the truth" (1.Pr. 2). While he ultimately dismisses and even parodies Gnostic perspectives, Irenaeus knows that Gnostics are a concern because they offer something like the truth wrapped in shiny packaging; they seem to answer important questions and make their adherents feel important. In not cohering to the "Rule of Truth" about the nature of the one God who created all things, the Gnostics veer away from truly knowing God and what it means to be human.

In the five books of *Against the Heresies*, Irenaeus covers a lot of ground. In Book 1, he outlines several "Gnostic" heresies, taking specific aim at the latest manifestations in the Valentinian school of thought and Marcionism, and he identifies their root in the figure of Simon Magus. Irenaeus expects that his explanations of the heresies will unmask them as obviously fraudulent. In Book 2, he shifts into his refutation project, painstakingly working through the doctrines he has just outlined to test their rationality and consistency. In Book 3, Irenaeus's refutation turns toward scriptural exegesis, here, focusing broadly on the Gospels. Book 4, the longest of the five, refutes the teachings of the Gnostics by offering an exposition on the parables in the Gospels. Book 5 rounds out the rest of Jesus's sayings and includes a foray into the letters of Paul. The extensive, exhaustive, and often repetitive nature of *Against the Heresies* amounts to an exegetical scorched earth strategy that is meant to overwhelm Irenaeus's audience with an arsenal of information to prepare his readers for confrontations with heretics.

The root of all heresies

Irenaeus viewed the heresies of his time as a many-headed hydra (1.30.14). He lumped all heresies under one term, "Gnostic," with the one root, Simon Magus, and created a genealogy of heresy over against the Apostolic tradition and succession (1.23.1–2). Labeling all divergences as "Gnostic" was an ill fit even though Irenaeus knew quite well that Marcion was very different than the Valentinian Ptolemy. Then, as now, the use of the term "Gnostic" is of "limited convenience."[7] It is easy to dismiss those first- and second-century perspectives classified as "Gnostic" as ridiculous or obviously flawed in their reading of Scripture, but these views were at the very least an attempt to make sense of evil and suffering in the world in light of the existence of a divine realm.[8] In general, the core of the Gnostic perspective is knowledge of what is unknowable for most: the nature of divinity and the origin of all that is.

Tapping into the rhythm of the *Pleroma*, the "fullness" of all that is divine, the Gnostics glean knowledge of a cadre of thirty quasi-sexual pairs of Aeons that emanate other pairs in a cascading hierarchy, having now recovered from the disaster that caused the physical world, provoking salvific insight in some humans. The uttermost pair, Abyss and Silence, emanated another masculine-feminine pair, Mind (*Nous*) and Truth (*Aletheia*), who then produced two further pairs, Word (*Logos*) and Life (*Zoe*) and Man (*Anthropos*) and Church (*Ecclesia*), and so on, until the hierarchy reached the number of fullness at thirty Aeons (1.1.1–2).[9] The pre-cosmic shaking of this divine realm occurred when one of the lowest Aeons, Wisdom (*Sophia*), desired contemplation of the ultimately inaccessible Abyss. This inappropriate desire caused her to break her pairing with "the Desired" (*Theletos*), commit an act of violence to obtain her desire, and thus suffer a twisting of her essence. In order to remedy the situation, Abyss emitted Limit (*horos*) to purify Wisdom, restore her to the divine fold, and eject Wisdom's damaging desire out of the Pleroma (1.2.4). After Wisdom's restoration, the Abyss emitted another pair, Christ and Holy Spirit, "to fix and consolidate the Pleroma, to teach the incomprehensibility of the father and the nature of spiritual 'rest'" (1.2.5). However, Christ took pity on Wisdom's expelled "shapeless, ugly Desire" (*Achamoth*), gave her substantial form, and sent the Savior who gave her the knowledge to create the material, psychic, and spiritual. Achamoth gave birth to the Demiurge who created the evil material world (1.4.1).

Minns points out that while Irenaeus mercilessly pokes at a system like Ptolemy's,[10] it was an attempt to explain the manifold sufferings and mysteries of human experience.[11] This system, however, struck Irenaeus as inherently problematic. How can something be both utterly distant from the crudeness of matter and evil and yet still be responsible for it? How can the Pleroma offer true access to knowledge of divinity and hope for humanity?

Aside from the Valentinians, Irenaeus addresses several other heresies in varying degrees of depth, such as Docetism, the Ebionites, and the Encratites, but Marcionism is his other main target. The Valentinians and Marcion rejected the creator God of the Old Testament but for differing reasons. This shallow similarity, however, was enough for Irenaeus to throw them into the same heretical heap. Marcion was particularly provocative for early Christians because he was the one who "openly dared to circumcise the scriptures and attack God more shamelessly than all others" (1.27.4). In other words, he interpreted the Scriptures in light of his divergent theological presuppositions and cut away anything that reflected the Old Testament God as having any connection to Jesus Christ (1.27.2).[12] Partially due to Marcion, the early Christian community's preserving and passing around of the Gospels and the letters of Paul soon became the project of clarifying the proper bounds of the canon.

The "Rule of Truth"

Before the established canon of Scripture and ecumenical councils, how did early Christians distinguish between what was truly their faith and what was error? Irenaeus helps us answer this question in his description of and deference to the "Rule of Truth" (*kanōn tēs alētheias*) in *Against the Heresies*.[13] For Irenaeus, this Rule refers to the fullness of what one can know about the one God who is Creator and Father of Jesus Christ who became incarnate for the sake of humanity's salvation as revealed by the Holy Spirit through the unified witness of Scripture.[14] The heretics cannot seem to agree on even one point whereas the church follows the one Lord, Jesus Christ, as the "one and only true teacher" and his teachings, unified as one body of truth (4.35.4). For Irenaeus, this is the "true Gnosis":

> [t]he teaching of the apostles, and the ancient institution of the church, spread throughout the entire world, and the distinctive mark of the body of Christ in accordance with the successions of bishops, to whom the apostles entrusted each local church, and the unfeigned preservation, coming down

to us, of the scriptures, with a complete collection allowing for neither addition nor subtraction; a reading without falsification and, in conformity with the scriptures, an interpretation that is legitimate, careful, without danger or blasphemy (4.33.8).

For Irenaeus, the God of the Old Testament who created all things must be the same God of the new covenant in Christ. The Rule of Truth, then, comprises Scriptural truth and is not complete without a full account of this covenantal narrative.[15] The Rule of Truth was vital for Irenaeus because without it one could be taken in by fancy and slippery interpretations of the Scriptures and be, before one knows it, "led captive, far from the truth" (1.3.6). What the apostles taught, we have; there is no secret teaching available to some and not to others. Key for Irenaeus's defense of the Rule of Truth as apostolic is that the Truth is accessible ("manifest in the whole world") and equally available ("present in every church to be perceived by all who wish to see the truth") (3.3.1).

Irenaeus distinguished Christianity from those perspectives that assumed and required exclusive access. Here we get a glimpse of the bishop of Lyons among the Celts: "Many barbarian peoples who believe in Christ assent to this sequence [succession], and possess salvation, written without paper or ink by the Spirit in their hearts, diligently observe the ancient tradition" (3.4.2). Irenaeus is so confident in the transformative and grounding nature of the Rule of Truth that he believes that, if the heretics came and spoke to the Celts in their language, they would refuse to listen because they know the difference between the apostolic tradition and the "lying inventions" that have deceived so many (3.4.2).[16]

Creator and creation

Central to Irenaeus's understanding of the Rule of Truth is his strict demarcation of an ontological boundary separating God as creator and everything else as creation. While the Gnostic system seems to have a multiplicity of categories between Abyss and the material world, Irenaeus discerns a problematic continuity in their system, a chain of being from the top of the Aeon hierarchy all the way down to the basest form of physicality.[17] For Irenaeus, this continuity means that the salvation offered by the Gnostics is illegitimate. One of Irenaeus's most significant contributions to orthodoxy is his understanding that the creator God is the one God, the simple God who "is unified, not composite, without diversity of members, completely similar and equal to himself, since he is all Mind, all Spirit, all Mentality, all Thought, all Word, all Hearing, all Eye, all Light, and entirely the source of every good thing ..." (2.13.3). In God there is no separation or instability; God is perfectly free and always was, is, and will be. Irenaeus contrasts the tragic creating of the Demiurge with the loving creating of the God who "freely made everything, not moved by another but on his own initiative" (2.1.1, cf. 4.20.1–2). God as not coerced and non-coercive is central to Irenaeus's understanding of God's relationship with creation. God's creation does not bind or contain God.

For Irenaeus, the Creator/creation distinction makes it possible for humans to be saved and for God to be the kind of God who saves. If creation is an accident or a tragedy that separates humans from God then what kind of hope does Christ offer in revealing divinity? Thus, Irenaeus cannot entertain the Gnostic doctrine of the three classes of human beings as material, psychic, and pneumatic (the Gnostics)[18] and draws a hard ontological line: "God makes, man is made. He who makes is always the same, while he who is made has a beginning, a middle, and an end, and ought to receive growth" (4.11.2). This definitive boundary line does not mean that God is distant from us. On the contrary, it is because God is creator that we know God to be the giver of all good things and because God is immutable, "God will never cease to benefit and enrich man, nor will man cease receiving benefit and wealth from God" (4.11.2). God is a good creator and that goodness is always in our favor, is always extended to us, and will never waver.

The mutability of humanity is intrinsic and God's plan was always that humans would become more like the image of God in Christ. Like other early Christian writers after him, Irenaeus differentiates (rather inconsistently) between the "image" and the "likeness" of God in humans. Irenaeus thought of the image—somehow both bodily and intellectual—as that with which every human is born; it is what makes us truly human. The likeness is the *telos* of humanity, that is, to be like Christ. Adam lost that likeness for all humans and only Christ could bring about a re-creation allowing humanity to regain what was lost. Thus, any division of humanity into classes with divergent access to divinity undermines God's created intent for humanity. Irenaeus's joining together of anthropology and soteriology sets him apart from other theologians of his time and charts a course for orthodox theology toward a more developed Christology and fuller understanding of God's economy.[19]

Recapitulation: God's covenantal plan

Recapitulation, which "corrects and perfects" humanity and "inaugurates and consummates a new humanity," is one of Irenaeus's most significant contributions to early Christian theology.[20] For Irenaeus, God's economy is a grand story that has a direction and an end. God's plan is therefore operative via three formative movements for humanity: the creation of Adam to the incarnation, the incarnation until the second coming of Christ, and the second coming into eternity. A good God who created a good creation underlies Irenaeus's entire theological paradigm. Humanity was created mutable and in need of development in order to attain the intended shape for all humanity: the perfection of Christ. Thus the "the economy of creation was also necessarily an economy of salvation."[21]

Christ had to be divine and human (3.19.1–3) because he "recapitulated in himself what he had formed" (4.6.2). The creator is the one who re-creates and is the only one who can. And, according to Irenaeus, whatever the Gnostics say, Scripture is clear on this point and would not testify to Christ as they do "if he were a mere man like all the others" (3.19.2). Irenaeus's insistence on Christ as human *like us* and human *for us* meant that he established important parameters for later Christology debates, especially about Mary: "she was the human being who guaranteed that our Saviour was a human being and guaranteed that his humanity was one with the humanity we all share in Adam: literally the same flesh."[22] Without Mary's flesh constituting Christ's flesh, there is no salvation (3.22.2–4; 4.19.1). Christ's incarnation therefore showed all humans our future (3.20.2). Christ had to live human, die human, and rise human so that all humans can access true human life, death, and resurrection in Christ (4.14.2; 5.36.1).[23]

Irenaeus argues that Adam represented all humanity in creation and sin; now Christ, as the new Adam, represents all humanity in re-creation and freedom. It should not be a surprise, then, given God's engagement with humanity from creation into eternity, that Irenaeus made specific claims about Christ's second coming and the rest of eternity. His unabashed belief that the kingdom of God was coming in a rigidly literal sense in which the just would rise and reign with Christ for a thousand years, a belief known as Millenarianism (Latin) or Chiliasm (Greek), caused no small amount of embarrassment to later theologians (cf. 5.28.3–4, 35.1–2).[24] Osborn advises us not to dismiss Irenaeus's eschatology as an "embarrassing postscript" at the end of *Against the Heresies* but to appreciate it as a "necessary consequence of a creator God who so surrounds all things … and loves his creature that he comes incarnate to restore its failings."[25]

Conclusion

The reception of *Against the Heresies* says a great deal about the impact of Irenaeus's theology. His emphasis on succession and on Mary would seem to recommend him solidly to Catholics, but the bishop of Lyons was important for the Reformers and later Protestants as well. Paul Parvis outlines a kind of "conversational" history of the publishing of *Against the Heresies* and demonstrates how each author claimed Irenaeus.[26] The conflicted Catholic Erasmus of Rotterdam edited the first but hasty version of the text in 1526, followed soon after with a more careful edition in 1570 by Gallasius (Nicolas des Gallars), a close associate of Calvin.[27] Less than thirty years later, the Franciscan Friar François Feuardent responded to this Protestant edition by publishing an edition in 1596. Later, in the eighteenth century Irenaeus again brokered a "conversation" between Protestant and Catholic, this time between the Anglican John Ernest Grabe in 1702 and the Benedictine René Massuet who published an edition in 1710 in response to the weaknesses he saw in Grabe's. These were followed by another edition by an Anglican, W. Wigan Harvey, in 1857. That Irenaeus and this work in particular kept an inter-denominational conversation of sorts going on even during some of the sharpest and most bitter debates between Protestants and Catholics is a testament to Irenaeus's lasting importance in Christianity. Protestants and Catholics alike have valued Irenaeus's strong creation theology, his concern for the purity of the "truth," and his appreciation for making strong connections between creation, incarnation, and eternity. *Against the Heresies* proved to be a fruitful, if difficult, meeting point for debate between Catholics and Protestants as they all sought to embrace the same tradition and battle through vital questions for faith and life.

Notes

1. Dating Irenaeus is notoriously difficult. Speculation on his date of birth varies from 98 CE to as late as 147 CE. According to Eric Osborn, a date sometime between 130 and 140 CE makes the most sense (*Irenaeus of*

Lyons [Cambridge: Cambridge University Press, 2001], 2). As for his death, Irenaeus is celebrated as a martyr but the tradition behind this is shaky at best. The earliest evidence for this tradition that the bishop of Lyons was martyred during the persecution of Septimus Severus in 202 or 203 CE is found in Jerome's commentary on Isaiah (c. 410). According to Osborn, this suggests that the tradition of Irenaeus's martyrdom may have been an interpolation from Gallic traditions about the persecutions in Lyons.

2.   Sara Parvis and Paul Foster, "Introduction," in *Irenaeus: Life, Scripture, Legacy*, eds Sara Parvis and Paul Foster (Minneapolis: Fortress, 2012), 1.

3.   Paul Parvis, "Who was Irenaeus? An Introduction to the Man and His Work" in *Irenaeus: Life, Scripture, Legacy*, 15. In *Against the Heresies*, Irenaeus says that he lives with the Celts and most of the time uses the "language of barbarians" (1.Pr. 3). There are Latin names alongside the Greek names among the martyrs but no Celtic names. However, Irenaeus indicates that there was a small Celtic contingent in the church (Osborn, *Irenaeus of Lyons*, 2; Denis Minns, *Irenaeus: An Introduction* [London: New York: T&T Clark, 2010], 3–4).

4.   Like the later *Demonstration of the Apostolic Preaching*, *Against the Heresies* was written sometime in the last two decades of the second century. It was composed in Greek but only survives in its entirety in a Latin translation from around the year 380 CE (Osborn, *Irenaeus of Lyons*, 1). The dates of the Latin translation, the earliest and only extant version of *Against the Heresies*, are also contested. Considering the popularity of the work, it is a mystery as to why the original Greek version did not survive. In any case, the Latin translation existed before 421 CE (when Augustine quotes from it). (Minns, *Irenaeus*, 6).

5.   Osborn references *AH* 1.10.1 (*Irenaeus of Lyons*, 6).

6.   The best full translation of *Against the Heresies* is still that of Alexander Roberts and James Donaldson in Volume 1 of the Ante-Nicene Fathers series from 1885: *The Apostolic Fathers, Justin Martyr, and Irenaeus*. Although Dominic J. Unger has translated the first three Books for the Ancient Christian Writers series, there is no indication of when Books 4 and 5 will be completed. Robert M. Grant offers a careful abridged translation, which is the translation used here. See Robert M. Grant, *Irenaeus of Lyons* (London; New York: Routledge, 1997).

7.   Minns, *Irenaeus*, 20.

8.   *Against the Heresies* was one of the few resources from Late Antiquity that had offered any access to Gnosticism until 1945 when a large library of fifty-two texts were discovered in Coptic translation at Nag Hammadi in Egypt. Was Irenaeus accurate in his characterizations? The scholarly debate rages on this point. According to Paul Parvis, "On the whole, Irenaeus has a reasonably clear understanding of *what* the Gnostics are

saying, though very little understanding of *why* they are saying it—and perhaps very little desire to understand" ("Who was Irenaeus?" 16).

9. Minns, *Irenaeus*, 22.

10. See *AH* 1.11.4 for Irenaeus's famous and amusing parody of the hierarchy of Melons descending from the Pre-principle "Gourd."

11. Minns, *Irenaeus*, 25.

12. Irenaeus takes Marcion to task throughout *Against the Heresies* in his modeling of reading the Old Testament (e.g. 4.15.1–2).

13. Whether he called it the Rule of Truth or, more commonly, the "Rule of Faith" from *Demonstration*, Minns notes that "rule" is a confusing translation for what Irenaeus called "a measuring rod of *truth* not only because it is used to gauge the truth, but also because to do so accurately it must itself be true" (*Irenaeus*, 11).

14. Irenaeus outlines the theological content of the Rule of Truth in various places but one of the fullest renderings can be found in *AH* 1.10.1.

15. Parvis, "Who was Irenaeus?" 20.

16. Irenaeus accused the Gnostics several times of taking advantage of those who are unable to discern their true designs of manipulation and destruction (1.Pr. I), such as Mark the Magician who uses trickery during the Eucharist to seduce women for sexual favors and their fortunes (1.13.1–7). The quasi-sexual cosmic pairs and the popularity of Gnostic groups with women has led to much discussion about whether Gnosticism was more open to women's leadership and participation than mainstream Christianity. According to Sara Parvis, it was important to Irenaeus to defend the space for women within mainstream Christianity ("Irenaeus, Women, and Tradition," in *Irenaeus: Life, Scripture, Legacy*, 159–60).

17. Minns notes that this is because the Gnostics are trying to account for the "change" in God from non-creator to creator (*Irenaeus*, 28).

18. Minns, *Irenaeus*, 24.

19. Osborn, *Irenaeus of Lyons*, 212. Along those theological anthropological and soteriological lines, Irenaeus emphasizes some kind of a material presence in the Eucharist that nourishes us and identifies us as members in the undeniably physically resurrected Christ, but how to interpret said presence has been a matter for great debate. For example, Luther, Calvin, and Grabe understood Irenaeus's earthly element as the bread, while the Benedictine René Massuet took Irenaeus to mean the body of Christ (*Irenaeus of Lyons*, 134).

20. Osborn, *Irenaeus of Lyons*, 97.

21. Minns, *Irenaeus*, 101.

22. Minns, *Irenaeus*, 104.

23. Irenaeus provides an important foundation and framework for the later discussions of atonement. His writings assume a variety of views of how

Christ accomplished redemption from the Christus Victor emphasis that dominated the early Church (4.21.1, 24.1; 5.21.1) to a foundation for an understanding of Christ's death as satisfaction (5.14.1, 17.3, 19.1).

24. Minns, *Irenaeus*, 140.
25. Osborn, *Irenaeus of Lyons*, 139–40.
26. See Paul Parvis, "Packaging Irenaeus: *Adversus haereses* and Its Editions" in *Irenaeus: Life, Scripture, Legacy*, 183–97.
27. Parvis observes: "Calvin himself—dead since 1564—would have approved. He had read Irenaeus by at least 1542, often cited him, and probably himself owned a copy of Erasmus's second edition of 1528" ("Packaging Irenaeus," 186).

Select Bibliography

Primary source

Grant, Robert. *Irenaeus of Lyons*. London; New York: Routledge, 1997.

Secondary sources

Behr, John. *Irenaeus of Lyons: Identifying Christianity*. Oxford: Oxford University Press, 2013.

Minns, Denis. *Irenaeus: An Introduction*. London: New York: T&T Clark, 2010.

Osborn, Eric. *Irenaeus of Lyons*. Cambridge: Cambridge University Press, 2001.

Parvis, Sara and Paul Foster, eds. *Irenaeus: Life, Scripture, Legacy*. Minneapolis: Fortress, 2012.

Wingren, Gustaf. *Man and the Incarnation: A Study in the Biblical Theology of Irenaeus*, trans. Ross Mackenzie. Eugene, OR: Wipf and Stock, 2004.

1.5

On First Principles[1] (c. 229–230 CE)

Origen of Alexandria (c.185–254 CE)

Figure 1.5 Origen of Alexandria

Introduction

Origen of Alexandria was a philosopher and a theologian, a teacher and a preacher, a prolific writer and a lover of the church. He was also a center of controversy during his lifetime and even more so after his death. Indeed, as the first to present a systematic and philosophical theology (*On First Principles*) and the producer of many important commentaries and countless homilies, Origen loomed large over Christian thought for centuries. Origen's fervent dedication to the interpretation and exposition of Scripture has left behind a rich legacy of pre-Nicene theology and stimulating exegesis.

While Origen is interpreting a shared and sacred text, it is best to approach his work as an intercultural exchange. He spoke a different language, wrote pre-Nicaea, and operated under some assumptions that are difficult for modern minds to even consider. His church was a persecuted church. It was a community struggling against the smooth infiltration of Gnosticism, but also enlivened by such minds as Tertullian, Irenaeus, and Justin Martyr.

Unfortunately, because of Origen's repeated post-mortem fallings from favor, precious little of his work remains. Most of what is extant comes down to us via translation. In particular, Rufinus of Aquileia (c. 340–410) has done posterity a priceless service in preserving Origen's work (*On First Principles*, the *Commentary on the Epistle to the Romans*, and many of his homilies) in translations from Greek into Latin. There is some debate over how much we are to trust Rufinus's translation. Even though consensus is likely never to be reached on the finer points, Rufinus proves himself in general to be a conscientious interpreter who communicates the sense of Origen's complex theology, even if he blunts the knife-edge of the Alexandrian's knack for nuance and brevity.

Thanks to Gregory Nazianzen (c. 329–389/390) and Basil of Caesarea's (329/330–379) diligent efforts in compiling an anthology of Origen's texts, the *Philocalia*, we have large sections of *On First Principles* preserved in the Greek. Add selections from Jerome, Justinian and others who quote Origen in a polemical context, and it means we have material to compare to Rufinus's translation. Utterly convinced of Origen's orthodoxy, Rufinus had no issue reorienting Origen's more controversial passages. He banked on Origen as a man of the church who, had he lived in the fourth century, would not have proposed unacceptable doctrines such as the pre-existence of souls, which was by Rufinus's time not a matter up for debate (see Rufinus's preface 2–3). *On First Principles* was the main battleground upon which vicious quarrels about Origen were often fought until he was condemned centuries after his death at the Second Council of Constantinople in 553 CE.

On First Principles is an early work for Origen in the sense that it was completed while he was serving as a *didaskalos*, a teacher for catechumens, before his falling out with Demetrius, the bishop of Alexandria. This break precipitated Origen's permanent relocation to Caesarea (between 216/217–231/232, the latter date being more certain).[2] One must not conflate "early" with immature, however. Origen was in his early 40s when he wrote *On First Principles* and, by this point, already a thoughtful and careful scholar who knew well what was at stake. Having witnessed his father's martyrdom while still a teenager, the threat and the grief of persecution remained with Origen throughout his life. He encouraged those facing martyrdom and even succumbed to death as a result of injuries inflicted when he was tortured on the rack three years previously. Origen knew the church needed tools to thrive and even to survive. *On First Principles* was his compendium that addressed important questions of cosmology and narrative in order to meet that need.

It is most productive to think of the four books of *On First Principles* as fundamentally structured according to a series of cycles that each return to set theological themes.[3] Origen begins with the doctrine of God and then follows a chain of topics from there—the Son, the Holy Spirit, rational beings, and the material world. Weaving a complex and connective theological narrative, he proceeds through each topic in his circle back to the doctrine of God for a total of four cycles. The core of *On First Principles* consists of two extended versions of this cycle, while the preface and concluding chapter of the last book are telescoped versions of the cycle. The Alexandrian encourages important questions and admits the limit of his knowledge throughout the work, creating a hospitable atmosphere for those keen to learn. Drawing from the New Testament and Irenaeus, Origen constructs a framework in *On First Principles* that outlines the divine plan for redemption. This redemptive narrative is grounded in an immaterial God's engagement with the material by which God justly and benevolently preserves the free will of all rational beings, all of which hinges upon the centrality of the person and work of Christ.

Cycle 1: Christ as the whole of truth

In his preface to *On First Principles*, Origen offers an outline of what he sees as his task: to expound on the Christian confidence that the human search for truth and the exercise of the good and blessed life is wrapped up in the person of Christ (*Princ.* preface 1–2). For Origen, this foundational truth is not limited to the Gospels or even to the New Testament; the truth of Christ courses through the books of Moses and the prophets as well. It is a basic truth borne from a commitment to the Holy Spirit's inspiration of Scripture. The outline Origen gives in his preface of the doctrines of the church begins with the Father, the Son, and the Holy Spirit and God's revelation to humanity. He then speaks briefly of the difficult journey of the rational soul, and of the creation and end of the material world. Origen's preface is brief, but it sets the tone for the rest of *On First Principles* and clearly demarcates where—or more appropriately, on whom—the Alexandrian places the entry point to revelation. For Origen, anything that can be or ever will be known about God hinges on the Incarnation of the Son of God.

Cycle 2: The immaterial and the material

The first extended cyclical iteration extends from the beginning of book 1 to book 2, chapter 3. It is clear that, for Origen, any consideration of theology begins with the nature of God. Thus he begins the cycle again with the Father, the Son, and the Holy Spirit. One theme that runs throughout Origen's treatment of the Trinity is that God is immaterial and is, as such, inherently other than the material.[4] While Scripture clearly describes God in material terms, Origen explains that the way God "consumes" is not the way a fire consumes (*Princ.* 1.1.2) and, importantly, when God begets it is not in the same way as humans beget (*Princ.* 1.2.4). In short, the created order lacks the capacity to comprehend or measure God (*Princ.* 1.1.5). Led by the thought of his time, Origen insisted that God, as immaterial, is simple intellectual existence, admitting no addition, delay in operation, limit, composition, intermixture, or diversity (*Princ.* 1.1.6). Origen locates these descriptors as coinciding with the scriptural use of the term "invisible" (Col 1:15; John 1:18), which leads him to consider the relationship between the Father and the Son as one of "knowing" and not of "seeing." Using the language of Scripture, Origen links the Father and Son at the same level of likeness: the Son is not an emanation but the "visible image of the invisible God" and the "express image of his substance" (*Princ.* 1.2.6; 1.2.8). The way one "sees" God is not the way humans see because "to see and be seen is the property of bodies" (*Princ.* 1.1.8). In short, Christ as the image of the invisible God makes God understood and known to humanity.

In Origen's section on Christ we find him wrestling with Christ's divine nature as Word and Wisdom. The triumph of Origen's Christology is his concept of eternal generation, which "allows the Father to be the cause of the Son's begetting and the Spirit's procession, but in such a way that, in distinction from all other created beings, they share in the Father's eternal and incorporeal existence."[5] For Origen, the Son of God as Wisdom does not minimize him to an attribute or indicate a lack of substantial existence. On the contrary, Origen comments on the impossibility that God could exist for one moment without begetting this hypostatic (substantial) wisdom (*Princ.* 1.2.2–3). Origen, then, decouples generation from temporal succession: there was never a time when the Wisdom of God was not (*Princ.* 1.2.9). It is this Wisdom who assumed human nature so as to fulfill the divine plan (as only the Word and Wisdom of God could do, see *Princ.* 1.2.4) to bring restoration to the entire created order. Origen's Christology provides the theoretical basis for Nicene orthodoxy, and his insistence on the two distinct natures of Christ in unity anticipates Chalcedon.[6]

While all rational beings (*logikoi*) are partakers of the word of God (*logos theou*), only the saints partake of the Holy Spirit (*Princ.* 1.3.5–8). Origen is careful not to ascribe to the Holy Spirit a higher honor than to the Father or the Son, but explains how God works everything in unity and distinction for the benefit of humanity: the Father gives life, the participation in Christ as reason (*logos*) makes all rational, and the Holy Spirit, through Christ, bestows a grace put into operation by the Father that allows for those who do not share the essence of God to participate in God's holiness (*Princ.* 1.3.7–8). This is often referred to as the "economy of salvation," the way God manages history for the salvation of the world. The theme that arises in this first extended cycle on the Trinity is that Origen conceives of God as one completely other, but also completely committed to restoring the created order and to aiding the saints in their progress toward that renewal. Even though Origen does not have the benefit of the language to describe God that is familiar to us through the Creeds of the Church (because that language was developed and defined in the fourth century), he sets the intellectual and theological foundations for the Creeds.

Origen conceives of the progress of the saint back to God as one that is destined for an ever-increasing loving desire and ability to hold fast to God (*Princ.* 1.3.8). For Origen, falling away from God is tragic, whether it is the fall of all pre-existent rational souls or the gradual fall of those who do not cling to God. In this section of *On First Principles*, Origen raises one of his most speculative and controversial themes. His starting points arise from Scripture but his conclusions were regarded as exceeding the parameters of Scripture. The first comes from an encounter Jesus and his disciples had with a man who was born blind. The disciples asked Jesus, "Rabbi, who sinned, this man or his parents, that he was born blind?" (Jn 9.2). What modern audiences usually miss in the disciple's question is that in much of antiquity, the question of when a soul begins to exist was not a closed one. For many, both Jews and Greeks, the souls of human beings preexisted the moment of conception and were united with the physical body in the womb of the mother. Furthermore, both the disciples and everyone else around them—Jew or gentile—accepted without question that every deformity or congenital illness was a sign of divine disfavor due to sin. For Origen, the fact that a baby was born infirm, blind in this case, also indicates the presence of sin in the pre-existent soul. Origen's second starting point comes from Paul's declaration that, at the end, God will be "all in all" (1 Cor. 15:28). What does that mean? If God is "all in all," is there a place (e.g., hell) or a condition (e.g., eternal separation from God) that is not included in that statement? And if so, how, then, is God truly to be "all in all," "everything in everything"?

In order for us to understand how Origen sees these two passages as bringing together the beginning and the end of time, we have to keep in mind two foundational aspects of his thought. First, unlike the Gnostics who thrived during this time, Origen insisted that the material world is not evil. Origen conjectured that the fall into bodies is a gracious move on God's part to allow humanity the capacity for the process of purification that will ultimately bring about restoration. Second, Origen's entire theological vision is built upon divine providence working *with* the free will of all rational beings for the sake of their progress. For Origen it is vital that no rational beings, whether angels, demons, opposing powers, or humans, are coerced *either* to fall *or* to ascend. Rather, the nature of rational beings is to be rational and so to decide for themselves. In this way, God is also safeguarded against the charge of being unjust and the architect of evil (*Princ.* 1.5.3). If necessity binds rational beings to a given station then God's goodness and justice are replaced by a capricious favoritism (*Princ.* 1.7.4; 1.8.2). Origen is committed to an always free will, a non-coercive God, and a heart alive to what may at first seem to be undeserved suffering (such as the hardships faced by the man born blind). Though Origen views suffering as always deserved, it is both punishment and education at once. He proposes the pre-existence of souls and the ascent and descent of rational beings as indicative of the return movement of the cosmos toward God being "all in all" (*Princ.* 1.8.1–4; 2.1.2).

In God, beginning and end converge such that when he considers the end of all things, he considers also the beginning of all things; and when he considers the beginning of all things, he considers also the end of all things (*Princ.* 1.6.2; 2.1.1–3). Origen clearly notes that, within this cosmology, humans can descend to be demons or ascend to be angels and, similarly, demons can ascend to become human—the transformative possibilities of descent and ascent pertain to every rational being since all share beginning and end.[7] Origen is nothing if not thoroughly logical, which got him into a good bit of trouble.

Origen's speculation about the pre-existence of souls and his proposal that rational beings were united to physical bodies for the purposes of purification and restoration were rejected by most Christian traditions even during Origen's own time. On the other hand, the principle of the freedom of the will as definitive of rational beings continues to be foundational for almost all Christian traditions, whether Eastern Orthodox, Roman Catholic, or Protestant. In the aftermath of the Protestant Reformation, however, the relationship between human will and the will of God will be debated greatly, especially among the Reformed and Arminian traditions.

Cycle 3: The just and good in relation to the material world

With book 2, chapter 4 we find Origen embarking on his third iteration of the cyclical pattern of *On First Principles*. This second extended cycle ends just before the last chapter of the final book (*Princ.* 4.4). In *Princ.* 2.4.1 Origen continues his construction of a framework for the Christian faith by returning to the Trinity once again, this time to address the error of those who would read Scripture and rebuff the idea that the God of the Old and New Testaments is the same (*Princ.* 2.4.1–4; 2.7.1–3). Marcion (and others) could not conceive of the same God as completely just and completely good. Origen draws upon arguments from the second cycle about God's immaterial and non-coercive nature to reorient the mistaken definitions of what is "just" and "good." For Origen, as two aspects of God's character, goodness and justice are not mutually exclusive or in opposition (*Princ.* 2.5.1–4). Rather, both are in full effect in the mystery of the Incarnation. Origen confesses his befuddlement and marvels at how Jesus Christ can seem so human and at other times so divine (*Princ.* 2.6.2). He contributes richly to Christology through his exploration of what it means for Jesus to have a human soul; that the Son of God assumes a human soul along with human flesh is necessary for the salvation of the cosmos (*Princ.* 2.6.3).

The theme of God's justice and goodness emerges in this third cycle with regard to the relationship between God and the material world. In this context, Origen expounds at length on the precious commodity of free will, which is a key theme not only in *On First Principles* but also throughout his work. This chapter is by far the lengthiest and, fortunately, it is largely preserved in the *Philocalia*. Origen's easy confidence is evident here as he delivers to his reader God's perspective. God views free will within a cosmological frame. Since God reckons not only our temporal existence but also our souls, in the context of the endless world, there is room for instruction and prescribed remedies to work (*Princ.* 3.1.13). There are two images that dominate Origen's view of God's relationship with the cosmos: that of the material world as a classroom (with Christ as teacher, see *Princ.* 2.11.4–7) designed to aid rational souls in their journey back to God, and that of God as a physician of souls who will "do no harm," but instead will do what is needed to restore health, even if it causes suffering in the short term (*Princ.* 2.10.6; 3.1.11,13). This second image of the physician renders judgment as primarily a means of purgation and eventual restoration.[8]

Origen carefully wades through passages in Scripture that seem to imply God shows favoritism or worse. He reconstructs a perspective of God's providence that draws upon his earlier work on God as just and good. For instance, Origen takes on the account of Jacob and Esau (*Princ.* 2.9.7) and the hardening of Pharaoh's heart (*Princ.* 3.1.7–10) to illustrate the thoroughgoing commitment of God to preserve free will, not simply as a matter of principle but also for the sake of the redemptive instruction of every soul. The soul is the principle of movement and therefore is in a constant tug of war between good and evil (*Princ.* 3.3.5; 3.4.3).

In this second extended cycle, Origen again addresses the creation of the material world. He links back to his discussion of the limits of human knowledge (*Princ.* 3.5.2), the unchangeable nature of God (*Princ.* 3.5.3), and the cosmological effect of free will (*Princ.* 3.5.4–5). He also draws upon several passages from across the scope of Scripture to bring more depth to his discussion of the material world and its end (*Princ.* 3.6.1ff). Because the beginning and end are intimately related for Origen, he poses the important question of what was lost in the fall and what will be regained with the consummation of the world. He affirms the truth of Plato's tenet that "the highest good is to become as far as possible like God" (*Theaet.*

176B), arguing that this wisdom was not original to Plato but actually comes from Moses (*Princ.* 3.6.1). Humans were created in the image and likeness of God, but it was the likeness (perfection of God) that was lost in the beginning and will be regained in the end. Some, especially among more recent Protestant traditions, see in this cosmic recapitulation and consummation a "universal salvation" that does not account fully for the scriptural warnings of eternal divine punishment for those who refuse God's grace. Nonetheless, others, including Orthodox, Catholic, and Protestant theologians, find in Origen's eschatology a reassurance that the end spells a transformation into incorruptibility and unity with Christ (*Princ.* 3.6.4).

This third cycle harkens back to the brief first cycle where Origen hints toward a fuller discussion of the interpretation of Scripture. Again, we have the benefit of a large section preserved in Greek in the *Philocalia*. Origen begins with an apology that measures the truth of Scripture according to the incomparable spread of Christian teaching, even though it has cost many their possessions and their lives (*Princ.* 4.1.1–2). We see the thrust of Origen's theology—that Christ is the hinge upon which the whole cosmos hangs—repeated in the context of Scripture's univocal affirmation that "God has really become man and delivered to men the doctrines of salvation" (*Princ.* 4.1.2). The salient point for Origen is that, while there are many sacred books, these ones are the result of the inspiration of the Holy Spirit, who has a plan of revelation and succession that requires an interpretation guided by the revealed one himself—Christ (*Princ.* 4.2.2).

In his approach to Scripture, Origen recognizes a three-fold (*somatic, psychic, pneumatic*) interpretation specifically given by God for the salvation of humanity and fitted to each Christian's need for edification (*Princ.* 4.2.4). While some have suggested mistakenly that Origen dismissed the "plain" or "literal" reading of Scripture,[9] the fact is that Origen always begins with the literal words of Scripture and argues that, even in their simplest form, they are efficacious and carry the meaning of salvation. He refers to this level as the *somatic* sense (from *soma*, the Greek word for "body") and, in doing so, underscores the importance of materiality for Christianity. Origen, however, recognizes that, as Paul prayed for the Ephesians (1:8), there are higher levels of understanding: through the *psychic* sense (from *psyche*, the Greek word for "soul") of Scripture one progresses by continuous education and progress in piety; and through the *pneumatic* sense (from *pneuma*, the Greek word for "spirit") one allows the Holy Spirit to reveal divine truth not readily apparent. Origen's approach to Scripture is radical, especially considering how the purveyors of Gnosticism at the time snubbed any approach to truth that did not treat materiality as evil.

Cycle 4: There and back again: Christ is central

In the fourth and final brief cycle, Origen returns to the centrality of the person of Christ. This time, Origen expands upon the relationship between the persons of the Trinity, specifically, the Son to the Father. Because of his reading of Proverbs 8:22, Origen has to deal with the Son as "created," a consideration that caused no small amount of controversy, especially given the development of Arianism which, two generations after Origen's death, taught that the Son is a creature, though the first and highest. Origen's use of "created" (*ktisma*), however, is best understood in connection with his doctrine of the Son's eternal generation. This concept sets the Son apart from the material world as eternally God and demonstrates that Origen meant something very different from what his later accusers thought him to mean. While Arians would come to say that "there was a time when he (the Son) was not," Origen maintains his own aphorism: there can never be a time when the Son was not (*Princ.* 4.4.1). He transitions smoothly from an economic description of the Trinity to discuss the shape and scope of Christ's presence with humanity and inquires into the union of divinity and humanity in Christ (*Princ.* 4.4.2–4). He ends by considering human participation in the image and likeness of God (*Princ.* 4.4.9–10).

Conclusion

As a pastor of a diverse community and a scholar, Origen was the first to attempt a synthesis of Christian teaching that would be foundational for all Christian thought to follow. Origen embraced a theological perspective that was expansive and all encompassing. He was not uncomfortable with persistent paradoxes or tensions if he was faced with mystery. For Origen, the Christian narrative that hinges upon Christ addresses all of reality. Origen was under no illusion that there were easy answers to many of the questions raised by students or the problems set forth by those deemed heretics, but he was determined that this not halt vigorous inquiry. *On First*

Principles has endured not merely because of the author's prominence or as a locus of controversy, but mostly because those questions and problems have continued to echo through the caverns of Christian thought.

Notes

1. Translated from *De principiis, Peri Archon*; all references to this work (Origen, *On First Principles* [trans. G.W. Butterworth. Torchbook; ed. Henri de Lubac; Gloucester, MA: Peter Smith, 1973]) shall be noted by employing in-text parenthetical citations.
2. Ronald E. Heine, *Origen: Scholarship in the Service of the Church* (Oxford: Oxford University Press, 2010), 83. Recent scholarship often utilizes the work on Origen's chronology done by Pierre Nautin, *Origène: Sa vie et son œuvre* (Paris: Beauchesne, 1977).
3. See Joseph W. Trigg, *Origen* (New York: Routledge, 1998), 22, for the scholarly consensus and an extended description of this structure.
4. Heine notes that while Origen does not present a complete doctrine of the three Persons, he speaks about the unity and immateriality of the Godhead along with the separate functions of the three persons, and there are suggestions that he thought about it on the model of the economic Trinity (*Scholarship*, 137).
5. Trigg, *Origen*, 24. See *Princ.* 1.2.2.
6. Athanasius cites *Princ.* 4.4.1 in *On the Decrees of the Synod of Nicaea* 27.1–2.
7. Justinian preserves this in the Greek and Jerome also paraphrases it. See also *Princ.* 1.7.5 and 3.6.5.
8. The Alexandrian speculated on a concept that seemed too close to the transmigration (or reincarnation) of souls for those who would make Origen's doctrines a battleground in later centuries (*Princ.* 2.10.8).
9. What Origen means by this is a type of "literal" or "plain" reading which minimizes the law and prophets by denying the Christological frame of reference (as he accuses the Jews of doing), or results in anthropomorphizing God or embracing absurdity, or one that undercuts the moral underpinning of the rest of the witness of Scripture (see *Princ.* 3.2). In other words, yes, take the words "plainly," but they must always be read in the larger context of the full canon of Scripture. Such a canonical approach demands a Christological reading while also deeming certain "literal" readings theologically inappropriate (e.g., OT references to God require him to have physical lips to speak, a nose to smell, and feet to walk) or morally problematic because one statement or story is isolated and pitted against the larger testimony of scripture.

Select Bibliography

Primary source

Origen. *On First Principles*. Translated by G.W. Butterworth. Torchbook ed., with an introduction by Henri de Lubac. Gloucester, MA: Peter Smith, 1966; reprint 1973.

Secondary sources

Crouzel, Henri. *Origen: The Life and Thought of the First Great Theologian*. Translated by A.S. Worrall. San Francisco, HarperCollins, 1989.

Heine, Ronald E. *Origen: Scholarship in the Service of the Church*. Oxford: Oxford University Press, 2010.

McGuckin, John Anthony. *The Westminster Handbook to Origen*. Louisville: Westminster John Knox, 2004.

Scott, Mark S.M. *Journey Back to God: Origen on the Problem of Evil*. New York: Oxford University Press, 2012.

Trigg, Joseph W. *Origen*. New York: Routledge, 1998.

1.6

Against Praxeas[1] (c. 213 CE)

Tertullian (c. 160–c. 220/5 CE)

Figure 1.6 Tertullian

Introduction

Tertullian is often called the father of Latin theology. He was the first Latin theologian of the early church and his lasting influence on Western Christianity is second only to St. Augustine (354–430 CE). Tertullian wrote the treatise *Adversus Praxean*, or *Against Praxeas*, to counter the teachings of

Praxeas (probably a pseudonym of a Roman figure) who advocated a monarchian understanding of God, denying the deity of the Son and of the Holy Spirit. *Against Praxeas* remains to this day a key text for the Christian understanding of who God is, for it is in this treatise that we first encounter terms like "sacrament," "Trinity," "person," "substance," and "satisfaction" in their Christian, theological sense.

Tertullian

Septimius Tertullianus grew up a pagan in Roman Carthage in the latter half of the second century CE and received the standard Greek and Latin education of his time. He studied rhetoric, philosophy, and medicine before converting to Christianity in his thirties. He almost never spoke of his early life, and the portrait that we have comes from Eusebius and Jerome in the late fourth century. According to Jerome, Tertullian was an ordained presbyter in the church at Carthage (*De vir. ill.* 53), while Eusebius mentions that his father was a proconsular centurion, and identified Tertullian with the Roman jurist Tertullianus (H.E. 2.2.4). These assumptions have informed much of the discussion of Tertullian as a person and of the nature of his work, especially during the first three-quarters of the twentieth century. As a result, many introductory treatments of historical theology present Tertullian as a legalist (presumably a remnant of his training in jurisprudence) and an uncompromising puritan whose rigorism forced him to break with the Catholic Church at the end of the second century and find a more passionate expression in the charismatic but schismatic movement known as Montanism (or, "the New Prophecy"). Tertullian's affiliation with Montanism, in turn, leads some to interpret his work and thought after c. 206 CE as a movement further into rigorism and separatism.

Most of the assumptions have been challenged successfully, including the idea that his father was a centurion, that Tertullian was a priest, and that he should be identified with the Roman jurist. Beginning with Timothy D. Barnes's critical study in 1971, a more complex narrative of Tertullian's life has emerged, and a more accurate chronology of his works has shed much needed light on the development of his thought. At the end, a different portrait emerges, crucial in understanding Tertullian's arguments and the positions for which he advocated so forcefully.[2]

Tertullian belonged to the educated elite of second-century Carthage and wrote in both Latin and Greek. Of Tertullian's writings, thirty-one treatises are accepted as genuine, while a number have not survived. As one considers the totality of his writing career, it becomes evident that through the years Tertullian's thinking about issues deepened and even changed. Following the conventions of his time, Tertullian wrote from a rhetorical perspective, which means that, unlike many of his contemporary Christian writers, he did not write treatises as much as he wrote prescriptions and advocacy papers. Conscious of his audience and aiming to win an argument, Tertullian wrote passionately and often used stark language that sometimes seems trenchant, often sarcastic, with no room for tepidity. Before we can engage *Against Praxeas*, three principles that underlie Tertullian's theology must be noted.

Preliminary principles

Tertullian's rhetorical flourish and witty aphorisms make his writing quite memorable and eminently quotable. Perhaps one of his most often (mis) quoted aphorisms comes from his treatise *On the Prescription of Heretics* (7.9): "What indeed has Athens to do with Jerusalem? What concord is there between the Academy and the Church?" Some have interpreted this statement to be a rejection of "reason" as antithetical to "faith." This is not the case at all. Tertullian's point is *not* that Christians ought not study philosophy, or that Christian faith is indifferent—worse yet, contrary—to reason. Tertullian did not simply abandon "Athens" for "Jerusalem." Nor did he equate Athens with "reason" and Jerusalem with "faith." His was not an anti-rationalist argument for faith but quite the opposite, a radically rationalist point of view that rejects falsehood of any kind.

For Tertullian, the question is not one of reason versus faith as sources of authority but rather a question of two different sorts of reason. "One is the reason of 'Athens'; the other the reason of 'Jerusalem.' One could be called 'dialectic reason' the other would then be 'historical reason.'"[3] "Athens" begins with the theoretically possible, the philosophically necessary, and argues that reason ought to conform to that. "Jerusalem," on the other hand, begins with what has actually occurred, as revealed in Scripture, and argues that reason ought to conform to the historical event.

Take the resurrection from the dead for example: "Athens" begins with the theoretical impossibility of resurrection: the dead do not rise to life. Therefore, it stands to reason that Jesus did not rise from the dead, and every narrative that claims he did needs to be rejected as impossible. "Jerusalem," on the other hand, begins with the historical event that Jesus did rise from the dead as described in Scripture and reasons for the resurrection of the dead (cf. 1 Cor. 15:32). Tertullian uses the same language of paradox in *On the Flesh of Christ* (5.4) when he presents the story of Jesus: "The Son of God was born: there is no shame, because it is shameful. And the Son of God died: this is believable because it is unfitting. And, having been buried, he rose again: it is certain because it is impossible."[4] Tertullian's argument is *not*, as has often been misquoted, "I believe because it is absurd" (*credo quia absurdum est*) but rather, "It is believable, because it is foolish" (*credible est, quia ineptum est*). Tertullian stands in a long tradition of antiquity that argues some stories are so improbable that it is reasonable to believe them (Aristotle, *Rhetoric* 2.23.22). The fact is that, in spite of how improbable a statement, a doctrine, or a notion may seem to contemporary philosophical presuppositions, "reason" has to conform to the historical event, not the other way around. The starting point is always the narrative of Scripture, not the categories humans can conceive *a priori* as true or false. This was one of Tertullian's first principles, and it is key in considering his argument against Praxeas and his description of the Trinity. This priority of God's self-revelation in Scripture, defended by Tertullian, remains one of the foundations of the Reformation and the starting points of Protestant theology.

A second principle is the authority and simplicity of Scripture. Like most other early Christian writers, Tertullian used Scripture in almost every chapter of every work.[5] As Geoffrey Dunn points out, "Tertullian's stated hermeneutic was his belief in the simplicity of Scripture. It could interpret itself, he claimed at one point, and had a method of its own, such that all apparent inconsistency could be explained (*Against Praxeas* 18.2). Indeed, the principle he put forward was that one text of Scripture must always be interpreted in the light of a greater number of texts (*Against Praxeas* 20.2), and that later texts must agree with earlier ones (*Against Praxeas* 20.3)."[6]

For Tertullian, all of Scripture spoke about Christ, and the Incarnation interpreted all of Scripture. Jesus's life and teachings were the definitive interpretive lens of both Old and New Testaments. Thus, Tertullian at times argued for an allegorical (or typological, or spiritual) interpretation of a scriptural passage, whereas at other times he advanced a more literal interpretation.

The third principle is the place of the received teaching of the Church, the *Rule of Faith* (*regula fidei*), a creedal statement of the Church's traditional teaching regarding who God is and how God has acted in history. Tertullian's most eloquent use of the Rule is found in *Against Praxeas* 2.2. Like Paul who charged Timothy to pass the faith on to reliable people who, in turn, would

TVllius Ausoniæ columénque, decúsque, Superbæ
    Tertulliano est Africa.
Illi verborum fœlicia flumina manant,
    Et melle sermo purior.
Hic gravis, & rerum divino pondere major,
    Minor licet facundia.
Hic Christum sonat, ille Deos, & nomina cassa
    Divinitatis indiga.
Res potior verbis, præcellunt sacra profanis,
    Quantum favillis sidera.
Ergo Sidonio cedat, licet aureus ore,
    Tertulliano Tullius,
Tullius ille siet Romanis, dummodò nobis
    Legatur hic ter Tullius.

Figure 1.7 Codex of Tertullian's Apologetics

be able to teach others what he had received himself (2 Tim 2:2), Tertullian stressed that the teachings of the Church were originally laid down by Christ, who delivered them to the apostles who, in turn, handed them over to the rest of the churches (*Apology* 19, 47; *Against Marcion*, V.3.1).[7] This was also one of the key criteria by which the earliest Christians evaluated which books were to be included in the canon of Scriptures as well as the truthfulness of the teaching of those who passed the faith on to subsequent generations.

Since the Reformation, the relationship between Scripture and Tradition has been much debated. For the most part, Protestants share Tertullian's confidence in the authority and simplicity of Scripture but (especially since the mid-nineteenth century) tend to shy away from emphasizing tradition. Much of this reaction stems from deeply rooted reactions to the traditionalism that eighteenth- and nineteenth-century Protestants saw in the Roman Catholic Church and which they feared replaced the centrality of Scripture. Jaroslav Pelikan has summarized well the relationship between traditionalism and the faith of the Church as presented in the Rule by noting that, "Tradition is the living faith of dead people... [while] traditionalism is the dead faith of living people who fear that if anything changes, the whole enterprise will crumble." It is traditionalism, Pelikan added, "that gives tradition such a bad name."[8] Indeed, the *Rule of Faith* Tertullian speaks about is the living faith of the diachronic Church (see also, *On the Prescription of Heretics* 19–21; 37).

How many Gods? The case *Against Praxeas*

In second-century Rome, a movement had arisen among Christian communities who insisted that in order to understand who God is and how the Father relates to Christ and the Holy Spirit, one must hold firm to the particular understanding of the oneness of God that comes from the Old Testament and the Jewish tradition. Yet, what set Christians apart from the beginning was the veneration they gave to Christ in their language of worship. This was a language and an idiom they inherited from the New Testament exaltation of Christ as the one in whom "dwells the fullness of the Godhead" (Col. 2:9), and who is "the reflection of God's glory and the exact imprint of God's very being" (Heb. 1:3).

Reacting against the prevailing religious ideas of their time that accepted the plurality of gods, some Christians insisted that the only way to reconcile what they saw as an apparent conflict between a long-received tradition of monotheism and the veneration of Christ as God was to declare the monarchy (from the Greek *monos*, meaning 'single', and *arche*, 'rule') of the one, single, God who creates all things and who rules over all. The term "Monarchians," by which these Christians came to be known, encompasses a number of distinct understandings of how the singleness of God ought to be understood. Praxeas represented the modalist or *patripassian* (meaning, 'the Father suffers') circle who blurred any distinction between Father, Son, and Spirit. For the modalists, the one God appeared, spoke, and revealed himself in three different modes (or guises): sometimes as "Father," other times as "Son," and yet other times as "Holy Spirit." For the Monarchians, it was the Father himself who suffered and died on the cross (*Against Praxeas* 1.1, 5).

Tertullian develops his argument against Praxeas and the Monarchians along five lines (chapters 1–4, 5–14, 15–18, 19–28, and 29–31), all of which are informed by the core principles that undergird the entirety of his thought: that the *Rule of Faith* guides all biblical interpretation, including the relationship between philosophical reason and the understanding that is shaped by the witness of Scripture.

The first line of argumentation, *Against Praxeas* 1–4, begins with an introductory section in which Tertullian describes the circumstances under which the ideas represented by Praxeas were imported to Rome from Asia Minor. Tertullian underscores the dangers of Monarchianism in no uncertain terms: in one swift movement, because he misinterprets Scripture and relies exclusively on philosophical presuppositions about who God is, Praxeas has managed "two pieces of the devil's business: he drove out prophecy and introduced heresy: he put to flight the Paraclete (the Holy Spirit) and crucified the Father" (*Against Praxeas* 1.5). Tertullian then sets to the task of presenting the faith in the triune God as the faith of the Church.

The second chapter of *Against Praxeas* (2.1–5) is one of the most packed and theologically beautiful articulations of the faith of the earliest Church. Here, Tertullian counters the Monarchians by claiming that both Scripture and the *Rule of Faith* testify that God's self-revelation in creation, in the history of Israel, and in the life, death, and resurrection of Christ has always been as Father, Son, and Spirit. To describe this ordered self-revelation of God Tertullian uses the Greek word *oikonomia* (economy, or management of the affairs of the household) (*Against Praxeas* 2.1).[9] It is within this economy that God is self-identified distinctly as Father, Son, and Spirit, as trinity (*trinitas*),[10] yet one God: "Three, however not in quality (*status*) but in degree (*gradus*), not in substance (*substantia*), but in form (*forma*), not in power (*potestas*) but in its aspect (*species*; i.e., its manifestation), yet of one substance and one quality and one power" (*Against Praxeas* 2.4). The oneness of God is on the level of substance, quality, and power, whereas the distinctions are on the level of degree, form, and aspect because the economy of God is a trinity.[11]

The second line of argumentation encompasses chapters 5–14, and it is a detailed engagement with the scriptural account of the relationship between Father and Son, who is also the Word and the Wisdom of God. Tertullian addresses the objections that came from either side of the monarchian camp. Standing opposed to the modalists, some of the other monarchian groups— who followed Valentinus—argued that the Father and Son are indeed two separate beings, the Father having brought forth a Son either by direct generation or by *probole*, a "projection" of the divine self at some moment in time (*Against Praxeas* 8.1–2). The camp represented by Praxeas rejected such a theory of generation because it resulted in two gods—or three, if one accounts for the Holy Spirit. Tertullian turned to Scripture to show that both sides are wrong. Against the Valentinians Tertullian asserts that since in Scripture the Son is identified as the *Logos* (Word), and Wisdom of God (Jn 1:1, 2; Prov. 8:22ff), and since *logos* in the Greek designates "reason" as well as "discourse," there can never be a time when God, who is rational—indeed, Reason itself—would be without God's reason, that is, God's *Logos* (*Against Praxeas* 5.2–5). The Father was never alone, without the Son (*Against Praxeas* 5.7). Beginning with Genesis 1:1 and working his way through the Psalms, the Proverbs, and the Prophets, Tertullian arrives at the many instances where the New Testament speaks of the Son as God (e.g., Jn 1:1,2; Phil 2:6), including Jesus's own statements that "I am in the Father" (Jn 14:11) and "I and the Father are one" (Jn 10:30), to find language appropriate to describe the plurality in the Godhead. He uses the word person (*persona*) to describe how Father and Son and Spirit were distinct but not separate (*Against Praxeas* 7.9; 9.1; 11.7, 10).[12] At times, Tertullian's analogies fall short of the concepts and language later Christian theology will use to describe the relationship of equality among the divine Persons of the Trinity because he tends to emphasize the priority of the Father, even stating that the Father is the whole substance of who God is, whereas the Son is a derived and inferior portion of the whole (*Against Praxeas* 9.2).

As a third argument against Praxeas's modalism (chapters 15–18), Tertullian focuses on the evangelical declaration that "No one has ever seen God" (Jn 1:18) and Paul's statement that God has neither been seen "nor can he be seen" (1 Tim 6:16). If it is true, as the Scriptures attest, that God cannot be seen, asks Tertullian, who was the Word who was made flesh (Jn 1:14) (*Against Praxeas* 15.4)? Who was the one whom John and the disciples touched and heard and handled (1 Jn 1.1ff) (*Against Praxeas* 15.5)? Who walked with Adam in the garden (Gen 3:8–9) and whom did the Patriarchs see (Gen 18 *et pass.*)? Tertullian argues that the very statements of Jesus in which he identifies the Father as other than himself (e.g., Jn 10:30), and even Peter's declaration that Jesus is "the Son of God" (Mt 14:33; Jn 1:49), show that the Father is different from the Son. The one who cannot be seen is the Father, while the one who is seen throughout history is the Son (*Against Praxeas* 15). In fact, the Father has always worked through the agency of the Son through whom he made everything (*Against Praxeas* 16.7).

In his fourth line of argument, chapters 19–28, Tertullian returns to the principle that Scripture needs to be interpreted by Scripture and focuses on the meager biblical support for the monarchian arguments and their misinterpretation of the biblical witness. The faction whom Praxeas represents finds support in only three passages: "I am God and beside me there is no other" (Is 45:5), "I and the Father are one" (Jn 1:30) and, most importantly, "Anyone who has seen me has seen the Father ... I am in the Father and the Father is in me" (Jn 14: 9–11) (*Against Praxeas* 20). In a brilliant and patient move, Tertullian turns first to the Gospel of John and then to Matthew and to Luke to show the plethora of passages in which the Father and Son are spoken of as distinct persons, including Jesus's own statements in which he speaks of the Father as of a different person (*Against Praxeas* 21–24). The phrase "I and the Father are one" immediately betrays two distinct centers of attribution: the one who speaks, "I," and the "Father." Furthermore, if one pays close attention to the very words Jesus uses to indicate his relationship with the Father, argues Tertullian, Praxeas's argument is thoroughly defeated, for Jesus uses the word *unum* ("we are one [thing]"), indicating the unity of essence, and not *unus* ("we are the same [person]") which would indicate singularity of number (*Against Praxeas* 22.10–11);[13] and even though the gospel was written in Greek and not in Latin, the same holds true in both languages.

Tertullian's Christology also flows from this Trinitarian position. From the beginning of the treatise, Tertullian has insisted that the primary impediment in Praxeas's understanding of the true God of the Bible is his insistence on ignoring the economy of God's self-revelation in history (*Against Praxeas* 3.1). The Incarnation shows us that the lens by which the economy—indeed all of history—is to be understood is Christ. Christians are to turn to the very person of the Word who was made flesh and through him to interpret the Old Testament. Against the monarchian assertion that the term "Son" indicated only the flesh, the human Jesus, while the term "Father" indicated the spirit, who is God himself (*Against Praxeas* 27.1), Tertullian argued that the divine Word became incarnate and was clothed with flesh without a transfiguration or change of substance (*Against Praxeas* 27.6–7). Any such mixture of flesh and divine spirit would mean that the incarnate Jesus is neither completely human nor completely divine (*Against Praxeas* 27.8). On the contrary, Tertullian presents as a principle of faith that Jesus is one person in whom are conjoined two natures: one human and one divine (*Against Praxeas* 27.11).

In the last argument against Praxeas, chapters 29–31, Tertullian draws out the implications of the monarchian position, namely, if there is no distinction between Father and Son, then, the one who suffered and died on the Cross has to be the Father himself. Tertullian calls this *patripassianism* blasphemous because, on the one hand, it ascribes possibility to the divine nature (meaning that God becomes an object to be acted upon), while at the same time it makes the Father himself "a curse for us" (Gal. 3:13) (*Against Praxeas* 29). Scripture insists, says Tertullian, that the one who suffered on the Cross, the one who was forsaken by the Father, raised from the dead, ascended into heaven, and is seated at the Father's right hand, is the Son and not the Father himself. It is the Son whom Stephen saw, and it is he who pours forth the gift of the Holy Spirit, whose mission is to interpret the economy of God to all who are willing to receive him (*Against Praxeas* 30). Monarchians held firmly to conceptions of God that were formed before the coming of Christ and, thus, could not understand the fullness of God's self-revelation.

Tertullian ends by concluding that understanding God as triune is what separates Christianity from Judaism (*Against Praxeas* 31).

Conclusion

One cannot overstate the importance of Tertullian for Christian theology, nor underestimate his brilliance. Rooted in the principles of the authority and simplicity of Scripture, Tertullian was willing to struggle with various notions of truth, reason, and even divine nature that permeated the culture in which he lived. In doing so, he provides for Christians of all times a new understanding of the relationship between reason and faith. In *Against Praxeas* Tertullian gave us much more than certain terms with which to describe God, such as "economy," "Trinity," "person," or "substance"—he gave us the language by which we may understand the very notion of God. Unity and distinction are no longer antithetical. Tertullian was absolutely convinced that the faith that was handed down from Christ and the apostles was "once for all entrusted to God's holy people" (Jude 1:3) and that this faith was complete. This *Rule of Faith* provided the framework not only for understanding who God is but also how we ought to interpret the very Scriptures that contained the Rule. And for Tertullian, like almost every other early Christian theologian, the hermeneutical key to understanding God and ourselves was Jesus Christ, God's own self-revelation. Even though the Old Testament pointed towards the Messiah and testified to him, after the Incarnation—or rather, because of it—Christians turn to Christ to find the means by which to interpret not only the New Testament but also the Old. Thinking about God has to begin with the history of the appearance of God in the person of Christ.

Notes

1. Translated from *Adversus Praxean.*
2. Timothy D. Barnes, *Tertullian: A Historical and Literary Study.* Oxford: Clarendon Press, 1971, rev. edn. 1985; William Tabbernee, *Montanist Inscriptions and Testimonia: Epigraphic Sources Illustrating the History of Montanism* (Macon, GA: Mercer University Press, 1997); David Rankin, *Tertullian and the Church* (Cambridge: Cambridge University Press, 1995); Eric Osborn, *Tertullian: First Theologian of the West* (Cambridge: Cambridge University Press, 1997).
3. Justo L. González, "Athens and Jerusalem Revisited: Reason and Authority in Tertullian," *Church History* 43 (1974), 22.
4. Tertullian, *De carne Christi* 5.4.
5. The only exceptions were his apologetic works that were written for a pagan audience; Geoffrey D. Dunn, *Tertullian*, in *The Early Church Fathers* (New York: Routledge, 2004), 19.
6. Dunn, *Tertullian*, 22.
7. In Latin, the word used for "passing on the faith" is *tradere*, which means to hand over for safekeeping—we get the word *tradition* from that root.
8. Pelikan, Jaroslav J. *The Vindication of Tradition: The 1983 Jefferson Lecture in the Humanities* (New Haven: Yale University Press, 1986), 65.
9. The term *economy* appears twelve times in *Against Praxeas.*
10. It is here, in *Against Praxeas* 2.4, that the term trinity (*trinitas*) is used to describe the Christian understanding of who God is.

11. See, Dunn, *Tertullian*, 36. Tertullian uses the term *substance* and its derivatives forty-nine times in the treatise.
12. Tertullian uses the term *persona* thirty-two times in *Against Praxeas* to describe Father, Son, and Spirit.
13. One may think here of the motto of the American seal, *E pluribus unum*, "out of many one." The *unum* indicated the unity of the Nation, not the singularity of persons.

Select Bibliography

Primary source

Tertullian. *Against Praxeas*. Edited and translated by Ernest Evans. London: SPCK, 1948. (Available also online at: www.tertullian.org/articles/evans_praxeas_eng.htm)

Secondary sources

Barnes, Timothy D. *Tertullian: A Historical and Literary Study*, rev. ed. Oxford: Clarendon Press, 1985.

Dunn, Geoffrey D. *Tertullian*. *The Early Church Fathers*. New York: Routledge, 2004.

González, Justo L. "Athens and Jerusalem Revisited: Reason and Authority in Tertullian," *Church History* 43 (1974), 17–25.

Osborn, Eric. *Tertullian: First Theologian of the West*. Cambridge: Cambridge University Press, 1997.

Rankin, David. *Tertullian and the Church*. Cambridge: Cambridge University Press, 1995.

1.7

On the Unity of the Catholic Church (c. 251 CE)

Cyprian of Carthage (c. 202– September 14, 258 CE)

Introduction

We do not know much about Thacius Caecilius Cyprianus before his conversion and meteoric rise to bishop of the most important city in North Africa.[1] Born into a wealthy family, it is likely that he became a teacher of rhetoric after the requisite pagan education. A mere two years or so after his conversion and baptism at the Easter Vigil in c. 246 CE, Cyprian was elected bishop of Carthage after the death of Donatus in c. 248.[2] Cyprian did not have much time to warm the episcopal chair before the new Emperor Decius issued an imperial edict in late 249–250, requiring all to sacrifice to the Roman gods. Decius was flush with his triumph over Emperor Philip at Verona and desired to ensure the success of his reign. Such an edict, of course, posed a significant problem for Christians. During the yearlong persecution that ensued, some bishops like Fabian of Rome were martyred while others like Dionysius of Alexandria and Cyprian went into hiding. After his short reign as emperor, Decius and his son died in battle with the Goths and Trebonianus Gallus (June 251–253) succeeded him. The apparent cessation of persecution that followed gave the wounded church time to work through difficult questions at councils in Rome and Carthage in 251 about what to do with those who had lapsed (fallen) by sacrificing (*sacrificati*), burning incense (*thurificati*), or gaining a certificate in proof of sacrifice illegally (*libellatici*).[3]

It is in this divisive aftermath of persecution that Cyprian penned *On the Unity of the Catholic Church* (*De catholicae ecclesiae unitate*).[4]

However, there was little time for the church to settle into addressing these questions before the clergy was subjected to the consequences of a joint edict by Valerian and Gallienus in August 257 requiring that "those who do not follow the Roman religion ought to recognize Roman ceremonies."[5] When he was summoned before the proconsul of Africa and called upon to give up names of presbyters, Cyprian refused and was exiled. Valerian strengthened his edict with a decree in 258 calling for immediate punishment of clergy as well as confiscation of property and stripping of status for those of wealth like Cyprian who did not sacrifice to the gods. As a result, the bishop of Carthage was called back from exile in order to face a new trial. On September 14, 258, Cyprian appeared before the proconsul at Utica, refused to offer sacrifice to the gods, and, as was his right as a Roman citizen, was sentenced to execution by beheading.[6]

Unity and authority: *On the Unity of the Catholic Church* 4–5

Cyprian opens *On Unity* 4 with Matt 16:18–19:

> The Lord speaks to Peter: "I tell you that you are Peter, and on that rock I will build my Church, and the gates of the underworld will not prevail against her. I will give you the keys of the kingdom of heaven, and whatever you will bind upon earth will have been bound even in heaven, and what you will loose upon earth will have been loosed even in heaven."

There are two sets of manuscripts that contain different versions of Cyprian's exegesis of this passage and of John 20:21 in *On Unity* 4–5. While both versions of *On Unity* demonstrate a similar conclusion on Cyprian's part—that Christ commands the unity of the church—his emphasis does shift to accommodate contextual needs.

The earliest version is the *Primacy Text* (*PT*), thus named because it speaks of a primacy given to Peter by Christ. The later *Received Text* (*RT*) refers to the version that was believed to be the only version of *On Unity* until the *PT* was rediscovered in 1563.[7] Since each version offers a different take on the authority of the bishop vis-à-vis Peter, it is no wonder that there was considerable debate during and after the Protestant Reformation regarding what Cyprian does or does not say about the primacy of the bishop of Rome.[8] The text-critical work of Maurice Bévenot, however, brought about consensus that both versions were indeed written by Cyprian, the first (*PT*) in 251 CE (at the time of *Letter* 55) and the second (*RT*) at the time of his dispute with Stephen of Rome around 256 CE (at the time of *Letters* 72–73).[9] The language of the *Received Text* is therefore edited to downplay the emphasis on the primacy of Peter for obvious reasons.[10]

The *Primacy Text* affirms that bishops have equal power and honor but that their unity begins from the "starting point" that is Peter.[11] Cyprian's concern here is less about the importance of Peter than it is about how the unity of the Church is revealed to the world. He identifies the common ancestor of the episcopal family tree in Peter, so that the Holy Spirit's preservation of the oneness of the familial legacy is recognizable and accessible in one's bishop, regardless of geographical location. For Cyprian, unity is a cooperative and familial endeavor. The bishop is under the "foremost obligation to grasp tightly this unity and to assert our title to it, with the object of proving that the episcopate in itself is one and indivisible" and the church member faithfully participates in this oneness.[12] According to Cyprian, there is no conception of the Church as divided; the "one body and one Spirit, one hope of your calling, one Lord, one faith, one baptism, one God" (cf. Eph 4:4–6) admits no division.

In the shorter *Received Text* (*RT*) version of *On Unity* 4, Cyprian omits much of the direct Petrine primacy language. He quotes Jesus after his resurrection charging Peter to "Feed my sheep" (John 21:17) and lodges the construction of the Church and the establishment of the source of episcopal authority (the "one Chair") with Christ: "Upon [Peter] [Christ] builds his Church, and to him he hands over in trust his sheep to be fed and, although he might assign to all the apostles equal power, he however established one Chair and ordained by his own authority that Chair as the source of unity and its guiding principle."[13] In the *RT*, Cyprian's language shifts away from Peter as the source toward Christ as the one establishing the episcopal family tree. Peter is identified as being granted the "first place," but this is very specifically to mark the unity of the Church: "one Church was exemplified by one Chair."[14] The same admonition of unity as a cooperative and familial endeavor between bishop and the faithful appears in the *RT*.[15]

Instead of an ecclesiological reliance on Rome as the guarantor of the unity of the Church, Peter's Chair instead represents the diffuse but unified authority of any bishop who manifests the "widespread increase of [the Church's] fruitfulness" that characterizes the many boughs of the firmly rooted episcopal tree.[16] Snapping a bough from the tree only succeeds in cutting off any hope of its fruitfulness; it does not fundamentally hurt the tree. Peter represents the unity of the source (Christ) that sustains the fruitfulness of the Church. In one of the most arresting passages in *On Unity*, Cyprian draws upon various images from nature to locate the maternal source of life in the Church as the body of Christ:

> Thus also the Church, when the light of the Lord is poured forth, though she sheds her rays of light throughout the whole world, nevertheless the light is one that is spread everywhere, but the unity is not cut off from the body. She extends her boughs into the whole world with an abundance of fruitful growth, she opens wide her streams that flow forth bountifully, nevertheless one is her head and source, and the one Mother is rich with the offspring of her fertility. From her womb we are born, by her milk we are nurtured, by her spirit we are given life.[17]

For Cyprian, the unity of the Church is life itself and bishops tend to its cultivation on behalf of Christ. The Church is the body of Christ, its source unwavering, its unity unbroken, and its fruitfulness unceasing. There is no life for the bough that splits from the tree.[18]

The Eucharist: practical matters and practicality matters

After the imperial persecution had ceased and he was able to return to Carthage, Cyprian had to consider various difficult issues. For Cyprian, all three categories of the lapsed (*sacrificati*, *thurificati*, and *libellatici*) had apostatized. Therefore, the central question was under what terms the lapsed could be readmitted to the Eucharist, if at all. This was the context of the first version of *On Unity*.[19]

Cyprian was unequivocal about the apostasy of these actions even under duress. At the same time, however, the Carthaginian bishop was a pragmatist who did not want to make hasty decisions about anyone's readmission until God granted peace to the church as a whole, especially if another bout of persecutions was around the corner.[20] Thus, Cyprian determined to postpone any official policy for reconciliation of the lapsed until after the cessation of persecution. Some in Carthage submitted to Cyprian's decision on the matter, but this deferment proved to be unsatisfactory for many others who challenged whether a bishop had the authority to hinder the reconciliation of those already granted it by a confessor.[21] Although, as Burns points out, for Cyprian, "neither the confessors and martyrs, nor even the bishop ... should presume to decide such a momentous and far-reaching question alone."[22] In other words, the whole body of Christ needed to be involved in the body-business of reconciling the body. In the meantime, the lapsed were "to remain in a state of repentance, desirous of receiving the Eucharist but cut off from actually receiving it."[23] For Cyprian, eating the meat offered to the gods was to unify oneself with them and to nullify the unity that came with the Eucharist. Offering incense as propitiation or publicly denying your baptism was no better.

Novatian, along with the Roman clergy and confessors, initially supported Cyprian's position and lobbied forcefully against those who stood against the bishop of Carthage. However, after the persecution ended, Cyprian modified his position at the Council of Carthage in 251 in order to come into accord with the bishop of Rome, Cornelius, thus accepting a distinction between those who sacrificed and those who gained a *libellus* through some other means. There was some variety in the severity of penance required for the lapsed but, for the most part, all agreed that there was a path back into communion. Novatian recoiled, adamant that whether one sacrificed, burned incense, or bribed one's way out of appeasing the gods it did not matter, it all amounted to apostasy and readmitting the lapsed to the Eucharist was therefore out of the question. While the Council of Carthage brought resolution for those who were in limbo regarding readmittance into communion, it also spelled the end of discussion on how rigorist was too rigorist: "the permanence of Novatian's schism was sealed, and his rival Church in his eyes legitimated."[24] The resulting splintering of the episcopal succession at Rome between Cornelius and Novatian fed into the later dispute between Cyprian and Pope Stephen about how to negotiate the invalidity of the sacraments outside of the church, that is, whether or not to re-baptize those who had been baptized into a heretical and schismatic group. Cyprian's approach in the previous controversy over the lapsed directly informed his stance in this later controversy.

Cyprian prioritized unity and the Roman presbyter prioritized his rigorist position and refused to accept Cornelius as bishop.[25] Novatian sided instead with the rigorist group in Carthage against Cyprian. A council called by Cornelius in Rome and another in Carthage in 253 solidified Rome and North Africa's definitive stance against the rigorists. Novatian was therefore condemned and excommunicated. For Cyprian, the Eucharist was the sustaining food of the one body of Christ and therefore a schismatic "bishop" such as Novatian could not preside at the Eucharist as one who had rent the "garment" of Christ asunder.[26] That food was not sustaining the one body and therefore did not come with the accompanying sustaining grace.

According to Cyprian, since Novatian and the other rigorists had torn apart the body and therefore could not celebrate the Eucharist, they also could not baptize new believers into the one body of which they were not a part. Therefore those "baptized" by Novatian and company needed to be "re-baptized," which was, for Cyprian, really their only baptism since the first was not valid. In Cyprian's mind, the reason Novatian and his followers were unable "to give salvation to their adherents was that they had no communion with the corporate body of Christ so that they could not transmit the grace that they pretended."[27] Bishops in their disparate geographical locations functioned as the collective head of the body of Christ. If one was cut off from that collective, then they were incapable of being sustained by Christ and participating in the life of the body of Christ:

> For Cyprian there can be no salvation outside the Church as he has theologically defined it. For him Novatian can be no valid bishop because, cut off from the network of bishops in mutual recognition and intercommunion, he has no organic link either with the forgiveness or with the grace given to the Church in Mt 16:18 and Jn 20:20–23.[28]

Stephen, on the other hand, considered Cyprian's perspective to be an innovation (even though it was typical of North African practice) and determined that only the laying on of hands and prayer by the bishop was needed.[29] Cyprian revised *On Unity* 4–5 during the baptismal controversy with Stephen. That he did this represents both the consistency of his ecclesiology and his understanding of how the practical reality of the church can help refine that ecclesiology.

Heresy and schism

While the boundary line between heresy and schism was not clear at this time,[30] Cyprian's objections to the rigorists and the laxists were primarily ecclesiological rather than a matter of false teaching.[31] In his view, schismatics like the Novatianists align themselves with the work of Satan when they break unity.[32] In fact, Satan himself is the author of heresies and schisms. He twists the truth and tears apart the unity of the Church by deceiving people into thinking they could be groomed to lead others toward the light, but instead they introduce "night instead of day, destruction for salvation, hopelessness under the guise of hope, betrayal under the cloak of trust, Antichrist under the name of Christ."[33] Walking in the "footsteps of the Christ who conquers" in obedience guards against such deceivers.[34] Obedience to Christ is basic for a Christian, like standing upright and walking without stumbling: "Casually staggering towards salvation does nothing to achieve the end of treading salvation's true path."[35]

Cyprian judged ludicrous the idea that there could be a counterfeit (schismatic) bride. Not only can Christ tell the difference, the bride of Christ is easily identified as watcher, protector, and mother; there is no reason to question her purity and purpose. Dissociating oneself from the Church is to buy into a lie and to lose everything as a result: "He is a foreigner, he is deconsecrated [profanus], and he is an enemy. He cannot have God as his Father who does not have the Church as his Mother."[36] For Cyprian, heresy and schism is akin to breaking union with the bride by committing adultery (breaking apart the family and abandoning all claims to its rights and privileges)[37] as well as to breaking ties with the people of God by effectively becoming a traitor. The schismatic is not only a traitor but a traitor who mounts an attack against Christ himself.[38] Of course these attacks can never succeed; the Church's foundation is indestructible and held together by the *sacramenta* that in turn steadfastly hold all who cling to the triune faith.[39] The schismatic who "rends and splits Christ's Church" cannot grasp the garment of Christ; they only succeed in letting salvation slip through their fingers.[40] Cyprian's understanding of the unity of the Church is grounded in the Christian eschatological responsibility to be alert and obedient. There is work to be done, promises for Christ to fulfill, and rewards for vigilance to claim (cf. Luke 12:35–37 and Matt 5:16).[41]

Conclusion

Credited with the theological mortar that laid the foundation of the hierarchical church polity based on Roman Carthage, Cyprian may not be the most obvious choice for a Protestant to read. With Cyprian we see an interpretation of church governance that does not seem to be based on Pauline or Johannine models, but the bishop of Carthage has served as a key partner in ecclesiological conversations throughout history and specifically in post-Reformation conversations between Protestants and Catholics. In the 1559 edition of the *Institutes of the Christian Religion*, Calvin references Cyprian thirty-one times—most of the time on the subject of the Church. Aza Goudriaan observes that Calvin specifically cites *On Unity* three times, always with approval, and quotes an extensive portion of the famous *On Unity* 5 twice. According to Goudriaan, Calvin and other Reformers valued Cyprian for his focus on the close union between church members and Christ and thought him a vital source from which to draw for polemics against the assumption of hierarchy among bishops.[42] Cyprian wrote *On Unity* for the Carthaginians who were caught between two compelling but ecclesially destructive approaches: the reconciliatory laxists and the rigorist followers of Novatian. While *On Unity* addresses the particular issues of the third century church at Carthage and in the post-persecution context of Western Christianity more generally, *On Unity* is a timeless classic of ecclesiology. Cyprian's clarion call for the unity of the Church amidst conflict has often served as a guide for the Western Church ever since, from Augustine to John Calvin.

Notes

1.   Pontius's *Life of Cyprian* (a defense against critics of Cyprian that includes an account of his martyrdom) and the *Consular Acts* (*Acta Proconsularia*) of *Carthage*, along with a few bits and pieces from Jerome and Augustine, make up the little that we know about the bishop of Carthage (c. 248–258 CE).
2.   J. Patout Burns Jr. observes that the laity must have overridden the objections of the majority of presbyters who certainly would not have been keen on a newly baptized Christian taking on the responsibility as leader, not only of the bishops of Proconsular Africa, but also over all of Latin Africa as far west as the Atlantic (*Cyprian the Bishop* [London and New York: Routledge, 2002], 1).
3.   The administration of the edict involved all imperial subjects mounting the hill to the temple of the Capitoline Triad where one offered meat to be sacrificed to the priest and poured out a libation of wine or offered incense to the emperor's image. Then, the petitioner declared to the commissioners that the sacrifice was completed and a *libellus* was signed and witnessed (Allen Brent, *St Cyprian of Carthage: On the Church Select Treatises*, Popular Patristics Series 32 [Crestwood, NY: St Vladimir's Seminary Press, 2006], 20).
4.   Just prior to *On Unity*, Cyprian wrote *On the Fallen* (*De lapsis*) to address the laxists and their eager grasping of reconciliation with the church through obtaining *libelli pacis* issued by African confessors. As Brent notes, *Letters* 33, 43, 55 and 59 provide context for both *On the Fallen* and *On Unity* (*St Cyprian*, 145). The controversy over the lapsed that was the context for *On Unity* fed directly into Cyprian's later controversy with Stephen of Rome (b. 254–257 CE) over the rebaptism of heretics and schismatics.

5. Herbert Musurillo, *The Acts of the Christian Martyrs: Introduction?, Text and Translations* (Oxford: Clarendon, 1972), 172 [*Acta Procons.* 3.4]) quoted in Brent, *St Cyprian*, 15.
6. Brent, *St Cyprian*, 17.
7. Russel Murray, "Assessing the Primacy: A Contemporary Contribution from the Writings of St. Cyprian of Carthage" *Journal of Ecumenical Studies* 47 (2012): 44.
8. Both Protestants and Catholics found a compatriot in Cyprian and took sides in the manuscript debate depending on their assumptions. In 1896 Anglican E.W. Benson claimed that the "papalist" version (*PT*) of *On Unity* 4–5 was a forgery. While Dom John Chapman called the forgery thesis into question and was the first to establish the existence of alternative texts, the Protestant Ulrich Wickert also called the *PT* fraudulent based on his rendering of how Cyprian viewed Peter, "Introduction: Cyprian's Stature and Influence" in *Cyprian of Carthage: Studies in His Life, Language, and Thought*, eds Henk Bakker, Paul van Geest and Hans van Loon (Leuven: Peeters, 2010, 9–18).
9. Brent, *St Cyprian*, 150. Karl Shuve notes that Bévenot's conclusion relies "largely on philological analysis of *primatus* . . . which should be understood to denote the symbolic 'starting point' of unity rather than the absolute priority of the Roman bishop above all others" ("Cyprian of Carthage's Writings from the Rebaptism Controversy: Two Revisionary Proposals Reconsidered" *The Journal of Theological Studies* 61 [2010]: 638).
10. Murray, "Assessing the Primacy," 54.
11. Cyprian *On Unity* 4 (*PT*) (Brent, 152–53).
12. Cyprian *On Unity* 5 (*PT*) (Brent, 153–54).
13. Cyprian *On Unity* 4 (*RT*) (Brent, 152).
14. Cyprian *On Unity* 4 (*RT*) (Brent, 152).
15. Cyprian *On Unity* 4 (*RT*) (Brent, 153).
16. Cyprian *On Unity* 5 (Brent, 154–55).
17. Cyprian *On Unity* 5 (Brent, 155). Later, Cyprian will contrast the fertility of the Church which results in the birth of life and salvation with those who are born of the devil, that is, those who give birth to heresy and schism (*On Unity* 12 [Brent, 164–65]), who have no access to the truth or promises of God (*On Unity* 11 [Brent, 162–63]).
18. Cyprian *On Unity* 23 (Brent, 178).
19. Burns, *Cyprian the Bishop*, 5.
20. Burns, *Cyprian the Bishop*, 3.
21. Cyprian says a great deal about what marks a true confessor and the damage that can come from their pride, see *On Unity* 21 (Brent, 175–76).
22. Burns, *Cyprian the Bishop*, 3.

23. See Brent on how Cyprian shifts his approach toward the lapsed over time, *St Cyprian*, 22.
24. Brent, *St Cyprian*, 23.
25. For a discussion on the contested election of the bishop of Rome after Fabian's death, see Burns, *Cyprian the Bishop*, 6–8.
26. See Cyprian *On Unity* 6–8 (Brent 157–60).
27. Brent, *St Cyprian*, 32.
28. Brent, *St Cyprian*, 38.
29. The positions of the Novatianist and laxist churches on penance revived the question of rebaptism in Africa (Burns, *Cyprian the Bishop*, 9). Church tradition would eventually reject Cyprian's perspective that the sacrament was invalid because of the bishop's heretical or schismatic status.
30. For a discussion of Cyprian's use of "heresy" and "schism," see Geoffrey D. Dunn, "Heresy and Schism According to Cyprian of Carthage" *Journal of Theological Studies* 55 (2004): 551–74. According to Dunn, "What we find in Cyprian is a refusal to separate belief and practice: deviant belief would lead to a break in the unity and a break in unity would prevent any unity of belief. In more modern terms, for Cyprian there could be no heresy without schism and no schism without heresy" (560).
31. As Qoheleth observes in Ecclesiastes 1:9: "What has been will be again, what has been done will be done again; there is nothing new under the sun." Long after Cyprian, Protestants will have similar struggles in terms of the tension between ecclesiastical unity and doctrinal purity. Prioritizing the dual concerns for the "unity and purity" is a broadly ecclesiological problem and it is no wonder that the Reformers consulted Cyprian on the unity of the Church and how he dealt with schismatics.
32. Cyprian *On Unity* 1 (Brent, 147).
33. Cyprian *On Unity* 3 (Brent, 148–49).
34. Cyprian *On Unity* 2 (Brent, 147–48). Cf. Matt 7:24–25.
35. Cyprian *On Unity* 2 (Brent, 148).
36. Cyprian *On Unity* 6 (Brent, 157).
37. Cyprian speaks of how Christ gives us his peace as our inheritance and "promises all the gifts that he has pledged, and his rewards, on condition of the preservation of his peace. If we are heirs of Christ, let us abide in Christ's peace" (*On Unity* 24 [Brent, 179]).
38. Cyprian later returns to his assessment of a schism as open hostility against the church by identifying a schismatic like Novatian as "an enemy of the altar, a rebel against Christ's sacrifice, of bad faith instead of faithfulness, guilty of sacrilege instead of proper religious practice, a disobedient servant, an undutiful son, a brother who is one's enemy" who "dares to set up a different altar against the bishops and priests of God whom he has treated despicably and has abandoned" (*On Unity* 17 [Brent, 170–71]).

39. Cyprian *On Unity* 6 (Brent, 157).
40. Cyprian *On Unity* 7 (Brent, 158). For a discussion on Cyprian's image of the "garment of Christ" in *On Unity*, see Burns, *Cyprian the Bishop*, 95.
41. Cyprian *On Unity* 27 (Brent, 181).
42. Aza Goudriaan, "Cyprian's *De ecclesiae catholicae unitate*: Why Did the Reformed Theologians Consider it a Useful Book (1559–1655)?" in *Cyprian of Carthage*, 227–28. For a discussion on the relevance of Cyprian for Lutherans in particular, see also Robert J.H. Mayes, "The Lord's Supper in the Theology of Cyprian of Carthage" *Concordia Theological Quarterly* 74 (2010): 307–324.

Select Bibliography

Primary source

Cyprian of Carthage, *On the Unity of the Catholic Church*. In Allen Brent, *St Cyprian of Carthage: On the Church Select Treatises*. Popular Patristics Series 32. Crestwood, NY: St Vladimir's Seminary Press, 2006.

Secondary sources

Bakker, Henk, Paul van Geest and Hans van Loon, eds. *Cyprian of Carthage: Studies in His Life, Language, and Thought*. Leuven: Peeters, 2010.

Burns, J. Patout. *Cyprian the Bishop*. London and New York: Routledge, 2002.

Dunn, Geoffrey D. *Cyprian and the Bishops of Rome: Questions of Papal Primacy in the Early Church*. Early Christian Studies 11. Strathfield, Australia: St. Paul's, 2007.

Sage, Michael M. *Cyprian*, Patristic Monograph Series 1. Cambridge, MA: Philadelphia Patristic Foundation, 1975.

1.8

On the Incarnation[1]
(c. 328–335 CE)
Athanasius
(c. 295–299–2 May 373 CE)

Introduction

For forty-six years, Athanasius (c. 295–May 2, 373 CE) was bishop of the ancient city of Alexandria, a major center of culture and learning and a melting pot of peoples and civilizations, including a large Jewish population. It was also the home of some of the greatest minds in early Christianity such as Clement and Origen. Athanasius was born at the very end of the third century, as the Church was about to enter the most dramatic period of social and political change in its history. The fourth century was a period of change and strife, including what is known as the Great Persecution (303–311), Emperor Constantine's acknowledgement of the Christian Church as a welcomed partner in the administration of the Empire (c. 312), and the articulation of a refined incarnational and trinitarian theology at the Second Council of Constantinople (381).

Little is known about Athanasius's family, but the earliest traditions of his life indicate he was perhaps born to a rich pagan family.[2] According to this account, Athanasius was baptized early in life and taken under the care of Alexander, the bishop of Alexandria. There, under the tutelage of Bishop Alexander, Athanasius received a classical as well as an exceptional biblical education. Until his death, the thrust of the Alexandrian's thought and the shape of his life was the study of the Scriptures.

Figure 1.8 Statue of Athanasius

As a young man, Athanasius was ordained a deacon and rose to be the bishop's principle "scribe," that is, his secretary and speechwriter. It was in this capacity that Athanasius joined Bishop Alexander at an ecumenical council, called by the Emperor Constantine and held at Nicaea, in 325 CE. Athanasius played a pivotal role in the theological discussions of the council.[3] In the decades that followed, Athanasius's Christocentrism and emphasis on redemptive history left a permanent imprint on the theology of the Church. Indeed, "no history of Christian doctrine may omit the name of Athanasius of Alexandria."[4]

Leading up to Nicaea

Around the year 318, a debate arose in Alexandria concerning the Person of Christ. For centuries, Christians had worshiped Christ as God, but what exactly is the relationship between the Father and the Son? How can the eternal God have a Son, or the eternal Son a Father? These were discussions on which Christians needed to come to a consensus.

One of the pre-eminent theological teachers and preachers in Alexandria was Arius (c. 250–336), a priest in the district of Baucalis. Arius did not deny the Son's divinity but he did not acknowledge him to be of the same "kind" of divinity as God the Father. Arius presumed a graded hierarchy of transcendence that would admit degree of existence, based on both scriptural and philosophical grounds. Phrases such as "only-begotten" (John 3:16) posed particularly knotty challenges, especially in light of one of the most frequently cited and hotly debated passages of Scripture, Proverbs 8.22–31. In Proverbs 8 Wisdom (which many Christian writers of the time identified with the *Word*, or *Logos*, of God in John 1:1–3) speaks in her own voice and declares: "The LORD brought me forth as the first of his works." For Arius and his followers, the Scriptures were clear that "there was a time when the Son was not"—a slogan that became their rallying cry.

Bishop Alexander and those around him saw this as a clear affront to the Christian faith. Such an understanding of the relationship between Father and Son not only challenged the eternal character and being of the Son, but also challenged the strict categories of Creator and creation and thereby the very core of salvation itself.

By the fall of 324, what had begun as a theological debate in Alexandria had spread throughout the eastern part of the Roman Empire and was dividing Christians. As soon as he secured the throne of the empire from his last rival, Emperor Constantine called for the bishops of the Empire to gather at what has come to be known as the First Ecumenical Council to deal with and come to an agreement on issues of Christian practice and theology. Among the issues discussed were the date of Easter, the transfer of bishops between sees, and, most importantly, the Arian controversy. Arius and his supporters were anathematized (or denounced as heretics) and exiled. The resulting statement is known as the Creed of Nicaea and affirmed that the Father and Son shared the same essence (the term they used was the rather ambiguous *homoousios,* meaning "of the same essence," but it was possible to also be interpreted as "of similar essence").

The aftermath of Nicaea

Athanasius found himself at the center of this tenuous, even divisive, state of ecclesiastical affairs. While only a young priest at Nicaea, Athanasius was Alexander's indispensable secretary and carried his theological voice. When Alexander died in 328, Athanasius had barely reached the canonical age of thirty and was elected to the episcopacy of the powerful see of Alexandria amidst great turmoil. From the beginning, his election was contested by the Meletians, a rigorist group that Athanasius inherited as opponents from his predecessor. He was also accused (wrongfully) of murder and of halting corn shipments from Egypt. Athanasius had no quarter for the challenges, which led to a litany of charges of violence alongside the seeming illegality of his ascension. He also refused Constantine's request to readmit Arius to communion, further antagonizing opponents. Arius died in 336 CE, but the debate did not die with him. In the years that followed, Athanasius became one of the most important theological voices. His understanding of Christ remained largely consistent throughout his career even as he endured six exiles that left him outside of his see for seventeen of his forty-six years as bishop.

After his first theological venture in the double treatise *Against the Greeks—On the Incarnation* (c. 328–335), Athanasius continued to be a prolific writer, especially during his exiles in the desert where he undertook some of his most famous work of ascetic meditation in the *Life of Antony* (c. 356) and the first treatise on the Holy Spirit in *Letters to Serapion* (c. 357–359), in which he unequivocally attributes *homoousios* to the Holy Spirit (attributed directly to the Holy Spirit in I.27 and attributed to the Son and "likewise" to the Spirit in III.1). Since *homoousios* is not found in the Scriptures, it was an embattled term in the long aftermath of Nicaea. Central to the debate was the question of who was adhering most closely to scriptural language and narrative. On this front, as well as on many others, Athanasius argued that *homoousios* was the safeguard of scriptural language. Prior to what has been called his "Golden Decade" (346–356), Nicaea and the creed did not figure prominently in Athanasius's defense. But a crucial shift occurred in the early 350s with the *Defense of the Nicene Creed* (c. 352–353), in which he leans upon the importance of the twenty-five-year-old creed as the mainstay of orthodoxy against the "Arian" heresy.[5] Athanasius's unwavering commitment to his cause helped to propel Nicaea to a level of ecumenical significance that would be firmly established by the end of the fourth century.

As far as Athanasius's polemical works go, the obvious difference between *Against the Greeks—On the Incarnation* and *Orations Against the Arians* (c. 339–46) is the notable addition in the latter of explicitly "anti-Arian" language. But these two works also illustrate the development of Athanasius's trinitarian thought: in the former, the Holy Spirit is largely absent, while in the latter Athanasius's trinitarian formulation is more comprehensive. After a long life saturated with controversy and tireless activism for Nicene orthodoxy, Athanasius died May 2, 373. The tentative rapprochement at the end of Athanasius's life did not mark the end of the difficulties for the pro-Nicene Alexandrian bishops; his successor Peter ended up in exile as well.

The weight of Athanasius's response to those whom he would describe collectively as "Arians"[6] rested upon his interpretation of the incarnation. Key for Athanasius was the question of what was needed for the redemption of humanity. The Word took a human body so that humanity would be re-created and deified. This redemption could only be accomplished by God the Son, the Word—otherwise the Christian faith lacked coherence. Underlying the whole salvific project is God's love for humanity. God loved, so he condescended. God loved, so he emptied himself. God loved, so he deified.

The narrative of "Athanasius *contra mundum*" has dominated his reception within Church tradition until recently, when his traditionally unimpeachable reputation has come under heavy critique.[7] Some modern theologians have also called into question his treatment of the humanity and divinity of the incarnate Christ, saying that it has the potential to slide into either Apollinarianism or Nestorianism. Athanasius may have been working with a more limited terminology, but the trajectory of his theology from his earliest to his later works, such as his *Letter to Epictetus* (c. 372), leans heavily in the direction of the single subjectivity of Christ and the vital importance of both the human and the divine natures, anticipating Cyril of Alexandria's (b. 412–44) formulation of Christological predication.

On the Incarnation

While *On the Incarnation* is often presented alone, *Against the Greeks—On the Incarnation* is really one apology (hence the phrase "double treatise") that offers different entry points and organizes arguments depending on what context is being addressed. Dating the double treatise has proven difficult because of the marked absence of any reference to "Arianism," but in recent scholarship it is generally accepted that it was composed during Athanasius's early years as bishop of Alexandria. *Against the Greeks—On the Incarnation* (c. 328–335) can be classified as apologetic in the tradition of Justin, Tertullian, and Origen, but *On the Incarnation* goes well beyond arguing the case for Christianity against paganism and constructs a theological framework for why God became human.[8] Because of this framework and its lasting influence, *On the Incarnation* will be the focus here.

The central claim of *On the Incarnation* is clear: as a result of the fall, humanity needed a savior and the incarnation was God's response to that need. In the opening chapter of *On the Incarnation*, Athanasius indicates that the purpose of the treatise is to build upon his claims in *Against the Greeks* to answer the question of why the Word of God would come in bodily form. He begins with an exploration of the method of creation so as to both distinguish the Christian account of creation from other competing accounts and to

Figure 1.9 Icon of Athanasius

illustrate how the re-creation of the world will take place through the one who originally created it (*De Inc.* 1–3). For Athanasius, the redemptive history that hangs upon the structure of creation, re-creation, and the resurrection is organized as a framework of ascent and descent. Athanasius highlights how humans are distinguished from all else in creation with the "impress of his own image, a share in the reasonable being of the very Word himself" (*De Inc.* 3). This is important because the fall precipitated a "de-creation," a corruptive descent into the non-existence from whence humanity came, that only the creator could stop and reverse: "it was our sorry case that caused the Word to come down, our transgression that called out his love for us, so that he made haste to help us and to appear among us. It is we who were the cause of his taking human form, and for our salvation that in his great love he was both born and manifested in a human body" (*De Inc.* 4). The proper teleological orientation of humanity is that of ascent, and sin is the movement in the opposite direction away from the essence of true humanity. Only the descent of the Word could affect the necessary inversion of fallen humanity back toward ascent.[9] Even as the Word found humanity hurtling toward non-existence, the Word was sustaining humanity's possibility for redemption by having created it in his incorruptible image (*De Inc.* 5).

God's dilemma and solution

In order to illustrate the need for the complete solution that is the incarnation of the Word, Athanasius advances the fall as presenting God with a dilemma. Of course, for Athanasius, God was never in a situation of wringing his hands about what to do; instead, this exercise of the imagination illuminates his conception of the inseparability of who God is and what God does. When faced with the results of the fall, God would not change the rules mid-game by sweeping away the law of death to which humanity and the rest of creation succumbed. The reasoning for this is not that God is intransigent, but that such a reversal would be "unfitting and unworthy" of God's character (*De Inc.* 6). Athanasius concludes that repentance would not be sufficient to mitigate the results of the fall because humanity's transgression was no mere misstep but a binding descent into corruption. Humanity was in such a state of descent that it could be characterized as "de-creation." Thus, it was not a "what" but a "who" that was needed to bring the corrupt to incorruption because only the Word would be able to exercise re-creation and put a stop to the downward spiral of humanity into death (*De Inc.* 7).

The Word of God entering the world he created was an act of love and revelation. Humanity, made in his image, was suffering and dying: "All this he saw and, pitying our race, moved with compassion for our limitation, unable to endure that death should have the mastery, rather than that his creatures should perish and the world of his Father for us men come to naught, He took to himself a body, a human body even as our own" (*De Inc.* 8). The reality and complete humanness of the Word's body is necessary, according to Athanasius, because only his voluntary death and the "grace of his resurrection" would reverse the corruption and descent of humanity and put it back on the trajectory of life and freedom from the bondage of death (*De Inc.* 8). Athanasius proclaims the sacrifice of Christ's body as a new beginning, the re-creation of the world that brings the hope of resurrection (*De Inc.* 10). But, if humans were just going to fall, why create them in the image of God in the first place?

Athanasius's answer is that creation itself was a grace (*De Inc.* 11). As Peter Leithart notes, this conception of creation itself as an activity of God's grace has its detractors among Protestants, specifically the Reformed tradition, that extend the law-gospel distinction back into Eden.[10] Athanasius, however, is convinced that the presence of the image of God in humanity and the Word's enabling creation to point to a creator (Rom 1:18–20) marks the *telos* of creation in communion with God. Thus creation itself is an act of grace, and God certainly would not abandon or destroy those with whom he had once shared his image (*De Inc.* 13). Of course this means that only the image of God himself could broker the necessary freedom for humanity: "Men could not have done it, for they are only made after the Image; nor could angels have done it, for they are not the images of God. The Word of God came into his own Person, because it was he alone, the Image of the Father, who could recreate man made after the Image" (*De Inc.* 13). In order to illustrate this, Athanasius imagines a portrait having been destroyed by stains; when faced with the dilemma of what to do, the artist does not throw away the canvas, but instead has the subject sit for it again and "the likeness is re-drawn on the same material" (*De Inc.* 14). The solution to the dilemma of the fall was never in question; God loved humanity and unflinchingly responded with the necessary, gracious, and pedagogical salvific accommodation that is the embodied Word (*De Inc.* 14–15).

Athanasius presents the incarnation as the manifestly gracious activity of God that purposes to reveal God specifically to human senses (*De Inc.* 16). The Word's thirty-three years on earth was an accommodation, a quest for humanity to know God in the flesh. Athanasius anticipates the question of sufficiency regarding this tactic of God revealing himself somatically, answering that the Word's human body was not a limitation but an instrument (in Greek, *organon*) so as to be the revelation that humanity needed.[11] The Word's body did not defile him; instead, the Word's union with it sanctified the body (*De Inc.* 17, 43–44). It was fitting that the Word become flesh as the ultimate act of self-revealing and love for humanity.

The crux of the matter

The death of Christ on the cross as a "monument of victory" is central for Athanasius (*De Inc.* 19). The incarnation was both the revealing of the Word to humanity and the facilitation of his sacrifice on behalf of humanity (*De Inc.* 20). Again, Athanasius anticipates the valid questions raised by the Word's act of surrender, such as why his death had to be a shameful rather than an honorable spectacle. The bishop's answer was that the Word was no ordinary man and his sacrifice could be no ordinary death. The incarnation had one intended outcome: the Word would die publicly and at the hand of enemy action so as to defeat death and corruption and bring about the resurrection of the body (*De Inc.* 21–24). In sum, the death Christ died was oriented specifically for the sake of humanity. Those who eagerly meet death with full confidence of its impotence are proven right: "Death has become like a tyrant who has been completely conquered by the legitimate monarch; bound hand and foot as he now is, the passers-by jeer at him, hitting him and abusing him, no longer afraid of his cruelty and rage, because of the king who has conquered him. So has death been conquered and branded for what it is by the Savior on the cross" (*De Inc.* 27). His resurrection was the seal of proof that the needed re-creation was complete (*De Inc.* 26).

The triumph

The tone of *On the Incarnation* becomes increasingly triumphal as Athanasius exults in the continuing work of the resurrected Savior amidst humanity: "This is the work of One Who lives, not of one dead; and, more than that, it is the work of God" (*De Inc.* 30). God's ongoing activity in the world demonstrates the veracity of the extent of God's solution to the dilemma of the fall. Building upon this proof, Athanasius follows with a refutation of the Jews and the Greeks in turn. In response to the Jews, Athanasius argues from

Scripture (Isaiah 53 figures prominently) for the need of a savior, a need that was not fulfilled by any of the earlier kings or prophets, and the unique fittingness of the Incarnation to meet this need (*De Inc.* 33–40).

His refutation of the Gentiles takes a different tack by arguing within their own framework to prove that the Incarnation was not unfitting or ridiculous. Taking his lead from Paul in Acts 17, Athanasius argues on behalf of humanity that it was not unbecoming for the Word to dwell in man to manifest the truth of God (*De Inc.* 42). As humanity is part of the whole of the universe, then "if it were unfitting for Him thus to indwell the part, it would be equally so for Him to exist within the whole" (*De Inc.* 42). Thus, if a human body is off-limits, then so is every form of embodiment. Since the Word's purpose was "to heal and to teach suffering men" in the first place, it is only fitting that he embody that which he comes to save (*De Inc.* 43).

Athanasius's refutation of the Gentiles continues with a second argument from the effect that the Word's death and resurrection has had upon the present situation of the world and the circumstances in which humans find themselves.[12] The bishop calls the Greeks to observe that idols have been abandoned, oracles have ceased, and magic has been destroyed (*De Inc.* 46–47). If his interlocutors do not believe his rendition of events, then there is no denying the observable experience of those who practice chastity and are martyrs who "despise death," "take heed to the things that do not die," "look past the things of time and gaze on things eternal," "think nothing of earthly glory," and "aspire only to immortality." This is the most powerful testimony and Athanasius even invites the testing of this power (*De Inc.* 47–48).

Athanasius intensifies his refutation of the Greeks by reiterating that God is transcendent but can be perceived through his works, and Christ's work is God's work. Now reaching the climax, Athanasius again answers the main question of the double treatise: why did the Word of God become incarnate? Athanasius avers, "He, indeed, assumed humanity that we might become God (in Greek, *theopoiēthōmen*). He manifested himself by means of a body in order that we might perceive the mind of the unseen Father. He endured shame from men that we might inherit immortality. He himself was unhurt by this, for he is impassible and incorruptible; but by his own impassibility he kept and healed the suffering men on whose account he thus endured" (*De Inc.* 54). Athanasius's view of salvation is the concept of *theopoiesis* (deification); by this he does not mean that humans become gods like God, as he is quite clear about the distinction between Creator and creation, but that by participation in the Word humanity can be free from sin and know God. As Leithart observes, *theopoiesis* is Athanasius's conception of the completion of humanity and the proper way to be human: "Deification in Athanasius's telling does not involve an ascent beyond embodied existence any more than it involves transcendence of creatureliness. Deification is about proper use of flesh, not about the destruction of flesh."[13]

Conclusion

Athanasius's ability to express complex truths helped to articulate plainly what was really at stake: the work of Christ for our salvation. His approach is undeniably pastoral and his theology was undeniably biblical. He interpreted his world through a framework saturated with Scripture, whether in current events that affected the Church at large or the Empire or in his personal struggles. His staunch defense of *homoousios* and the attack upon the "Arians" as distorters of Scripture arise from his unwavering belief in the truth of the Bible. Athanasius's commitment to the Nicene faith was an apologetic for the requisite confession of the veracity and efficaciousness of the Incarnation in light of the truth of Scripture.

Notes

1. Translated from *De Incarnatione Verbi Dei.*
2. The earliest account of Athanasius's life comes from the Arabic *History of the Patriarchs of Alexandria* (tenth century) and likely is more legend than fact. See Khaled Anatolios, *Athanasius*, The Early Church Fathers (London: Routledge, 2004), 3.
3. *Ecumenical* means world-wide. Even from the beginning of the Christian movement, there had been numerous local councils (including the one described in Acts 15), but the Council of 325 was the first one in which representatives from almost all the major Christian centers and churches had gathered together.
4. David M. Gwynn, *Athanasius of Alexandria: Bishop, Theologian, Ascetic, Father* (Oxford: Oxford University Press, 2012), 55.
5. Gwynn, *Athanasius*, 43.
6. Athanasius, along with Marcellus of Ancyra, was largely responsible for the historical reception of the lingering debate after Nicaea as between "orthodoxy" and the "Arians." This is, of course, a gross oversimplification,

but an effective way to wage what could be called both a defense and an offense.

7.   See Timothy D. Barnes, *Athanasius and Constantius: Theology and Politics in the Constantinian Empire* (Cambridge, MA: Harvard, 1993).

8.   James D. Ernest, *The Bible in Athanasius of Alexandria*. The Bible in Ancient Christianity 2 (Leiden: Brill, 2004), 43.

9.   Athanasius defines evil as "non-being, the negation and antithesis of good" (*De Inc.* 4) and sin as "de-creation." See Anatolios, *Athanasius*, 44–51. The sinful state of humanity has left it with only death and corruption. As Thomas G. Weinandy notes, Athanasius does not present anything akin to the developed notion of original sin in Augustine, but this does not mean sin does not figure any less prominently in his theology. The plight of humanity is what precipitated the incarnation as the only solution (*Athanasius: A Theological Introduction* [Aldershot: Ashgate, 2007], 31–32).

10. Leithart identifies Michael Horton as particularly decisive on this point within the Reformed tradition, with a subtler version of the nature/grace dichotomy being typical of Protestant soteriology (*Athanasius* [Grand Rapids: Baker, 2011], 100).

11. This section has caused some controversy. But accusations of Nestorian or Apollinarian leanings, as Leithart observes, do not accurately portray the "robust" christological framework that is present: "Having assumed flesh *for us*, that flesh becomes a property of the Word, not an external possession or detached instrument, but as proper to the Word as his being the Word of the Father. That is what Athanasius means when he writes of an 'impassible sufferer,' the impassible Word on the cross. Jesus's death on the cross is the voluntary act of the Word who has taken all our anguish to himself and made it *his*." See Leithart, *Athanasius*, 122–26, 145.

12. According to Anatolios, the triumphal tone of *De Incarnatione* helps date the work before Athanasius's first exile (*Athanasius*, 12).

13. Leithart, *Athanasius*, 160.

Selected Bibliography

Primary source

Athanasius. *On the Incarnation*. Popular Patristics Series 3. Crestwood, NY: St. Vladimir's Seminary Press, 1977.

Secondary sources

Anatolios, Khaled. *Athanasius*. The Early Church Fathers. London: Routledge, 2004.

Gwynn, David M. *Athanasius of Alexandria: Bishop, Theologian, Ascetic, Father*. Oxford: Oxford University Press, 2012.

Leithart, Peter J. *Athanasius*. Grand Rapids: Baker, 2011.

Weinandy, Thomas G. *Athanasius: A Theological Introduction*. Aldershot: Ashgate, 2007.

1.9

To Ablabius: On Not Three Gods[1] (late 380s CE)
Gregory of Nyssa (c. 335–c. 395 CE)

Five Theological Orations, Orations 27–31[2] (c. 380 CE)
Gregory of Nazianzus, or, Gregory the Theologian (c. 329–c. 390 CE)

Introduction

Gregory of Nyssa and Gregory of Nazianzus, along with Basil of Caesarea, are known collectively as the Cappadocian Fathers. Their contributions to the construction of early Christian dogma, piety, intellectualism, and ascetic expression cannot be overestimated. They played important roles in the establishment of theological language and thought at a time when it was not yet clear what was orthodox.

Figure 1.10 Image of Gregory of Nyssa

While Christian discussions about God predate Arius, the period designated as the "Trinitarian Controversy" begins around 318 CE and continues for about a century. The conflict between what narrowed into the pro-Nicene and anti-Nicene ("Arian") parties continued to rage after Nicaea's affirmation of Father and Son as *homoousios* (same essence) against Arius's graded hierarchy of divinity in 325. When the pro-Nicene Theodosius I became emperor, he issued a series of edicts that set the stage for a pro-Nicene Council of Constantinople in May of 381 where 150 eastern bishops reconfirmed Nicaea and anathematized anything against the full divinity of the Son and Holy Spirit. Basil was instrumental in his advocacy of the pro-Nicene cause but died just before the council in 379. The pro-Nicene party turned to Gregory Nazianzen to fill the vacancy.[3] Nazianzen and Nyssen secured Nicene orthodoxy through the former's oratory campaigns, favor with the court, and unofficial leadership of Constantinople, combined with the latter's reputation in Constantinople, administration of ecclesiastical affairs, and literary works.

During this volatile period of trinitarian deliberation, the overarching question for Nyssen and Nazianzen was how to conceive of God as one undivided essence as well as three distinct persons. The construction of one *ousia* and three *hypostases* was invaluable because affirmation of being underlies both Greek terms and locates the unity at the level of being while preserving the distinction of the Trinity from all other being. In the tumultuous aftermath of Nicaea, Gregory of Nyssa and Gregory of Nazianzus together secured the future of Nicene orthodoxy.

Gregory of Nyssa, *To Ablabius: On Not Three Gods (AdAbl)*[4]

"We are not tritheists," Gregory reminds Ablabius. Packaged in this response is a dizzying combination of conceptions of God's nature, how God relates to the world, and then more specifically how a triune God relates *in se* and *ad extra*, that is, in itself (immanent Trinity) and toward the outside (economic Trinity).[5] *AdAbl* exhibits well the original and synthetic mind of Gregory of Nyssa. It is a short work, but it was vastly influential in its specific contribution to the methodology of speaking of God. A theologian, a philosopher, and a bishop, Gregory of Nyssa seamlessly weaves together the confessional with learned philosophical accuracy. His project in *AdAbl* is thus a deeply theological one. Speaking of God is a science and an art, but it is also a practice.

The central question of the letter is to ask why we can speak of three men as concrete subjects (as in Peter, James, and John), but not of three gods (149). Once Gregory has established that neither polytheism nor the ousting of the Son and Spirit from the divine nature are acceptable, he turns toward a correction of language: human nature is one and, thus, it is not proper to speak of many human natures (150–51). In this way, Gregory sets up his premise for understanding the divine nature. For Gregory, God is a unity and is known in distinction:

> But through the perceived peculiarities, the topic of the *hypostases* admits distinction and is viewed in number according to combination. But the nature is one; it is united to itself, undivided, a precisely undivided unit, not increased through addition, not decreased through subtraction, but being one and remaining one, even if it would appear in a multitude ... (151).

In short, he presents a theology that declares essence ineffable but still embraces speaking of God.[6]

The overarching approach of *AdAbl* is one of synthesis between Christology and the doctrine of the Trinity. For Gregory, these discussions cannot be separate. At stake in the discussion of speaking of God is certainly a concern for proper terminology and the theological undergirding of trinitarian discourse, but there is also the weighty question of how humans relate to this God. For the Nyssen, there is no need to jettison the idea of the immanent triune God in order to preserve "God with us." What a proper articulation of the immanent and economic Trinity provides for Gregory is the ability to speak of God in a way suitable for humans. The inability to circumscribe or define God's nature does not portend an epistemological or confessional brick wall; there are ways to know and to speak of God.

"From," "Through," and "By"

God's substance is transcendent, but that God interacts with creation quells any fear that it is improper to speak of God. Indeed, it should compel speech (154). This speech, however, is limited to activity not nature, one activity that starts *from* (*ek*) the Father, proceeds *through* (*dia*) the Son and is completed *by* (*en*) the Holy Spirit. There is no action if it did not start or proceed or if it is not completed: the one action enacted in diverse unified activity, one divine life, "activated by the Holy Spirit, prepared by the Son, and produced by the Father's will" (155). Gregory continues: "Therefore, then, the holy Trinity works every activity according to the manner stated, not divided according to the number of the *hypostases*, but one certain motion and disposition of goodwill occurs, proceeding from the Father through the Son to the Spirit" (155). The Nyssen certainly cites Scripture as his reference and guide, so how does his argument work in an example such as that comparing Genesis 8:25 and Romans 8:6, both of which state that God judges the earth as the judge of all, and John 5:22, which states that God judges no one? Gregory says that Scripture does not contradict itself but shows the truth of the "unity of activity." God gives all judgment, the Son judges, and the Holy Spirit is the perfection of that judgment (156).

The unity points to the interrelatedness of God but also to how distinction is understood and perceived as not three gods but one. The activity points to the perceived distinction in relation to the world but also to how the activity has a definitive origination, procession, and completion as reflected in the distinction in the Godhead. For Gregory, distinction of "cause and causality" does not result in separation or difference in nature. In the Trinity, difference is located in dependence: "There is the one which depends on the first, and there is that one which is through that one which depends on the first" (160).[7] The Son is "from the cause" and therefore retains distinction as the "only-begotten," and the Spirit is not hindered in God-nature by the Son's mediation. Gregory qualifies his description of the interrelatedness of the Trinity by pointing out that even "cause" and "from a cause" are descriptors and do not indicate essence. He is careful not to collapse the triune God into a monad or speak of God's activities (*energeia*), observed in the distinction of the *hypostases*, in such a way that compromises the unity of essence. Confessing the transcendence of God does not come at the expense of God's engagement with the world.

Speaking of God

Gregory takes his cues for thinking of and speaking about God's nature from the Bible: "But we, following the suggestions of Scripture, have learned that the divine nature is unnamable and unutterable" (152). No descriptor or title can in any way encapsulate the divine nature, but this does not mean there is nothing to say. Those names "invented from human usage" demonstrate something important about God: a desire for humanity to observe and name God's activity (152). Gregory expects that these names will be congruent with accepted custom, no doubt, but as humans are compelled to speak of God they will meet the mystery with a sense of discovery and delight at the possibilities. For Gregory, "language is, then, one might say, both imperfect and appropriate."[8]

This capacity to speak offers epistemic and experiential access to God. As long as the descriptors do not intend to encompass God's substance or imply plurality, one can feel free to name aspects of God in the singular. Gregory gives some examples—good, holy, savior, judge—and leaves the list open for an undetermined number of descriptors, as long as they are given by one who is beholding God's activity (159). Here is an opportunity for creativity that is based on the human capacity to behold God's activity and offers a way to engage with God's identity and to shape Christian speaking of God. For Gregory, the infinite cannot be defined and the finite mind cannot comprehend the infinite (158). Our perspectives are finite and reflective caution is requisite.

Gregory's approach to speaking of God can be summarized as a posture of humility toward God and others. Speaking of the triune God is a

Figure 1.11 Gregory of Nyssa

participatory act where humanity communally and individually engages with Scripture, invented custom, and the experience of God interacting with the world and with the life of the mind and heart. For the Nyssen, speaking of God must flow from a fully trinitarian perspective, otherwise one either says too much and falls into error or says too little and remains distant from the divine.

Gregory of Nazianzus, *Five Theological Orations*

In his famous five orations (Orations 27–31), probably given in the summer or autumn of 380 CE, Gregory's oratory prowess in conjunction with his commitment to a careful and scriptural trinitarian terminology threw a strong anti-Nicene contingent into disarray and simultaneously empowered the weary and outnumbered pro-Nicene camp. While he did not write any treatises dedicated to dealing with the controversies of his day, Nazianzen modeled an integration of preaching and theology.[9] He distinguishes himself in the history of trinitarian thought as one who emphasized the harmony of unity and diversity in the Godhead: "For Gregory, the generative nature of God eternally produces the triunity as the perfection of divine existence."[10]

"Discussion of theology is not for everyone": *Oration* 27[11]

For Gregory, context is everything. Theology is not to be treated casually or by the untransformed person. This does not mean, however, that Nazianzen is propagating an elitist theology; on the contrary, it is for the sake of those doing the theologizing to prepare themselves properly: "For one who is not pure to lay hold of pure things is dangerous, just as it is for weak eyes to look at the sun's brightness" (*Or.* 27.3). He promotes what he considers to be a balanced approach to theology that is keen to investigate but that is cognizant of human limitation. However, Gregory exhorts, "it is more important that we should remember God than that we should breathe. . . it is not continual remembrance of God I seek to discourage, but continual discussion of theology. I am not opposed either to theology, as if it were a breach of piety, but only to its untimely practice, or to the instruction in it, except when this goes to excess" (*Or.* 27.4).

Gregory is concerned not just with the content and method of theological discourse, but also with the theologian as one who is continually being transformed. He assails his interlocutors with a list of questions to reveal whether or not what they are offering promotes the tangible outcroppings of Christian piety—feeding the poor, showing hospitality, prayer, etc. He deems it scandalous that, for his opponents, true piety has become optional and they are concerned only with fame and not the wellbeing of others. It is important to note that this construction of his interlocutors is fundamental to Gregory's rhetorical approach and should not necessarily be taken at face value. The disqualifying of one's opponent from the debate by discrediting their participation as a valid conversation partner is a common and effective rhetorical tool in ancient polemic.

"To know God is hard": *Oration* 28

Now that the matter of context and character has been firmly established, Gregory expounds upon the doctrine of God. The first thing he makes clear is that even the highest of experiences (his own included) with the majesty of God barely scratch the surface of the Divine Being. Nazianzen's basis for this discussion is very similar to Nyssen's, that is, the clear demarcation between Creator and created that irrevocably places human comprehension of the essence of God within a bounded set. Humans have bodies and language; God does not have a body and is not confined to language. Thus, "to tell of God is not possible ... but to know him is even less possible" (*Or.* 28.4). To claim encompassing knowledge of creation, even of our own selves, is beyond our purview (he expounds at length on this starting in *Or.* 28.22). Nazianzen states it well: "Conviction, you see, of a thing's existence is quite different from knowledge of *what* it is" (*Or.* 28.5).

Gregory goes to great lengths to explain that it is not possible to ascribe corporeality to God or assume corporeality can access the divine nature. It is not biblical, for one thing, nor does the "verdict of our fold" (i.e., tradition) affirm it (*Or.* 28:9). Here he gives a brief lesson on how terminology operates. God is incorporeal, but in saying this Gregory does not assume it offers us all-encompassing access to God's essential being. Descriptors such as "unoriginate" or "immutable" can be predicated of divinity but the full reality of God is left a mystery still. Where Nazianzen is more practical than Nyssen is in the strength of his affirmation of identifying God as subject: "an inquirer into the nature of a real being cannot stop short at saying what it is *not* but must add to his denials a positive affirmation" (*Or.* 28.9).

Gregory does not lose sight, however, of a God who deeply loves creation and does not hide behind inaccessibility. He points to the titles ascribed to God in Scripture—Spirit, fire, light, love, and so forth—and notes that the human mind cannot think of these titles without material reference. The desire to know does not overturn the inability to grasp what cannot be known (*Or.* 28.13). He points to those who "knew" God in the Bible—Enoch, Abraham, Elijah, Peter, and John, to name but a few—as examples of the pinnacle of knowledge but that even these men did not have knowledge in its fullest sense.[12] Gregory reminds us that theology is difficult and truth is an unending quest: "All truth, all philosophy, to be sure, is obscure, hard to trace out" (*Or.* 28:21). With the conclusion of *Oration* 28, Gregory's rhetoric is reminiscent of when the Lord finally spoke to Job and bombarded him with questions about the created order. The point is clear: human knowledge is so limited and God is so far beyond the created order that access is only granted through God's gracious revelation; and this should bring us to reverent silence and thus with Job declare, "I will say no more" (Job 40:5).

"He remained what he was; what he was not, he assumed": *Oration* 29–30

Gregory opens his two orations on the Son by first establishing that no division is admitted in the Godhead and the method of parentage of the Son is not coincident with human generation but is eternal and incorporeal (*Or.* 29.2). He then shifts to a question and answer format to refute the opposition. In this section, he considers how the Son and Spirit can be co-eternal with God but not identified as origin (*Or.* 29.3), as well as how the voluntary begetting of the Son does not involve change within the Godhead (*Or.* 29.4–6). Harkening back to his "Job-like" exposition on the limitations of human knowing, he places this begetting as one of those truths that humans cannot fathom (*Or.* 29.8). Simply put, God is not like us and God's begetting is not like our begetting.

Gregory marks the problem of subordination of the Son as both an attempt to maintain equality by connecting two "unequals" (*Or.* 29.14) and an affirmation that the nature of the Father *qua* cause is superior to the Son (*Or.* 29.15). In response to the question of whether "Father" is a designation of substance or activity, he offers another option altogether: "'Father' designates neither the substance nor the activity, but the relationship, the manner of being, which holds good between the Father and the Son" (*Or.* 29.16). Gregory "tolerates" questions from his interlocutors for a while but then assails his opponents with examples from Scripture that affirm the Son as properly God (*Or.* 29.17). And if, perchance, an opponent would fight back with scriptural proof of their own of the Son's subordination, Gregory illustrates how expressions of divinity should be predicated of the Godhead and those "lowlier" should be predicated of the incarnate Christ for the sake of our salvation (*Or.* 29.18). Scorning the incarnate Christ scorns the transcendent: "He remained what he was; what he was not, he assumed" (*Or.* 29.19). For Gregory, the Incarnation invites paradox and ends in mystery and our only response is faith: "Faith, in fact, is what gives fullness to our reasoning" (*Or.* 29.21).

In *Oration* 30, Gregory continues with an expanded examination of the Scripture that he had brought to bear in the preceding oration. His solution for speaking properly of Christ is to allocate the "more distinctly divine" expressions to the Godhead and the "humbler and more human" to the human—"God passible for our sake over against sin" (*Or.* 30.1). So, Gregory does just that, he addresses difficult passages raised by opponents and explores the titles of the Son (*Or.* 30.20–21), bouncing back and forth between Old and New Testaments in order to do so. The key for Gregory of Nazianzus is the Son's voluntary appropriation of the stuff of human existence for the sake of our salvation.

"We shall extol the Spirit; we shall not be afraid": *Oration* 31

Gregory structures this oration in a fashion similar to *Oration* 29, but this time he addresses opponents' questions about the Spirit. In response to the question of whether or not the Holy Spirit is ingenerate or begotten, he puts forth another option, "procession," as a midway term of sorts: "Insofar as he proceeds from the Father, he is no creature; inasmuch as he is not begotten, he is no Son; and to the extent that procession is the mean between ingeneracy and generacy, he is God" (*Or.* 31.8). As to what this proceeding actually is, Gregory leaves that to mystery.

For Gregory, it is imperative that speaking of God informs worship (*Or.* 31.17) and he takes particular offense at the accusation that the concepts he is setting forth are not in the Bible (*Or.* 31.21). Thus, he engages in a discussion of how to read Scripture in which he rebuffs an overly literal reading of Scripture that would map corporeality onto God (*Or.* 31.22). Gregory points toward two transformations of the human way of life in history, the covenant that brought about the transition from idols to the Law and the covenant enacting the transition from Law to Gospel. He identifies a shared feature in both covenants: God is not a despot and will not use force (*Or.* 31.25). He draws upon the image of a physician or a schoolmaster to explain how God persuades and does not coerce.[13] Gregory of Nazianzus uses Scripture's outlining of the covenants to illustrate how in current times this progress has brought the church to a clearer manifestation of the Holy Spirit than before (*Or.* 31.26).

Conclusion

Modern theology has had ample opportunity in recent years to re-think, re-imagine and re-evaluate the trinitarian tradition and, as a result, Gregory of Nyssa and Gregory of Nazianzus have received new attention. Scholars such as T. F. Torrence and Robert W. Jenson demonstrate just how important the reception of the Cappadocians on trinitarian matters is to the history of Protestant systematic theology.[14] Fresh engagement with the two Cappadocians includes many Protestant voices that are taking part in the groundswell of rereading the Cappadocians as well as in the re-energized consideration of Nicaea and its aftermath.[15] The Gregorys gave us shared language to speak about God and confess God's commitment to creation through Christ. Their particular way of doing this that marshals the entire Bible to such a strong degree exhibits a versatile and wide-ranging understanding of Scripture that is fruitful for considerations of God. This commitment to Scripture's central role in speaking of God, along with their dynamic entwining of the conceptions of Trinity and Christology, demonstrates Gregory of Nyssa and Gregory of Nazianzus to be valuable resources for the continuing theological endeavor of speaking of God.

Notes

1. Translated from *Ad Ablabium*; all references to this work (Gregory of Nyssa, *To Ablabius: Concerning We Should Not Think of Saying That There are Not Three Gods in The Trinitarian Controversy* [trans. William G. Rusch; Minneapolis: Fortress, 1980], 149–161) shall be noted by employing in-text citations.
2. All references to this work (Lionel Wickham and Frederick Williams, trans., *On God and Christ: St Gregory of Nazianzus,* The Five Theological Orations *and* Two Letters to Cledonius [Popular Patristic Series; Crestwood, NY: St. Vladimir's Seminary Press], 2002) shall be noted by employing in-text citations.
3. "Gregory's short tenure in Constantinople was both the most arduous and the most fruitful period of his life, and nothing short of decisive for the course of Trinitarian orthodoxy," Christopher A. Beeley, *Gregory of Nazianzus on the Trinity and the Knowledge of God: In Your Light We Shall See Light* (Oxford: Oxford University Press, 2008), 34.
4. There is a wide range of opinions regarding the time Gregory of Nyssa wrote *On Not Three Gods* (*AdAbl*). Based upon the confident serenity of the letter and the synthetic approach proffered in the work, it is most likely from later in Gregory's life. See Guilio Maspero, *Trinity and Man: Gregory of Nyssa's* Ad Ablabium. SVC 86 (Leiden: Brill, 2007), xix–xxii, and Lucian Turcescu, *Gregory of Nyssa and the Concept of Divine Persons* (Oxford: Oxford University Press, 2005), 64.
5. Though foreign to Gregory, this construction of the Trinity *in se* and *ad extra* that has become a fixture in modern trinitarian thought is, generally speaking, a helpful way to capture the breadth and relevance of the Cappadocian's treatment of the Trinity. But, as with any interpretive move, it is important to recognize it as such and continue to interrogate its usefulness.
6. Gregory of Nyssa has his own brand of apophatism. See Scot Douglass, *Theology of the Gap: Cappadocian Language Theory and the Trinitarian*

Controversy, AUS 235 (New York: Peter Lang, 2005) and Ari Ojell, "Apophatic Theology" in *The Brill Dictionary of Gregory of Nyssa*, eds, Lucas Francisco Mateo-Seco and Giulio Maspero and trans. Seth Cherney, *Supplements to Vigilae Christianae* 99 (Leiden: Brill, 2010), 68–73.

7. We should not identify these "relations of origin" with the filioque since Gregory's conception of the Father and the Son is that they do not form one principle like that in Western doctrine. For Gregory, the proper cause of the Holy Spirit is the Father. Turcescu, *Gregory of Nyssa*, 68.

8. Morwenna Ludlow, *Gregory of Nyssa, Ancient and (Post)Modern* (Oxford: Oxford University Press, 2007), 235.

9. Frances M. Young with Andrew Teal, *From Nicaea to Chalcedon: A Guide to the Literature and its Background*, 2nd ed. (Grand Rapids: Baker, 2010), 162.

10. Lewis Ayres, *Nicaea and Its Legacy: An Approach to Fourth-Century Trinitarian Theology* (Oxford: Oxford University Press, 2004), 244–45.

11. A read-through of Nazianzen's orations offers a taste of what it might have been like to be in the audience. Sometimes harsh and other times inspiring, Nazianzen here mounts an oratorical assault against those whom he calls "grotesque and preposterous word-gamesters" as those who peddle a false and useless knowledge (*Or.* 27.1). It is not entirely clear who his opponents were but they may have included homoians, heterousians (Eunomians), and homoiousians.

12. *Or.* 28.18–20.

13. It is likely that these images are draw directly from Origen.

14. Morwenna Ludlow, *Gregory of Nyssa: Ancient and (Post)modern* (Oxford: Oxford University Press, 2007), 15–50.

15. E.g., Colin E. Gunton, *The Promise of Trinitarian Theology* (Edinburgh: T&T Clark, 1997); Thomas F. Torrance, *Trinitarian Perspectives: Toward Doctrinal Agreement* (Edinburgh: T&T Clark, 1994); Jean Zizioulas, *Being as Communion: Studies in Personhood and the Church* (Crestwood, NY: St. Vladimir's Seminary Press 1985).

Select Bibliography

Primary sources

Gregory of Nyssa, *To Ablabius: Concerning We Should Not Think of Saying That There are Not Three Gods* in *The Trinitarian Controversy.* 149–161. Translated by William G. Rusch. Minneapolis: Fortress, 1980.

Wickham, Lionel and Frederick Williams, trans. *On God and Christ: St Gregory of Nazianzus*, The Five Theological Orations *and* Two Letters to

Cledonius. Popular Patristic Series. Crestwood, NY: St. Vladimir's Seminary Press, 2002.

Secondary sources

Beeley, Christopher A. *Gregory of Nazianzus on the Trinity and the Knowledge of God: In Your Light We Shall See Light*. Oxford: Oxford University Press, 2008.

Coakley, Sarah, ed. *Re-Thinking Gregory of Nyssa*. Oxford: Blackwell, 2003.

Daley, Brian E. *Gregory of Nazianzus*. The Early Church Fathers. London: Routledge, 2006.

Ludlow, Morwenna. *Gregory of Nyssa, Ancient and (Post)Modern*. Oxford: Oxford University Press, 2007.

Mateo-Seco, Lucas Francisco and Giulio Maspero, eds. *The Brill Dictionary of Gregory of Nyssa*. Translated by Seth Cherney. *Supplements to Vigilae Christianae* 99. Leiden: Brill, 2010.

Meredith, Anthony. *The Cappadocians*. Crestwood, NY: St. Vladimir's Seminary Press, 1995.

1.10

On Wealth and Poverty (388–389 CE)

John Chrysostom (c. 349– September 14, 407 CE)

Introduction

John, known as Chrysostom (meaning, *golden-mouthed*) because of his eloquence, was born to Christian parents in the Syrian city of Antioch around the year 349. This was a period of remarkable change in the Roman Empire. Even though Christianity was ascending, it was not yet the dominant religion, and it struggled to compete with traditional Greek, Roman, and the variety of local religions that dotted the empire. At a young age, John joined Theodore and Maximus—who later became bishops of Mopsuestia and Seleucia in Isauria respectively—in the school of the renowned pagan rhetorician Libanius. There, John studied philosophy, literature, and rhetoric. In his late teenage years (c. 367), John joined his friends at the *asketerion*, the famous theological seminary in Antioch, where he continued his studies in biblical exegesis and theology under Diodore and asceticism under Carterius. Around 371, John was ordained a lector and soon thereafter moved to the mountains near Antioch to lead the life of rigorous asceticism as an *anchorite* (a hermit). Perhaps because of his poor health, he returned to Antioch and was ordained a priest in 386 and served in the city for the next twelve years. When the Archbishop of the capital city of Constantinople died suddenly in 397, John was put forward as a candidate for the position and was consecrated to the See on February 26, 398. As the Archbishop of Constantinople, John

Figure 1.12 Statue of St. John Chrysostom

continued holding Christians accountable for the plight of the poor and spoke frequently against the excesses he saw in the capital. Through a series of political and ecclesiastical developments, his popularity with those in power and vested interests waned and Chrysostom was eventually removed from his See and sent into exile in 404. He died on September 14, 407, on his way to the Black Sea.

Of John's years in Antioch, over 900 sermons have survived, and many more have been lost to us. This was a turbulent time in the empire as the city of Antioch found itself at the center of a rebellion that drew the ire of the emperor Theodosius. Many of Antioch's citizens, who fled the city for the mountains and uninhabited places of the surrounding environs, died on the way and the city itself faced increasing economic difficulties: "In the city itself the baths and theatre were shut; the usually bustling market-place was empty. Only the churches were full. Throughout this period John preached on Saturdays and Sundays in the morning and on weekdays in the afternoon."[1] It was during this time that John's eloquent preaching and reputation for the care of the poor of the city gained him the sobriquet of "Chrysostom."

The seven homilies on wealth and poverty[2]

As the new year 388 (or 389) dawned, John Chrysostom, still a priest in the church of Antioch, took the opportunity of the feast of the Saturnalia to inaugurate a series of sermons on Luke 16:14–31, the parable of Lazarus and the rich man. Chrysostom delivered his sermons probably within the span of the year, interrupting his schedule in order to accommodate the liturgical year, the various feasts of saints, martyrs, or the "occasional" natural catastrophe, such as a devastating earthquake that hit Antioch between his fifth and sixth sermons. Throughout his preaching career in Antioch as well as in Constantinople, the homilies of St. John are dominated by his care for the poor and their plight, and the responsibility of the rich (especially those within the Church) to give alms generously and without distinction. Chrysostom's picture of the poor was always set against the prosperous marketplace of late antiquity, a picture that accentuated the chasm between the classes and the sharp social distinctions present in the city.

John Chrysostom follows in a great line of early writers who exhorted Christians, especially wealthy Christians, to pay more attention to their souls and divest themselves from attachments to material wealth. Throughout the early church period, the argument was made again and again that it is the attitude one has towards wealth and poverty, not wealth itself that marks a rich person. What seems to be of utmost concern to most early Christian writers is not so much wealth or poverty as such, but the attitude one has towards wealth and poverty. Early Christian theologians and writers were highly concerned with the venality and unreliability of wealthy Christians.[3] This attitude, of course, was not without parallels in the biblical prescriptions that taught that freedom from passionate attachments (including material possessions) was part of the ideal life (1 Cor. 6:12, 7:29–31; Phil 4:11–12; 1 Jn 2:15–16).[4]

Chrysostom develops similar themes in these homilies. In the first sermon, based on Luke 16:19–21, he lays out the plan for the series and invites his audience to explore the lives of the two men; this sermon was given in the wake of the Saturnalia, the Roman festival of the god Saturn, which the city had just celebrated in extravagant form. Throughout the sermon, Chrysostom draws parallels between the lives of the two protagonists and those of his audience, and brings into focus the moral character of the two men. The second sermon focuses on Luke 16:22–24 and concentrates on the death of the protagonists, allowing the true character of each to be revealed. Throughout this sermon Chrysostom encourages his audience to move beyond the surface reading of a dichotomy between rich and poor—even healthy and sick—in the "earthly" condition of the two, and search for the spiritual meaning of the story. The rich "must hold their property as stewards for the poor, and must share their wealth without regard to the moral qualities of those who are in need."[5] As one moves through these sermons, we must bear in mind that in fourth-century Antioch (as in our time) this was not an easy argument to make, nor one that resonated well with the affluent members of Chrysostom's congregation.

The next two of the homilies also follow closely the divisions in the biblical narrative: the third concentrating on verses 24–26, the rich man's first petition that Lazarus bring him a drop of water and the fourth on the second petition, verses 27–31, that Lazarus visit his brothers. The last three sermons move away from the account in the gospel of Luke but still deal with issues of class differentiation, wealth and poverty, returning to the theme of Lazarus and the rich man in the seventh and final sermon through the text of Matthew 7:13–14: "Enter through the narrow gate." Here, Chrysostom reprimands his audience for their unhealthy attitude and reminds them that Lazarus entered God's rest and blessedness through the narrow path, while the rich man, who took the easy route, ended up in "the inexorable judgments, that unquenchable fire, and the undying worm" (Mk 9:48) (p. 125).

Stewardship and God's gift

The first sermon, then, deals with the lives of the two men. Following the biblical narrative, Chrysostom juxtaposes the luxury of the one and the poverty of the other, the life of self-indulgence (the true unrighteousness in this story) against the life of patient suffering. Chrysostom is very careful to note that there was nothing intrinsically evil or unrighteous or vile in wealth itself, or righteous and good in poverty, as such. He is very careful not to trivialize one or vulgarize the other. On the contrary, he insists that both states are neutral—one is not a sign of divine favor, the other of divine punishment. For Chrysostom, it is how one responds within the condition one finds oneself that truly matters: "Many people admire [Lazarus] for this reason only, that he was poor, but I can show that he endured chastisements nine in number, imposed not to punish him, but to make him more glorious; and indeed this came about" (p. 29).[6] The same held true for the rich man who by his indifference to the plight of his poor neighbor "became hard-hearted and more reckless even than that unjust judge who knew neither fear of God nor shame before man" (p. 21). This is a theme Chrysostom continues in the second homily: "Let us learn from this man not to call the rich [fortunate] nor the poor unfortunate. Rather, if we are to tell the truth, the rich man is not the one who has collected many possessions but the one who needs few possessions; and the poor man is not the one who has no possessions but the one who has many desires" (p. 40).

Now in this, the second homily, the time has come for Chrysostom to move to the heart of the matter, having seen what he calls the "virtuous disposition" of his audience. It was in death that the veil of confusion, of temporality, of self-imposed ignorance and deceit was finally lifted and the true character of each was revealed. The evangelist is clear: in this new and eternal condition, freed from pretense and oppression, it is the rich man who became a suppliant: "Father [Abraham], have mercy on me, and send Lazarus to dip the end of his finger in water and let a drop fall into my mouth" (pp. 47–48). The conclusion is clear, says Chrysostom, "the situation was reversed, and everyone learned who was really the poor man" (p. 46).

But for Chrysostom, this trope of irony is not a jubilant eschatological moment of social reversal. As he follows the biblical narrative, John is very aware that he ought not pander to the factions within his own congregation by making either poverty itself a means of salvation or wealth a reason for eternal damnation. Chrysostom neither lingers voyeuristically on the suffering Lazarus nor delights in the plight of the rich man. On the contrary, he is both quick and careful to anticipate the objection: "Why should the rich man suffer such a terrible fate? What is his crime? Did he do something evil to Lazarus? Did he steal from him? Did he oppress, punish, or abuse him? Is he condemned only because he is rich, or is God a respecter of persons, for Abraham, too, was a wealthy man?"

All these objections, argues Chrysostom, miss the point of the story: "Indeed Lazarus suffered no injustice from the rich man; for the rich man did not take Lazarus' money," but his offense was much greater: it was the crime of *indifference*. For though he did not take Lazarus' money, the rich man failed to share his own: "See the man and his works," declares John, "indeed this too is theft, not to share one's possessions" (p. 49ff).

Chrysostom introduces God in *propria persona* to pass judgment: "I sent the poor man Lazarus to your gate to teach you virtue and to receive your love [and] you ignored [him]" (p. 48). Unlike the righteous Abraham who was proactive in generosity and quick to extend hospitality, who "hunted out those who were going past and brought them into his own house," the rich man of our story overlooked even the one who was lying inside his own gate. Chrysostom turns to Malachi 3:8–10 to find support for his case: "Accusing the Jews through the prophet, God says, 'The earth has brought forth her increase, and you have not brought forth your tithes; but the theft of the poor is in your houses.' Since you have not given the accustomed offering, he says, you have stolen the goods of the poor" (p. 49). Not sharing one's own possessions is indeed theft.

Chrysostom insists that like Israel of old, each of us, individually, and as a Church community, is called to be stewards of God's wealth—the image he uses is that of the imperial *oikonomos*, the household steward—and we are called to distribute it to those in need: "For our money is the Lord's, however we may have gathered it . . . This is why God has allowed you to have more: not for you to waste on prostitutes, drink, fancy food, expensive clothes, and all the other kinds of indolence, but for you to distribute to those in need" (pp. 49–50) without distinction or limitations.

"The rich must hold their property as stewards for the poor," writes Catherine Ross in her introduction to Chrysostom's *Wealth and Poverty*.[7] But what does it mean to be stewards *for* (not *of*) the poor? To be sure, for Chrysostom, in the late fourth century, such stewardship included patronage and almsgiving, but it did not stop there, that was merely the beginning:

> Against the ostentatious display that was both the basis and the articulation of status [in fourth century Antioch, as it is in our time], . . . Chrysostom sketched an alternative economic system in which the rich had to acknowledge

their indebtedness precisely to those who were poor and insignificant in the eyes of the world. His message was one of mutuality. He obtained this mutuality by investing the very poor, who had previously been excluded from patron–client relations because they had nothing to contribute [like Lazarus], with a valuable commodity, namely, special access to God.[8]

The key here is to see how Chrysostom lifts up the very poor from the status of the *invisible* to the necessary. This, of course, is not an ontological argument, rather, it is one based on an inversion of the ancient motif of "worthiness." Rather than accepting the Roman axiom that "the good person is the rich person," Chrysostom inverts the relationship so that "the rich person is the good person."

Friendship with God

Throughout his life—both as a priest in Antioch and as a bishop in Constantinople—wealthy Christians found it difficult to be around Chrysostom, for he always challenged them to take care of the poor. Chrysostom's prodigious energy was not limited to warnings against the practices of the wealthy. He insisted that action be taken, and his own life as monk, priest and, eventually, bishop exemplified this reflective purgation he demanded of others.

Chrysostom focused on the rich man in the story to provide an alternative for his own congregation. The rich man's life was oriented by indifference: he would step in and out of his house, perhaps many times during the day, and yet he would not even notice Lazarus laying at his doorsteps. As such, his orientation was one of not simply indifference, but a self-referential, *blind* indifference: "If we suppose that he passed the man by on the first day, he would probably have felt some pity on the second day;" says St. John, "if he overlooked him even on that day, he surely ought to have been moved on the third or the fourth or the day after that, even if he were more cruel than the wild beast. But he felt no such emotion ..." (p. 21). Throughout these sermons, Chrysostom invited his audience to see the daily routine of this man; to see him stepping over the threshold of his courtyard where the suppliant Lazarus would lay incapable of uttering the customary words to entreat for the alms that never came, to see him going to the marketplace, even perhaps the Temple to offer sacrifices for his sins, putting his alms in the box of the poor (though Chrysostom is certain that the latter would never happen, since he did not take care of the one who was at his doorstep) and coming back to his home, after a day full of social and religious observance only to walk past Lazarus once more and enter his house "clean" and "satisfied," ready for another lavish banquet, "communion" with his friends. The rich man in Jesus's parable is not simply a heuristic device, Chrysostom argues in these homilies—he is us.

But such a telling of the story can be seen as a bit unfair to this unnamed rich man (and, by extension to us, too). For in the then commonly accepted practice of patronage, the rich man could raise an objection and argue that he had no obligation to take care of Lazarus. Lazarus had nothing to offer back. Lazarus could not be a true client. The relationship was broken because the sick and dying Lazarus, due to his sickness and his inability to follow and offer loyalty, praise, and prestige to his patron, had already broken the bonds of the patron–client relationship himself—for there is no reciprocity.

In his prescriptions for the care of the poor Chrysostom uses the language of "gift," "grace," and "abundance." He exhorts his congregation to give without the imposition of limitations on those who receive. He notes that Abraham did not ask an account of the stranger's life, nor did he require them to change their ways but "he simply welcomed all who were passing by. For if you wish to show kindness, you must not require an accounting of a person's life, but merely correct his poverty and fill his need" (p. 52). And he concludes:

> The almsgiver is a harbor for those in necessity: a harbor receives all who have encountered shipwreck, and frees them from danger; whether they are bad or good or whatever they are who are in danger, it escorts them into its own shelter. So you likewise, when you see on earth the man who has encountered the shipwreck of poverty, do not judge him, do not seek an account of his life, but free him from his misfortune (p. 52).

This is the particularly Christian move from "reciprocity" to "gift" and from "patronage" to *friendship*.

Conclusion

In her *God Knows There's Need: Christian Responses to Poverty*, Susan Holman mentions that even John Calvin "built his vision for the diaconate on Chrysostom's writings," but, notes Holman, not many Presbyterians know that.[9] At its most basic expression, Christianity is a *religio* (from the Latin *relegare*, meaning "to bind together"). All Christians—whether Protestant, Roman Catholic or Eastern Orthodox—understand Christianity as a community, a group, a family, bound together by bonds of faith and practice that stem from the relationship with God and bear witness to it. As such, questions of wealth and poverty, social responsibility, and the relationship between the rich and the poor in our societies have occupied the thinking of countless Christians. This attention to the plight of the poor and the Church's unique responsibility for those in need is not new; rather, it has been part of the very identity of Christianity from its earliest times (e.g., Acts 6:1–7).

Following the example of the Apostles in the book of Acts and the mandate of Jesus's teaching in the Gospels, John Chrysostom offered for the Church a new axis of orientation—both for his time and ours. Lazarus is not simply "an object lesson" manufactured by God for the benefit of the Church. Rather, Lazarus becomes the mirror within which the Church can see herself as she truly is: a suppliant at the doorsteps of God. For Chrysostom, the locus of our friendship with God and the lens through which Christians are called to see the world is found in a meal, in God's banquet set for us: the *Eucharist*. Unlike the feasts the rich man of the story set for his flatterers and clients, only an earshot away from the distressed Lazarus, John looks at the banquet that Jesus set and notes that it was indeed within the context of that meal that the Lord told those who had gathered around him that they were no longer servants but chosen friends (Jn 15:14–15).

It is hard to overstate the influence of John Chrysostom on the theology and life of Christianity. Along with Basil the Great and Gregory of Nazianzus, Chrysostom is considered as one of the Three Hierarchs, the most respected theological voices whose Christian insight and influence continues to impact most of our theological inquiry to this day.

Notes

1. Wendy Mayer and Pauline Allen, *John Chrysostom* (London: Routledge, 2000), 7.
2. A fuller version of this essay can be found in Mark Husbands and Jeffrey P. Greenman (eds), *Ancient Faith for the Church's Future* (Downers Grove: InterVarsity Press, 2008), 156–68.
3. Cf. Clement, *Who is the Rich Man that Shall be Saved?* 7, 11–12, 14–15, 20.
4. For an excellent short essay see Rebecca H. Weaver, "Wealth and Poverty in the Early Church," *Interpretation* 41.4 (October 1987), 368–81.
5. St. John Chrysostom, *On Wealth and Poverty*, transl. and introduction Catharine P. Roth (Crestwood, NY: St Vladimir's Seminary Press, 1999) 12. Henceforth, references will be to pages of this edition.

6.   And he enumerates them: "he was poor, he was ill, he had no one to help him. He remained in a house which could have relieved all his troubles but he was granted no word of comfort. He saw the man who neglected him enjoying such luxury, and not only enjoying luxury but living in wickedness without suffering any misfortune. He could not look to any other Lazarus or comfort himself with any philosophy or resurrection. Along with the evils I have mentioned, he obtained a bad reputation among the mass of people because of his misfortunes. Not for two or three days but for his whole life he saw himself in this situation and the rich man in the opposite" (p. 37).
7.   St. John Chrysostom, *On Wealth and Poverty*, 12.
8.   Blake Leyerle, "John Chrysostom on Almsgiving and the Use of Money," *HTR* 87:1 (1994): 41.
9.   Susan R. Holman, *God Knows There's Need: Christian Responses to Poverty* (New York: Oxford University Press, 2009), 4ff. See also Bonnie Pattison, *Poverty in the Theology of John Calvin* (Eugene, OR: Pickwick, 2006).

Select Bibliography

Primary source

St. John Chrysostom, *On Wealth and Poverty*. Translated and introduced by Catharine P. Roth. Crestwood, NY: St Vladimir's Seminary Press, 1999.

Secondary sources

Holman, Susan R., ed. *Wealth and Poverty in Early Church and Society*. Grand Rapids: Baker Academic, 2008.

Holman, Susan R. *God Knows There's Need: Christian Responses to Poverty*. New York: Oxford University Press, 2009.

Leyerle, Blake. "John Chrysostom on Almsgiving and the Use of Money." *Harvard Theological Review* 87:1 (1994): 29–47.

Mayer, Wendy, and Pauline Allen. *John Chrysostom*. London: Routledge, 2000.

Rhee, Helen. *Loving the Poor, Saving the Rich: Wealth, Poverty, and Early Christian Formation*. Grand Rapids: Baker Academic, 2012.

Weaver, Rebecca H. "Wealth and Poverty in the Early Church," *Interpretation* 41.4 (October 1987): 368–81.

1.11

On the Unity of Christ[1] (438 CE)

Cyril of Alexandria (c. 378–June 27, 444 CE)

Introduction

Cyril stands as one of the most important figures during one of the most important periods of the history of early Christianity. He was born in the period historians call "Late Antiquity," a transitional period from the world of classical antiquity to that of Medieval Europe and the Middle Ages. In the West, Cyril's contemporary and fellow North African bishop, Augustine of Hippo Regius, is still one of the best-known representatives of this period of theological, socioeconomic, and political change. A brilliant theologian and a shrewd politician, Cyril is almost singularly responsible for the nuances of the Christian understanding of the relationship between the human and divine natures of Christ, as well as for the "grammar" that interprets the Incarnation for Western and Eastern Christians alike.

Cyril was born c. 378 in Alexandria, the second most important city in the Roman Empire in this period.[2] By the end of the fourth century, Alexandria's economic, social, philosophical, and ecclesiastical dominance was superintended by both the Byzantine City Governor and the Patriarch of the city. Cyril's maternal uncle, Theophilus, was Patriarch of Alexandria from 385 until his death in 412. From around the age of twelve onwards, Cyril came under the tutelage of his uncle who provided for him the best classical and Christian education of the time. Cyril was trained in grammar and

Figure 1.13 Icon of Cyril

rhetoric, philosophy and mathematics, as well as Christian theology and the Scriptures. His knowledge of the Bible was profound and the Scriptures informed all of Cyril's theological vision.

At the age of twenty-five, in 403, Cyril was ordained a *lector* (reader) in the church, and it was in his capacity as a theological and administrative assistant of the Patriarch that Cyril attended the Synod of Oak (403), one of the most important Church councils of that era. It was at the Synod of Oak that Cyril experienced first-hand the rough-and-tumble world of ecclesiastical politics as well as the need for theological clarity and coherence in both teaching and preaching.

When Theophilus died in the fall of 412, Cyril was consecrated his successor; and even though the election was highly, even violently contested, Cyril prevailed with the support of the local church. During

Cyril's thirty-two years as bishop of Alexandria, the city experienced in multiple ways the immensity of the transition from a millennium-old pagan city to the Christendom of the early Byzantine period. The old order was passing away. Traditional Hellenes (pagans) were losing their influence and were constantly at odds—often violently—with the rising Christian plurality that tended to dominate civic life. The same was true for the large Jewish population of Alexandria. Like his uncle before him, Cyril was not simply an ecclesiastical authority but engaged actively in politics and civic life.

Christianity in Alexandria followed in the centuries-long tradition of exceptional philosophical education and intellectual rigor that had made the city the envy of the ancient world. By the second century Alexandria had become the most important center of Christian life and thought far surpassing any other city. Clement (c. 150–216) was one of the earliest Christian teachers and the most articulate philosophical mind of the second century, while Origen (c. 184/185–253/254) towered over all and his influence continued to be at the core of Christian theology for centuries to come. In the generation just prior to Cyril's, Athanasius (c. 296–373) had fought against the heresy of the Arians and had set the theological framework for our understanding of the Incarnation and the Trinity. And Cyril was prepared well to become the inheritor of this intellectual tradition. In addition to his theological and philosophical acumen, Cyril also possessed a deep appreciation and knowledge of the Bible. He was a prolific commentator of Scripture, producing in-depth works on almost all the books of the Bible (many of which have survived to our time) as well as a plethora of theological works. Much of Cyril's profound engagement with the Bible, however, has been overshadowed by his works on Christology produced on the occasion of the debate with Nestorius, the Bishop of Constantinople. Through his letters and treatises, Cyril shaped our understanding of the Incarnation and gave Christians the language by which to understand the relationship between the human and divine natures of Christ. The most famous of his treatises on Christology is *On the Unity of Christ*.

Cyril wrote *On the Unity of Christ* c. 428 at the end of almost a decade of grueling debates on the very nature of language, of understanding how Christians ought to interpret the Incarnation, and of the process of salvation itself. The occasion for most of this debate came in the year 428, when "a storm broke over the universal Church whose proportions could hardly have been envisaged by those then involved. It was a crisis that forced the whole of Christianity to examine the fundamentals of its beliefs about Jesus, and set in train no less than three ecumenical councils (Ephesus 431; Chalcedon 451; Constantinople II 553)."[3]

The Christological debates

In 428, the emperor summoned a monk called Nestorius from Syrian Antioch to become the new Patriarch of Constantinople.[4] Nestorius was a brilliant theologian in his own right and came from a long tradition of Antiochene theologians such as Diodore of Tarsus, John Chrysostom, and Theodore of Mopsuestia.

At the time Nestorius assumed the patriarchal throne of Constantinople, the theological environment was highly charged. In the latter decades of the fourth century, a fierce debate had arisen on whether the divine Logos had assumed a complete human nature during the Incarnation or only a human body and life. Everyone accepted that "the Word became flesh" (John 1:14), but disagreed on what "flesh" actually meant. Did the divine Logos change from his eternal divinity to *become* a complete human being, with a human body, a human soul (understood as life), and a human mind, or did he simply *assume* a human body and life, "flesh," as the apostle John called it? Was the Incarnation a "clothing" of the divine Logos with the "garment" of the human flesh, or did the Word truly become a human being? All agreed that during the Incarnation Jesus indeed possessed a body like ours, and that he also possessed all the elements of our human life, from our physiology to our emotions, summed up in the word "soul." But did the incarnate Logos, Jesus, also possess both the divine mind of the Word as well as a human mind? Did Jesus have two minds? Did he possess two centers of reasoning, one divine and one human? And if this was the case, how could the human mind of Jesus ever retain its own integrity without being completely and irretrievably subsumed into the overwhelming presence of the divine Mind? The most famous proponent for the position that during the Incarnation the divine Logos assumed only human "flesh" and not a human mind was Apollinaris of Laodicea.

This was at its core a discussion not only on technical aspects of anthropology but, primarily, one of soteriology. What was at stake was nothing less than the process of human salvation. For, if the Logos did not assume our human nature completely, flesh, soul, as well as mind during the Incarnation, how can our minds be redeemed? Or is the human mind excluded from the Incarnation of the Word? Ever since the earliest decades, it has been a first principle of Christian thought that "whatever part of the human being was not assumed by Christ, that part was not redeemed."[5] How can the human mind, then, the human reason with all its power and importance be redeemed, if Christ ignored it and rejected it during the Incarnation?

The debate ended with a condemnation of Apollinaris during the Second Ecumenical Council at Constantinople in 381. The Church agreed universally that "the Word became flesh" (John 1:14) meant that at the Incarnation the Word became a true human being for our salvation, that he was truly made one of us, like us in all things except sin, assuming true and complete humanity, in flesh, soul, and mind.

But if this is true, how is one to understand Jesus's suffering and death? The divine nature is immutable and impassible. How then did the Incarnate Word thirst and suffer and die? Apollinarianism had provided a conceptual solution to this dilemma: since the Incarnation was only a "clothing" of the divine Logos with flesh, just like a garment, the sufferings and death belonged to that "garment," the part of the human nature assumed by the Word, leaving the divine unaffected. The divine remained immutable and impassible as the human "flesh" of Jesus suffered and died. Even though the Church had rejected Apollinarianism, the relationship between Jesus's human and divine natures during the Incarnation still needed to be worked out. For one could confess Jesus to be truly human and truly divine at the same time, but how can two antithetical natures come together in one Person? How can a truly divine being suffer and die?

Two natures, one person?

Because they had seen how dangerous Apollinarianism was for Christian soteriology, the Antiochene theologians wanted to safeguard the humanity of Jesus during the Incarnation and not allow the divine nature of the Word to be seen as overwhelming the human nature. In addition, so as to preserve the integrity of both of Christ's natures and not allow the Word's divine nature to be compromised either, the Antiochenes preferred to speak of the Incarnation as a *union* (Gk: συνάφεια), a "conjoining" or "association" of the divine Logos with the man Jesus of Nazareth.[6] Along with his fellow Antiochenes, Nestorius insisted that the biblical narrative made it clear that Jesus's struggles were real and his frailties true: he hungered, thirsted, suffered, and died. Yet, at the same time, divine transcendence, immutability, and impassibility are also essential in the Incarnation, for Jesus was also truly God. Jesus was both God and a human being. Each nature possesses (or, rather, expresses) its own *idioms* (properties) and they each have to be protected fully. As Jesus's true human suffering has to be maintained for the Incarnation to be a truly human event, so does the impassibility of God have to be maintained throughout as a first principle of Christian theology. A confusion of the natures or an alteration of the properties would have dire consequences for both our understanding of the Incarnation and of the Trinity. Nestorius contended that, if we "grant that ... [the Son] accepted suffering, you evacuate him of *impassibility* and of *immortality*, and of being consubstantial (*homoousios*) with the Father, because he acquired a change of nature, seeing that [the Son] accepts and [the Father] accepts not [these sufferings]."[7] Nestorius presented a threefold argument for the immutability of God: First, being transcendent, God is all perfect, immutable in himself, and thus cannot change. Second, God must also be immutable in relation to the Incarnation, for if any change was effected upon God by virtue of the Incarnation, then the incarnate one, he who is "man," is no longer God but whatever God has been changed into. And third, "the Son must be immutable for the sake of the human nature, i.e., a change in the Son becoming man effects a change in the humanity as well, rendering it no longer an authentic humanity."[8]

In his attempt to protect the full humanity of Christ, Nestorius began from an anthropomorphic interpretation of the Incarnation; but that meant that he "could not conceptually unite Jesus's full divinity and full humanity in an *ontological union* for fear that such a union necessitated that the human experiences of the Son of God jeopardize the integrity of his divine status."[9] Conceptually, Nestorius imagined the two natures as separate *before* the incarnation: the divine nature, on the one hand, expressing the divine attributes, such as transcendence, immutability, impassibility, etc., and the human nature, on the other, in all its limited, passible, and mutable expression. Because of this, he conceived the incarnational process as a concretion, the coming together or the joining of the two antithetical and incompatible natures in a common Person, Jesus of Nazareth. This conceptualization allowed Nestorius to ascribe to each of the two natures what belongs to it by definition, suffering and death, to the human nature, for example, glory and the miraculous to the divine and yet see the one Person of Jesus as the one in whom these two natures come together in an ontological conjoining. The problem, however, was that because he had mentally separated the two natures of Christ prior to the Incarnation,

Nestorius could not possibly conceive them as becoming ontologically one without destroying them in the process.[10] By doing so, Nestorius was seeing the Incarnation as a "phenotypical," a functional, an economic "hybrid," a meta-person, a real prosopic unity, but not a true Person. The two natures remained always asymptotically conjoined and the Incarnation was never truly a unity.

On the Unity of Christ

Cyril's understanding of the Incarnation ran counter to Nestorius's for two reasons: first, the language of "union" as "association" seemed to be very close to the understanding of what happened with the prophets of the Old Testament, where the Spirit of God inspired or "indwelt" the prophets, and Jesus, as the incarnation of the divine Word, was fundamentally different from that reality. Second, the asymptotic relationship between the human and divine natures described by the language of Nestorius meant that the Logos did not actually become human thus putting in jeopardy the complete reconciliation of God and humanity in the person of Jesus.

Written in the form of a dialogue between two unnamed interlocutors, A and B—where A provides the authoritative answers and B simply responds or poses new questions—*On the Unity of Christ* represents Cyril's mature and precise thought on the Incarnation as intimately related to salvation. Cyril insisted that in the incarnation, "the divine Lord truly experiences all that is genuinely human, in order to transform that which is mortal into the immortal."[11] Cyril accused the Antiochenes of being driven by Greek metaphysics and Jewish hermeneutics. He insisted that they were too dependent on preconceived notions of rationality, too ready to accept philosophical logic as the measure of what is and what is not fitting to God. As a result, they "are wholly incapable of grasping the profundity of the mystery, for they think it is foolishness on our part to say that Christ died for the life of the world."[12]

Instead of seeing the Incarnation as a union of two pre-existing, antithetical natures, Cyril understood that the two natures are a *unity* rather than a *union*. As an astute philosopher and theologian, Cyril understood that Christian concepts and language about God must enter the realm of paradox, resisting the application of logic alone as a guide. When we ask the question of how we are to understand the relationship between the one to whom the human predicates apply (birth, being the son of Mary, having a rational body, etc.,) and the Son, the Second Person of the Trinity, there are two possible answers: the first is a *connection of identity*; the other sees the human predicates as *added* to the divine being, carefully maintaining the distinction between the predicates that are substantial in the cases of all other humans but are not substantial predicates in the case of Christ. Proceeding from an anthropomorphic understanding of the Incarnation, Nestorius followed the second option, ascribing inferences of human attributes and properties (manhood, birth, thirst, suffering, death, etc.) to the *Person* of Jesus, but only at the level of the human nature, never to the divine. Through this additive relationship Nestorius could say that Christ indeed died on the cross because the human nature of the "*common Person*" suffered the death, and we can also say, at the same time, that the divine did not suffer, because the center for divine and human activities are their existing natures.

Cyril insisted on the other possible answer, namely, the relationship of identity. In Cyril's vocabulary, the term for "person" is *hypostasis* (or *physis*), signifying a singular subject of unity and attribution in Christ: the Second Person of the Trinity *is* the person of Jesus Christ.[13] For Cyril, all predicates, whether those assigning human or divine attributes to the person, can truly be said of the single person, Jesus of Nazareth, the incarnate Logos. Instead of conceptualizing the Incarnation as a *concretion* or conjoining of two antithetical natures with incompatible characteristics and trying to explain how such a union can occur, Cyril turned to the narrative of the incarnation as found in Scripture for the answer. "The Word who is God has become a human being," he argued in *On the Unity of Christ*, "but has retained all the while the virtues of his proper nature . . . Nonetheless he made the limits of the human nature his own, and all the things that pertain to it, and for this reason he is called Christ even though he cannot be thought of as anointed when we consider him specifically as God or when we speak about his divine nature."[14] And again, commenting on Gal 2:19–20 and Heb 13:12 he noted how Scripture insists that "it was 'his own body' and 'his own flesh' which was given up for us. We must not say, then, that the flesh and blood was that of another son apart from him, understood as separate and honored by a mere conjunction, having an alien glory, someone who did not have pre-eminence substantially, but only as if the name of Sonship and that of Godhead which is above every name were thrown over him like a mask [(that is, something *prosopic*)] or a cloak."[15]

Cyril's articulation of the relationship of the properties of each nature (what is termed, *communicatio idiomatum*, or *communication of idioms*) insisted that, in the Incarnation, the divine and human attributes were not predicated of their respective natures, but of the single person of the Son according to the *hypostasis*: "This Jesus is one and single."[16] Such a reading of the communication of idioms ensured two fundamental precepts of human salvation: first, that it was indeed the *Son of God*, the Second Person of the Trinity, who experienced suffering, and, second, that it was *true* human suffering that the Son of God experienced.[17] This meant "the Incarnation is not the compositional union of natures [(as was the case in the Nestorian prosopic union)] but the person of the Son taking on a new manner or mode of existence."[18] Cyril knew full well that God must be "at work among creatures, not merely playacting on the stage of the world, and that work is a mysterious but inexorable transformation of the human life of his disciples into something radically new ... The incarnation was fundamentally a time-bound act of rescue for the human race, one that had to be contextualized in a larger scheme of God's eternal philanthropy and providence for the world."[19]

If, then, suffering and death are located in the one single subject, Jesus, and not in the human nature alone, while the divine nature remained unaffected, how could that happen? How could the eternal, divine Logos enter human suffering and die? Would this not make God an object to be acted upon by those who put him to death? For it is yet another first principle of Christian theology that God is always a subject, an acting agent, not an object to be acted upon. Cyril's response to the apparent conundrum is thoroughly biblical as it is brilliant. By refusing to accept the limitations of philosophical logic and Aristotelian empirical views of identity, Cyril was able to see the paradox of the Incarnation: "The Only Begotten Word of God has saved us by putting on our likeness. Suffering in the flesh, and rising from the dead, he revealed our nature as greater than death or corruption."[20] Turning to John 10:18, where Jesus declared that, "No one takes [my life] from me, but I lay it down of my own accord. I have power to lay it down, and I have power to take it up again," Cyril understood that Christ never ceased to be the acting agent, the subject who allowed himself to enter the reality of our limitations, even death, not out of necessity of nature. On the contrary, even in death "The Word remained what he was even when he became flesh, so that he who is over all, and yet came among all through his humanity, should keep in himself his transcendence of all and remain above all the limitations of the creation."[21]

Commenting on Hebrews 1:3 and Philippians 2:5–7, Cyril insisted that the economy of the Incarnation reveals the paradox of the divine Word's suffering and death: "In this way he humbled himself, *economically* submitting himself to the limitations of the human nature ... Just as we say that the flesh became his very own, in the same way the weakness of that flesh became his very own in an *economic* appropriation according to the terms of the *unity*."[22]

This unity, then, did not change or alter or confuse the divine and the human natures of Christ, and yet, paradoxically, in a manner "he alone knows," it reveals the one and only subject, the eternal Son, who became flesh for us and our salvation: "To the same one we attribute both the divine and human characteristics, and we also say that to the same one belongs the birth and the suffering on the cross since he appropriated everything that belonged to his own flesh, while even remaining impassible in the nature of the Godhead."[23] Otherwise, "if the flesh that is united to him, ineffably and in a way that transcends thought or speech, did not become the very flesh of the Word, directly, then how could it be understood as life-giving?"[24]

Conclusion

A theologian of our time, Stanley Hauerwas, once wrote that even though what Christians believe is wonderfully simple, to say what is simple is not easy.[25] It is surprisingly simple for Christians to proclaim as an article of faith with the Evangelist John that "In the beginning was the Word, and the Word was with God, and the Word was God" (Jn 1:1) and that this Word became flesh for us and our salvation. Yet, it is quite a bit more difficult to explain *how* the eternal Word through whom all things were made (Jn 1:3) became a human being. Did he cease to be God, and if so, how? Or is this confession simply a pious affirmation one ought not examine too closely? Every attempt we make to speak properly of God leads us into the deep paradox of our faith: we speak of the ineffable. As human beings we try to describe that which is not our own experience—the Incarnation of God. As we have seen in the debate between Cyril and Nestorius, ancient Christians refused to be driven either into premature silence about the God who revealed himself in Jesus, or to accept dominant philosophical presuppositions as true and sufficient to speak of God.

In latter Protestant debates on the person of Christ, especially those between Lutherans and the Reformed, attempts at clarifying our understanding of the *communication of idioms* resulted in further refinement into a number of *genera* that seek to clarify the relationship between concretion and abstraction. In spite of the technical clarifications of Protestant Scholasticism, in an attempt to protect the divine nature of Christ from human suffering and death, many contemporary Christians are prone to Nestorianism (and it seems that some Protestant traditions are more prone to this than other Creedal communions).[26]

As we have seen, Cyril provides a necessary corrective. Cyril recognized that when one begins to describe the Incarnation by holding fast to philosophical assumptions and commitments to what is "fitting" to God, to what the attributes or idioms of the divine nature are and to how they are to be joined to their antithetical human nature, one is always led to conceptualize the Incarnation of the Word as either a concretion that can never reveal a true humanity or an unacceptable confusion and alteration of both natures. On the contrary, because he begun with Christ and the narrative of Scripture, not with philosophical concepts, Cyril was able to conceive the paradox of the Incarnation and to see in the Person of Jesus the Word incarnate. In this way, Cyril established for us yet another first principle in Christian theology, namely, the Christocentric nature of theology: all Christian speech about God (which is what *theology* is) ought to begin with the Person of Jesus.

All Christians in our time, whether Catholic, Orthodox, or Protestant stand in historic continuity with the Christological expression of Cyril and the three ecumenical councils (Ephesus 431; Chalcedon 451; Constantinople II 553) that affirmed his Christology as the Orthodox theology of the Church.

Notes

1. Translated from *Quod unus sit Christus*.
2. Since the first quarter of the fourth century, the center of gravity of the Roman Empire had shifted from Rome to New Rome (as Constantinople was officially known). In 324 CE, Emperor Constantine re-founded the city of Byzantium—an ancient colony of Megara—as the new capital of the empire for a variety of reasons. By the end of the fourth century, administrative and economic power, as well as ecclesiastical influence had been shifting to the new capital. In spite of this shift, Alexandria retained its place of influence and prestige as the "second city" of the empire.
3. St. Cyril of Alexandria, *On The Unity of Christ*, transl. and introduction John Anthony McGuckin (Crestwood: St. Vladimir's Seminary Press, 2000), 15.
4. For a detailed history and analysis of the so-called Nestorian controversy, see John A. McGuckin, *Saint Cyril of Alexandria and the Christological Controversy*. Crestwood: St. Vladimir's Seminary Press, 2004.
5. The principle that "whatever was not assumed [by Christ] was not saved" (*quod non est assumptum non est sanatum*), which was most clearly formulated by Gregory of Nazianzus in Epistle 101 (*Against Apollinarius*) had been accepted as a first principle of Christology from the time of Irenaeus, Tertullian, and Origen.

6. McGuckin, *On The Unity of Christ*, 18.
7. Nestorius, *The Bazaar of Heracleides*, eds C.R. Driver and L. Hodgson (Oxford: Clarendon Press, 1925), 39 (as well as 91–95). My emphasis.
8. Nestorius, *The Bazaar of Heracleides*, 16, 26–27. See also, Thomas G. Weinandy, *Does God Suffer?* (Edinburgh: T&T Clark, 2000) 177, nt. 8.
9. Weinandy, *Does God Suffer*, 175.
10. For a more detailed presentation of the issues at hand, see George Kalantzis, "Is There Room for Two? Cyril's Single Subjectivity and the Prosopic Union." *St. Vladimir's Theological Quarterly* 52, no. 1 (2008), 95–110.
11. McGuckin, *On The Unity of Christ*, 34.
12. McGuckin, *On The Unity of Christ*, 130.
13. See, Weinandy, *Does God Suffer*; for further discussion of the issue, see also T.G. Weinandy, *Does God Change? The Word's Becoming in the Incarnation* (Petersham: St. Bede's Publications, 1985) and John Lamont, "Aquinas on Divine Simplicity," *Monist* 80.4 (1997): 521–539.
14. McGuckin, *On The Unity of Christ*, 67.
15. McGuckin, *On The Unity of Christ*, 128.
16. McGuckin, *On The Unity of Christ*, 87.
17. Weinandy, *Does God Suffer?*, 203.
18. Weinandy, *Does God Suffer?*, 200.
19. McGuckin, *On The Unity of Christ*, 34–37.
20. McGuckin, *On The Unity of Christ*, 130.
21. McGuckin, *On The Unity of Christ*, 128–29.
22. McGuckin, *On The Unity of Christ*, 86, 107. Emphasis added.
23. McGuckin, *On The Unity of Christ*, 133.
24. McGuckin, *On The Unity of Christ*, 131.
25. Ben Quash, Michael Ward, and Stanley Hauerwas, *Heresies and How to Avoid Them: Why It Matters What Christians Believe* (Peabody: Hendrickson, 2007), x.
26. For a good description, see Richard A. Muller, *Dictionary of Latin and Greek Theological Terms: Drawn Principally from Protestant Scholastic Theology* (Grand Rapids: Baker Book House, 1985), 72–74.

Select Bibliography

Primary sources

Cyril of Alexandria: Select Letters. Edited and translated by Lionel R. Wickham. Oxford: Clarendon Press, 1983.

St. Cyril of Alexandria. *On The Unity of Christ.* Translated and introduced by John Anthony McGuckin. Crestwood: St. Vladimir's Seminary Press, 2000.

Secondary sources

Kalantzis, George. "Is There Room for Two? Cyril's Single Subjectivity and the Prosopic Union." *St. Vladimir's Theological Quarterly* 52.1 (2008), 95–110.

McGuckin, John A. *Saint Cyril of Alexandria and the Christological Controversy.* Crestwood: St. Vladimir's Seminary Press, 2004.

Russell, Norman. *Cyril of Alexandria*, in *The Early Church Fathers*. London: Routledge, 2000.

Weinandy, Thomas G. and Daniel A. Keating, eds. *The Theology of St. Cyril of Alexandria: A Critical Appreciation*. London: T&T Clark, 2003.

1.12

Confessions[1] (c. 397–401 CE)
Augustine of Hippo (Nov. 13, 354–Aug. 28, 430 CE)

Introduction

Augustine wrote the *Confessions* relatively early in his storied career as bishop of the North African city of Hippo Regius. He was known for his keen theological and philosophical mind, abundant writings, and some very famous controversies (most notably with Pelagius and with the Donatists). Now in his mid-forties and only recently a bishop, Augustine wrote the *Confessions* about ten years after his mother Monica's death. Why write such a personal work at the beginning of his career? First, Augustine faced detractors because of both his extended time with the dualistic and non-Catholic Manichees and the indiscretions of his youth.[2] Instead of ignoring the complaints against him or writing a straightforward defense, Augustine chose authenticity, opening his life and showing a commitment to disclosure uncharacteristic of much of Late Antique writing.

Augustine's road was long and full of detours, some of which were very painful and all of which prompted him to be humbly grateful for being guided back on track. Dictating the *Confessions* would have been an emotional journey for Augustine, speaking aloud the things in his own heart. The resulting warmth and vulnerability in the *Confessions* has made this work a beloved Christian classic.

What is the *Confessions*?

The short answer to this very complex and popular question is that the *Confessions* is a great many things. It is a dialogue with God, a retrospective, a story, a philosophical exercise, a defense, a theological journal, a meditation on scripture, and what Peter Brown calls a "therapy of self-examination"—all at the same time.[3] Also, the *Confessions* is not easily outlined; it has too much verve and not enough chronology for that. Even if Augustine's discourses on memory or time or his fascinating allegorical read of Genesis seem tangential, they are not.

While there is a discernible shift with Book 10 and again with Books 11–13 from the more narrative-focused Books 1–9, it is clear that Augustine means for all thirteen books to work together as a cohesive whole. For this reason, the approach here will be to begin by asking the questions: (1) What did Augustine mean by "confession"? (2) Why did he feel the need to set out on this journey? (3) What does he think it accomplishes? From there we will look at some of the events that Augustine chooses to include that mark his search for truth and the substantial role Monica plays throughout the narrative. Finally, we will turn to Augustine's encounter with God and Scripture.

Confession: "Our heart is unquiet until it rests in you"

For Augustine, confession is the process of coming to know who we are in light of God's knowing of us and, then, armed with that self-knowledge, submitting ourselves wholly to God in worship. Broadly speaking, the *Confessions* is structured around this understanding of confession. Many of the books open with prayer, and often Augustine slips into prayer when it feels right for him to do so—at times giving thanks and at other times humbly confessing sin and asking for God's mercy. Acknowledging that humanity is shaped to praise God by virtue of being created, he prays: "You arouse us so that praising you may bring us joy, because you have made us and drawn us to yourself, and our heart is unquiet until it rests in you" (I.1, 1). Augustine's restless heart propels him, during his pre-Christian years, to search for a mentor in Manichaeism, for camaraderie among friends, for sexual fulfillment, and for answers in Neoplatonism, all of which, he

Figure 1.14 *Confessions*—Augustine

concludes, were indicative of his restless heart pointing him toward God all along. Augustine goes through the arduous process of filtering through his past for his own sake as well as for the sake of the reader. Primarily, however, he wades through his youthful indiscretions and his moral failings because he wants to love God: "Out of love for loving you I do this, recalling my most wicked ways and thinking over the past with bitterness so that you may grow ever sweeter to me" (II.1, 1). Throughout the *Confessions,* Augustine notes that God was present, even guiding him, through his wanderings and periods of willful arrogance.

Augustine's understanding of confession is predicated on a central question in Book 1: Who is God?[4] Wrestling with this question was at the core of his difficulties with embracing the faith of the Church. A notion that was particularly difficult for him to shake was the assumption that Christianity imaged God as having a body.[5] Throughout the *Confessions* Augustine explains how this erroneous assertion prevented him from reading the Scriptures correctly. It was not until he encountered the works of the Neoplatonists of his time, Plotinus and Porphyry, that he was able to come to grips with the immateriality of God. For Augustine, this was the last step before encountering the Word of John 1, the final stage in his search for truth. The Incarnation was crucial for Augustine; in Christ the immaterial God was accessible and the Scriptures, previously dismissed, became the unassuming trove of truth.

Searching for truth: "Let us love you and run to you"

From the perspective of a young Augustine, his life seemed a series of largely futile searches for truth and fulfillment. When he revisits his youth, one can almost see Augustine shaking his head and heaving his shoulders in a sigh. Throughout his first thirty years, Augustine consistently desired to be part of the in-crowd and even fabricated stories about himself to make it happen. Unfortunately, he also consistently chose the wrong friends. He calls them his "companions" in "Babylon" with whom he "wallowed in its filth as though basking amid cinnamon and precious ointments" (II.3, 8).

One night Augustine and his friends trespassed onto a farmer's property and stole a bunch of pears. They did not need the pears nor did they even eat them; instead, they took the pears and pelted them at a bunch of pigs. While some might interpret this as a harmless youthful prank, a "boys will be boys" moment that even elicits a chuckle, Augustine's recollection of the event fills him with disgust. Such a response might seem an overreaction. For Augustine, however, the theft was evidence that his moral compass was severely compromised and that the pleasure of the action was in doing what was not allowed: "Look upon my heart, O God, look upon this heart of mine" (II.4, 9). This moment looms large for Augustine as a spot-on exposé of the depth of his wickedness, for he did evil for no reason: "The malice was loathsome, and I loved it. I was in love with my own ruin, in love with decay: not with the thing for which I was falling into decay but with decay itself" (II.4, 9). A little wickedness among friends is, for Augustine, a symptom of the basic human propensity to lead others to ruin.[6]

At twenty-nine, Augustine learned a valuable lesson in his search for truth: never meet your idols. The famous Faustus was coming to Carthage in 383, and, after nine years of flirting with Manichaeism, Augustine felt that he needed his encounter with the superstar Manichee to be definitive. While Faustus was gracious enough, his insufficient education and humble admission of ignorance snuffed out any spark for Manichaeism that remained in Augustine.[7] His disappointment with Manichaeism, his newfound respect for the epistemological doubt of Academic skepticism, and his distrust of the philosophers to deal properly with his soul, led to Augustine reengaging with the Catholic faith with help from Ambrose of Milan.[8] Gradually, as we see in Book 6, Augustine warmed to the Church and Scripture, even if his belief vacillated.

The famous "conversion" in Book 8 is not a conversion to Christianity but to a particular brand of Christian devotion: asceticism.[9] Augustine needed to be freed from the weight of the "bonds" of his slavery to his desire (for sex, for admiration, and for success). He was reluctant to surrender, even in the face of the beautiful truth he met in Christ and Scripture, because he thought himself too weak. Even though he had publicly proclaimed his faith and was baptized, he now knew just how much he wanted to be free to love in truth: "Come, Lord, arouse us and call us back, kindle us and seize us, prove to us how sweet you are in your burning tenderness; let us love you and run to you" (VIII.4, 9). Augustine craved freedom but was a prisoner still.

One day in July 386 at a house in Milan where they were guests, Augustine and his former student and friend Alypius received a surprise visit from Ponticianus, a high-ranking official, who told them about the famous Egyptian ascetic Antony. The story had a profound effect on Augustine because he had chosen to continue satisfying his lust rather than receive chastity. After Ponticianus's departure, Augustine's discomfort swelled to a climax and he retreated outside to the garden. Poor Alypius followed, not knowing what was going on except that his friend seemed grievously disturbed and overwhelmed with interior struggle. Augustine's agony was the result of hesitation; he knew he had to face a choice, the choice of Deuteronomy 30, to choose life or death: "I shrank from dying to death and living to life, for ingrained evil was more powerful in me than new-grafted good" (VIII.11, 25). He faltered in his choice, embarrassed at his weakness of indecision. Finally, he threw himself beneath a fig tree sobbing uncontrollably. Then he heard a child's voice chanting over and over again, "Pick it up and read, pick it up and read" (VIII.12, 29). The disruption broke the spell of his weeping and its meaning in that instant was clear to him: like Antony, he was to pick up the Scriptures and trust God to call him forth from his slavery into freedom. He rushed back to an astonished but patient Alypius, seized a codex of Paul's writings, and opened it to Romans 13:13–14: "Not in dissipation and drunkenness, nor in debauchery and lewdness, nor in arguing and jealousy; but put on the Lord Jesus Christ, and make no provision for the flesh or the gratification of your desires" (VIII.12, 29). Now that he had chosen continence, the clouds of doubt parted and peace settled upon him. He was free.

Monica and grief: "So deeply was she engrafted into my heart"

While Augustine mentions several people who either helped him in his journey back to God (Cicero, the Platonists, and Ponticianus) or journeyed along with him (his long-time friend Nebridius, Alypius, and his son Adeodatus), it is clear from the *Confessions* that his mother Monica is his mainstay. Augustine compares Monica's longsuffering tenacity and trust in his eventual conversion to God's guardianship of his life. Thus, Augustine understands his whole life as a return to its true shape as orchestrated by God and perceived by Monica even in the womb. Monica physically travailed to bring him into the world, but Augustine notes with grateful awe that "with far more anxious solicitude did she give birth to me in the spirit than ever she had in the flesh" (V.9, 16). Augustine's relationship with his mother was not perfect; at times he chafed under the pressure of her sometimes myopic and rigid vision for his life. In remembering Monica, though, Augustine recognizes her voice as God's voice (more than once in his *Confessions*, he wrestles with God being silent, only to realize later that God *had* been speaking through Monica)—she was the beacon that helped guide him on his return.

It is notable that, when Augustine revisits a loss in the *Confessions*, he views his management of grief as indicative of his spiritual health. In Book 4, Augustine relays how he responded to the death of an unnamed friend. His grief consumed him and he was miserable. Attempting to stem the tide of his emotions, Augustine tried everything from games to sex, to no avail. What he concludes is that he had not loved his friend well and therefore could not grieve well. Augustine expresses a similar sentiment on being compelled to send away his common-law wife and mother to his only son, Adeodatus, in the hopes of finding a suitable marriage eventually. Augustine writes: "So deeply was she engrafted into my heart that it was left torn and wounded and trailing blood" (VI.15, 25). His pain at the loss of this relationship drove him to give into desperate lusts and immediately run into the arms of another woman in hopes of abating his misery.

Augustine's remembrance of Monica's death in Book 9, however, strikes a different tone. Certainly there are still tears and open expression of grief, but gone is the weight of death and the retreat into bad habits for consolation. He is compelled to speak about his mother and his last moments with her at the port of Ostia on the Tiber. It does not read like a eulogy as much as a window into the last sweet moment of intimacy between two people who encountered beauty and truth together. The scene is idyllic; Augustine and Monica gazing out a window overlooking a garden and resting from their journey in one another's company. Together they search for truth with hearts open to one another and God. They pondered eternal life and experienced a moment of transcendence, a taste of the resurrection to come. Five days later Monica took ill, after nine days she was dead. Augustine's sorrow, while keenly felt—"bereft of her comfort, so great a comfort, my soul was wounded"—was checked by the reality that Monica's state was not one of misery or extinction (IX.12, 30). He was learning to grieve differently now, experiencing the pain of loss but tempering it with the hope of resurrection.

Augustine and scripture: "I read on and on, all afire"

Upon his first encounter with Scripture Augustine, like many well-educated early Christians, was not impressed:

> when I studied the Bible and compared it with Cicero's dignified prose, it seemed to me unworthy. My swollen pride recoiled from its style and my intelligence failed to penetrate to its inner meaning. Scripture is a reality that grows along with little children, but I disdained to be a little child and in my high and mighty arrogance regarded myself as grown up (III.5, 9).

As Augustine's story shows, becoming like a child and having humility before God and Scripture are not easy. He was much more impressed with the smooth-talking Manicheans and their seemingly rational concerns about the Bible. The *Confessions* must be read not only as Augustine's journey back to God, but also as his journey back to Scripture.

In Book 7, Augustine explains how the Neoplatonists gave him the last push he needed to embrace Scripture and the Catholic faith. Plotinus and Porphyry helped him come to grips with the immateriality of God, giving him a foundation upon which to understand the Trinity and the Incarnation. The Neoplatonists compelled Augustine to begin that difficult interior journey into himself, but Augustine had to come face to face with Christ and the heavy chains of his sin: "I was drawn toward you by your beauty but swiftly dragged away from you by my own weight, swept back headlong and groaning onto these things below myself" (VII.17, 23).[10] His questions about the nature of God and evil began to fall into place, but the strength to enjoy God was elusive until he embraced Christ as his mediator.[11] Augustine's encounter with Christ cannot be separated from his encounter with Scripture. So, with "intense eagerness," he devoured Paul, shaking his head at his former Manichaean-informed assumption that Paul contradicted the Law and the Prophets, and found himself trembling before the truth of Christ's deliverance (VII.21, 27).

One could accurately sum up the *Confessions* as Augustine's search for true love. That his sex drive ruled him was especially problematic at several points in his life, such as when he began his schooling in Carthage, "where the din of scandalous love-affairs raged cauldron-like around me" (III.1, 1). Most often Augustine's response to desire, grief, and loneliness was the unhealthy catharsis of becoming enthralled with the drama of theatrical shows or falling into bed with another woman. Reading Cicero's *Hortensius* (no longer extant) at eighteen was enough to stoke his desire for philosophy as the "love for wisdom" that would eventually lead him to the books of the Platonists and finally to Scripture.[12] Thus, we should not be surprised that throughout the *Confessions* Augustine is deeply moved by what he reads in the Bible. In Book 9, for instance, in the midst of Augustine reading through Psalm 4, he writes this: "I read on and on, all afire, but I could find no way to help those dead, dead folk among whom I had once been numbered. I had been a lethal nuisance, bitter and blind and baying against honey-sweet scriptures distilled from heaven's honey, scriptures luminous by your light" (IX.4, 11). The *Confessions* brims with biblical allusions and quotations because Augustine is remembering and reengaging with Scripture. This is a particular contribution of the *Confessions*, that one can see Augustine drawing that biblical engagement to the forefront and mapping it onto the work. This is why his reading of Genesis in Books 11–13 cannot be separated from the rest of the *Confessions*. Augustine brings us along with him in his encounter with Scripture, coming back to lingering questions and delving into biblical interpretation because he has found true love.

Books 11–13 of the *Confessions* presents Augustine's reading of the beginning of Genesis. The books are Trinitarian in shape—Book 11 focuses on the Father, Book 12 on the Son, and Book 13 on the Holy Spirit—but Augustine does not adhere slavishly to that structure.[13] Instead, in coming to the text, Augustine trusts that what he will find will reveal who God is—a return to that central question in Book 1. He is refreshingly frank and realistic when it comes to responding to Genesis 1. He wishes he could grab Moses and beg him to explain creation to find out if he was really telling the truth. Obviously this is not possible, even if we might all wish it to be. As he considers passages such as "In the beginning God made heaven and earth" and "the earth was invisible and unorganized," Augustine leans upon his knowledge of God drawn from the whole witness of Scripture to explore the range of possibilities that are theologically and textually tenable.

That God is the author of the truth of Scripture is a core belief that Augustine shared with his fellow early Christian writers. Thus, he assumes that there will be multiple interpretations of the text and that even the author might not have grasped the full range of meanings. Augustine's confidence in the text is fueled by a confidence in the Incarnation and in the truth of who God is, rather than by some particular ability he has to access the mind of Moses. Augustine refuses to dismiss the universal accessibility of Scripture: "Indeed, once it is true, it is no longer their property. If they love it because it is true, then it belongs to me as well as to them, because it is a common bounty for all lovers of truth" (XII.25, 34). For Augustine, it is for each interpreter to do their best to draw upon the truth of the text and recognize that there is a range of possibilities within the bounds of orthodox theology.

Conclusion

The *Confessions* read as Augustine's love letter to God, the God who saved him from the Manichees, from the pressures of the world, and most importantly from himself. In Book 10, Augustine describes his journey of confession as a process in which he recollects himself and sees himself collected, the mess of his earlier disordered life brought into unity once God liberated him from his captivity to other loves.[14] As Augustine looks back on his winding road and knows that God's guidance has not ceased, there emerges a deuteronomic sense to his project—a remembering and a call to remember at the same time. The *Confessions* is not merely a retrospective; it is a meditation on his life in the presence of God. For Augustine, this means a tour through some difficult and personal things in order to see the goodness of God and to deal with events and aspects of himself that may have taken on a new sense of meaning. The best way to read this text is to let Augustine guide the tour and to enjoy the ride.

There is power in confession, power in speaking the truth about ourselves, and even more power in that confession and truth-speaking to have God as one's witness. Confession is an immensely personal event. Augustine cracked open his life—the painful and embarrassing bits, warts and all—and had a face-to-face conversation about it with God. Augustine looms over the history of Christian theology with a long shadow. But while some giant thinkers of the past resist access, Augustine does the opposite: He throws open the doors of his life in an exercise of access that is a confession of need and praise.

Notes

1. Translated from *Confessiones*; all references to this work (Augustine, *The Confessions* [trans. Maria Boulding; New York: Vintage, 1998]) shall be noted by employing in-text citations.
2. For more on Augustine's Manichaeism, see Peter Brown's masterful biography *Augustine of Hippo: A Biography*, new ed. (Berkeley: University of California Press, 2000), 35–49.
3. Brown, *Augustine*, 175.
4. Augustine finds words terribly confining, but "woe betide those who fail to speak" and do not describe God, see *Conf.* I.4, 4.
5. Augustine discusses his difficulty with this in several places, see *Conf.* IV.15, 26–29.
6. Another example of this was his association with the "Wreckers" in Carthage, a gang of young men known for their vandalism. Augustine turned up his nose at their hazing of younger students but still had friendly associations with them (III.3, 6).
7. *Conf.* V.4, 10–V.7, 13.
8. *Conf.* V.13, 23–V.14, 24. Augustine was more impressed with Ambrose than he had been with Faustus. The bishop had enough skill to be admired that Augustine found himself regularly going to church to hear him even though he was not yet interested in the content.
9. Garry Wills, *Augustine's* Confessions: *A Biography* (Princeton: Princeton University Press, 2011), 58–59.
10. For an exploration of Augustine's conception of a Christian "ascension narrative" and how it compares to that of Neoplatonism, see John Peter Kenney, *The Mysticism of Saint Augustine: Rereading the* Confessions (New York: Routledge, 2005); about Augustine's journey with Platonism in general, see Brian Dobell, *Augustine's Intellectual Conversion: The Journey from Platonism to Christianity* (Cambridge: Cambridge University Press, 2009).

11. On Christ as mediator: *Conf.* X.42, 67–43, 69: "For our sake he stood to you as both victor and victim, and victor because victim; for us he stood to you as priest and sacrifice, and priest because sacrifice, making us sons and daughters to you instead of servants by being born of you to serve us" (X.43, 69).

12. *Conf.* III.4, 8–9.

13. Garry Wills notes that Genesis is fundamental to the structure of the *Confessions*: "Episodes in Genesis lie behind key events in Augustine's life . . . The God who made the world is still remaking Augustine by his secret providence and graces. Furthermore, Augustine finds the mystery of the Trinity implicit in the creation story, and the Trinity has also been haunting the entire book" (*Augustine's* Confessions, 13).

14. *Conf.* X.29, 40.

Select Bibliography

Primary source

Augustine, *The Confessions*, trans. Maria Boulding (New York: Vintage, 1998).

Secondary sources

Brown, Peter. *Augustine of Hippo: A Biography*, new ed. (Berkeley: University of California Press, 2000).

Kenney, John Peter. *The Mysticism of Saint Augustine: Rereading the* Confessions (New York: Routledge, 2005).

Quinn, John M. *A Companion to the* Confessions *of St. Augustine* (New York: Peter Lang, 2002).

Wills, Garry. *Augustine's* Confessions: *A Biography* (Princeton: Princeton University Press, 2011).

Part II

The Medieval Period

Introduction to the Medieval Period (500–1500)

Hans Madueme

If the medieval tradition vanished today, Protestants would hardly notice—most of them anyway. Not too long ago, it was common practice to disparage this era as the "Dark Ages," an intellectual desert that signifies the total collapse of all genuine knowledge and learning (while its alternate name, the "Middle Ages," is marginally better, it also connotes a nondescript, inferior time between the collapse of the Roman empire and the resurgence of classical learning during the Renaissance).

But such assumptions are profoundly misleading, if not downright false. In the essays that follow, the intellectual seriousness of medieval theology is never in doubt. These were theologians on a mission, intoxicated by God as they aimed to have their minds saturated in divine things. They longed to know and experience God intellectually, devotionally, even mystically. The different ways that thinkers tended to prioritize one of these aspirations over the others stimulated the vigorous diversity of the period. Those differences were also the source of theological controversy.

Medieval Christians were not so different from Christians today. What motivated so many of the classic medieval debates was how to render God more real in the lives of needy people, such as through holy communion. We see in early medieval arguments that the Eucharistic bread and wine became the literal body and blood of Jesus Christ. The intimations of this position were already there in Gregory the Great (c. 540–604) and the Venerable Bede (672–735), but they were more explicitly defended in Paschasius Radbertus (785–865). Others claimed instead that the elements were transformed spiritually *not* physically (e.g., Berengar of Tours, 999–1088). The Fourth Lateran Council in 1215 ratified the former position; not mainly for arcane, technical reasons—though such existed—but because the winning side was convinced that an overtly sacramental Eucharist ministers Christ more vividly to believers. There was a similar rationale for the cult of the saints, prayers to the Virgin Mary, and pilgrimages to holy relics; such controversial practices sometimes obscured the key *pastoral* motivations, chief of which was rendering God's grace more accessible and existentially meaningful to Christians.

Medieval theology emerged in a Roman Empire divided into East (Greek) and West (Latin). By the time Constantine became emperor in 324 CE, he ruled the whole empire and decided to move his imperial seat to the east in Byzantium (later called Constantinople). The Roman Empire would eventually collapse in the fifth and sixth century as a result of the barbarian invasions. Partly because of linguistic, cultural, and political differences, but also because of mounting theological differences (e.g., the *filioque* controversy), the Eastern and Western regions drifted apart. In time, two very different theological traditions developed.

Byzantine theology became the theology of the Eastern Church (now the Eastern Orthodox Church). Theologians in this tradition adopted an "apophatic" mode of theology, where the emphasis is on the incomprehensibility of God. They despised theological creativity; early church fathers like Athanasius and Cyril of Alexandria were considered normative (thus Byzantine theology lacks much doctrinal development beyond the patristic fathers). The early ecumenical Councils were seen as final and non-negotiable; that is true for Nicaea (325), Constantinople (381), Ephesus (431), and Chalcedon (451), but also for the final three Councils—Constantinople II (553), defending two-nature Christology; Constantinople III (680–681), affirming two-wills Christology; and Nicaea II (787), which starred John of Damascus. John ended the iconoclast controversy by arguing on the basis of the incarnation that Christians may *venerate* but not *worship* icons. However, these last three Councils were almost exclusively an Eastern affair; Latin medieval theology in the West followed a different path.

In the wake of the collapsing Roman Empire, the attention of Western Europeans was directed at surviving the invasions; theology was focused on the existential needs of embattled people. But by the year 1000, medieval Europe was undergoing a number of significant cultural transformations, including in the area of philosophy. The Crusades brought Christians into contact with Greek philosophical texts that had been preserved by Arabic nations. The relationship between theology and philosophy was now a fertile area of creative thinking. No longer satisfied to recycle old insights from earlier ages, theologians sought to demonstrate the rational coherence of the faith. Nevertheless, the frequent citation of Augustine betrayed a longing to show that medieval theology was still in continuity with Augustine's teachings. In their quest for intellectual sophistication, "faith" and "reason" became two hubs of a new intellectual project.

That was how the scholastic approach to theology was born. When we hear about medieval "scholasticism," we imagine scoliotic scholars secluded in ivory towers, fighting over how many angels can dance on the head of a pin. This canard has a grain of truth, but reality was far more complicated. One of the first significant scholastic theologians, Anselm of Canterbury (1033–1109), confessed in his *Proslogion*: "I believe, in order that I may understand" (*credo ut intelligam*); theology to his mind is "faith seeking understanding" (*fides quaerens intellectum*). Anselm was no rationalist; faith was indispensable to rational thought.

Yet such concerns triggered fierce debates. Can genuine theology exist without divine, spiritual illumination? Can we have any knowledge of God without loving him first? Is reason possible without faith? Not only are these questions alive and well within Christianity today, they were discussed by Augustine in the patristic era, and further explored by medieval theologians. The clash between Abelard and Bernard could serve as the epitaph for an era. Peter Abelard (c. 1079–1142) belonged to the period of "early scholasticism" (~500–1200); in his work *Sic et Non* he developed a new way of doing theology by contrasting different theological views in the patristic tradition (his dialectical approach influenced Peter Lombard's *Sentences*, a book that became required reading for medieval university students). Abelard's views were condemned as heresy—more than once!—thanks in no small part to Bernard of Clairvaux (c. 1090–1153). Bernard denounced Abelard's theological approach. Abelard was studying what others had said about God; real theology, Clairvaux argued, was knowing God.

These tensions between loving God *devotionally* and studying theology *academically* continued throughout the period of "high scholasticism" (~thirteenth century). The polarities appear in the contrast between the medieval universities and monasteries. Put too simply, monks meditated on God and pondered divine things, while the schoolmen forged theology in the heat of intellectual debate. But the lines were always blurred. Certainly, Franciscan monks, named after Francis of Assisi, were suspicious of scholasticism and devoted themselves to Christian piety and a life of poverty. They were a "mendicant" order (Lat. *mendicans*, beggar). But there was another mendicant order—the Dominicans (named after Dominic)—that did not reject academic learning. They paved the way for the towering figure of Thomas Aquinas, a Dominican monk whose prolific works blended citations from Scripture, patristic authors, and Aristotle.

By the thirteenth century, the intellectual scene had shifted dramatically. If Augustine had been the patron saint for early scholasticism, Aristotle was now the rage. His voluminous writings covered topics ranging from physics and biology to ethics and metaphysics. Major universities in Europe revised their curricula to make room for the Aristotelian philosophy. These shifts came with plenty of controversy: many revised their theology in light of Aristotle, while others rejected his pagan philosophy (the University of Paris issued multiple bans against Aristotle's works). Aquinas' theology became significant in how it appropriated Aristotle in a rich and compelling way. In the process, he revolutionized the medieval intellectual landscape forever and developed new ways of relating faith and reason.

Alas it was not to endure. The delicate balance between faith and reason began unraveling during "late scholasticism" (~1300–1500). Realism had been the dominant paradigm of the medieval period, but that consensus was overturned by nominalists like John Duns Scotus (1265–1308) and William of Ockham (c. 1285–1347). God's creation, they believed, did not reflect a transcendent rational order as realists had thought. Reason was more fragile, less trustworthy; faith in God's revelation became the decisive factor. The resulting picture was a rather arbitrary world, one in which society was shaped fundamentally by our own choices not by a higher, external order. Perhaps it was inevitable, in retrospect, that someone like Marsillius of Padua (c. 1275–c. 1342) would pen an incendiary political tract that vested authority in the people rather than the church (or the pope). But Marsillius was merely tending the garden; nominalism—many would argue—had already planted the seeds of modern democracy, science, and Protestant Reformation.

Change was in the air, even revolution. Through it all, however, one always discerned the abiding concern to know God. Medieval mystics like Meister Eckhart (1260–1328), advocates of popular piety like Thomas à Kempis (c. 1380–1471), and heretics like John Wycliffe (c. 1328–1384)—all these authors, in different ways, were trying to storm the gates of heaven. They wanted to bring reform to a languishing medieval church. Many decades later, an Augustinian monk faced his accusers at the Diet of Worms, and said, according to tradition: "I cannot do otherwise, here I stand, may God help me." Not only was Martin Luther standing in the presence of distinguished European royalty, he was standing ineluctably in the churning stream of early church and medieval theology, rejecting large parts of that earlier tradition no doubt, but also drawing out treasures old and new.

List of Classic Works of the Medieval Period

Boethius, *The Consolation of Philosophy* or *Sacred Works*, 523
Pope Gregory I, *The Rule for Pastors*, 591
Benedict of Nursia, *The Rule of St. Benedict*, late fifth century.
Dionysios the Areopagite, *Divine Names*, c. 650
Bede, *Homilies on the Gospels*, c. 700
John of Damascus, *The Fountain of Wisdom*, 717
Rabanus Maurus, *Veneration of the Holy Cross*, early eighth century
Paschasius Radbertus, *On the Body and Blood of the Lord*, 831–833
Peter Damian, *On Divine Omnipotence*, 1065
Anselm, *An Example of Meditation on the Reason for Faith*, 1075–1076
Peter Abelard, *Yes and No [Sic et Non]*, 1100
Bernard of Clairvaux, *On Loving God*, 1115
William of St. Thierry, *On Contemplating God*, 1121–1124
Anonymous, *The Play of Adam*, 1125–1175
Aelred of Rievaulx, *The Mirror of Charity*, 1142
Hildegard of Bingen, *Scivias*, 1142–1151
Bonaventure, *The Mind's Road to God* or *The Tree of Life*, 1200
Gilbert of Poitiers, *Commentaria in Boethii opuscula sacra*, c. twelfth century
William of Auvergne, *Teaching on God in the Mode of Wisdom (Magisterium)*, 1220–1240
Vincent of Beauvais, *Great Mirror*, 1244
Clare of Assisi, *The Rule of St. Clare*, 1253
Roger Bacon, *Greater Work (Opus Majus)*, 1267
Duns Scotus, *Ordinatio*, late twelfth century

St. Gertrude, *The Herald of Divine Love*, late twelfth century
Arnaud Cogul, *A French Peasant's Theology of God*, 1320
John Wycliffe, *On the Truthfulness of Holy Scripture*, 1377–1378
Catherine of Siena, *On Receiving the Eucharist*, c. 1378
Julian of Norwich, *Revelations of Divine Love*, 1395
Giovanni De Cauli, *Meditations on the Life of Christ*, late thirteenth century
John Huss, *The Church*, c. 1400
Jean Gerson, *The Art of Dying Well*, 1430–1435
Margery Kempe, *The Book of Margery Kempe*, 1438

2.1

Pastoral Care[1] (c. 590 CE)
Gregory the Great
(c. 540–604 CE)

The author's life and work

Gregory, later called "the Great," was born around 540 CE to an aristocratic family in Rome. Educated in law, he became prefect of the city when still in his early thirties, but after his father's death in 574 he became a monk and converted the family mansion into a monastery. In 578, he was ordained a deacon and in the following year was sent to Constantinople as the bishop's ambassador to the emperor. Though he spent several years in the east, he never learned Greek. In 585, he returned to Rome and five years later he was elected as the city's bishop. Gregory did not want this promotion, and he did his utmost to avoid it, but on September 3, 590, he was consecrated in spite of his objections. It was he who first described himself as the "servant of the servants of God," a title which is still borne by the popes today.

Gregory found himself having to organize the civil government of Rome, which had broken down, and he was soon in control of much of Italy. The emperor in Constantinople was unable to offer effective aid to resist the Lombards, who had invaded Italy in 568, and Gregory stepped into the breach, becoming the first "pope" to exercise significant secular authority. Gregory realized that the Roman Empire was gone for good, and he did all he could to strengthen ties with the churches in Spain and Gaul, bringing them more firmly under Roman ecclesiastical control. He organized a successful mission to the English, which led to their gradual conversion after 597. His attempts to reform the church along monastic lines were less

Figure 2.1 Gregory the Great

successful, but they provided a pattern that gradually imposed itself in the later Middle Ages.

As a writer, Gregory was not particularly prolific or original, but his practical bent ensured that his works would be widely read. He produced a commentary on 1 Samuel and sermons on Ezekiel, the Song of Songs, and the Gospels.[2] An enormous number of his letters survive and give us a good picture of his pontificate. The most famous of these are the ones he sent to Augustine, the first archbishop of Canterbury, in which he outlined how the newly-established English church should be organized.[3] His most ambitious work was an allegorical study of the book of Job, which is a profound study of the meaning of suffering and how it has been redeemed in Christ, the suffering servant and judge of all mankind, by his death on the cross. It quickly became a theological classic and has remained one in spite of its allegorical reading of the Biblical text.[4]

Gregory's most influential work was his *Liber regulae pastoralis*, or *Pastoral Care*, which he wrote shortly after becoming a bishop and which became the standard textbook for bishops and other pastors for the next millennium. Even in his lifetime it was translated into Greek (an almost unheard of honor for a Latin writer) and the first English translation was made by King Alfred the Great (871–899). In 813 a series of synods convened by the Emperor Charlemagne made study of the book obligatory for all bishops in his empire, and within a generation it had become customary to give a copy of it to every bishop at his consecration. The medieval church was shaped in Gregory's mold largely because of this work, and, although times have changed, its principles remain just as valid today as when he first penned them.

Gregory died on March 12, 604, his greatness universally acknowledged. He was soon recognized as one of the four doctors of the Western church (the others being Ambrose, Jerome, and Augustine), and his works were widely read. John Calvin admired his insight into the nature of spiritual leadership and bemoaned the way it had been lost in the church of his time.[5] Today, his reputation rests mainly on his political achievements and his spiritual writings are less well known than they once were, but his place as one of the great leaders of Western Christendom remains secure.

Pastoral Care

The book of *Pastoral Care* was composed by Gregory shortly after taking up the office of bishop. He wrote it in response to John, archbishop of Ravenna, who rebuked him for his reluctance to take on this responsibility, and it is in effect an explanation of why he did not want it. The inspiration for his approach came from Gregory of Nazianzus (d. 390) who wrote a similar treatise shortly after being ordained as a presbyter, a role he did not want either (*Flight to Pontus*, or *Oration* 2).[6] Since Gregory of Rome did not know Greek, he must have read his namesake's work in translation, but the numerous quotations and allusions to it that are scattered throughout the book make it perfectly clear where he got his inspiration from.

Divided into four parts, the book examines different aspects of the bishop's life and work in the following order: (1) The qualifications required for becoming a bishop. (2) The lifestyle that ought to characterize a ruler of the church. (3) The art of preaching, which Gregory regarded as the bishop's primary pastoral duty, and (4) A brief final reminder that the bishop, having performed his duties according to the prescribed rule, must always remain humble and remember his own unworthiness for a task that cannot be accomplished apart from the grace of God.

1 A bishop is a spiritual doctor

Gregory begins by saying that the care of souls is the art of arts, a phrase taken from Gregory of Nazianzus, and he compares it to the calling of a medical doctor. A good doctor is careful when it comes to treating his patient's illnesses and hesitates to offer medicines that may end up doing more harm than good. The pastor must likewise be highly skilled, because curing the soul of its diseases is far more difficult than curing the body. The sins of the soul are hidden and hard to discern, yet there are many who think they can deal with them even though they have had no special training to do so. Gregory adds that God will deal severely with these blind guides, though he recognizes that those who listen to them are also responsible for accepting the leading of people who do not know what they are doing.

Gregory insists that whoever assumes pastoral responsibility must practice what he preaches. It is perfectly possible to know the theory but not to live by it. The consequences of such behavior are potentially disastrous. In his words: "No one does more harm in the Church than he, who having the title or rank of holiness, acts evilly."[7] Gregory refers to the example of Jesus, who shrank from accepting the earthly kingdom that his followers offered him.[8] Instead, Jesus chose to suffer and die so that we might learn from his example to flee the temptations of the world, but not to fear its dangers. His life shows us that adversity is to be welcomed and prosperity feared because of the temptations it brings. Saul and David both accepted earthly glory, but they were puffed up with pride and suffered because of it.

2 The responsibilities of high office

Gregory knows that people who take on administrative responsibilities find it hard to concentrate on their own spiritual development and may be led into sin as a result. On the other hand, there are men who are endowed with the gift of government who prefer to turn away from responsibility. When they do that, they not only deprive others of their gifts, but they risk losing them because of their selfishness. Those who have received gifts are expected to use them for the benefit of others, and if they refuse to help their neighbors in this way they will suffer for their negligence. Gregory concludes that the truly humble are those who refuse leadership roles until they are summoned to take them up by a direct command from God.

For Gregory, the highest responsibility of the leader is to preach, and he says that there are some preachers who have quite rightly desired that ministry and others who have been unable to escape it. He cites the examples of Jeremiah, who protested without resisting the call of God, and Isaiah, who accepted the call but then had to be cleansed by a coal from the altar before he could take up his appointed task.

3 The character of a church leader

Gregory analyzes the character of those who seek high office in the Church when they do not deserve it. Anyone who wants a bishopric merely for the prestige it conveys has misunderstood it and will bring it into disrepute if he gets what he wants. Such people fool themselves into thinking that they will be able to achieve great things, but they are deceiving themselves. Thinking they have deserved the position they have obtained, once they are installed in it, the desire to do good tends to atrophy because they have no idea of the stress they will be under and lack the spiritual depth to resist and overcome the forces ranged against them.

The man who is put in charge of others must die to himself, renounce worldly riches and success, rise above petty desires, and learn to praise and condemn the deeds of others in the right degree. Everything he does must serve as an example to others. Above all, he cannot reconcile people to God if he has not been reconciled himself, and for that reason he must pay heed to his own sins, repent of them and seek forgiveness before setting out to minister to others. Those whose prayer life is weak or non-existent, who have no consciousness of their own need for forgiveness, who lack discernment, who busy themselves by poking their noses into other people's business, and who worry about nothing but the affairs of this world are totally unsuited to the task of pastoral care. Consumed by lust, they are diseased in their souls and quite unable to help anyone get closer to God. Only those who have overcome their worldly feelings and desires are fit for the service of God, and only they should be chosen and appointed to be leaders of the flock of Christ.

4 A bishop's spiritual life

Gregory says that a shepherd of God's flock "should be pure in thought, exemplary in conduct, discreet in keeping silence, profitable in speech, in sympathy a near neighbor to everyone, in contemplation exalted above all others, a humble companion to those who lead good lives [and] erect in his zeal for righteousness against the vices of sinners."[9]

That a bishop must be pure in thought is Gregory's first concern. Any temptation to lewd or dissolute behavior must be resolutely resisted by bowing to the dictates of reason, which Gregory regarded as a sure protection against excess and depravity. Furthermore, purity of thought meant keeping the examples of the patriarchs and saints firmly in mind. Their lives should guide ours and point us to a deeper understanding of the mind of God himself. Ultimately the presence of that mind in our hearts must rule and control our lives, inspiring in us a right "fear of the Lord" and giving bishops the strength to resist the forces that would destroy their ministry.

5 A bishop's public behavior

Right thoughts necessarily lead to right conduct, and Gregory expects bishops to set an example to others in this respect. The priestly sacrifices outlined in the Old Testament serve as an example of how bishops should behave, keeping the service of God always foremost in their minds and not allowing any earthly consideration to distract them from it. He uses the colors of the priest's garments as an allegory to expound the different characteristics that a bishop ought to display, the emphasis at all times being on the acquisition and application of heavenly wisdom.

A bishop must know when to speak out and when to keep quiet. Because of his position, he will be told things in confidence, and he must never betray that. If he talks too much, people will stop listening to what he says. Though he guards his tongue, he will not be afraid to use it when issues of justice and truth are at stake. In human terms, the bishop is called to be the voice of the Lord and must learn from the prophets of old how to stand fast and fulfill his calling.

A bishop must be detached enough from his own concerns to be able to reach out in sympathy with those of others. Gregory takes the Apostle Paul as his model. Though Paul was a man of prayer, he did not hesitate to get involved in affairs of everyday life, and he even counseled married couples about how they should live together. He behaved like a Jew when dealing with Jews, not because he had abandoned his faith in Christ (which is how most people in Gregory's time thought of Jews), but because he was reaching out to them in sympathy. Gregory goes on to talk about Moses, who alternated between contemplating the glory of God in the tabernacle and ministering to the needs of the people. Finally, he upholds Jesus, who "engaged in prayer on the mountain and worked miracles in the towns."[10]

A good bishop should see himself as the companion of those who lead good lives, not trying to set himself up above them. Yet he must assert his authority when dealing with the wicked. Gregory believed that all men were created equal but had fallen into different degrees of inferiority according to the seriousness of their sins. For that reason, he says, some have been appointed to rule over others, but they must also be genuinely superior to those under them. He is well aware of the temptation to pride in rulers, and he spends a great deal of time warning his readers against the dangers of flattery, power, and worldly prestige. As he puts it: "Let rulers uphold externally what they undertake for the service of others, and internally retain their fear in their estimation of themselves."[11] On no account should he allow his exercise of authority to become a lust for domination, but neither should he succumb to favoritism or overlook the sins of those close to him, as Eli overlooked the misdeeds of his own sons.[12] A deep knowledge of the Holy Scriptures is the key to such success. They chastise us like a rod but uphold us like a staff, which is why David said: "Your rod and staff have comforted me."[13]

6 The right balance between public service and private spirituality

The good bishop must also maintain the right balance between concern for the external affairs of his office and dedication to the inner life of prayer and worship. Those who devote themselves too much to the burdens of their office are soon weighed down by them, and, although they think they are laboring for the benefit of their flock, they are merely wearing themselves out and doing their people no good at all. Learning to delegate his responsibilities to trustworthy subordinates, the leader can be free to pursue spiritual things. His real function is to share those things with his congregation, but he can only do so if he has something to give them. On the other hand, there are bishops who are so otherworldly that they neglect the duties of the office. This must be avoided, because it brings them into disrepute and does nothing to pastor the flock.

The ruler of the church must not be a people-pleaser, trying to keep folks happy according to their own wants and desires. Instead, he should consider what the Bible says they ought to want, and, like a good physician, he should insist on giving them that, whether they appreciate it at the time or not. Only when people develop a love for the truth will they grow spiritually, and this must be in the forefront of the bishop's mind at all times.

Bishops must also realize that vices can pass themselves off as virtues, as when a stingy person claims to be thrifty. This kind of self-deception leads to apparently meritorious acts becoming instruments of damnation, because their real purpose is very different from what appears on the surface. Above all else, a bishop must seek to become discerning and to act with prudence. He goes beneath the surface and finds out what is really going on before passing judgment on particular actions. If he discovers ignorance, he points out what the people concerned are doing wrong, and shows them how they must change. Gregory does not underestimate the difficulty in doing this, as we see from his remark that: "when the mind of the teacher is incited to reprove, it is very difficult not to break forth sometimes into expressions that should have been avoided."[14] When that happens, Gregory advises repentance and restoration in the sight of God, something which is all the more important given that his excesses were committed out of a right desire for the truth to prevail.

Bishops must spend time meditating on the Scriptures, which should be their constant guide and companion. Referring to the image of the Old Testament priests, he tells his readers that just as they carried the ark of the covenant in ancient times, so the bishops of the church have a similar responsibility to guard the truth of the Gospel. The outward forms of the new covenant in Christ are different from what they were under the law of Moses, but the underlying spiritual meaning is the same and must be honored by a bishop who wants to please both God and the people he is called to rule over.

7 The art of preaching

Gregory believes that preaching should be geared to the edification of the hearers, seeking to inculcate virtues in them and not encouraging the growth of the contrary vices. For instance, he says that marriage should be preached to those who cannot contain themselves, but not in a way that will unsettle those who have no difficulty suppressing their sexual desires. In appreciating this, the modern reader must realize that Gregory lived in a society where sexual license was closely associated with paganism and where marriage was more of a social contract than a love affair. Similarly, Gregory insisted that generosity should be encouraged without falling into prodigality and thrift is to be taught without succumbing to miserliness.

The preacher must also be aware that many people are torn by contrary desires and not assume that only one of them is causing them trouble. As a result, balanced treatment is essential in order to avoid seeing them lurch from one extreme to the other. Sometimes it will be necessary to overlook minor sins because there are more serious ones to be dealt with first and the lesser ones can be left until a later time. Weak Christians should not be confused with teaching that is too deep for them to absorb, and the good preacher must lead his flock one step at a time. Finally, Gregory comes back to where he began, concluding his message with the words: "every preacher should make himself heard rather by deeds than by words, and ... by his righteous way of life should imprint footsteps for men to tread in, rather than show them by word the way to go."[15]

8 The need for God's grace

Gregory insists that all the pastor's efforts are worthless unless they are blessed and guided by the grace of God. Frequently, after a preacher has delivered a successful sermon, he will be impressed by his own performance, but this kind of pride must be avoided. No servant of God should exalt himself, and when he has done well he must be especially careful to remind himself that he can do nothing without the grace of God. As Gregory puts it, the eye of the soul "should look to the good not that it has done, but that which it has neglected to do, so that while the heart becomes contrite in recalling its weakness, it may be the more solidly established in the eyes of the Author of humility."[16] This is the portrait of the true pastor, concludes Gregory, and the only way that his labors for the Lord will not be in vain.

Conclusion

Gregory's *Pastoral Rule* became and remained one of the most important books of the Middle Ages. Every time reformers sought to bring the church back to its primitive purity, it would be revived as a standard textbook and eventually a copy was given to every new bishop at his consecration. By the sixteenth century his reputation was such that it survived the Reformation intact and he was regarded as the last of the "good" popes before the corruptions of later times set in. Almost every Protestant manual of preaching and pastoral care reflected his influence, though he was seldom mentioned by name. The most outstanding work of this kind is undoubtedly Richard Baxter's *Reformed Pastor*, which picks up the same themes that Gregory dealt with and applied them to the conditions of seventeenth-century England.[17] Times and circumstances had changed, but the fundamental spiritual lessons that the good pastor has to learn were exactly the same as they had always been, and in the ministry of the Puritans Gregory's counsels found a new and fruitful application to the spiritual health of the church.

Notes

1. Translated from *Liber Regulae Pastoralis,* also known as *Cura Pastoralis* and *Regula Pastoralis*; references to the work (Gregory the Great, *Pastoral Care* [trans. and ed. Henry Davis; Westminster, MD: Newman Press, 1950]) shall be noted employing in-text parenthetical citations.

2. E.g., see Mark DelCogliano, ed. and trans., *Gregory the Great: On the Song of Songs,* Cistercian Studies 244 (Collegeville, MN: Cistercian Publications, 2012).

3. See John R.C. Martyn, ed. and trans., *The Letters of Gregory the Great,* 3 vols., Medieval Sources in Translation 40 (Toronto: Pontifical Institute of Medieval Studies, 2004).

4. Gregory the Great, *Moralia in Job,* ed. M. Adriaen, CCSL, 143, 3 vols. (Turnhout: Brepols, 1979–1985).

5. John Calvin, *Institutes of the Christian Religion* IV.iv.3; IV.vii.4. Calvin does not refer specifically to the *Pastoral Care,* but covers the same ground as it does.

6. Cf. Gregory of Nazianzus, "In Defence of His Flight to Pontus," in *Orations and Letters,* NPNF Second Series, vol. 7 (Peabody, MA: Hendrickson, 1994), 204–227.

7. I, 2, p. 24. All quotes are from the Davis translation.

8. He cites John 6:15.
9. II, 1, p. 45.
10. II, 5, p. 58.
11. II, 6, p. 64.
12. He quotes 1 Sam. 2:29.
13. Ps. 23:4.
14. II, 10, p. 85.
15. III, 40, p. 232.
16. IV, 1, p. 237.
17. Richard Baxter, *The Reformed Pastor* (Edinburgh: Banner of Truth, 1981).

Select Bibliography

Primary sources

Gregorii Magni *Regula Pastoralis*, edited by F. Rommel, 2 vols., Paris: Cerf, 1992.

Gregory the Great, *Pastoral Care*, translated and edited by Henry Davis, Westminster, MD: Newman Press, 1950.

Gregory the Great, *The Book of Pastoral Rule*, translated and edited by George E. Demacopoulos, Crestwood, NY: St Vladimir's Seminary Press, 2007.

Secondary sources

Cavadini, J.C., *Gregory the Great: A Symposium,* Notre Dame, IN: University of Notre Dame Press, 1995.

Evans, G.R., *The Thought of Gregory the Great*, Cambridge: Cambridge University Press, 1986.

Markus, R.A., *Gregory the Great and His World*, Cambridge: Cambridge University Press, 1997.

Richards, Jeffrey, *Consul of God. The Life and Times of Gregory the Great*, London: Routledge and Kegan Paul, 1980.

Straw, C.E., *Gregory the Great: Perfection in Imperfection*, Berkeley: University of California Press, 1988.

2.2

Ecclesiastical History of the English People[1] (731 CE)

Bede (672/3–735 CE)

The author's life and work

Bede was born to a humble English family in Northumbria, probably in 673 CE, and entered the monastery at Jarrow while still a boy. He remained there for the rest of his life and never ventured further than York, less than 100 miles to the south. Although his physical world was very sheltered and provincial, this did not prevent him from becoming the most learned man of his age and one of the greatest Englishmen of all time.

Christianity had come to the English only two generations before Bede was born and in many parts of the country its implantation was more recent still. Competition between monks sent from Rome and monks radiating out from the Celtic monastery of Iona had produced two different kinds of churches among the English. The most noticeable difference between the two was the way they calculated the date of Easter. The Celts followed the pattern laid down at the first council of Nicaea in 325, whereas the Romans used a modified version adopted at Rome in 457. The Roman party triumphed at the synod of Whitby in 664. Though Bede was always a staunch champion of their cause, he also had a great admiration for the scholarship of the Irish monks, from whom he learned (and borrowed) a great deal.

In his engagement with the Easter controversy, Bede developed a life-long interest in chronology and the computation of time, and it was he who was largely responsible for introducing the Christian era of dating, which had originally been invented by Dionysius Exiguus more than a century before Bede was born. The great popularity of Bede's writings, which quickly spread all across Western Europe and often remained standard works in their fields for centuries, displayed his success as an historian.

Bede made the most of the monastery library at Jarrow, which was extremely well stocked. He wrote several biblical commentaries, which are noted for the clear and judicious interpretation of the texts, and a number of didactic works on subjects ranging from correct spelling to the calculation of time. He was the author of a hagiographical biography of Cuthbert, the saintly bishop of Lindisfarne who was still alive in Bede's youth, and of liturgical works describing the Old Testament tabernacle and temple. We also have a selection of his sermons and poems.

Bede's greatest achievements, however, were in the field of history, in which he excelled. Aside from two chronicles and an account of the abbots of his own monastery, his most important work is undoubtedly his *Ecclesiastical History of the English People*, a monumental study of the origins of England and one of the most important sources for our knowledge of its history and development. Inevitably, the text reflects Bede's own background and prejudices, but these do not detract from the value of the work as a whole, and his concern for dating makes it largely accurate as well as informative. It remains the most widely read book written in medieval England and without it we would know far less than we do about the conversion of the English to Christianity. Modern scholars mine his work for details of social and political history, which tends to distort its main purpose, which was theological. Bede was following Luke, the author of the Acts of the Apostles, in telling how the great commission that Jesus had given to his disciples when he ascended into heaven had been fulfilled in England. It is a missionary history, not unlike those written in the nineteenth and twentieth centuries by the pioneers who took the gospel to Africa and Asia, and it must be read as such.

Despite Bede's Englishness and the pride that he took in his national origins, he wrote exclusively in Latin. There is a suggestion that he may have translated the Gospel of John into English, but if he did, it has not survived. Bede died at Jarrow on May 26, 735, and was buried there. Around 1050, his body was taken to Durham and since 1370 it has lain in the cathedral of that city. But Bede's real monument is nothing less than England itself, the nation to which he gave a collective consciousness centuries before it was politically united and which continues to honor his memory as one of the greatest men it has ever produced.

Ecclesiastical History of the English People

The history opens with a preface and dedication to King Ceolwulf of Northumbria (729–737). Bede tells that he had already sent his manuscript to the king because of the latter's interest in the history of his people, and that now he sends it again, in the hope that it might be copied and preserved for posterity. His inspiration for writing came from Albinus, abbot of the monastery of Saints Peter and Paul at Canterbury (709–732), to whom he owed much of his source material. He also acknowledges his great debt to Nothelm, who became archbishop of Canterbury in 735. Nothelm had been to Rome and consulted the papal archives, copying valuable documents there to which Bede had no access. Bede also relates that he relied heavily on information supplied to him by bishops and monks in other parts of England, and that he had consulted the *Life of St. Cuthbert* at Lindisfarne as well as spoken to those who had known Cuthbert personally. However, only in dealing with his native Northumbria did he feel confident that he knew the facts himself, and he pleads with his readers to excuse him if he has misinterpreted them. His aim, he says, is to get as close to the truth as possible and to record for future generations how the English nation had been won for Christ.

1 The challenge of Christian mission

Bede begins with a description of the British Isles,[2] which is surprisingly accurate and tells us that they are inhabited by four nations—the English, the British (Welsh), the Picts (in Scotland), and the Irish. Each of these speaks its own language, but they are united by the common use of Latin, the language of the Church, which gathers all nations to itself. The particular characteristics of each nation have been brought together in the bosom of the Church, and in this respect the British example is a microcosm of the worldwide spread of the Gospel. Bede had a strong sense that the British peoples were specially chosen by God, and he used every opportunity he had to link their history with that of Christ. Britain first appeared in history when it was invaded by Julius Caesar, the reformer of the Roman calendar, something that was an important consideration for Bede. That invasion was followed a century later by another, more permanent one. Bede points out that Britain became Roman at the same time as the famine in Syria foretold by the prophet Agabus took place, thereby linking the event to the beginnings of Christianity (cf. Acts 11:28). The discovery of Britain and the coming of Christ into the world were thus parallel events, and for someone who believed in predestination as strongly as Bede did, that could not have been an accident.

Christians first appeared in Britain sometime in the mid to late second century, which is probably historically correct, even though Bede's description of it is not. Nevertheless, although he often got the facts wrong (to varying degrees, it should be added) the general drift of his account is fairly accurate. When we remember that his main interest was in the progress of evangelization, not in politics, we can appreciate that he had a good sense of what transpired.

Persecution came to Britain during the reign of Diocletian (285–305), as it did to the rest of the Roman Empire, and the country produced its first martyr in the person of Alban, a Roman soldier stationed at Verulamium (now St Albans). Bede understood the importance of martyrdom as a witness to the truth of the Christian faith, and so he tells the story in great detail. Alban stood firm in the face of death, miracles occurred, and the onlookers were moved to worship the true God instead of their pagan idols. The blood of martyrs was truly the seed of the Church, and Britain was converted by the strength of their witness.

After that, Britain was caught up in the dynastic quarrels of the Roman Empire and in the spread of heresy. Bede mentions the presence of Arianism, but does not dwell on it because it was of little importance in Britain. Nevertheless, it opened the door to other forms of false teaching, one of which originated with the British monk Pelagius. He taught that human beings could save themselves without the help of God's grace and was condemned by the great St. Augustine, but in Britain his ideas were popular and undermined the state.[3] The Romans also withdrew at this time, and the country was invaded by the Irish and the Picts. Managing to rally their forces, the British beat back their enemies, but they foolishly invited the Angles and Saxons to come and assist them. Seeing the weakness of the Britons, the Anglo-Saxons soon set out to conquer them and subdue the country, which Bede saw as God's just punishment on the Britons for their Pelagianism.

Meanwhile, help arrived from the continent in the shape of Germanus of Auxerre, a Gallic prelate, who turned up in Britain to rid the country of heresy and restore order. This was no easy task and Germanus had to return a second time, but, although he dispatched the remaining Pelagians, his attempts to unite the Britons proved to be in vain. As soon as he left, they started quarreling again and fell prey to the Anglo-Saxon invaders. As Bede saw it, the Britons compounded their sins by refusing to evangelize the newcomers, whom he believed had been called by God and sent to Britain in order to hear the gospel which had not yet reached their homeland in north Germany.

At this point there is a considerable gap in the history, which begins again with the mission of Augustine, sent by Gregory the Great to convert the English, who by then were well-established in Britain. Augustine landed in 597 and was well-received by the king of Kent, whose wife was already a Christian. The king was soon converted and his people followed in what we would now recognize as a typical tribal conversion. Augustine was clearly delighted with his success and reported it back to Gregory, sending him a list of nine questions about how to proceed in building up the church. Bede records these questions and Gregory's replies in great detail, and they reveal the extent to which Kentish society had been turned upside down by the advent of the gospel.

2 Conversion and spiritual warfare

Bede's second book relates the progress of the mission from its beginnings to its first major setback a generation or so after Augustine's landing. Bede begins by relating the death of Pope Gregory I in 604, an event which allows him to write a long and admiring obituary of the man whom he called the Apostle to the English. It is in the course of this obituary that Bede recounts the famous legend, according to which Gregory happened to see two blond boys being sold in the slave market at Rome, and when he asked the slave traders where such beautiful youths had come from, he was told that they were Angles. "Not Angles but angels" was Gregory's famous reply, and from that day on he determined to evangelize the English. While Augustine came to evangelize the Angles instead of Gregory, Bede says that Gregory would have come himself had he not become pope.

The obituary is important because it expresses the feelings that Bede and perhaps most of the English had for the man and the church that had sent them the gospel. Only those who have been brought out of darkness into light can fully appreciate what that means. Whether the incident recorded actually happened or not (and Bede had his doubts about that), he expressed the heartfelt gratitude of an entire nation, which for centuries remained devoted to Rome above and beyond any claim to jurisdiction that the papacy might make.

Bede then goes on to recount the attempts made by Augustine to win over the British bishops, whom he wanted to help him in his work of evangelizing the English. It was at this point that the ritual differences between the British and the Roman churches surfaced, the most important of them being the different methods used to calculate the date of Easter.[4] Reading between the lines, it is possible to see that Augustine was probably high-handed and intolerant of his British counterparts, who in turn may well have suspected that his approach was a trick to get them to submit to Anglo-Saxon political control. On the surface, the issues were purely ecclesiastical, but underneath there were other currents which neither side seems to have been able to recognize and deal with.

Bede then goes on to explain how Augustine set up a hierarchy of bishops in England and how the Easter controversy began to color relations not only with the Welsh but with the Irish as well. He also relates how paganism revived after the death of the king of Kent who had embraced Christianity, and the conversion was revealed to have been more superficial than Augustine had imagined. Meanwhile, the gospel was spreading to the north, and in 625 King Edwin of Northumbria was baptized by Paulinus, whom Augustine had consecrated as bishop and intended to install in York. Once again, we find that the king's wife had been a Christian all along and that it was through her good offices that Paulinus gained entry to the Northumbrian court. The conversion of great men through the intercession of their wives is a recurring theme in missionary tales, but Bede was intent on demonstrating what powerful support she enjoyed from the Church.

In spite of all this arm-twisting, Edwin seems to have resisted until he had a vision when he was in exile in East Anglia. Bede records this as proof that true conversion is a work of God, not of man, however highly placed that man may be, and shows that it was only when Edwin was convicted of his sinfulness and turned to Christ as a repentant sinner that he became a child of God.

Once converted, Edwin lost no time introducing Christianity into his kingdom and destroying the remains of paganism. A similar movement spread to East Anglia and Lincolnshire, where Paulinus also had a successful preaching ministry. Bede makes sure that his readers know that most of these people were baptized on Easter day, a reminder of just how important the controversy over that day was. For the next few years things went well, but in 633 Edwin was killed in battle, his kingdom relapsed into paganism, and it looked as though all the gains of the previous decade had suddenly been lost. The first phase of the English mission had come to an end.

3 The struggle for the gospel

After the death of King Edwin, paganism revived and the Britons seized the country until they were repulsed by the saintly King Oswald. Oswald prayed before battle and set up a wooden cross as his standard, which in later years was credited with performing many miracles. Once more we see the familiar pattern—the authenticity of Oswald's faith is guaranteed by the miraculous results it was able to obtain.

Oswald wanted to continue the Christianization of his kingdom, and to do so he appealed to the Irish, among whom he himself had been converted. This led to a prolonged period in which the Irish Church, complete with its rites and customs regarding the celebration of Easter, took over Northumbria. The Irish sent him Aidan, who became the bishop of Lindisfarne and directed the work of evangelization from there. That Bede's history praises Aidan as a great saint in spite of his divergent customs and differences over the date of Easter says much for his success and for Bede's understanding of the priority which must be given to the gospel.

Aidan brought with him many monks from Iona, whose history and evangelistic efforts among the Picts Bede then proceeds to recount. Between them, Aidan and Oswald settled Northumbria as a Christian kingdom which would no longer revert to its pagan past.

While this was going on in the north, the south of England was being progressively won for Christ by dedicated missionaries sent from Rome. The West Saxons became Christians in 635, and five years later Kent was restored to the Church. Oswald was involved in at least some of this, and Bede makes a point of mentioning the importance of Irish influence as well. Oswald was eventually killed in battle, but the site of his death was recognized as a place where miracles would occur, and soon people were being healed at his tomb. Bede recounts all these things at great length in order to demonstrate that the power of a great saint is not extinguished by his death but takes on a new and higher spiritual form.

The next few chapters continue the story of internecine warfare among the rulers of Northumbria, broken by the adventures and miracles performed by Aidan. Bede then goes on to tell the story of the conversion of East Anglia, which was marked by similar struggles, miracles, and Irish influence. After that he turns his attention briefly to the conversion of Mercia in 653 and the re-conversion of Essex, which was thanks to the missionary evangelism of Cedd. In all these places, monasteries were quickly founded and endowed by grateful kings and people.

Though Irish influence continued in Northumbria after Aidan's death, the controversy over Easter would not go away. In 664, it came to a head, and, at a great synod held at Whitby, the king opted for the Roman rule. The leading Irishmen withdrew in protest, but many others stayed on and Irish influence continued at the grassroots level. Bede describes the debate held at the synod in great detail, rehearsing the arguments used by both sides to defend their position. The truth was that the Irish observed the calculations authorized by the first council of Nicaea in 325, whereas Rome had modified these in 457, but nobody seemed to be aware of that. Instead, they used spurious arguments from the Bible to bolster their position, and Rome won because it could claim greater universality. In the years that followed, the Irish gradually accepted this, but Iona held out until 715. At Bede's death in 735, only the British (Welsh) were still using the old system, which they did not surrender until 768, and this may explain why he regarded them as uniquely recalcitrant and obnoxious.

4 Consolidating spiritual victory

In 668 Theodore of Tarsus was consecrated as archbishop of Canterbury, an event that was of cardinal importance for Bede. Theodore was a Greek and something of a surprise choice for England, but his pontificate was a great success and laid the foundation for the future growth of the church. Bede was aware of his own debt to him because, without Theodore's encouragement, his own monasteries of Wearmouth and Jarrow would not have had the library resources that distinguished them, nor would learning have been nearly as prized in the church as it was. Both his mentors, Albinus and Nothelm, had studied under Theodore, and so at this point we are entering Bede's own time.

Spared the need to do primary evangelism, Theodore lost no time in visiting every corner of England in order to establish the liturgy and worship of the local churches on a sound footing. He spread the knowledge of the Scriptures and the use of sacred church music and appointed saintly men to bishoprics.

The rest of the book tells the story of the different bishops who succeeded one another in sees that were by now firmly established, recounts how the last remaining pockets of paganism were won over, and how the bodies and relics of the early English saints were performing miracles at their various shrines. The synods of Hereford (673) and Hatfield (680) are recorded in detail as is the life and death of Queen Etheldreda, who founded the convent at Ely that is now the cathedral there. Bede then goes on to relate the death of Hilda, the abbess of Whitby (680), and he gives a detailed account of the singer-poet Caedmon, who was one of the first men to write hymns in English.

Bede gives a great deal of space to the career and death of Cuthbert, the great abbot of Lindisfarne and one of Bede's heroes. The usual details of a holy life and a sanctified afterlife marked by miracles performed at his tomb are all recorded in detail as a fitting climax and end to the first generation of settled church life in England.

After recounting the death of Cuthbert, Bede tells the story of the English Church in his own lifetime. He devotes much space to the life and miracles of Bishop John of Hexham (687–706) who later became archbishop of York and whom Bede knew personally. He also tells of pilgrimages to Rome and of new missionary endeavors to the Germanic cousins of the English on the continent. England was now in a position to give to others that which it had received, and Bede was enthusiastic at the prospect of an English mission to northern Europe.

Conclusion

Bede's *History* is a remarkable work that has stood the test of time and is still the major source for the events it describes. Its breadth of vision, its accuracy, and its general fairness to all sides put it in a class of its own, and it is generally recognized today as the greatest work of its kind to have been produced in the Middle Ages. It is theologically important because it places human history in the hand of a providential God, who created the nation of England long before the country had any political unity to speak of. Bede shows how great men can influence the course of events and how people who turn away from the true doctrine of Christ will pay a high price for their apostasy. His blow-by-blow account of the evangelization of an entire people, with its bursts of success followed by setbacks, records a pattern that has been repeated time and again in the missionary history of the Church.

At the time of the Reformation, Bede's sense that his nation had been specially called by God was a great encouragement to those who believed that God was calling them to fulfill the promises which he had made to his people a thousand years before. Bede wrote of a Christianity that owed a great debt to the missionary vision of Gregory the Great, the last "good" pope, but that also drew on non-Roman sources for its vitality. This was a message that appealed to the mainline Protestants of the sixteenth and seventeenth centuries who wanted to show that English Christianity had retained the best of its ancient inheritance but was also open to reform in the light of God's Word.

It was only in the nineteenth century, however, that Bede really came into his own in the Protestant world. The spread of the Gospel to the far corners of the world, much of it undertaken by British and American missionaries, was the fulfillment of his spiritual vision for the special calling of the English people. That approach has gone out of fashion in our post-imperial and post-colonial world, but Bede's emphasis on God's purposes in building his Church remains an inspiration to Christian missionaries even today.

Notes

1. Translated from *Historia ecclesiastica gentis Anglorum*.
2. Throughout this essay, "Britain" refers to Roman Britain or *Britannia*, i.e., those parts of Great Britain ruled by the Roman Empire between 43 and 410 CE.
3. Hugh Williams, *Christianity in Early Britain* (Oxford: Clarendon Press, 1912); Charles Thomas, *Christianity in Roman Britain to AD 500* (California: University of California Press, 1981).
4. Cf. Alden A. Mosshammer, *The Easter Computus and the Origins of the Christian Era* (Oxford: Oxford University Press, 2008).

Select Bibliography

Primary sources

Bede, *Ecclesiastical History of the English People*, London: Penguin, 1955.
Bede's Ecclesiastical History of the English People, edited by B. Colgrave and R. A.B. Mynors, Oxford: Clarendon Press, 1969.
Bede, *Ecclesiastical History of the English People*, Oxford: Oxford University Press, 1994.
Venerable Bede, *Venerabilis Baedae Historiam Ecclesiasticam Gentis Anglorum*, ed. C. Plummer, 2 vols., Oxford, 1896.

Secondary sources

Blair, Peter Hunter, *The World of Bede*, Cambridge: Cambridge University Press, 1970.

Brown, G.H., *A Companion to Bede*, Woodbridge: Boydell and Brewer, 2009.

DeGregorio, S., *The Cambridge Companion to Bede*, Cambridge: Cambridge University Press, 2010.

Wallace-Hadrill, J.M., *Bede's* Ecclesiastical History of the English People. *A Historical Commentary*, Oxford: Clarendon Press, 1988.

Ward, Benedicta, *The Venerable Bede*, London: Geoffrey Chapman, 1990.

Wright, J.R., *A Companion to Bede*, Grand Rapids: Eerdmans, 2008.

2.3

The Orthodox Faith[1] (c. 743 CE)

John of Damascus (c. 650/675–749 CE)

The author's life and work

St. John Damascene was born in Damascus to a prominent local family sometime between 650 and 675 CE. His background was Semitic, but Greek had been the language of the local elite since the time of Alexander the Great. His ancestors had served the Roman Empire and remained faithful to the imperial version of Christianity even when most of Syria became Monophysite in the late fifth and early sixth centuries. It was his grandfather who, as prefect of the city, handed it over to the invading Muslim Arabs in 635, and was rewarded by securing a post in the new administration. Young John thus had a good grounding in Arabic and Islam, as well as in Greek and Christianity—a unique combination.

Spiritually speaking, John owed allegiance to the emperor in Constantinople and the church of the (eastern) Roman Empire, though he never set foot there. His administrative career was cut short when the caliph Abd al-Malik (685–705) turned against the Christians and Arabized his civil service. John withdrew to the monastery of Mar Saba near Jerusalem and spent the rest of his life as a monk. His subsequent career was one of a teacher and church official, which allowed him time and gave him the resources to write on a wide range of theological topics.

Figure 2.2 John of Damascus

His career took an unexpected turn after 726 when the Emperor Leo III (717–741) instigated a controversy over icons, which he regarded as vestiges of paganism. John, who must have known how similar this was to Islam, took up his pen in defense of icons, which he regarded as a Christological issue. If the Son of God had become a man, it must have been possible to paint a picture of him, and on that basis icons ought to have a place in Christian worship. John did not live to see the end of the controversy, but his views triumphed at the second council of Nicaea in 787 and have been the foundation of Orthodox iconology ever since.

Among John's writings there is a treatise on fasting, a commentary on the Pauline epistles, a few sermons (one of which contains a Muslim–Christian dialogue on the incarnation of Christ), and some hagiographical works. For the most part, John copied and extracted passages from earlier writers, so that his originality is more obvious from the choice and arrangement of his material rather than from its content. His chief work is *The Source of Knowledge*, which he wrote in three parts and later revised. Both the original text and the later revision of all three parts have survived. The first part is devoted to philosophy and is little more than an adaptation of a Christian revision of Porphyry's introduction to the subject. The second part is a catalog of heresies, most of which is derived from Epiphanius, though with some other sources and a few original contributions by himself.

It is the third part of this work, the *Exposition of the faith*, on which John's fame as a theologian rests. In it he attempted to describe the Christian faith in a comprehensive and systematic way, borrowing a great deal from earlier sources but shaping the material in an original way. It has a fair claim to being called the first systematic theology ever to have been written. In the twelfth century it was translated into Latin by Burgundio of Pisa (d. 1193) and later subdivided into four parts, corresponding to the division of Peter Lombard's *Sentences*. It became widely known in the West where it exercised considerable influence on the development of medieval theology. In the Eastern churches, it remains a fundamental theological textbook, occupying a position not unlike that of Calvin's *Institutes* among Reformed Protestants. Written before the period of standard systematic theologies, when *The Orthodox Faith* underwent modification to match the format of Lombard's *Sentences*, its character as a systematic theology was established. As a result, it significantly influenced later scholastic theology in the Middle Ages, the Reformation era, and beyond.

Although he lived to a great old age, the exact date of John's death is unknown. It was probably shortly before the overthrow of the Damascus caliphate in 750, but as with the date of his birth, that can only be a conjecture.

The orthodox faith

1 Knowing God as three in one

John begins his exposition of the Christian faith with the doctrine of God and the Trinity, which he regards as fundamental to the rest. He was the first

Christian theologian to write against a backdrop of Islam, and so what he has to say about this is of particular importance for mission and inter-faith dialogue today. Starting with a quotation from Scripture (John 1:18), John tells us that God is unknowable. Only the Son and the Holy Spirit know the Father, who is hidden even from the angels. But God did not leave us in ignorance, because he planted knowledge of him in every human being and spoke directly to us through the prophets. Finally, in Jesus Christ, he showed us as much of himself as we are able to grasp. Everything we need to know about him is contained in Holy Scripture, and what is beyond our understanding he has kept hidden from us.

In theology we must distinguish between what we know in our minds and what we can express in words. We know that by nature God is totally different from any of his creatures and we have no access to his inner being. We do not even know how it was possible for him to become a man in the womb of the Virgin Mary. When we talk about him, we are forced to use words familiar to us and recognize that they cannot express the fullness of his divinity. For example, we sometimes talk about God as if he had hands and feet, and we describe the persons of the Trinity as "begotten" and "proceeding." Holy Scripture authorizes us to do this, but the words still fall far short of the reality behind them.

Everyone has an innate knowledge of the existence of God. We know that he must exist because of the nature of the created order. Everything has a cause, and is mutable. The First Cause must be greater than any of his creatures, including human beings and angels, and he must also be immutable: this is the God who reveals himself to us. We can deduce from our own observations that God must be incorporeal and motionless, since he created bodies and set them in motion, but we cannot describe what his being is like. The only thing that is comprehensible about him is his infinity and incomprehensibility! Even to say that he is good, just, and wise merely describes the qualities of his nature and says nothing about that nature itself.

That there is only one God is plainly demonstrated by Scripture, but for those who do not accept that testimony, we may say that there can only be one totally perfect and infinite being. If there were more than one being claiming to be God, there would have to be some difference between them, but that would make at least one of them imperfect, and so not really divine. Furthermore, the universe would not hold together if it had more than one ruler.

The one God is rational because he possesses the faculty of Reason (*logos*).[2] There was never a time when that was not true, and the divine reason could not separate itself from him because there is nowhere for it to go. At the same time, his Word (*logos*) is an expression of his mind and can be distinguished from it. But because it proceeds from the perfect mind it is also perfect and must be regarded as such. In the same way, the Word must possess a spirit, since otherwise it could not be uttered. The Spirit is the breath that makes speech possible. In the case of human beings, this spirit comes from the air we breathe, but in the case of God it must come from inside himself, since there is nowhere else that it could come from. In that case, it is just as perfect as God and his Word are. Even the Old Testament speaks of God's Word and Spirit, so Jews have no excuse for not believing in them.[3]

The one eternal, infinite, and incomprehensible God subsists in three persons, who are united without confusion and distinguished without being separated from each other. The Father is unbegotten, without cause or origin. The Son is the only-begotten of the Father, consubstantial with him and co-eternal. There was never a time when he did not exist, because then the Father would not have been Father and it is blasphemous to suggest that.

We also believe that the Holy Spirit is a third person, proceeding from the Father and resting in the Son. There is a difference between procession and generation, but what that difference is remains beyond the scope of our understanding. What we know is that all three persons are perfect in their divinity and that they all possess the same powers and attributes. We speak of the Father as being Father of the Son, and we speak of the Son as the Son of the Father because he derives from the Father. We also speak of the Holy Spirit as the Spirit of the Father and the Son, although he derives from the Father and not from the Son. We do not, however, speak of the Son of the Spirit, because the Son does not derive from him.

John tells us that God is "simple." This means that when we describe him as eternal, good, and so on, we are not describing qualities that are part of him but realities that characterize his being as a whole. The names of God speak of his being and his energy, which is how we understand him. A second category of names (like "Lord" and "King") describe his relationship to other things and not his actual being. All these names and attributes apply equally to the three persons of the Trinity. The incarnation of the Son, however, is unique to him.

When the Bible uses body language to talk about God, it does so in order to make us understand what God's character is like. These words are analogies pointing us towards heavenly things that cannot be expressed otherwise. But at the same time, the God-Word also took a human body and dwelt on earth. In relation to his creatures, God is the one who made them, who preserves them in being, and who restores them to the state he originally wanted them to enjoy.

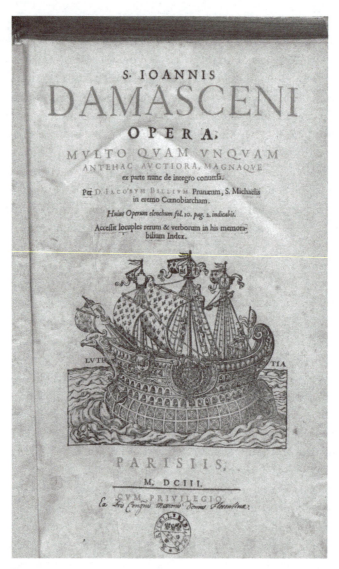

Figure 2.3 Icon of John of Damascus

God cannot be located in any particular place because he does not have a body. He can be compared to the mind, which has a distinct identity but no physical place in which it can be found. God is his own place, filling all things and penetrating the whole of creation without being part of it. Furthermore, he is everywhere present in the fullness of his being and cannot be divided up into parts. Other spiritual beings like angels and souls are finite, but they are like the mind in not being confined to a particular place.

2 The importance of creation

Having dealt at length with the doctrine of God, John goes on to expound the doctrine of creation, including the nature of humanity. He begins by defining the word "age" (*aiôn*), explaining that it can mean many different things. Eternity is the sum of the ages, all of which are caught up in God.

God created the world because he was not content merely to contemplate himself. He wanted others to share in his goodness, and so he created other beings, both visible and invisible. Humans are a combination of both.

The highest of the creatures are the angels, and John gives a detailed description of them. Angels are intelligent, rational beings and also immortal, though their immortality is given to them by grace and not by nature. Dionysius the Areopagite has explained their hierarchies and Gregory of Nazianzus claims that they were created before anything else was made.[4]

The devil and his angels were also made good, but they chose to rebel and desert God. This is the essence of evil, which is ultimately the absence of what is good.[5]

While touching on the visible creation, John is more concerned to discuss the nature of heaven. He mixes biblical quotations with secular Greek learning, seeking to prove the truth of the latter by reference to the former. He claims that there are seven heavens, each of which is higher than the next and governed by one of the planets. He devotes a long chapter to an examination of the planets, placing Saturn at the top and the moon at the bottom.[6] He also gives details of the four seasons, starting with the spring in which, he claims, God created all things. He even gives us the signs of the zodiac, beginning with Aries and ending with Pisces, and explains how the planets traverse them, saying that the moon goes faster than the others because it is the lowest of the planets! On the other hand, John is firmly against astrology and says quite plainly that the stars have no control over our lives. He makes a partial exception for comets, which foretell the death of kings, and for the star that the wise men saw, which was not in the natural order of creation.

John describes the air and the winds that compose it, as well as water and the seas with their currents, followed by the earth and its fruits. All these chapters give us what is essentially the sum of ancient scientific knowledge, referring occasionally to the Bible for support. He describes the Garden of Eden as a paradise of perfect climate and conditions made for the enjoyment of Adam and Eve. He mentions the two trees, of life and of knowledge, remarking that the latter was for the mature only. God forbade Adam to eat from it because he did not want him to be weighed down with the cares of this world, but Adam disobeyed. The tree of life, on the other hand, was reserved for those who were meant to enjoy eternal life. John was aware that some people interpreted the Garden literally and others figuratively, but states that both opinions are valid, because man is a combination of body and soul and thus has need of both.

After describing the Garden, John comes to the creation of the human race, which God reserved for last because he wanted man to be a mixture of the spiritual and material. The human body and soul were created at the same time, not one after the other, and the latter was endowed with God's image and likeness. According to John, the image refers to the human mind and free will, whereas the likeness pertains to virtue. The man thus created was good and sinless, not in the sense that he was incapable of sinning but in the sense that, if he were to sin, he would have to do so of his own free will. In this life, man was meant to live like an animal, needing food and sleep and so on, but in the life to come he would become like God, not by taking on the divine being but by participating in the divine glory.

John goes on to talk at length about pleasure, pain, and the different activities of the rational soul—fear, anger, imagination, sensation, thought, memory, conception and articulation, passion, and energy. John covers most of these somewhat cursorily, repeating generally received opinion, but he devotes more space to the last one because of the theological arguments about the nature of the human will of Christ. John explains that although Jesus possessed a human will because as a man he had a rational soul like other men, the fact that he was the second person of the Godhead gave him the ability to control these human forces and use them in ways consistent with the will of God.

The culmination of his teaching about creation is a lengthy discourse on the eternal questions of predestination and free will. John starts the discussion by distinguishing between actions that are voluntary and actions that are not, pointing out that there are some things that are both. Children, for example, perform voluntary actions but without choosing to do so, and the same is true of adults in certain circumstances. He then goes on to consider what the nature and limitations of free will are. On the one hand, he says that God is the cause of all things, but that man is obviously endowed with free will and can choose to obey or disobey divine commands.

According to John, God maintains his universe in being and is aware of what will happen in the future, but does not predetermine it because he did not want evil to come into his creation. Nevertheless, it was God's will that the obedience of Adam and Eve should be tested, although he cannot be held responsible for their failure to rise to the challenge.

3 The need of salvation

After delineating the Christian doctrines of God and creation, John moves on to consider how they intersect with one another in the Incarnation of Christ. He expounds the logic of God's plan of salvation, saying that after the fall of Adam he did his utmost to show mankind the way to live, until finally he sent the Redeemer, a man without sin because he was God, to resolve the problem of human disobedience once and for all.

Using biblical texts and framing his remarks in the language of the Nicene Creed, John describes the virgin birth of Christ. He defends the Chalcedonian doctrine of the one divine person in two natures, explaining how each nature interacts with the other. He compares the three persons in the one substance of God with the one person in two natures, showing how the doctrine of the Trinity coheres with Christology. He shows how one divine person can be united with a human nature in its entirety, without having to forgo a human mind or soul (*anhypostasis*), before demonstrating how the incarnate Son acts as a single person (*enhypostasis*).

John knew that the theology in his time tended to over-emphasize Christ's divinity at the expense of his humanity, so that when dealing with the death of Christ and his descent into hell, he concentrated on the reality of Christ's human suffering to a greater degree than had been common before his time. His Christology is perhaps best described as one of balance, presenting the Chalcedonian doctrine in the best possible light at a time when it was under attack both from other Christians and from Muslims.

4 The future consummation of all things

Dealing at some length with the resurrection of Christ, John eventually turns to the resurrection of all mankind. His eschatological focus leads him to discuss the theme of evil in the world and he upholds the sovereignty of God over any form of dualism. John sees the present age of the church as an eternal Sabbath, making special observance of the day unnecessary. Virginity is superior to marriage, but marriage is not condemned and is even encouraged for those unable to remain celibate. The Antichrist will come at the end of time, but John says that he will come to the Jews, not to Christians, and (interestingly) does not identify him with Muhammad. Finally, the resurrection will reunite our souls and bodies in a new and incorruptible form, and the devil and all his servants will be consigned to everlasting damnation. After that, the saints will dwell in eternal light, praising God and enjoying him forever as they were always meant to do.

Conclusion

John of Damascus can fairly claim to have written the first systematic theology, and as such he exercised considerable influence on men like Peter Lombard four centuries after his death. Unfortunately though, as a Greek theologian, John's theology got caught up in the debates between the Western and the Eastern churches in the later Middle Ages and was increasingly marginalized as a result. At the time of the Reformation his work was little known and largely unread by either Protestants or Catholics. It was not until the nineteenth century that his Christology became important to Protestant thought when Friedrich Schleiermacher picked up John's discussion of *enhypostasis* and used it to argue for a perfect God-consciousness of Christ.[7] John's distinction allowed Schleiermacher to retain a robust conception of the full humanity of Jesus while also retaining the notion that Jesus is enhypostatically the person of the Logos (the perfect God-consciousness).[8] Since that time there has been a renewal of interest in his work, and today he is being rediscovered both as a bridging figure between East and West and as a Christian theologian who had to confront the challenge of Islam when it was still a new and largely unknown religion. In both these respects, his writings are now regarded as being of considerable relevance and we may expect to see a renewal of interest in him in the next generation.

Notes

1. Translated from *Ekdosis akribēs tēs orthodoxou pisteōs*.
2. The Greek word *logos* can mean both "reason" and "speech" or "word." Both meanings are intended here.
3. John cites Ps. 119:89, 107:30, 104:30 and 33:30 as well as Job 33:4 to prove this point.
4. "Dionysius the Areopagite" was the pseudonym of a sixth-century monk who was probably of Syrian origin. The source is his *De caelesti hierarchia*, 6. Also Gregory of Nazianzus, *Oratio 2*.
5. For an account of the privation theory of evil in the early church, see Tatha Wiley, *Original Sin: Origins, Developments, Contemporary Meanings* (Mahwah, NJ: Paulist, 2002), 37–100; see also, Donald A. Cress,

"Augustine's Privation Account of Evil: A Defense," *Augustinian Studies* 20 (1989): 109–128. For broader discussion within the Protestant tradition, see Henri Blocher, *Evil and the Cross: An Analytical Look at the Problem of Pain* (Grand Rapids: Kregel, 2004), 26–35.

6. The days of the week also correspond to the seven planets, but the order is curious. Following John, we must read the week backwards, skipping a day as follows: Saturday, Thursday, Tuesday, Sunday, Friday, Wednesday, Monday. We order them in reverse because we rise from the lower to the higher.

7. Friedrich Schleiermacher, *The Christian Faith*, ed. and trans. H.R. Mackintosh and J.S. Stewart (London: T&T Clark, 1999 edition), 402.

8. See Allen Jorgensen, *The Appeal to Experience in the Christologies of Friedrich Schleiermacher and Karl Rahner* (New York: Peter Lang Publishing, 2007), pp. 112–114.

Select Bibliography

Primary sources

John of Damascus. *Ekdosis akribês tês orthodoxou pisteôs*, ed. by B. Kotter, *Die Schriften des Johannes von Damaskos*, Vol. 2. *Patristische Texte und Studien*, XII. Berlin: De Gruyter, 1973.

John of Damascus. *Exposition of the Orthodox Faith*, translated by S.D.F. Salmond, Oxford: J. Parker, 1899. Reprinted in *Library of Nicene and Post-Nicene Fathers, Series II*, Volume 9, eds P. Schaff and H. Wace. Peabody, MA: Hendrickson, 1994.

John of Damascus. *Writings*, ed. F.H. Chase, Washington, DC: Catholic University of America Press, 1999.

Secondary sources

Blancy, Alain. "Protestantism and the Seventh Ecumenical Council: Towards a Reformed Theology of the Icon," pp. 35–45 in *Icons: Windows On Eternity*, eds Helmut Brenske and Stefan Brenske. Hannover: Carl Albrecht Verlag, 2001.

Cross, Richard. "Perichoresis, Deification, and Christological Predication in John of Damascus." *Mediaeval Studies* 62 (2000): 69–124.

Louth, Andrew. *St John Damascene. Tradition and Originality in Byzantine Theology*. Oxford: Oxford University Press, 2002.

Martin, Edward. *A History of the Iconoclastic Controversy*. London: SPCK, 1978.

2.4

Why did God become man? (Cur Deus homo) (1096–1098 CE)

Anselm of Canterbury (c. 1033–1109 CE)

The author's life and work

Anselm was born around 1033 at Aosta, in what is now northwestern Italy. As a young man, he went to live with his mother's family in Burgundy and from there he was attracted to the monastery of Bec in Normandy. He became a monk, and around 1070 he was elected prior of the monastery following Lanfranc's promotion to the archbishopric of Canterbury in the newly-conquered Norman kingdom of England. Anselm remained at Bec where he became abbot in 1078. When Lanfranc died in 1089, the Canterbury chapter wanted Anselm to succeed him, but King William II held things up for four years. It was while he was in England to visit Chester that Anselm was finally asked to become archbishop, a post which he accepted against his better judgment.

From then on he was in almost constant quarrels with the king, who was notably non-religious. In 1097 he was exiled and went to Italy, but when William II died in 1100 he returned to Canterbury. Unfortunately, he soon fell out with the new king, Henry I, and was sent into exile again in 1103. He finally returned in 1107 and died at Canterbury on April 21, 1109. Anselm got into trouble because he was a firm defender of the rights of the church, but in the end he was forced to compromise with the kings, who were too powerful to be ignored. Though not English himself,

Figure 2.4 Anselm

and unfamiliar with the language, he attracted devoted followers in England, one of whom, the monk Eadmer, wrote a detailed biography of his hero that remains a standard source for our knowledge of Anselm's life and career.

As a writer, Anselm is known for the originality and brilliance of his thought. While still at Bec, he wrote two important philosophical works, the *Monologion* and the *Proslogion*, in the second of which he outlined and defended the so-called "ontological" proof for the existence of God. According to Anselm, God is a being higher than any other that can be thought to exist. This view has often been refuted in different ways, but it keeps resurfacing and is still widely admired today.[1] It was during his first exile that he finished his famous work on the atonement of the Son of God, known to us as *Cur Deus Homo* which may be translated either as a question (*Why did God become man?*) or as a statement (*Why God became man*). It was also during his stay in the south of Italy that he engaged in debate with the Eastern church over the double procession of the Holy Spirit, and he wrote a definitive tract on the subject which shows a clear grasp of biblical exegesis.

Why God became man

The treatise opens with a letter to Pope Urban II (1088–1099) and a preface that helps us date its composition. Anselm tells us that he began writing in England before he was expelled (in 1097) and the work must have been completed before the pope's death, when Anselm was still in exile. *Cur Deus Homo* consists of two books of roughly equal length, each of them subdivided into a number of short chapters. In his preface, Anselm tells us that the first book aims to answer the objections of unbelievers who regard the Christian faith as irrational. The second book presupposes that the world knows nothing about Christ and argues that human beings were destined for an immortality that only a God-man could bring about. Anselm specifically stated that he wanted the preface and the chapter headings of the entire work to be included at the beginning, so that readers could decide what parts of it they wanted to read.

Faith must seek understanding

Anselm was reluctant to go beyond the teaching of the Bible and the church fathers, but he recognized that many people found them difficult to understand. His starting point was faith in Christ, something which he presumed he had in common with his readers. Theological disputation he regarded as a means of elucidating truth, which is why he insisted that faith must come first. In his mind, the truth could only be discerned by those who sought it in the right spirit. The life, death, and resurrection of Jesus were universally agreed matters of faith among Christians, and it was by contemplating them that a deeper appreciation of the mind of God could be attained.

But although this was true in principle, Anselm was reluctant to pursue it too far in practice. There would always be things about God that were mysterious and beyond human understanding, even if it was possible to expound the logic of what has been revealed to us in Scripture. Anselm insisted that everything he said should be supported by evidence from the Bible and the church fathers, who remained his fundamental authorities.

The Son of God had to become a man

The first and most fundamental problem that confronted Anselm was the objection, often made by unbelievers, that the Incarnation of the Son of God is unworthy of him because it tries to contain the infinite within the limits of the finite. Is such a thing possible without reducing God to something less than he truly is? For Anselm, the debate was as much about God's honor as about his nature, but in his mind the two went together. God was worthy of honor because of his infinite being and power. Any restriction placed on these was bound to diminish him, or so it was thought, and if this were the case, the Incarnation of the Son, if it were possible at all, could only weaken God and not strengthen him.

Anselm answered this argument by saying that the Incarnation magnifies God because it shows us what he is able to do. The fact that he decided to save us in this way is not a sign of his inherent weakness but of his greatness. God can transcend the contradictions of the human mind in order to transform us into his image and likeness in a way that we cannot do for ourselves.

The second problem that Anselm had to deal with was the objection that the Incarnation must be a myth because it is not logically necessary. The God who made the world could surely redeem it without entering it himself. He could easily have sent an angel or created a sinless man and charged him with the task of saving the human race. Why then did Christians insist that he did not do so?

Anselm's answer to this objection was that God could not let his highest creature perish without fulfilling his plan. After the fall, that plan could not be put into effect without direct divine intervention, which is why the Son became incarnate. To the suggestion that it would have been better for an angel or another man to have done that, Anselm replied that the human race would then be enslaved to that angel or man as its redeemer, and not be in communion with God.

Equally difficult in Anselm's mind was the question of how the Son could have been a "ransom" for our sins. Why was God forced to pay a ransom to Satan in order to deliver the human race from the bondage of sin? The devil is not more powerful than God and has no right to claim such a reward, so why should God defer to him in this way? Surely God could have set us free by disposing of the devil, which would have made the Incarnation, and all that it entailed in terms of suffering and death, an irrelevance. Even if man deserves to be punished for his rebellion, it is not Satan's place to punish him, but God's. Satan has no right to ensnare man in sin, and has only done so because God has permitted it as our punishment for disobeying him. He is not entitled to his ransom, so why did God give him one? Anselm did not really have an answer to this, but took refuge in an appeal to God's will, which passes human understanding. The very existence of evil is a mystery, so we can hardly expect that the ways in which God dealt with it will be any clearer in our minds.

Agreeing with his critics that God cannot be diminished in any way, Anselm concluded that the Son could not suffer and die for our sins in his divine nature. He became a man because he had to acquire a nature that was able to suffer and die. Far from detracting from the honor and glory of God, this act did the opposite—it exalted human nature and raised it to the level of the divine.

Of course that observation did not answer the further question—was it right for a sinless man to take the burden of human sinfulness on himself and die for it? To put it a different way, was God obliged to condemn an innocent man in order to save the guilty? To this objection, Anselm replied that God did not force his Son to die for sinful human beings. The Son took this task upon himself, of his own free will. It was not Christ's obedience to his Father's will that forced him to give up his life, but the rejection he suffered from those who could not tolerate the presence of a man who was fully obedient to God's will.

It was because of this all-pervasive spirit of obedience that it can be argued that the Father sent his Son to die, because he told him to do things that led inexorably to his death. The Bible explains this by saying that he learnt obedience by his sufferings (Heb. 5:8). Jesus told his disciples that he had come to do the will of his Father, which Anselm interpreted to mean that his desire to do the right thing did not spring from his humanity but from his divinity. When the Bible tells us that God did not spare his Son but handed him over to death, Anselm understood it to be saying that God did not release him from his obedience (Rom. 8:32). For this reason, it was impossible for the Son to escape from suffering and death once he had surrendered his will to that of the Father.

Anselm went on to claim that the Father wanted a man capable of achieving the restoration of the human race to die in order to bring that about. The death of a sinless man was necessary because of the seriousness of sin, which has cut the human race off from God. Only someone who was

Figure 2.5 From *Meditations of St. Anselm*

not personally implicated in human sin and guilt could achieve the necessary reconciliation. This point does not entirely exclude the possibility that someone else could have suffered and died on the cross, but there are difficulties that make it unlikely. First of all, there is no other sinless person, and the Father would have had to create one specially for the task, which would not have been easy to do, given that the man in question would have to be a real human being, and therefore somehow connected to sinful humanity. As it happened, the Son volunteered to do the Father's will, making any alternative arrangement unnecessary.

The Son was not forced to do his Father's will, argued Anselm, and thus he could have avoided death if that was his desire. However, if the Son had chosen that option, the human race would not have been saved. Jesus went to his death of his own free will, as he told his disciples (see John 10:17).

In the final analysis, Anselm argued that the Father acquiesced in the Son's desire to suffer and die, because he understood that what the Son wanted to do was praiseworthy in itself. Without his voluntary sacrifice, we would not have been saved, and how could the Father have failed to desire that salvation? His forgiveness of our sins is absolutely necessary if we are to enjoy eternal life, but that forgiveness will only be granted if and when sin is paid for, which is what the Son took upon himself to achieve.

The meaning of forgiveness

Once he explained the logic of the Incarnation, Anselm shifted his discussion to a consideration of the principles underlying God's forgiveness. His first assertion is that the essence of sin is the refusal to give God what is owed to him. To disobey God is to deny him what he is entitled to. Disobedience is possible for angels as well as for human beings, and, as long as no compensation is offered for it, those who are guilty remain in a state of debt. Furthermore, it is not enough simply to give back what is owed. The guilty parties must return the debt with interest, because not only have they taken what does not belong to them but they have insulted the honor of God. This aspect of the matter is unfamiliar to modern minds but reflects something that was of great importance in the medieval world. Worth was not measured so much in financial terms or in quantities, but rather in terms of honor. A nobleman might be quite poor but his status entitled him to a certain respect, and if that were not accorded to him there could be serious trouble. God was in a category of his own, of course, but the basic principle still applied and the only question was what level of compensation would be adequate to remove the offense caused to him.

Having established that point, Anselm went on to ask whether God can forgive a sin out of mercy alone, without demanding any compensation for it. To us, this may seem like the essence of his forgiveness, but to Anselm such a solution was unthinkable. To his mind, if there was no compensation for sin, the only way to put matters right was to punish it. If God were to forgive it without compensation or punishment, the sin would not have been put right, and God cannot tolerate such disorder in his kingdom. Forgiveness without some kind of recompense would also imply that there is no real difference between sinners and non-sinners, since the sinners would all be forgiven automatically, and it would look as if nothing had ever gone wrong. The righteous are those who keep the law of God, and so forgiveness without compensation would mean that sinners were freer than the sinless are, because they would take no responsibility for their actions and suffer no consequences. Only God is in that position, because only he is above wrongdoing by nature. It makes no sense to say that sinners are more like God than others are, and so Anselm is forced to conclude that some form of payment for sin is necessary.

The creature cannot take something away from the Creator and not pay him for it. God cannot tolerate such an insult to his honor, because if he did, the universe would fall into chaos. The punishment of a sinner upholds God's honor because it shows that sinners belong to him whether they want to or not. Mankind cannot be saved without compensation for sin, and Anselm argues that the compensation ought to be proportionate to the offense. The insult inflicted on God's honor by human sin is too great for any human action to be able to repay. What man stole from God cannot be repaid, creating an impossible dilemma. Man cannot be happy until the debt is cleared, but he cannot be excused simply because he is unable to pay it back. Logically, he is eternally condemned, which is why the Son of God had to come into the world to save him. Only in that way could the conundrum be resolved and mankind set free from the consequences of our disobedience to the will of God.

The cost of reconciliation with God

Anselm begins his discussion of the reconciliation of God and man by asserting that human beings were originally made righteous in order that they should be happy. This assumption was common to ancient philosophical thinking and is not particularly surprising, but Anselm draws the conclusion that if we had not sinned we would have been immortal, an idea that does not necessarily follow from the original premise.

To Anselm's mind, salvation in Christ is a restoration of the happiness we lost by the fall, and he therefore concluded that if it were to be genuine, we would have to come back with the same body that we originally had. To him, that was the logic of resurrection, and it will be in that renewed body that God will bring his work of creation to perfection. This cannot happen, however, unless and until compensation is paid for the offense caused to God by our sin.

Anselm did not doubt that this restoration would occur, but he insisted that God could not be compelled to bring it about. Our salvation can only be an act of his free grace, and the fact that he extends it to us despite our unworthiness makes it an act that is worthy of him. The difficulty is that only somebody who can make sufficient payment for our sins is able to offer the required compensation, and in the nature of the case no creature can do that. Once that line of reasoning is accepted, it follows that God himself must pay the price for the sins of his rational creatures and the only way he can do that is by becoming a man. Therein lies the logic and significance of the Incarnation.

Once he established this position, Anselm went on to demonstrate the inexorable logic of the Christology defined at the council of Chalcedon in AD 451 and accepted ever since as orthodox in the Western Church. Chalcedon had stated that the incarnate Christ is one person in two natures, one divine and the other human. Anselm defended this Christology by arguing that the God-man must be complete in both natures, since otherwise he would not be identical to either of them. He cannot be part God and part man, because if he were, he would be a third kind of being. The incarnate God must also be a single person with two natures, because if he were not, the recompense would not be made. It makes no sense to say that God can somehow pay himself back in simply his divine nature—the eternal Son of God owes nothing, and his divine nature is free from any taint because it is sinless both in fact and in principle. Therefore, the divine Son only becomes able to make recompense by becoming a man (i.e., taking on a full human nature) and then, as a human (particular but uniquely able to represent the universal) he is able to pay the debt owed to God in the human nature that he has assumed.

Could the Father have created a human nature for his Son in heaven and sent him into the world in order to suffer and die for us? Anselm rejected that possibility because he believed that if God wants to save the existing human race, as he evidently does, he has to take the Son's human nature from that race and not create a new one afresh. This sounds obvious to us today, but it evidently did not appear like that to Anselm, who thought that he had to argue the case, not least because of the Christian belief in the virginal conception of Jesus.

It was for this reason that Anselm treated his readers to a lengthy discourse on the four possible ways in which God could create a man. The first and most familiar of these is the usual method of the natural intercourse between a man and a woman. But if he had done that in the case of Jesus, Jesus would not have been the incarnate Son of God. As an alternative to that, God can create a man from nothing, as he did with Adam, but if he had done so in this case, Jesus would have been the first creature of a distinct, non-Adamic human race. Thirdly, God can create a human being from a man alone, which is how Eve came into being, but the logic behind her creation does not lend itself to the creation of another male. Finally, he can create a man from a woman alone, something which he had not done until the coming of Christ, but which occurred uniquely in his case. As far as Anselm was concerned, this last option was preferable, partly because of its uniqueness, which befits the equally unique Incarnation, and partly because it includes women in the hope of salvation. To understand why this mattered to him, we must appreciate that the medieval world generally believed that sin had entered the human race by the disobedience of the first woman, and that this belief led many to devalue the feminine. In opting for a virginal conception, therefore, God was honoring women and reassuring them that they too would be saved in Christ.

More controversially, Anselm claimed that the incarnate Son of God did not have to die because of his human nature, but that he chose to do so. Anselm believed that Jesus could have lived for ever as a man, but he did not come into the world for that reason. The fact that he shared our finite existence during his earthly life, with all its inherent limitations, does not mean that he was unhappy in the way that we are, nor does it imply that he suffered from ignorance in the way that other mortals do. God the Son took on mortality for a purpose and he always knew exactly what he was doing and why. Here the modern reader is confronted with a dilemma. We can accept that God had a purpose in sending his Son into the world, but not that Jesus could have lived for ever if he had chosen to do so. Humanity has always been mortal by nature and sooner or later Jesus would have completed the ordinary life cycle. A man who had been fully accepted by his contemporaries as one of them could hardly have lived for millennia without being seen to be different!

When he comes to the question of the adequacy or sufficiency of Christ's sacrifice, Anselm explained that the death of Christ outweighs all conceivable sin because it is the perfect offering of the perfect person. So much is this the case that it even pays the price of the sins of those who put him to death! At this point however, Anselm's rigorous and thoroughly orthodox logic began to desert him. He explained how God made a sinless man out of sinful matter, a miracle which he regarded as greater than that of the original creation, but which was a fanciful conclusion because matter is not in itself sinful. Here Anselm fell under the spell of ancient dualistic thinking, which was still very powerful in the Christian world.

Still thinking along these lines, Anselm went so far as to claim that there has always been at least one human being who was not completely cut off from God, and that Adam and Eve had a part to play in their own reconciliation to him, though he was honest enough to admit that there is nothing to that effect in Scripture. He also speculated that the devil cannot be saved because that would require the death of a God-angel, and angels cannot die.

Anselm may have been right in his musings about the devil, but we cannot accept his belief that some small portion of the human race was left unaffected by the fall. Nevertheless, in spite of these defects, Anselm went a long way towards demonstrating that there is a logic to the Incarnation and the subsequent salvation of the human race which demonstrates the truth of the Old and New Testaments. To sum up his argument, what the Bible tells us is what had to be, and Anselm regards this as proof that our minds and God's revelation match one another and form a coherent whole.

Conclusion

Anselm's greatness, both as a philosopher and as a theologian, has never been disputed, and he is more popular and widely read today than he has ever been. For many centuries his theological genius was acknowledged but he was little read. He has often been overshadowed by his more prolific successors, and particularly by Thomas Aquinas, even though many of his ideas remained fundamental in Western theology and influenced both Catholics and Protestants. His belief that faith and reason should co-operate rather than compete with one another remains attractive, even if many of his solutions have been superseded. His doctrine of the atonement, often known today as the "satisfaction theory," remains the cornerstone of subsequent analysis, although it was augmented and reinterpreted by the Protestant Reformers. Similarly, his defense of the double procession of the Holy Spirit is still valuable today and ought to be more widely known than it is. Modern theologians like Karl Barth have used him as a guide for doing their own theology, and the fecundity of his mind is such that he is likely to go on playing that role for a long time to come.[2] Few men have had a deeper or more productive influence on the church than Anselm, whose writings remain as fresh and attractive as when they were first written.

Notes

1. E.g., see Alvin Plantinga, ed., *The Ontological Argument from St. Anselm to Contemporary Philosophers* (Garden City, NY: Doubleday, 1965).
2. E.g., see Karl Barth, *Anselm: Fides Quaerens Intellectum: Anselm's Proof of the Existence of God in the Context of His Theological Scheme* (London: SCM, 1975).

Select Bibliography

Primary sources

Anselm of Canterbury, *The Major Works*, Oxford: Oxford University Press, 1998, pp. 260–356.

Anselme de Cantorbéry, *Pourquoi Dieu s'est fait homme*, edited and translated into French by R. Roques, Paris: Cerf, 1963.

Secondary sources

Eadmer, *The Life of St Anselm*, edited with notes and translation by R.W. Southern. Oxford: Oxford University Press, 1962.

Evans, G.R. *Anselm*. London: Geoffrey Chapman, 1989.

Evans, G.R. *Anselm and Talking about God*. Oxford: Oxford University Press, 1978.

Hopkins, Jasper. *A Companion to the Study of St Anselm*. Minneapolis: University of Minnesota Press, 1972.

Southern, R.W. *Saint Anselm. A Portrait in a Landscape*. Cambridge: Cambridge University Press, 1990.

2.5

The Song of Songs (1136–1153) Bernard of Clairvaux (c. 1090–1153)

The author's life and work

Bernard was born about 1090 near Dijon, in Burgundy. As a young man, he and several of his family and companions became monks at Cîteaux, a monastery founded in 1098 with the deliberate intention of reforming the monastic life. The addition of so many new members at Cîteaux was concerning, and in 1115 Bernard was sent to start a new foundation at a place he named "clear valley" (Clairvaux). After a rocky start, Clairvaux soon prospered and Bernard was able to launch the new monastic order all over Western Europe; the order was called "Cistercian" after the mother house of Cîteaux. By the time he died, he had directly or indirectly founded 343 monasteries, and Clairvaux itself had over 700 monks.

Although Bernard lived a cloistered life, he was closely connected to the politics of his time. He was particularly supportive of crusading, and in 1128 secured recognition at the synod of Troyes for the crusader order of the Knights Templar. He also became deeply involved in papal affairs to the point where one of his pupils was elected pope as Eugenius III (1145–1153). By that time he was preaching a second crusade to the Holy Land, but, although his appeal was successful, the crusade itself turned out a disaster and he took the blame, somewhat unfairly.

In theological matters he became embroiled in controversy with Peter Abelard and also with Gilbert de la Porrée, because Bernard regarded their Trinitarian views as heretical. He visited Italy several times and played a major part in ending quarrels that had broken out over the papal succession.

Figure 2.6 Saint Bernard of Clairvaux

In these activities it was inevitable that Bernard would gain enemies as well as admirers, but he felt that it was his duty to stand for what was right and forced himself to get involved in the controversies that were threatening the unity of the Church.

With a notable work on the love of God that has become a classic of spiritual writing, Bernard's writings mainly consist of occasional tracts. A number of his sermons survive along with 530 letters. Bernard died at Clairvaux on August 20, 1153, and was buried there, but when the monastery was dissolved in 1792 his remains were transferred to Troyes cathedral where they are buried to this day.

Sermons on the Song of Songs

Bernard's eighty-six sermons on the Song of Songs cover only the first two chapters and the first five verses of chapter three, or about 40 percent of the whole text, but they remain one of the classic and best-loved expositions of this most enigmatic part of the Old Testament. As divided up in the Cistercian Publications edition, the first twenty sermons cover no more than the first three verses of the first chapter. Sermons 21–46, in the second volume, cover the remainder of that chapter (fourteen verses), sermons 47–66 (the third volume) take us down to chapter 2:15, another fifteen verses, and the last volume, containing sermons 67–86, brings us to chapter 3:5, only seven verses! It is thus apparent that Bernard spent longer on some portions of the text than he did on others, and along the way there are many references and detours through other parts of the Bible. The text being expounded is the Song of Songs but the context is Scripture as a whole and the reader must always bear that in mind.

An allegory of divine love

It is impossible to understand Bernard's sermons without realizing that for him, the Song of Songs was an allegory of divine love. This view was universal in the early church and the majority opinion until the nineteenth century, when modern critical scholarship began to take the literal sense more seriously. Today, allegory is often derided and regarded as an unacceptable way to read the Bible, but while that may be true of many parts of Scripture, the Song of Songs is a special case. It is clearly a love poem and not the literal reporting of history; the only question is whether it refers exclusively to what the church fathers called "carnal love" or whether there is a spiritual dimension to it as well.

Because they regarded erotic love as a poor substitute for devotion to Christ, the church fathers and the medieval scholars who succeeded them generally had a low view of such "carnal love." In this they had both Jesus and the Apostle Paul on their side, something which many in the modern church find hard to admit. In the minds of the fathers, the Song of Songs would not have been part of Scripture if it had been no more than a carnal love song, because all Scripture speaks of Christ. It was therefore not only natural but necessary for them to find a Christological meaning in the text. This was supported by the New Testament witness to Christ as the bridegroom and the church as the bride, and it seemed natural to them to apply that imagery to the Song. The bride was interpreted either as the church or as the soul of the individual believer, but the two merged into one another and both interpretations could easily be accepted as valid.

Figure 2.7 Stained glass representing St. Bernard of Clairvaux

The allegorical interpretation had the added advantage of integrating the Song into the rest of the Bible, which Bernard does with great success. A poem about carnal love would have little bearing on most of the rest of Scripture, but once it is seen in the light of Christ, the connections become both numerous and clear. Instead of appearing as an oddity, the Song of Songs became a central text for understanding the love of God for his people and the meaning of the Bible as a whole. This interpretation, though not widely accepted today, may have more to say for it than modern critics have allowed. Without recommending allegory as a general method for biblical interpretation, it may nevertheless be possible to rescue it in this particular case and recognize its value alongside, if not instead of, the literal sense. In any case, Bernard's approach must be understood by his readers before they begin, otherwise they will not appreciate the depth and importance of what he has to say.

The believer's experience of Christ

The Song of Songs which is Solomon's. Let him kiss me with the kisses of his mouth! For your love is better than wine; your anointing oils are fragrant; your name is oil poured out; therefore virgins love you.

(Song 1:1–3 ESV)

The first twenty of Bernard's sermons are an exposition of the above text. Bernard begins by making it clear that he intends to give his monastic brothers solid food instead of the milk which they had hitherto been accustomed to receiving.[1] In his words: "Solomon has bread to give that is splendid and delicious ... Let us bring it forth then, if you please, and break it."[2] They had already tasted the wisdom of Ecclesiastes and learned from him to shun the empty pleasures of this life. They had also feasted on the Proverbs, learning thereby how to live a moral and upright life in the world. Now it is time for them to rise higher and taste the heavenly manna by contemplating what it means to have fellowship with God.

Who is it who said: "Let him kiss me with the kisses of his mouth"? How can we tell who is speaking and about what? The name Solomon means "peace" and the kiss is the sign of peace. This is not just any song, of which there are many in the Old Testament, but the Song of Songs, the greatest and most exalted song of them all: "We must conclude then that it was a special divine impulse that inspired these songs of his that now celebrate the praises of Christ and his Church, the gift of holy love, the sacrament of endless union with God."[3] When we turn to Christ he puts a new song into our hearts and onto our lips, and this is it. There are many psalms that are called songs of ascent because they take us up on high, but this Song is sung by those who have arrived at the heavenly gates.

Bernard then examines the different meanings of the kiss. There is no greater desire than to long for the kiss of Christ, which warms our frigid hearts and sets our soul ablaze with love for him. Even the prophets of old longed for his coming and hoped like the aged Simeon that they would live to see it (Luke 2:25–34). The holy kiss was bestowed on the world for two reasons—to strengthen the faith of those who were waiting and to show them that the mediator between God and man was himself a man, Jesus Christ.

There are other kisses, of the hands and of the feet, as well as of the mouth, but it is the last of these which is the greatest. We begin with the feet and move up to touch his gracious hand, but then we proceed to the most intimate relationship of all. The kiss of the feet is that of conversion, the kiss of the hand is that of guidance in the Christian life, and the kiss of the mouth is that of mystical union with Christ, which is reserved only for a few.

Having examined the different types of kiss, Bernard goes on to consider the four different kinds of spirit, because it is with his Spirit that Christ kisses us. As he develops this theme, he brings in God's power, mercy and judgment as he examines the way God works in our lives in order to bring us to perfection. Bernard talks of intimacy with God and shows how this is expressed both in our prayers and in the psalms, but above all in the work of the Holy Spirit, who is the kiss of the mouth personified. It is his kiss "that enables us not only to know God but to love the Father, who is never fully known until he is perfectly loved."[4]

Christ the bridegroom and his bride

After finishing his exposition of the kiss, Bernard returns to the main theme of the Song and examines the relationship between the bride and the bridegroom. Bernard read the phrase: "Your love is better than wine" as: "Your breasts are better than wine" and he points out that it is not clear who said this. First he assumes that it was the bride, and interprets the phrase as referring to her desire to rest in the arms of her beloved. But then he takes the opposite track and suggests that it may have been the groom who spoke them. As his bride's breasts are filled with the love of God, so he is attracted more deeply to her and thanks to his embrace she will conceive the fruits of righteousness in her womb. Finally, they may be the words of onlookers who remind the bride that the breasts with which she will feed her young are more important than the heady wine of mystical contemplation—spirituality must be practical!

Having settled on that, Bernard develops the theme of the bride's breasts still further, with special attention being paid to the grace of spiritual anointing given by the presence of the Holy Spirit. He goes on to expound this theme at great length, with thanksgiving for Christ's saving work, an exposition of the grace of loving kindness, and another one on our thanksgiving and God's glory. The theme of anointing is then taken further with a sermon on the relationship between the Church and the Jews, for whom God's anointing was a sacred rite before he moves on in the text to a discussion of the name of Jesus.

The love of God is sweet, wise and strong. We are to love God with all our heart, with all our soul, with all our mind and with all our strength. Even carnal love can be used for God's glory when it is purged of sensual desire, focuses on the imitation of Christ, and yearns for spiritual fulfillment in him.

The Christian life

Having warmed to his theme, Bernard enters into the plot of the Song. "Draw me after you; let us run" (Song 1:4)—he interprets these words as the love of the bride, that is the Church, for Christ. She who asks to be drawn wants to be drawn; the pull of the bridegroom is not resisted. She longs to follow her Master and rest in the sweet perfume of his ointments. The attractions of the bridegroom are his four cardinal virtues, which are wisdom, righteousness, holiness, and redemption (1 Cor 1:30). Bernard expounds these, reminding us that the Church is powerless until she is anointed with them.

Christ the king has brought his bride into his chambers, the source of the sweet fragrance, which is the goal of our striving (Song 1:4). There are two distinct rooms in the king's palace, one being the room of spices and the other the room of ointment. In the former, the rough herbs are pounded until they bring out their fragrance—this is spiritual discipline. In the latter, the raw spice is refined and purified so as to become useful in the service of God.

The believer's love for Christ

Sermon 24 was delivered on Bernard's return from Rome in 1138, and is devoted to his reflections on the success of that visit. He picks up his exposition of the Song where he left off and explains why the righteous love the bridegroom. This means that they practice what they preach, because faith without works is dead, and the loss of faith is the loss of love for God. The bride knows that she is "black but beautiful."[5] She had apparently been taunted for this, but rather than strike back, she blesses the daughters of Jerusalem who have mocked her and moves on. She is not referring here to her past life of sin, because if she were, she would have spoken in the past tense. On the contrary, she is describing her current state, lowly and dark in the eyes of the world but beautiful, because she shines with the light of the heavenly king in her heart.

By expounding the meaning of the tents of Kedar—which stand for the sinful places of this world—Bernard continues this theme. The bride must dwell there and share the sorrows of the world, but she is never destitute. Bernard interrupts his flow here with a long lament on the death of the monk Gerard, whose absence has left a gaping hole in his heart. That is what it means to be full of love in the tents of Kedar, where that love can never find its perfect fulfillment. He contrasts the tents of Kedar with the curtains of

Solomon, whom Bernard takes as a type of Christ. The bride tells her critics not to look at her, but to focus on Christ, who has made her far more than she could ever be or become in herself.

The Christian's spiritual warfare

Bernard knows that there is a problem of discord in the Church ("my mother's sons were angry with me" [Song 1:6]) which he attempts to deal with. He discusses the vineyards which the bride has been given to look after and says that these are mystical places that demand very careful self-control. There are different ways of seeing God, who makes himself known to his flock in different ways at different times. Christ adapts his grace to the needs of each one of us because he knows and loves us as we are. The mystical noontide is the height of our experience of him, but it carries its own demands. There are some things we must seek after and other things we must avoid, and Bernard guides us through these.

Sermon 34, based on verse 8, is a discourse on true humility. If the bride does not know where to find her bridegroom, she should follow in the tracks left by the flock because he will be at their head. Bernard explains how the bridegroom reproaches his bride in order to increase her devotion. She is to acquire knowledge of both God and herself because ignorance of God leads to despair and spoils the beauty of the bride.

Bernard describes the devil and his power and contrasts that with the beautiful face of the bride (Song 1:10). He explains how the mind and faith contribute to contemplation and how God the Father corrects us along our spiritual journey. The bundle of myrrh in verse 13 brings Bernard naturally to the sufferings of Christ and he compares his resurrection to the sweet grapes of Engedi in verse 14. In verse 15 the lovers mend their quarrel and return to their first love; Bernard concludes the chapter with a sermon on the beauties of contemplation in the house of God. Spiritual warfare is thus both individual and collective. Every believer experiences it, but victory and peace are attained only in the fellowship of the Church.

The blessings of Christ

Bernard's sermons on chapter 2 begin with a discourse about the flower of the field ("rose of Sharon" in English Bibles) and the lily of the valleys.

Bernard understands the flowers as the blessings of Christ with which he rewards the humble. The lily is found among thorns, just as the soul is found amid the sins of this world. Christ is compared to an apple tree, humble in appearance but the only one to bear fruit for the bride's enjoyment. From the orchard, Bernard moves on to the banqueting house, which he equates with the Church on the day of Pentecost when the disciples seemed to be full of new wine after inordinate feasting (Acts 2:13–15). This leads him to discourse further on the nature of love in both affection and action.

The bride is soon lost in the sleep of contemplation, from which she is not to be unduly roused, because there is no substitute for spending time alone with God. Bernard points out that hearing precedes seeing—the voice of the beloved calls out and then the bride sees him coming in great haste and glory (Song 2:8). The bridegroom is compared to a gazelle because the Word of God "runs swiftly" (Ps. 147:15). He stands behind a wall (verse 9), concealing himself but partially revealing himself to us as well. Bernard concludes from this that we must all watch and wait for the bridegroom to come, and that when he does, he will reward us according to our deserts.

Reminiscent of the words of Jesus to his disciples as he saw his betrayer coming, the bridegroom tells the bride to make haste. God humbles himself before us to the point of sounding like a turtledove in our land and the green figs remind the bride not to loiter on her way to the vineyards, for the harvest season is coming. The clefts of the rock in verse 14 are the protecting arms of Christ and we must rest in him. The foxes of temptation are destroying the vineyard of our life and we must catch them before they root everything up. In our day, says Bernard, these foxes are the heretics who are doubly dangerous for that reason.

The believer's union with Christ

Bernard preached that the bride bears witness to the bridegroom, and, in her, others sense his fragrance. The bridegroom cares only for his bride, and she is totally devoted to him. All the bridegroom's attributes are lilies, and the bride feeds among them. The bride cannot bear to be parted from her beloved, a theme that Bernard applies to both the Church and the synagogue, though in different ways. He also applies it to the individual soul which may seek Christ, yet only to be disappointed. The bridegroom cannot be found on earth because he has ascended into heaven, but the wandering bride is found by faithful watchmen, of whom there are too few. Angels and men work together when they go in search of the bride, but the bride's only concern when they find her is to see her beloved once more.

At the heart of our union with Christ is the relationship between the Word of God and the soul of the believer. For the soul, being is living, but for the Word, being is living in blessedness. Bernard explains how the soul can always return to the Word to be reformed and restored. The greatest good is to seek God and be sought by him, which the soul needs but the Word does not. Bernard lists seven reasons why the soul seeks the Word. He praises the modesty of the bride and counsels us as to the times and places that are best suited to prayer. At this point Bernard breaks off, and the unfinished sermon series comes to an end, but we have heard enough to know that it is only in perfect union with Christ, pictured in the ideal relationship between the bridegroom and the bride, that the Christian life finds its meaning and achieves its purpose.

Conclusion

All Bernard's writings are characterized by a simplicity and reverence that appealed to his first readers and that still make him attractive today. He was one of the most popular medieval writers in the sixteenth century and was frequently quoted by Martin Luther and John Calvin among others. His emphasis on the importance of personal devotion was very influential in later medieval spirituality, and this was the foundation of his popularity with the Reformers. They were aware of the severe criticisms of the allegorical method of biblical interpretation that had been made by Erasmus and other humanist scholars of the Renaissance and they admitted that Bernard often went to excess. Yet so valuable was his treatment of the Christian life that it outweighed his defects as an exegete. Time and again they quoted Bernard or referred to him as someone who had the right spirit and was in tune with the true meaning of the Bible, even if they were forced to dispute his reading of particular verses.

In later times, opposition to allegory increased in the Protestant world, and today few people would take his exegesis of the Song of Songs seriously. But as a guide to the Christian life and to what it means to be united with Christ, Bernard continues to attract readers and his sermons have never gone out of print. They remain an outstanding example of the power of monastic spirituality and can still be read with profit by those who want a closer walk with God in their own lives.

Notes

1. See 1 Cor. 3:1–2; Heb. 5:12–14.
2. Sermon 1, Vol. 1, p. 1 of the Cistercian edition, from which all quotes are taken.
3. Sermon 1, Vol. 1, p. 5.
4. Sermon 8, Vol. 1, p. 52.
5. Song 1:5.

Select Bibliography

Primary sources

Bernard of Clairvaux. *Opera I-II*. Edited by J. Leclercq, C.H. Talbot and H. Roques. Rome: Editiones Cistercienses, 1957.

Bernard of Clairvaux. *On the Song of Songs*. 4 vols. Translated by K. Walsh and I.M. Edmonds. Kalamazoo, MI: Cistercian Publications, 1971–80.

Secondary sources

Evans, G.R. *Bernard of Clairvaux*. Oxford: Oxford University Press, 2000.

Gilson, E. *The Mystical Theology of St Bernard*. London: Sheed and Ward, 1940.

Lane, A.N.S. *Calvin and Bernard of Clairvaux*. Princeton, NJ: Princeton Theological Seminary, 1996.

Maguire, B.P. *The Difficult Saint*. Kalamazoo, MI: Cistercian Publications, 1991.

Posset, F. *Pater Bernhardus. Martin Luther and Bernard of Clairvaux*. Kalamazoo, MI: Cistercian Publications, 1999.

Ward, B., ed. *The Influence of St Bernard*. Oxford: SLG Press, 1976.

2.6

Sentences[1] (c. 1150)
Peter Lombard (c. 1100–1160)

The author's life and work

Peter Lombard was born near Novara in Lombardy sometime shortly before 1100. He does not appear in the historical record until he was already a grown man with an established reputation, and nothing is known of his early life or education. We first hear of him in 1136, the year he went to Paris after a brief stay in Reims. By 1144 he was already a famous teacher there, probably in the cathedral school of Notre Dame. After that, he was frequently consulted on theological matters, and took part, along with Bernard of Clairvaux, in the condemnation of Gilbert de la Porrée for his unorthodox Trinitarian teachings at the council of Reims in 1148.

In 1154 Peter went to Rome, where he had occasion to see the newly translated *Orthodox Faith* of John of Damascus, parts of which he later incorporated in his *Sentences*. He became bishop of Paris in 1159, but died a year later on July 20, 1160. He was buried in the church of St Marcel, but his tomb was desecrated in 1793, during the French revolution, and the church was later demolished.

Peter was the author of a number of works in addition to his monumental *Sentences*. He wrote a gloss on the Psalter, probably during his stay at Reims. His next gloss was on the Pauline Epistles, which draws on a large range of patristic sources and moves away from strict commentary to a kind of nascent systematic theology. It contains a number of theological treatises on different themes that were later incorporated into the *Sentences*. In addition, at least thirty-five of his sermons have survived, covering a variety of Old and New Testament texts.

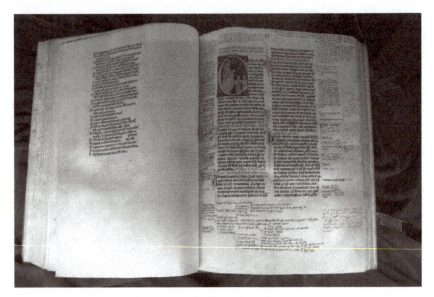

Figure 2.8 From *The Sentences* by Peter Lombard

All of these works, however, pale in comparison to the *Sentences*, a vast compilation of theological source material that became the standard textbook of theology for the rest of the Middle Ages. After the rise of the universities, no candidate for a doctorate in theology could take his degree without writing a commentary on them, and even Martin Luther did so. They were not replaced until after the Reformation, but then they sank into an oblivion from which they have never recovered. Twentieth-century scholarship revived some interest in his work, but the first full English translation did not appear until 2007–2010, and it is too early to tell whether this apparent renewal of interest will have any noticeable long-term effect.

The Sentences

There are four books, logically divided according to theme. The first deals with God the Trinity, the second with creation, the third with Christology and the fourth with what the Lombard[2] calls the "signs" of God's grace. The first three books correspond to the divisions made in John of Damascus's *Orthodox Faith*, whereas the last (and longest) is more diverse, reflecting theological developments in the Western Church that had not troubled the

East in John's time. Each book consists of a number of sections known as "distinctions" which are in turn subdivided into chapters. (There are a total of 182 distinctions and 933 chapters in the entire work.) The *Sentences* is not a book in the usual sense, but more like a theological encyclopedia that groups sources together under different headings and organizes them in a systematic way. It was the first compilation of its kind to circulate in Western Europe, though its format closely resembles that of Gratian's *Concordantia Discordantium Canonum* or *Decretum*, which was put together in about 1140 and performed much the same function for canon lawyers as the *Sentences* did for theologians.[3]

Peter Lombard never intended to be original and has often been criticized for this. In the sense that his work is largely a series of extracts from earlier writers, that is true, but Peter's historical importance lies in the nature of the selections he made and the way he arranged them—which was indeed original. For more than 350 years after his death, every theological student in Western Europe studied his extracts, but very few read the works from which they were taken. Thus, the impression of Augustine and the other church fathers that circulated among medieval theologians as late as the time of the Reformation was largely derived from the Lombard, and even Calvin, in his *Institutes*, takes knowledge of the *Sentences* for granted. In that sense, and for that reason, Peter Lombard must be considered one of the most influential theologians of all time.

The inner life of the Trinity

Focusing on God the Trinity, Peter gives a general introduction that he borrowed from Augustine's treatise *On Christian Doctrine* (*De Doctrina Christiana*). He explains the difference between things and signs (i.e., words that mean something different from what they say on the surface) and says that the study of Holy Scripture is about one or other of these. This forms the basis for his examination of the Trinity, which he finds not only in both the Old and New Testaments but also in the existence of so-called "vestiges" of it in the created order. Among other things, Peter mentions the Augustinian doctrine of the image and likeness of God in the human soul, which he saw as Trinitarian. He touches briefly on the person of the Father, who owes his existence to no other principle, before going on to consider the generation of the Son. For the most part, Peter repeats the teaching of the ancient creeds, though he also considers some underlying theological issues, such as whether the Father begat the Son voluntarily or of necessity. This question seems strange to us, but it is really about the identity of the first person of the Godhead and had been a major point of dispute in the fourth century. If the Father had always been Father, then the generation of the Son would have been necessary. If it was not necessary, then the Father must have chosen to give birth to a Son. At stake is the nature of divine freedom, which inevitably impinges on the nature of human freedom as well.

Peter also asks whether the power to generate the Son is something that belongs to the Father alone and therefore makes him greater than the Son. He cannot accept such a conclusion because it would make the Son less than fully God, but asking it forces him to consider what the true nature of theological language is. Once again, he is dealing with a question that had lain at the heart of the ancient debates from which the church's creeds emerged. While the original circumstances in which the early creeds were written had long passed, Peter had to show his contemporaries that these ancient ecclesial confessions still mattered. Underlying the ancient debates were philosophical issues about the being of God that were of perennial importance. Peter chose his material and expounded it in a way that brought this dimension out, and in the process he demonstrated why systematic theology was a necessary foundation for understanding the Christian Gospel.

The oneness of God

Only after discussing the Trinity does Peter go on to consider the unity of the divine essence and its attributes. This is significant because it is the opposite of what was to come later and reflects a more traditional (and less philosophical) approach to theology than we normally associate with the Middle Ages. In this respect, Peter denies that God is a substance, insisting that such language is used of him only because we are incapable of finding anything better. He also insists that God's being is uniform and simple, so that no part of him is greater or less than any other part. Peter then goes on to discuss the individuality of the persons in God, maintaining that they are co-eternal with his being and beyond human description. He concludes with a refutation of the main heresies that had forced the Church to define its doctrine in this area.

The importance of the Holy Spirit

Somewhat surprisingly, Peter devotes a large amount of space to examining the person and work of the Holy Spirit. This subject had never before been covered in such detail, though he found most of what he needed in different sources. He begins by defining who the Holy Spirit is and concludes with Augustine that he is properly called the love of the Father and the Son. In light of this, he considers the so-called "double procession" of the Holy Spirit, in other words—does the Holy Spirit proceed from the Son as well as from the Father? Peter notes the difference of opinion between the Western and Eastern churches, but believes that it is a matter of words rather than of substance, on which both branches of the Church are agreed. Given that the matter was rapidly becoming a major bone of contention between East and West, this conclusion is a remarkable one. It has always been influential in Western theological thinking, but not in the East, which takes the question more seriously and still regards it as the main doctrinal difference separating the two churches.[4] Peter concludes with an explanation of the difference between generation and procession. What this difference represents in God is beyond our understanding, but it is important to maintain it so that we do not confuse the Son with the Holy Spirit or *vice versa*.

Peter then turns to the work of the Holy Spirit on earth, concentrating on his gifts and also on the fact that he was sent. The sending is common to the Son and the Spirit, both of whom came into the world from the Father, though that does not make either of them inferior to him. The Holy Spirit is the love by which we learn to love our neighbors, and spiritual gifts are given in and through him, because in the final analysis, he himself is the gift of God to us.

Personhood in God

Peter returns to the Trinity in distinction 19, where he expounds the eternal equality of the three persons in God and their mutual relations. He then goes on to explain how we can consider each person separately without losing sight of the overall unity of the Godhead, before continuing with an extended discussion of the names of God and the meaning of the word "person". This leads to a detailed analysis of the attributes of the persons and how they must be distinguished from the unity of the divine substance. Peter's insistence on this was influential not only in making the Trinity a central topic of discussion in the twelfth-century church but in determining the lines along which that discussion would proceed.

The attributes of God

From distinction 29 onwards, Peter considers more purely philosophical matters, starting with the relationship between time and eternity. The principal attributes of God come into focus as he examines how they apply to each of the persons individually and in relation to each other. He also examines whether the attributes are synonymous with the divine nature or whether they can be distinguished from it. He concludes that they cannot be separated because to do so would be to diminish the fullness of the divine being. God cannot be partially good or holy, so that even if these qualities can be named, they cannot be isolated from the nature of his being.

Peter then asks whether God's foreknowledge is the cause of things that happen and whether it is limited or fallible in any way. He examines whether a predestined person can lose salvation or a reprobate gain it, and concludes that this is not possible because God's decree is eternal. God cannot change his mind, learn new things, or forget what he already knows for precisely the same reason. Peter's interest in these questions derives from Augustine, but it was common in his time and provided an important incentive for further discussion of the issues involved. From his time until the Protestant Reformation and later, predestination was seldom off the theological agenda, and the near-universal familiarity with the Lombard must be credited with helping to maintain such a high level of interest over so long a period.

According to Peter, God expresses his will in commands of various kinds, but these must not be mistaken for his eternal purpose. Individual commands are given in time for particular reasons, but God's will is eternal and can never be broken or denied. Even things that are evil find their place in his purposes, though he cannot be held responsible for their existence. When we say that things are done "against God's will" what we mean is that they are done against his commands, not against his eternal purpose. Protestant theology would recycle this distinction as the difference between the "secret" and the "revealed" will of God, and it is not hard to see how in essence it goes back to the teaching of the Lombard.

The identity of angels

Peter deals at great length with angels, a reminder to us of how important they are in the overall scheme of creation. Peter claims that they were created at the same time as the material order, though at the beginning the matter of each was formless. He then discusses what qualities the angels had when they were made, and whether they were all equal to one another. (They were not.) He insists that they were all created good and that they possessed wisdom and the love of God. Though angels did not originally enjoy the blessedness of heaven, after some of them fell the others were confirmed in their loyalty by God's grace and given the blessedness they now possess. The angels, therefore, enjoy heaven by grace and not because of their spiritual nature.

Peter then goes on to expound the fall of the angels, saying that both greater and lesser angels rebelled against God, including one of the highest of them all (Lucifer). He discusses what happened to them after their fall, where they are now, and what power Lucifer has been permitted to wield in their fallen state. Much of this is purely speculative, but it is important nevertheless, because as Peter realized, evil cannot be reduced to human disobedience of God. It has a spiritual power behind it that can only be dealt with in a spiritual way, a point which undergirds the need for a divine incarnation as the only means by which it can be defeated.

The creation of the material world

After dealing with the angels, Peter turns to the material creation. He rejects the view that everything was made at once, and explains how material objects were created at particular intervals of time. This is an important means of establishing a hierarchy of importance in the created order, which is essential if we are to understand the place of human beings in the plan of God.

In dealing with the six days of creation, Peter explains the different usages of the word "day" in Scripture, but opts for a twenty-four hour period because of the repetition of evening and morning. He accepts the usual medieval cosmology, which reminds us that his approach was essentially pre-scientific in spite of the acuteness of some of his observations, and offers his own suggestions as to why animals and plants were made the way they were.

Human beings as the crown of creation

Peter deals next with the creation of human beings. Starting with Adam, he concentrates on the meaning of the image and likeness of God in him. That takes him on to the soul and the nature of the paradise in which Adam was placed. He devotes a full distinction to the creation of woman, saying among other things that Eve's soul was given to her directly by God and not derived from Adam's, because one soul cannot give birth to another. Peter did not intend it, but his statement amounted to an affirmation that women were equal to men as creatures of God, something that could not be taken for granted in his day.

In examining the state of mankind before the fall, Peter says that Adam's body was both mortal and immortal—mortal by nature but immortal by grace, and that after he sinned it was simply dead. On the question of whether Adam could have lived forever in paradise without eating from the tree of life, Peter remains agnostic, citing different opinions held by the church fathers and refraining from taking a position himself. He does, however, say that the procreation of children was planned in paradise but not carried out before the fall.

Sin and the fall

Peter devotes the second half of his second book to the question of sin—how it originated, what it is, and whether it can be avoided or resisted. Peter naturally begins with the devil's motivation to tempt Adam, which he thinks was jealousy, and then discusses the Genesis story of the fall in great detail. Temptation came to both the man and the woman, and both are equally responsible for the result. The notion that Eve was responsible for Adam's fall was implicitly rejected, with potentially great consequences for the status of women in both the church and society.

According to Peter, human beings have free choice in a limited sense, but cannot escape sin which corrupts their will at every turn. True freedom is a gift of God's grace and not a by-product of our human nature. Grace comes to us in two ways, first as an unmerited gift of God and then as part of our growth in him, in which we learn to desire and ask for it. By grace we come to appreciate what is good, and that is necessary before faith can take effect. Even those who never think about goodness have some understanding of the concept, and they recognize it when they meet it. Grace sets the will free to do good, and faith deserves justification. Grace is not merit, but produces it. When spiritual virtue is at work in our lives our wills are set free to choose what is right. Here the Lombard's teaching is clearly at variance with that of the Reformers, whose insistence on justification by faith alone and the total depravity of the human will were a conscious rejection of it.

Adam and Eve passed on their sin to their descendants, and we call it "original sin." Peter explains that this is not an act but an inclination which is present in all of us. Peter believed that original sin is passed on not through the soul but through the flesh and is remitted in baptism. Though the inclination to sin is inherited, actual sins are the work of particular individuals. Peter discusses the difference between intention and act, pointing out that the gravest sins are in the will and not in the acts that follow from it. If much of this sounds familiar to us now, it is because Peter established the theological framework within which these questions would be debated for centuries to come. The Protestant Reformers came up with different answers in some cases, but they worked within a mental universe that the Lombard had constructed.

The incarnation of Christ

Peter's exposition of the doctrines of God, creation, and the fall of mankind were all conceived as preparatory to his Christology. Peter explains why it was the Son who took on human nature and not the Father or the Holy Spirit. He also explains how Christ's human flesh was preserved from sin, appealing to Augustine for confirmation that the Virgin Mary was sinless when she conceived her son. Peter does not say how that happened, but his quotations suggest that Mary was purified at the annunciation and not at her own human birth. This was an important step in the direction of later Catholic Mariology, but it is noticeable how far short it falls of modern Roman Catholic teaching, which claims that Mary was sinless from her conception.[5]

Peter's presentation of the Incarnation is thoroughly traditional, following the creeds of the ancient church without question. The main interest of his Christology lies in his willingness to speculate on matters that were seldom if ever mentioned before. For example, Peter discusses whether the Son could have become incarnate as a woman and offers reasons why that was impossible. He also examines the relationship of Christ's humanity to his divinity at the different stages of his earthly life, and explains how Jesus could grow in the former while remaining unchanged in the latter.

Defining the sacraments

Peter is noted for having given the most comprehensive explanation of the sacraments to be found in any theologian before the Reformation. He did not invent the term "sacrament" but he was responsible for numbering them as seven, a classification that has passed into modern Roman Catholic theology but has been rejected by Protestants.

He deals first with baptism, including the interesting question of what happens to those who receive it unworthily. He then gives a brief exposition of confirmation, before proceeding to holy communion. Peter gives a detailed explanation of transubstantiation and insists on the real presence of Christ in the sacrament. Perhaps somewhat surprisingly, Peter devotes nine distinctions to the question of penance, which he equates with repentance. He pays special attention to the power of the priest to pronounce absolution. Here again we can perceive a yawning chasm between his theology and that of the Reformers, whose concentration on the sacraments and their significance owes a great deal to his exposition of them. Had Peter not codified the "sacraments" it is probable that the Reformation would have looked quite different, and it is possible that the controversies that were to erupt over baptism and holy communion would either not have occurred, or else would have been resolved differently.

After dealing briefly with extreme unction and holy orders, Peter goes into a long discussion of matrimony, considering all the restrictions and limitations placed on it by nature and custom. Here again, the differences between pre- and post-Reformation practices are especially obvious.

The resurrection of the dead

Peter concludes his systematic theology with the resurrection of the dead and says that we shall return with uncorrupted and incorruptible bodies. After death, he says that souls go to a place of "reception" but says nothing about purgatory. However, he believes that prayers for the dead are beneficial and recommends them as a comfort to those awaiting the final resurrection. He gives a full description of the last judgment, saying that the saints will assist Christ in it, and then describes both heaven and hell. He speculates as to whether there will be any communication between the blessed and the wicked and ends by quoting Jerome to the effect that the blessed will not be disturbed by the sight of the wicked being punished, but will give thanks to God that they have been spared a similar fate.

Conclusion

Peter's achievement was recognized at the Fourth Lateran Council in 1215, and from then on nobody could teach theology in a university or higher school of learning unless he had written and defended a dissertation on some aspect of the *Sentences*. Even Martin Luther did this, and the Lombard's work was the common reference point for all sides in the debates of the Reformation. The Protestants rejected many of his conclusions but they were forced to adopt many of his methods. This was especially true of John Calvin, whose four-volume *Institutes of the Christian Religion* was designed to replace the *Sentences* in Protestant circles. Time and again, the reader of the *Institutes* is brought face-to-face with the "master of the *Sentences*" as Calvin called him, and they cannot be understood without a knowledge of the Lombard's teaching.

Once Protestant theology found its feet, however, the *Sentences* faded into oblivion and it would not be until the twenty-first century that translations into English and French would begin to appear. As a result Peter Lombard is now the greatest unknown influence on the Reformation and it may be supposed that greater familiarity with his writings will significantly affect the way we read the Reformers in the future.

Notes

1. Translated from *Libri Quattuor Sententiarum*.
2. Peter Lombard was born in the north of Italy in an area that once belonged to the Lombards. That was the reason he received the surname "the Lombard."
3. For more on Gratian and his influence in twelfth century canon law, see Anders Winroth, *The Making of Gratian's* Decretum (Cambridge: Cambridge University Press, 2000) and Stephen Kuttner, *Gratian and the Schools of Law, 1140–1234* (London: Variorum Reprints, 1983).
4. Cf. A. Edward Siecienski, *The Filioque: History of a Doctrinal Controversy* (Oxford: Oxford University Press, 2010).
5. The historical debate is summarized in René Laurentin, *Queen of Heaven: A Short Treatise on Marian Theology*, trans. Gordon Smith (Dublin: Clonmore & Reynolds, 1956), 11–73.

Select Bibliography

Primary sources

Magistri Petri Lombardi. *Sententiae in Quattuor Libris Distinctae.* 2 vols. Grottaferrata: Editiones Collegii S. Bonaventurae ad Claras Aquas, 1971–1981.
Peter Lombard. *The Sentences.* 4 vols. Translated by Giulio Silano. Toronto: Pontifical Institute of Mediaeval Studies, 2007–10.

Secondary sources

Colish, M.L. *Peter Lombard.* 2 vols. Leiden: Brill, 1994.

Evans, G.R., ed. *Medieval Commentaries on the* Sentences *of Peter Lombard: Current Research I.* Leiden: Brill, 2002.

Rosemann, P.W. *Peter Lombard.* Oxford: Oxford University Press, 2004.

2.7

The Trinity[1] (1162–1173)
Richard of St. Victor
(c. 1125–1173)

The author's life and works

Richard of St. Victor was born somewhere on the English-Scottish border, probably around 1125. We first hear of him as a monk in Paris, where he joined the famous monastery of St. Victor, which was then one of the leading intellectual centers of Western Europe thanks to the work of Hugh of St. Victor, who died in 1141. Whether Richard ever studied under Hugh is questionable, since he must have been very young when Hugh died and may not have entered the monastery before then, but there is no doubt about the influence of Hugh's writings on him. Richard became subprior of the monastery in 1159 and prior in 1162, though he was forced to serve under the abbot Ernisius, who was unequal to the task. An appeal to the pope led to a papal visitation, and after some time Ernisius was removed. Richard was commended for the part he played in this, but received no material reward. He remained in close contact with England throughout his time in Paris, where he died on March 10, 1173.

Richard wrote on a great variety of subjects, often lifting material from earlier sources but also putting his own independent stamp on them. Many of his surviving tracts and letters were written in response to specific requests from his students, and they give us a clear insight into the mentality of his time. In his later years he reworked some of his earlier material and gradually drifted away from the teaching of his mentor Hugh, factors that help us to date his works, at least in relative terms.

His exegetical writings deal mainly with difficulties in Scripture, but he wrote a commentary on the book of Revelation and a book on Ezekiel's vision, which demonstrate his interest in supernatural phenomena. He also wrote mystical, contemplative works on the Psalms and the Song of Songs, as well as a book of "exceptions," or extracts, in which he cites a large number of historical sources to support his biblical interpretations. Richard is also the author of a book on Emmanuel, in which he outlines the Old Testament prophecies that foretold the coming of Christ.

Among his more substantial works, *Benjamin Minor* and *Benjamin Major* stand out for their teaching on the art of contemplation. Taking the story of Jacob and his sons as his scriptural text, Richard uses it to develop his ideas about the psychology that underlies particular virtues and vices. From there he goes on to talk about the relationship of body, mind, and spirit, intending to inculcate the basic principles of the art of contemplation into his students. In *Benjamin Major* he concentrates on the practice of prayer, but quickly moves on from there to a more general consideration of mystical theology, which he tries to describe as a coherent system of thought.

Richard also wrote a commentary on Ezekiel which is noteworthy for being illustrated. His greatest work, however, is his treatise on the Trinity, for which he is best known today. His originality consists of his largely psychological approach to his subject matter. He was deeply interested in the inner workings of the human mind and tried to apply his knowledge to theological issues. Like other medieval writers, he borrowed freely from his predecessors and had no wish to contradict or replace any of them, but his original approach meant that in many cases his interpretation of the inherited tradition was quite different from what had become standard in his day.

Richard's theological method derived from Anselm. He sought to apply reason to the difficulties posed by theological questions, though without subordinating theology to logic in the way that Peter Abelard was accused of doing. The marriage of faith and reason that characterizes the Anselmian tradition was breaking down in Richard's time, but his works had a great impact on the development of medieval mysticism. He influenced the early Franciscans, especially Bonaventure, for whom he was a second Augustine and his understanding of personhood had a considerable impact on Thomas Aquinas.

On the Trinity

Richard's treatise *On the Trinity* (*De Trinitate*) consists of six books, each of which contains twenty-five chapters (usually only a paragraph long), plus a prologue in which he explains his purpose and method. Richard begins his study by appealing to the three theological virtues—faith, hope and love. His opening line is the famous quote from Habakkuk, *via* the Apostle Paul: "The just shall live by faith" (Rom 1:17, citing Hab 2:4). But he quickly adds that hope cannot exist without faith, and love cannot exist without hope, and that without love we can do nothing (1 Cor 13:3). Richard's contention is that it is by means of hope and love that we rise from faith towards divine knowledge, and it is through divine knowledge that we attain eternal life. His approach is to rise from the lower to the higher, from a good beginning to a perfect end. He tells us that Christ ascended into heaven in order to draw us after him, and that the Holy Spirit subsequently descended in order to make that possible. It is our duty and privilege to go up to heaven with him, at least in our thoughts, because we cannot yet ascend bodily. Richard analyzes the three heavens through which we must pass before attaining to the perfection of mystical contemplation: immortality, or the region of the human spirit; incorruptibility, or the region of the angelic spirit; and finally eternity, which is the region of the divine Spirit (see 2 Cor 12:2). The level of spiritual difficulty increases for each stage of heaven. Thus, we are presently able to ascend to the first heaven; we can reach the second heaven with the help of virtue (on the strength of our merits); and the third heaven, where God alone dwells, can only be accessed by contemplation.

What God is

We acquire knowledge, according to Richard, in three ways—by experience, reason and belief. Each of these represents a higher stage of contemplation, and Richard quotes Isaiah to remind us that unless we believe we shall not understand (Isa 57:15). No convictions are held more strongly than those that are based on faith, and Richard intends to discuss eternal truths that we are expected to believe. His approach to these truths, however, will rely on logical reasoning rather than on quoting traditional authorities.

Repeating the orthodox Trinitarian doctrine,[2] Richard also adds that although he has often been told to believe it, he has never discovered on what arguments the doctrine is based. It is his intention to look for these, even if he fails to find them. His first premise is that every kind of being can be understood in a threefold way. Any being that is not eternal is not self-generating but has a cause outside itself. A self-generating being is by definition eternal, and such a being must exist, because if it does not, there would be no source for the other beings in the world. It is however possible to imagine a being which is eternal but not self-generating. The rays of the sun, for example, co-exist with the sun itself but depend on it for their being. In this treatise, says Richard, it is with these two modes of being in eternity, and only with them, that he is concerned.

Richard begins his analysis of the different grades of being that we can observe on earth and argues that the supreme being must be capable of producing all of them. For example, it is clear that a rational substance is higher than a non-rational one, which means that the supreme being must be rational. This supreme substance must also be complete in itself, lacking nothing and possessing everything in perfection, because otherwise it would be possible for some other substance to surpass it. Its power and wisdom must be equal to each other, since if they are not, its actions would be distorted.

It is impossible for anything else to share the nature of the supreme substance, because what is absolute cannot become relative and what is relative cannot become absolute. This supreme substance is what we call God. There can only be one God, and so it follows that everything that exists must derive from him, everything he needs must be present in him, and everything he is must correspond to his power and wisdom.

God is all-powerful because he can do whatever he chooses. However, God cannot do anything that would involve loss of power (e.g., destroy himself). There is no knowledge or understanding higher than he is, so he knows everything, and because he can do whatever he wishes, he has the power to use his wisdom in any way he chooses. Logically, there can only be one omnipotent being, which is why there can only be one God.

What God is like

The first and most fundamental of God's attributes is that he is self-existent and therefore uncreated. An uncreated, self-existing being must also be eternal, otherwise he would be subject to time which would be greater than he is. Furthermore, his perfect wisdom cannot contain any falsehood, and since he is pure truth he must be eternal, since truth is always the same.

Incorruptible and immutable describe God, because he cannot lose what he is, and any change in his perfection would of necessity be a loss of something. God is both everlasting in time and eternal beyond time because he cannot be any different from what he is, even if the circumstances in which he manifests himself change. He is also immeasurable because he is infinite. In time and space we call this his magnitude, but in eternity it is his infinity, though there is no actual difference between them, just as there is no difference between being everlasting and being eternal.

Each of these attributes necessitates the others, so that a being who has one of them must have them all. God is the only such being, and everything that has been created has been made out of nothing. Richard then concludes this section by showing that there are other ways of demonstrating the same conclusion. To be created means dwelling in time, which is the measurement of change, but as this does not apply to God, he must dwell outside time. To be measurable is to be comparable to something else, but as there is nothing for God to be compared with, he must be immeasurable. The divine attributes cannot be given to other beings, but God can allow them to share in his power and wisdom by being present and active in them.

After considering the natural properties of the divine being, Richard moves on to divine virtues and affections. God is good in relation to himself, and because of that, he is the supreme good in relation to everything else. Similarly, he is perfectly happy with his being, and so he must also be the supreme happiness in relation to all other beings. To be good and happy is to be like God, and the less like him a thing is, the less good and happy it will be.

The divine substance is incomprehensible. We can tell by comparing created things with each other what imperfection is like because we are aware of both quantity and quality and can see that they are variable. In God, however, this is not possible because his quantity is infinite and his quality is immeasurable. Furthermore, God is incomprehensible in every place and at every time, because time and space are limitations that he does not fit into.

When we speak of God's activity, we are talking about things that he wills and does. When we speak about his permission, we are talking about things that he allows others to do. In either case, God remains in supreme control because he possesses everything that exists and anything that does not exist as well. Richard concludes his exposition by saying that the divine properties that are eternal and uncreated are one and the same in his being.

Who God is

Richard moves on from his exposition of the divine substance and its attributes to consider the plurality and properties of the three divine persons. He argues that where supreme good exists, supreme love must also be found, because love is the highest good. To be satisfied with oneself, as God undoubtedly is, is not the same as love, which reaches out to others. God can love his creation, but that love is not perfect because it is a case of the absolute loving the relative. The fullness of the divine love cannot be communicated to any single creature, nor can any creature measure up to the infinity of the divine love for it. For the divine love to be fully manifested, as it must be if it is perfect, it requires a being capable of receiving and of sharing it. That being can only be God, which proves that there must be a plurality of persons in the Godhead.

Moreover, the fullness of divine happiness confirms the same principle, as does the fullness of divine glory. None of these attributes would have any meaning if there were no plurality of persons to share them. To wit, the necessity of the existence of a plurality in God is confirmed by a threefold testimony, and a triple cord will not be broken (Eccl 4:12).

Richard demonstrates that each of the divine persons must possess the divine attributes in their fullness and perfection, otherwise they would not be fully divine themselves. The divine persons are not three separate parts of God, but are each fully divine. Here he draws on a distinction between persons and substance. God is three persons in one substance, whereas a man is one person in two substances (body and soul).

Richard then moves from the necessity of a plurality in God to the necessity of a Trinity. Perfect love must manifest itself not only in mutual adoration but in a desire to share that love with another, and thus a third person becomes necessary for the love to be perfect. The same applies by extension to the supreme good and the supreme glory. It seems that the fullness of power and wisdom can subsist in a single person, and that happiness requires only two, but perfect goodness requires a third. Therefore, there is a Trinity in God who is the perfect good. Centuries later, another Richard—Richard Swinburne, a twentieth century philosopher and theologian—has used the same reasoning in his work *The Christian God* to argue for the necessity of three persons in the Trinity.[3]

Richard appeals to our experience of love and fellowship as indicating that there are vestiges of the divine Trinity in human life. Once that is established, he returns to the themes of equality and simplicity, and shows how each member of the Trinity must be fully God in order to share in these attributes.

Who the individual persons of the Trinity are

Richard goes on to tackle the problem that the Trinity seems incomprehensible to human minds. He states that there are many things in life that are incomprehensible, yet either experience or reason shows them to be true. There is, however, a real difficulty with the term *persona* (person) because it has been defined in many different ways. Richard ignores the Greek word *hypostasis* but concentrates on its Latin equivalent, which is *subsistentia* (subsistence). He does not deny that this word describes the threeness in God, but dislikes it because its meaning is not generally understood, whereas *persona* is. Richard then goes on to state that the word *persona* was given to the fathers of the Church by the Holy Spirit as a definition of God's threeness. A person is not a substance, because it is an individual, not a species. It refers to some*one*, not to some*thing*. There can be many *personae* (persons) but only one *substantia* (substance), as is true of God, just as there can be more than one substance in a single person, as is true of human beings.

Richard then embarks on an analysis of the word *existentia* (existence), which means "to subsist out of something" or "to possess substantial being." Existence can, therefore, be distinguished by the origin of a thing or by its nature, but in God the nature is identical, so any difference of existence in him must be determined by origin alone. In the divine nature there are forms of existence that are common to several persons (e.g., eternality) and forms that are incommunicable (e.g., the Son's Incarnation; only the Son 'becomes' man). The former are properties of the divine substance, the latter are properties of the divine persons. In God, a person is really nothing other than an incommunicable existence, of which there can be many in a single substance (i.e., Father, Son, and Spirit).

Richard defines a "person" first in terms of creation and then in terms of God. He shows that personhood is common to God and mankind, in spite of the difference of substance, and concludes by saying that the divine nature differs from other natures because one of its properties is the ability to accommodate a plurality of persons within it.

How the persons relate to each other

Having laid the groundwork for defining the individual persons of the Trinity, Richard goes on to consider their individual properties. The first person to be considered is the one who is self-existing, a property which is clearly distinct from those of the two persons who derive from another source. Richard says that one person must be self-existing, but only one. A person who proceeds from another person may do so directly, indirectly, or both at the same time, and Richard goes on to state that there must be one person whose procession from the self-existent one is direct. He then says that there must be another person who proceeds both directly and indirectly, but that there cannot be a person who proceeds only indirectly.

Richard demonstrates at great length how there can only be one person per mode of procession and explains again how there can be only one self-existent person, and one person who proceeds from one and who also has another person proceeding from him. He argues that there is no room for a fourth person in the divine nature because three exhausts all the relational possibilities in God.

Towards the end of his exposition, he introduces the theme of love and considers the role of the difference in personal properties. Only one of the persons has a completely gratuitous love, only one has a completely received love, and only one can combine the two in a single person. The last chapters of the book are a demonstration of why there can be no fourth person. The giving and receiving love of God is not a work of grace but part of the divine nature. God's love belongs equally to all three persons, but it is revealed in different ways according to the personal property of each of them.

The names of the divine persons

The last book takes up the remaining question of what names should be given to each of the divine persons. Nothing in God is attributable to grace; everything belongs to his nature. The relationship of Father to Son is peculiarly appropriate for the person who proceeds directly from the self-existent one, though the names themselves are conventional rather than necessary. The unbegotten person has a different relationship to the third person in the Trinity than he has to the second, because he does not have twin sons. The one who proceeds from both the Father and the Son must be called something else, and this is the Holy Spirit, who personifies the nature of the divine.

Richard examines why the Son is called the image of God and the Word, and why the Holy Spirit is called the Gift. He also discusses why the power of God is sometimes attributed to the Father, the wisdom of God to the Son, and the goodness of God to the Holy Spirit.

Turning then to focus on the relationship of the Father to the Son in the context of generation and on the Holy Spirit, Richard considers here the one who proceeds apart from generation. Richard explores how these words help us to distinguish one person from the others, but also shows how they cohere in the one divine substance. In the end, he returns to the Catholic faith of the creeds from which he started, and claims that he has demonstrated by rational argument that what the Church confesses is what must necessarily be present in the inner life of God.

Conclusion

In the later Middle Ages, Richard's influence can be seen most clearly in mystical writings like *The Cloud of Unknowing*, which is essentially a rendering of the *Benjamin Minor* into Middle English. His writings were still popular at the time of the Reformation,[4] but the Renaissance humanists had little appreciation for him and he faded into relative oblivion among both Protestants and Catholics. Not even the great revival of interest in medieval theology that took place in the late nineteenth and early twentieth centuries altered this picture very much. Karl Barth, for example, though he was strongly attracted to Anselm, had little or nothing to say about Richard, and the same is true of most modern theologians. But there have been some exceptions, such as Colin Gunton, who represents certain recent theologians who have found Richard's contribution as a stimulating way to advance their own conceptions.[5] Only very recently have his writings begun to appear in translation, and there is some hope that the revival of interest in Trinitarian theology will lead to a growing appreciation of Richard, whose understanding of the doctrine is unparalleled in medieval literature.[6]

Notes

1. Translated from *De Trinitate*.
2. The Athanasian creed was recited daily by the brothers of St. Victor. Grover Zinn, "Introduction" in *Richard of St. Victor*, trans. Grover Zinn (New York: Paulist Press, 1979), 46.
3. Richard Swinburne, *The Christian God* (Oxford: Oxford University Press, 1994), 190ff.
4. Cf. Declan Mariom and Rik van Nieuwenhove, "Theology of the Trinity from Richard of St. Victor to the Reformation," in *An Introduction the Trinity* (Cambridge: Cambridge University Press, 2010), 96–141.
5. E.g., Colin Gunton, *The Promise of Trinitarian Theology*, 2nd edition (Edinburgh: T&T Clark, 1997), 91–92. See also T.F. Torrance, *Theological Science* (Edinburgh: T&T Clark, 1996), 306.

6. For an excellent recent volume, see N. Den Bok, *Communicating the Most High: A Systematic Study of Person and Trinity in the Theology of Richard of St Victor*, Bibliotheca Victorina, 7 (Turnhout: Brepols, 1997).

Select Bibliography

Primary sources

Richard de Saint-Victor. *De Trinitate*. Edited by J. Ribaillier. Paris: Vrin, 1958.

Richard of St. Victor. *On the Trinity*. Translated by C. Evans. In *Trinity and Creation: A Selection of Works of Hugh, Richard and Adam of St Victor*, edited by B.T. Coolman and D.M. Coulter, Turnhout: Brepols, 2010.

Secondary sources

Chase, S. *Angelic Wisdom: The Cherubim and the Grace of Angelic Contemplation in Richard of St Victor*. Notre Dame: University of Notre Dame Press, 1995.

Coulter, D.M. *Per Visibilia ad Invisibilia: Theological Method in Richard of St Victor*. Turnhout: Brepols, 2006.

Cousins, Ewert. "A Theology of Interpersonal Relations." *Thought* 45 (1970): 56–82.

Den Bok, N. *Communicating the Most High: A Systematic Study of Person and Trinity in the Theology of Richard of St Victor*. Bibliotheca Victorina 7. Turnhout: Brepols, 1997.

Zinn, Grover. "Introduction" in *Richard of St. Victor: The Book of the Patriarchs, The Mystical Ark, Book Three of the Trinity*. Translated by Grover Zinn. The Classics of Western Spirituality. New York: Paulist Press, 1979.

2.8

Summa Theologica (c. 1267–1273)

Thomas Aquinas (1225–1274)

The author's life and works

Thomas was born in the southern Italian town of Aquino around 1225. He received his early education at the famous Benedictine monastery of Monte Cassino and later in Naples, where he decided to join the newly-created Dominican order of mendicant friars. He studied for a time with Albert the Great (1200–1280) who appreciated his genius and lived long enough to defend his former pupil from attacks made on him after his death.

By 1252 Aquinas was in Paris, where he taught at the Dominican convent and began his writing career. He produced a commentary on Peter Lombard's *Sentences*, wrote a philosophical treatise on the theme of "being," and composed commentaries on Isaiah and Matthew. Around 1259, he began to work on his *Summa* against the Gentiles, in which he tried to demonstrate the truth of the Christian faith by rational argument alone. His formal audience was composed of Jews and Muslims, but in reality the book was probably destined mainly for Christian students in Spain and southern Italy where they were familiar with Islamic beliefs and had to counter them.

The book was not finished until 1264, because he went back to Italy for several years, teaching in different places and organizing the schools of his order. While in Italy he began work on his great *Summa Theologica*, which eventually extended to five huge volumes but was still not finished when he died. He was back in Paris in 1269, but returned to Naples three years later. On December 6, 1272, he had a mystical vision of God, after which he

Figure 2.9 Altar of San Domenico in Ascoli depicting St. Thomas Aquinas

repudiated all his books and never wrote another word. He was on his way to attend the Second Council of Lyon when he died of a stroke on March 7, 1274.

Thomas Aquinas was revered for his theological precision, his personal piety, and the great clarity of his expositions. He was not above writing manuals for the common people, which made him better known than most scholars normally are. His body was eventually buried in the church of St. Sernin in Toulouse but was moved to the Jacobin church in the same city as recently as 1974. He was not widely read at the time of the Reformation, but in 1567 Pope Pius V declared him to be a doctor of the church and Pope Leo XIII made his *Summa* the basic theological textbook for Catholic students in 1879. That led to a revival of interest in his theological method, which combined the work of Aristotle, and to some extent Plato, with Scripture. Neo-Thomism became the dominant school of Catholic thought in the early twentieth century, though it was eclipsed by the Second Vatican council (1962–65). Nevertheless, his writings are still of great interest, not least to some conservative Protestants who have rediscovered him in recent years.

Summa Theologica

Thomas Aquinas' *Summa Theologica* (or *Theologiae*) is without any doubt one of the most monumental books ever written by a Christian theologian. It is a systematic attempt to cover every theological question from every conceivable angle and to provide the definitive answer based on a synthesis of Scripture, tradition, and reason. Nothing as ambitious as this had been attempted before and it is probably true to say that nothing as ambitious has been attempted since. It is virtually impossible to read it all at one time, and those unfamiliar with it will probably need some sort of introductory guide before they attempt it. Peter Kreeft's *Summa of the Summa* is a good place to start, but the beginner must be warned that in 500 pages of text, even Dr. Kreeft manages to cover only about a third of the entire work and to reproduce roughly 15 percent of the original text![1] Only when we consider that Aquinas wrote all this by the time he was forty-six years old, that he left it unfinished, that it is by no means his only work, and that for 200 years after his death it had to be copied out by hand—only then—can we get some idea of the immensity and grandeur of his achievement.

Formally, the *Summa* is divided into three parts, but it is better to think of them as four, because the second part is split into two. In general terms, the first part deals with the doctrine of God, the second part with morals, and the third part with Christology. The second part is subdivided into morals in general and morals as they apply to specific circumstances.

The organization of the work bears some resemblance to that of Peter Lombard's *Sentences*, but the second part is greatly expanded and deals only with human behavior, the section on creation having been put in the first part. Instead of distinctions there are questions—119 in the first part, 114 in the first half of the second part, 189 in the second half, and 90 in the third part, for a total of 512. It should be remembered, however, that these questions are further subdivided into "articles," some of which are long enough to be treatises in their own right. In the end, Aquinas produced a work that is substantially different from the Lombard's *Sentences*, both in style and in content. Whereas the *Sentences* are systematically arranged quotations from other authors supplemented by commentary, the *Summa* is a wholly original work in which quotations from other writers may be used to support the arguments being made but do not determine the work's overall shape.

It is clear that Aquinas intended to write a scientific treatise, justifying theology as a serious academic discipline whose function is to complete and perfect what can be discovered by the human mind. Unlike the Lombard, who quoted only the Bible and Christian authors, Aquinas did not hesitate to cite pagan philosophers, and especially Aristotle, whose authority in the secular sphere of knowledge he fully respected. His argument was that pagan philosophy had much to contribute at the purely human level, but that it did not (and could not) give a complete picture of reality, which depended on divine revelation. That required theology, as revealed in Scripture and developed by the Fathers of the church, sources which Aquinas quoted with the same ease as he quoted Aristotle.

The doctrine of God

The *Summa* starts off with an extended exposition of the unique essence of God. This is in sharp contrast to Peter Lombard, who put the Trinity first, and came back to the divine unity only later. For Aquinas, the philosophical issue of the existence of God and the nature of theology as a science had to come first. Only when that was demonstrated by an appeal to both reason and revelation would it be possible to go on to consider a truth that could only be known by the latter. He considers the basic attributes of the divine essence, and demonstrates why each of them is logically necessary. He quotes scriptural verses in support of his arguments but seeks to prove them by rational analysis and does not rely on the authority of revelation alone.

Aquinas then brings up the issue of ideas and asks whether everything God knows properly belongs in that category. From there he goes on to discuss God's will, his love, his righteousness, his mercy, and his providence. That leads him naturally to the question of predestination and the book of life in which the names of the elect are written. Thus, we see how rational argument ends up in an appeal to the truths of revelation which put the findings of reason in their proper perspective and show what they mean in the mind of God.

This inductive method, beginning with reason and moving on to revelation, characterizes Aquinas' method and can be seen very clearly in his discussion of the Trinity. He expounds the doctrine without mentioning the term to start off with. Instead, he defines what a person is, goes on to discuss the plurality of persons in God, asks whether there are only three of them, and then distinguishes between what belongs to God's oneness and what is said of his threeness. The word "Trinity" first appears in a discussion in which he concludes that it cannot be known by natural deduction. From there he examines each of the persons in turn, with an extra question about the image of God pertaining to the Son and two questions on the name of the Holy Spirit, which is both Love and Gift, as Augustine said. In other words, after demonstrating that the Trinity can only be known by divine revelation, he proceeds to analyze what that revelation says about it, using the same principles that he employed in his earlier analysis of what can be known about God by unaided human reason.

Thomas relates the persons to the divine essence, and discusses various aspects of the persons—how they relate to the divine attributes, to the mental acts of God, and so on. This section ends with a discussion of the sending of the Son and of the Holy Spirit by the Father. Once again, what can be known about God by rational deduction is supplemented by divine self-revelation to give a full and perfect picture of reality.

The importance of creation

Thomas argues that God is the First Cause of all things and asks whether creation is as eternal as he is, whether time was created simultaneously with the first creatures, and whether the differences among the creatures were intended by God. He then goes on to discuss the nature of evil and how it originated. Most of this is pure speculation, though Aquinas does not hesitate to quote divine revelation in trying to answer questions that the revelation does not raise. In other words, questions arising from human curiosity and the desire to know are answered by both logic and divine pronouncements that support that logic, once again demonstrating how revelation reaches out to human reason and perfects its understanding.

After dealing with the material world, Thomas turns to a consideration of angels, including demons. It is easy for modern readers to miss the significance of this, but for Aquinas the existence of a celestial hierarchy was of paramount importance because it was among them that the great issues of good and evil arose.

Having dealt with the material and the spiritual worlds, Thomas then discusses the creation of human beings, who combine the two. He explains how our intellect apprehends things and how the rational soul can understand both what is in it and what is above it. He includes an extended discussion of the image of God and what attributes were given to the first humans by virtue of their creation.

Finally, Thomas turns to the issue of order in the universe, and asks how it is governed by God. He concludes with a picture of a coherent universe in which God and man are united by their common possession of reason and their common participation in the order that reason brings to both the material and the spiritual world.

The characteristics of human nature

Thomas devotes considerable space to an examination of human nature, explaining how much of what we do depends on circumstances and analyzing what the role of the human will is. As he sees it, it is the moral dimension of human actions that most clearly reveals what it means to be created in the image of God. Our capacity for morality makes us like God and explains our need to know him, since without that knowledge our moral sense lacks the direction it requires.

From this basic moral sense, Thomas moves on to consider human passions, first in general terms and then with respect to particular feelings. He examines where they come from, how they are related to one another, whether they are good or bad, and whether some are more fundamental than others. He then goes on to talk first about love, its cause and effects, then of hatred, and lust. There is also an extended discussion of enjoyment and whether it is good or bad. He repeats this procedure in examining the phenomena of sadness, hope and despair, fear, boldness, and anger.

Natural virtue and the need of grace

When Aquinas comes to his examination of virtues, he distinguishes between intellectual and moral types, comparing the latter to the passions and examining distinctions between them. He lists the cardinal virtues as prudence, justice (righteousness), fortitude, and temperance. All the other virtues derive from or consist of these in one way or another, and Thomas sets out to determine precisely how. Opinions differ about how successful he was, but no one can doubt his intentions and there are many who have been persuaded by his arguments. Aquinas wanted to integrate the ethics of Aristotle with the spiritual teaching of the Bible, which he believed made it possible to achieve the virtuous life that the pagan philosophers sought but could not obtain on their own. For that, they needed divine grace, to which Aquinas now turns.

He examines the theological virtues of faith, hope, and love, which must be distinguished from the intellectual and moral ones, though they cannot be separated from them. He then considers where these virtues come from, how they are manifested, how they are related to one another, whether they are equal to each other, and whether they last beyond the end of this life. He wraps up this section with a discussion of gifts, blessings, and the fruits of the Holy Spirit, once more demonstrating how natural qualities can and must be supplemented by the infusion of supernatural grace.

The character of sin

Aquinas begins by asking whether vice is the opposite of virtue and whether sin and virtue can co-exist in the same person or act. In practice they often do, but this is an unstable situation because of the incompatibility that exists between them. We have a duty to apply virtue to the eradication of sin, something which can be initiated by the human will but only achieved by divine grace. He then goes on to distinguish different types of sin and compares them with one another before asking what the subject of sin is. Is it located in the will, the senses or the mind? He asks whether sins have a cause and whether ignorance is a sin, a cause of sin, or something that mitigates sin. He examines the interrelationships between the will, the passions, and the weakness of the flesh as potential causes of sin and then goes on to consider the role of spiritual wickedness in causing sin, and the role of external forces, including God himself, the devil and other people.

He saves the topic of original sin for last, which leads him to examine how one sin can lead to others. He then looks at the effects of sin, which corrupts human nature and leaves a stain on the soul. He concludes his analysis with a discussion of guilt and the differences between moral and venial (forgivable) sins.

Law and grace as remedies for sin

Having examined the nature and effects of sin, Aquinas turns to the remedies for it. He starts with the different kinds of law—eternal law, natural law, and human law. He looks at how law can change and devotes the next eight questions to a consideration of the Old Testament, dividing its legal precepts into moral, ceremonial, and judicial categories that were to become the standard way of reading the Law of Moses until the rise of modern critical scholarship. He then goes on to the "new law" of the Gospel and compares it with the Old Testament before describing it in detail.[2]

Having covered the different kinds of law, Thomas points out why grace is necessary and tries to define what it is. He asks whether it can be divided into different types, where it comes from, and what its effects are, particularly in the justification of the ungodly. This leads him to discuss the issue of merit and he shows that ultimately all human merit depends on the grace of God.

The alternation of virtues and vices is intended to clarify what they are in practical terms, with the intention of persuading people to accept that the former are more rational and therefore more desirable than the latter. Virtue is conformity to God's plan and purpose for his creation, whereas vice is rebellion against God and therefore destructive of those who have rejected the light of both divine and human reason.

Justice

Aquinas discusses the question of justice at great length, examining its relationship to law, what constitutes injustice, and so on. He aims to provide practical insights for his readers and not simply a theoretical investigation into the nature of justice. In this respect, the structure of the *Summa* allows the reader to explore individual issues related to the overall question without having to read an entire book on the subject. So, for instance, in questions 64–78, Aquinas deals with various injustices, examining the problem of the unjust judge, false accusation, sins like perjury committed by the accused, and other abuses in court cases.

In many ways, it is this part of the *Summa* that has had the greatest influence on later generations. It became and has remained the foundation of moral theology, which presupposes that good behavior and the divine will are two sides of the same rational coin. Aquinas was careful to insist that human virtue was unachievable without God's assistance, but his account of moral action leaned in the direction of a form of salvation by works that is neatly summed up in the popular phrase: "God helps those who help themselves." The Protestant Reformers rejected this. They denied that human virtue had any value in the sight of God, whose grace is sufficient to save even the worst of sinners. However, it must be said that many Protestants continued to believe in the value of virtuous works for sanctification, which they distinguished from justification, which was by faith alone. As a result, Thomist concepts of virtue and vice have played almost as important a role among Protestants as they have among Catholics, despite the Reformers' attempts to get away from them.

Christology and the sacraments

The third part of the *Summa* is the shortest and is unfinished. In some Latin editions it is followed by an extended supplement of ninety-nine further questions, dealing mainly with the sacraments and eschatology, but these are of a later date and are not included in the most recent Latin edition, which has an accompanying English translation.

First come twenty-six questions dealing with various aspects of Christ's Incarnation. Aquinas starts by considering the appropriateness of a divine Incarnation and goes on to examine how it occurred. He looks at it from the standpoint of the Son of God and also from that of the man Jesus Christ. He then details the order in which the Son took on the different parts of human nature and then goes on to consider all the usual questions relating to his human soul and its capacities. After that, Thomas looks at the submission of the Son to the Father and considers whether the incarnate Christ could pray, be a priest, be adopted by the Father, be predestined, or be worshiped. He then examines Christ's role as mediator between God and man.

There is an extended discussion on the human life of Christ which begins with four questions relating to the Virgin Mary, four more on the conception of Christ in her womb, three on his birth and circumcision, two on his baptism, and six on his earthly ministry, including the temptations and his transfiguration.

The next section deals with his passion, death, resurrection, ascension, heavenly session, and final judgment. The order and content follow the classical creeds and explain their meaning and implications in detail. Most of what Aquinas says can be found in earlier writers, and here he is perhaps as close to Peter Lombard as he ever gets. Nevertheless, he deals with each of his chosen topics in such comprehensive and exhaustive detail that he cannot really be compared with any of his predecessors. His encyclopedic treatment was intended to be the last word on the subject, and for many it has been.

Aquinas next moves on to the sacraments, beginning with their nature and number before going on to look specifically at baptism, confirmation, the Eucharist (including the questions of transubstantiation and the real presence of Christ), and penance.

Conclusion

The *Summa* ends abruptly at this point, and we can only guess what the complete work would have looked like. The influence of the Lombard's *Sentences* is obvious and the *Summa* was originally conceived as an extended commentary on that earlier work, but its structure and contents go far beyond anything that Peter Lombard could have envisaged. Thomas Aquinas laid the foundations for a philosophical theology that in different ways has remained foundational for the discipline ever since. His belief that there is an essential harmony between divine revelation and natural science remains fundamental to the Christian tradition, even when theologians have interpreted it differently. His categories and use of terms like "nature" and "grace" have entered the Western tradition and the relationship between them has been the source of continuing debate over the centuries. He continues to be regarded as the ultimate source of so-called "natural theology," the fortunes of which have waxed and waned over time.

In the sixteenth century, he was little read because his methods and his reliance on Aristotle were being increasingly questioned by the Renaissance humanists of that time. The Roman Catholic Church continued to honor him and to advocate his theology as the antidote to what it perceived to be Protestant and secular heresy. Within the Protestant world, reactions to him varied accordingly. Some theologians, particularly the so-called Protestant Scholastics of the seventeenth century, tried to create an alternative systematics by using the categories of Aquinas but giving them a different content.[3] In more recent times, that tendency can be seen at its fullest in the philosophical theology of Herman Dooyeweerd and those associated with his Dutch school of "neo-Calvinism."[4] This pattern is likewise seen in the "neo-Thomism" of the Roman Catholic Church: it enjoyed a revival in the early twentieth century but is now largely a spent force.[5]

Mainstream Protestantism, on the other hand, sometimes rejected Aquinas by denying his assertion that grace perfects nature and showing suspicion toward natural theology. In the twentieth century that reaction reached its highest level in the work of Karl Barth, who deliberately set out to construct an alternative that was grounded exclusively in divine revelation. In return, Barth was frequently criticized by neo-Thomists, who claimed that he lacked an adequate doctrine of creation.

In general, it must be said that although sympathy for Aquinas has never been great in Protestant circles, it has not been possible to ignore him either. For better or for worse, much Protestant theology has been conceived and written in opposition to his methods and ideas, and Protestants cannot understand their own traditions without coming to grips with the work of a man who, perhaps more than any other single individual, represents everything about medieval theology that they were protesting against.[6]

Notes

1.   Peter Kreeft, *A Summa of the* Summa (San Francisco: Ignatius Press, 1990).
2.   This is where Dr. Kreeft's *Summa of the* Summa breaks off.
3.   For an excellent example of how often this happens in Reformed Theology, see the monumental work Richard Muller, *Post-Reformation Reformed*

Dogmatics: The Rise and Development of Reformed Orthodoxy, 4 vols, 2nd ed. (Grand Rapids: Baker Academic, 2003).

4. Herman Dooyeweerd, *A New Critique of Theoretical Thought*, trans. David H. Freeman, William S. Young, and H. De Jongste, 4 vols. (Jordan Station, Ontario: Paideia Press, 1984). For an introduction to Dooyeweerd, see Leendert Kalsbeek, *Contours of a Christian Philosophy* (Toronto: Wedge, 1975).

5. Etienne Gilson was instrumental in helping resurrect Aquinas in the twentieth century (for example, see his *Being and Some Philosophers*, 2d ed. [Toronto: Pontifical Institute of Medieval Studies, 1952]). For other sources, see also Craig Paterson and Matthew S. Pugh, eds., *Analytical Thomism: Traditions in Dialogue* (Aldershot, UK: Ashgate, 2006); John F.X. Knasas, *Being and Some Twentieth-Century Thomists* (New York: Fordham University Press, 2003).

6. For more on the Thomistic revival, see Fergus Kerr, *After Aquinas: Versions of Thomism* (Malden, MA: Blackwell, 2002); Peter S. Eardley and Carl N. Still, *Aquinas: A Guide for the Perplexed* (New York: Continuum, 2010); Matthew Levering, *Scripture and Metaphysics: Aquinas and the Renewal of Trinitarian Theology* (Oxford: Blackwell, 2004); Hans Boersma, *Nouvelle Théologie and Sacramental Ontology: A Return to Mystery* (Oxford: Oxford University Press, 2009).

Select Bibliography

Primary sources

Thomas Aquinas. *Summa Theologica*. Edited and translated. 61 vols. London: Blackfriars, 1964–76.

Thomas Aquinas. *Summa Theologica. A Concise Translation*. Edited by T. McDermott. London: Eyre and Spottiswoode, 1989.

Secondary sources

Copleston, F.C. *Aquinas. An Introduction to the Life and Work of the Great Medieval Thinker*. London: Penguin, 1955.

Davies, Brian, *The Thought of Thomas Aquinas*. Oxford: Oxford University Press, 1992.

Emery, G., *The Trinitarian Theology of St Thomas Aquinas*. Oxford: Oxford University Press, 2007.

Kreeft, Peter, ed. *Summa of the* Summa. San Francisco: Ignatius, 1990.

Pieper, Josef, *Guide to Thomas Aquinas*. New York: Pantheon, 1962.

2.9

The Defender of the Peace[1] (1324)

Marsilius of Padua (c. 1275–c. 1342)

The author's life and work

Marsilius of Padua (Marsiglio da Padova) was born in the Italian university city after which he is named, sometime around 1275. He studied medicine and was a soldier for a time, but in 1311 he went to Paris where he taught natural science. He gained such a high reputation that only two years later he was elected rector of the university, a post which he held for the statutory term. Little more is heard of him before 1324, when he wrote his famous *Defensor pacis* (*The defender of the peace*).

The circumstances which led to Marsilius writing the book were complex. Following a struggle between the king of France and the papacy, the French managed to prevent the newly-elected Pope Clement V from going to Rome, and Clement was forced to establish himself at Avignon (1305). About the time that Marsilius went to Paris, Clement called a church council which met at Vienne (1311–1313) and undertook a major revision and expansion of the church's canon law. Papal determination to recover lost ground was continued and intensified under John XXII (1316–1334), who was a close ally of the French king.

Matters came to a head because although Ludwig (Louis) of Bavaria had been elected Holy Roman Emperor in 1314, his ambitions were seen as a threat to the papacy and the pope refused to crown him. In 1323, the kingdom of Naples, allied with the papacy and the French, tried to conquer Milan, which was under Bavarian protection. Ludwig sent an army into Italy, whereupon the pope excommunicated him and demanded that he relinquish the imperial throne.

Defying the pope, Ludwig claimed that the pope had no authority in secular affairs. It was at this juncture that Marsilius sprang to his support. Two years after *Defensor pacis* was published, it was condemned by the pope and Marsilius was declared a heretic. He was forced to flee to Bavaria, where Ludwig took him in and made him a member of his court circle.

Marsilius' subsequent career was bound up with Ludwig's fortunes. He was appointed imperial vicar in Bavaria during Ludwig's absence in Italy (1328–1329) and persecuted the clergy there who remained loyal to John XXII. After Ludwig's return, he was rewarded with the archbishopric of Milan, but that was an empty title which the pope never recognized.

During these years he continued to write in defense of lay sovereignty and against the claims of the papacy. In a treatise entitled *De translatione imperii* (*The transfer of the empire*), he maintained that the emperor alone had jurisdiction in matrimonial affairs, and not the pope, a view which would famously resurface in England when Henry VIII wanted to annul his first marriage in the late 1520s. He also wrote a second version of the *Defensor pacis*, known today as the *Defensor minor*, which was even more strident than the original in its denunciation of the papal claims.

Marsilius died in about 1342, but his book became famous as the main source of intellectual opposition to the papacy. As papal power declined, the arguments Marsilius made became obsolete and his work was less widely read. In modern times he has been relatively little studied, except among medievalists, who continue to see him as one of the leading representatives of the new Aristotelian school of philosophy that was challenging the church establishment in the late thirteenth and early fourteenth centuries. Nevertheless, his historical importance is assured since it was his book, more than any other, which gave the secular rulers of the time the ammunition they needed to defeat what they saw as the excessive claims being made for papal jurisdiction in non-church matters.[2]

The Defender of the Peace

The book is divided into three discourses of uneven length. The first discourse contains nineteen sections or chapters, the second thirty and the third only three. Marsilius makes it clear in the first chapter of the first discourse that this arrangement was planned from the beginning for a specific purpose, so we can safely assume that the disparate lengths are not due to a failure to complete the work or to a subsequent editor who combined originally independent treatises into a single whole.

The origin and nature of civil society

Marsilius begins this discourse with a number of quotes from the church fathers and the scriptures, especially the New Testament, arguing to the effect that peace ought to be the normal and most desired condition of mankind. But all too often discord breaks out, peace is destroyed, and civil society ceases to function. Turning to the philosophers and historians of antiquity, Marsilius cites them both as witnesses of civil strife (Sallust) and as guides for what should prevail (Aristotle, Plato, and Cicero). Unfortunately, the wisdom of the ancients has become powerless because a perverted opinion has taken hold, which assumes that there is a higher power that can work miracles above and beyond the usual forces of cause and effect. Marsilius does not say what that is, but promises his readers that he will reveal it in due course.

He then returns to the New Testament, quoting various texts from the Gospels and Epistles of Paul and James to the effect that he must tell the truth and point out what the Christian world should do to support the Emperor Ludwig in his desire to bring peace to God's people on earth. He defines what he means by the "tranquility" of a city or kingdom, which for his purposes differ only in relative size. As Marsilius understands it, tranquility is "that good condition of a city or realm, in which each of its parts is enabled perfectly to perform the operations appropriate to it according to reason and the way it has been established."[3]

The third chapter outlines how civil societies came into being. As a true disciple of the ancient Greeks, Marsilius takes the city as the ideal model, tracing its origins back to the household and the development of neighborhoods. The purpose of the city was to find a way in which human communities could live well. Human beings must seek the good life on two different levels, the earthly and the heavenly. While philosophers knew about the first of these but not the second, within the sphere of their competence their opinions are still valid.

Marsilius distinguishes between the common people and the elite, which he defines in six categories—agriculture, industry, the military, finance, religion, and government. As civilization developed, human beings discovered different kinds of production and creativity, which they put to good use. But in order to ensure that they did not go to excess or privilege one kind of activity over others, government and a system of justice were instituted to provide the regulation needed to ensure the right balance among all these elements. A distinctive military order was established so as to defend the emerging society from enemies that would try to destroy it. Bankers are also necessary in order to budget resources, so that in hard times there will be enough to meet the people's requirements and in good years resources will be conserved and not squandered.

The one order in society that is hard to account for is that of the priesthood. What is it for? It may be a good thing to worship God, but is a special class of people needed for this? In actual fact, however, all societies have set up a religious establishment, even if its leaders do not believe in the official religion, "in order thereby to induce in men a reverence and fear of God and a desire to avoid the vices and cultivate the virtues."[4] As a result of this, all societies have some kind of priesthood, but Christian priests are superior to the others because they have a true understanding of God and of the kingdom of heaven, and so will give people the right guidance in such matters. Of course, Marsilius was catering here to the general prejudice of Christendom, and it would soon become apparent, not least to the Christian priests themselves, that there was no real justification for this statement.

Why civil society is necessary

Looking back to Adam, who was created in the image of God, Marsilius sees one who was originally sinless. Had Adam remained in that state of innocence, civil government would not have been necessary, nor would there have been any religion as we know it. But because Adam fell from grace, this happy state of affairs never developed. But God took pity on his fallen creatures and sent them guides to give them rites and ceremonies by which they might atone for their sins, appease his wrath, and turn back to him. In particular, he revealed himself to the Jewish nation. After many centuries, he sent his Son Jesus Christ to preach the Gospel, which would earn the grace of eternal happiness for those who believed and followed it. Christians are promised blessedness in the next life and, with the help of sacraments and the teachings that go with them, they will receive strength to live a meritorious life here on earth. It is for that purpose that a Christian priesthood has been instituted, so that we may learn how to obtain eternal salvation.

Within the context of the earthly city, each social order has been created for a particular purpose and must fulfill its function for the good of the whole. They are necessary because of the deficiencies of our human nature, but for the most part they have been brought into being by legislators, although on very rare occasions God has intervened directly.

Marsilius examines the character of the legislators who govern civil society and says that they are of two types—the well-ordered and the flawed. Well-ordered states may be monarchies, aristocracies, or representative democracies; flawed ones will be tyrannies, oligarchies, or popular democracies (i.e., subject to mob rule). Without question Marsilius recognizes that he is here following what Aristotle says in his *Politics*. He goes on to discuss the ways in which these different types of regimes can be established and maintained in being, basing himself once more on Aristotle but with a nod in the direction of Christian writers like Augustine, who saw such things as being ultimately under the controlling hand of God.

The ideal ruler

According to Marsilius, any well-ordered state must be governed by law, which performs the dual function of instructing us in what is right and commanding us to observe it. Teachers are needed for the first of these functions and enforcers for the second. In theory, laws should be conducive to living a good and moral life, and legislators who are guided by a knowledge of God will try to ensure that this is so. But there is no necessary correspondence between law and virtue, and in flawed societies the law itself may be unjust.

Debating whether it is better to have a state ruled by a just man or to be subject to just laws, Marsilius concludes that it is better to be subject to law because no man, however good he may be, is entirely free from passion or bias, and every human judge will be ignorant to some degree. Here again, he is following Aristotle, whom he actually refers to as "divine."[5] When a society is ordered by human decisions and not by divine decrees (as ancient Israel was), it must find a way of choosing its governors, and popular election is the best method. People chosen in that way have no authority other than that of their electors, in whose interests they must labor and to whom they are ultimately responsible.

Marsilius recognizes that some people will say that he is painting too ideal a picture because, in reality, human beings are stupid and ignorant of their own best interests and incapable of electing the best men as their legislators. Marsilius agrees with this to some extent, but he denies that all the citizenry can be put in this category. He claims that most people are sensible enough most of the time, and while they may not have the expertise needed to legislate themselves, they have the discernment to choose men who do have the expertise and to elect them to exercise it in their place. It is certainly to everyone's advantage to entrust law-making to a virtuous minority, but the citizens in general have the ability to judge who they are and should be trusted with electing them.

The ideal ruler, according to Marsilius, should possess two basic qualities—prudence and moral virtue. In addition to this, he should also have the ability to discern what is fair, what judges call "equity" and philosophers *epieikeia*. He should also have an army at his disposal for enforcing law and order when necessary. The chief ruler of the state should also be chosen by popular election, mandated by the legislators but open to the entire citizenry. In this way, there will be a clear distinction between the legislative and the executive branches of government, but each one will be chosen by the citizenry and be responsible to it.

Marsilius then goes on to debate whether rulers should be hereditary or not, and comes down on the side of the hereditary principle for a number of reasons. To his mind, hereditary succession is more likely to produce good rulers because they will come from good stock, be trained in government from birth, and be independent of the pressures of factions within the state. He does, however, recognize that the method is not foolproof, and recommends that popular confirmation of office should be sought and a means of deposing an unsuitable ruler developed.

Every state should be headed by a single individual who is ultimately responsible for its welfare, otherwise chaos and irresponsibility will take over. Marsilius suggests ways in which the powers granted to this ruler can be monitored and kept in check and insists again that no one is above the law. In the final chapter of this discourse, he sums up what he has said about legislators, the ruler, and the proper establishment of civil order, before going on to fulfill the promise he made at the beginning, to explain why this has broken down in his own time in a peculiar and particularly intractable way.

The mission of Christ in the world

The breakdown of the civil order is explained, according to Marsilius, by going back to the life and example of Jesus Christ, who had told his disciples to preach his message to the entire world and had equipped them for that task. Jesus had given them the right to teach the Gospel, to celebrate the sacraments, and the power to forgive sins in his name. But in addition to this, another kind of priestly authority has developed over time. This was not of divine origin, but was originally bestowed on the priesthood by human authority, mainly in order to avoid disorders that might lead to scandal. This authority allowed the priests to set up one of their number above the others. It was his particular responsibility to ensure that worship was conducted in the right way and that there were funds available to keep the priestly order viable. Marsilius had little idea of the true origin of the Christian priesthood and his interpretation of it is largely a form of propaganda directed against the abuses he saw in his own time, but in the absence of historical knowledge generally, his theory had more plausibility then than it has today.

Among the disciples whom Jesus commissioned one stood out above the rest. This was Peter, who became the first bishop of Rome, and was martyred there along with the Apostle Paul. Because of what they see as a definite pre-eminence given to Peter, his successors in Rome have claimed superiority, not just over all other bishops and priests, but over secular rulers as well. They claim that when he legalized Christianity in the fourth century, the Emperor Constantine granted them this authority and that as vicars of Christ on earth they have the right to exercise jurisdiction over all those who are subject to him. That includes all kings and lords of this earth (see Rev 19:16). The bishops of Rome have thus usurped powers that properly belong to secular rulers. The result has been widespread social disorder and the loss of the kind of peace that in normal circumstances ought to prevail among Christians. It was for this reason, Marsilius argued, that the Christian world is in such disarray and the pope's usurped authority must be repelled if peace is to be restored.

How the papacy has usurped civil authority

The second discourse is three times as long as the first, but the focus is clear throughout. It is a massive attack on the powers claimed by the papacy in the name of the institutional church, which has become identified with the priestly hierarchy and is no longer thought of as the assembly of the whole people of God. Marsilius sees the key to the problem in the need to distinguish what is "temporal" from what is "spiritual." "Spiritual" has come to be a term used for the officials of the institutional church, which is not at all what it is supposed to mean. The result is that the priesthood has claimed exemption from temporal jurisdiction when it ought to be subject to it in civil affairs.

The papacy has usurped secular authority without the consent of the people, according to Marsilius, and the popes do not see that they should be subject to human laws because they have been appointed by God. Furthermore, it has developed an entire body of canon law in order to justify its claims, when a simple reading of the New Testament will soon show that they are unwarranted. Indeed, says Marsilius in chapter 4, if the popes were really determined to follow Christ, they would renounce temporal authority, just as he did! The witness of the apostles and church fathers is exactly the same, but the popes ignore it because it does not suit them to follow their example.

The need to separate church and state

Marsilius balances his analysis of the power of the priesthood and the nature of the spiritual realm with an equally robust discussion of the secular sphere, followed by an attempt to explain how the two are related. He grants that priests have the right to exercise spiritual authority within their appointed sphere, and accepts that it is they who must decide who should be excommunicated for heresy. But whether heretics (and unbelievers, such as Jews) should be allowed to remain in the state is for the secular ruler to decide. In practice, they have almost always been more tolerant than the Church and have refused to enforce divine laws by civil sanction. In Marsilius' view this is the right approach, which the priests ought to accept as valid in the secular sphere.

Such questions as who should be canonized as a saint and whether the clergy should be forced to embrace celibacy are then broached. His somewhat surprising conclusion is that saints should not be canonized without secular consent, though quite why this should be so is not properly explained. More understandably, he also thinks that priests should be allowed to marry as they were in the early church, unless there is a good reason for not permitting it.

Because Christ instituted poverty as the rule for his servants on earth, Marsilius reasons that priests are to be cut off from worldly interests so as to be free to preach the gospel to all. This argument takes up four long chapters, in which he covers every aspect of the question from both Scripture and practical experience, showing that a priesthood that has compromised with the world has lost its spiritual authority, not enhanced it.

Next, the authority of the priesthood is dissected as Marsilius distinguishes what is essential to it from what is purely accidental. Just as the apostles were all equal to each other, so are their successors, the modern bishops, and the priests as well. Ordination confers an authority that can be exercised anywhere, subject to mutual agreement and convenience, and priests should be chosen by the people assembled together. In particular, secular rulers should have the right to reject ecclesiastical appointments and to submit the pope's decisions to the judgment of the people. Needless to say, all of this was deeply subversive of the established order in both church and state, and Marsilius' proposals could not have appeared as anything less than revolutionary.

In his consideration of the character of spiritual authority, Marsilius explains how the papacy came to make its particular claims, and then goes on to insist on the supremacy of Holy Scripture to every other law. The interpretation of disputed parts of Scripture must be determined by general councils of the Church and not by any individual, but the power to convene such councils has always belonged to the secular ruler and not the pope. Furthermore, he argues that no bishop has the power to excommunicate a priest or exercise any temporal jurisdiction, unless it has been delegated to him by the state. Here Marsilius reflects the confusion between church and state that prevailed in his time and his solution to it must be regarded as inadequate. Excommunication was a spiritual penalty that had secular consequences, but it could not legitimately be administered by anyone outside the Church.

It is not that Marsilius was blind to the advantages of having a central church organization and of recognizing one bishop and local church as having authority over the rest. However, he rejected the view that such a primacy can claim scriptural authority, and he did not see why there was any objective reason for that role belonging to the Roman bishop and church. Nevertheless, he did admit that since custom and tradition has focused on Rome, changing that would probably be impossible.[6] Even so, he argued that the primacy should be one of honor and dignity, not one of superior authority that would allow the pope to become a dictator. Marsilius quickly returns to that theme, which takes him four chapters to develop. He details all the complaints and abuses that have occurred in his own time and that have led to the conditions that prompted him to write this discourse.

Returning to the question of the episcopate, Marsilius picks up the objection to his view that all priests are equal. He goes through the case that is made for the superiority of bishops over the clergy before replying to each of the points in turn. He returns to some objections raised in connection with his earlier concern that the papacy does not believe itself to be under the jurisdiction of human laws, and explains why the claims made that Scripture gives coercive jurisdiction to bishops are misinterpretations of the text. The same goes for the claim that the papacy has inherited the rights and privileges of the ancient Roman emperors, which he says is false.

How civil peace can be established

In sharp contrast to the second discourse, the third is very short and is presented as a summary of the other two, from which no fewer than forty-two conclusions will be drawn. The first, and most important, is "that in order to gain eternal beatitude, it is necessary to believe only in the truth of divine or canonical Scripture, what follows from it with any kind of necessity, and the interpretation of it that has been made by a common council of the faithful, if this is put to an individual in due fashion."[7]

Conclusion

When men like John Wycliffe, Jan Hus, and Martin Luther rebelled against the authority of Rome, they were routinely denounced as Marsilians, which gives some indication of the influence his reputation had, though whether he influenced the Reformers directly is doubtful.[8] It is nonetheless clear from reading his work that it prefigures the platform of the Reformation in an uncanny way. The importance given to secular rulers, the effective separation of church and state, the rejection of papal claims, and even the abandonment of clerical celibacy are all ideas taken from Marsilius, and had he not made the case for them it is unlikely that the first Protestants would have been able to implement them as quickly and as successfully as they did. Even if they never read Marsilius, they owed him a great deal, and the post-Reformation church looked much more like what he envisaged than did, ironically, the one in which he himself lived.

Notes

1. Translated from *Defensor Pacis*.
2. For Marsilius as a key precursor to the Reformation, see Joan Lockwood O'Donovan, *Theology of Law and Authority in the English Reformation* (Atlanta: Scholars Press for Emory University, 1991), 11–28.
3. I,2.3, p. 13 (All quotations are from the edition of A. Brett.)
4. I,5.11, p. 28.
5. I,11.2, p. 57.

6. It must be remembered that when Marsilius was writing this, the papacy was in exile at Avignon and not in Rome at all.
7. III,2,1, p. 547.
8. See Margaret Harvey, "Condemnation of John Wyclif, 1377," *The English Historical Review* 113.451 (1998): 326; Thomas M. Izbicki, "The Reception of Marsilius" in *A Companion to Marsilius of Padua*, eds Gerson Moreno-Riano and Cary Nederman (Leiden: Brill, 2011), 320; Bernd Mayerhofer, "Marsilius of Padua," in *Philosophers of Peace*, ed. Peter Cornelius Mayer-Tasch (Munich: Herbert Utz Verlag, 2007), 43.

Select Bibliography

Primary sources

Marsilius of Padua, *Defensor Pacis*, edited by R. Scholtz. Hannover: Hahn, 1932–3.

Marsilius of Padua. *Defensor pacis*. Translation and introduction by Alan Gewirth. Toronto: University of Toronto Press, 1980.

Marsilius of Padua. *The Defender of the Peace*, edited by Annabel Brett. Cambridge: Cambridge University Press, 2005.

Secondary sources

Garnett, G., *Marsilius of Padua and "the truth of history."* Oxford: Oxford University Press, 2006.

Lee, H.Y., *Political Representation in the Later Middle Ages: Marsilius in Context.* New York: Peter Lang, 2008.

Nederman, C.I., *Community and Consent: The Secular Political Theory of Marsiglio of Padua's* Defensor pacis. Lanham, MD: Rowman and Littlefield, 1995.

Riaño, G.M., ed., *The World of Marsilius of Padua.* Turnhout: Brepols, 2006.

2.10

Predestination, God's Foreknowledge and Future Contingents (before 1324 CE)

William of Ockham (c. 1285–1347 CE)

The author's life and work

William of Ockham was born in the English village of that name (near Guildford, Surrey) sometime around 1287. About 1300 he entered the Franciscan order, where he received his basic philosophical education. He was ordained a subdeacon in 1306, but his subsequent movements are obscure. He may have gone to Paris in about 1310, but he was certainly lecturing on Peter Lombard's *Sentences* in Oxford in 1317–1319, and likely followed that with a series of lectures on the Bible.

From 1321 to 1324 he taught in a Franciscan school, probably in London but perhaps in Oxford: this was an opportunity that allowed him to produce a number of important books. At this time, he wrote commentaries on Aristotle and the first five of his seven collections of disputations known as the *Quodlibeta septem*. He also wrote a lengthy textbook on logic, and possibly began work on his subsequent treatises on the Eucharist. It was during these years that he developed his view that only substances and their qualities were universal concepts, and not accidents like quantity, relation, time, or place. The implications of this radical view for eucharistic doctrine

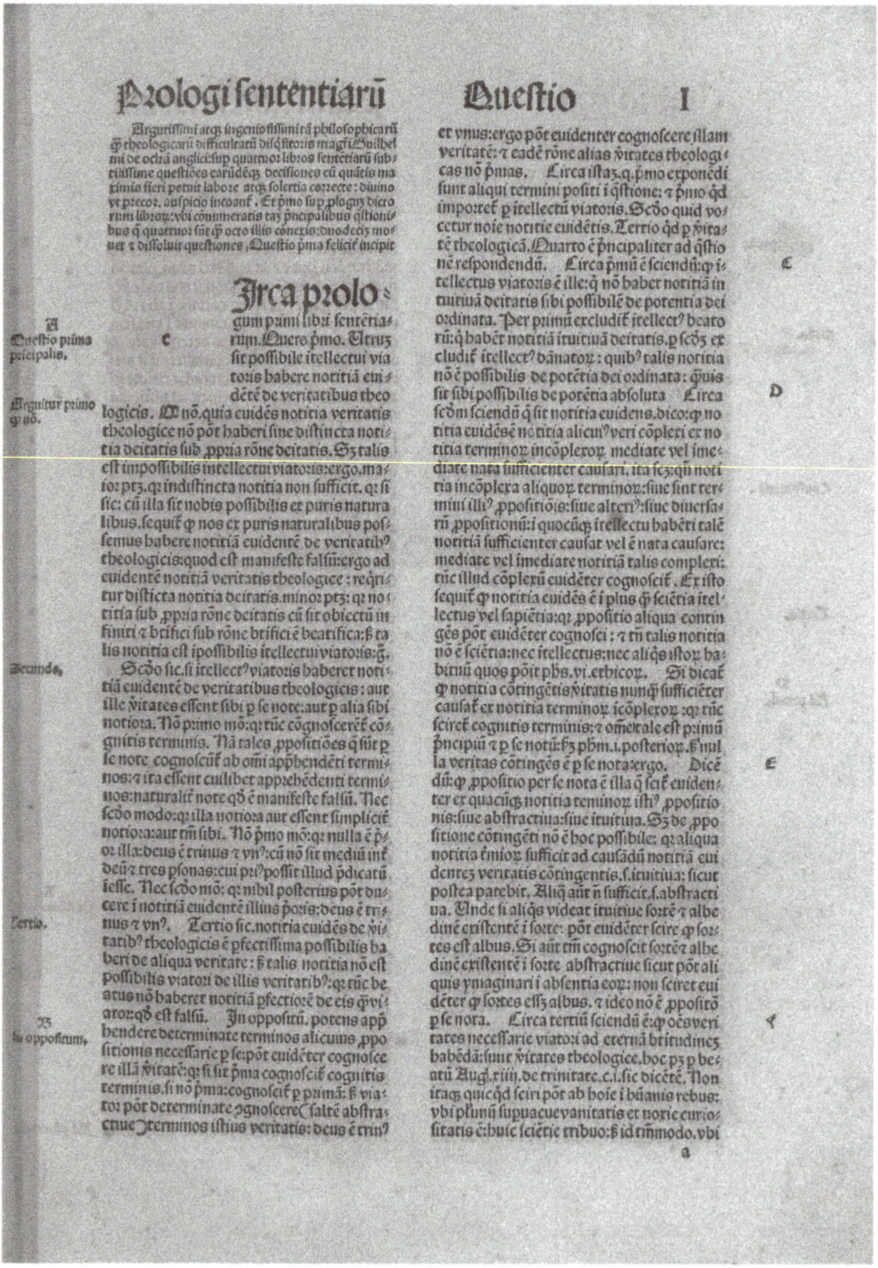
Prologi sententiarũ Questio I

Figure 2.10 William of Ockham

were soon noticed, and Ockham was summoned to a provincial chapter of the Franciscan order sometime in 1323 in order to explain his views.

Ockham was clearly suspected of heresy, because in 1324 he was called to Avignon to answer questions about his lectures on the *Sentences*. The investigation was conducted by John Lutterell, a former chancellor of Oxford, who may have developed an animosity towards Ockham from their time in the university together. Whatever the case, the commission of inquiry was unable to convict Ockham and he would have been cleared had he not taken the step, along with several of his brother Franciscans, of accusing the pope of heresy because of his views on the poverty of Christ.

This was the provocation the pope needed to condemn him, and in 1328 Ockham fled with his companions to the court of Ludwig of Bavaria, where he joined Marsilius of Padua and others who opposed the papacy. He remained there until his death on April 10, 1347. William's exile transformed him from a philosophical theologian into a political activist, and the last two decades of his life saw the production of a large number of works upholding the authority of the secular state and denouncing the pretensions of the papacy. Though he was closely associated with Marsilius of Padua during this period, William was more conservative in the positions he took and continued to hold the papacy in reverence, despite the aberrations of John XXII.

As a theologian, William believed that philosophy was the handmaid of theology and could be used to resolve a number of difficult theological problems. His views were similar to those of John Duns Scotus (1265–1308), but he refused to regard abstract concepts as substances in the way that Scotus had done. His main achievement was to combine five basic principles in a new synthesis that became the charter of what is now called "nominalism" and eventually displaced the earlier ("realist") philosophy that had dominated the universities up to his time. These principles may be listed as follows:

1 Only God is transcendent (absolute) and necessary; everything else is contingent (relative) and essentially unnecessary.

2 God's power must be distinguished between *potentia absoluta*, or the capacity to do whatever he wishes, and *potentia ordinata*, or the power revealed in his will and decrees. The former is necessary but the latter is not and depends on God's decisions. The order one sees in creation is the result of his promise to maintain it; it is not inherent in the creation itself.

3 The laws of nature and grace are contingent on God's will. Natural forces operate as he chooses and not by some inner power of their

own. Similarly, the sacraments are efficacious because he wills them to be, not because of any virtue they possess in themselves.

4 The fundamental realities of the external world are substances and their qualities. Given that the world is composed of individual things, one must explain how they are related to each other and why they can be classified into species and universals.

5 The simplest explanation of things is the best one. The truth may be more complicated, but that has to be demonstrated and not assumed. It is this principle that has come to be called "Ockham's razor."

Ockham's influence on nominalism is generally recognized, although it took time for his ideas to be widely accepted. On the eve of the Reformation, the great minds of the time were mostly Ockhamists, and they influenced men like Martin Luther, even though Luther was critical of many of Ockham's views.[1] Interest in him subsequently declined, but it has revived in the past generation when his importance for modern linguistic theory and semiotics has been acknowledged.

Predestination, God's foreknowledge, and future contingents

William of Ockham's treatise on predestination is very short, but it is densely packed and translators are forced to supply a good deal of connecting phraseology in order for the reader to make sense of it. Even then, it is far from easy going and every word has to be pondered carefully.

Predestination is a doctrine found in the New Testament, but it was first developed by Augustine (354–430) as part of his campaign against the heretic Pelagius, who believed that human beings had the free will to co-operate with God in achieving their own salvation. After that, it entered the mainstream of Christian doctrine, at least in the Western Church, though it was never uncontroversial. Christians could hardly deny that a sovereign God must be in control of events, and so everything that happens can only happen according to his will, either because he has actively caused it himself or because he has allowed some inferior power to cause it instead.

For Christians there are two underlying difficulties with the doctrine of predestination. The first is the existence of free will. God has made spiritual creatures, both angels and human beings, with the ability to make choices. The most serious of these is the ability to disobey God and create what is commonly called "evil." The second difficulty with predestination follows on from the first, because God tolerates the existence of evil, but he has not caused it and is not responsible for it. To what extent can we say that God willed its existence? Does he control it, and if so, why does he not simply do away with it?

Theologians have argued these matters for centuries, and some have been tempted to deny predestination because it appears to negate the reality of human freedom. Unfortunately, they can only do this at the cost of denying God's sovereignty, which effectively means that he cannot be relied on to save us. Of course, most anti-predestinarian theologians deny that. Yet the question lingers: if human beings are free to decide whether to be saved or not, what power does God have? Am I free to choose some aspects of salvation that suit me, or do I have to take the whole package? In the end, the idea of predestination often wins out, partly because it is more consistent with classic conceptions of the being and majesty of God and partly because it is the only way one might be sure that our salvation is complete and irrevocable.

William of Ockham knew all this, but had to deal with the problem because of the way it impinged on the growing acceptance of Aristotelian philosophy as the basis for what is now called the natural sciences. Aristotle believed in determinism. According to him, everything that happens must take place and there is nothing we can do to stop or to change it. The human will is essentially an illusion, because we have to do whatever we actually do. Ockham rejected that conclusion, and so his treatise is basically a defense of the Christian doctrine of predestination that establishes that it is not deterministic but allows for genuine freedom of choice on the part of human beings.

As far as the past is concerned, the argument over predestination is essentially irrelevant, in Ockham's view. What has already happened can be assumed to be necessary, not in the sense that it could never have been otherwise but in the sense that it is now an established fact and cannot be changed. For example, when Jesus went to his death in Jerusalem, he told Peter that Peter would deny him three times. As long as that was a prediction, it could have been altered. Jesus might have added something like: "If you accompany me to Jerusalem, you will deny me three times," allowing for the possibility that Peter might not go with him to the city. In that case, he would not have denied Jesus because the opportunity to do so would not have arisen.

Of course, Peter did go with Jesus and he did deny him three times (e.g., John 18:15–27), so there is no point arguing now about what might have happened had he not done so. The potential for any alternative course of action no longer exists and so the question of predestination and Peter's free will is now irrelevant. But what if someone were to say to me that I shall deny Christ tomorrow? Talking about the future and the question of free will suddenly becomes very pertinent indeed. If I am a follower of Jesus as Peter was, do I have the power to make the prediction false? God told Jonah that he would destroy Nineveh (see Jonah 3:4), but in the end he spared the city because its people repented. Did the Ninevites change God's will or was that what he secretly intended all along (as Jonah suspected)?

The possibility that some other factor may intervene to prevent the realization of a particular plan of action is called "contingency." Even today, we may make plans to have a picnic in the park next Saturday but have a plan B up our sleeves in case it rains—this is known as "contingency planning" and every sensible person does it all the time. But how does God see this? Presumably he must know whether it will rain or not—because he controls the weather—but he is not telling us. This is his foreknowledge, which he must have because he dwells outside time and space and so has no concept of the "future" in the way that creatures have.

Humans, on the other hand, are free to make alternative plans or not, knowing that if they fail to do so they will have to suffer the consequences if the gamble does not pay off. If people choose not to plan ahead, they are taking a risk, but God may have intended this in order to teach them a lesson. If so, then his foreknowledge is also predestination. People do not know it, but afterwards they may look back and recognize what has happened—they took a risk, lost out, and know better for next time, so that they can say that all things work together for good for those who love God, even when the things concerned involve suffering (cf. Rom 8:28).

This is where Ockham comes in. He asks five questions which help him resolve the issue. After the first question he comes up with nine assumptions that guide him as he works his way through the final four.

1. Is it possible to lose salvation?

Can someone who is currently predestined to be saved lose his salvation by sinning? If it is impossible for him to lose it, whatever he does, there would be no point in having him make moral choices of any kind, since they would make no difference. But people do make moral choices, so the issue must be more complex than that. Let us suppose therefore that a predestined man can sin and lose his salvation. If he is still predestined to be saved, then he is predestined and reprobate at the same time. In this case, the present will be different from the past, but the future remains unclear. If he dies without repenting, one can say that he was never really predestined—he only thought he was, or other people somehow assumed it, but his death in a state of sin reveals that they were wrong.

Augustine would reject this line of argument, because to his mind a man is either predestined or reprobate by definition, and nothing can change that fact. If a predestined man falls away or a reprobate one professes faith, these things are illusory and change nothing. As long as one believes that predestination and foreknowledge are objective, eternal realities, says Ockham, they can never solve this dilemma and human free will must remain a delusion. At this point, Ockham pauses to consider some objections that might be raised to what he has just said.

First, it may be argued that someone who is in a state of charity is predestined because of that and that charity cannot be destroyed. Ockham replies that this is false because there is no reason to suppose that someone in a state of charity is necessarily predestined. Secondly, it may be objected that if something is true now it will always be true of the past. Therefore if a man is predestined now, it will always be true to say that he was predestined at a particular point in time, but since predestination is the gift of eternal life, what is true of it at any point in time must always be true of it. Ockham replies that predestination involves the future as well as the past and present and is therefore always contingent. It may be true if nothing occurs to change it, but we have no guarantee that nothing will.

Ockham goes on to deal with more objections that are based on the character of God. For example, the argument is made that if God is eternal, then predestination must also be eternal (and therefore unalterable), but Ockham argues that predestination is essentially a temporal concept and therefore subject to change in the future. It is subject to contingency, which is part of God's eternal decree on the subject. A man who is truly predestined will be predestined from eternity because he is predestined to live forever with God, who dwells in eternity. But if he sins and loses his salvation, he shows that he was never really predestined and the proposition to the effect that he is turns out to have been false all along.

With respect to prophecy in the Bible, Ockham says that all prophecies were made contingently and must be so understood, giving the story of Jonah as a classic example of how that works.

Ockham's assumptions

After going through these points, Ockham pauses to establish nine assumptions or presuppositions on this subject. They may be listed as follows:

1 Neither active predestination nor active reprobation is a real thing distinct from God and his relations.

2 All propositions relating to predestination and reprobation are contingent.

3 Some propositions refer to the present where they may be true, but this tells us nothing about the past or the future.

4 No proposition about the present that concerns predestination or reprobation has necessarily been true in the past.

5 God does not know contradictions, so statements about predestination that may or may not be true are not statements about what he knows.

6 We cannot say precisely how God knows future contingents, but he certainly does know them, albeit in a contingent way, so that different choices remain open.

7 God knows everything, whether it is true or not, so that what he knows cannot be equated with the truth.

8 Some propositions regarding predestination and reprobation are complex and must not be taken as simple statements of fact. For example, to say that the predestined cannot be damned is true, but it does not guarantee that any particular person is eternally predestined to begin with.

9 Cause and effect can apply to real things, but they can also apply to logical inferences, and this is the case in statements made about predestination and reprobation. It is this aspect that Ockham will go on to discuss in greater detail and which forms the substance of his work.

2. Does God know everything that will come to pass?

The question Ockham discusses is whether, in the case of future contingents, God has a predetermined knowledge that one part of an apparent contradiction is necessarily and immutably true. First he rehearses the arguments as follows:

1 Neither truth nor falsehood is predetermined in future contingents, so God does not know for sure what will happen.

2 If it were, our discussions about what might happen would be pointless.

3 If it were, God would not be all-powerful because he would not be able to change it.

4 If something is not predetermined God cannot really know it.

Next, he goes on to answer them, point by point, as follows:

1 Assumptions 5 and 6 (above), taken together, answer this adequately.

2 What God knows he knows contingently, so our discussions have their validity.

3 God is not bound by determinism, so this argument is not valid.

4 The future is contingent and predetermined in that context, and God knows this.

Ockham moves on to argue that God has certain and infallible knowledge, and that he is not deceived if things do not work out according to the original plan. Once again, his argument hinges on the assertion that future knowledge is contingent, and that because God knows what all the contingencies are, he is ready for anything!

The third part of the argument claims that God does not have immutable knowledge of future contingents, and Ockham goes through all the various implications of this, refuting each one along the same lines. The argument that God must be able to know more than he actually does, because although contingencies can work out in different ways they will not in fact do so, is refuted by Ockham on the grounds that God knows what is true, not what is false, and so the argument is not valid. Similarly, God's knowledge cannot increase or decrease because what is true is always true. Fundamentally, Ockham is arguing that God's perspective on things is different from ours, so that what humans see as a series of contingencies he sees as a pattern of truth that does not change.

To the argument that God must have necessary knowledge about future contingents, Ockham again replies that the word "necessary" does not apply to God, who is above necessity and free from it. As he puts it: "The divine essence itself is one single necessary and immutable cognition of all things, complexes as well as non-complexes, necessary and contingent."[2] The argument that everything that is possible is mutable means that everything that is immutable must be necessary is not valid when applied to God, who is immutable but above and beyond necessity. In brief, the arguments used to compromise or deny God's infinite knowledge are flawed in their premises and therefore also in their conclusions.

3. Is the will an independent agent?

This question concerns external acts of the will, both of God and of man. If the will does something, can it do the opposite at the same time? Can it turn around and do the opposite later on, or cancel out what it has already done?

In answering this, Ockham refers back to Duns Scotus, who argued that in the case of the human (created) will, it is quite possible to do one thing and think the opposite at the same time, so that the will retains the capacity for contradicting itself. Ockham dissents from this opinion, because he believes that although a created will can reverse itself, it can only do so in the sequence of time because one act must follow another. In God, where there is no time, such a thing is inconceivable, but again, Ockham says that God acts contingently, so his will may appear to change from the standpoint of the outside observer, but in fact it does not do so.

4. Is predestination inherent in nature or willed by God?

This question asks whether there is some innate cause in the predestined and in the reprobate which determines their fate. Ockham denies this and uses baptism as an example, because in baptism a child receives divine merit without having done anything to deserve it. On the other hand, if by "cause" we mean the consequence of a particular action, then it is possible to say that, logically speaking, sin will lead to reprobation and perseverance in faith will lead to predestination. But this is a sequence of logic, not of fact, because everyone is born reprobate without having done anything to deserve it, and God saves people by grace, not by their works.

5. Is change possible?

This question asks whether it is possible for the statement "Peter is predestined" to be succeeded by the statement "Peter is reprobate," both being equally true at the time they were uttered.

Ockham says that this is not possible, because if Peter is predestined he is eternally predestined and that is not subject to change over time. The difficulty is that one cannot know for sure that it is true at any particular point in time, so that if Peter sins and loses his salvation, the truth is that he was never saved in the first place and was always reprobate. If people make assertions about what is unknowable, then it is only to be expected that they may be falsified. As before, Ockham concentrates on showing that the question is faulty to begin with, and he ends by saying that the entire difficulty with predestination is that it starts with the wrong assumptions and therefore comes to the wrong conclusions.

Conclusion

Ockham's preoccupation with predestination and its implications led him to develop the idea to a degree previously unknown. He detached it from the saving grace of God and applied it to the general workings of the universe, a shift in perspective that inevitably led him to equate it with determinism. But, as Ockham shows, our knowledge is limited and faulty, so that even if determinism is true, we cannot know what it is. This line of reasoning had a powerful impact on the Protestant Reformers.[3] Luther claimed that he belonged to "Ockham's school," though what he meant by that is unclear. Calvin and his followers became famous for the weight they put on predestination, and the many controversies that have ensued within the Protestant world have largely been due to the confusion of that doctrine with determinism in line with the speculations of Ockham. Even though he has seldom been mentioned by name, William of Ockham has dominated Protestant theological thought for centuries, and the questions he raised remain fundamental to modern debates on this subject.[4]

Notes

1. Cf. R.P. Desharnais, *The History of the Distinction between God's Absolute and Ordained Power and Its Influence on Martin Luther* (Ph.D. diss., Catholic University of America, 1966); and more generally, Heiko Oberman, "*Via Antiqua* and *Via Moderna*: Late Medieval Prolegomena to Early Reformation Thought," *Journal of the History of Ideas* 48 (1987): 23–40.
2. Question 2, article 4, part 1, p. 67 (in the translation by Adams and Kretzmann).
3. See Heiko O. Oberman, *The Harvest of Medieval Theology: Gabriel Biel and Late Medieval Nominalism*, 3rd ed. (Durham, NC: Labyrinth Press, 1983).
4. See Steven Ozment, *The Age of Reform, 1250–1550: An Intellectual and Religious History of Late Medieval and Reformation Europe* (New Haven: Yale University Press, 1980), esp. 55–63; Alister McGrath, *The Intellectual Origins of the European Reformation*, 2nd ed. (Oxford: Blackwell, 2004), 67–115.

Select Bibliography

Primary sources

William of Ockham. *Opera philosophica et theologica II: Tractatus de praedestinatione et de praescientia Dei et de futuris contingentibus.* New York: Franciscan Institute Publications, 1970.

William of Ockham. *Predestination, God's foreknowledge, and future contingents*, translated by M.M. Adams and N. Kretzmann. 2nd ed. Indianapolis, IN: Hackett, 1983.

Secondary sources

Adams, Marilyn McCord. *William of Ockham.* Vol. II. Notre Dame, IN: University of Notre Dame Press, 1987.

Chang, S.C. *William of Ockham's View on Human Capability.* Frankfurt am Main: Peter Lang, 2010.

Courtenay, W.J. *Ockham and Ockhamism: Studies in the Dissemination and Impact of his Thought.* Leiden: Brill, 2008.

Klocker, H. *William of Ockham and the Divine Freedom.* Milwaukee, WI: Marquette University Press, 1992.

Maurer, A.A. *The Philosophy of William of Ockham in the Light of his Principles.* Toronto: Pontifical Institute of Mediaeval Studies, 1999.

Spade, P.V. *The Cambridge Companion to Ockham.* Cambridge: Cambridge University Press, 1999.

2.11

On the Truth of Holy Scripture[1] (1377–1378)
John Wycliffe (c. 1328–1384)

The author's life and work

John Wycliffe (or Wyclif) was probably born at Wycliffe in North Yorkshire sometime in or shortly before 1328. He was almost certainly ordained in 1351, when he must have been at least twenty-three years old. By that time he was in Oxford, where he was connected with Merton College for at least some of the time and was master of Balliol by the end of 1360. For the next twenty years, he alternated between periods of residence at Oxford and the care of the three parishes that he was appointed to—Fillingham (1361–1368), Ludgershall (1368–1374), and Lutterworth (1374–1384).

At some point in the early 1370s Wycliffe entered the king's service, and in 1374 he went on a mission to Bruges to discuss clerical taxation with papal officials there. In September 1376 John of Gaunt, the king's brother, summoned him to appear before the king's council, apparently because he saw Wycliffe as an ally in his struggles against the church. On February 19, 1377, Wycliffe was called before the archbishop of Canterbury and charged with seditious preaching. Gaunt accompanied him to his trial, but a public riot ensued and it had to be abandoned. It seems that his offenses were politically motivated and had mainly to do with his denial of papal privileges and ecclesiastical immunities.

On May 22, 1377, Wycliffe's views were condemned by Pope Gregory XI, who ordered a full investigation of his teaching. The condemnation was based entirely on Wycliffe's book *De civili dominio* (*The civil power*), but by the time it reached England, the king had died and was succeeded by his grandson Richard II, under a regency in which John of Gaunt played a prominent part. An attempt to have him censured by the University of Oxford failed, but he was forced to appear in London to defend himself early in 1378. Once again, the investigation was disrupted by protesting Londoners and nothing came of it.

In the years that followed, the political situation deteriorated to the point that in 1381 the peasants rose in revolt, sacking Gaunt's palace and killing the archbishop of Canterbury. Wycliffe discussed it in his book on blasphemy (*De blasphemia*), but although it is clear that he sympathized with the rebels, he does not seem to have been involved with them. He had already been condemned at Oxford in May 1381, and John of Gaunt had ordered him to be silent, which may have affected Wycliffe's reaction to the peasants a month later. In any case, he withdrew to Lutterworth sometime before the end of 1381 and died there on December 31, 1384.

After the peasants' revolt, the new archbishop of Canterbury determined to take action against Wycliffe, which he did by condemning twenty-four propositions supposedly taken from his works: ten as heretical and fourteen as erroneous. These propositions were vigorously condemned throughout England, but it is unclear how many of them were actually held by Wycliffe and he himself was never censured by name. Only after his death was a list of 267 articles, extracted from his writings, formally condemned by the council of Constance (May 4, 1415). Later still, his body was exhumed and burnt in a crackdown on his disciples and their preaching (1428).

Wycliffe is generally regarded as the founder of the so-called Lollard movement, whose adherents preached in the vernacular and translated the Bible into English. He had a reputation as a translator himself, but it is now thought that he played no part in producing either of the two "Wycliffite" versions of the Bible that appeared in 1384 and 1388 respectively.[2] Nevertheless, there is no doubt that he had enormous influence on the church, both in England and on the continent. The Lollards survived until the Reformation, though in a greatly weakened state, and Wycliffe was the recognized inspiration for the Bohemian reformer Jan Hus, who in turn influenced Martin Luther. The Bohemian connection is particularly significant, and many of Wycliffe's works only survive in manuscripts copied by his followers there.

Wycliffe's early writings were mostly philosophical, following the then dominant Aristotelian school of thought. Later he turned to theology, writing on the creation of man and on the Incarnation of Christ. He also composed a gloss on the entire Bible, though it was not original and only parts of it now survive. He developed a considerable interest in law, which can be seen in his *Summa theologiae*, a work in twelve books that discusses divine law as well as human lordship before and after the fall. The seventh book is a treatise on the church and is followed by others on the power of the king and of the pope. Towards the end of *Summa theologiae* are books on simony, apostasy (in which he expounds his eucharistic doctrine), and blasphemy. His work on the truth of Holy Scripture is the sixth book of his *Summa*, which seems to have been put together from smaller tracts and cannot have been completed before 1378.

Unlike William of Ockham, Wycliffe was a "realist" in philosophical matters, and therefore a conservative in the climate of his time. He was a strong believer in predestination and in the invisible church, to which the visible institution on earth bears only partial resemblance. Maintaining that Scripture alone is the source of the church's law, Wycliffe's position has earned him the epithet of having been the "morning star" of the Protestant Reformation, though that is an exaggeration. More significant in his own time were his reservations about transubstantiation, which he found philosophically incoherent. While he never went to the point of denying it completely, many of his followers did and he became posthumously associated with their views.

The Truth of Holy Scripture

John Wycliffe's important treatise on the truth of Holy Scripture lies at the heart of his theological concerns and was probably the most influential of his writings at the time of the Reformation. It was originally in three parts, but the recent English translation divides it into four, and that is the order followed in this analysis. There are thirty-two chapters in all, and since these are numbered consecutively throughout the work, it is easy to see how the Latin text differs from the translation:

Parts of the text	Translation	Latin
Part One: The Truth of Scripture	1–8	1–15
Part Two: The Authority of Scripture	9–15	
Part Three: The Divine Origin of Scripture	16–19	16–24
Part Four: Scripture as the Law of Christendom	20–32	25–32

It should be said that the translation is an abridgement of the original, but nothing essential has been left out and it can be used with confidence, although the translator's separation of the first eight chapters from the next seven may lead the unwary reader to forget that for Wycliffe and his contemporaries, the truth and the authority of the Scriptures were one and the same thing.

1. The Truth of Scripture

Wycliffe begins his dissertation with a clear statement of the importance of Scripture as follows: "Scripture is the foundation of every Catholic opinion, and within it resides the very salvation of the faithful. Moreover, it is the exemplar and mirror designed to examine and extinguish every sort of error or heretical evil. Surely even a small error in this principle could bring about the death of the Church."[3] He accepts that this view is not universally shared and goes on to deal with some of the major objections to it. The first of these is that the Bible uses obscure metaphorical language, which Augustine warned his readers not to imitate. Wycliffe accepts this as a matter of fact, but goes on to say that its forms of speech are appropriate to the subject matter and should be interpreted accordingly. Providing several examples, he concludes with the assertion that the writings of the Greek philosophers ought to be corrected by Scripture and not the other way round.

From there he goes on to clarify the matter even further, by explaining how the Bible uses earthly things to describe heavenly realities. For example, Christ is compared to a lion, not because he is an animal but because many of the characteristics of lions are similar to attributes found in him. He also gives an extended discussion of the use of mystical senses, parables, and the like, and pleads for interpreters to figure out what the author's intended meaning was before commenting on it. Wycliffe states quite clearly that the Bible often uses figurative language drawn from nature, but that this should not be confused with making statements about natural science.

He distinguishes five levels of Scripture and four senses of interpretation. The first category appears to be original with him, but the second has been taken over from traditional usage.[4] The five levels are: (1) the Bible is the Book of Life; (2) truths are written in the Book of Life in a way that is intelligible to ordinary people; (3) these truths are to be believed in light of their proper form; (4) Scripture must be interpreted in a way that is congruent with the natural light given to the rational human soul; and (5) Scripture contains words and signs designed to lead us to a deeper understanding of its fundamental truths, as Augustine said. The four senses are the literal, the allegorical, the moral or tropological, and the anagogical: "The letter teaches the deeds, the allegory what you should believe, the moral what you should do, the anagogue that for which you ought to strive."[5]

Particular passages of Scripture ought to be read in the light of the whole, so as to avoid taking things out of context, and Wycliffe shows how misunderstandings of Scripture lead to heresy.

2. The authority of Scripture

In the second part of his dissertation, Wycliffe defends the authority of the Scriptures against those who would attack them and claim that they lead people into error. The interpreter must first learn to understand the inner logic of Scripture and read it in that light. God speaks in many different ways, but his self-revelation is never contradictory. Those who think that it is have misunderstood it and failed to interpret it properly.

Accurate interpretation requires understanding the authority of the Old Testament as the law of God given to his people and fulfilled by Jesus. Wycliffe is quite clear that God is the ultimate author of the text, even though he used human scribes to write it down. As he puts it: "It is pointless to quarrel over who was the scribe, or the composer of the manuscript, or the reed-pen of the Lord whom God infused with such knowledge. For it is sufficient to believe that God spoke the given knowledge through some of his saints in particular and through individuals generally."[6]

Thanks to the preference which Jerome, the translator of the Latin Vulgate Bible, had for the Hebrew text over the Greek one, Wycliffe is well aware of the problem posed by the so-called "apocryphal" books of the Old Testament. He deals with these by saying that everyone should agree on the canonicity of the Hebrew Bible and accept that Jerome's translation is an exact rendering of its meaning. That there are corruptions in the manuscripts available to him he does not deny, but he attributes them to the laziness and incompetence of the Church's copyists and not to any differences in the texts themselves. (It is interesting to note that Wycliffe saw no need to learn Hebrew or Greek.)

Wycliffe then deals with the objection that there are many things said in Scripture which are paralleled in secular writings. He does not deny this, but says that the presence of such material in the Bible gives it a sacred authority in that context that they otherwise do not have outside of Scripture. Similarly, he knows that there were many Gospels written besides the four that we now recognize, but trusts the decision of the early church, which knew how these books were written, as to which of them we should receive as canonical. Many of the apocryphal books, he admits, may be Holy Scripture because they have life-giving properties, but he sees no need to make them canonical since we have enough to go on already.

As many before him, Wycliffe locates the source of false readings in human pride. As he puts it:

> It appears that our own theologians walk into the lecture hall one day dressed as sheep with the purpose of commending the law of Scripture, and all of a sudden acquire the teeth of foxes, adding to this the tail of a viper. They say that Holy Scripture is for the most part impossible and even blasphemous when read according to the literal, verbal, and fleshly sense.[7]

Wycliffe did not feel bound to the literal sense to the exclusion of all other meanings, but he did not agree that the literal sense was unprofitable, because God would not have inspired a text that would tend to lead people astray.

Wycliffe goes on to defend the primacy of truth in interpretation. Every biblical statement must be read in that light, so that if, for example, we are going to say that Christ is a creature, we must add that this applies only to his human nature.[8] The fathers of the early church quite rightly refused to accept terminology that had no scriptural support unless and until it could be shown that its meaning was clear from the text. In that case, the demands of the truth made it possible and even necessary to accept them. Nowadays, says Wycliffe, theologians invent all kinds of technical terms that have no biblical basis and that cannot be shown to be in agreement with the meaning of the text. Because of that, adherence to the truth today means that we must reject them.

Knowing how and when it is appropriate to speak the truth is a skill, and Scripture is a pastoral tool that must be used with great care and discernment for the discipline and building up of the people of God. To those who accuse him of trying to subvert the Church by appealing over its head to Scripture, Wycliffe replies: "In publicly proclaiming the love and veneration I have for my Mother, the Roman Church, I am seeking to protect her privileges and her insignia, and taking care to see that they are thus secured."[9] In other words, the Church has nothing to fear from the proclamation of the truth.

In the last chapter of this part, Wycliffe returns to the authority of Scripture and argues that it is greater than any human authority because it comes straight from God. As he says: "Since the entirety of Holy Scripture is the word of the Lord, no testimony could possibly be better, more certain, or more efficacious. For if God, who cannot lie, has spoken something in his own Scripture, which is itself a mirror of his will, then it is true."[10] Wycliffe goes on to apply this to every part of the text, which he says is equally and fully authoritative in everything it says. But although it is all equally true, there are some truths that are more fundamental than others and we must recognize this in our teaching and application of the text.

Furthermore, the writings of the church fathers or the letters of the pope cannot be accorded an authority equal to that of Scripture. Rather, Christians must make sure that what they say is in accordance with the sacred text before they claim authority for it, because if it is not, it must be rejected.

3. The divine origin of Scripture

Wycliffe begins this section with a startling assertion that Christ uttered the grossest falsehoods knowing that people would deliberately misunderstand him. This is why he called himself the good shepherd, the door, the Alpha and the Omega, and the true vine—none of which is literally true. It seems obvious, therefore, that he must be refuted and his law condemned as not only wrong but blasphemous, because he claimed that it came from God. Wycliffe is saying this in order to shock his hearers into considering what the nature of truth is. To speak metaphorically is not the same thing as lying, and the faithful interpreter of Scripture must not fall into the trap of thinking that it is. God's mind is greater than ours and we must rise to meet it, not try to drag him down to the limitations of our own foolish literalism.

He pursues this theme by distinguishing between what he calls "sacred subtleties" and blatant lies. It is here that he applies the four senses of interpretation that he mentioned near the beginning of the work, showing how each of them has its place in interpreting the text but that none of them is sufficient by itself to provide a satisfactory general hermeneutic. Wycliffe points out that there are different ways of expressing truth. He then goes on to a detailed examination of the Old Testament prophets and their use of signs to indicate what God is saying to his people.

4. Scripture as the law of Christendom

The fourth and longest part of the dissertation is at once the most practical and the most political. Wycliffe appeals to the law of Christ, the teaching of the Gospel, as the basis for the Christian Church and tells his readers that they should love it in the same way that they love the one who gave it. As Christ is the prince of peace, so his teachings are the way of peace and should be followed if peace is what they really desire. In the Old Testament, the Law of Moses was mixed with human traditions and became a burden to the people whom Jesus had redeemed to new life. Later on, Muhammad weakened the Christian world by introducing a system of law that runs contrary to the gospel, and now the same error has been committed by the leaders of the Church. If they do not recognize this and take steps to cleanse the Church of these accretions, they shall fall under their weight, just as the Jews of old, and lose the message that Christ came to bring.

Rather, Wycliffe explains, our first duty must be to foster the preaching of God's Word, because if it is not preached it will not be heard, and if it is not heard it will not be obeyed. Every Christian has a duty to do this and to seek to win others for Christ, but the responsibility falls most heavily on the priesthood because it has been appointed and set aside for that purpose. Even the sacraments cannot be understood without the preaching of the Word, which they confirm and illustrate, and the abuses seen in the Church are often due to the neglect of this essential task.

Wycliffe takes two chapters to outline the Bible's rules governing the ministry of the clergy. The Scriptures tell priests how they ought to live and give them clear guidance as to what they ought to teach. In Wycliffe's view, it is the duty of a pastor to preach everything contained in the Bible, including such truths as the threats of eternal damnation for those who reject his message. There was a certain anti-intellectual strain in the church and not everyone thought that it was necessary for a priest to be a theologian as well, but Wycliffe had no time for that argument. In his words: "Every Christian must be a theologian, as I have demonstrated elsewhere. For it is essential that every Christian learn the faith of the Church, either through infused knowledge, or along with this, knowledge acquired from human teachers. Otherwise, he would not be a person of faith, and faith is the highest theology of all."[11]

Laymen, who are persons of faith, then, are allowed to pass judgment on the clergy, who are not above the law in temporal matters. They can seize church property if necessary, not least because Christ commanded his followers to be poor and to forsake the riches of this world. On the other hand, they also have a duty to protect the church, as Scripture indicates.

In his consideration of the Mosaic law, which he divides into ceremonial and moral elements, he states that the ceremonial has been abolished in

Christ but the moral remains as valid as ever, and indeed has been reinforced by the coming of Christ. With this distinction in mind, the principles of the Old Testament law ought to be applied in the Church. Wycliffe argues that rites like circumcision have been abolished but that moral principles like the prohibition of murder, adultery, and theft have not. Sometimes the law can be read in a mystical sense, drawing out a spiritual application from what appears on the surface to be a physical command or prohibition. What believers have to remember is that Christ is the fulfillment of the law and they must therefore interpret whatever it says in the light of that.

Finally, Wycliffe goes on to talk about heresy, which is particularly interesting considering the accusations that were being made against him at the time he was writing these words. Wycliffe's definition of heresy is simple—whatever goes against Holy Scripture is false, and if it is taught in the Church, that teaching is heretical. Although he does not explicitly say so, the subversive character of this assertion is clear. Wycliffe was being accused of heresy, not because what he was saying was unscriptural but because it went against the teachings of the institutional Church. Wycliffe's claim was that those teachings could not be found in Scripture, and so the implication must be that they and those who propagate them are heretical, and he is not. With that, the dissertation comes to an end.

Conclusion

Wycliffe's historical reputation has been controversial and is marked by confessional bias, with Protestants claiming him as their own and Catholics refuting that claim. In the sixteenth century he was admired by the Reformers but not read in any depth, and interest in his work remained low until the nineteenth century. Then, partly in reaction to the growth of Anglo-Catholicism, a number of scholars and devotees recovered his writings and published them, often for the first time. After that, interest subsided once more, but now it appears to be reviving again, though there is still no satisfactory edition of his works, some of which remain untranslated to this day.

In the nineteenth century, Wycliffe was hailed as "the morning star of the Reformation" and his (undeserved) reputation as a Bible translator has been perpetuated by modern evangelical missionaries who treat him as a kind of patron saint. Scholars have not found it difficult to refute such exaggerated claims for him, but in spite of everything, he did make a significant contribution to what was to become standard Protestant orthodoxy. He died protesting the doctrine of transubstantiation, but more importantly, he promoted the principle of *sola Scriptura* (Scripture alone) as the only true source of Christian doctrine. His biblicism makes him an authentic forerunner of later Protestantism, and it is significant that when the Reformation came his surviving followers (the Lollards in England and the Hussites in Bohemia) readily identified themselves with it.

Notes

1. Translated from *De veritate Sacrae Scripturae*.
2. For more on this story, see Alister McGrath, *In the Beginning: The Story of the King James Bible and How It Changed a Nation, a Language, and a Culture* (New York: Anchor Books, 2001), 19–23.
3. Chapter 1, 1–2, p. 41 (in the Levy translation, from which all quotations are taken).
4. See Henri de Lubac, *Medieval Exegesis: The Four Senses of Scripture*, 3 vols. (Grand Rapids: Eerdmans, 1998–2009).
5. Chapter 6, 119, p. 104.
6. Chapter 10, 218, p. 151.
7. Chapter 12, 272, p. 173.
8. This was the Arian reading of Prov. 8:22.
9. Chapter 14, 368, p. 196.
10. Chapter 15, 377, p. 200.
11. Chapter 24, 233–34, p. 300.

Select Bibliography

Primary sources

Wyclif, John. *De veritate Sacrae Scripturae*, edited by R. Buddensieg. London: Wyclif Society, 1905.

Wyclif, John. *On the truth of Holy Scripture*, translated by I.C. Levy. Kalamazoo, MI: Medieval Institute Press, 2001.

Secondary sources

Cowell, R.H. *John Wyclif: Translator of the Bible and Reformer*. London: Charles H. Kelly, 1898.

Evans, G.R. *John Wyclif: Myth and Reality.* Oxford: Lion Hudson, 2005.

Kenny, A. *Wyclif.* Oxford: Oxford University Press, 1985.

Lahey, S.E. *John Wyclif.* Oxford: Oxford University Press, 2009.

Levy, I.C. *Companion to John Wyclif: Late Medieval Theologian.* Leiden: Brill, 2006.

2.12

The Imitation of Christ[1] (c. 1427 CE)

Thomas à Kempis (c. 1380–1471 CE)

The author's life and work

Thomas Hemerken (or Hemerlein) was born at Kempen, in the lower Rhineland, around 1380. In 1392 he went to nearby Deventer to study, remaining there for seven years. During that time he came into contact with the Brethren of the Common Life, a new kind of semi-monastic order started by Gerhard Groote and known for its espousal of the so-called *devotio moderna,* or new devotion. Essentially, Groote wanted families to live together in community and practice the monastic virtues as best as they could. Celibacy was obviously replaced by chastity within marriage, but otherwise much of the monastic round of prayer and work was taken over and adapted for community use.

Thomas did not join the Brethren, but he remained a devoted follower of their principles and his work may fairly be regarded as having been inspired by their ideals and example. He wrote a biography of Groote and another of his colleague Florentius Radewijns, which shows how deeply attached to them he was.

On leaving Deventer in 1399, Thomas went to Zwolle, where his older brother John had become the prior of Mount St. Agnes monastery. He took his vows there as a monk in 1406, but he was not ordained as a priest until 1413. He became subprior of the monastery in 1429, where he spent the rest

Figure 2.11 Thomas à Kempis

of his life in contemplation, writing and copying manuscripts. Four copies of the Bible made by him survive, among much else. He died on July 25, 1471, and was buried in the church of St. Michael in Zwolle.

Though he wrote a number of short books on the subject of devotion to Christ, none has attained the fame or the popularity of *The Imitation of Christ*, which remains a spiritual classic and is still widely read for devotional purposes. We do not know exactly when it was written, but it seems to have been about 1427. Certainly we know that by 1450 over 250 manuscript copies had been made, which suggests that it had been in circulation for some time. It was printed for the first time in 1471, the year Thomas died. It consists of three books (or four if the section on Holy Communion in the third book is regarded as a separate section) and is quite repetitive in places. Some scholars have suggested that the parts were written by different people, or perhaps by Thomas at different times, and later pieced together, but lack of evidence makes it impossible to be certain about this.

Perhaps the most interesting thing about *The Imitation of Christ* is that it is probably more popular among Protestants than among Roman Catholics, though he has always appealed to both. It is undoubtedly the most widely-read medieval book and has been translated into any number of languages. Interestingly, despite its popularity, the book has not often been commented on or studied, and there has been relatively little scholarly research on Thomas as a person. He remains a shadowy figure, and the uneventfulness of his life makes it difficult to write a substantial biography. Nevertheless, his influence on generations of Christians has been profound and, despite the changes in theological emphasis that have occurred over the centuries, his little book has never gone out of fashion.

The Imitation of Christ

1. A personal relationship with Christ

At the heart of Thomas' theology is the conviction that we must imitate the life of Christ above everything else. Being a Christian is more about having the love of God in our hearts than it is about academic learning, because knowledge and ignorance are primarily spiritual phenomena. The study of theology can be just as worldly a pursuit as anything else, and if we do not model our lives after that of Christ, it almost certainly will be. Even the most highly educated people know relatively little, and the learning that we have ought to make us humble, not proud of our accomplishments. Great teachers appear from time to time and may have a considerable impact, but the love of Christ remains with us forever. For that reason, God does not concern himself with the extent of our knowledge but rather with the degree to which we apply it in our lives.

The Truth in Jesus Christ must reveal himself to us if we are to know him; he cannot be discovered by investigation, however thorough or well-meaning. To understand him, we must be reconciled to God, since only then will we have the spiritual depth we need in order to grasp who he is and what he means. Thomas did not speak in terms of a personal relationship with God in Christ, but that is what he was talking about. Today this has become a commonplace, but it is indicative of the state of late medieval theology that, although personal intimacy with Christ could certainly be advocated (as Thomas did), it was not so universally taken for granted that a book like his would be considered unremarkable. Thus, his book was memorable and continues to have a wide audience.

From Thomas' standpoint, the chief business of the Christian is to discern the difference between perfection and imperfection, and to do the best to eradicate the latter from our lives. He deplored the fact that people are often more prepared to solve the problems of the world than they are to get to grips with their own personal difficulties. Whereas today we might think that a concentration on things external to ourselves is preferable to any form of self-centeredness, for Thomas it was a way of avoiding the most important issues we have to face.

2. The love of God

At the heart of Thomas' perception of reality was the spirit of love. Whatever we do must be done in that spirit, otherwise it will be tainted with the desires of this world. The first and greatest object of our love is God himself. Pleasing him will be the first aim of the person who is full of love, and our attitude towards other people will be governed by the quality of our love for God. Putting up with other people is not easy because nobody is perfect. We all see what is wrong with others, but tend to forget that we also have our faults and that others may find us equally difficult. According to Thomas, this is why God tells us that we must bear one another's burdens and do what we can to support and edify them, not tear them down by our criticisms.

At the same time, Thomas was concerned not to become too involved with other people, because if we do, our faults will be all too apparent and we shall lose our respect for one another. It is better for us to reserve our most intimate thoughts for our relationship with God, who understands our true motives and is aware of everything we think, say, and do. When dealing with other people, we must first of all obey the authorities who have been set up over us, even when we think that we know better than they do. We all think that our opinions are better than those of others, but sometimes we have to let them go in order to maintain good relations. This is no bad thing, because in the final analysis we are called to put our trust in Jesus Christ, who will draw us closer to himself and share his mind with us, giving us an understanding of things that is greater than any human wisdom can attain.

3. The importance of wisdom

Wisdom, for Thomas, was both the goal of love and the means by which it is expressed. If we have an opportunity to express our opinions, we should take care to do so in a way that edifies others, so that the body of Christ can grow together to maturity. Wisdom is not subject to emotional whims but disciplines human feelings and keeps them under control. It follows from this that the pursuit of wisdom must be a major preoccupation of anyone who wants to exhibit the true love of God. It is obvious that living a good life in accordance with his will is an essential part of that, and Thomas insisted that the way to know what we should do must be found by reading Holy Scripture along with other godly literature. For him, it was not so much the author(s) as the content that was most important. He was not particularly interested in the veneration of the saints for their own sake, but was more concerned with the soundness of the message which they conveyed. Truth is the same regardless of who expresses it, and it is the truth that should undergird the mind and behavior of the Christian. This is especially important to remember when we read the Bible, which is God's Word written. It is all too easy to get caught up in the minutiae of obscure details and ignore the basic message, but we must learn to submit ourselves to that message so that we may grow in the knowledge and love of God.

The greatest dangers on the pathway towards wisdom, Thomas warned, were the ones posed by the temptations that assail us, and he devoted a good deal of space to dealing with this problem. It is common for people to try to flee temptation completely, but they only succeed in falling more deeply into it. Temptation comes from outside ourselves and we cannot prevent it, but we can (and must) learn to confront it and fight against it. The sooner we can recognize it and knock it on the head, the better. If we let it grow and develop, its power over us will increase and we shall be unable to escape from it. That said, individuals feel the power of temptation differently. Some people experience it more when they are young; for others, it increases with age. Perhaps most people live with it more or less constantly throughout their lives. God understands this and is able to deal with each one of us according to our own particular needs. Knowing this will prevent us from falling into despair when temptation comes. He knows how much we can endure and moderates the temptations that come to us so as to prepare us for the life of heaven towards which he is leading us.

4. The life of contemplation

Thomas lived in a world where it was officially believed that the supreme expression of the love of God was the monastic life, to which he himself was committed.[2] Thomas subscribed to that ideal, but he knew that it was not easy to live up to it in practice. The lives of the saints are full of reminders that they were constantly under spiritual attack, not least when they were deep in prayer and meditation. Monks live at a level of intensity that makes them more vulnerable in this respect than most other people, and they must always guard against the wiles of the devil. If we are engaged in a serious attempt to imitate Christ we must set aside time for prayer and be prepared to humble ourselves in the presence of God, seeking his help to overcome our weaknesses and lead us into a deeper communion with Christ.

In the second book, Thomas explains that humility must govern everything we do. When people upbraid us for our failings we ought to rejoice, because it points the way towards greater humility, and we cannot progress in the spiritual life until we recognize that we are the lowliest of all.

At the heart of Thomas' approach to self-discipline was his sense that death was an ever-imminent reality and human life was best lived preparing for it. The spiritual exercises and self-denial demanded of the monk were a foretaste of the ultimate abandonment of worldly things that death would bring. Nothing in this world can contribute to our eternal salvation, because we cannot take it with us. It is therefore necessary that we prioritize spiritual devotions whose fruits will carry over into the next life and justify us before God when we stand in his presence on the day of judgment.

5. The inner life of the soul

This is the main theme of the second book of *The Imitation of Christ* and it is significant because the soul is the seat of the mind, the will and the emotions. If we devote all these to God, then Christ will come and dwell in us. Indeed, Christ must be the only one we admit into our lives in this way, because only he can give us the healing and reconciliation with God that we need. Only in him can we rise above the cares and desires of this world and be fully at peace with God.

The way to achieve this condition is to be honest in our desires and intentions. We have to be set free from earthly passions in order to live the Christian life. Thomas uses the model of an iron cast into the fire. When put to the test, the iron loses its rust and burns with new life. In the same way, the person who turns to Christ will find that his old nature is stripped away and that he is born again as a new creation in Christ.

6. A good conscience

A person who seeks to imitate Christ must not trust his own judgment, but must examine himself and do all he can to suppress the sins of his own flesh. The essential characteristic of the truly spiritual man is a good conscience, which we can acquire if we love and fear God. If our love is pure, we shall be indifferent to both the approval and the criticism of others because we shall know that our hearts are right with God. Here we can detect echoes of what was to become one of the major themes of the Reformation, namely, the witness of a clear conscience in the presence of God.

Having Christ close to us and strengthening our conscience is the foundation of true happiness. Apart from intimacy with Christ, we are spiritually dry and unable to bear the kind of fruit that he demands of us. The person who loves Jesus and ignores his own desires is truly blessed; if he submits his own will to that of God, he will know what the friendship of Christ means. Obedience to his commands is the way in which a clear conscience is expressed and our relationship with him is maintained.

In the third book, Thomas takes 1 Corinthians 13 as the charter for the Christian life lived in love and humility. If we learn to be patient and accept that whatever happens to us will turn out in the end for our good, our consciences will remain clear and we shall never be distracted or disappointed in our love for God.

7. Carrying the cross

He will never abandon us, even if there are times when we will wonder whether he is still present and active in our lives. Even the greatest saints have been put through trials when they have felt abandoned by God. This is not because they have sinned but because God is testing them and teaching them to wait patiently for him to act. And for the same reason, we too will experience such times of spiritual dryness. God wants us to appreciate him and to long for him to come into our lives. We ought to be grateful when we are blessed and patient when we are not, because in whatever state we find ourselves, God will draw us nearer to himself and affirm us in and through our humility.

Times of trial are necessary in order to distinguish those who say they love God from those who really do. It is easy to be pious when things are going our way, but much harder when we are confronted with reversals and challenges. It is then that we must take up our cross, as Jesus said, and follow him. The cross is our salvation and our life. The cross protects us from our spiritual enemies and blesses us with the strength of purpose that will bring us to perfect holiness. If we are crucified with Christ we shall live, because by his life we shall be changed. Here Thomas echoes the teaching of St. Paul and takes us to the heart of the matter. It was because God loved the world that he sent his Son to die for us, and it was in love that the Son bore our sins on the cross. The least we can do is to humble ourselves before him and imitate his example. If we suffer with him, we shall also reign with him in glory, and Thomas goes so far as to say that unless we suffer, we shall not be worthy of that reward. His justification for that view is that if there were something better than suffering, God would have revealed it to us. In fact however, this is the way he has chosen and the pattern that he expects us to follow if we want to live with him in his kingdom.

8. The consolation of Christ's presence

In the third book of *The Imitation of Christ*, Thomas developed the theme of the spiritual consolation that the believer receives from God by hearing the voice of Christ speaking directly to him. He did not use the later language of what the Reformers called the "inner witness of the Holy Spirit," but that is what he was talking about.[3] As he understood it, there is no greater consolation for the believer than hearing the voice of Christ speaking directly to his soul, and that voice is the voice of the Spirit bearing witness with our spirit that we are children of God.

Thomas was aware that the Truth speaks to us in ways that go beyond words, but he also knew that the living voice of Christ was entirely consistent with the written word of Scripture. This consistency holds because the experience of the prophets and apostles was the same as ours, and they were given the task of recording their knowledge of God for our benefit. Because of this, we can memorize what they said and take it to heart. In doing this, we are arming ourselves for the fight against the evil spiritual forces that we are bound to encounter along our earthly journey to the kingdom of heaven.

9. Trust and obedience

The true child of God will always listen to the voice of Christ and obey his commands, whether he understands their purpose or not. This is where obedience merges with trust to form the essence of Christian discipleship. God's purposes are often unclear to us, and we have to believe that he knows what he is doing in our lives. If we cast our burdens on him and seek his consolation he will draw us closer to himself and will give us what we need when the time is right. If we are suffering, then we must accept that this is for our good, even when we cannot see what that good is. We cannot rely on our own strength, but must renounce it and trust in Christ's power instead. At the same time, we must count our blessings, which even in the hardest times are always very great. Worrying about trivial matters gets us nowhere, and it is only by concentrating on God's loving purposes that we shall find the peace of mind that we so desire.

Thomas warned his readers that they would face many problems in this life but that whatever happened, they must learn to call on God for assistance and deliverance. The pleasures and rewards of this life are of no value to those facing death, and the comfort that other people offer is weak and insufficient. Only God can meet our needs, and only when we are in eternity ourselves will we fully understand how he has provided for us. Eternal life is a blessing beyond compare, and when we enter into it everything we have been and done beforehand will pale into insignificance. The Christian knows this already, and his best defense against the temptations of this life is to recognize how trivial and unimportant they are. We are deserving of nothing but punishment, and God's consolation is the greatest gift we can ever receive.

Using the medieval language of nature and grace, Thomas explains how we are torn between the desires of this world and the rewards of the next, and he urges his readers to forsake the former and pursue the latter. If we put God first, everything else will follow from that, and we shall receive the promises that Christ has made to all those who faithfully follow him.

10. The sacrament of Holy Communion

The supreme manifestation of the love of God was the sacrament of Holy Communion, Thomas claimed, to which the last eighteen chapters of the third book of *The Imitation of Christ* are dedicated. As Thomas understood it, it was in the sacrament that believers received the body and blood of Christ. He was not especially concerned about the doctrine of transubstantiation, though he doubtless believed it, but rather with the impact that receiving the consecrated elements has on those who participate in the Lord's Supper. Unusually for a man of his time, he actually said that it was unnecessary to go into specific detail about the nature of the consecrated elements; what mattered was that we should approach and consume them in the right spirit. It is in Holy Communion, said Thomas, that God demonstrates the depth of his love and goodness towards us, and we should approach the sacred feast in a spirit of gratitude and thanksgiving. Thomas believed that Christians should communicate frequently in order to receive the promised blessing, though he also insisted that those who approached the Table must do so worthily.

Even more significantly, Thomas admonished those who were called to celebrate and administer Holy Communion that they too were expected to be worthy of their high calling. This was an increasingly important matter in the late medieval church, where the scandalous behavior of many priests was becoming a matter of public knowledge and gossip.

What strikes us most today is the strong emphasis that Thomas placed on the need for prospective communicants to prepare themselves adequately beforehand. This would also be a significant element of Reformation teaching, but it has declined in recent times, and Thomas' admonitions have become pertinent once more.[4]

In the end, what mattered most to Thomas was that Holy Communion was the ultimate demonstration of Christ's self-offering on behalf of his people, a reminder to us that if we are to imitate him as we ought, we too must offer ourselves for his service.

Conclusion

Thomas à Kempis is important because he is the best-known exponent of the spiritual life as this was understood in the generation before the Reformation, and generations of both Protestants and Roman Catholics have taken him to heart. His work reminds us that there was a deep spiritual renewal in progress when Martin Luther began to preach, and that it was because there was such a spiritual hunger that the Protestant message was so well received. But it also reminds us that the distance between Protestants and Catholics, which in later times would loom large, was initially not all that great. A devout person could find himself in either camp, according to political circumstances, and many did. Some went back and forth, some sat on the fence and others never really decided one way or the other. That this was possible is due in no small measure to the kind of devotional theology that Thomas represented. His was the pilgrim way of the ordinary believer seeking to get closer to God, and much of what he says can be found, not only in the Reformers but especially in the Puritans. Though he was seldom mentioned by name, his impact was enormous, and he remains the one medieval writer who is still widely read today.

Notes

1. Translated from *De imitatione Christi*.
2. On monasticism generally, see Greg Peters, *The Story of Monasticism* (Grand Rapids: Baker Academic, 2015). For the story of Christian spirituality in the monastic period, see David H. Farmer, "Saints and Mystics of the Medieval West: 11th to 16th Centuries," in *The Story of*

Christian Spirituality: Two Thousand Years, from East to West, ed. Gordon
Mursell (Minneapolis: Fortress Press, 2001), 89–124.

3. On the inner witness of the Spirit, see Bernard Ramm, *The Witness of the
    Spirit: An Essay on the Contemporary Relevance of the Internal Witness of
    the Holy Spirit* (Grand Rapids: Eerdmans, 1959).

4. For general background see Edward Foley, *From Age to Age: How
    Christians Have Celebrated the Eucharist*, rev. and exp. (Collegeville,
    Liturgical Press, 2008), ch. 6; or, for a more focused study, see Lee Palmer
    Wandel, *The Eucharist in the Reformation: Incarnation and Liturgy*
    (Cambridge: Cambridge University Press, 2005).

Select Bibliography

Primary sources

Thomas à Kempis. *De imitatione Christi*, edited by T. Lupo. Vatican City:
    Libreria Editirice Vaticana, 1982.

Thomas à Kempis. *The imitation of Christ*, translated by A. Croft and H. Bolton.
    Peabody, MA: Hendrickson, 2004.

Secondary sources

Becker, K.H. *From the Treasure-house of Scripture: An Analysis of Scriptural
    Sources in* De imitatione Christi. Turnhout: Brepols, 2002.

De Montmorency, J.E.G., *Thomas à Kempis: His Age and Book*. London:
    Methuen, 1906.

Fuller, Ross. *The Brotherhood of the Common Life and its Influence*. Albany, NY:
    State University of New York Press, 1995.

Preston, G.H., *Studies in Thomas à Kempis in the Light of Today*. London:
    Mowbray, 1912.

Part III

The Reformation Period

Introduction to the Reformation Period (1500–1600)

Hans Madueme

In 1517, according to tradition, Martin Luther affixed his ninety-five theses to a church door in Wittenberg. The iconic moment unleashed a series of events that would turn the world upside down. I write this introduction on the eve of 2017, five hundred years since the beginning of the Protestant Reformation. Half a millennium later its effects continue to reverberate across the globe; countless Protestant denominations and millions of Christians from all nations and ethnicities trace their roots back to this period of church history.

Luther himself moved in a different world. He was an Augustinian monk whose deepest assumptions were shaped by medieval and patristic concerns. Like many men and women of his day, his earlier training led him to believe that with God's help he could earn salvation by doing good works. But he was haunted by the knowledge that he would never measure up. God was holy—his sins would find him out. Deliverance came through Scripture when he discovered, based on his study of Galatians and (especially) Romans, that his own uneven attempts at righteousness would not make him acceptable before a holy God. Obeying the Law perfectly is a fool's errand. The truth that had eluded him was now a bright light shining; sinners are justified by God's grace *through faith apart from works* (he would later describe the experience as being "reborn," as if "going through open doors into paradise"). To those who believe the gospel, Luther finally concluded, God imputes the righteousness of Christ, an "alien" righteousness which is not their own, but received as a gift from God.

In the late medieval church, the common prescribed remedy for people weighed down by their sins was to confess to a priest, receive forgiveness, and perform a good deed (a "penance"). Doing penance was the condition of having your sins wiped clean. But there was a back door; you could bypass some or all of that penance by giving money to the church (an "indulgence"). The selling of indulgences became a lucrative practice for some greedy popes and their bishops. In Luther's mind, however, the entire system was not only corrupt, it reeked of "works-righteousness." He wrote the ninety-five theses as a blast against the selling of indulgences, not knowing his actions would open Pandora's box and bring down the full wrath of the papal authorities.

We forget too easily that Luther never intended to launch a new church or denomination. The very idea would have repelled him. He wanted to bring reform to the late medieval church and its many abuses. Even before Luther, others throughout Europe had been pleading for reform, men like John Wycliffe (d. 1384) and Jan Hus (d. 1415) who died for the sake of the gospel as they understood it, and movements like "Modern Devotion," where laypeople in the Netherlands—most famously, Thomas à Kempis (d. 1471)— urged each other to pursue lives of simple piety. Renaissance humanists were also part of the reform effort, speaking out against abuses in the church. They also stressed getting back to the original sources, retrieving the wisdom of classical ancient literature, including Holy Scripture in the original languages (Desiderius Erasmus published the first Greek New Testament in 1516). Much of Luther's agenda resonated with the humanists—even if his theology ended up too radical for most of them. These reform movements paved the way for Luther's message, as did the recent invention of the printing press, church taxation, and widespread corruption in ecclesiastical leadership—none of these factors made the Reformation inevitable, but they left a disillusioned laity primed to hear dissenting voices.

Much to the chagrin of the Catholic hierarchy, Luther would not stand down. Given one final chance to retract his views at the Diet of Worms (1521), he was unrepentant and sealed his fate. In the meantime, on the Catholic side, attempts were made to curb church abuses and thus outmaneuver Luther. Ignatius of Loyola (1491–1556), a former knight who had been wounded in battle, founded the militant Society of Jesus. Loyola and his fellow Jesuits worked aggressively both to reform the Catholic church and to root out any Protestant heretics. Pope Paul III called together the Council of Trent—a series of meetings in Trent, Italy (1545–1563)—which gave institutional power to what became the Catholic "Counter-Reformation." Far from resolving the crisis, however, these moves only widened the divide between Roman Catholic teaching and the early Protestant movement.

Luther persevered in defending justification by grace through faith, the priority of Scripture over tradition, and related doctrines. As long as the Reformation kept a united front, the break with Roman Catholicism was a price worth paying. Unhappily for Luther, however, it was not long before his own movement was threatened by the machinations of more reckless agitators. Sometimes known as the "Radical Reformation," these sectarian groups seemed to sprout like weeds all over Europe; they were restless souls emboldened by the spirit of reform, but impatient with the moderation of the Reformers.

Andreas Bodenstein von Karlstadt (c. 1480–1541), for instance, one of Luther's colleagues at the University of Wittenberg, appealed to the inner voice of the Holy Spirit over institutional authority. Thomas Müntzer (c. 1490–1525) raised the stakes with sectarian and violent rhetoric, preaching political revolt in the city of Mühlhausen, Germany; Müntzer and others were eventually executed in 1525 for sedition. That same year in Zurich, Conrad Grebel (c. 1500–1526) and a group of enthusiasts had rejected infant baptism as unbiblical and began rebaptizing each other—in defiance of the church authorities. Although these first "Anabaptists" were killed, often by intentional drowning, eccentric Anabaptist groups just kept multiplying. In 1527, Michael Sattler (c. 1490–1527) produced the *Schleitheim Confession* to reflect the beliefs of Anabaptists. Yet many were stamped out, sometimes horrifically, until Menno Simons (1496–1561), a former priest, founded peaceful Anabaptist communities—the "Mennonites"—in the Netherlands and in Northern Germany.

Unlike their radical counterparts, mainstream Reformers accepted the existing political structures. Once the Reformation was in full swing they relied on the protection of princes and magistrates (hence, the "magisterial" Reformers). In addition to the emerging "Lutherans," Martin Luther's writings influenced other Reformers longing for church renewal. Among them was Huldrych Zwingli (1484–1531), a Swiss pastor who was more radical than Luther; he swept aside practices like praying to the saints and enforced stripping down the liturgy and removing all images from worship. He soon became the leader of the Reformed wing of the Reformation. At a meeting in Marburg, Germany, October 1–3, 1529, Luther and Zwingli met to iron out their differences and unite the fledgling movement. However, this historic opportunity collapsed when the two men could not agree on the meaning of the Eucharist; thus the two traditions—Lutheran and Reformed—went their separate ways.

Many pastors joined Zwingli's Reformed tradition, leaders like Heinrich Bullinger (1504–1575), Martin Bucer (1491–1551), Johannes Oecolampadius (1482–1531), and John Knox (c. 1513–1572). But pride of place belongs to the Frenchman John Calvin (1509–1564)—Zwingli laid the foundation, Calvin built the castle. His theology of the Eucharist struck a balance between the insights of Luther and Zwingli. Even as a busy pastor, he wrote prolifically. Calvin is best known for his *Institutes of the Christian Religion*, a work that went through multiple editions and became an instant classic. Calvin's genius was his ability to fuse rhetorical power, uncanny rigor, and exegetical fidelity as he expounded key tenets of the Reformation. Under his leadership, the city of Geneva where he devoted most of his ministry became a rallying point for Protestant Reformers.

The British Isles would also catch the spirit of Reformation. Spurred on by his marital problems, King Henry VIII brought the Church of England to Protestantism and away from papal interference. The Anglican tradition held together elements from Lutheran, Reformed, and also Catholic theology. But much of it was Reformed in character, due in no small part to Thomas Cranmer (1489–1556). In 1549, when Cranmer was Archbishop of Canterbury, he crafted the *Book of Common Prayer* to function as the national liturgy. Some years later (1553), he produced a summary of Anglican doctrine, the *Forty-Two Articles* (the *Thirty-Nine Articles* of the Church of England draw extensively from Cranmer's work). Nonetheless, early Puritans complained about the lingering Catholicism; in their minds, the Anglican Church had not completed its reformation. By next century, persecuted and under duress, a number of these Puritans would flee to New England in search of the city upon a hill.

Doctrinal conflicts over the correct interpretation of holy writ left an ongoing subtext of bitter disputes and misunderstandings. The medieval church certainly enjoyed its own share of theological controversy, but with the fracturing of the church in the Reformation those problems loomed large. By the end of the sixteenth century, the Reformation was essentially over. The separate factions of the Protestant movement drew up confessional statements that would guide their different traditions. The first major Protestant confession was the Lutheran *Augsburg Confession* (1530), later supplemented by the *Formula of Concord* (1577); among the Reformed groups, the *Second Helvetic Confession* (1566) and the *Heidelberg Catechism* (1563) are two of the many statements that were commissioned. And virtually all these confessions were forged in the heat of religious conflict (conflict that would only continue into the next century).

Evidently the Reformation was a time of intense religious feeling and conviction. In light of the historical record, should Protestants be applauding, or hanging their heads in shame? Many have asked that question—what had been for medieval believers a single, unified, Catholic church was fractured irreversibly into a cacophony of disparate and divided groups. To complicate matters, the Reformation has also been praised and blamed for notable features of the modern world ranging from capitalism and natural science to modernity, the privatization of religion, and secularization. Roman Catholic thinkers might be forgiven for claiming that Luther and his fellow Reformers had irreparably damaged the unity of the church. But Protestant men and women, heirs of Martin Luther, often remain convinced that the Reformers were recovering the abiding apostolic witness preserved in the medieval and patristic tradition.

List of Classic Works of the Reformation Period

Desiderius Erasmus, *In Praise of Folly*, 1509

Martin Luther, *95 Theses*, 1517

Johannes Oecolampadius, *Canonici indocti*, 1519

Martin Luther, *A Treatise on Good Works*, 1520

Martin Luther, *On the Babylonian Captivity of the Church*, 1520

Thomas Müntzer, *Prague Manifesto*, 1521

Philipp Melanchthon, *Loci Communes (Common Places in Theology)*, 1521

Huldrych Zwingli, *The Clarity and Certainty of the Word of God*, 1522

Desiderius Erasmus, *The Freedom of the Will*, 1524

Thomas Müntzer, *A Manifest Exposé of False Faith*, 1524

Katharina Schütz Zell, *Letter to the Suffering Women of the Community of Kentzingen, Who Believe in Christ, Sisters with Me in Jesus Christ*, 1524

Huldrych Zwingli, *Commentary on True and False Religion*, 1525

Johann Eck, *Enchiridion of Commonplaces against Luther and other Enemies of the Church*, 1525

Martin Luther, *On the Bondage of the Will*, 1525

William Tyndale, *A Pathway into the Holy Scripture*, 1525–1532

William Tyndale, *The Obedience of a Christian Man*, 1528

Menno Simons, *The Spiritual Resurrection*, 1536

John Calvin, *Institutes of the Christian Religion*, 1536–1560 (diff. eds)

Marie Dentière, *Epistle to Marguerite de Navarre*, 1539

Benedetto da Mantova, *The Benefit of Christ's Death*, c. 1540

Thomas Cranmer, *Exhortation and Litany*, 1544

Martin Bucer, *On the Kingdom of Christ*, c. 1550

John Knox, *A Treatise on Prayer*, 1553

John Knox, *History of the Reformation in Scotland*, 1559

Guido de Brès, *Belgic Confession*, c. 1560

Heinrich Bullinger, *Decades (House Book)*, c. 1560
Peter Martyr Vermigli, *A Dialogue on the Two Natures of Christ*, c. 1560
Olympia Morata, *The Complete Writings of an Italian Heretic*, 1562
John Jewel, *An Apology of the Church of England*, 1562
Zacharius Ursinus, *Heidelberg Catechism*, 1563
Pope Pius IV, *The Profession of the Faith of Trent*, 1564
Theodore Beza, *Tractationes theologicae*, 1573
John of the Cross, *Dark Night of the Soul*, c. 1577–1579
Book of Concord, 1580
Martin Chemnitz, *The Apology of the Formula of Concord*, 1583
Teresa of Ávila, *Way of Perfection*, 1583
William Whitaker, *Disputation on Holy Scripture*, 1588
Richard Hooker, *Treatise on the Laws of Ecclesiastical Polity*, 1594–1597

3.1

The Handbook of the Christian Soldier[1] (1501)
Desiderius Erasmus of Rotterdam (1467–1536)

Introduction

Enchiridion militis christiani, or *The Handbook of the Christian Soldier*, was written by the leading intellectual and educator of the sixteenth century, Erasmus of Rotterdam (1467–1536). This popular "how to" spiritual manual for laity serves as a valuable mirror for Erasmus' theology and spirituality but also for people's religiosity before the sixteenth century Reformations. Reflecting Christians' real-life concerns and aspirations for living in accordance with their faith, it gives a precious perspective on how theology can be translated into guidelines for daily life.

The humanist educator

The Dutch author was one of the most influential intellectuals in early modern Europe. Through his prolific scholarship, as well as his vast correspondence, traveling, networking and personal connections, his presence was known widely throughout Europe. A true citizen of the world, Erasmus gained exceptional fluency in Latin and high aptitude in Greek, using both extensively in his work.

Figure 3.1 Erasmus

He rose to his position from humble beginnings. Erasmus was born in Gouda, Holland, on October 27, 1467, out of wedlock. His father Roger was a priest and his mother Margaret a widow. They sent off young Erasmus and his older brother to a grammar school (Deventer) where he learned his Latin. Erasmus was later taken into the care of the Brethren of the Common Life in Hertogenbusch, where he learned their unique semi-monastic spiritual model for laity. After their father's death, the impoverished brothers were steered towards monastic life. Soon after, while still a teenager, Erasmus begrudgingly took the vows of an Augustinian Canon Regular at Steyn near Gouda. Despite his distaste and initial lack of calling for a monk's life, the studious atmosphere in the company of like-minded men proved a positive stimulus for this man prone to intellectual excellence. The *Handbook* reveals the deep influence of his monastic experiences as well as his preference for a spiritual life beyond the monastery walls.

Erasmus was tireless with his pen. His writing projects included retranslating both Greek and patristic works, producing critical editions of the Latin and Greek fathers, and crafting many humanist textbooks and guidebooks for laity. A known satirist with a very sharp wit, he was not afraid to expose the folly and corruption he witnessed in the Catholic church. But, even unto his death, he never broke ties with it. Erasmus was deeply religious and remained confident that the church could be genuinely reformed from the inside, starting with the individuals. He did not join the German monk Martin Luther's efforts at theological reform, though to a degree he was supportive from a distance. However, he did contribute to the Reformations in a profound way with his brand-new critical edition of the New Testament.

The significance of Erasmus' annotated New Testament edition that replaced the problematic Latin text of the *Vulgata* cannot be overstated. His work transformed for good the world of biblical interpretation, provided a critical tool for Luther and other Reformers, and paved the way for Luther's groundbreaking vernacular translation of the New Testament for German speaking Christians. The *Handbook* was one of Erasmus' rare theological and anthropological texts, serving as the foundation for the prefaces he wrote to his edition of the New Testament; there he was transparent about his disputes with the contemporary scholastics. The clash between Erasmus and Luther on the question of human free will in relation to grace was yet to come; that debate would eventually obscure their more fundamental disagreement on biblical interpretation and making God's Word available to the masses.

The treatise: in response to a lady's request . . .

The *Handbook* saw many editions. It was first published in 1503, with Erasmus' early writings, and again in 1515 in two different books. The 1518 edition became a bestseller, its vernacular translation an oasis in the desert for Christians looking for spiritual guidance. The stimulus for the work came from an unnamed lady pleading for Erasmus' help for the spiritual education and reform of her husband with questionable morals. Erasmus thus writes what he calls a "method of morals" for the man, a Christian soldier, giving practical advice for "what," "why" and "how to" improve one's Christian conduct. The manual sheds light on Erasmus' own spiritual and vocational journey: the man once upon a time forced into monastic life now dismisses monastic religiosity and all reliance on rituals and erudition as futile and snobbish. Instead, one should aspire to live in accordance with Christ's Spirit and embrace the "philosophy of Christ" (*philosophia Christi*), as he later comes to call it. "If only a moderate danger to religion lurked in ceremonies," he writes in frustration, "yet nowhere do I condemn a moderate degree of ceremony; but I cannot endure that holiness from stem to stern ... should be thought to lie in them" (CWE 66:19). Many of our human rituals are trivial in the face of the transient nature of this life and the state in which every human is born into and leaves this world: naked, with nothing.

Christ stands instead as the only and sufficient model; his cross gives the right perspective on life for all Christians who should be different from others. Erasmus points to "the word of God" and its study as "the helmet of salvation and the sword of the Spirit," reminding readers that one should "approach the sacred Scriptures with washed hands," meaning "the purity of mind," so that the "manna" would not "pass immediately into the bowels of emotions" (CWE 66: 37, 34). In other words, once people appropriated the gospel *internally*, once they reoriented their practical lives toward goodness, then true, spiritual transformation could be expected.[2] Erasmus greatly desired the reform of the church, and he believed it would begin with the transformation of individuals.

In his Foreword, Erasmus confides in doctor Paul Volz, the abbot of Hugshofen, that he was content with this work dealing with a matter of importance: people's piety and daily lives. Anticipating its dismissal as "unlearned" by the ignorant puffy scholarly-types, he defends himself: "It [the Handbook] need not equip men for the wrestling-schools of the Sorbonne if it equips them for the tranquility proper to a Christian. It need not contribute to theological discussion provided it contributes to the life that befits a theologian" (CWE 66:8–9).

There is nothing simple about striving towards goodness, which is the highest goal in life for everyone. Erasmus writes: "For one thing, it is an element of goodness to have a sincere desire to be good .... This must be one's first purpose all one's life long, and repeated attempts will one day succeed. A man [or a woman, we imagine Erasmus means] who has really learnt the way has a good part of a complicated journey already behind him [her]" (CWE 66:8). Instead of losing ourselves in the sometimes silly details and footnotes that preoccupy theologians, it is more important to remember that: ". . . the good life is everybody's business, and Christ wished the way to it to be accessible to all men [women], not beset with impenetrable labyrinths of argument but open to sincere faith, to love unfeigned, and their companion, the hope that is not put to shame" (CWE 66:9).

Erasmus sets out to teach practical morals so that all Christians can live properly informed religious lives. In retrospect, however, the humanist's expectations are guarded with cynicism. His thinking about women in particular betrays a heavy patriarchal hand, starting with the association of women with sinful lust: "The carnal passions are our Eve, whose glance the clever serpent attracts daily. When she has been corrupted, she proceeds to tempt her spouse to participate with her in the evil." Erasmus' views on women are not only offensive but they distort his doctrine of salvation by making it fully available only to men; to his mind, men's honor is a consequence of women's dishonor. Even the anticipated "new" woman, the "female warrior" who "by the power of faith" crushes the serpent's head, will experience the ultimate curse, subjection to men: "[W]hen by God's authority Sara's honour was diminished, Abraham's honour was enhanced, and from then on she did not call him husband, but lord" (CWE 66:48–49). Already in his *Handbook* Erasmus' misogynist views are apparent, as he worries that the woman as "the carnal part of man [humanity]" brings along many temptations: "This is our Eve, through whom the cunning serpent lures our mind towards deadly pleasures" (CWE 66:25). At such moments, modern readers glimpse the theology of a man who lacked the good fortune of knowing women as equal partners, for he was left vulnerable to the intellectually woeful concept of women's essential inferiority as human beings.

Erasmus has a lot to say about the deadly pleasures. The *Handbook* addresses the vices Christians should particularly gird themselves against—pride, greed, hatred, and destructive lustiness and wrong desires. The manual gives detailed advice on navigating the perils of these omnipresent temptations. Drawing widely on Greek characters, philosophy, church fathers, and the apostle Paul, Erasmus lifts up the value of contemplating scriptural truth, accompanied by earnest prayer. The key is to be prepared and ready to resume battle when you stumble (and you will, he promises).

On Christian life as a warfare: harness yourself!

The path toward goodness is an adventure fraught with danger. Erasmus explains, "I hammered out an 'enchiridion,' that is, a sort of a dagger, which you should never put aside, not even at table or in bed, so that ... you will not allow yourself to be overcome at any moment by that ambusher when you are totally unarmed." Erasmus admits that the book is small, "but if you know how to use it rightly together with the shield of faith, you will easily withstand the violent onslaught of the enemy and will not receive a mortal wound." In the end, believers can expect to be transported by Christ to "everlasting peace and perfect tranquility." "In the meantime, however, all hope of salvation must be placed in this armor" (CWE 66:38).

Heaven belongs to those who fight, whereas the wicked (and lazy) will find no peace. Once Christians profess their faith through baptism, the battle has begun and they can rely on God's assistance. Prayer and knowledge of scripture serve as the main armor for the Christian who should never cease from war but go boldly into it, remembering that peace and happiness come from God alone: "Jesus Christ is the author of wisdom and indeed wisdom itself, the true light that alone scatters the night of worldly stupidity" (CWE 66:38).

For starters, Erasmus reasoned, you need to know yourself. You need to understand the fierce dynamic between your two "divergent natures"; the inner and outer human were once upon a time "joined in happy concord" but are now in warfare because of sin. Betraying the obvious influence of Plato's dualistic philosophy, Erasmus adores the soul as a godlike being and is rather dismissive of the lower, bodily part of the human being: "If the body had not been added to you, you would be a divinity; if the mind had not been bestowed upon you, you would be a beast" (CWE 66:41). Erasmus insisted that, *because* of the body the human being is like an animal, prone to fleshly sins. Mercifully, it is the soul, assisted by reason, who serves as the great arbiter and must choose whether to stay clear or to give in to bodily temptations. Erasmus writes:

> Therefore the spirit makes us gods, the flesh makes us brute animals. The soul constitutes us as human beings; the spirit makes us religious, the flesh irreligious, the soul neither the one nor the other. The spirit seeks heavenly things, the flesh seeks pleasure, the soul what is necessary. The spirit elevates

us to heaven, the flesh drags us down to hell, the soul has no charge imputed to it (CWE 66:52).

Erasmus illustrates these realities with examples from daily life and clarifies the distinction between natural (base) and virtuous (divine). For instance, love of family members or friends should not be confused with a virtue but rather recognized as something natural that is in accordance with the flesh and basic ways of being human—and so regardless of original sin. One should not "disguise a vice of nature with the name of virtue, calling depression gravity, harshness sternness, envy zeal, stinginess frugality, adulation friendliness, or scurrility wit" (CWE 66:45). At the same time, religious practices such as prayer, fasting, and good deeds are usually "spiritual" *but not always*; when done for personal gain and glory, such practices are inspired by the flesh and are nothing to boast about. Erasmus wishes to deflate the balloon of false pompous religiosity.

How does one then know what is godly and what is carnal? "Your soul stands at the crossroads" (CWE 66:52). The responsibility lies with the soul to discern these things. The soul knows when prayer is effective and when it is just a mumbling of words; the soul knows that attending to the needs of the neighbor in need is far more spiritual than self-serving ascetic practices. In short, the soul knows how to name things appropriately and keep the believer on the right track, viz., living after the wisdom of Christ.

The *Handbook* assumes human beings will tend to make good moral choices and thus restrain society from utter chaos. This basic optimism reflects an appreciation of free will that thrust Erasmus right into the middle of medieval debates going back to the famous clash between Augustine and Pelagius. Their debate on how to relate the grace of God and human free choice was resurrected in Erasmus and Luther. Erasmus argues for the necessity of the freedom of will against fatalism and determinism (*On Freedom of the Will*), whereas Luther underscores the necessity of grace and God's work in salvation to steer clear from any mentality of "works righteousness" (*On the Bondage of the Will*).[3] Both men appreciated the immensity of God's grace and both understood God's ways as beyond human comprehension; however, a fundamental distrust clouded their ability to speak in unison on this most important matter. True, they disagreed over the church's role and authority in biblical interpretation, but those differences were exacerbated by harsh polemics, mutual animosity spinning out of control. It was a missed opportunity between two gifted men.

Erasmus' rules: always prepared!

Let us summarize the basic principles of Erasmus's *Handbook*: (1) prayer and knowledge are the armor Christians need for their life journey; (2) the Christian source of knowledge is found in the God-authored Scriptures; (3) the divinely inspired Scriptures provide the Christian with the right kind of wisdom, true not worldly wisdom; (4) the Christian's ability to know anything reflects the duality of human nature: divided into spirit and flesh, human beings know both outwardly and, with the eye of the soul, also inwardly. The latter kind of knowing is necessary for true wisdom and the successful fight against sin in this world.

Erasmus iterates over twenty rules for ordering Christian life. The first rule is the most important: believe in Christ—who is wisdom itself—and the divinely inspired Truth in Scripture:

> Since faith is the only avenue to Christ, it is fitting that the first rule should be
> to understand fully what the Scriptures tell us about Christ and his Spirit, and
> to believe this not only by mere lip service, nor coldly or listlessly or hesitantly,
> as does the common lot of Christians, but with your whole heart, with the
> deep and unshaken conviction that there is not one tiniest detail contained
> therein that does not pertain to your salvation (CWE 66:55).

The second rule calls Christians to "enter upon the road of salvation not hesitantly or timidly" but with a "gladiatorial heart," unlike the "sluggard shilly-shallies" who let worldly fretting and pleasures wear them down (CWE 66:56). The third and fourth rules lift up Christ's example. Since the devil is always lurking to pull Christians away from Christ and his teachings, Christians need to set their eyes on Christ alone and love and desire nothing but Christ. They should hate and abhor all sin and flee from it, and never let their guard down. The rules provide a game plan to fight temptations.

The main thing is for Christians to live in perfect piety after Christ's own example (Rules 5–13). Becoming different from others, followers of Christ steer away from the visible and worldly towards the cross of Christ, where true honor is revealed. For Erasmus, it is of utmost importance that we know ourselves and our weaknesses in order to nip temptations in the bud. Whether one responds with hate, defiance, by simply fleeing the situation, with a prayer, or by quoting from the Scriptures, the key is not to be taken by surprise and always to fight as if it were the last battle. There is no room for arrogance: all glory belongs to God whose assistance in temptations is vital, and under whose constructive plan the temptations actually work out for the holy edification of the Christian.

After the first thirteen rules, Erasmus moves on to coaching how to uproot basic vices from one's life and replace them with virtues and good manners (Rules 14–20). Christians should never take sin or vice lightly, whether it is vainglory, pride, boasting, wantonness, murder, fornication, theft, or incest. Without falling in despair, Christian warriors need to pick themselves up after every bitter battle. Their chief remedy, the cross of Christ, provides milk for the weary soul. The reality of the cross is to be expected in the life of the followers of Christ. They should consider all sin and worldly hardship in light of the marvel of human nature as the temple of the Holy Spirit: humans are gentle and noble creatures, heirs to immortality, whose minds are a place of the Spirit's indwelling. This knowledge should give them confidence to choose Christ over the Devil, and steer clear from sin-induced filth and pestilence. The rules end reminding the reader of the transitory nature of this life and the impossibility of fully recovering from sin, while keeping in sight the heavenly reward.

A word on the vices: Christ as the remedy

Erasmus has firm ideas about certain sins and vices, especially those of a sexual nature, avarice, and the swelling of the head (i.e., arrogance). Erasmus addresses people in different stations of life about the thorn of human existence—*lust*, which threatens to make the most divine creation no different from brute beasts, swine, goats, dogs, and always leaves a sting in one's conscience. For example, he chastises the priest who "should come into physical contact with the stinking flesh of a harlot." For the woman, he writes that "nothing becomes this sex more than modesty." He reminds the married man of the honesty of keeping the marital bed undefiled. An old man overly engaged in "sensual pleasure" gets a verbal spanking: "If it is something to be pitied and repressed in young men, in an old man it is truly monstrous and utterly ridiculous … Among all the monstrosities of life there is nothing more grotesque than an old man's lust" (CWE 66:116–117). Avarice, stirred by the Devil, leads one to desire riches more than Christ, thus committing idolatry. According to Erasmus, we can focus on the infinite things from God that bring true satisfaction by remembering that we are born into this world naked, and we leave it in the same condition. The same is true with arrogance: swelling of mind can be kept in control by simply recalling one's filthy birth and future end in the bed of worms. One should also, following the model of Christ's love, overcome arrogance with meekness, evil with goodness, and malice with kindness. In Erasmus' opinion, wrath and desire for vengeance are childish signs of weakness, unbecoming for a noble follower of Christ. Speaking in anger or hurting another person only serves to hurt or embarrass; the tell-tale signs of flaming eyes, pale cheeks, dry mouth, foaming lips, quivering voice, none of it makes a positive impression. It is far wiser to "stay cool" (in the contemporary expression).

Erasmus warns the reader to avoid occasions to sin by using moderation in everything (e.g., sleeping, eating, or drinking), and to pray purely and often, especially at the time of temptation. One should never remain idle and unarmed but rather stay steadfast in meditation and the study of scripture, learning from the model of Christ and godly Christians known for their holiness.

The *Handbook* was written quickly, since Erasmus feared he was in competition with other teachers of models for religious life: making unflattering comparisons to Jewish religiosity, Erasmus warns of the "superstitious fraternity among the religious" who "after filling his mind with mere quibbles and thorny problems that nobody could solve, they bind him to some petty observances, of human, not divine, origin, and plunge the poor fellow into a kind of Judaism, teaching him how to tremble, not how to love" (CWE 66:127). Of the monastic path *per se* he concludes: "I personally do not urge you to adopt it, nor yet do I urge you against it. I merely advise you to identify with piety not with diet, or dress ..." Most importantly, "Associate with those in whom you have seen Christ's true image" (CWE 66:127).[4] They should make friends with the Apostle Paul and study him night and day. Proper learning should be engaged for piety's sake, not for glory or fame.

The book ends with greetings to the reader, whom Erasmus addresses as his dear brother and a friend. The book written for the benefit of the soul's health for all Christian people is signed off in Saint Andomers, 1501.

Conclusion

Erasmus of Rotterdam sparked spiritual and moral reforms in the sixteenth century and beyond. His *Handbook* for Christian living had its particular impact in the shaping of Protestant theology and how it was lived out in practice: the Reformers would eventually counter his theological optimism and offer their counter-manuals. Protestant Catechisms were designed to teach their congregants the principles of Christian living with an explicit emphasis on God's grace as the "sole" actor in all matters pertaining to holiness and goodness. At precisely this point, whatever core theological differences remained, the *Handbook* manifests Erasmus' shared passion with the Reformers: "A very important part of Christianity is to want to be a Christian with all one's heart and soul" (CWE 66:46).

Notes

1. Translated from *Enchiridion militis christiani*; the edition used here (=CWE): *The Handbook of the Christian Soldier/Enchiridion militis christiani,* ed. and trans. Charles Fantazzi, in: *Collected Works of Erasmus: Spiritualia,* ed. John O'Malley, Vol. 66 (Toronto: University of Toronto Press, 1988), 1–127. Hereafter, all references to this work shall be noted by employing in-text citations.
2. Erasmus used the term "philosophia Christi" in his 1516 *Paracelsis* and his introduction to the New Testament, and then again more formally in his letter to the abbot of Hugshofen, Paul Volz, which accompanied the 1518 edition of the *Enchiridion* as its preface.
3. The longstanding debate started through correspondence in 1517 and led Erasmus, whom Luther called "Pelagian," to match Luther's aggressive tone with his 1526 *Hyperaspistes.*
4. Erasmus' views on the inferiority of Jewish religion are similar to most Reformers, including Luther, who condemned Judaism in favor of Christian faith and biblical interpretation.

Select Bibliography

Primary sources

Collected Works of Erasmus, Vol. 66: Spiritualia: Enchiridion, De contemptu Mundi, De Vidua Christiana. Edited by John W. O'Malley. Toronto: University of Toronto Press, 1988 [=CWE]

The Handbook of the Christian Soldier/Enchiridion militis christiani, ed. and trans. Charles Fantazzi, in *Collected Works of Erasmus: Spiritualia,* ed. John O'Malley, Vol. 66: 1–127 Toronto: University of Toronto Press, 1988.

The Handbook of the Christian Soldier/Enchiridion militis christiani, from CWE, in *The Erasmus Reader*, ed. Erika Rummel. Toronto: University of Toronto Press 1997, 138–154.

Leclerc, Jean, ed. *Desiderii Erasmi Roterodami opera omnia*. 10 vol. Leiden: Peter Vander Aa, 1703–1706.

Rummel, Erika, ed. *The Erasmus Reader*. Toronto: University of Toronto Press, 1990.

Secondary sources

Cornelis, Augustijn. *Erasmus: His Life, Works, and Influence*, trans. J.C. Grayson. Toronto: University of Toronto Press, 1991.

Halkin, Léon-E. *Erasmus: A Critical Biography*, trans. John Tonkin. Oxford: Blackwell, 1993.

McConica, James. *Erasmus*. Oxford: Oxford University Press, 1991.

Rummel, Erika. *Erasmus and His Catholic Critics*, 2 vols. Bibliotheca Humanistica et Reformatorica, 45. Nieuwkoop: De Graaf Publishers, 1989.

3.2

The Freedom of a Christian (1520)

Martin Luther (1483–1546)

Introduction

"Many people have considered Christian faith an easy thing." With these words the German Reformer, monk, and university professor Martin Luther began his most influential 1520 Reformation treatise (343).[1] In the pages of *The Freedom of a Christian*, Luther ambitiously wished to educate the whole of Christendom in Christian faith, starting with the head of the church: he sent his Latin work with a letter to Pope Leo X who was on the verge of excommunicating the troublesome monk (334–343). In his "token of peace and good hope," and feeling sorry (or so he said) for Leo who had the misfortune of serving as the pope "in these times," Luther appealed to the pope to give him a fair hearing (343). In fact, Luther argued, the true problems in the church lay not with Luther, but in corrupt practices, false teachings, and the ungodliness of its leaders.

To the Christian Nobility, The Babylonian Captivity, and *The Freedom of a Christian* are three major Reformation works written within months of each other that launched an unprecedented attack on papal authority, central sacramental teachings, and practices of the Roman Catholic Church. In them, Luther calls for lay leaders to rise against what he deemed as misuses of the gospel. With a redefinition of Christian freedom and a repositioning of biblical arguments for equality, dignity, and the freedom of every person, *The Freedom of a Christian* conveyed an emancipatory message with serious political implications, which did not go unnoticed. Luther's theological

Figure 3.2 Martin Luther

vision of God's grace becoming real "for us" through faith and "through us" in love offered a particular justice-oriented paradigm for life. Existential freedom of conscience combined with compassionate accountability for fellow creatures became, in Luther's model, the foundation for love-based ethics and spirituality.

The reformer and his passion: reformation and freedom

Martin Luther was a theological freedom fighter. His reforms fought to secure the freedom of conscience for every child of God. This agenda thrust him forward as the leader of the Reformation that unfolded. But we should not overstate Luther's attitude: he was quintessentially a medieval man whose concerns for the freedom of a "Christian" remained limited in scope to his known reality, the Christian tradition. Luther was also nervous about advocating practical steps with political ramifications—he feared chaos. While conservative as a social reformer, as a *theological* reformer Luther was bold and revolutionary. He was emboldened to act out of the freedom of his own conscience, galvanized by the Holy Scriptures which he had interpreted anew. Luther was burning with the conviction that the gospel of Christ was about freedom beyond human imagination: freedom from the binds of God's wrath, eternal punishment, death, and damnation. At the basis of this freedom he saw Christ's person and work; the price for human freedom in the scope of eternity was already paid when Jesus of Nazareth died on the cross. Luther gained these insights when lecturing from the Bible (first on the Psalms, then on Romans, Galatians, and Hebrews, 1513–1518).

The turning point came with Luther's lectures on Paul's letter to the Romans from which he gained an exclusive new focus: grace "only," faith "only," and Christ "only" saved human beings from their otherwise inherited damned condition.[2] Feeling like he had entered paradise with this new discovery, Luther would begin to read all of scripture Christ-centrically to unfold this most remarkable revelation: because of Christ, grace, forgiveness, and holiness were free and available for all in equal need of divine intervention. This insight gave Luther the peace of mind he had hungered for as a monk and now wished at all costs to make available to others as well. He showed no patience for those who did not share his experience or were not convinced by his arguments, which he amassed profusely in writing, preaching, conversation, debating, and counseling.[3]

A word of caution regarding Luther's theological discovery is in order: Luther's extreme Christ-centric reading of the Scriptures—including the Hebrew Bible—would come to bolster his polemics against the Jewish faith as anti-Christ and anti-Christian, as law-based and thus futile. His ignorance of Judaism, his tainted anti-Jewish sources, and his Christ-biased biblical interpretation led the man who in other ways exhibited a great capacity for compassion to commit serious transgressions by writing in hateful words. Luther defended single-mindedly his jewel conviction of God's saving grace by faith alone and was unwilling to entertain differences of opinion. After all, Abraham and Sarah—whom he considered his faith ancestors—had already experienced this grace, and so Luther expected everybody urgently to convert when encountering his discovery regarding matters of salvation. As with any other historical theologian, contemporary readers must reckon with these facts when separating the wheat from the chaff in Luther's legacy.[4]

While still an Augustinian monk, and recently inaugurated professor of the Bible at the University of Wittenberg (1512), Luther presented his legendary *Ninety-Five Theses* in 1517 as a call to attention. Several teachings and practices had begun to irk him. First, the abject poverty of the people in striking contrast to the indulgence sales funding the most opulent building project of the time, that of St Peter's basilica. Second, the abusive selling of the indulgences that led ordinary Christians to spend what little they had on faulty premises of absolution, purchasing relief from acts of penance or from presumed divine punishment rather than pursuing a life of repentance and service to one another. Third, the illusion that the authority behind any declaration of forgiveness depended on the office of the pope, a pope whom Luther tried to alert to the problems in his pasture and who, in Luther's opinion, really should have been sharing from his riches for the benefit of his sheep. Luther would soon conclude that the indulgences were worthless, their selling based on false premises; good deeds for the benefit of one's neighbor were a much better option. (If the leader of the Christian church, the pope, was not willing to show a good example here, Luther concluded, he would need to be reminded of the human character of his office and of the mission he was expected to lead: a fair and even distribution of the graces afforded to and through the church.) The source of forgiveness was not in papal hands; only God could forgive, while people were mediators in bringing this message home to one another. Any practices or teachings that put a prerequisite on God's grace needed to be corrected.

What began for Luther as a seemingly simple concern ended up as a complex set of issues put on the table, including questions about the basic premises for knowledge of God and the rules of theology. In the 1518 *Heidelberg Disputation* prepared for a hearing with his Augustinian peers, the monk presented a controversial recipe for theology and God-knowledge: from the experience of suffering and naming reality "as is," a theologian of the cross could come to discern the surprising truth that God makes sinners lovable apart from human effort or worth. He inverted traditional thinking about the role of good works and the ability to use free will to do what was expected in a Christian life. He argued regarding salvation that human beings are free only in a passive capacity; that is, they can only receive what God wills for them. However good they may seem to us, human works actually correspond to mortal sins. In a similar fashion, human beings are so tortured by sin and perversion that God's work within their lives can appear alien; God's law torments and condemns with its accusation until the grace of the gospel exalts and brings faith, hope, and salvation.[5] The only chance for human beings is Christ who comes to dwell within, by faith, and leads them into good deeds and to a glimpse of God's unambiguous presence. Luther concludes with a most poignant argument (article 28) that God creates good and makes sinners pleasing by loving them first. A true theologian worth her salt is the kind who sees God through this apparent absence and recognizes God's invisible work in human suffering and brokenness.[6]

Luther's main concern was freedom—freedom of the individual conscience in particular and freedom of every Christian to interpret Scripture. The gospel, in his reading, was primarily about forgiveness and the love of God that belonged to all, *for free*, as a matter of faith. Having written and debated within his university and monastic order, Luther then sharpened his criticism and confronted in writing some of the central teachings and practices of his church.

The first in the series of Reformation calls was his address *To the Christian Nobility*, published in August 1520, in German. Calling the secular leaders to protect the gospel, he exposed three problematic assumptions—first, that the pope should be above council. In the spirit of the Council of Constance, Luther argued that the highest authority belongs in the hands of the general council. Second, that the primary authority to interpret scripture belonged to the pope. Quite the contrary, as Luther demanded, the word of God belongs to every man and woman. Third, Luther took exception to the notion that clergy were in any way above laity. Luther appealed instead to a level playing field, emphasizing the equality among baptized Christians as far more important.[7] In his next tract, published in Latin on October 6, 1520, he targeted Roman Catholic theology in *The Babylonian Captivity of the Church*. Characterizing the gospel as a prisoner of the institutional church, Luther began to lay out his renewed understanding of the sacraments, including their purpose, effectiveness and number; he leveled specific critique at the doctrine of transubstantiation and the practice of officiating Masses for the dead. In his criticism of the Mass, he ridiculed fasting rules, pilgrimages, relics and devotion to saints, clergy celibacy, and the primacy of the pope. In so doing, he was burning bridges with the Roman Catholic Church. Luther then turned to the Christian men and women in need of guidance and comfort.[8]

Reformation theology became the possession of lay people in his popular treatise *The Freedom of a Christian,* published in November, 1520, in Latin first, with *An Open Letter to the Pope Leo X*. The widely spread German translation effectively sealed Luther as the leader of the new movement— even in circles and for purposes he was not prepared for, such as the coming uprisings of the peasants (1525).[9] A common theme in these works is Luther's critique of teachings and practices that in his view compromised the gospel message and caused undue burdens on individuals' consciences (and purses). Forgiveness, mercy, and salvation were gifts from God and received in faith alone, he argued, and the evidence of these gifts should show in a Christian's life, and thus in the life of the church. Christian community should be known for the qualities of love, compassion, and service to the other after the example of Christ, rather than for greed, corruption, and abuse of power. The bottom line was to protect the gospel; Christian men, women, and children needed comfort and liberation from being bound by human-made traditions. Given what was at stake, no price was too high for Luther on the path he had taken, though he did not know all that would unfold as a direct or indirect result of his preaching, teaching, and writing.

Already considered a troublemaker and identified as a "heretic" due to public debates (Augsburg 1518, Leipzig 1519), Luther was officially excommunicated by papal bull on January 3, 1521, the same year the Diet of Worms would condemn him as an outlaw (May 25, 1521). When defending his works in front of the emperor and the German princes, he appealed to Scripture and the voice of his own conscience. His words hit a chord in the hearts of Christians dealing with similar issues and who were willing to join him to protect the gospel and Christian faith. The compassionate and widely read treatise *The Freedom of a Christian* served as a major stimulus for evangelical teachings taking root among people from different walks of life during the vulnerable years when evangelicals' faith was under attack and far from secured.

Freedom in faith, service in love

"I am sending you this little treatise dedicated to you as a token of peace and good hope," Luther wrote in his accompanying letter to Pope Leo X (343). "It is a small book if you regard its size. Unless I am mistaken, however, it contains the whole of Christian life in a brief form, provided you grasp its meaning. I am a poor man and have no other gift to offer, and you do not need to be enriched by any other but a spiritual gift" (343).[10]

The gist of the book, dedicated to his friend Mühlphordt, Mayor of Zwickau (333), is found in his statement: "One thing, and only one thing, is necessary for Christian life, righteousness, and freedom. The one thing is the most holy Word of God, the gospel of Christ" (345). He offered in its pages a masterful exposition of the Christian life through the lens of the gospel and faith, addressing such themes as human nature, the law and gospel in Christian life, the change caused by the Word, justification by faith and the indwelling of Christ, the work of the Holy Spirit and works of love, and the nature of Christian faith-based freedom, both in the scope of eternity as well as in this life.

The key statement in the text characterizes the two-fold reality of Christian life: freedom in faith and bondage to the Spirit for love. "A Christian is a perfectly free lord of all, subject to none. A Christian is a perfectly dutiful servant of all, subject to all" (344). This duality describes how men and women relate to God and to their neighbors in this world. At its foundation, the treatise is Luther's teaching on justification and the Christian life: when Christ becomes the subject of our being, life from then on is shaped by the experience of liberation and the resulting compassionate responsibility for justice.[11]

The dimensions of human life: two natures, two realms

Much like his medieval contemporaries, Luther believed that human beings live in two dimensions, a spiritual dimension with regard to their souls (their inner persons), and a fleshly dimension with regard to their bodies (their outer persons) (344–345). Christians must find conformity between the inner and outer person in order to experience freedom and to exemplify conduct shaped by neighborly love. The inner person becomes righteous and free through God's Word and keeps the outer person under control through "reasonable discipline" of the body and subjecting it to the Spirit (358, 369). While he recognizes the many temptations that beset our physical senses, Luther does not simplistically equate flesh and sin with bodiliness. Writing that "only ungodliness and unbelief of heart, and no outer work, make him [her] a guilty and damnable servant of sin" (347), Luther points out that the "flesh" is most detrimental in its spiritual manifestation when involving the soul, the central agent in human life. In Luther's explanation of the mystery of salvation, faith that saves belongs to the realm of the soul, and saving faith that manifests in bodily existence also depends on the soul.

Luther typically casts human existence into two fundamental realms. He uses the expression *coram Deo* (before God) for all matters pertaining to salvation and our relationship to God, and he uses *coram hominibus* (before humans) for our temporal relations with other creatures. *Coram hominibus* we experience incompleteness, failures, and progress, whereas *coram Deo* we are either beneficiaries of Christ's perfect holiness or completely doomed because of sin. Christians deal with this duality in their daily lives through the work of the Word, which both reveals what is missing and gives what is needed for the soul to receive the gift of grace.

Faith alone, word alone: dynamics of law and gospel

Luther paints a bleak picture of original sin and our inability to resist sin, but in the process he underscores the vital work of God's Word. He argues, "One thing, and only one thing, is necessary for Christian life, righteousness, and freedom. That one thing is the most holy Word of God, the gospel of Christ" (345). The "Word" has many nuances for Luther, but typically when he writes of the Word he means "the gospel of God concerning his [God's] Son, who was made flesh, suffered, rose from the dead, and was glorified through the Spirit who sanctifies." In short, the Word is Christ. The Word also creates the faith that brings human beings into personal communion with God: "faith alone is the saving and efficacious use of the Word of God" (see Romans 10:9) (346).

Reflecting the basic duality within human experience, the Word also has two dimensions: In commandments and promises the Word speaks to the alternating human experience of despair and hope. The law works first to humble and to bring men and women to recognize the nothingness in themselves; the gospel then arrives bringing hope. The law is necessary because of sin, human beings unable to obey even God's basic command to "believe." The law makes human beings realize their sin of unbelief as the most terrible disobedience against God, provoking them to repent, receiving the promise of God's Word in saving faith. Luther writes about this dynamic: "We must bring forth the voice of the law that men [human beings] may be made to fear and come to a knowledge of their sins and so be converted to repentance and a better life. But we must not stop with that . . . we must also preach the word of grace and the promise of forgiveness by which faith is taught and aroused" (364). Ultimately, as Luther puts it, "To preach Christ means to feed the soul, make it righteous, set it free, and save it" (346).

Salvation by faith: oneness with God

Faith is a divine gift. It returns to God what is God's (351). "Therefore true faith in Christ is a treasure beyond comparison," urged Luther, a treasure "which brings with it complete salvation" (347). Luther never deviated from his central message: "No other work makes a Christian" (347). He writes,

"Therefore it is clear that, as the soul needs only the Word of God for its life and righteousness, so it is justified by faith alone and not any works" (346). The man or woman who has faith possesses the whole world and will be glorified by God (351). Like his experience of the Word, Luther's notion of faith is quite mystical. Together they hold a key to Luther's theology.

Luther points to the dynamic of faith and Word when explaining the mystery of reconciliation, our justification before God. Faith acts in three ways. First, faith draws human beings to God with the "most tender spiritual touch," the Word. Faith then gives God what God wants, namely, righteousness. Finally, faith unites the soul with Christ (348). Faith shields Christians from sin, death, and damnation, and then—in a glorious exchange—it enables them instead to receive grace, life, and salvation (351). In Luther's soteriology, faith is exclusively the engine—"a Christian has all that he [she] needs in faith and needs no works to justify him [her]" (349), and it is always so with the Word that brings things home. God is the doer, the one who makes human beings holy, and he accomplishes this wonder through his own Word.

Human works can never unite us to God. Such a miracle requires the mystical work of the Word. "Just as the heated iron glows like fire because of the union of fire with it," Luther explains, "so the Word imparts its qualities to the soul." The power is in the Word: "If a touch of Christ healed, how much more will this most tender spiritual touch, this absorbing of the Word, communicate to the soul all things that belong to God. This, then, is how through faith alone without works the soul is justified by the Word of God, sanctified, made true, peaceful, and free, filled with every blessing" (349). Luther is a Word-mystic and his notion of justification is profoundly mystical.

Justification as forgiveness and transformation

Luther is famous for his doctrine of justification by faith. The word "justification" in his usage refers to sinners made right with God, forgiven and restored to a personal relationship with God. One aspect of justification is the forgiveness of sins, known in Lutheran language as "forensic" justification. It is the reality of being "declared not guilty" and thus free from the punishments of original sin. The other aspect of justification is "effective" justification. The sinner is wonderfully transformed as Christ enters her life;

Christ brings along all of his goodness and removes all of her sins. In the words of Luther: the "happy exchange"!

Justified life, however, does not imply a problem-free (that is, sin-free) life. Justification does not render some human beings "better" than their neighbors. Rather, forgiven persons remain in this life vulnerable, faltering, and lacking free will to choose right; they must discipline themselves and work at their human relations (the *coram hominibus* reality). At the same time, a person justified is fully transformed, internally, with holiness and righteousness from Christ (the *coram Deo* reality) (358–359). The justified are thus appropriately named after Christ who dwells in them—Christians are like Christ (368).

The fundamental tension in Christian life is captured in Luther's insight that human beings are simultaneously righteous and sinners, *simul iustus et peccator*. On their own, everyone is a sinner, while *in Christ* everyone is a saint. Righteousness has two dimensions. Righteousness is grounded in the passive, "alien" righteousness of Christ. In their own, "proper" righteousness human beings can make progress in baby steps. Proper righteousness implies a need for action and an experience of incompleteness, whereas alien righteousness is mystical and complete, effected by the Word alone regardless of human works or desire. Luther portrays the Christian life as rooted in God's free gift of grace, while simultaneously calling for active participation in God's work in this world, for the benefit of others: mostly because God's Spirit cannot be idle!

On good works in the Christian life: not to be rejected!

The question of the role of good works in the Christian life was heavily debated among Protestants in Luther's time and beyond. Luther's point was clear: "We do not, therefore, reject good works; on the contrary, we cherish and teach them as much as possible" (363). Good works belong to the Christian life but they do not save anybody or make anybody better or holier (just as evil works do not make a person actually wicked). Rather, good works are expected as a natural outcome of the gift of righteousness, and one "must do such works freely only to please God" (360).

Because of faith, the soul can be expected to love God (359). Faith gives the right attitude so that "our hearts will be filled by the Holy Spirit with the love which makes us free, joyful, almighty workers and conquerors over all tribulations, servants of our neighbors, and yet lords of all" (367). Good works prompted by faith are pleasing to God. Christ is the real subject in these works; from him comes the faith that justifies, makes holy, and effects the kind of response God desires (361). The good works that God wants, then, are inspired by love after the model of Christ (369).

Conformity with Christ, dwelling in Christ

Having unraveled all the theological complexities in his treatise, Luther returns to basic spiritual teaching. Christian life is about Jesus. Ordinary men and women, Luther promises, can expect to be mystically conformed to Christ; they will serve others as Christ did because they are in union with that same Christ: "Surely we are named after Christ, not because he is absent from us, but because he dwells in us, that is, because we believe in him and are Christs one to another and do to our neighbors as Christ does to us." Because of Christ, his followers are to live not in themselves but in Christ and their neighbor (368): "Otherwise he [she] is not a Christian. He [she] lives in Christ through faith, in his [her] neighbor through love. By faith he [she] is caught up beyond himself [herself] into God. By love he [she] descends beneath himself [herself] into his [her] neighbor. Yet he [she] always remains in God and in his [God's] love" (371).

Luther drills home the gift-nature of holiness and salvation, the indispensable role of faith, and the mystical outcome of the process that gives the human being a "form of God": "So a Christian like Christ his [her] head, is filled and made rich by faith and should be content with this form of God which he [she] has obtained by faith. This faith is one's life, righteousness, and salvation, making one acceptable to God; and so one "should increase this faith until it is made perfect . . ." (366). These realities cannot be rationally explained, but are a matter of divine truth and belief. Luther advises his readers to pray that God would make them *theodidacti*, taught by God (as in John 6:45). Being taught by God makes people humble and inspires them to live not in themselves but in Christ through faith and in their neighbors through love (376–377).

How Christians live out this tension between freedom and responsibility in their daily lives is a challenge for which they need constant guidance from the Spirit. *The Freedom of a Christian* underscores the agency of God's Word and the Holy Spirit while stressing the importance of active faith and love. Freedom is the fertile ground for such extroverted spirituality.

Radical bondage: passivity of the will, activity of God

Luther's understanding of justification and the Christian life presupposes a radical view of the human will and its bondage to sin. Luther agreed with Augustine that human nature is fatally compromised since the fall, so that people always incline to want the wrong things. On this opinion he never wavered. This perspective lies at the root of every statement Luther made about the God–human relationship, and thus about sin and grace. Luther articulated this view especially in *The Freedom of a Christian*, and later gave a sustained defense in *On the Bondage of the Will* (1525), which is a heated response to Erasmus of Rotterdam who strongly defended human freedom in response to Luther's 1520 works.[12] Luther considered these two works among his most important writings, and both have made an enormous impact not only in scholarly debates on the vexing topic of free will and grace but also in the lives of Christians trying to find a balance between receiving and giving.

Conclusion

The Freedom of a Christian offers a theological vision for Christian living. The treatise continues arguments made earlier in the *Ninety-Five Theses* about God's grace as the basis for salvation and forgiveness. It also spells out why this vision matters, for those existentially and spiritually liberated by God's Word and made holy by God's own act are humbly bound to one another socially and relationally. The universal need for forgiveness and liberation should guarantee solidarity among God's people who stand together equally in need of God's grace. Luther writes, "Just as our neighbor is in need and lacks that in which we abound, so we were in need before God and lacked his [God's] mercy." Just as Christ came to our help, we should hurry freely to help our neighbors (367). True freedom, a divine gift, is undeserved and comes from having our consciences liberated. In Luther's prescription, this kind of liberation does not lead to anarchy—even if it should be used "constantly and consistently in the sight of and despite the tyrants"—but to profound love, compassion, and commitment to the neighbor's benefit. Freedom feeds justice (374, 367).

This beloved text gives a profound sense of who Luther was as a theologian, what he believed as a Christian, and what drove his Reformation vision. In the shadow of Luther's most outrageous argument about the absolute bondage of will, his most far-reaching vision was probably his view of justice arising from Christian freedom. If the later Lutheran tradition sometimes overemphasizes passivity of faith in salvation, it does so at the expense of the active vision Luther had for a Christian life. Those "passively" justified by faith in Christ were expected to be "actively" working towards justice in the world with the same love that liberated them in the first place. Furthermore, Luther offers individuals and communities a compelling recipe for emotional, social, spiritual, and political well-being based on the experience of freedom. He casts a vision of Christian life, redemption, holiness, and justice—all of these powerfully rooted in a love that is divine in nature and fertile with a freedom beyond words. *The Freedom of a Christian* demonstrates how happiness and freedom, love and equality, compassion and justice are all inter-related, and it makes a theological argument for the deep correspondence between inner freedom and outer responsibilities. These seeds that Luther sowed were revolutionary in his day, but no less for our time as they can still set the world on fire.

Notes

1. Translated from *Von der Freiheit eines Christenmenschen*; hereafter, all references to this work (Martin Luther, *The Freedom of a Christian* in *Luther's Works—American Edition* [55 vols.; eds. Jaroslav Pelikan and Helmut T. Lehman; Philadelphia: Fortress Press, 1957], 33:333–77) shall be noted by employing in-text citations.
2. With Romans 3:28 in particular, Luther in his translation emphasized the exclusive power of grace to save, adding the word "sola" in the verse as a theological clarification of this vital point: ". . . a person is justified by faith *alone* apart from works . . ."
3. In his *Preface to the Complete Edition of Luther's Latin Writings* (LW 34:327–338), Luther describes how he moved from hating the very concept of "righteousness of God" to seeing it in new light with the help of the apostle Paul's letter to the Romans, chapter 1 verse 17 in particular: "There I began to understand that the righteousness of God is that by

which the righteous lives by a gift of God, namely by faith. And this is the meaning: the righteousness of God is revealed by the gospel, namely, the passive righteousness with which merciful God justifies us by faith, as it is written, 'He who through faith is righteous shall live.' Here I felt that I was altogether born again and had entered paradise itself through open gates." (LW 34:336–337 [337]).

4. See *Martin Luther, the Bible, and the Jewish People: A Reader*, eds. Brooks Schramm and Kirsi I. Stjerna (Minneapolis: Fortress Press, 2012).

5. Here Luther seeks to make the point about the difference between the effect of the law and the gospel, both of which work for the benefit of the Christian. Later Luther will talk about the different uses of law: The terrifying function of the law to condemn and annihilate human pride serves the purpose of bringing one to God and is not to be confused with the "civil law" that orders human life in society or the "third" or "pedagogical" use of the law that guides the moral life of the justified person.

6. *Heidelberg Disputation*, 1518, LW 31:39–58; WA 1, 353–374, passim; particularly articles 3–10 on the law and good works, articles 14–16 on free will, articles 19–21 on the theologian of the cross, and articles 25–28 on justification and presence of Christ.

7. *To the Christian Nobility of the German Nation Concerning the Reform of the Christian Estate*, 1520, LW 44: 123–217; WA 6 (381) 404–469.

8. *The Babylonian Captivity of the Church*, WA 6, 497–573; LW 36, 11–126.

9. The peasants suffering from poverty and oppression had initially great hopes for Luther to support their cause; Luther, however, while sympathetic to their fair demands for justice, condemned any action leading to anarchy and did not intervene to prevent the bloody suppression of the revolts. Unlike the apocalyptic leader from Saxon-Anhalt, Thomas Müntzer (c. 1489–1525), Luther did not wish to assume the role of a political reformer.

10. *An Open Letter to Pope Leo X*, dated September 6, 1520; LW 34: 334–343; WA 7, 42–49, *Epistola Lutheriana ad Leonem Decimum summum pontificem*.

11. According to John Witte Jr., "Luther's *Freedom of a Christian* thus became, in effect, his *Dignitatis Humanae*—his bold new declaration on human nature and human freedom that described all Christians in his world regardless of their 'dignity or lack of dignity,' as conventionally defined. Pope and prince, noble and pauper, man and woman, slave and free—all persons in Christendom, Luther declared, share equally in a doubly paradoxical nature . . . A theory of human dignity that fails to take into account the combined depravity and sanctity of the human person is theologically deficient, and politically dangerous." See "The Freedom of a

Christian: Martin Luther's Reformation of Law & Liberty," by John Witte, Jr. http://cslr.law.emory.edu/fileadmin/media/PDFs/Lectures/Witte_Freedom_Christian.pdf, based on Dr. Witte's "Snuggs Lectures" at the University of Tulsa, March 7–8, 2005. Accessed 5/16/12.

12. *The Bondage of the Will*, LW 33. See more with Erasmus' *Enchiridion*.

Select Bibliography

Primary sources

Luther, Martin. *D. Martin Luthers Werke: Kritische Gesamtausgabe. Schriften.* [65 vols.] Weimar: H. Böhlaus Nachfolger, 1883–1993: *Von der Freiheit eines Christenmenschen*, WA 7, 20–38; *Mar. Lutheri tractatus de libertate christiana*, 1520, WA 7, 49–73.

Luther, Martin. *Gesammelte Werke* CD-ROM. Ed. Kurt Aland. Digitale Bibliothek 63. Berlin: Direct Media, 2002.

Luther, Martin. *Lateinisch-Deutsche Studienausgabe*, Band 2: Christusglaube und Rechtfertigung, hrsg. Johannes Schilling, Leipzig: Martin Luther Evangelische Verlagsanstalt, 2006: *Epistola Lutheriana ad Leonem Decimum summum pontificem. Tractatus de libertate christiana/Brief Luthers an Papst Leo X. Abhandlung über die christliche Freiheit,* 1520, übersetzung Fidel Radle.

Luther, Martin. *The Freedom of a Christian* in *Luther's Works—American Edition*, edited by Jaroslav Pelikan and Helmut T. Lehman, 55 vols., 31: 329–77. Philadelphia: Fortress Press, 1957.

Luther, Martin. *Martin Luther's Basic Theological Writings.* Edited by Timothy F. Lull and William R. Russell. 2nd ed. Minneapolis: Fortress Press, 2005, 387–411.

Luther, Martin. *Luther's Spirituality.* The Classics of Western Spirituality. Edited and translated by Philip D.W. Krey and Peter D.S. Krey. New York: Paulist Press, 2007.

Luther, Martin. *The Freedom of a Christian. Luther Study Edition.* Edited and translated by Mark D. Tranvik. Minneapolis: Fortress Press, 2008.

Secondary sources

Mannermaa, Tuomo. *Two Kinds of Love. Martin Luther's Religious World.* Edited and translated, with a preface, by Kirsi Stjerna. Epilogue by Juhani Forsberg, translated by Stjerna. Minneapolis: Fortress Press, 2010.

Mannermaa, Tuomo. *Christ Present in Faith: Luther's View of Justification.* Edited with Introduction and Bibliography by Kirsi Stjerna. Minneapolis: Fortress Press, 2005.

Oberman, Heiko. *Luther, Man Between God and the Devil.* New Haven: Yale University Press, 1989.

Witte Jr., John. "The Freedom of a Christian: Martin Luther's Reformation of Law & Liberty." http://cslr.law.emory.edu/fileadmin/media/PDFs/Lectures/Witte_Freedom_Christian.pdf, based on Dr. Witte's "Snuggs Lectures" at the University of Tulsa, March 7–8, 2005. Accessed 5/16/12.

3·3

The Large Catechism (1529)
Martin Luther (1483–1546)

Introduction: the book on Christian love

Martin Luther did not invent "the catechism," but he wrote some of the most successful ones: his *Small Catechism* and *Large Catechism* from 1529 were adopted into use immediately and were eventually in the Lutherans' *Book of Concord* (1580) as well as in their Church Orders. As a summation of Luther's most characteristic theology, the *Large Catechism* is pedagogically savvy and has been instrumental in steering Lutheran theology, church life and spirituality through generations.[1]

A few words about the catechisms

In the years 1522–1530 at least thirty catechisms were published. The market was hot. Not happy with the theology of the new catechisms, Luther finally wrote his own after eye-opening visits to the emerging evangelical congregations (1528–1529). Theologically uninformed people needed more than a new translation of the New Testament. Manuals were needed for teaching, preaching, praying, and practicing the sacraments. In response to this "deplorable state," Luther wrote his catechisms in the spring of 1529. In those vulnerable years before the 1580 *Book of Concord*, catechisms provided theological vision and practical direction toward building inter-Lutheran unity; they also helped in the now re-activated mission against the devil, death, and all that threatened the well-being of Christians. As Luther writes:

Nothing is so powerfully effective against the devil, the world, the flesh, and all evil thoughts as to occupy one's self with God's word, to speak about it and meditate upon it. For this reason alone you should gladly read, recite, ponder, and practice the catechism (Preface to LC 381:10–11, 1530 edition).

Luther's two catechisms, dubbed at the time as the "Lay Bible," made the Word available for men and women in every walk of life. The *Small Catechism* was an instant best-seller. Written in "question and answer" format and published in broadsheets with accompanying woodcuts, it spelled out the essential teachings of faith with the words of the Creed, the Ten Commandments, and the Lord's Prayer, and with instruction on the sacraments. The *Large Catechism*, written in both German and Latin and revised immediately after its first publication, was intended to benefit the parish clergy as well as deepen the education of Christians in general. Luther writes, "I am also a doctor and a preacher, just as learned and experienced as all of them who are so high and mighty. Nevertheless, each morning and whenever else I have time, I do as a child who is being taught the catechism and I read and recite word for word the Lord's Prayer, the Ten Commandments, the Creed, the Psalms, etc." Even Luther needed mother's milk: "I must still read and study the catechism daily, and yet I cannot master it as I wish, but must remain a child and pupil of catechism—and I also do so gladly" (Preface to LC 380:7–8).

Luther is most known for his radical emphasis on grace as a gift with which one receives a faith that alone brings humans into a restored relationship with God. At the same time he underscores the centrality of "active" love in the Christian life. The Christians' call to live in, out, with, and for love is laid out wonderfully in his *Large Catechism*, the handbook on Christian faith and love. Luther begins with the Commandments, before centering on the Creed, especially its chief teaching of Christ's redeeming work. With that lens, he unfolds the meaning of the Lord's Prayer and ends with the exposition of the theology and practice of the only two necessary means of grace, Holy Baptism and the Sacrament of the Altar.[2]

Observations on the commandments, Creed, and prayer

Who is your God? In his vision of the God of the Bible as the one who creates, redeems, and sanctifies, Luther presents God in a personal relationship with human beings. Luther strategically begins with the

Commandments so as to counter misconceptions that evangelicals had no use for law in their over-infatuation with the gospel. He gives advice for how to orient one's life in the tension of law and gospel and intentionally to seek a godly way of life.

The first three commandments set parameters for the basic "I–God" relationship. Luther explains: "A 'god' is the term for that to which we are to look for all good and in which we are to find refuge in all need. Therefore, to have a god is nothing else than to trust and believe in that one with your whole heart . . . Anything on which your heart relies and depends, I say, that is really your God" (LC 386:2–3). The first commandment is thus vital: "if the heart is right with God and we keep this commandment, all the rest will follow on their own" (LC 392:48).

Love of God entails fear, respect, and honor. This is only possible with the help of God's own Word, "the treasure that makes everything holy" (LC 399:92). Keeping the Word in one's heart, lips and ears (LC 400:100), in light of the commandments, one is called to respect not only God (commandments 1–3) but one's neighbor—their person, reputation, possessions, and integrity (commandments 7–10).

The commandments guiding family relations are essential for Luther: in his married experience, there are enough challenges and opportunities to strive towards holiness in the ordinary family life; no monasteries are needed for spiritual discipline (LC 401:112). Household chores and parent–child responsibilities outdo the "holiness and austere life of all the monks" (LC 406:146). True happiness begins from a happy household where faith and love rule. A former monk married to an ex-nun Katharina von Bora (1525) and a blessed father of six children, Luther describes parenthood as a holy vocation: "God has given this walk of life, fatherhood and motherhood, a special position of honor, higher than that of any other walk of life under it" (LC 400:105). Young people are to love and honor their parents: "It must therefore be impressed on young people that they revere their parents as God's representatives, and to remember that, however lowly, poor, feeble, and eccentric they may be, they are still their mother and father, given by God. They are not to be deprived of their honor because of their ways or failures" (LC 401:108, also 402:116). Likewise, obedience is the "great, good, and holy work" of children (LC 401:112). Marriage itself is praised as the most honorable walk of life, protected by the sixth commandment: one must not dishonor one's spouse with adultery (LC 413:200) but cherish the spouse given by God (LC 415:219). God is involved in all aspects of marriage and parenting; these vocations are both the cradle of holiness and also the gravest of temptations.

Commandments 7–10 cover basic human affairs in light of the expectation of love and respect for the other. Holy life entails no stealing or coveting after what belongs to others; whether it is house, spouse, possessions, honor, or anything else, such coveting is "sinful and forbidden" (LC 425:293). The command against coveting also forbids hurtful use of words that can rob one of honor. With a "Mind your own business" motto (LC 420–425) Luther admonishes: "So you see that we are absolutely forbidden to speak evil of our neighbor" (LC 422:274; also LC 424). He goes on to say that, "There is nothing around or in us that can do greater good or greater harm in temporal or spiritual matters than the tongue, although it is the smallest and weakest member" (LC 425:291). To ignore those in need would be similarly devastating: "But beware of how you deal with the poor" because "if you arrogantly turn away those who need your aid . . . . 'they will cry out to heaven' and 'they will reach God, who watches over poor troubled hearts'" (LC 419:246).

The Commandments are overwhelming, "but the Creed brings pure grace and makes us righteous and acceptable to God. Through this knowledge we come to love and delight in all the commandments" (LC 440: 68). Most importantly, the Creed gives us words to answer the question, who is our God? "I believe in the Father, who created me, I believe in God the Son, who has redeemed me; I believe in the Holy Spirit, who makes me holy" (LC 432:7, also 440:67). These three statements of "I believe" correspond to the three articles of the Creed.

With the first article, Luther underscores God's omnipotent, sustaining work that is all-inclusive: "I hold and believe that I am God's creature, that is, that he [God] has given me and constantly sustains my body, soul, and life, my members great and small, all my senses, my reason and understanding, and the like; my food and drink, clothing, nourishment, spouse and children, servants, house and farm, etc. Besides, he [God] makes all creation help provide the benefits and necessities of life," from sun, moon, and stars to fish and grain and clothing (LC 432:13–16). Since everything is given and protected by this God, people are expected to "love, praise, and thank God," serving their Lord without ceasing (LC 433:19). We need to know what we have received from and what we owe to God (LC 433:24).

The second article, "And I believe in Jesus Christ, his only Son, our Lord," is the pivotal confession of faith: "Indeed, the entire gospel that we preach depends on the proper understanding of this article. Upon it all our salvation and blessedness are based, and it is so rich and broad that we can never learn it fully" (LC 435:33). Luther understood the second article to be saying, "I believe that Jesus Christ, true Son of God, has become my Lord." He reminds catechumens that the single word "Lord" implies forgiveness, protection, and salvation. "What is it 'to become a Lord'?" asks Luther. "It means that he has redeemed and released me from sin" (LC 434:27). Christ, the lord, has "brought us back from the devil to God, from death to life, from sin to righteousness, and keeps us there" (LC 434: 31). Without Jesus's lordship, we would remain under the wrath of God and we would be condemned by God's own law (LC 435:33). In his introduction to the second article, Luther admonishes that it "should humble and terrify all of us" finite beings. The holiness it reveals is overwhelming and requires a grateful response (LC 432:23). "For this reason we ought daily to practice this article, impress it upon our minds, and remember it in everything we see and in every blessing that comes our way" (LC 433:22).

The third article of the Creed talks about the consequence of Jesus's lordship in our lives. "I believe in the Holy Spirit" means "I believe that the Holy Spirit makes me holy" (LC 436:40). That is the office of the Holy Spirit who "has made us holy and still makes us holy" (LC 435:36). Luther simplifies: "Therefore being made holy is nothing else than bringing us to the Lord Christ to receive the blessing, to which we could not have come by ourselves" (LC 436:39).

The Creed names particular venues for grace and holiness: "I believe in the Holy Spirit, one holy Christian church, the community of saints, the forgiveness of sins, the resurrection of the flesh, and the life everlasting. Amen" (LC 435:34, 436:36–37). However, the Word remains the key. In the first place, we could not come to Christ or believe what he has accomplished for us unless these were "bestowed on our heart through the preaching of the gospel by the Holy Spirit" (LC 436:38). To bring this gift to people, "God has caused the Word to be published and proclaimed, in which he [God] has given the Holy Spirit to offer and apply to us this treasure, this redemption" (LC 436:38–39). In the second place, the collaboration between the Holy Spirit and the Word is vital: "for where Christ is not preached, there is no Holy Spirit to create, call, and gather the Christian church, apart from which no one can come to the Lord Christ" (LC 436:45). In the third place, the church is crucial for "making us holy" as the place where the Word is preached.

People need church as a channel of grace, according to Luther. The church consists of people who form a holy community of saints and sinners: "I believe that there is on earth a holy little flock and community of pure saints under one head, Christ. It is called together by the Holy Spirit in one faith, mind, and understanding" (LC 437:51). The main purpose of the church is the proclamation of forgiveness; there the church promotes holiness. The forgiveness of sins "takes place through the holy sacraments and absolution as well as through all the comforting words of the entire gospel" (LC 438:54). While Luther's position may seem exclusive, it points to the importance of the regular dose of Word and Spirit for the daily experience of forgiveness (LC 438:56, 58).

How does the salvation become ours? According to Luther, it "is the office and work of the Holy Spirit, to begin and daily increase holiness on earth through these two means, the Christian church and the forgiveness of sins" (LC 439:59). When the Word is preached in the community, faith is stirred and increased, with the affirmation of the forgiveness of sins (LC 439:62). This is so willed by God who created human beings to make them holy (LC 439:64). The Creed, Luther points out, "tells us what God does for us and gives to us" (LC 440:67).

Observations on prayer

The Lord's Prayer is the abbreviation of the entire gospel. Since nobody can keep the Ten Commandments perfectly because of the devil and the world, "nothing is so necessary as to call upon God incessantly." It is a Christian duty to "drum" prayers into God's ears so that God "may give, preserve, and increase in us faith." The Lord's Prayer is given for this purpose (LC 440–441:2–3, 5, 8). As a matter of obedience and respect of God as our parent (LC 442:13, 443:18), and because the wicked human heart wants to flee from God, "the most necessary thing is to exhort and encourage people to pray, as Christ and the apostles also did" (LC 441:4).

Prayers are heard (LC 456:119). With this certainty we should use the Lord's Prayer to address all human needs (LC 440:2, 444:30). The first three petitions call attention to God's holiness, power, and presence, and remind of the importance of respecting God as God is (LC 445:39). The petitions 4 and 5 call attention to the universally felt need for forgiveness and to God's generosity. Honoring the first commandment and making God's name holy among us—by striving for godly living and teaching—involves asking for "many and great things" from God (LC 447:56, 445:39). The fourth petition, "Give us today our daily bread," encompasses our entire life (LC 450:73). We pray for forgiveness, knowing that even before we prayed, God gave us the gospel, and with it forgiveness—which we can only accept, not earn (LC 452:88). Petitions 6 and 7 address the ways to resist in prayer the many temptations Christians encounter (LC 445:109, 111).

Observations on sacraments

It was important for Protestants to articulate their view on the sacraments. With Augustine's criteria, Luther lifts up tangible means of grace that include both the Word and the elements.[3] From Scripture, he draws Jesus's command and promise for only two specific practices, two early Christian practices: baptism and the Lord's Supper. Luther came to dismiss the Catholic tradition's other five sacraments: confession, confirmation, marriage, ordination, and the last unction. Protestant congregations were marked by the celebration of two rather than seven sacraments, the promotion of clergy marriage, and the distribution of both bread and chalice to laity in the Lord's Supper. Luther affirms the importance of sacraments for Christian ministry. They are not, however, absolutes for salvation; the Word alone is.

Luther regarded baptism as "excellent, glorious and exalted" (LC 457:7). He writes, "No greater jewel, therefore, can adorn our body and soul than baptism, for through it we become completely holy and blessed, which no other kind of life and no work on earth can acquire" (LC 462:46).

As in the early church, baptism incorporates us into a communion of believers and thereby grants forgiveness and a new life. Luther disagrees most vehemently with the practice of "believer's baptism." One of the main arguments for infant baptism is that baptism's validity cannot depend on human faith or work (LC 462:49). Rather, baptism generates and nurtures the kind of faith that saves. We bring children to baptism with the "hope that [they] may believe, and we pray God to grant [them] faith. But we do not baptize on this basis, but solely on the command of God" (LC 462:57). The argument he offers is startling: "even if infants did not believe—which, however, is not the case, as we have proved—still baptism would be valid and no one should rebaptize them" (LC 463:55). Ultimately, baptism is God's own work: God's Word baptizes with God's water, after God's own commandment and promise.

"What is baptism?" Luther reiterates "that it is not simply plain water, but water placed in the setting of God's Word and commandment and made holy by them. It is nothing else than God's water, not that the water itself is nobler than other water but that God's Word and commandment are added to it" (LC, 458:14). The water is blessed because of the Word and the Holy Spirit that convey through it all that is God's own (LC 457–459, 462:60). As "truly God's own act" (LC 457:10), baptism results in new birth and a new life in humility and confidence in Christ (LC 460:27). Given their chronic experience of *simul iustus et peccator* [simultaneously just and sinful], "let all

Christians regard their baptism as the daily garment that they are to wear all the time." Baptized Christians will continue, in repentance, to suppress "the old creature" and "practice the work that makes us Christians" (LC 466:84–85). Baptism is a gift beyond human comprehension: "In baptism, therefore, every Christian has enough to study and practice all his or her life. Christians always have enough to do to believe firmly what baptism promises and brings—victory over death and the devil (celebrated in exorcism), forgiveness of sin, God's grace, the entire Christ, and the Holy Spirit with [his] gifts" (LC 461:41–42).

With respect to the Lord's Supper, Luther's main grievances had to do with the Catholic teachings of the enhanced role of clergy, their exclusive right to receive communion in both kinds and so denying the chalice from laity, and the practice of "performing" Mass without the congregation, sometimes for a monetary compensation (selling of private Mass). He introduced significant changes into people's religious lives by insisting that communion be served to all and regularly, without force (LC 471:40, 45). Meant for frequent, communal use, the Lord's Supper replaced the sacrament of confession in importance (LC 470–71:39). Repentance, Luther argued, should characterize the entire Christian life and is a proper preparation for communion, the "daily food and sustenance" for the strengthening of faith (LC 469:24–25).

These benefits can only be received in faith (LC 470:33–35) by "those who feel their weakness." The Lord's Supper works as "a precious antidote against the poison in their systems," because the communicant receives not only forgiveness from Christ's lips" but also God's grace and the Spirit's gifts (LC 474:70). This reality happens, without a doubt, because of God's Word; the faith of the recipient or of the one who administers the sacrament is irrelevant (LC 473:64): "Even though a scoundrel receives or administers the sacrament, it is the true sacrament (that is, Christ's body and blood ... For it is not founded on human holiness but on the Word of God" (LC 468:16). Therefore, just as in our baptism, "we come as poor, miserable people, precisely because we are unworthy" (LC 473:61).

Luther emphasizes Christ's real presence in the sacrament. He distinguishes his view from the Catholic doctrine of transubstantiation (which teaches an ontological change in elements) and, even more strongly, from the Zwinglian view of the sacrament as a sign of Christ's spiritual presence.[4] Needless to say, Luther was most opposed to the celebration of remembrance of Christ's work, a view held by the so-called radicals. (The next generation of Reformers, with Jean Calvin, would propose yet another solution. This issue has remained a source of great division among Protestants; only recently have different denominations found enough common ground for table fellowship and sharing in ministry.) Luther's ultimate concern all along was not necessarily to explain the "how" but to emphasize the reality and real benefits of Christ's work "for us."

Observations on confession and repentance

Rather than thinking of confession as a third sacrament, Luther saw it as a mode of living for the baptized. He writes, "Therefore, when I exhort you to go to confession, I am doing nothing but exhorting you to be a Christian" (LC 479:32).[5] Given the nature of sin in human life, repentance cannot be reduced to one ritual, just as no amount of confessing would ever count for all transgressions. Therefore, "by divine ordinance Christ himself has placed absolution in the mouths of his Christian community and commanded us to absolve one another from sins" (LC 477:14). Being Christian, in other words, means that we "are to confess our guilt before one another and forgive one another before we come to God and ask for forgiveness. Now, all of us are debtors to one another; therefore we should and we may confess publicly in everyone's presence, no one being afraid of anyone else" (LC 477:10). Confession also has existential or psychological import, especially in the form of "secret confession that takes place privately before a single brother or sister," not least at times when "some particular issue weighs on us or attacks us, eating away at us" (LC 477:13). In Luther's summary, the "essence of a genuinely Christian life" is to repent and pray for God's grace (LC 477:9).

Conclusion

Luther's central concerns are the Christian freedom of conscience and the equality of all sinners, for we are all beggars in need of God's grace. His *Large Catechism* targets the incessant human need for forgiveness, just as it unfolds God's support system for the feeble sinner. It presents a theological vision for who God is as well as a model for spiritual living as a saint and a sinner in this world. The *Large Catechism* stands out as a book of love as much as a book of faith, as it suggests ways to orient one's life in loving service to others in response to God's gracious love.

Notes

1. Translated from *der Grosse Katechismus*; hereafter, all references to this work (*The Large Catechism*, in *The Book of Concord* [eds. Robert Kolb and Timothy J. Wengert; Minneapolis: Fortress Press, 2000], 377–480) shall be noted by employing in-text citations.
2. Exhortation to Confession in the 1529 revision of the work was not consistently included in the ensuing editions.
3. "It is the Word, I say, that makes this a sacrament and distinguishes it from ordinary bread and wine, so that it is called and truly is Christ's body and blood. For it is said, 'Accedat verbum ad elementum et fit sacramentum,' that is, 'When the Word is joined to the external element, it becomes a sacrament'" (LC 468:10). See also LC 458:18.
4. Any chances for a unified front for Protestants ended relatively early on in Zwingli's and Luther's inability to find a middle ground in their convictions regarding Christ's presence in the sacrament (most notably at the 1529 Marburg Colloquy).
5. Already in his Ninety-Five Theses, Luther stated that Christian life is spent in repentance.

Select Bibliography

Primary sources

Luther, Martin. *Der Große Katechismus.* In: Luther, Martin. *D. Martin Luthers Werke: Kritische Gesamtausgabe. Schriften.* [65 vols.] Weimar: H. Böhlaus Nachfolger, 1883–1993: Vol. 30:1, 125–238.

Luther, Martin. *Gesammelte Werke* CD-ROM. Ed. Kurt Aland. Digitale Bibliothek 63. Berlin: Direct Media, 2002.

Luther, Martin. *The Large Catechism.* In: *The Book of Concord*, eds Robert Kolb and Timothy J. Wengert. Minneapolis: Fortress Press, 2000, 377–480.

Secondary sources

Arand, Charles P. *That I May Be His Own: An Overview of Luther's Catechisms.* St. Louis: Concordia, 2000.

Peters, Albrecht. *Commentary on Luther's Catechisms, Baptism and Lord's Supper.* Trans. Thomas Trapp. St. Louis: Concordia Publishing House, 2012.

Stjerna, Kirsi. *No Greater Jewel. Martin Luther on Baptism.* Augsburg Press, 2009.

Wengert, Timothy J. *Martin Luther's Catechisms. Forming the Faith.* Fortress Press, 2009.

3·4

The Institutes of the Christian Religion[1] (1559)
John Calvin (1509–1564)

Introduction

The *Institutes of the Christian Religion* stands among the most influential single works from the Reformation century. In a systematic fashion, it offers a comprehensive presentation of Christian doctrine from a Protestant perspective. The originally catechetical treatise developed over the years into a sophisticated tome that was published in revised versions in French and Latin. With an international impact, it solidified the French author Jean Calvin's stature as the principal reformer and a theological authority next to Martin Luther. In the following, highlights from the latest edition of 1559 are introduced with an eye to the mystical dimensions of Calvin's theology.

A catechism to educate

Jean Calvin, born in 1509 in Noyon, France, wrote his *Institutes* for the first time in 1536 as a twenty-six-year old scholar and before entering ministry. During the violent times and persecution of the Huguenots, he wanted to educate his fellow French men and women on the basics of Christian faith. He presented his brand-new French catechism to King Francis I, appealing to his benevolence to end the violence against the French Protestants.

While Calvin set out to write a rudimentary handbook of the Christian faith for his fellow French Protestants, in the process of writing he discerned

Figure 3.3 Calvin

the need to furnish the King with a description of the doctrine "that so inflames the rage of those madmen who are this day, with fire and sword, troubling your kingdom. For I fear not to declare, that what I have here given may be regarded as a summary of the very doctrine which, they vociferate, ought to be punished with confiscation, exile, imprisonment, and flames, as well as exterminated by land and sea . . ."[2] Quite boldly, Calvin reminds his majesty of his duty to investigate the cause worthy of his throne. After all, "The characteristic of a true sovereign is, to acknowledge that, in the administration of his kingdom, he is a minister of God."[3] These words from the exile witness to Calvin's security in his faith and the stamina he showed as a reformer before he died on May 27, 1564, in Geneva.

The original catechetical work in Latin from 1536 had only six chapters: on the Decalogue, the Apostles' Creed, the Lord's Prayer, the Sacraments, the false sacraments, and Christian freedom. The text grew three sizes larger for its Latin edition of 1539, translated into French in 1541. Calvin continued to perfect his book: after its 1543 expanded Latin version, and its French translation in 1545, and yet another Latin (fourth) edition in 1550 and another in French in 1551, Calvin finally completed the definitive edition in Latin in 1559, which was translated into French in 1560. In its many translations the *Institutes* came to establish Calvin as the leading reformer with an international audience. As Calvin trained, supported, and directed

Protestants from his base of operations in Geneva, the portable single-volume would have carriers in different corners of the globe.[4]

Calvin's personal journey

Calvin converted to Protestant faith in 1533–1534 under the influence of the famous Circle of Meaux, sponsored by the king's older sister Marguerite. As a classically trained humanist and a lawyer who had flirted with theological studies, he conversed with the cutting edge French scholars and artists with reforming tendencies, all of whom were led into exile after two striking events. The first was the "Affair of the Posters" (October 17, 1534), in which the Mass was blasphemed in posters plastered around the royal castle, and the second was the "Cop Affair," in which the new university rector preached a sermon with evangelical undertones. Violence against the Huguenots culminated in the St. Bartholomew's Day massacre (August 23, 1537) of thousands of Huguenots, including those attending the royal wedding of Marguerite's Protestant grandson Henry and a Catholic princess Margaret of Valois. The peace was restored with Henry's (IV) accession to the throne and official return to the Catholic faith. The fate of the Protestants (with the Confession of La Rochelle from 1559) remained precarious until the moderately tolerant Edict of Nantes (April 13, 1598) and beyond. It was during these bloody times in French Reformation history that Calvin emerged as a leading voice for evangelical faith from his new home in Geneva, which under his leadership became the stronghold of the Reformation.

On a lay-over in Geneva *en route* to Strasbourg, Calvin—considered a French refugee—was seized by a newly protestant preacher William Farel who saw in him a "Godsend." Calvin arrived on the scene in 1536 when Catholics had already been ordered to leave the previous year; he brought a number of reforms but with a heavy hand, and as a result he was asked to leave in 1538. After some happy years as a scholar in Strasbourg (1538–1541), Calvin was called back by the Genevans. This time, with a firm hand and faithful preaching, Calvin established himself as the indisputable leader of reforms. During the years 1541–1564, Geneva was under Calvin's diligent if at times intimidating care. Life was ordered under the supervision of the Consistory and with all-encompassing "Ordinances." Calvin rose to such a leadership position on account of the power of his *Institutes*, his forceful convictions, convincing commentary on the scriptures, and the unique context for his call. Together with his German associate Phillip Melanchthon, he remained hopeful of a joint Protestant confession; however, the debate over Christ's presence in the Lord's Supper proved insurmountable.[5]

The foundation: at the mercy of the sovereign God

The *Institutes* is divided into four books. The first book addresses the goodness of God and creation in contrast to sin, as well as the knowledge of God; the second book elaborates on the providential goodness of God the Redeemer in the person and work of Christ; the third book targets the divine work of the Holy Spirit in the election, justification, and sanctification of the elect; the fourth book's subject matter is the (true) Church, its proclamation, and the sacraments of baptism and the Lord's Supper as means for God's goodness. The explanation of the Ten Commandments, the Lord's Prayer, and the Creeds are fleshed out within the books that build on Calvin's central vision of the sovereignty of God and fallible human beings' grace-based relationship with God. From several different angles, the four books develop the premise that salvation comes irresistibly by God's free promise and election, resulting in a life characterized by active repentance and producing good fruits for the glory of God.

At the root of Calvin's theology is his appreciation of the absolute sovereign goodness of the Creator. In concert with the early church's doctrine of the triune God of creation, redemption, and continued grace (ICR Book I, ch. XIII), Calvin's fundamental teaching is that not only the creation of human beings, but also their sustained well-being and, significantly, their salvation ultimately rests in the hands of the omniscient triune God. This is the foundation for the most famous teaching associated with Calvin, that of election and predestination (ICR Book III, chs. XXI–XXIV in particular). Similarly, his anthropology is based on the conviction that God's universal omnipotence manifests in the particulars of one's personal life. That God's hidden hand is involved in every life, every moment, and every turn of events is for Calvin a sweet insight filled with comfort and promise.

Knowledge of God and of self: in creation, within, and in Scripture

Calvin begins his book with reflection on wisdom and two-fold knowledge: knowledge of self and knowledge of God are essentially related (ICR, Book

I, ch. I, 1). One's self-knowledge is a step towards proper knowing of God, and thus happiness. At the same time, contemplating God's sovereign greatness reveals our finitude and need for God (ICR Book I, chs. I-III). The good news is that the one and only creature called the image of God, which Calvin portrays as a microcosm of creation, has received the necessary facilities to know the Creator (ICR Book I, ch. V, 3), such as reason and free will, with the original God-given righteousness (ICR Book I, ch. XV, passim). The bad news is that sin has damaged these faculties and compromised one's ability to know God or oneself. The clouded human awareness of God is useless without divine restoration (ICR Book I, chs. IV-V). Worse, degenerated human beings are blinded by innate self-love (ICR B II, ch. I, 1–2).

Most damaging is the depravity of the freedom of will and the slavery to sin, both of which underlie humanity's chronic ignorance of divine matters (ICR Book II, ch. II). This point stands even if some "residue of intelligence and judgment" remains. For instance, the natural gift of reason, "by which [human] man discerns between good and evil," while not "entirely destroyed," is weakened to a "shapeless ruin" (ICR Book II, ch. II, 12). Calvin is adamant that "free will does not enable any man [human] to perform good works, unless he [she] is assisted by grace" (ICR Book II, ch. II, 6).

Stupid curiosity and indulging in vain speculation are of no use and offer no way out of this predicament (ICR Book I, ch. IV, passim); revelation from the Scriptures is needed. Creation also offers constant clues about the Creator's existence and will, both within and outside the *imago Dei*'s being (ICR Book I, ch. V, 3 and passim): "That there exists in the human mind, and indeed by natural instinct, some sense of Deity, we hold to be beyond dispute" (ICR III, Ch. 1, 1). Calvin teaches that "a sense of Deity (*sensus divinitatis*) is indelibly engraved on the human heart," as if fixed "in our very bones" (ICR Book I, ch. III, 3), even for the wicked to experience: the fear of God is unavoidable, at least on some level (ICR Book I, ch.III, 3).

In tune with the medieval mystics, Calvin teaches that this *sensus divinitatis* waits to be discovered under the debris of sin, a flicker that can be re-ignited and recovered. This happens through the revelation of Scripture: the spectacles of Scripture provide a corrected vision by which to make sense of God's self-revelation in creation, but it is always these inspired words of the prophets, apostles, etc., which enables one to most faithfully lead a Christian life (ICR Book I, ch. IX, 1–13). Knowledge of God in this sense is intimately linked with saving faith (ICR Book III, ch. II) as "a knowledge of the divine favor, and a full persuasion of its truth" (ICR Book III, ch. II, 12, 28). The faith saves not as a human work but because of the free promise of God, with the certainty of salvation for the elect (ICR Book III, ch. II, 2, 6, 16, 19, 24, 29, passim). Accordingly, it "arms and fortifies itself with the word of God" (ICR Book III, ch. II, 21). Calvin describes the effect: "As soon as the minutest particle of faith is instilled into our minds, we begin to behold the face of God placid, serene, and propitious; far off, indeed, but still so distinctly as to assure us that there is no delusion in it . . ." (ICR Book III, ch. II, 19). Like a hand reaching out to receive a gift, faith is the "hand of the soul" which is empowered by the Spirit to receive the Gospel offered in Christ. This living faith, then, has four effects: "(1) Repentance, (2) a Christian life, (3) Justification, and (4) Prayer," and these four represent the sanctification that follows for those who have received God's promise through his Son and by His Spirit (ICR Aphorisms, Book III, see Aphorisms 44, 47).

Sanctification and repentance: in the company of the Holy Spirit

Calvin understands the Christian's life as sanctified; that is, as life with the Spirit: "Hence the Spirit is called the Spirit of sanctification, because he quickens and cherishes us . . . because he is the seed and root of heavenly life in us" (ICR Book III, ch. I, 2). This life is not for everyone but those who are, first, elected, and second, justified. At its foundation, it involves an experience of regeneration, and an ongoing life of active repentance and good works (ICR Book III, ch. V, in sum Book III ch. VII). None of this is possible without the Holy Spirit.

First of all, like a divine energy, the Holy Spirit draws people to the Scriptures to have their minds illuminated regarding God's will and their own condition. Second, the Holy Spirit personally leads one to Christ and produces the benefits of redemption (ICR Book I, ch. VII, 1–5). Only the soul drawn, illuminated, and elevated by the Spirit's mystical work "receives as it were a new eye" and can "contemplate heavenly mysteries, by the splendor of which it was previously dazzled" (ICR Book III, ch. II, 34). Third, the Holy Spirit effects a "total" renewal of the person from a state of "total" perversion (Book II, ch. III, 1, passim).

The divine stimulus of grace and "quickening" by the Holy Spirit are needed to awaken people from their sluggishness and blind inertia (ICR Book II, ch. II, 1),[6] and to enable them to live a sanctified life (ICR Book III, ch. II, 1–2). With the concepts of repentance and regeneration, also referred to as mortification of the flesh and quickening of the soul, Calvin describes the Spirit-led damage-control needed for sanctified life (ICR Book III,

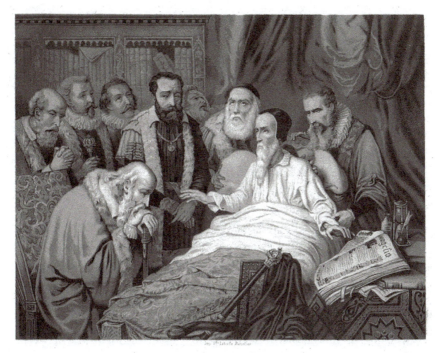

ÚLTIMOS MOMENTOS DE CALVINO

Figure 3.4 Calvin at his death bed

ch. III). The goal of regeneration is nothing less than union with God and loving service of one's neighbor. Calvin underscores the personal work of the Holy Spirit in both. After all, "the Holy Spirit is the bond by which Christ effectually binds us to himself" (ICR Book III, ch. I, 1) and brings us into a sacred marriage with Christ. Furthermore, the Spirit renews our vigor by adopting us with the sprinkling of the Spirit. At the core of regenerate life is the union with Christ through the Spirit's constant work (ICR Book III, ch. I, 3).

The Spirit leads believers through the stages of repentance, starting with the hatred of sin, which gives one "access to the knowledge of Christ, who manifests himself to none but miserable and afflicted sinners." To "stand in Christ" means to actively cultivate repentance throughout one's entire life (ICR Book III, ch. III, 20): "In one word, then, by repentance I understand regeneration ['une regeneration spirituelle'] the only aim of which is to form in us anew the image of God" (ICR Book III, ch. III, 9). On their way to the heavenly goal, to see God face to face, Christians are to engage in warfare to abolish carnal pollution and to grow in conformity with Christ, so that "the nearer any one approaches in resemblance to God, the more does the image of God appear in him." (ICR Book III, ch. III, 9).

Predestination and justification: the ultimate comfort

Only four chapters in the *Institutes* are devoted to the issue of predestination (ICR Book III, chs. XXI–XXIV). Acknowledging human depravity and bondage to sin, and emphasizing the constant work of God's Spirit, Calvin underscores that the salvation of men and women is entirely in God's hands. Calvin follows the path set by Augustine and the early church's councils that decided against the teaching of free will in salvific matters (contra Pelagius and others). In light of the experience of persecuted Protestants, Calvin's doctrine of predestination is ultimately about divine comfort and security in God. The burden is lifted from the individual's shoulders: God's grace alone makes one fit to be chosen, in accordance with the eternal hidden degree of the omnipotent God (ICR Book III, ch. XXIV, 1 and passim).

Speaking of the eternal hidden degree, Calvin distinguishes between prescience and predestination. He reminds that "all things always were, and ever continue, under his [God's] eye; that to his knowledge there is no past or future, but all things are present." God's prescience, which could be described as God's immediate contemplation of all that is in "the whole circuit of the world," is distinct from pre-determination. By predestination, Calvin understands God's eternal decree of election according to which "some are preordained to eternal life, others to eternal damnation" (ICR Book III, ch. XXI, 5). The election happens through the preaching of God's word and its illumination by God's Spirit, and results in the elect's justification and sanctification. The efficient cause in all this is God's mercy, the material cause is Christ, and the final cause is that God's people would glorify God. Through and through, "our election is connected with our calling" (Book III, ch. XXIV, 6). Resurrection is the final goal, which the elect should anticipate secure in God's own promise.

Calvin's understanding of justification is inseparable from his teaching of predestination. The elect who are personally engrafted into the life of Christ receive his righteousness (ICR Aphorisms, Book III, 52).[7] Calvin writes:

> This whole may be thus summed up: Christ given to us by the kindness of God is apprehended and possessed by faith, by means of which we obtain in particular a twofold benefit; first, being reconciled by the righteousness of

Christ, God becomes, instead of a judge, an indulgent Father; and, secondly, being sanctified by his Spirit, we aspire to integrity and purity of life (Book III, ch. XI, 1, also Aphorisms Book III, 53).

As with Luther, the interpretative tradition has neglected a crucial insight on the nature of justification and its Christological basis in Calvin's theology, namely, the mystical dimension. Calvin is convinced that justification means more than the declaration of forgiveness. Using words like "communicate" and "partakers," Calvin explains how Christ in his divine righteousness not only "covers your sins" in the eyes of God but even effects "that all which is his is made yours, you become a member of him, and hence one with him." With the gifts of resurrection and eternal life, Christ himself is communicated to the elect as the author of salvation (ICR Book III, ch II, 24): "We expect salvation from him—not because he stands aloof from us, but because engrafting us into his body he not only makes us partakers of all his benefits, but also of himself" (ICR Book II, ch. XI-XIV). In such intimate union with Christ, the elect have the grounding for holiness and a sanctified life.

On the basis of the mystical communication of Christ and his benefits and the ongoing union with the Spirit, believers can live a regenerated life in holiness. In the guidance of the Holy Spirit and in ongoing repentance, they can aim to become increasingly Christ-like in this life. The church and its sacraments are given as a means for this journey.

On church and sacraments: union in faith

The doctrine of election and the presence of the Holy Spirit are the grounding for Calvin's understanding of the Church: a community of grace and salvation, instituted for preaching and administering the sacraments (ICR Book IV, chs I-IV). All Christians are called to preach and serve the sacraments in the common ministry of all believers. Ministry is handled through the equal-yet-distinct offices of the elders, pastors, teachers and deacons; the hierarchy between clergy and laity is diminished (ICR Book IV, ch. III, 8). For the church and its ministry, proclamation of the Word is of primary importance, while the same grace is mediated through sacraments.

Sacraments are not seen as crucial for salvation, only faith is. They are celebrated as testimonies to God's grace received in the Word (ICR Book IV, ch. XIV). Consisting of word and external sign (ICR Book IV, ch. XIV, 4), sacraments rest on God's promise, Calvin reminds. They also entail participation in the community of faith that one joined in the first sacrament, baptism (ICR Book IV, ch. IV, 5). Theologically, baptism is the initiatory sign of a covenant that engrafts the baptized into Christ, while practically it joins new members into the fellowship of the children of God. Children need baptism for the washing of forgiveness and mortification of the flesh; it signals entrance into the school of faith, the mother church, that then molds its children in the Christian life of faith (ICR Book IV, ch. XV and XVI on infant baptism). Those marked with baptism as the people of God are true partakers of Christ's blessings, Calvin concludes (ICR Book IV, ch. XV, 1; Aphorisms Book IV, 83).

The Lord's Supper demands more of Calvin's attention (ICR Book IV, ch. XVII). He holds that the sacred mystery of the Lord's Supper, instituted by Christ (ICR Book IV, ch. XVII, 1), consists of the corporeal signs of bread and wine, and of spiritual truth (ICR Book IV, ch. IV, 11). The Lord's Supper is a "spiritual feast" that preserves the elect, aids in confirming their faith towards God, and serves as a confession and exhortation in relation to others (ICR Book IV, ch. 84–85). In the aftermath of the breakup between Zwingli and Luther, Calvin takes the middle way. He is one with Luther in rejecting any notion of the Lord's Supper as a repeated sacrifice and the doctrine of transubstantiation, but Calvin does not find the ubiquity of Christ satisfactory to explain Christ's presence or the benefits of the sacrament for the believer. If anything, the ubiquity *of the Holy Spirit* is the distinctive emphasis of Calvin. While the risen humanity of Jesus is at the right hand of the Father, the believer "ascends" to encounter Jesus in faith. This "spiritual presence" takes place through Christ's divinity, unlimited by time and place. The fullness of Christ's presence is celebrated in Christ's resurrection, in the ecstasy of the worshipper's faith, and through the Holy Spirit's influence in the daily life, as well as in the sacraments.[8]

Calvin defends his view of the nature of Christ's presence as far from "obscure" or "absurd" but "in perfect accordance with Scriptures." As he argues, "The presence of Christ in the Supper we must hold to be such as neither affixes him to the element of bread, nor encloses him in bread, nor circumscribes him in any way." Rather, when Christ "called himself the bread of life, he did not take that appellation from the sacrament ... he made us partakers of his divine immortality" (ICR Book IV, ch. XVII, 19). The blessings of Christ's sacrifice become ours through the gospel and by participation in the Supper where "Christ offers himself to us with all his blessings, and we receive him in faith" (ICR, Book IV, ch. XVII, 4–5). What is "signified" in this Supper is truly received by believers only. This is the work of the Spirit, incomprehensible to the human mind (ICR, Book IV, ch.

XVII, 10). With a mystical insight, Calvin teaches that the Spirit makes the believer present to Christ through participation in the sacrament, in the *mysterion*. Reminiscent of Luther in his justification doctrine, Calvin's exposition of the Supper points to the mystical, personal union Christ offers to his own.

Conclusion

Calvin was instrumental in the survival of Protestant faith in the French-speaking lands in the midst of much bloodshed and grief, even if he was in exile from his home in France. In addition to teaching and preaching with an international influence from his base in Geneva, he offered protection for the persecuted and organized a mission with trained doctors, pastors, deacons, and elders in different contexts in Europe. He bolstered the spirits of persons in key positions through both personal visitation and vigorous correspondence. In solidarity with those persecuted for their Protestant faith, he developed a theological vision for Christian living and the mission of the church. Beyond the *Institutes*, Calvin left sermons, letters, catechetical material, commentaries, and confessional texts that show the breadth of his theological acumen, the fruits of his faithful scriptural exegesis, and his expansive vision as an educator in the Christian faith. He remains most recognized for his role as the Reformer of Europe and the author of the *Institutes*, his theological testament, designed to convince the reader. As Elsie McKee once said, "he demands serious attention—there are no lazy readers of the *Institutes*!"[9] But the experience is worth it.

Notes

1. Translated from *Institutio christianae religionis*; the edition used here: John Calvin, *Institutes of the Christian Religion*, trans. Henry Beveridge (Grand Rapids, MI: Wm. B. Eerdmans Publishing Company, 1989 [1845]). Hereafter, this work is quoted as ICR.
2. ICR, 3–4.
3. Ibid., 4.
4. For Calvin's life, see Bruce Gordon, *Calvin* (Yale University Press, 2011).
5. Melanchthon and Calvin were approaching an agreement on the wording regarding the Lord's Supper on the basis of the Altered Augsburg Confession, crafted autonomously by Melanchthon.

6.   See ICR Book II, ch. II, 1. On human depravity, sin and lack of freedom, ICR Book II, chs. I-III.
7.   "They are justified by faith who, shut out from the righteousness of works, receive the righteousness of Christ. Such are the elect of God" (ICR Aphorisms, Book III, 52).
8.   See David Steinmetz, *Calvin in Context* (Oxford University Press, 2010), 126–127, here summarized.
9.   Originally published as an online essay by Elsie McKee, "Reflections," in her introduction to *Ad Fontes: A Primer in Reformed Theology*. It has since been taken offline, nevertheless Dr. McKee graciously has given permission to still use it.

Select Bibliography

Primary sources

Calvino, Ioanne. *Institutio Christianae Religionis*. Genevæ, 1559. 564 pp. Available in Logos.com.

Ioannis Calvini opera quae supersunt omnia. Edited by G. Baum, E. Cunitz and E. Reuss. 59 vols. *Corpus Reformatorum* 29–87. Brunswick: Schwetschke, 1863–1900.

Calvin, John. *Institutes of the Christian Religion*. Translated by Henry Beveridge, 1845. Grand Rapids, MI: Eerdmans, 1989. Available online in Christian Classics Ethereal Library, www.ccel.org/ccel/calvin/institutes/

McNeill, John T., ed., *Calvin: Institutes of the Christian Religion*, 2 vols., Library of Christian Classics. Nashville: Westminster John Knox, 1960.

Secondary sources

Gerrish, Brian A. *Grace and Gratitude: The Eucharist Theology of John Calvin*. Minneapolis: Fortress, 1993. (Digitalized by University of Michigan 2009.)

Gordon, Bruce. *Calvin*. New Haven: Yale University Press, 2011.

Jones, Serene. *Calvin and the Rhetoric of Piety*. Columbia Series in Reformed Theology. Nashville: Westminster John Knox, 1995.

Parker, T.H.L. *Calvin: An Introduction to His Thought*. Nashville: Westminster John Knox, 1995.

Steinmetz, David C. *Calvin in Context*. New York: Oxford University Press, 1995.

Steinmetz, David C. "The Theology of John Calvin." Pages 113–129 in *Cambridge Companion to Reformation Theology*. Edited by David Bagchi and David C. Steinmetz. Cambridge: Cambridge University Press, 2004.

3.5

A Foundation and Plain Instruction of the Saving and God-Pleasing Teaching of Jesus Christ, Briefly Compiled from the Word of God and Again with Great Diligence Read Over and Improved (1558)

Menno Simons (1496–1561)

Introduction

Menno Simons' major work *Foundation of Christian Doctrine* (1539, expanded and revised, 1558) is the most important doctrinal work from the first generation Anabaptist tradition. Menno Simons rose to leadership in a tender time in Anabaptist history. After violent actions from and against the so-called radicals in Germany and the Dutch lands, a voice of reason and peace was needed. A young priest Menno Simons came to shepherd the fragmented Anabaptist groups back to their original non-violent roots. As a fugitive missionary, he became the uniting theological voice among the

Figure 3.5 Menno Simons

Anabaptists, who at the time were without a confessional standing, and most importantly so with this *Foundation of Christian Doctrine*.[1]

The fugitive leader's peaceful vision

Menno Simons was born in January 1496 in East Friesland (modern day Netherlands) and was ordained into Catholic priesthood in 1524. He served in parish ministry from 1524 to 1531 (at the village of Pingjum) and between 1531 and 1536 (in his home town of Witmarsum). During this time as a parish pastor, he grew bothered both by the violent treatment of Anabaptist Christians and the sacramental practices and teachings of the Catholic church. From 1525 onwards, he began studying the Bible for himself, very much influenced by Luther's writings (e.g., Luther's 1520 *On Christian Freedom* and his 1518 *Seven Articles*). He embraced the Protestants' argument of the Bible as the primary authority and its interpretation belonging to all. He began to disassociate himself from the Catholic teaching of sacraments and he even doubted the validity of his calling as a priest in the church he no longer recognized as the institution for salvation.

Several turning points led him to take leadership in defense of the persecuted Anabaptists: the 1531 execution of a rebaptized Christian (Sicke Snijder of Leeuwarden) and in 1535 his own brother's death with an Anabaptist group (associated with the Munsterites) attempting to take over the Oldeklooster. Menno continued to serve in his priestly office for nine months, while preaching with Anabaptist convictions. He began to examine the biblical grounds for infant baptism and argued that the Catholic Church's practice of baptism was not biblical. Proclaiming his new conviction that unbaptized children are just as saved as baptized ones, Menno publicly renounced his Catholic faith. He was rebaptized by a Friesian Anabaptist Obbe Philips and installed as the elder (bishop) leader for the Anabaptists in the province of Groningen in 1537. Now a fugitive himself, Menno married Geertruid, a beguine. His travels from South Netherlands (1536–1543) extended to the Rhineland in Germany (1543–1546) and Danish Holstein (1546–1561). As a mediator and a missionary, the preacher of repentance pulled together different factions of Anabaptists with his peaceful vision. He led the majority of the European Anabaptists to disengage from the aggressive factions (such as the apocalyptic Munsterites who had failed in their efforts to establish a theocratic new Jerusalem in the town of Munster). Menno continued his ministry until his death on January 31, 1561, near Ordesloe, Holstein.[2]

On the Foundation of Christian Doctrine: The plain teachings of the NT

A prolific author, Menno sought to write for common people. His *Foundation of Christian Doctrine* became the most important doctrinal work from the first generation Anabaptist tradition. It helped to restore the original

Anabaptist vision on practical holiness. Its teaching on the Church's role in the lives of people called for intense repentance and demonstrates Menno's pastoral concern for the salvation and well-being of others; it was for that reason that he emphasized the teaching of the sacraments and regenerate life. Menno desired to explicate a message of peace and salvation, effective sacramental ministry, and the importance of proclaiming the "plain" word.

Menno's theology explicitly rests on what he reads from the New Testament; if a teaching is not there, it should not be taught or believed. Infant baptism, taking oaths, military service, killing another person, or marrying someone outside the church, for instance, were not in line with the New Testament's teachings, whereas salvation by grace and justification by faith without works was at the heart of the matter. Likewise, Menno considered both believer's baptism and the need to live the Christian life in constant repentance as part of the "plain word," as was the New Testament teaching on the true presence of Christ in and behind the relations in the church, in ethical action, and in the community life of the regenerate, the separation of state and church, and the call for non-violence for all Christians. In the plain meaning of the New Testament, believers were called to active faith, which meant repentance and love of God and one another. Love was the sign of a believer, just as it was the sign of the church; indeed, a true church must be willing to suffer to the point of martyrdom.

The book begins with a preface, in which Menno describes his own process of discernment and conversion. Following the logic of I Corinthians 3:11, Menno articulated the basic principle, his motto of faith: No one can lay any other foundation than the one already laid, which is Jesus Christ. Menno's work is essentially Christ-centric. From this foundation he urges believers to courage and the persecuted to perseverance. Reminding readers of the importance of biblical authority, Menno then proceeds to address central issues in three parts: biblical preaching, sanctification, and sacraments.

Throughout his *Foundation of Christian Doctrine*, Menno is cautious to hold to the Word of God, yet confident in proclaiming that Word to the world. Menno reminds the true church of its active, obedient faith; a faith in which it baptizes, a faith that rebukes all broken Christian traditions for their infidelity to a true communion with Christ Jesus, and a faith that requests peace from the sinful world for the faithful church of Christ.

The *Foundation* seeks to provide a theological framework for the entire life of the church, with an apocalyptic eschatology and a highly developed theology of the cross (and of its glory), and a willingness to suffer with Christ. A common refrain echoes throughout the *Foundation*: a call to rightly understand God, the Scriptures, the sacraments (baptism and the Lord's Supper), the church and its calling to peace. Menno writes:

> ...there is but one church of Christ ... having but a single Gospel, faith, baptism, Supper, and service; traveling on the same road and leading a pious, unblamable life, as the Scriptures teach. All then who do not have the pure, unmixed Word of God, genuine active faith, together with the Lord's holy baptism and Supper, in spirit and power, and walk the broad road of the flesh: these are not the congregation and the church of Christ.[3]

These basic marks of Christian life inform the Church: "... take heed what the Word of the Lord teaches you, and observe the true doctrine of Christ, the true teachers, the true sacraments, the true church, and the true Christian life which is of God ..." (FCD 152). The fullness of God's grace is promised to the church that obeys and loves Christ: "In brief, without love it is all in vain that we believe, baptize, celebrate the Lord's Supper, prophesy, and suffer" (FCD 149). Love is the starting point and at the heart of Menno's exploration of the tenets of his theology, viz. God, the Scriptures, baptism, the Lord's Supper, the church and peace.

God

Complete union with God is the foundational Christian hope and goal. Menno's *Foundation* has little room for paradox in this regard. God is either present or not present. Humanity is either faithful or unfaithful. One is either united with God or not united: "We must be in Christ and Christ in us; we must be moved by His Spirit, and abide in His holy Word outwardly and inwardly. Otherwise we have no God" (FCD 191). Union with God is the cornerstone upon which all else depends.[4]

Union with God casts out all sin and error. When Christians "become one with the Spirit, doctrine, and example of Christ as the Scriptures teach," then God the Almighty will keep "the pious, God-fearing hearts" in grace and preserve them from errors that would lead them away from divine love (FCD 201). With God there is no sin; therefore, where human lives are united with God, they will be united with the absence of sin. Proper obedience to Christ the leader, then, implies active striving for righteousness (FCD 157). As Christ is the embodiment of holy living, Christians must live as Christ lives (FCD 187).

Mercy is God's inclination toward the penitent: God "is long-suffering, gracious, and merciful, and pardons" all who sincerely seek for grace (FCD 106). The cost of grace is a life of repentance without which God's mercy avails nothing (FCD 114). Whereas there is no hope for a humanity that seeks its own way, all those who repent from the world and are joined to God through Christ are given every grace and mercy of the true God. Repentance is a must for the forgiveness of sins and reception of Christ's merits: "Read and search the whole Scriptures, the true doctrine and testimony of the holy prophets, evangelists, and apostles, and you will discover most clearly that this godly repentance is to be earnestly received and practiced, and that without it no one can receive grace, enter into the kingdom of heaven, nor have any hope forever" (FCD 112). Scripture insists that one continue to believe and confess, and to live "a pious an irreproachable life" with a "sincere, regenerating, vigorous faith in Christ Jesus," with pure love and obedience (FCD 108, 114).

The Scriptures

Menno calls for believers to "read and search the whole Scriptures," for in them we find the only trustworthy guide to know God. This essential teaching underscores the importance of attaining the plain understanding of the Word: in such reading Christ's Spirit guides believers and conforms their lives with the doctrine of the early church's apostles (FCD 108 and 192, 186). The Scriptures provide the guide for Christian faith and living, and they also give the narrative of the true, suffering church, the glory of which is in its status as the true bride of Christ (FCD 190–191).

Baptism

Menno's *Foundation* teaches directly on the sacraments of baptism and the Lord's Supper. In seeking for the plain understanding of faith through the Scriptures, the sacrament of baptism serves as a statement of faith and a commitment to living a new life in Christ: "Here we have the Lord's commandment concerning baptism … that the Gospel must first be preached, and then those baptized who believe it" (FCD 120). The Word and will of God requires that, in order to bear witness to Christ, a Christian be prepared to "forsake their homes, possessions, lands, and lives and to suffer hunger, affliction, oppression, persecution, the cross and death" (FCD 121–122). As a profession of faith, including death to the world, baptism is reserved for those who would truly live in and suffer with Christ. This personal profession of faith is the fulfillment of the Word of God (FCD 129). A renewing, regenerating, active faith is vital (FCD 139). Menno explicitly refutes Luther's teaching of infant faith and baptism (FCD 121, 126).

Rejecting any "passive" faith or infant baptism, Menno writes: "Young children are without understanding and unteachable; therefore baptism cannot be administered to them without perverting the ordinance of the Lord, misusing His exalted name, and doing violence to His holy Word" (FCD 120). Children are actually excused from the necessity of baptism on two grounds: Firstly, children are not awake to faith or sin (FCD 121–122); secondly, Jesus has promised the kingdom of God to little children with whom God has established a covenant for salvation (FCD 133). Far from serving as a source of grace, baptism is rather a statement of faith and a commitment to obedience: "Through [Jesus] alone we boast to have gained grace, favor, and the forgiveness of our sins with God our Father, and not by baptism, whether we are children or believers." It was the "sweet smelling sacrifice" of Christ's blood that brought the pardon and washing away of sins, not water baptism (FCD 130). In other words, the water has no significance in itself, but when joined to the Word of God through active and understanding faith it becomes salvation for the believing Christian. The

Figure 3.6 Menno Simons

new birth comes from "the power of the divine Word received through faith." The promise of Jesus Christ is effective only with faith and in love manifesting in obedience (FCD 123).

The Lord's Supper

The sacrament of the Lord's Supper is a reminder for the church of Jesus Christ, "a living and impressive sign" that drives believers to live as God's saints. It signifies God's kindness and the love of God's church, as well as the communion of Christ's flesh and blood. It is the table where the penitent and regenerated sit, rather than at the devil's table (FCD 142). Thus, the Lord's Supper is not a service from God to the church, or an occasion where people passively receive Christ through perishable elements. Quite the opposite; Christ has ordained the Supper to nurture the penitents to believe and to follow Christ, in fear and love, while actively mortifying their flesh. The Supper symbolizes how the recipients walk in love and union with their neighbors, and it is a foretaste of the resurrection and life eternal (FCD 158).

Menno's *Foundation* underscored four points about the "proper" understanding of the Lord's Supper (FCD 143). First, Christians are not to confuse bread and wine with Christ's actual body and blood. Because Christ is eternal and has ascended to the Father, his body and blood cannot be confined to perishable elements on earth. The sign signifies the reality, i.e., the perishable bread and wine signify the imperishable body and blood. Second, the broken body and blood of Christ are signified in order to remind the church of the greatest love of God for humanity, proved by the death of Christ for his friends. Third, the sharing of one bread and wine binds the church together in one meal, one body, one faith. When the church is united in love between believers, God is rightly honored for the love shown by the cross of Christ. Lastly, by living in unity in the love of Christ who gave himself for the church, the true church is united with God through Christ and thereby experiences true spiritual communion with the body and blood of Jesus.

When the true church communes with Christ by faith, love and obedience—not by the means of bread and wine (which would be idolatry) (FCD 148)—the Lord's Supper is a true communion with Christ's body and blood. Since Christ is sitting at the right hand of his Father, he cannot be "masticated" or "confined" in an element:

> But where the Lord's church, the dear disciples of Christ, have met in Christ's name to partake of the holy Supper in true faith, love, and obedience, there the outward perishable man eats and drinks perishable bread and wine, and

the inner imperishable [hu]man of the heart eats in a spiritual sense the imperishable body and blood of Christ which cannot be eaten nor digested (FCD 153–154).

Communion with the body and blood of Christ occurs when a believer is "with unity" in Christ, in the obedience of faith, and apart from sin. Christ can only commune with righteousness, and thus with the truly penitent and faithful (FCD 150)—never the wicked (FCD 149). The Lord's Supper is true only for those living as *the Lord's church* (FCD 142). It is a gift of reconciliation for the suffering church (FCD 155).

The Church

Menno teaches that whenever the Gospel is reduced to cheap grace, humanity is led away *from* God *in* Christ rather than *to* God *through* Christ. Menno has specific culprits in mind: "They (Lutheran and Zwinglian reformers) preach nothing but the grace, the favor, the mercy, and the love of God before their covetous, proud, showy, impure, drunken, and impenitent church, little realizing that the whole Scriptures testify that such folk cannot inherit the kingdom of God. They strengthen the hands of the wicked so that no one repents of his wickedness, as the prophet complains" (FCD 167).

The true church neither condemns nor judges those outside the church, but proclaims the judgment of God as plainly understood through the Scriptures; the church is bound to uphold God's Word and to proclaim God's truth, in its obedience to God (FCD 173). The true church is an awake, active, obedient church. Christ's sheep and the children of the Spirit are to hear Christ's voice and follow" (FCD 172). The gospel is worthless to those who persist in sin. It is not enough to trust God's goodness; one must live in a manner worthy of God's goodness. Faith without works is dead. A regenerated, irreproachable life is possible and necessary. An unconverted, wicked person deserves to be called a Christian no more than a fig! In such cases, "It is in vain that we are called Christians, that Christ died, that we are born in the day of grace, and baptized with water, if we do not walk according to His law, counsel, admonition, will, and command and are not obedient to His Word" (FCD 110–111).

The true church is that body living in obedient, penitent faith. Salvation and deliverance from sin is granted to those who die to sin (FCD 188). If one has forsaken sin, sin should be missing from one's life. Salvation is yoked with obedience (FCD 191) as the necessary way to walk after Christ, in perseverance even through suffering (FCD 189). Menno warns: True

Christian service and leadership, "if rightly served . . . is full of labor, poverty, trouble, care, reproach, misery, sorrow, cross, and pain" (FCD 172). This is the reality for those striving imperfectly for perfection: They are to die for sin and be born of God—and they are to be unable to sin (FCD 122). The true church will suffer the pain of the cross on account of persons who fall away from the church, just as Christ was condemned on account of sin that was not his own (FCD 177).

Peace

The true church, according to Menno, is a persecuted church because it lives in union with the persecuted Christ. This church will only defend itself with the Word of the Lord and will succeed even against the gates of hell: "All who are moved by the Spirit of Christ know of no sword but the Word of the Lord. Their weapons are powerful, fervent prayer, a long-suffering and patient heart, strong, immovable faith, a living hope, and an unblamable life, as was said" (FCD 175). God triumphs through patience, therefore, the attacks of the world are not ultimate threats to the life of the church (FCD 174). Violent use of power serves as tangible evidence of separation from God and the church; wherever violence is present, God's church is absent (FCD 175). God rules through peace in Christ; to be anti-peace is to be anti-Christ (FCD 190–191). Thus, God's peace requires that the church shun the violent anti-Christ (FCD 158–159).

Conclusion

Menno was not the founder of the Anabaptist tradition(s), but he rose to leadership in a decisive time for the future of the movement. His name lives on in the Mennonite tradition, while his theological legacy is found in his *Foundation of Christian Doctrine*. Menno's work points to a deep, emotional reliance on (comm)union with God in Christ Jesus, who serves as the ultimate means of grace to the world. Menno struggles to establish a plain understanding of Christian faith in keeping with the Reformation principle of *sola scriptura*, yet he also develops strong and creative understandings of baptism and the Lord's Supper from his "plain reading" of the biblical witness. Far from being cheap in his valuation of grace, Menno builds the framework of a church that strives to live in a manner worthy of the Gospel and a church that finds strength in the peace of God and rejects violent power. That model continues to offer an appealing counterculture in the contemporary world plagued with unimaginable forms of violence.[5]

Notes

1. *Menno Simons. The Complete Writings.* Translator Leonard Verduin, editor John Christian Wenger (Scottsdale, PA: Mennonite Publishing House, 1956).
2. See, e.g., Hans Joachim Hillerbrand, *Menno Simons, Molder of a Tradition* (Christian Century Foundation, 1961).
3. Menno Simons, "Foundation of Christian Doctrine," in *The Complete Writings of Menno Simons*, trans. Leonard Verduin, ed. John Christian Wenger (Scottsdale, PA: Herald Press, 1956), 191. Hereafter, all uses will be denoted as FCD through in-text citations.
4. 1 Corinthians 3:11.
5. For examples from contemporary theologians writing against violence, see Stanley Hauerwas, *War and the American Difference: Theological Reflections on Violence and National Identity* (Grand Rapids, MI: Baker Academic, 2011).

Select Bibliography

Primary sources

Ein Fundament unde klare awisinge van de heylsame unde Godtfellyghe leere Jesu Christi uth Godes woort mit gueder corte vervatet under wederumme mit grooter vlyte averghelesen unde ghebetert (1558).
Dat Fundament der Christlycken Leere. Door Menno Simons op dat alder correckste geschreven/ ende wtghegheven / Anno M.D.XXXIX. Ende nu nae het alder outste exemplaer wederom herdruckt (1616).
Menno Simons. The Complete Writings. Translated by Leonard Verduin. Edited by John Christian Wenger. Scottsdale, PA: Mennonite Publishing House, 1956. Available online in Christian Classics Ethereal library http://www.ccel. org/ccel/simon/works1.html

Secondary sources

Bender, Harold S. *Menno Simons 1536–1936.* Mennonite Publishing House, Scottsdale, PA, 1936.

Bender, Harold S. and John Horsch. *Menno Simons' Life and Writings. A Quadricentennial Tribute 1536–1936.* Wipf & Stock, 2003.

Hillerbrand, Hans Joachim. *Menno Simons, Molder of a Tradition: A Memorial Tribute to a Notable Reformation Leader on the Occasion of the 400th Anniversary of his Death.* Christian Century Foundation, 1961.

Voolstra, Sjouke. *Menno Simons. His Image and Message.* Bethel College, 1997.

3.6

Women Writers of the Sixteenth Century

Argula von Grumbach (1492?–1563?), Katharina Schütz Zell (1498–1562), and Elisabeth Cruciger (c. 1500–1535)

Introduction

Women in the sixteenth century played a significant role in the spreading of evangelical theology through their personal lives and vocations, without necessarily writing famous texts for publication. Those who did write tended to incur criticism, before often sinking into obscurity. In light of what we know today of the varied roles and writing activities of women during the Reformation period, women's contributions to the theological tradition need to be assessed with a renewed vision of what qualifies as "significant."

In a world where theology and public ministry were ostensibly a male prerogative and where basic gender roles remained largely unchanged as a result of the Reformations, women of learning were scorned as trafficking in intellectual un-chastity. After all, most women lacked access to education; they were bereft of female models to shepherd them into leadership roles as teachers and writers. Convents were closed in the wake of the newly glorified

Figure 3.7 Medal depicting Argula von Grumbach

calling to marriage and motherhood, which only served to re-enforce women's exclusion from the pulpit and classroom. Protestant women were also discouraged from aspiring to the calling of a mystic or a visionary, as many of their medieval foremothers had done, producing volumes of theological texts.

Protestant women were expected to find satisfaction in the noble calling of motherhood, which was as glorious as that of the priests and bishops (at least in theory). However, it was through their own definition of motherhood that some women emerged as theological writers. With or without biological children of their own, Protestant women took up roles as mothers of the church and thereby could become public theologians in a variety of ways. The rediscovery of these sources has expanded the range of Protestant literature available for theological reflection.[1]

Women's texts introduced: letters of defense and consolation

Women's texts open new windows into the theological tradition and the study of it. The genres women employed included letters, guidebooks or manuals to their children, songs or hymns and poems, biblical interpretations, or autobiographical pieces and diaries. Letters were the most efficient and diverse tool; while private in character, a letter could be used to advise, console, defend, teach, urge, admonish, record, reminiscence, interpret scripture, and mediate. In addition, letters were often published. Private letters between women may have been intended for publication and were often crafted with a larger audience in mind and with an agenda. Of the many examples, consider the following: a Bavarian noble lady Argula von Grumbach wrote a widely circulated letter against the University of Ingolstadt in defense of a student accused of Lutheran heresy; a pastor's wife and author in Strasbourg, Katharine Schütz Zell, wrote a feisty letter in defense of clergy marriage, including her own; a learned Calvinist from Italy, Olimpia Morata, wrote to her sisters about the importance of education and to Anna of Guise in France about the responsibility of the ruler to take risks in defending the persecuted; a married ex-nun/historian from Geneva, Marie Dentière, penned a letter to Queen Marguerite de Navarra, which included an explosive "defense of women" and their rights in the church; a "church mother" and a noble ruler Elisabeth von Braunschweig wrote to her subjects as their "territorial mother," informing them of the new Lutheran faith to be installed in their land. Clearly, these letters were employed politically, theologically, spiritually, and personally. (We cannot, however, give an account of the contents of each.)

In what follows, three pieces authored by women are introduced: (1) a letter by Argula von Grumbach from Ingolstadt, Germany; (2) a letter by Katharina Schütz Zell from Strasbourg; and (3) a hymn by Elisabeth Cruziger from Wittenberg, Germany. Instead of reflecting on the core theology of these women's texts, the aim here is to illuminate in more general terms how women in different contexts applied and developed particular brands of Protestant theology; attention is also given to how they defended—explicitly or implicitly—a woman's place in theological conversation. These works from the hands of the Reformation mothers belong to the canon of matristics, still in formation and expanding as new discoveries are being made.

Argula von Grumbach: defending Lutheran "heresy"

Argula von Grumbach (1492?–1563?) from Bavaria was a noblewoman and a mother of small children who became famous when writing letters to challenge the University of Ingolstadt and the professors' attack on a young student accused of Lutheran heresy. She considered this an urgent cause for public debate. Argula alone rose to defend Arsacius Seehofer who was found in possession of texts from Wittenberg. Argula demanded the university men to prove to her, from scripture, why they considered the young man—or Luther, for that matter—heretical. Dismissed as a desperate "bitch" by the faculty, she was penalized through her husband who, after losing his position, raised his hand against his wife. Argula described this apparent spousal abuse as her husband persecuting the Christ in her. Undeterred, Argula continued her letter campaign, writing to the University, to her town, and to noble men in positions of authority. Her published letters from 1523–1524 made her the best known female Lutheran and a best-selling pamphleteer.[2]

Argula's published works include a number of letters from 1523. On September 20, she wrote a letter to the University of Ingolstadt (printed in fourteen editions) and another to Duke Wilhelm (IV). The following month (October 28), she was corresponding with the Mayor and the City Council of Ingolstadt; and from December 1, her correspondence extended to the Count Palatine Johann von Simmern and to Fredrick the Wise. Later that month (December), she sent a letter to Count Adam von Thering. On June 29, 1524, after writing to the city of Regensburg, she was attacked in an anonymous student-authored poem.

As a Protestant writer, Argula argued about and with the Word. Her authorization arose from the Bible she knew thoroughly—in addition to her "von Stauff" status—and her ultimate concern was the proper interpretation of it. First of all, she explicitly defended Protestant theology and teachers: "What do Luther or Melanchthon teach you but the word of God? You condemn them without having refuted them ... For my part, I have to confess, in the name of God and my soul's salvation, that if I were to deny Luther and Melanchthon's writing I would be denying God and his word ...."[3] The issue at stake was the integrity of God's own Word—the source of truth—and she understood it. She proves that time and again in her writings, which were generously infused with biblical references:

> I beseech you for the sake of God, and exhort you by God's judgment and righteousness, to tell me in writing which of the articles written by Martin or Melanchthon you consider heretical. In German not a single one seems heretical to me. And the fact is that a great deal has been published in German, and I've read it all ... I have always wanted to find out the truth ... I don't intend to bury my talent, if the Lord gives me grace.[4]

She was writing as a woman, but first and foremost, as a Christian theologian in the priesthood of all believers who embraced the ultimate primacy of the scriptures. "What I have written to you is no woman's chit-chat, but the word of God; and (I write) as a member of the Christian Church, against which the gates of Hell cannot prevail ... God give us his grace, that we all may be saved, and may (God) rule us according to his will. Now may his grace carry the day."[5] On the basis of this scriptural foundation and her deep conviction that Christian faith is meant to be confessed, she was able to break free from the confines set for women in her time: "Yes, and whereas I have written on my own, a hundred women would emerge to write against them. For there are many who are able and better read than I am; as a result they might well come to be called 'a school for women' .... We have to confess publicly ..."[6] Luther deemed the Bavarian lady a brave instrument of Christ, a true and exemplary confessor of faith.[7]

In addition to the principles of *sola scriptura* and the priesthood of all believers, characteristic Lutheran convictions were important theological themes for Argula. She was confident that salvation is not earned but received as a gift of faith. Salvation is based on Christ's work. The Holy Spirit is active and present even beyond institutional church structures, blowing fresh winds that enabled and authorized new voices to proclaim the Word to unexpected places. Most uniquely, perhaps, her radar tracks a topic of utmost theological importance, viz., justice and Christian freedom. Theology, as she sees it, is less about minute articulation of divisive doctrines and more about compassion and defending the vulnerable. She confessed with passion: "I am prepared to lose everything—even life and limb. May God stand by me! Of myself I can do nothing but sin." Furthermore, "I had intended to keep my writing private; now I see that God wishes to have it made public. That I am now abused for this is a good indication that it is of God ..."[8]

Katharina Schütz Zell: Defending Protestant reforms of marriage

Katharina Schütz Zell (1498–1562), a pastor's wife from Strasbourg, wrote with similar confidence and compassion as she developed her distinct theological voice through several treatises that made her one of the most published women in her century.[9] Looking back on her life, she wrote:

> Since then the Lord drew me from my mother's womb and taught me from my youth, I have diligently busied myself with His church and its household

affairs, working gladly and constantly. I have dealt faithfully according to the measure of my understanding and the graces given to me, without deception ... So, constantly, joyously, and strongly, with all good will have I given my body, strength, honor, and goods for you, dear Strasbourg; I have made them a footstool for you .... My devout husband too was very heartily glad to allow this; and he also loved me very much for it ... And I also have loved and served you, Strasbourg, from my youth, as I still also do in my old age and almost sixty years ...[10]

Katharina's Protestant theological perspectives were formed during her marriage to the newly Protestant pastor Mathew Zell in Strasbourg. She had married with a strong sense of calling to the office of a pastor's spouse. As a "church mother" (her own term), she relished the ability to minister to the people through different means—for example, through hospitality in her own house, through hosting ecumenical table discussions between different confessional parties, through caring for the sick and the imprisoned, and through offering refuge and shelter to those in need. She used letters in particular to offer consolation and advice beyond her city, to defend Protestant changes to doctrines and practices of the church, and to critique both Catholics and fellow-Protestants when needed; she also shared abundantly her insights into biblical interpretation. Towards the end of her life, she even preached and officiated at funerals; her own death prevented her from suffering the otherwise inevitable punishment for these transgressions.

Katharina's first text (not the first published, though) was a highly polemical defense of clergy marriage in general—and her own in particular—and of the goodness of marriage *per se*. Another important text comes from the aging Katharina who wished to remind her beloved Strasbourgians of the earlier generations' ecumenical orientation and to caution them against the rigid and divisive confessionalism of the newer generation. Christian love-based fellowship should overcome any doctrinal, or personal, disputes. Katharina's own theology was infused with and oriented by her gift of compassion, which she demonstrated amply in words and deeds.

Katharina wrote more—e.g., texts with pastoral care intent, catechetical orientation—and always with robust biblical interpretation and autobiographical themes. Last but not least, she provided a lasting tool for her dear citizens of Strasbourg: a hymnbook. The hymnbook, built on the first edition of the Bohemian Brethren's hymns, was the first of its kind published in German. With an expansive and inclusive vision for lay theology, she wrote: "I found such an understanding of the work of God in this songbook that I want all people to understand it. Indeed, I ought much rather to call it a teaching, prayer, and praise book than a songbook. However, the little word 'song' is well and properly spoken, for the greatest praise of God is expressed in song."[11]

Interim conclusions: power of the compassionate word

Both Argula and Katharina were driven inexorably by the principle of "sola scriptura." There lay their empowerment and call to intervene when they saw the gospel in jeopardy. For instance, Argula wrote to Duke Wilhelm: "The word of God alone should—and must—rule all things. They call it Luther's word; yet the words are not Luther's but God's."[12]

Both theologians wrote on the basis of their personal transformative experience of Christ's redeeming work. They were unabashedly Protestant in their proclamation of the doctrine of justification by grace and by faith alone, and applied that in their ministries. For instance, Katharina Schütz Zell wrote in her explanation of the Lord's Prayer that "the basic source of consolation for sick souls is true teaching; that Christians are made right with God solely by Christ's grace."[13]

Both Katharina and Argula lived out their understanding of their call as those baptized into the priesthood of all believers and took significant risks in that calling in the service of God's word. A significant stimulus was their compassionate theological convictions that compelled them to act against the injustice and violence they witnessed. Argula chastised the professors of Ingolstadt: "How in God's name can you and your university expect to prevail, when you deploy such foolish violence against the word of God . . . I am compelled as a Christian to write to you."[14] Katharina Schütz Zell wrote against her enemies:

> Thus I cannot excuse myself and persuade my conscience that I should be silent about these very great devilish lies that have been said and published about me, as I have been silent until now. Yes, just as the commandment to love my neighbor does not allow me to excuse myself from acting, so also I cannot excuse myself for the following reason. That is, it is proper to (and part of) being a Christian to suffer, but it is not at all proper for him to be silent, for that silence is half a confession that the lies are true.[15]

She wished to live by the principle of forgiveness: "I forgive all people as I believe God also forgives me."[16]

Their evangelical theology was expansive and practical: the freedom of conscience promised in the gospel called Christians to overlook doctrinal and confessional differences, and to eradicate injustice. The very source of their compassionate theology and courageous Christian action was their unflappable experience of God as loving omnipresence and justice, present for all and in every life circumstance. Such theology fueled their action.

A special feature of Argula's and Katharina's writing is the special calling they embraced as Protestant women and lay theologians: motherhood. This was true of several other women as well. They wrote theology as church mothers, caring for those left in their care, and this meant stretching their maternal calling beyond their private households.[17] Katharina Zell lost her infant to death but devoted her maternal care to the whole city of Strasbourg, a city filled with her children. She writes: "Since I was ten years old I have been a church mother, a nurturer of the pulpit and school."[18] Motherhood in the church became her entrance to the world of theology, church leadership, and ecumenical ministry.[19] Generally speaking, the calling of motherhood replaced the mystical experiences and supernatural visions that had been the main authorization for medieval women's theological writing. Motherhood, strongly promoted by reformers as an exclusive calling and holiness for women, was reinterpreted by women themselves in a much more expansive direction. Thus, rather than confining women to their private homes, the experience of motherhood became the very calling for these women to step out into the world and more publicly take care of business—such as theology.

Elisabeth Cruziger: teaching with a hymn

Music and hymns have been most effective transmitters of Protestant theology among people—more so than any single doctrinal treatise. As a result, let us conclude by considering Elisabeth Cruziger and her hymn "Herr Christ, der einig Gotts Sohn," "Lord Christ, the Only Son of God," which is still sung in various languages in Protestant circles.

Little is known about Elisabeth beyond the basics: around 1500, Elisabeth (née Elisabeth von Meseritz or Moseritz) Cruziger (also spelled Kreuziger, Creutzier, Cruzer, Crützigeryn) was born into a noble Polish family in Meseritz (near the Polish border). She was a nun in the cloister of Marienbusch in Treptow (Riga) where she enjoyed higher education, especially in Latin and the Bible. Hearing Lutheran reformer Johann Bugenhagen's sermons led her to Wittenberg in 1521. There, in 1524, she married a reformer named Caspar Cruciger, Luther's close associate. After a few years in Magdeburg, where Caspar served as a pastor and a teacher, the couple returned to Wittenberg in 1528. While Caspar taught at the University of Wittenberg, Elisabeth carved her own space as an active pastor's wife and a "Seelsorgerin"—pastoral care provider—in her community. She was a friend of Martin Luther and later mother-in-law to Luther's son Hans, as her daughter Elisabeth became Hans' second wife.

Elisabeth was lauded for her musical gifts, and she became the writer of the first published Lutheran hymn. Her hymn was included in the hymnal printed in 1524 in Wittenberg, *Geystlich Gesangk Buchleyn,* edited by Johann Walter, to be used in worship according to Luther's original design. However, Elisabeth's work was published anonymously until 1531. This has caused some confusion in identifying the true author of the hymn.[20]

The frame for Elisabeth's work came most probably from a medieval Latin hymn sung at Christmas time (by Aurelius Prudentius) and a melody from a secular song (from Wolflin Lochamer's collection of songs, printed in mid-fifteenth century Nürnberg). Her rendition became a beloved hymn for use in Protestant worship and religious life. Through this hymn, Elisabeth thus continued to speak as a theologian, even if she was a lay woman. With her hymn Elisabeth provided a musical interpretation of Lutheran Christology and Luther's theology of salvation, in words that enabled lay people to sing about their faith experience.

The hymn offers a poetic explanation of the atonement in terms of the early church's central doctrinal statements on Christ's two natures. The glory is explicitly given to the whole Trinity who, because of Christ—the center of the hymn's message—attends to the cries of mortals. Because of Jesus, the adored, salvation is assured. Because of Jesus, one can stand "in faith" and "unshaken," no matter what. The words echo medieval Jesus-mysticism, rarely if ever found in the compositions of the first-generation Lutherans, as well as unflappable trust in the work of the Word of God in leading the vulnerable human being into eternity.

In Elisabeth's words:

(1) "The only Son from heaven, foretold by ancient seers, by God the Father given, in human form appears. No sphere his light confining, no star so brightly shining as he, our Morning Star. (2) Oh, time of God appointed, oh, bright and holy morn! He comes, the king anointed, he Christ, the virgin born, grim death to vanquish for us, to open heav'n before us and bring us life

again. (3) Awaken, Lord, our spirit to know and love you more, in faith to stand unshaken, in spirit to adore, that we, through this world moving, each glimpse of heaven proving, may reap its fullness there. (4) O Father, here before you with God the Holy Ghost, and Jesus, we adore you, O pride of angel host; before you mortals lowly cry, 'Holy, holy, holy, O blessed Trinity!'"[21]

The great Lutheran composer Johann Sebastian Bach, in a later generation, came to find these words inspiring.[22]

Conclusion

Protestant women in the sixteenth century wrote without visions or mystical experiences or scholastic training. They stretched the domestic calling designed for women as mothers to include the caretaking of the Word and with the Word. Typically compelled by a specific situation, guided by their love and knowledge of the scriptures, and empowered by their sense of Christian duty in regards to the gospel, women writers emerged as scriptural and situational theologians; they were knowledgeable of Protestant theological principles and as such can be recognized as genuine reformers. The "mothers" interpreted scripture for themselves and for others whose wellbeing depended on them, creatively using literary genres available for them. They also put evangelical theology into practice in their own contexts, most characteristically in their defense of the vulnerable and the suffering or in their catechesis. If there is one word to characterize sixteenth century women's theology it is compassion. Women wrote, sang, and acted as Protestant Reformers without mystical visions or degrees in theology but with deep wells of compassion and wisdom.

Notes

1. See Kirsi Stjerna, *Women and the Reformation* (Wiley Blackwell, 2009) for biographical introductions and theological interpretation, and for methodological discussion, as well as bibliographical information. For a pioneering study, see Roland Bainton, *Women of the Reformation in Germany and Italy* (Minneapolis: Augsburg Publishing House, 1971).
2. See Paul Matheson, ed., *Argula von Grumbach: A Woman's Voice in the Reformation* (Edinburgh: T&T Clark 1995).
3. See Matheson, *Argula*, 76–77.

4. See Matheson, *Argula*, 86–87.
5. Matheson, *Argula*, 90. Later she testifies: "I am called a follower of Luther, but I am not. I was baptized in the name of Christ; it is him I confess and not Luther. But I confess that Martin, too, as a faithful Christian, confesses him" (1523 letter to Adam von Thering, the Count Palatine's Administrator in Neuburg). Matheson, *Argula*, 145.
6. Matheson, Argula, 120–121.
7. On Luther and Argula, see Bainton, *Women*, 106–109; WABr 4:706; 2:509. Also Matheson, *Argula*, 18, 21, footnotes 48, 58; WABr 3: 247/25–34 21; WABr 3:235; 4:605.
8. Matheson, Argula, 149.
9. Elsie McKee, ed., *Katharina Schütz Zell: The Life and Thought of a Sixteenth-Century Reformer*, Vol. 1: *The Writings* and Vol. 2: *A Critical Edition* (Leiden: Brill 1999); Katharina Schütz Zell, *Church Mother: The Writings of a Protestant Reformer in Sixteenth-Century Germany*, edited and translated by Elsie McKee (Chicago: University of Chicago Press 2006).
10. McKee, *Katharina*, 224–225.
11. Zell, *Church Mother*, 93; also, see 82–92, 82–96.
12. Matheson, *Argula*, 101 (and also, 108).
13. McKee, *Katharina*, 128.
14. Matheson, *Argula,* 75, 77.mc.
15. McKee, *Katharina*, 64.
16. McKee, *Katharina*, 82.
17. See Kirsi Stjerna, *Women and the Reformation*, 32–39.
18. McKee, *Katharina*, 226.
19. McKee, *Katharina*, 226. See also ibid., 15–16.
20. See Mary Jane Haemig, "Elisabeth Cruciger (1500?–1535): The Case of the Disappearing Hymn Writer," *The Sixteenth Century Journal* 32.1 (Spring, 2001): 21–44.
21. Quoted from Evangelical Lutheran Worship (Minneapolis: Augsburg Fortress Press, 2006), Hymn # 309.
22. See Johann Sebastian Bach Cantatas, EKG 46, BWV 132/6 (1715). See www.bach-cantatas.com/Lib/Kreuziger.htm.

Select Bibliography

Primary sources

McKee, Elsie, ed. *Katharina Schütz Zell. The Life and Thought of a Sixteenth-Century Reformer.* Vol. 1: *The Writings*; Vol. 2: *A Critical Edition.* Leiden: Brill, 1999.

Schütz Zell, Katharina. *Church Mother: The Writings of a Protestant Reformer in Sixteenth-Century Germany.* Edited and translated by Elsie McKee. Chicago: The University of Chicago Press, 2006.

Secondary sources

Bainton, Roland. *Women of the Reformation in Germany and Italy.* Minneapolis: Augsburg Publishing House, 1971.

Haemig, Mary Jane. "Elisabeth Cruciger (1500?–1535): The Case of the Disappearing Hymn Writer." *The Sixteenth Century Journal* 32.1 (Spring, 2001): 21–44.

Matheson, Paul, ed. *Argula von Grumbach: A Woman's Voice in the Reformation.* Edinburgh: T&T Clark, 1995.

Stjerna, Kirsi. *Women and the Reformation.* Malden, Oxford: Wiley Blackwell, 2009. This volume also contains bibliographical references to Argula von Grumbach's and Katharina Zell's works.

3·7

The Reformation Confessions

Michael Sattler—*Schleitheim Confession* (1527)

Philip Melanchthon—*Augsburg Confession* (1530)

Zacharius Ursinus—*Heidelberg Catechism* (1563)

Introduction

Different confessions were written by Protestants as mission statements, manifestos, and teaching tools. Since the sixteenth century, the confessional texts have shaped the theological identities, self-understandings, and mutual relations among the Christian factions that mushroomed in the aftermath of the Reformation. In what follows, three confessions are introduced: the *Schleitheim Confession* of the Radical Protestants (the earliest of the confessions), the *Augsburg Confession* of the Lutherans (the first Protestant confession accepted in the Holy Roman Empire), and the *Heidelberg Catechism* of the Reformed tradition (the most ecumenical and widely embraced confession).

A few words on the confessing evangelicals

Confessions are documents of courage and conviction born in times of turmoil. They typically argue from scripture for a particular vision, one that clarifies the confessing group's identity in the face of opposition. The writers of the confessions showed admirable certainty for their beliefs and were even willing to die for them.[1] Historically speaking, the word "confession" is associated with a courageous living out of one's conviction about the gospel. The word "confessing" belongs also in liturgy: traditionally Christians have sought to repent and pray for forgiveness through confessing their sins. Confessing is always about action, about repentance, and about reinvigorated efforts to re-cultivate the vineyard with the Word,[2] starting with one's soul.

All Protestants could be considered "radical" for the changes they promoted in theological emphasis and practice. Reorientation of gospel-centered preaching and a renewed emphasis on the individual led to a serious reconsideration of the teachings and practices of the church. The church's authority, sacraments, and Mass lay at the heart of the debate between the different parties. Specifically, however, the term "radical" labeled those Protestant groups that took to heart the Reformation principles of "sola scriptura" and "priesthood of all believers," emphatically practicing lay and prophetic leadership and seeking to separate from the "world" in Spirit-filled following of Christ. Further, these "radicals" departed from the pan-Christian practice of infant baptism. The different shades of "radical" are manifest most clearly in the various positions on the meaning of sacraments, baptism, and the Holy Supper in particular. Interestingly, each view was argued from the same scriptures that "authorized" the Reformers when they began. Study of the confessional texts in light of their context allows contemporary readers to relate and reclaim the radical gospel of emancipation imbedded in different confessions.

Michael Sattler, *The Schleitheim Confession*, 1527

The most important historic confession for the varied radical groups was adopted in a Swiss Brethren Conference on February 24, 1527. Titled the "Brotherly Union of a Number of Children of God concerning Seven Articles," this foundational document for the Anabaptist movement was

Figure 3.8 The radicals confess

written by a German ex-Benedictine monk Michael Sattler of Stauffen (c 1490–1527) in Breisgau, Germany, under precarious circumstances that eventually led to his martyrdom.

A leader in the Anabaptist movement, Sattler had first become influenced by Luther's and Zwingli's teaching at the University of Freiburg. The radical

Reformation ideas spread through the Black Forest and the invasion of his monastery by rebelling peasants in May 1525 contributed to his growing unease with the monastic lifestyle. After studying Paul's letters, he abandoned his monk's robes and married Margaretha, an ex-beguine. While leading a congregation in Horb, Sattler became instrumental in the Schleitheim conference, which took place on February 24, 1527, and laid out teachings acceptable for the different Anabaptist factions.

At great risk, the Anabaptist factions gathered in Schleitheim to put forward their most distinctive principles. In the words of the cover letter accompanying the printed articles, "The articles we have dealt with, and in which we have been united, are these: baptism, ban, the breaking of bread, separation from abomination, shepherds in the congregation, the sword, the oath."[3] Sattler and his wife were subsequently put on trial with several charges issued against him and the Anabaptist groups in general: e.g., breaking the imperial law in denying infant baptism, attacking the doctrine of transubstantiation and the proper practice of the Lord's Supper as well as rejecting the sacrament of unction, Mary and the saints, oaths, and governmental offices. Further, Sattler's personal decision to leave his monastic order and his appeal for non-resistance to the approaching Turkish armies was scrutinized in the worst possible light. The writer of the Schleitheim Confession was burned to death after undergoing a gruesome torture that included tongue cutting, bodily mutilation, and being dragged behind a wagon. Sattler was killed on May 20, 1527, as a warning to others. His wife was drowned eight days later.[4]

Seven articles: the non-negotiables

The articles written in Schleitheim spell out the fundamental principles for Christian living that have shaped the different Brethren communities over the ages: the rejection of infant baptism, separation of Christians from the world, and prohibition on Christians taking arms or giving oaths.

The cover letter addresses the "brothers and sisters in the Lord" gathered in Schleitheim. With a concern for the consolation and the assurance of the conscience, readers are urged to follow "the true implanted members of Christ" instead of following the "false brethren" (Denck, Hubmaier, Hut, Bucer) into lawlessness under the false assumption that no harm would face the "believers".[5] The Seven Articles address:

1 the teaching and practice of baptism;
2 the importance of the ban and excommunication;

3 teaching and practice of the Lord's supper;

4 the necessary separation of Christians from the world;

5 the expectations pertaining to pastors;

6 the refusal to allow Christians to carry a sword or a sword-bearing office; and

7 the prohibition against making oaths.

Translations of the text were already in circulation by its first printing in 1527, and later editions in other languages helped it to become a foundational text for different communities.[6]

The Articles begin with a foundational statement about believer's baptism:

> Baptism shall be given to all those who have learned repentance and amendment of life, and who believe truly that their sins are taken away by Christ, and to all those who walk in the resurrection of Jesus Christ, and wish to be buried with him in death, so that they may be resurrected with him, and to all those who with this significance request it [baptism] of us and demand it for themselves. This excludes all infant baptism, the highest and chief abomination of the Pope. In this you have the foundation and testimony of the apostles (Matt. 28, Mark 16, Acts 2, 8, 16, 19). This we wish to hold simply, yet firmly and with assurance.[7]

The first recorded adult baptism took place in Zurich, when Conrad Grebel baptized George Blaurock on January 21, 1525. Since rebaptism was outlawed in Zurich and throughout the Holy Roman Empire, those practicing it possibly faced the penalty of death.

In adult baptism, communities witnessed their personal faith and celebrated their union in the one body of the Christ-led church. The third article explains how the Eucharist benefits these baptized: "All those who wish to break one bread in remembrance of the broken body of Christ, and all who wish to drink of one drink as a remembrance of the shed blood of Christ, shall be united beforehand by baptism in one body of Christ which is the church of God and whose head is Christ."[8] The cup of Christ benefits those who walk in the light with a clean conscience and who belong to the one body united in Christ. Remembrance of Christ's sacrifice affects the desired oneness with Christ and one's fellow recipients. There is no reason to insist on a "reality" of Christ's presence or change in the elements.

The sacraments belong to those who belong to the body of Christ, who will not take oaths, serve in the military or in any office that involves using the sword or force. As stated in article four,

> For truly all creatures are in but two classes, good and bad, believing and unbelieving, darkness and light, the world and those who [have come] out of the world, God's temple and idols, Christ and Belial; and none can have part with the other. To us then the command of the Lord is clear when he calls upon us to be separate from the evil and thus he will be our God and we shall be his sons and daughters.[9]

In the spirit of the dualist anthropology, believers are urged to actively separate themselves from worldliness, for instance, by not holding civic offices, swearing by oaths, or drinking alcohol, as stated in article four: "From all these things we shall be separated and have no part with them for they are nothing but an abomination, and they are the cause of our being hated before our Christ Jesus, Who has set us free from the slavery of the flesh and fitted us for the service of God through the Spirit Whom He has given us."[10] This service requires absolute pacifism, after Christ's example. Article six reminds readers that Christian citizenship is in heaven, whereas governments belong in the realm of flesh. The sword held by worldly magistrates is ordained by God but belongs outside the perfection of Christ. In following Christ, mutual discipline is sufficient (a ban as a warning and excommunication for sinners). The only weapons Christians should be armed with are "the armor of God, with truth, righteousness, peace, faith, salvation and the Word of God."[11] Purity, integrity, and humility go hand in hand with the surrender to the godly order of things and separation from the worldly order. The leader's task is to maintain intra-communal disciplinary practice, and voluntary obedience to punishment is expected from all.

Pastoral leaders, according to article five, are to live beyond reproach in order to discipline others:

> This office shall be to read, to admonish and teach, to warn, to discipline, to ban in the church, to lead out in prayer for the advancement of all the brethren and sisters, to lift up the bread when it is to be broken, and in all things to see to the care of the body of Christ, in order that it may be built up and developed, and the mouth of the slanderer be stopped.[12]

Pastors own their call to God and to those they serve, and also need to be on good terms with those "outside the faith." In the case of a failure to live according to these standards, a new pastor is to be elected immediately "so that God's little flock and people may not be destroyed." The last article, the seventh, explains that swearing is never allowed because of Christ's own example: "He says, Your speech or word shall be yea and nay."[13]

These articles representing the "united" or "agreed upon" ("Vereinigung", "vereignigt") views were published with a cover letter and (a second cover letter) that included additional articles on congregational order. Seven articles flesh out the basic rules for communal life, worship, and Christian conduct: Directions are given for gathering at least three or four times a week, with readings and explanation (by the one with the best understanding of the text). Expectations for decent behavior are laid out with ordinances about the Lord's Supper for each meeting and about mutual admonishment, with warnings against gluttony and private possessions.

Philip Melanchthon, *The Augsburg Confession*, 1530

The Lutherans confess

After the 1517 posting of the ninety-five theses started an avalanche, Luther and his associates were on the hot seat as outlawed heretics after 1521. A forced return to the Catholic faith was envisioned at the Diet of Speyer in 1529, the same year any hopes for a German–Swiss alliance were lost after Luther and the Swiss reformer Uldrich Zwingli left the Marburg Colloquy without an agreement on the issue of Christ's presence in the Lord's Supper. Lutherans had an opportunity to defend their faith at the imperial Diet of Augsburg in 1530. With Luther in exile, his colleague Philip Melanchthon represented the Wittenberg theologians, drafting the Augsburg Confession of twenty-eight articles on the basis of previous collaborative documents. The document was read in German and presented in writing in Latin, only to be refuted by the imperial Catholic theologians. Melanchthon's quick *Apology of the Augsburg Confession* had no impact on the imperial decision.

The Augsburg Confession (CA), with its Apology, and with Luther's Catechisms, provided a much-needed unifier for Lutherans who in 1537 went to war against the imperial army. Though the Lutherans lost, the eventual 1555 Peace of Augsburg gave them the right to practice faith in accordance with the Augsburg Confession. However, ongoing intra-Lutheran controversies made necessary the 1577 Formula of Concord as a shared interpretation of the Augsburg Confession. In 1580, over 8,000 Lutherans signed the *Book of Concord*, which included the Augsburg Confession (1530), its Apology (1531), Luther's Small and Large Catechisms (1529), the ecumenical Creeds,

Figure 3.9 Philip Melanchthon

Melanchthon's *Treatise on the Power and Primacy of the Papacy* (1537), and Luther's *Smalcald Articles* (1537, in Latin) (the latter two documents originally written for the Lutheran Smalcald League).[14] Of all these, Luther's Catechisms and the Augsburg Confession, with the Creeds, continue to guide the doctrine and practice of the Lutheran church—both globally and locally.[15]

Twenty-eight articles: *sola gratia, sola fide*

With Luther's Catechisms, the Augsburg Confession continues to serve as the norm for Lutheran teaching, preaching, and ministry. The confession, comprising twenty-one articles on doctrine and seven on the proposed reforms, offers a particular lens to interpret the Scriptures—the ultimate authority—and the foundational faith statements of the early Church's Creeds.

The primary teaching in the Augsburg Confession pertains to salvation and is succinctly articulated in article 4: one is made right with God when one is declared forgiven for Christ's sake and when one is made one with God in faith through grace because of Christ. Justification served as the foundational doctrine, teaching that by justification "we receive forgiveness of sin and become righteous before God out of grace for Christ's sake through faith when we believe that Christ has suffered for us and that for his sake our sin is forgiven and righteousness and eternal life are given to us. For God will regard and reckon this faith as righteousness in his sight ..." (CA 4:1).[16]

The experience of Christians as being simultaneously sinners and saints, totally forgiven yet constantly faltering in this life, is the fundamental insight in the confession. It is coupled with a vision about the dual proclamation of the Word: God speaks to humans in both the word of the law and the word of the gospel, which together lead to repentance and good fruits.

The order of the articles conveys a particular theological vision: CA's articles 1–4 prove the fundamentally Trinitarian basis and God-centeredness of Lutheran theology. Articles 1, 3, and 17, respectively, affirm a faith in God the Creator of the universe, in Christ as God's Son whose work absolutely redeems humankind, and a hope that he shall return to judge and claim his own at the end of time. God alone is the source of human salvation and happiness, a gift that can only be received.

The justification doctrine (article 4) refers to the gracious giving of Godself: God restoring the faith lost in the Garden of Eden, Christ restoring the distorted image of God, God infusing the sinner with faith that is "alien," that is, not of our own origins but from the only source of grace—God—and making humans just, righteous, and holy. Not only is one declared forgiven as a favor of Christ, one also receives Christ in one's being as a gift. The terms used to distinguish these dimensions of justification, i.e., forensic and effective righteousness, would later be debated (as overemphasis on the forensic side of justification has diminished the appreciation of the mystical oneness with the savior, the latter of which Luther celebrated more than his confessional followers).

Article 2 and article 19 articulate a startling view of humanity in such bondage to sin that they cannot even want to save themselves. The root of the evil is in the human will, bound to follow wrong impulses. Because of the inherited distortion of the will and concupiscence, only grace can undo the damage. This view has deep roots in Augustine's reflections on freedom and sin, but is taken further in reaction to a perceived medieval semi-Pelagian preference that wished to retain a modest grace-assisted freedom to improve themselves.[17] The Lutheran confession stresses the absolute fallibility and inability of humans to better themselves, and underscores the glory of Christ.

Article 4 proclaims the pivotal statement: salvation and holiness are based on God's word and action, and are granted to human beings as a gift "earned" by the sacrifice of Jesus Christ. This is a matter of faith, engaging one into the realm of the Holy Spirit who, in this life, makes Christ's benefits available to human beings, and who kindles and nurtures the kind of faith that saves. For that, God has seen it wise to institute the church as a hospital for sinners with medicine in the form of sacraments.

Articles 5, 7–13 reason that the church is the primary place where the Word, the gospel of Jesus Christ, is proclaimed and where the sacraments are administered. Instituted by God, their effectiveness rests on God's word only. They are given for human benefit and flourishing. In preaching the Word, individuals hear the word of the law and the word of the gospel, face their finiteness, and receive the grace of forgiveness. This transformative experience rests on the gifts received in baptism and leads to a life of repentance and service to others (as stated in the junctional article 6).

Only after the preaching of the word can the sacraments of baptism and the Lord's Supper be given for the kindling, nurturing, and strengthening of one's faith. Only baptism and Communion are recognized to have the necessary biblical institution with Jesus's command and a promise of God's presence in the elements. Ordained ministry secures the preaching and sacraments made available to Christians who are all called to share the good news in their daily vocations.

Articles 6, 20, and 14–21 address Christian living in the world and in the church, with its sin-infused realities reiterating the point that salvation and peace with God rest in God's generosity and action. Justification by grace is not about cheap grace and nominal declaration of forgiveness but must instead lead to fruition. As stated in article 6, "Our teachers are falsely accused of forbidding Good Works" (CA 20:1). To the contrary, it is firmly believed that "our works cannot reconcile God or merit forgiveness of sins, grace, and justification, but that we obtain this only by faith when we believe that we are received into favor for Christ's sake" (CA 20:9). Any trust in human works would imply despising Christ (John 14:6): "But, although this doctrine is despised by the inexperienced, nevertheless God-fearing and anxious consciences find by experience that it brings the greatest consolation, because consciences cannot be set at rest through any works, but only by faith, when they take the sure ground that for Christ's sake they have a reconciled God" (CA 20, 15).

Faith itself is a work of receiving the forgiveness of sins, grace, and righteousness through the work of Christ alone; it leads to good works under the inspiration of the Holy Spirit (CA 20:27–29). At this point, the CA quotes Ambrose, saying, "Faith is the mother of a good will and right doing" and what is good in God's eyes (CA 20:30). Without the diligent work of the Holy Spirit, human beings only have capacity in ungodly affairs (20:31). With the active presence and agency of the Holy Spirit, humans have some freedom in the realm of civil righteousness (that is, aspiring to make right choices in the normal situations of earthly life), whereas they lack the power on their own "to work the righteousness of God, that is, spiritual righteousness" (i.e., human beings are not able to "make" themselves holy and worthy of God—only God can do that). The so-called "sanctification" in Lutheran understanding rests on the continuous work of the Holy Spirit (CA 19: 1–2).

The first twenty-one articles end with a discussion on how Lutherans should think of the saints, before proceeding with the last seven articles that address the issues around the reforms introduced. Allowing the clergy to marry and offering the cup to the laity are defended first and foremost. These were the most visible reforms in need of careful justification against hundreds years of practice. With clerical marriage, the celibate lifestyle and entire monastic calling were judged to be harmful, whereas ordinary daily life— including marriage and parenthood—was lifted up as a holy vocation, spiritual, and blessed (CA 22, 23, 24). Religious penitential practices of the Catholic church, such as fasting rules and mandatory ad verbatim confession, were abolished, along with the Catholic celebration of the Mass and any misconceptions of Christ's satisfaction being re-enacted. The emphasis moved to the experience of forgiveness and away from the minute narration of one's transgressions, which was seen as counterproductive (CA 25, 26, 27).

For the sake of unity and safeguarding proper doctrine, the office of bishop was preserved with the caveat that in the absence of good bishops other arrangements would be possible. The question of the papacy was left out of the discussion at this point (CA 28). That issue became an obvious watershed between Lutherans and Catholics, as did the overall vision for Christian life and holiness:

> For Christian perfection is to fear God earnestly with the whole heart and yet also to have a sincere confidence, faith, and trust that we have a gracious, merciful God because of Christ; that we may and should pray for and request from God whatever we need and confidently expect help from him in all affliction, according to each person's vocation and walk of life; and that meanwhile we should diligently do external good works and attend to our calling. This is true perfection and true service of God (CA 27:49).

Zacharius Ursinus, *The Heidelberg Catechism*, 1563

The reformed confess

A beloved confession of a most ecumenical spirit, the Heidelberg Catechism was printed in 1563 in Heidelberg. It was requested by Elector Frederick III of Palatinate, who was committed to the Reformation and was particularly frustrated with the conflict between the Lutherans and Calvinists/Reformed in his region and at the University of Heidelberg.[18]

Controversies were brewing between Gnesio-Lutherans and the Philippists[19] on the issue of Christ's presence in the Lord's Supper, with significant debates in 1560 leading to the Naumburg Princes' conference in 1561. The Elector wished to sponsor a unifying catechism in the region that had already embraced Protestant faith in the 1540s during the rule of his predecessors Frederick II and Ottheinrich; Ottheinrich had invested heavily in the Lutheran reformation (1556–1559). The Heidelberg Catechism (HC) was written at a time when neither the Lutheran nor Reformed side was dominant. However, it was modeled after the Augsburg Confession and benefited from the influence of Philip Melanchthon. After Melanchthon's death (1560), Geneva and Zurich provided leadership as the Palatine proceeded to eradicate remnants of "papist" piety.

Hopes for unity guided the leading authors of the Heidelberg Catechism: Zacharius Ursinus (1534–1584), a student and a friend of Melanchthon and a

Figure 3.10 Zacharius Ursinus

most notable defender of the text, and secondarily Caspar Olevianus (1536–1587), a professor at Heidelberg University and later Fredrick's court preacher.[20] With Ursinus' lead, and with the Elector's personal involvement, a tool was crafted for explicitly "Christian" (not Lutheran, not Reformed/Calvinist) education and preaching, with hopes of providing a unifying confessional text that would also be used for the instruction of the youth. The text resembles and draws from different Catechisms of the time; pastoral and personal in its affect, its conciliatory tone and framework echo the *Augsburg Confession*. The articles are oriented more towards spiritual concerns and convictions about salvation based on God's grace; distinctively Reformed perspectives like predestination and the Lord's Supper are far less prominent. Its preface, written by Fredrick III, explains that a "Christian" doctrine is at stake, and not merely a Lutheran or Reformed one. First published on January 19, 1563, and translated into Latin, it was immediately popular in the lives of Reformed communities. Confirmed in the synod of Dort in 1619, its strength lies in the fact that it is one of the most accommodating confessions and thus mediates across confessional boundaries.

One hundred and twenty nine questions: From Misery to Redemption to Gratitude

From Misery/Guilt to Redemption/Grace to Gratitude—that is the famously genius order of the 129 articles of the Heidelberg Catechism (HC). Using the catechetic "question and answer" method, the traditional parts in Christian education are employed: the Creed, the Law, the Prayer, and the Sacraments. The explanation starts with the Creeds. With an explicitly evangelical and soteriological orientation, and written in a devotional tone, tender words are offered for the pilgrim in this life who eagerly awaits the life to come due to the present experience of misery and struggle. While it wishes to present a "common platform" for Lutherans, Calvinists, Zwinglians, and Bullinger's followers,[21] the text avoids dwelling on contentious issues while not shying away from them either.

The catechism opens with the fundamental question to all humanity (HC 1): "What is your only comfort in life and in death?" The answer summarizes the Christian gospel about Jesus's work for every person's life: "That I belong—body and soul, in life and in death—not to myself but to my faithful Savior, Jesus Christ" who has redeemed and freed me and protects me so that without God's will "not a hair can fall from my head," but "indeed, that everything must fit his purpose for my salvation." By the Holy Spirit, God "assures me of eternal life, and makes me wholeheartedly willing and ready from now on to live for him [God]."[22] In the midst of life and death struggles, comfort comes from the knowledge that one belongs unambiguously to God who is in charge.

"How many things must you know to live and die happily in this comfort?" The answer is threefold: I need to know "first, how great my sin and misery are. Second, how I am delivered from all my sin and misery; and third, how I am to be thankful to God for such deliverance."[23] The main parts of the HC address these three stages in life: the human misery because of the damnation brought about by God's law and righteousness; the redemption because of the mediation of Christ and his righteousness; and the life lived in gratitude and blessed obedience with the help of the Holy Spirit.

(1) The first part, HC questions 3–11, explains the misery of human beings born in sin and, thus, unable to save themselves. Unable to meet the basic expectation to love God and neighbor, they incur the wrath of God whose majesty demands retribution for the offense. God's sovereign actions and Christ's redeeming work are underscored: On their own, human beings are totally corrupt, by their own fault. They are at the mercy of God who has to cause their rebirth through the Spirit, in order for all the righteousness to be met.

(2) The second part, questions 12–85, extrapolates the source and meaning of redemption from death to life. Deliverance to righteousness is explained from the work of "Our Lord Jesus Christ, who is freely given to us for complete redemption and righteousness" (HC 18). The gospel in this regard is the source for the truth about the saving faith, which includes knowledge, acceptance of God's revelation, and trust. It is the teaching of the Holy Spirit that "to me also God has given the forgiveness of sins, everlasting righteousness, and salvation, out of sheer grace solely for the sake of Christ's saving work" (HC 20). Faith that saves brings about forgiveness, which frees one to live in obedience and gratitude in anticipation of the resurrection and the life everlasting.

The Apostles' Creed gives the parameters for believing (HC 26–28) and for Christian identity (HC 32): a Christian is one who shares in Christ through faith and offers oneself as a living sacrifice to Christ. The central belief is that Christ's resurrection has overcome death and that his elect will share in his righteousness: "the resurrection of Christ is a sure pledge to us of our blessed resurrection" (HC 45). The catechism reminds the believer that the Holy Spirit, equally eternal as Christ and the Creator, is given to the elect especially to prepare them through true faith to share in Christ and in his benefits (HC 53). Furthermore, this Holy Spirit "comforts me and will abide with me forever." The experience of such forgiveness and grace is transformative: "I now feel in my heart the beginning of eternal joy, I shall possess, after this life, perfect blessedness" (HC 58).

The doctrine of predestination is best understood as an abiding presence of the Holy Spirit and confidence in the benefits received from the personal association with Christ. In accordance with God's own eternal decree (HC 26), the elect are the members of the community of Christ, under his judgment, and preparing for eternal life with him (HC 28, 54).[24] Nothing can separate them from God's grace. That is providence. That is what Christ accomplished.

The articles on election lead to discussion of the role of the Christian community, the church, and its sacraments. Sacraments in general bring forth faith and grant grace where needed, as "visible, holy signs and seals instituted by God" (HC 67). Specifically, the sacraments (cf. HC 20) are meant for the use of those grafted into Christ by faith (HC 65, 66). They are important for the sake of faith and the means through which the Holy Spirit works: "The Holy Spirit creates it [faith] in our hearts by the preaching of the holy gospel, and confirms it by the use of the holy sacraments" (HC 65). Furthermore, "the Holy Spirit teaches in the gospel and confirms by the holy sacraments that our whole salvation is rooted in the one sacrifice of Christ offered for us on the cross" (HC 66).

Baptism as the "water of rebirth" washes away sins. More than an empty sign, baptism, as the pledge of the spiritual washing, causes a rebirth of the Spirit and brings about forgiveness, renewal, and sanctification to the members of Christ (HC 70–75). Infants, who are incorporated by baptism into the covenant people of God, receive this rite as well (like circumcision in the Old Testament) (HC 72–73). The other sacrament ordered by Christ, the Lord's Supper (HC 75–82), is reserved for "feeding" those baptized into the community of believers. Christ has promised that he himself "feeds and nourishes my soul to everlasting life with his crucified body and shed blood as I receive from the hand of the minister and actually taste the bread and the cup of the Lord which are given to me as sure signs of the body and blood of Christ" (HC 75). The Catechism carefully explains how eating the bread and wine means not only embracing the passion of Christ but, for the elect, "it is to be so united more and more to his blessed body by the Holy Spirit dwelling both in Christ and in us" (HC 80–81). Just as in baptism the water is not changed into blood but remains a holy sign of the washing of sins, similarly in the Supper the element does not become Christ but "in accordance with the nature and usage of sacraments, it is called the body of Christ" (HC 78). The "eating" is for nourishment and effects the recipient's union with Christ and with his body, the church (HC 78, 75–79). The second part ends with a statement about the office of keys belonging to the task of gospel proclamation and Christian discipline (HC 83) and preparing for the kingdom of God (HC 84–85).

(3) Part three, questions 86–129, explains the importance of gratitude and obedience and describes the fundamentals for new life with the Holy Spirit. The work of the Church, the commandments regarding neighborly relations, and an ongoing relationship with God are all discussed as pillars that support a sanctified life in obedience and gratitude to the redeemer (HC 92–115). Ending with a short explanation of the Lord's Prayer (HC 116–129), the Catechism affirms the Christian privilege to call God "Father" (HC 120) and to end their prayers with a firm "Amen" (HC 129).

In all, the major statement of the Catechism that thematically runs throughout the whole text is found in the opening lines: One's comfort in life and death is in God, the omnipotent and ever-loving One, who frees humans *from* sin and *to* life with him. That message, delivered with an existential approach to life and death issues, has made HC a timelessly appealing tool for catechesis and spiritual formation that transcends confessional boundaries. The beloved confessional text continues to be translated in different languages for new generations around the globe.[25]

Of all the confessional writings resulting from the sixteenth century Reformations, the Catechisms may be considered the most influential: their format and language allowed them to be used effectively in both education and proclamation among laity and clergy, young and old, and they instilled the roots of the Reformed teachings for the long term. They are also the most ecumenical of the confessional writings as their heart is in the common concern for nurturing faith and love of God and one's neighbor.

Notes

1. After the Diet of Augsburg of 1555 and the "cuius regio, eius religio" principle, each territory/leader could choose between Catholic faith and the 1530 Augsburg Confessions. The Peace of Westphalia of 1648 brought similar rights for the Reformed. Anabaptists continued to suffer at the hands of Catholics, Reformed and Lutherans.

2. Referring to Scott Hendrix's thesis in his *Recultivating the Vineyard: The Reformation Agendas of Christianization* (Westminster John Knox, 2004).

3. The text quoted here is from Mark A. Noll, ed., *Confessions and Catechisms of the Reformation*, Grand Rapids, MI: Baker House, 1997, pp. 50–58 (with an Introduction, pp. 47–49), reproduced from John C. Wenger, ed., *The*

Doctrine of the Mennonites. Scottsdale, PA.: Mennonite Publishing House, 1952. "Ban" is a reference to excommunication.

4.   See C. Arnold Snyder, *The Life and Thought of Michael Sattler* (Scottsdale, PA: Herald Press, 1984); John H. Yoder, *The Legacy of Michael Sattler* (Scottsdale, PA: Herald Press, 1973).

5.   Noll, *Confessions and Catechisms*, 50.

6.   See Yoder, John Howard, *The Schleitheim Confession, 1527* (Herald Press, 1977), 28–54.

7.   Noll, *Confessions and Catechisms*, 51–52.

8.   Ibid., 52.

9.   Ibid., 53.

10. Ibid.

11. Ibid., 55.

12. Ibid., 53–54.

13. Ibid., 57.

14. See Robert Kolb and Timothy Wengert, eds., *The Book of Concord: The Confessions of the Evangelical Lutheran Church* (Minneapolis: Fortress Press, 2000); *Die Bekenntnisschriften der evangelisch-lutherischen Kirche* (BSLK). Göttingen 1930, 1998.

15. For historical information, see Günther Gassmann and Scott Hendrix, *The Fortress Introduction to the Lutheran Confessions* (Minneapolis: Fortress Press, 2000); Charles Arand, James Nestingen, and Robert Kolb, *The Lutheran Confessions: History and Theology of the Book of Concord* (Minneapolis: Fortress Press, 2012).

16. The text from the Latin version has a slightly different emphasis: "human beings cannot be justified before God by their own powers, merits, or works. But they are justified as a gift [*gratis*] of Christ through faith . . ."

17. Noll, *Confessions and Catechisms*, 53. See, e.g., Gerhard O. Forde, with Steven D. Paulson and James A. Nestingen, *The Captivation of the Will: Luther Vs. Erasmus on Freedom and Bondage* (Grand Rapids: Eerdmans, 2005). See also chapters in Kirsi Stjerna and Deanna A. Thompson, eds., *On the Apocalyptic and Human Agency: Conversations with Augustine of Hippo and Martin Luther* (Cambridge: Cambridge Scholars Publishing, 2014); Harry J. McSorley, *Luther: Right or Wrong? An Ecumenical-Theological Study of Luther's Major Work, The Bondage of the Will* (Minneapolis: Augsburg Publishing House, 1969).

18. Lyle D. Bierma, *Introduction to the Heidelberg Catechism: Sources, History, and Theology* (Grand Rapids, MI: Baker Academic, 2005).

19. The word "Gnesio" was used for those considering themselves as the most authentic bearers of his teachings, as opposed to the more conciliatory "Philippists" named after Melanchthon.

20. Recent scholarship identifies Ursinus as the main author. See Bierma, *Introduction to the Heidelberg Catechism*, 49–74.
21. Bierma, *Introduction to the Heidelberg Catechism*, 94.
22. Ibid., 95.
23. Ibid., 81.
24. See HC 1, 21, 32, 53, 56, 57, 58, 59 for references to election. On the Covenant, see HC 74, 77, 79, 82.
25. Amidst the friendly teaching, criticism is spelled out regarding the Catholic views on the Mass (HC 80) and the saints (HC 30, 94), justification by works (HC 62–64), baptism's regenerative powers (HC 72), the doctrine of transubstantiation (HC 78), and the worship of images (HC 97–98).

Select Bibliography

Noll, Mark A. *Confessions and Catechisms of the Reformation*. Grand Rapids, MI: Baker, 1997.

Primary sources on Schleitheim Confession

Wenger, John C., ed. *The Doctrine of the Mennonites*. Scottsdale, PA: Mennonite Publishing House, 1952.

Secondary sources on Scheitheim Confession

Bender, Harold S. *The Anabaptist Vision*. Scottsdale, PA: Herald Press, 1944.
Snyder, C. Arnold. *The Life and Thought of Michael Sattler*. Scottsdale, PA: Herald Press, 1984.
Yoder, John Howard, *The Schleitheim Confession, 1527*. Scottsdale, PA: Herald Press, 1977.

Primary sources on the Augsburg Confession

Die Bekenntnisschriften der evangelisch-lutherischen Kirche (BSLK). Göttingen 1930, 1998 (Latin/German).
Wengert, Timothy and Robert Kolb, eds. *The Book of Concord*. Minneapolis: Fortress Press, 2000. http://bookofconcord.org/augsburgconfession.php

Secondary sources on the Augsburg Confession

Arand, Charles, James Nestigen, and Robert Kolb. *The History and Theology of the Lutheran Confessions*. Minneapolis: Fortress Press, 2012.
Gassmann, Gunther and Scott Hendrix. *The Fortress Introduction to the Lutheran Confessions*. Minneapolis: Fortress Press, 1999.
Grane, Leif. *The Augsburg Confession: A Commentary*. Minneapolis: Fortress Press, 1987.

Primary sources on the Heidelberg Catechism

Catechismus, oder, christlicher underricht, wie der in den Kirchen und Schulen der churfürstlichen Pfaltz getrieben wirdt. Heidelberg: Johann Mayer, 1563.
Catechesis religionis christianae, quae traditur in ecclesiis et scholis Palatinatus. Heidelberg: Michael Schirat and Johann Mayer, 1563.
The Heidelberg Catechism: A New Translation for the Twenty-First Century. Translated by Lee C. Barrett III, with an Introduction. Cleveland, OH: The Pilgrim Press, 2007.
The Book of Confessions. Part 1 Pages 58–79 in The Constitution of the Presbyterian Church (USA). The Office of the General Assembly. The Heidelberg Catechism, 2004.

Secondary sources on the Heidelberg Catechism

Barth, Karl. *The Heidelberg Catechism for Today*. Richmond: John Knox Press, 1964.
Bierma, Lyle D. *Introduction to the Heidelberg Catechism: Sources, History, and Theology*. Grand Rapids: Baker Academic, 2005.
Our Only Comfort: A Comprehensive Commentary on the Heidelberg Catechism. 2 vols. Grand Rapids: Faith Alive Christian Resources, 2001.

3.8

The Book of Common Prayer[1] (1559)
Thomas Cranmer (1489–1556)

Introduction

The Book of Common Prayer of the Church of England belongs among the most theologically influential works with roots in the sixteenth century. A collection of books that "contains a whole history within it,"[2] it serves as a manifold manual and application of characteristically English theology. The book applies the theological vision expressed in the Thirty-Nine Articles of Religion (1563, 1571), the backbone of English Protestant theology, and aims to reach the hearts of the people through uniform prayer and liturgy.[3] The many editions of the prayer book speak to the tender process of one nation leaving the Catholic tradition in pursuit of their own kind of Protestant solution—one that has many different voices in the mix. Through its use in homes and in public prayer, the prayer book has yielded theological influence on a vast scale.[4] With Queen Elizabeth I being the indisputable mother of the English Reformation and the force behind the religious uniformity that was accomplished, the 1559 *Queen Elizabeth's Prayer Book* is offered here as a window into Reformation theology in England; it will be discussed in connection with the other significant editions from 1549, 1552 and 1662.

Figure 3.11 Thomas Cranmer

A few words on the history of the book: a queenly endorsed form of prayer

For the success of the English Reformation, a queen, a bishop, and a prayer book were needed on the chessboard. Archbishop Thomas Cranmer (1489–1556), Queen Elizabeth I (1533–1603), daughter of Henry VIII, and his second wife, Anne Boleyn, were the key players who secured the long-term employment of Protestant theology in England. They did so by developing a prayer book that provided liturgical unity in the midst of theological ambiguity and political uncertainty. Even if grave divides remained, Christian life in England became organized by the book that set up common liturgies for regular cyclical prayers, such as the Morning and Evening prayers, and other practices of the church (e.g., the sacraments of Eucharist and Baptism, rites for Confirmation, Marriage, Visitation and Communion of the Sick, Burial, and Thanksgiving of women after childbirth). The book, in different editions and translations, has accompanied people from cradle to grave.[5] It has fortified Christians across denominations with powerful prayers such as this evening prayer, with its Collects for Peace and Grace:

> O GOD, whiche are authour of peace, and lover of concord, in knowledge of whom standeth our eternal lyfe, whose service is perfect fredom: defend us thy humble servaunts, in al assaultes of our enemies, that we surely trusting in thy defence, may not feare the power of any adversaries: through the might of Jesu Christ our lord. Amen." (Seconde collecte for Peace). "O LORDE our heavenly father, almightie and everlastyng God, whiche hast safely broughte us to the begynnyng of thys day: defende us in the same wyth thy myghtye power, and graunte that this daie we fall into no synne, neither runne into any kinde of daunger, but that al our doinges may be ordred by thy governaunce to doe always that is rightuous in thy sighte: through Jesus Christe our LORDE. Amen." (Thirde collecte for Grace.)[6]

The prayer book went through multiple versions during different monarchies as several documents were tried between the excommunications of Henry (1533) and Elizabeth (1570): First the *Ten Articles* (1536) bending towards Lutheran theology, followed by Henry's *Six Articles* (1539) and the *King's Book* (1543), defending the essential Catholic teachings. The Six Articles reenforced withholding the cup from laity and the doctrine of transubstantiation in the Lord's Supper as well as clerical celibacy and monastic vows of chastity, private masses and call for confession for the enumeration of sins. In 1544, an edition of the revised English Litany was published, paving the way for a new prayer book during the reign of Edward VI (1547–1553): The first printing of the actual prayer book in 1549, to replace the existing medieval Latin rites, signaled the separation from Rome liturgically (a "divorce" already initiated by Henry VIII when he declared himself the head of "his" church in 1534).

The architect behind the book was the Archbishop of Canterbury, Thomas Cranmer. His original Forty-Two Articles from 1552 (written during the reign of Edward VI, the highpoint of Calvinist influence in England) were revised into the Thirty-Nine Articles of Religion (1563, finalized 1571) with the leadership of the new Archbishop of Canterbury, Matthew Parker.[7] The articles provide the theological map and foundation for the church in England, as evidenced in the issues addressed: the basic creedal teachings such as the doctrine of God; the interpretation of scripture (articles 1–8); issues pertaining to personal faith, sin, salvation and the doctrine of justification by faith, and the role of the church (articles 9–18); issues related to public faith and the institutional church, including worship, sacraments, and government (articles 19–31); miscellaneous topics on traditions, celibacy, excommunication, including a statement of the Roman bishop's lack of authority in England (articles 32–39). The articles, written in Latin and English, became the starter for the idiosyncratic character of the English church, which was "at home" between Catholic practices and extremist Calvinist theology. The leader towards unity was Queen Elizabeth I. When she ascended to the throne on the heels of her Catholic sister Mary's rule (1553–1558), she knew already the price of religious division within her own family. With the Act of Uniformity in 1558, which the Parliament passed on April 28, 1559, Elizabeth I extended an invitation to all England for uniform ways of worship and prayer and for regular church attendance—at least three times a year, one being Easter. Retaining much of the essentials in the pre-existing Latin manuals, and omitting extreme Protestant additions from an earlier edition, the 1559 prayer book set a course towards a moderately reformed Protestant mode of worship, prayer, and sacramental teaching, allowing some diversity in private faith.[8] It is noteworthy that "while it was proclaimed by parliament to constitute an 'Act of uniformity', its real effect was anything but. It came into being as a physical embodiment of a revolution in religious practice and in the politics of religion which we know as the Reformation."[9] That radicalness is camouflaged by the plentitude of collects and prayers that constitute the bulk of the book—such as the collect for the Second Sunday in Lent:

O GOD mercifull father, that dispisest not the syghing of a contrite hart, nor the desyre of suche as be sorowfull, mercyfully assiste our praiers, that we make before thee, in all our troubles, and adversities, whensoever they oppresse us, and graciouslye heare us, that those evelles, which the crafte and subtiltie of the devel, or man, worketh against us, be brought to noughte, and by the providence of thy goodnesse, they may be dispersed, that we thy Servauntes beyng hurt by no persecucions, may evermore geve thanckes to thee, in thy holy Church, through Jesus Christ our Lorde.[10]

On Cranmer's manual(s) from 1549 to 1559: The "middle of the way"

Drawing from medieval sources, Archbishop Cranmer designed a manual for the daily life of the church, Christian families, and individuals; services for Sundays, other occasions and daily use, the practice of the Lord's Supper (referred to as "Holy Communion"), Baptism, and other rites of the church[11] were accompanied by New Testament readings and the canticles.[12]

The Reformation took root in England through a reform of liturgical practices. Introducing several changes—both subtle and obvious—to the "form" of religious practices, Cranmer also provided for revisions of "content" that invoked Reformed theology. A distinctly Protestant theology came to shape his contemporaries' theological imagination through the Reformed liturgical framework. Influenced by his German ally Philip Melanchthon, Cranmer negotiated reforms with moderation. For instance, a number of beloved medieval saints' celebrations and traditional feast dates were eliminated (such as Corpus Christi and Holy Cross days), while the already familiar sources provided for rites of matrimony, confirmation, and visitation of the sick (in a simplified form). Baptism was preserved as a primary sacrament, while some of the gestures from the Catholic rite were maintained (such as exorcism, unction with oil, and blessing of the water font). In all of this, the role of faith was underscored.

Celebrating only two sacraments and rejecting the doctrine of transubstantiation, the document is unambiguously Protestant. The reality of the sacraments' effectiveness is honored, while the issue of "real" or "spiritual" presence is left open for interpretation. Cranmer personally preferred a metaphorical understanding of Christ's words, "this cup." In conversation with the Swiss Reformers and with the assistance of

Melanchthon, he articulated a semi-Calvinist viewpoint with room for various interpretations. Finding the proper wording for the rite of the Eucharist was a volatile issue and of such importance that the House of Commons had to become involved before the 1549 edition could be accepted.[13] The Office for the Dead underwent significant changes: the prayer for the deceased was omitted, with no references to purgatory. Similarly, the wording on the Mass and the sacrifice of the Mass changed noticeably. The conditions for forgiveness of sins gained a renewed focus on Christ's "once and for all" sacrifice, as liturgical formulations underscored the certainty of the absolution in the words of forgiveness alone.

If the first edition was still quite medieval Catholic in character, the Second Prayer Book from 1552 had a decidedly "Reformed" tone. Human beings' unworthiness gained a Protestant emphasis, whereas Catholic rites like exorcism by baptism, prayers for the dead, and communion at funerals were omitted as unnecessary. The so called Black Rubric was added: practical directions given in black ink advised communicants to receive the Lord's Supper not kneeling but

CRANMER RECANTING HIS RECANTATION.

Figure 3.12 Thomas Cranmer

sitting down so that they might resist superstitious veneration of the elements or allusions to the refuted doctrine of transubstantiation. The Eucharistic wording was distinct from both Lutherans' and Catholics' emphasis on the reality of Christ's presence.[14]

The 1552 edition was soon withdrawn upon the ascension to the throne of the Catholic Queen Mary I, daughter of Catherine of Aragon and Henry VIII. Many of the Catholic traditions were returned even with violent measures until the decks changed again at Mary's death. The mildly revised 1559 edition of the Prayer Book was adopted during the very first year of young Elizabeth's reign (1558–1603), daughter of Henry VIII and Anne Boleyn.[15] Presented and passed on April 28, 1559, by the Parliament, with a New Act of Uniformity, the book was signed by most of the 9,400 clergy involved (with only 189 refusing). The eager queen launched its use on May 12 that year, in her own chapel, before the official adoption of the book in England on St. John the Baptist's Sunday.

The content of the book: on doctrines and rubric

Some of the most notable features of the 1559 edition pertained to the rewording of the baptismal rite and the clarification on the Lord's Supper, including continued rejection of the doctrine of transubstantiation and now omitting the previously added Black Rubric on the manner of receiving the communion. Traditional vestments and externals were allowed, and the office of episcopacy was re-enforced. Earlier anti-papal statements were omitted while scripture prevailed as the highest authority. The monarch's authority in the affairs of religion was crucial: it was in the King's or Queen's power to decide, with the input of parliament. The wording includes a Prayer for the Queen's majesty, that she be led by the Holy Spirit.[16]

The wording of the sacramental rites required careful deliberation. Baptism was reaffirmed as central to ecclesial life, but the questions of who could baptize, when and how, had to be ironed out. Baptism should take place only on given Sundays—especially on Easter or Whitsuntide—or other designated holy days when most people in the church could attend to witness and testify (if occasion required) to the arrival of the newcomer, and also be reminded of their own baptismal profession to God. Since the baptism was for the building up of the congregation, home baptisms were discouraged, sans urgent reasons. Only English was to be used so that the maximum number of people could both hear and understand the word.

Jesus's command to go and teach and baptize the nations provided the rationale for baptism. The founding expectation was that the ritual brought about fullness of grace and a heavenly washing. The doctrine of election grounded the expectation that in baptism God brings about a "regeneration" or a rebirth for those whom the Holy Spirit comes to adopt as heirs of everlasting salvation. Incorporating the elect into the holy communion of faith, the merciful God leads them to partake in Christ's resurrection. Pre-existing faith was not required; the continuance of infant baptism was stipulated: "Almighty and everlasting God ... we geve thee humble thankes ... Geve thy holy spirit to these enfantes, that they may be borne againe, and be made heyres of everlasting salvacion, through our Lorde Jesus Christ."[17]

More Calvinistically oriented Protestants wished for a stronger wording on the "rebirth" being reserved for the "elect." The impact of election on the celebration of the sacraments and beyond would continue to stir debate in the years to come. Most famous was the challenge of the so called "Arminians" (after Jacobus Arminius) who believed salvation provided by God belonged to all ("universal salvation") versus those Calvinists who understood salvation belonged to the predestined elect only ("limited atonement"). Conclusions on salvation and predestination would have ramifications for how Christians imagined the church's foundation and identity, and also for how Christian life and ecclesial fellowship were conceived. Concerned by these issues as well as the administration of the sacraments, the so-called Puritans left the crown-led church that insisted on uniformity in religious form through use of the same prayer book. Eschewing this text as the means by which a shared identity among the English Protestants might be forged, the Puritans sought freedom to establish their own confessionally defined worship communities.

The wording on the sacrament of baptism explicates a foundational trust in God the Sovereign creator, redeemer, and sanctifier and continues the teaching of the early church's creeds. The prayer in the baptismal liturgy underscores the essentials:

> We yelde thee harty thankes most merciful father, that it hathe pleased thee to regenerate this enfant with thy holy spirite, to receive him for thine owne childe by adoption, and to incorporate him into thy holy congregation. And humbly we beseche thee to grauant that he being dead unto synne, and lyvin unto righteousness, and being buried with Christ in his death, maye crucify

the old man, and utterly abolyshe the whole bodye of synne, that as he is made partaker of the deathe of thy sonne, so he maye be partaker of hys resurrection, so that finally with the residue of thy holy congregacion he may be inheritour of thine everlasting kingdome. Through Christ our Lord. Amen.[18]

The liturgical forms employed are presented to promote unity for Christians in their shared faith in one God. The 1559 prayer book's call for unity in worship and sacraments would be particularly significant with the Lord's Supper, historically the most contested ritual.

Elizabeth's prayer book poignantly removed the Black Rubric about the proper form of receiving communion, thus showing deference to the traditionalists who were accustomed to kneeling. That revision, the relaxation of other "rules" about receiving, and a certain amount of ambiguity in the wording about the nature of Christ's presence, allowed individuals some personal freedom in approaching the gift. Different parties could come to the table together and make their own choices whether to kneel or stand when receiving, and how to discover Christ's presence for them. No trace of the doctrine of transubstantiation was to be tolerated; the use of regular bread was preferred as a new way of celebration with this renewed theology. Once altars were replaced with tables and the host was offered into communicants' hands (not mouths), people needed a reminder of the importance of a reverential participation in the ritual. Communicants were reminded that they were eating in remembrance of Jesus, after his own holy institution; that they were to remember his death and suffering as they drank from the cup for the forgiveness of sins.[19] People were urged to participate at least three times a year and to receive communion in both kinds—a change that required much education and positive enforcement. To safeguard against the practice of private masses and such, it was stipulated that communion could not take place without a proper number of participants for whom the rite was written and that the rite had to be performed in English. The use of vernacular language was essential for people to espouse the Reformed faith in their hearts and devotions. The power of the English prayer book breathes splendidly through its language, as exemplified in the prayers that constitute the liturgies for the sacraments.

With eloquent phrasing, the prayers present theologically complex formulations in comforting and elevating words for every worshipper to join in. Of all the sixteenth century "confessional" or founding denominational documents, the English prayer book surpasses others in its poetic beauty and sophistication. A post-communion prayer gives a flavor of how theology and poetry are united in the order for the Lord's Supper:

Almighty and everlastinge God, we most hartely thancke thee, for that thou doest vouchsafe to fede us, whiche have duly received these holy misteries, with the spiritual fode of the moste precious body and bloude of thy sonne, our saviour Jesus Christ, and doest assure us therby of thy favour and goodnes towarde us, and that we be very membres incorporate in thy mystical body, whiche is the blessed company of al faithfull people, and be also heyres through hope of thy everlasting, kingdom, ... We now most humbly besche thee, o hevenly father, so to assist us with thy grace, that we may continue in that holy felowship, and do all suche good works as thou hast prepared for us to walke in, throughe Jesus Christe our Lord, to whom with thee and the holy ghost be all honour and glory, wolrd without ende. Amen.[20]

The Elizabethan prayer book was creating a new religious culture. The negotiation between Catholic symbols and Reformed theology caused tension in the pews. For instance, as the use of the alb (a white, ankle-length garment) and the cope (cloth worn over the shoulders, fastened at the breast) were restored in Elizabeth's time, the more Calvinistically oriented Protestants reacted against such liturgical attire as it seemed too Catholic. Maintaining the episcopal office and equating resistance to the bishop to resistance to the monarch did not sit well with all the most explicitly Calvinist groups who wished for a clearer separation of powers and a different constitution of leadership in the church. Minority groups found irritating the retention of rituals such as the use of communion wafers, gestures of kneeling and bowing heads when communing, and using the sign of the cross at baptism. Nevertheless, some notable traditions were preserved: the practice of confirmation (in association with baptism) and the ritual for matrimony with the exchange and blessing of the rings—neither of which was considered a sacrament any longer. Rites for visiting the sick and the dying were continued, as was the "Thanksgiving of women after child birth" (aka churching of women): with Psalm 121, a woman was welcomed back to the community with a prayer, "O almighty God, which hast delivered this woman thy servaunte from the great paine and peril of children birthe: Graunt ... that she through thy help may bothe faithfully live, and walke in her vocation, according to they will ..."[21] The sacrament of extreme unction was abolished, yet the emphasis on good dying made rituals supporting those in illness and dying pertinent. Prayers for the dead were omitted though, which caused controversy.[22]

Eventually the clash between those favoring a closer resemblance with the Catholic tradition (the Laudians) and those in favor of more drastic purging of the rituals (the Puritans) led to civil wars in the years of uncertainty following the time of Elizabeth. As an example, in 1640 a petition was made to eliminate episcopacy entirely. Similarly, attempts were made to rid England of the prayer book and for fifteen years an alternate book was used ("A Directory for the Public Worship of God"). The prayer book, however, was already so much part of the culture and spirituality that it could not be erased. It was restored for use in 1662 by a royal decision.

Elizabeth's prayer book in its different editions and translations has continued to accompany people from cradle to grave.[23] Developed in the generation of Shakespeare, it shaped Protestant religious life in word and ritual, image and song. The introduction of music to the worship liturgy was sponsored by the Queen herself who commissioned glorious pieces for services held at her court. Regular congregational music came along gradually, mostly in the form of psalm and hymn singing.[24] The prayer book that was brought to the Americas in the 1600s was Elizabeth's.[25]

Conclusion

The development of the prayer book reflects the changing mood and personalities in the royal court and the fluctuating debates between different religious factions in England, i.e., both Catholicism and the various hues of Protestantism. The editions document the development of the theological identity of the Church of England.

The prayer book allowed a significant blending of traditions. While taking a clearly Protestant stand on the sacraments, the 1559 prayer book allowed room for a diversity of ways for individuals to participate and appreciate the gifts offered. The uniformity in form assured proper administration of the sacraments and their availability for all, just as it ensured the proclamation of the Word, foundations for the future of the church. With Queen Elizabeth's foresight and personal commitment to unity without forced unanimity, the prayer book became both a successful vehicle for internal ecumenicity in praxis and—what came later to be characterized as—a *via media* for theological engagement of various kinds. As both a symptom of and a catalyst for the Reformation, Brian Cummings concludes, "this is a book to live, love, and die to."[26]

Notes

1. See sixteenth-century printing in *The Boke of common praier, and administration of the Sacraments, and other rites and Ceremonies in the*

Churche of Englande (Londini, in officina Richardi Graftoni). Cum privilegio Regie Maiestatis. Anno, 1559. There are different editions of Book of Common Prayer, BOCP: 1549, 1552, 1559, 1662. In what follows, quotations are from the 1979 U.S. Book of Common Prayer.

2. Brian Cummings, ed., *The Book of Common Prayer: The Texts of 1549, 1559, and 1662* (Oxford: Oxford University Press, 2011), xvi, ix.

3. See Charles Hefling, "Introduction: Anglicans and Common Prayer" in *The Oxford Guide to the Book of Common Prayer: A Worldwide Survey*, eds Charles Hefling and Cynthia Shattuck (Oxford: Oxford University Press, 2006), 1–6. Helfing, 1–3, characterizes the BOCP as a library or a script or playbook for action.

4. See Leonel Michell, *Prayer Shapes Believing: A Theological Commentary on the Book of Common Prayer* (Wilton, CT: Morehouse Publishing, 1991).

5. E.g., its American edition, the Ratification of the BOCP, comes from 1789, with later revisions in 1892 and 1928. Available http://justus.anglican.org/resources/bcp/formatted_1979.htm

6. From Evening Prayer, in Elizabeth's Prayer Book, in Cummings, *Book of Common* Prayer, 111.

7. Whereas the *Thirty-Nine Articles* was clearly a Protestant document, in the subsequent church politics and constructive reinterpretations (e.g., with John Henry Newman) the theological configuration of the Anglican tradition became somewhat clouded. (Euan Cameron, personal communication, via email, 08/08/2013.)

8. See Judith Maltby, *Prayer Book and People in Elizabethan and Early Stuart England* (Cambridge: Cambridge University Press, 1998).

9. Cummings, *Book of Common Prayer*, xiii.

10. Ibid., 120.

11. Also included are rites and directions for baptism and confirmation, for marriage, for prayers for the sick and burial, and thanksgiving for women's recovery from childbirth.

12. Included are: Morning and Evening Prayer, Litany, Holy Communion; Baptism, Confirmation, Marriage, Prayers for the Sick, Funeral. In addition, there are biblical texts for the liturgical year: the Collect, the Epistle and Gospel texts, Old Testament and New Testament texts, Psalms, and Canticles.

13. Cummings, *Book of Common Prayer*, xxv, xxvii.

14. The authorship of the "Second Prayer Book" from 1552 (Edward VI's era) is not certain, while Cranmer's fingerprints are clear.

15. The contents of *An act for the uniformitye of Common prayer* (1662): A preface (1549); Of ceremonies, why some bee abolished, and some retained /1662; The order howe the Psalter is appointed to be read /1662; The table for the order of the Psalmes to bee sayde at Mornynge and

Evenyng prayer /1662; The order how the rest of holy Scripture is appointed to be read /1662; Proper Psalmes and lessons at Mornynge and Evening prayer, for sondays and certaine feastes and dayes /1662; An Almanacke /1662; The table and Kalendar for Psalmes and Lessons, with necessarie Rules, apperteyning to the same /1662; The ordre for Mornyng prayer and Evening prayer, throughout yere; The Letanie; The Collectes, Epistles, and Gospels, to bee used at the ministracion of the holy Communion, throughoute the yeare /1662; The order of the ministracion of the holy Communion; Baptisme both publique and private; Confirmacion, where also is a Catechisme for children; Matrimonie; Visitation of the sicke; The Communion of the sicke; Buriall; The thankesgeving of women after childe byrth; A Comminacion againste synners, wyth certayne prayers to be used diverse tymes in the yeare. See Cummings, *Book of Common Prayer*, 102–181. [1662 indicates parts included in the 1662 edition as well.]

16. "O Lord our hevenly father ... most hartely we beseche thee with thy favoure to beholde our mooste gracious soveraigne Lady Quene Elizabeth, and so replenyshe her with the grace of thy holy spirit, that she may alway incline to they wil, and walcke in thy waye." From Litany in Elizabeth's Prayer Book, in Cummings, *Book of Common* Prayer, 121.
17. Ibid., 143.
18. Ibid., 146.
19. The words of Exhortation: "I cal you in Christes behalf, I exhort you, as you love your owne Salvation, that ye wil be partakers of this holy Communion. And as the sonne of God, did vouchesafe to yelde up his soule by death upon the crosse for your healthe, even so it is youre duety to receyve the Communion together, in the remembraunce of his death as he hymselfe commaunded" (Cummings, *Book of Common Prayer*, 130–131)
20. From Communion in Elizabeth's Prayer Book, in ibid., 138.
21. From Thanksgiving of Women in Elizabeth's Prayer Book, in ibid., 176.
22. See Cummings, *Book of Common Prayer*, xxxvi–xxxvii.
23. "O Almightye God, ... have pitie upon us miserable synners, that nowe are vysited with great sicknesse, and mortalitie, that like as thou diddest then commaunde thyne angel to cease from punishing: So it may now please thee to withdraw from us this plague, and grevous syckenesse, through Jesus Christe oure Lorde. Amen" (from Litany, prayer at the time of sickness, in Elizabeth's Prayer Book, in Cummings, *Book of Common Prayer*, 123).
24. Ibid., xxxv. See ibid., xxiv–xli on the prayer book, ritual and performance.
25. The American edition, the Ratification of the BOCP, comes from 1789, revised in 1892 and 1928.
26. Cummings, *Book of Common Prayer*, xvii, xii.

Select Bibliography

Primary source

The Boke of common praier, and administration of the Sacraments, and other rites and Ceremonies in the Churche of Englande. Londini, in officina Richardi Graftoni. Cum privilegio Regie Maiestatis. Anno. 1559.

Cummings, Brian, ed., *The Book of Common Prayer, The Texts of 1549, 1559, and 1662.* Oxford: Oxford University Press, 2011, pp. 99–181. See also http://justus.anglican.org/resources/bcp/1559/BCP_1559.htm

Secondary sources

Hatchett, Marion J. *Commentary on the American Prayer Book.* New York: Seabury Press, 1995.

Hefling, Charles. "Introduction: Anglicans and Common Prayer." Pages 1–6 in *The Oxford Guide to the Book of Common Prayer: A Worldwide Survey.* Edited by Charles Hefling and Cynthia Shattuck. Oxford: Oxford University Press, 2006.

Maltby, Judith. *Prayer Book and People in Elizabethan and Early Stuart England.* Cambridge: Cambridge University Press, 1998.

Michell, Leonell. *Prayer Shapes Believing: A Theological Commentary on the Book of Common Prayer.* Wilton, CT: Morehouse Publishing, 1991.

3·9

Friendly Exegesis, that is, Exposition of the Matter of the Eucharist to Martin Luther[1] (1527)

Huldrych Zwingli (1484–1531)

Figure 3.13 Portrait of Zwingli

Introduction

The Swiss Reformer and humanist preacher Huldrych, or Ulrich Zwingli (1484–1531), established himself as a front-line reformer with his German counterpart Martin Luther; neither man would acknowledge any influence from the other, nor wish to collaborate. Amidst all of Zwingli's publications— including his articles on faith, treatises, letters or, his most distinctive craft, sermons—his lasting contribution to the divergent Protestant traditions hinges on the sacrament of the Lord's Supper. His "Friendly Exegesis, that is, Exposition of the Matter of the Eucharist to Martin Luther" from 1527 is "perhaps the most important independent statement of Zwingli on the Eucharist."[2]

Sermons and reforms in Zurich

Huldrych Zwingli entered ministry as a twenty-two-year-old pastor. After his first ministerial positions in Glarus and Einsiedeln, he was called as "people's priest" in Zurich in 1519. As a preacher, Zwingli, a trained humanist and an ex-soldier, became an outspoken critic of hiring Swiss soldiers for foreign service. He developed a method of exegesis suitable for his proclamation and preached without lectionaries. Preaching with the *sola scriptura* principle, and drawing from the church fathers, Zwingli effectively ignited and spearheaded Protestant reforms in Zurich. Zwingli's use of the scriptures infused his Reformation with vision and courage, as evident from his 1522 sermon "The Clarity and Certainty of the Word of God."

A particular event brought Zwingli to the larger consciousness of his contemporaries: On March 9, 1522, he preached in defense of a group of individuals who had broken the Lenten fast and snacked on pork sausage after a long day's work at the printer Christoph Froschauer's shop. Zwingli himself had declined the sausage but defended the men who were subject to punishment. In the midst of public inquiries, Zwingli defended them against unbiblical vows and customs in his sermon (published with the title "On the Choice and Freedom of Foods").[3] He defended Christian freedom from human ordinances, arguing that only rules explicitly grounded in the scriptures could be considered from God and thus binding. Unlike others who would eventually seek to flaunt or abuse this newly claimed "freedom," Zwingli's own restraint with the sausages shows his own tempered approach to these matters. Nevertheless, his fundamental concern was to secure genuine Christian liberty of conscience and action on non-binding matters: his points took off and others joined in demanding changes.

Zwingli was not the only preacher in town. So-called radicals were preaching the gospel too, demanding separation of faith matters from secular authority and the institutionalized church. They also took their radical views on the sacraments as demonstrations of faith. To clear his name from any association, Zwingli published his sermon "Divine and Human Righteousness" (1522). In addition to explicating the doctrine of salvation, he addressed several controversial practices, the practice of the Mass and the sacraments in particular. As the radical groups promoted believer's baptism against existing expectations, it was crucial for the people in Zurich to clarify their unified position. They also needed to decide how to practice the Lord's Supper, as well as the other holy rituals, in the spirit of Zwingli's gospel-centered preaching.

Bringing reforms to the attention of the citizens of Zurich, Zwingli emerged as the leading spokesperson in the decisive disputations on how Zurich should respond to the reforms. The watershed disputations on January 29, 1523, (600 attending) and on October 26–28 (900 attending) were both influenced by Zwingli's *67 Articles*, which became the charter of the Swiss Reformation. The first disputation targeted the radicals' practice of adult baptism, on the basis of biblical interpretation; other themes discussed included the notion of grace alone and the final authority of the Bible. This disputation led to the permission of priests to marry, removal of images, disbanding of monasteries, and the abolition of the Roman Catholic Mass. The second disputation condemned the Mass and images as unbiblical. The third, smaller disputation of 1524 resulted in a conservative reaction against the reforms already being implemented. Things were happening in 1525: New marriage laws were put in place (May) and the Mass was replaced with an evangelical service (April), with the Easter Service offered in German. Earlier that same year (January 18), the Zurich town council ordered infants to be baptized within eight days of birth, which prompted the first recorded rebaptism: on January 21, 1525, Conrad Grebel rebaptized George Blaurock, at Felix Manz's house. In March 1526, the town's council decreed punishments for the rebaptizers. Felix Manz became the first martyr on January 5, 1527, and more would follow. The milestone Diet of Speyer in 1529—reaffirming the edict from the Diet of Worms in 1521's decisions—demanded the evangelicals' return to the Catholic faith to rid the empire from "heretical" evangelicals. Both Luther's and Zwingli's followers protested, with little effect, earning the unifying label: "protestants". Both factions so named as

Protestants joined the Catholics in their persecution of the Anabaptists, whose practice of re-baptism made them guilty of a crime punishable by death.

Zwingli himself died on October 11, 1531, in the Battle of Kappel. As the Swiss cantons (twelve) went to a war over religious matters, Zwingli participated as a city pastor. As a warning for others, the Catholic troops quartered him. Shortly before his death, Zwingli had participated at the 1530 Diet of Augsburg, with his *Fidei Ratio*. Zwingli's work, presented together with Bucer's *Confessio Tetrapolitana* was overshadowed by the equally-rejected *Augsburg Confession* of the German evangelicals. Internal division between Catholics and Protestants in Switzerland continued, just as the gap between German and Swiss evangelicals grew larger.

Not so friendly but definitive

The text introduced here is not the most widely known for modern readers, but at the time of its first publication in 1527 it kindled furious responses from Luther and amplified the public debate on the sacraments. The lengthy and colorful piece sheds light on the vexed relationship Zwingli had with Luther, whose shadow he resented, as much as it addresses different aspects of the Eucharistic debate. Written at the time of Zwingli's high tide as a leader of reforms in Zurich, it presents most poignantly his distinct position on the Eucharist, as well as his Christological emphasis.[4]

The exegesis was written at a time when theological differences already fragmented the vulnerable Protestant communities of faith. A controversy around the Lord's Supper had already begun with Martin Luther in the 1520s when, against the church's established practice, he began demanding the laity's right for communion in both kinds (bread and wine) while also criticizing the Catholic teaching of transubstantiation. Rather than assume that when the rite was performed by a priest the consecrated elements *changed* in their substance into the blood and body of Christ, though their appearance as mere bread and wine remained the same, Luther focused on the promises of Christ for his real presence. Based on his reading of scripture, Luther emphasized the true presence of Christ in the Lord's Supper: while denying transubstantiation, by his personal promise as the High Priest Jesus was in, with, and under the elements. It cannot be emphasized enough how bold it was for anyone to digress from the traditional teaching he inherited. But once Luther raised questions about the sacraments, there was no one-size-fits-all alternative to the inherited tradition. The jury was still out, so to speak, for a satisfying rationale for Protestants to celebrate the Eucharistic ritual and Christ's presence there. Yes, celebrate the Supper. But what does it mean for Jesus to say "This is my body"? In five treatises on the sacrament, Luther's hot-headed colleague Andreas Karlstadt von Bodenstein put forward a startling argument that appeared confusingly close to Zwingli's position: Karlstadt argued that Christ's words "This is my body" referred simply to Christ's actual body at the time, nothing more, nothing less. Zwingli needed to state his exact viewpoint, urgently and unambiguously.

Zwingli's November 1524 "Letter to Matthew Alber Concerning the Lord's Supper" explicated, for the first time, his own formula for a "symbolic" interpretation of the sacraments; he saw them as "oaths of allegiance" and expressions of faith.[5] Zwingli drew increasing criticism not only from Catholics and Lutherans but also from the very people who had implemented his vision for worship reforms. His language of symbolism was met with unease. After his "Commentary on True and False Religion" in 1525, he wrote a "Subsidiary Essay on the Eucharist," which circulated widely among friend and foe: "Several references by colleagues of Luther and by Luther himself reveal the first energetic reaction of the Lutheran camp to Zwingli's Eucharistic thinking. Although directed primarily against Zwingli's Catholic opponents, this treatise became a major factor in the Eucharistic conflict between Luther and Zwingli."[6] A copy was sent to the German prince Philip of Hesse who made an effort to facilitate reconciliation between Luther and Zwingli at the Marburg Colloquy in 1529, but his attempt was in vain.

Figure 3.14 Zwingli on bronze doors

Confrontations

A Friendly Exegesis, that is, Exposition of the Matter of the Eucharist to Martin Luther was published by Zwingli in February 1527.[7] It consists of several essay-like parts.

In the preface, Zwingli addresses Luther first (238–242), before writing "To the Reader" (242–243). He clarifies his authority to speak: "I am influenced by a desire for that full liberty in the church in accordance with which Paul teaches that the individual has the right to speak in it, even if his seat is not among the prominent" (238). Anticipating objections from the reader, he writes: "I am not so dull, however simpleminded otherwise, good reader, as not to foresee what you are going to feel when you look upon this exposition of mine, written, if not against Luther, yet to him" (242). He wants to give the reader some perspective, so that he will not be judged too harshly: "Luther, therefore, has written against me by name before, and I against him, but without mentioning his name. Now I am going to answer him by name, but without abuse. If he is angry with me, it will be nothing new" (242). Zwingli is sad that Luther has not recognized the truth. Then follows the main text to flesh out Zwingli's most distinctive and essential viewpoints on Christ's presence in the Lord's Supper. "A Friendly Exegesis" begins with Zwingli's promise to rebut Luther from an exegetical basis, before offering his own solution.[8]

Zwingli begins by taking on Luther's unfair criticism of the Strasbourg Reformer Martin Bucer as falling into the "blasphemous monstrosity" known as "sacramentarianism" (246). Zwingli disagrees with Luther's hasty and vicious slandering of Bucer, even if the "Suermeri" are problematic to both.[9] "They form an evil just as troublesome to my party as to yours," Zwingli wrote (245). In his mind, Luther was making a fundamental error: "It appears that you either put the most important part of salvation in physically eating the body of Christ, or are carried beyond bounds by your feelings" (244). His basic argument against Luther's chastising of Bucer, the sacramentarians, Waldensians, and others, is this: the Word does not make anything "present" any more than knowledge does, and the Spirit does not bring about anything without the certainty of faith. Physical eating is not equivalent to what happens in the Eucharist (258). Criticizing Luther for making too much of the "word," he points out that "the apostles did not have the same view of the supper that we have," since "the apostles did not worship the host" (265). Furthermore, Zwingli draws evidence from the history of churches in Switzerland to demonstrate through various examples that "our ancestors had no feeling that they were eating the bodily flesh of Christ" and that the practice of Mass had been unknown (265).

Then follows the main quarrel: the precise meaning of the words "this" and "is." First of all, Christ's words "This is my body" [Mt. 26:26] should not be twisted but interpreted in light of the redeeming work of Christ: "The word 'this' indicates here that the body of Christ was slain for us" (265). Christ's atoning work is of essence, not imagining a tangible presence. Second, in accordance with Scripture, the word "is" needs to be understood as "signifies" (265). In other words, Zwingli's understanding of the Eucharistic celebration rejects a more literal interpretation of the scriptures— something he, like Luther, criticizes the Jews for—and believes that allegorical interpretation yields the true meaning (267).

Zwingli ridicules Luther's insistence on the "real" presence of Christ in the elements and his emphasis on the importance of "real" eating. There is no need to confuse eating for flesh, or bodily eating and spiritual feeding. It is more important, Zwingli argues, to understand the meaning of the Lord's Supper—or more importantly, Christ as Savior—for your life is much more important than what you think you are eating at the moment. The flesh does not understand or make one alive (269); rather, the Word does that, and the Word is a matter of belief. Whereas eating is a physical act, the significance of the sacrament is spiritual, belonging to the realm of the Spirit. Zwingli writes, "Eating the body of Christ, then, does not belong to the things that are breathed or instilled into the mind, for that which enlivens the mind and penetrates to it must be spirit; it shrinks from feeding upon body" (278). Zwingli wishes to separate chewing and believing. "Sarkophagia," flesh-eating, has no room in Zwingli's theological imagination of the sacrament of the altar.

Like Luther, Zwingli is a faith-exclusivist in terms of understanding salvation, righteousness-making, and the sacraments. Without faith, the sacraments would be of little use. Faith that saves is not taken into oneself by physical means but by the Spirit. Thus the word "signify" helps explain the benefit of the Lord's Supper for the believer for whom it is vital to understand the meaning of Christ's redeeming work (281). Internal righteousness is received as a gift in the faith that includes knowledge of Christ and it is the work of the kindling of the Holy Spirit (285). External righteousness involves exercising mercy in one's life and keeping faith (281). In either case, physical eating is relevant only in the meaning of "signify." Zwingli concludes the first part with an address to Luther: "You understand now that I am chiefly aiming to bring out here that the flesh of Christ profits nothing as far as eating is concerned." When Christ spoke the words "this is my body," he meant something other than giving his body for eating. To say anything else would be just absurd and not scriptural (286).

To say that Zwingli was unimpressed by Luther's treatment of the subject is an understatement. The titles of the next two parts are telling: "In Regard to the Things Luther Wrote in the Second Part against Carlstadt and the Fanatics" (287–298) and "As to the Things that Luther Wrote in his Book 'On the Adoration of the Sacrament'" (298–306). Zwingli wonders whether Luther was overwhelmed by other tasks with no time for careful thought, or perhaps his texts date back to "those infant days" (299).

Zwingli's humanist training shows in his close treatment of the Lord's Supper on the basis of his Christology. In his emphasis on God's sovereignty and Christ's divine nature, Zwingli suggests the concept "alloiosis" (exchange) as a logical way to explain the presence of the divine Christ for the adoration of the believer on earth. Echoing the decision of the ecumenical Council of Chalcedon (451 CE), Zwingli wishes to make a metaphysical point about Christ's super-human ability to exchange his own qualities for human beings' benefit. In his humanity, the resurrected Christ remains at the right hand of the Father; yet, in his divinity Christ can extend his presence as only God can. This is a matter of *spiritual* presence; Zwingli insists that while the human nature of Christ is limited by location, his divinity is not. Disregarding the term "alloiosis" only "handicaps people," Zwingli writes in response to Luther's ridicule. Luther's preferred notion of the "ubiquity" of Christ, which conveyed that Christ is omnipresent in human and divine nature everywhere, including the sacrament, would utterly confuse people about who Christ was, i.e., the true God. Zwingli mocks Luther: "you say the body of Christ is everywhere and fills all things as barley fills a sack (I can hardly help laughing, my dear Luther, whenever your sack is mentioned), you expand human nature to the measure of the divine." Luther's notion of ubiquity only served to revive old papal errors, Zwingli charges (303).

Then follows the piece titled "In regard to the Things that Luther Wrote in the Sermon against the Fanatics or Tricksters whom He Calls the Gushers" (306–319). Zwingli takes issue with Luther's claim, expressed in a sermon (WA 19:482:12–23), that the object of faith is that "we believe in fact that the body and blood of Christ are in the bread and wine." That is, the nature and role of faith is at stake. Puzzled by Luther's emphasis, Zwingli utters: "why, I ask, do you call faith what is only an opinion? The object of faith is the thing on which alone faith rests safely and wholesomely. Eating the body physically and materially is not such that we rest upon it alone unto salvation. Otherwise there would be two roads unto salvation, one, the death of Christ . . . the other, physical eating" (307). When it comes to the Eucharist, "The object of faith in this sacrament is the death of Christ for us, for which we come together to give thanks" (307). Luther makes too much of the manner of receiving gifts in the sacrament and forgets his own focus on the primacy of faith.

In the section titled "On the alloiosis of the Two Natures of Christ" (319–336) Zwingli returns to his infamous solution to the question of how Christ is or is not present in the Lord's Supper: "I have been so copious in its treatment as no doubt to have wearied the most patient reader. But the situation demanded it, lest I should seem to treat lightly a matter of great importance" (336). The issue deserving the utmost attention was a Christological one:

> For as humanity was put on by the Son of God that he who had been creator might duly become a sacrificial victim, and as this humanity, through the glory of the passion, death and cross, was raised to the throne of the supreme deity and sits at the right hand of God, so his divinity abides unchangeable, reigns alone, and alone governs all things. If through exchange of his natures we attribute such things to Christ the man, we ought to recognize without offense how this is done (336).

Zwingli was arguing for an alternate position, one distinct from the transubstantiation doctrine of the Roman Catholic Church, the memorialist doctrine of the "radical reformers," and Luther's doctrine of real presence. The people in Zurich found his solution most appealing.

The intriguing part that follows, "On Absurdities of Scripture" (337–350), written in the form of a dialogue between Luther and Zwingli, ends with Zwingli's conclusions. "Part Two" (330–364) zeroes in again on the explanation of the words of the Lord. Finally an "Epilogue to Luther" (364–367) and "To the Reader" (367–368) are followed by "To Follow Now the Things that Luther and his Followers Maintain without Authority from Scripture" (368), "On Images" (368–369) and "On Confession" (369). These lively writings illuminate the unresolvable tensions between the Reformers and reiterate Zwingli's main arguments.

Conclusion

The "Friendly Exegesis" transports the reader to the combustible theological debate between Luther and Zwingli who deploy the words alloiosis and ubiquity as cursive missiles. Considering each other's solutions utterly unsatisfactory, the men could not see what we can in retrospect. Seeking to defend the precious wonder that Christ the divine had become human to redeem humanity, and deeply passionate about unfolding this gift, their discord about the "how" in their respective Christologies proved irreconcilable. Looking at the fire that drove both men in their study of the Bible, passionate preaching, and brave reforms, we can see them on a shared mission. Their pastoral and academic concern was to bring the Word, Christ, authentically into people's lives for their good and for their church's spiritual wellbeing. Unfortunately, their feud over this most significant of holy rites, the sacrament that celebrates the mystery of the Word becoming flesh "for us" in this life, had serious ramifications in the larger Protestant story. The next generation of Reformers with Jean Calvin and others would pick up the pieces to continue the conversation and reinterpret the mysteries of God.

Notes

1. In: *Huldrych Zwingli, Writings. In Search of True Religion: Reformation, Pastoral and Eucharistic Writings.* 500th Anniversary Volume 2. Translated by H. Wayne Pipkin/E.J. Furcha. (Allison Park, PA: Pickwick Publications), 1984, 238–369. [In the following, text references are to this Pipkin volume.] In: *Huldreich Zwinglis Sämtliche Werke,* Volume V: 562–758. Edited by Emil Egli, et al. Corpus Reformatorum, vols. 88ff. Reprint: Zurich: Theologischer Verlag Zurich, 1983.

2. H. Wayne Pipkin, Introduction to Huldrych Zwingli's "Friendly Exegesis, that is, Exposition of the Matter of the Eucharist to Martin Luther," 1527, in *Huldrych Zwingli, Writings. In Search of True Religion: Reformation, Pastoral and Eucharistic Writings.* 500th Anniversary Volume 2. Translated by H. Wayne Pipkin/E.J. Furcha (Allison Park, PA: Pickwick Publications, 1984, 238–369), 236.

3. "Concerning Choice and Liberty Respecting Food" (1522, April 16) 70–112, in *Ulrich Zwingli, Early Writings.* Edited by Samuel Macauley Jackson. Durham: The Labyrinth Press, 70–112.

4. Pipkin, 236. "The Friendly Exegesis then is of importance for two main reasons. It is perhaps the decisive document from the Zwinglian side in the Eucharistic controversy. In addition, although imperfect in form, it sets forth with clarity the essence of the Eucharistic position of Zwingli, a spiritual view characterized by the immediacy of the presence of Christ to the believer in faith, and, thus, not at all the 'mere memorial' by which it is typically characterized." It was published in the 1527 original collection of Zwingli's works by Froschower. "It served to arouse the wrath of Luther to a fever pitch, though it advanced the Zwinglian cause in southern

Germany." It also gives the clearest exposition of Zwingli's Eucharist theology (Pipkin 236–237).

5. Pipkin, 129. Matthew Alber was Luther's associate.
6. Pipkin, 190.
7. Zwingli's 1527 Latin text was included in the *Opera Zwinglii* (from the sixteenth century) and was translated into English for the first time in 1984.
8. Pipkin, 243–286.
9. The Suermeri were branded by Luther as "the Gushers," whereas Zwingli referred to them as "Spiriteuseri" ("the Spiritizers").

Select Bibliography

Primary sources

Huldreich Zwinglis Sämtliche Werke, Berlin, Leipzig, Zurich, 1905.
Huldreich Zwingli's Werke, Zurich 1828–42.
Furcha, E.J. *Selected Writings of Huldrych Zwingli, i. The Defense of the Reformed Faith*. Allison Park, PA: Pickwick Publications, 1985.
Heller, C.N. *The Latin Works of Huldreich Zwingli*, iii. Philadelphia, 1929. Repr. as *Commentary on True and False Religion*. Durham: NC, 1981.
Hinke, W.J. *The Latin Works of Huldreich Zwingli*, ii. Philadelphia, 1922; repr. as *Zwingli on Providence and Other Essays*. Durham: NC, 1983.
Pipkin, H.W. *Selected Writings of Huldrych Zwingli, ii. In Search of True Religion: Reformation, Pastoral and Eucharistic Writings*. Allison Park, PA: Pickwick Publications, 1985.

Secondary sources

Furcha, E.J., and H.W. Pipkin. *Prophet Pastor Protestant*. Allison Park, PA: Pickwick Publications, 1984.
Jackson, S.M. *Huldreich Zwingli*. New York: G. P. Putnam's Sons, 1901.
Stephens, W.P. *Zwingli: An Introduction to His Thought*. Oxford: Oxford University Press, 1992.
Zwingliana, annual list of works on Zwingli, since 1972.

3.10

The Spiritual Exercises[1] (1548)

Ignatius of Loyola

Figure 3.15 Ignatius of Loyola

Introduction

The "Spiritual Exercises" of St. Ignatius of Loyola (1491–1556) is a "must read" for students of Christian spirituality. Embodying the core spiritual vision for reforms in the sixteenth-century Catholic Church, and with a renewed focus on the spiritual wellbeing of the person, the work rescinded the centuries-old ideal of rigorous devotional discipline for the sake of cultivating an individual disposition oriented toward enhanced communion with God and service to others. It offered both practical and mystical insights for spiritual discernment and developing a *habitus* of *imitatio Christi* in humility and service. Originally a significant counterpart to the Protestant Reformers' respective visions for a renewed Christian life, the timeless classic has found friends across the confessional boundaries who are spiritually hungry, seeking God's will and meaning in their lives.

A few words about the author: a pilgrim's program

Ignatius was born in 1491 to the noble family of Loyola in the Basque Country (the home of the Basque people, a region overlying the French and Spanish borders on the Atlantic coast). Following family tradition, Ignatius entered a military career to serve Emperor Charles V. His life path changed drastically after he was wounded in the battle of Pamplona. On his sick bed at home (August 1521–February 1522) he began to read the "Life of Christ" (by Ludolf of Saxony) and the lives of the saints. Soon after, he discerned a new call on his life. Detaching himself from wealth and any position of authority, he embarked on a pilgrimage to Jerusalem, where he landed in 1523. On the way there, he stopped at Montserrat, where he received a vision of Mary and the infant Jesus (1522), and at Manresa, where he supported himself by begging and hospital work (1522–1523). He began to engage in intense spiritual experiences involving acts of penance, fasting, and prayer. His vision and work for the *Spiritual Exercises* originates from this time and place, before his return to Europe from the Holy Land, though he added some last revisions of the work from Rome, 1539–1541.

Studying Latin and theology first in Alcala and then in Paris exposed him to the Protestant Reformation movement(s). Witnessing anti-Protestant actions that made people like John Calvin flee Paris (1534), Ignatius' response was to return to the ascetic model of service-oriented piety. With a vision to serve the church as its spiritual soldiers and in support of the papacy, Ignatius and his friends took vows of obedience, chastity, and poverty in 1539, and thus the Order Society of Jesus was founded, which was later approved as the Jesuit Order in 1540. Over the years, Ignatius established himself as a spiritual-soldier-scholar, an exemplary servant of the Catholic Church. He was a leader of Christian missions and education in all corners of the world, establishing a university tradition (and founding several universities himself) with a legacy lasting to the present day. The patron saint of soldiers, canonized in March 1622, has been acknowledged as a notable spiritual teacher through the ages. Even Protestants are finding ways to modify Ignatian exercises to match their respective practices for improved spiritual health.[2]

The *Exercises* applies theology to real life rather than aiming to be an academic treatise on systematic theology. It reads as a program book that consists of different parts: rules, texts, prayers and meditations, and theological reflection interwoven throughout. It is a text offering a structured and sustained exercise for a pilgrim in search of God's will in her life with steps involving prayer, meditation, and confession for a month-long retreat. Following the text faithfully, and preferably with spiritual direction, one can expect to reach new spiritual maturity and a clearer discernment of one's life and vocation. The path is practical, intentional and, ultimately, mystical—as the goal is an intensified personal relationship with God, a transformed sense of self, and greater clarity on the direction of one's life. Optimally, one would find a place detached from everyday responsibilities and free from the distractions of daily life and devote the suggested four weeks for this pilgrimage. If setting oneself apart for the entire month is not an option, the Exercises are flexible enough to be modified accordingly.[3]

Minimally, one needs to be able to focus on the exercises of the mind and soul, and to reach a particular state of humility. Ignatius' emphasis on discernment and humility reflects his personal conversion experience that compelled him to strip down to the basics and transform himself from a soldier with shiny armor on a horse to a poor man in robes walking on dusty roads. It also speaks of his major theological discovery: the finiteness of humanity, the omnipotence and the glory of the loving God, and the need to discern one's identity and direction in relation to Christ who is—and needs to be—at the center of everything.

Directions for discernment with Christ's will to conquer

Throughout the exercises, Ignatius points to a central theological reality, namely, that Christ acts in and for *others*, which effects transformation and salvation. The exercises are not the stimulus for Christ's action; they assist people in becoming more aware and in tune with the 'Christ-reality' and in conforming their will to that of Christ's. Christ conquered the world through his will; thus, Ignatius believes, this is the path for his followers (SE/Ganss, 147 [95]). Despite the obvious emphasis placed on personal devotion and the explicit molding of the will to Christ's, Ignatius underscores that the Divine Will is operative first and foremost; through the *Exercises*, it is Christ who communicates himself to the soul, inflaming the soul to praise God and orienting the contemplative person towards servitude and humility.[4]

Ignatius' "Directions" for a four-week schedule for spiritual discernment take one on a mystical path for a deeper self-recognition and awareness of God's will. Each of the four weeks is imbued with a certain set of expectations as well as advice on "consideration and contemplation" for designated topics. The first week is focused upon sin. The second week concerns the life of Christ up to and including Palm Sunday. The third week is used entirely to reflect upon the passion of Christ and death on the cross. The final week is set aside to consider Christ's resurrection and ascension. Ignatius suggests that a full hour be spent on each of the five exercises assigned per day, and that one be on guard against the temptation to shorten that length of time. During the four weeks of exercises, one learns to discipline the will and open one's being to God's work and use.

Some features are repeated throughout the exercises. The beginning exercise for the first week is repeated in the days and weeks to come, as it is the "Principle and Foundation" of the routine. It also expresses the basic goal, the premise for the exercises, and Ignatius's theological anthropological vision:

> Human beings are created to praise, reverence, and serve God our Lord, and by means of this to save their souls. The other things on the face of the earth are created for the human beings, to help them in working toward the end for which they are created. From this it follows that I should use these things to the extent that they help me toward my end, and rid myself of them to the extent that they hinder me. To do this, I must make myself indifferent to all created things ... I ought to desire and elect only the thing which is more conducive to the end for which I am created (SE/Ganss, 130 [23]).

According to this vision, the believer is in charge of her situation in creation, and is equipped to use the created good wisely. The exercises are meant to illuminate what is truly important and motivate the reader to get rid of excess or what proves to be a hindrance on the way towards the godly goal, which is attainable. An important step towards humility is that one makes oneself indifferent to all other created things. The exercises are geared to assist in attaining this state of indifference.

Another central piece in the system and crucial for the experience of humility is what Ignatius called the "Particular Examination of Conscience" (SE/Ganss, 130–131 [22–26]). Three times throughout the day—upon waking up in the morning, after the noontime meal, and after the evening meal—one is to examine one's conscience through an elaborate scheme by which the repentant would enumerate sins and place them on a chart. As part of the exercise, one is to write the letter "G" [in English version] seven times. The letter is to be written from the top to the bottom of the page, each time making the letter a little smaller as the space decreases to list one's offenses. The effect of this practice results in the retreatant being able to see their faults lessening as they progress through the week. This practice coupled with opportunities for confession and the reception of Holy Communion allows for a steady progress in the *Exercises*.

After these warm-ups follow the actual exercises. A flexible and uncomplicated compass is set for the exerciser to consider one's sinfulness, discern the longings of one's spirit, and draw guidance from designated texts from the Scriptures. After these exercises follow words on "Contemplation to Gain Love," which sets the goal of the journeyer (SE/Ganss, 176–177 [231–237]), practical help in the form of "Three Methods of Prayer (On the Ten Commandments, The Deadly Sins, Powers of the Soul, and the Bodily Sense) (SE/Ganss, 178–182 [238–260]), and reflections on "Mysteries on the Life of Christ Our Lord" (where the role of Mary is notable) (SE/Ganss, 183–200 [261–312)]. In the end comes the section on "Rules" (SE/Ganss, 201–214 [313–370]).

The Rules of spiritual engagement are meant to help the retreatant get the most of their experience and remove some of the many obstacles that stand in the way of spiritual progress. They effectively summarize Ignatius' agreement with the core teachings and practices of the Catholic Church of his time and draw a clear line in opposition to the Protestants' theological reform suggestions.

As an example, the first set of rules addresses the different movements of one's soul, with advice on how to discern the proper source of consolation and to prepare for times of desolation. After providing guidelines for discerning spirits, Ignatius gives particular rules governing how alms should be distributed and rules for understanding people's scruples (e.g., stepping on a cross made of straws [section 346]), providing strategies for how to respond against the various schemes "the enemy" uses against different people's vulnerabilities of conscience. The last set of rules, well-known to many, is titled, "To have the true sentiment which we ought to have in the church militant" (SE/Ganss, 211 [352)].

The first rule sets the basic expectation that persons should obey their holy Mother, the Church, in everything. They should praise the practice of confession to a priest, the reception of the Holy Sacrament once a year, and also the Mass. Religious orders, virginity, and monastic vows are to be praised as well as scholastic theology and the teachings of superiors. Praise belongs also to relics, saints, constitutions, and church edifices. This was and remains a significant barrier for many Protestants who nevertheless want to learn from Ignatius. In other words, all the practices and teachings that the Protestant Reformers came to criticize, abandon, or propose changes to are here re-instated as worthy of praise; they are holy practices that lead to higher spiritual goals than any "Reformed" practice could promise.

Ignatius' point is clear: his theological vision is "orthodox" in nature; that is, his vision is in disagreement with Protestant views, in full unanimity with the teachings of his mother church, and does not question the church's authority in ordering the life in the church. According to Ignatius, it was not the church but rather *the individual* who needed radical transformation. The thirteenth rule about obedience to the church expresses Ignatius' unflappable confidence in the role, power, and calling of the Church to work with Christ's Word for the benefit of its children:

> To be right in everything, we ought always to hold that the white which I see, is black, if the Hierarchical Church so decides it, believing that between Christ our Lord, the Bridegroom, and the Church, His Bride, there is the same Spirit which governs and directs us for the salvation of our souls. Because by the same Spirit and our Lord Who gave the ten Commandments, our holy Mother the Church is directed and governed. (Rule 13) (SE/Ganss, 213 [365]).

After the obedience clause, Ignatius addresses heavily debated theological issues having to do with Christian freedom in salvation matters: predestination, salvation by faith, and grace.

On predestination Ignatius says that, "Although there is much truth in the assertion that no one can save himself without being predestined and without having faith and grace; we must be very cautious in the manner of speaking and communicating with others about all these things." This caution is necessary for the sake of common people who might be misled into laziness with the misconception that all has been already decided for them (Rule 14–15) (SE/Ganss, 213 [366–367]). After all, Ignatius' rules are based on the belief that one can have an impact on one's faith and spiritual development, here and now; that one can make healthier decisions and improve not only one's own life but also the lives of others.

In the same vein, Ignatius criticizes, implicitly, the Protestant emphasis on justification by faith alone. He writes, "In the same way, we must be on our guard that by talking much and with much insistence of faith, without any distinction and explanation, occasion be not given to the people to be lazy and slothful in works, whether before faith is formed in charity or after" (Rule 16) (SE/Ganss, 213 [368]). It is then no surprise that Ignatius takes an Erasmian stand on the issue of liberty of will, in opposition to the teaching of Luther on the bondage of the will: "Likewise, we ought not to speak so much with insistence on grace that the poison of discarding liberty be engendered" (Rule 17) (SE/Ganss, 213 [369]).

Ignatius is concerned with laxity and negligence in the most important task for all Christians, i.e., active love of one's neighbors in response to God's love of them. Rule 18 summarizes his theological vision behind the *Exercises*:

> Although serving God our Lord much out of pure love is to be esteemed above all; we ought to praise much the fear of His Divine Majesty, because not only filial fear is a thing pious and most holy, but even servile fear—when the [hu]man reaches nothing else better or more useful—helps much to get out of mortal sin. And when he is out, he easily comes to filial fear, which is all acceptable and grateful to God our Lord: as being at one with the Divine Love.

The molding of one's will and exercising one's discernment has this mystical end-goal: oneness with Divine Love and praise of God as one's Father (SE/Ganss, 213–214 [370–371]).

Figure 3.16 St. Ignatius having a vision

These rules clearly align Ignatius with the teaching and practices of the Catholic Church, the tradition re-affirmed at the Council of Trent where Ignatius' theological contribution was evident.

On the spiritual theology of the Exercises: right relations, inside and out

How do I understand myself in relation to the Divine? That is the fundamental question driving Ignatius' reflection, since that was the question at the heart of his conversion experience. Ignatius found himself renewed as a result of the self-revelation that showed him his human finiteness and dependency on God's grandeur. In humility he found God—or was rather found by God—who showed him a new direction to his life. Right kind of knowledge is crucial, he learned.

Ignatius describes the constant battleground of the human soul, starting from the kinds of thoughts and ideas one is exposed to and that need discernment: "I assume that there are three kinds of thoughts within myself. That is, one kind is my own, which arises from my own freedom and desire; and the other two come from outside myself, the one from the good spirit and the other from the evil" (SE/Ganss, 132 [32]). Humans are in a position to choose between God and evil. Individuals need to be attentive in this very real warfare. Prayers, confession, and worship are meant to feed, inform, and guide the thoughts of the faithful. The *Exercises* apply Ignatius' basic theological insight concerning Christian reality and what one can do about it. Cultivating one's will is essential; it equals conformity with Christ's will.

An important part of knowing God is proper knowledge of one's self and, from there, acknowledging one's own sins and sinfulness. The Second Point of the *Exercises* urges the participant to weigh her sins. Rather than despairing, such soul-searching gives confidence about an enhanced relationship with God. Spiritual exercises open one's eyes and ears and heart and whole being to experience that relationship—an experience that humbles in its awesomeness and leads to concrete servitude. Love—love of God and love of the neighbor—is the divine force one encounters constantly and that transforms the seeker. Affection and gratitude are the best stimulus for active love of others in self-denial—that is the kind of rule Ignatius elaborates on, condoning it with his own positive experience (SE/Ganss, 147 [98]).

In the section entitled "Contemplation to Attain Divine Love," Ignatius offers a method: First, one is to remember, with affection, all the benefits received in creation and redemption. One is to consider particularly how much Christ has given and continues to want to give to "me" (SE/Ganss 176–177 [234]: "I will ponder with deep affection how much God our Lord has done for me, and how much he [God] has given me of what he possesses, and consequently how he [God], the same Lord, desires to give me even his very self, in accordance with his divine design" (SE/Ganss, 176–177 [234]). The contemplation continues on God's presence within creatures and labors for the benefit of human beings, all of which should stir loving emotions and gratitude (SE/Ganss 177 [235–237]).

Humanity's primary goal is to give their life to God in service, praise, and thanksgiving. This is a response to the gifts that have already been bestowed by a loving and gracious God. With humility as the underlying experience, a Christian's primary response is that of gratitude and a rekindled love that calls for action. In the "Second Week" under the "Second Part, Third Point," a prayer speaks to the dynamics of this process:

> Eternal Lord of all things, I make my offering, with your favor and help. I make it in the presence of your infinite Goodness, and of your glorious Mother, and of all the holy men and women in your heavenly court. I wish and desire, and it is my deliberate decision, provided only that it is for your greater service and praise, to imitate you in bearing all injuries and affronts, and any poverty, actual as well as spiritual, if your Most Holy Majesty desires to elect and receive me into such a life and state (SE/Ganss, 147 [98]).

The prayer verbalizes the desire to imitate Christ in actual and spiritual poverty. It articulates a desire to detach oneself from current and potential possessions and attachments. As a result, one then experiences "emptiness before God" and a need for God as the sinful self is emptied in order that the Infinite might be discovered anew. This Source of Life, rediscovered, is the alpha and the omega, that is, Love.

Conclusion

Pope Paul III approved the *Exercises* in 1548, and the work of Ignatius became a vital instrument in the papal-led reforms of the Catholic Church. His impact was significant through the decisions of the Council of Trent where most of the theological reforms and suggestions from the Protestants were either rejected, ignored, or countered, and medieval theological principles, spiritual practices, and structures were re-instated. For instance, the doctrine of justification by grace through faith alone was attacked from many directions, while many of the established spiritual practices were defended with an active model for individual piety. With Ignatius' *Exercises*, the mystical model was preserved for future generations. Likewise, in the spirit of humility and in line with the principle of detachment of one's own self and authority, Ignatius modeled absolute obedience to the Church and the papacy as its representative.

To the Protestant mind in the sixteenth century, when the battle wounds were still fresh, Ignatius' spiritual theology seemed outlandishly semi-Pelagian and threatened a return of the works righteousness mentality that the reformers had fought so hard against. Recent ecumenical work and re-examination of Martin Luther's mystical theology have unveiled some of the unfortunate, mutual misunderstandings on the meaning of grace and justification by faith, and common ground has been found with regard to the spiritual concerns (even if in many practical matters and with regard to the papal office, greater divides remain and traditions continue to "agree to disagree").

A renewed interest in Christian spirituality has ignited new generations to peruse the writings of Ignatius and other medieval Catholic saints (e.g., his female counterpart Teresa of Avila).[5] In this respect, a common ground is found for the Protestant Reformers and the Catholic teachers and their followers: the shared desire to follow Christ, who is reckoned as the only source of salvation, and whose very desire is to be united with the believer; thus the Incarnation, thus the cross, thus the resurrection. Ignatius's *Exercises* offers an invitation to join in a spiritual exploration to discover the mystical dimensions of life with Christ and to improve in one's following of Christ in daily life.

Notes

1. Translated from *Exercitia spiritualia*; the following edition was used: Ignatius of Loyola, *The Spiritual Exercises and Selected Works*, trans. and ed. George E. Ganss (New York: Paulist Press, 1991). Hereafter, all references are to this work, SE/Ganss, page number [section number].

2. See Philip Caraman, *Ignatius of Loyola* (London: Collins, 1990); and Andre Ravier, *Ignatius of Loyola and the Founding of the Society of Jesus* (San Francisco: Ignatius Press, 1987).

3. See e.g., William A.M. Peters, *The Spiritual Exercises of St Ignatius: Exposition and Interpretation* (Rome: Centrum Ignatianum Spiritualitatis, 1978).

4. See Juan Luis Segundo, *The Christ of the Ignatian Exercises* (London: Sheed & Ward, 1988).

5. The current Pope Francis only enhances the already growing contemporary interest in Ignatian spirituality, with important overlaps with contemporary psychology. For example, see how to "Find your Inner Iggy" and other articles in www.ignatianspirituality.com/what-is-ignatian-spirituality. See also: Timothy M. Gallagher, *The Discernment of Spirits: An Ignatian Guide for Everyday Life* (New York: Crossroads, 2005). Similarly, as an example of the renaissance of Teresan spirituality, see Rowan Williams, *Teresa of Avila* (London: Bloomsbury Academic, 2004); Peter Tyler, *Teresa of Avila: Doctor of the Soul* (London: Bloomsbury Academic, 2014).

Select Bibliography

Primary sources

Ignatius of Loyola. *Exercitia spiritualia.* Rome: Antonio Bladio, 1548.

Ignatius of Loyola. *Exercitia Spiritualia Sancti Ignati de Loyola et eorum Directoria.* Ed. A. Codina. Madrid/Matriti, Typis Successorum Rivadeneyrae, 1919.

Ignatius of Loyola. *The Spiritual Exercises and Selected Works.* Classics of Western Spirituality series. Translated and edited by George E. Ganss. New York: Paulist Press, 1991.

Available in English Online in the Christian Classics Ethereal Library: www.ccel.org/ccel/ignatius/exercises.html

Secondary sources

Caraman, Philip. *Ignatius of Loyola.* London: Collins, 1990.

Cusson, Gilles. *Biblical Theology and the Spiritual Exercises.* Translated by Mary Angela Roduit and George E. Ganss. St Louis: Institute of Jesuit Sources, 1988. (Translation of the original: Cusson, Pédagogie de l'expérience spirituelle personelle: Bible et Exercises Spirituels.)

Mottola, Anthony, translator. *Spiritual Exercises of Saint Ignatius.* Doubleday Image, 1964.

Peters, William A.M. *The Spiritual Exercises of St Ignatius: Exposition and Interpretation.* Rome: Centrum Ignatianum Spiritualitatis, 1978.

Ravier, Andre. *Ignatius of Loyola and the Founding of the Society of Jesus.* San Francisco: Ignatius Press, 1987.

Segundo, Juan Luis. *The Christ of the Ignatian Exercises.* London: Sheed & Ward, 1988.

Part IV

The Seventeenth and Eighteenth Centuries

Introduction to the Seventeenth and Eighteenth Centuries

Kelly M. Kapic

Obviously the sixteenth century is vitally important for understanding the Protestant tradition because that's when Protestantism emerged, growing out of earlier reforming efforts. However, what is not always appreciated is how the seventeenth and eighteenth centuries saw the growth and maturing of this movement as it addressed new questions and tried to organize its thinking and practice. Following sixteenth-century trajectories, in this period it becomes even more clear that "Protestantism" does not represent a single uniform tradition, but instead tradition*s*. Yet, amid the diversity there is this common Reformation heritage.

Non-Roman Catholic western approaches to theology and practice become more set in the early part of this period. Various communities carefully worked through how to incorporate distinctive Reformation emphases into their religious self-understanding. William Ames' work *The Marrow of Theology* (1623) was one such result that became a standard text for ministers being trained in England and America. Even more thoroughly Reformed and influential were *The Westminster Standards*, composed by the Westminster Assembly in the 1640s.

Many Protestants, however, did not agree with the distinctly Calvinistic thinking exemplified by Ames and Westminster. For example, Jacobus Arminius' *The Declaration of Sentiments* (1608) reflected the tensions already present in Protestantism that would grow in the following centuries: he certainly believed he was rightly reflecting the best of Reformation theology even if he was advocating positions which would be rejected by the *Canons of Dordrecht* (1618–1619) and the *Westminster Confession*.

These are two examples of different Protestant trajectories that formed during these centuries. Some emphasized the primacy of holy scripture and sought to make sure all remaining practices and beliefs had explicit biblical warrant: they self-consciously tried to continue the "purifying" of the Church (e.g., Puritans) that they believed had begun but was not completed in the sixteenth century. Others rallied around a distinctive view of the "priesthood of all believers," raising deep questions about the value and place of ecclesiastical structures and hierarchy. Madame Guyon's *A Short and Easy Method of Prayer* (1685) can be read as having these kinds of concern.

Older tensions don't diminish but instead often become even more exaggerated. For instance, while some believed the implications of Luther's call to "faith alone" had not yet been fully implemented, different voices responded with passionate pleas for moral renewal. They were convinced the Church had become too distracted by academic debates or simply morally lax, having lost concern for ethical development.

Within this diversity was a growing shared assumption, namely, that the individual was more central to Christianity than was the community. For example, the Baptist tinker John Bunyan, in his *Pilgrim's Progress*, portrayed each Christian as on a pathway filled with possibilities and dangers, pursuing a journey that required individual determination, wisdom, and personal dependence upon God. Others could help you along the way, but ultimately this was a journey followed by a solitary figure seeking the Lord.

Some scholars have noted that the "Enlightenment" and the experience of "Awakenings" provide a way to understand both the tensions and the similarities among Christian groups in this period, especially Protestants. One side drew increasing attention to the power of the intellect, the human faculty that alone could be trusted to make not simply scientific observations but also serve as the foundation for religious convictions. Such confidence in reason thus abstracted from faith and tradition could be used to undermine orthodoxy, as seen for example in the Unitarianism and Deism of this period. Rather than merely question divine revelation as a reliable source for reasonable religion, they reject it.

Yet not all in the Church feared this new-found confidence in the human mind: certain Christian advocates believed that a right use of reason and deduction was more than able to defend and uphold the ancient Christian faith. William Paley's *Natural Theology* provides an illuminating example of this attitude. Such advocates thought revelation and reason were complementary rather than in conflict. Sometimes these efforts defended a form of classic orthodoxy. John Wesley, for example, wrote *The Appeals to Men of Reason and Religion* to call people back to scripture, tradition, reason, *and* religious experience. At other times, however, those who tried to make reason work apart from revelation ended up taking supporters far from early creedal Christianity. The world was changing around the Church.

Yale theologian Hans Frei once observed of this massive transformation that, in the early Church and even through the Reformation, the *biblical* world was the horizon of the believer: current experience and belief was tested by the canon of sacred scripture. The seventeenth and eighteenth centuries saw a seismic alteration, he commented, because the biblical world was beginning to stand *under* the judgment of *the reader's experience*, rather than the other way around. The particular God of Abraham, Isaac, and Jacob was dethroned, replaced by a new optimism about uncovering an underlying "natural" or "Universal" religion. Inclined to trust reason and nature over revelation and tradition, these assumptions exerted incalculable pressures on Christian belief and practice, not only during the seventeenth and eighteenth centuries, but also by setting the trajectory that has continued to shape the modern western world. John Owen's *Pneumalogia* (*On the Holy Spirit*) should be read as a response to the expanding influence of rationalism (e.g., Socinianism) while also rejecting Christian overreactions that appeared to pit God's Spirit against God's creation (e.g., Quakers). No, Owen objected, God's Spirit is personal and active: the true Spirit of the Creator God and of the incarnate Christ delights to work in and through creation, rather than belittling it.

While sharing assumptions about the importance of the individual, other Protestants turned their attention from the mind to the heart. Philipp Jacob Spener's *Pia Desideria*, the classic example of this impulse, marks the rise of what becomes known as "pietism." Suspicious about Protestant Scholasticism, the value of received orthodoxy, and an ongoing emphasis on ecclesiology, this group feared intellectual assent had replaced the role of experience. They promoted the experiential love of God and neighbor, turning from doctrinal disputes toward personal practices of godliness.

Many of the "Awakenings" and the rise of devotional literature during this period emphasized the importance of the individual while seeking to focus on a more practical rather than intellectual faith. George Whitefield's *Sermons*, preached throughout Great Britain and the American colonies, urged listeners to make sure they personally experienced God's grace. It is estimated that Whitefield and Wesley were probably heard by millions of people in total, and their version of the emerging "evangelicalism"—the good and potentially problematic—would eventually spread beyond their original audience to be felt throughout the non-western world. For more on the global impact, we will need to wait for the eighteenth–nineteenth centuries. But when this message was heard in America, it resonated with the new identity being forged among those in this great experiment of a country. Part of the DNA of the American experience, from early on, was a tendency to value the practical. Anne Bradstreet exemplified a theologically astute version of this impulse. Through her *Poems* we discover the wonder of how she meditated on God's presence and action in daily life, filled with beauty and hardship.

These strong emphases on personal experience, however, introduced new complications, especially as one tried to figure out if one's subjective experience was from God or simply an emotional burst. Jonathan Edwards wrote his *Religious Affections* as an attempt to affirm the contemporary signs of renewal while also warning of potential abuses.

In all, these centuries show both a solidifying of certain Protestant perspectives while at the same time increasing the already-present tensions between different participants in this movement. The various versions of Protestantism were spreading, evolving, and adjusting to the new challenges of their own contexts.

List of Classic Works of the Seventeenth and Eighteenth Centuries

Johann Arndt, *True Christianity*, 1606

Jacobus Arminius, *Declaration of Sentiments*, 1608

Benedict Canfield, *Rule of Perfection*, 1609

Francisco Suárez, *Treatise on Laws*, 1613

Francis de Sales, *Love of God*, 1616

Hugo Grotius, *Truth of the Christian Religion*, 1622

Jakob Böhme, *Way to Christ*, 1622/24

John Donne, *Devotions upon Emergent Occasions*, 1624

William Ames, *Of Conscience, Its Power and Cases*, 1630

George Herbert, *The Temple*, 1633

Richard Sibbes, *A Description of Christ*, 1639

John Goodwin, *Imputatio Fidei, or a Treatise on Justification*, 1642

Thomas Browne, *Religio Medici*, 1642

Roger Williams, *Bloody Tenet of Persecution*, 1644

John Cotton, *Keys of the Kingdom of Heaven*, 1644

Richard Baxter, *The Saints' Everlasting Rest*, 1650

Jeremy Taylor, *Rule and Exercise of Holy Living and Holy Dying*, 1650

John Bunyan, *Grace Abounding to the Chief of Sinners*, 1666

John Milton, *Paradise Lost*, 1667

Margaret Fell, *Women's Speaking Justified*, 1667

Henry Scougal, *The Life of God in the Soul of Man*, c. 1670

Robert Barclay, *An Apology for the True Christian Divinity*, 1678

Francis Turretin, *Institutes of Elenctic Theology*, 1679–1685

Anne Bradstreet, *The Flesh and the Spirit* (poem), 1678

Brother Lawrence, *Practice of the Presence of God*, 1692

John Locke, *Reasonableness of Christianity*, 1695

William Law, *A Serious Call to a Devout and Holy Life*, 1728

Jonathan Edwards, *A History of the Work of Redemption*, 1739

Anne Dutton, *Letters on Spiritual Subjects*, 1740

Count von Zinzendorf, *Nine Public Lectures*, 1748

David Brainerd, *Diary of David Brainerd*, 1749

Jonathan Edwards, *Concerning the End For Which God Created the World*, 1749

George Whitefield, *The Works of George Whitefield*, c. 1750

John Wesley, *Notes on the New Testament*, 1755

Jean-Jacques Rousseau, *Creed of a Savoyard Priest*, 1762

John Wesley, *A Plain Account of Christian Perfection*, 1766

Isaac Backus, *An Appeal to the Public for Religious Liberty, Against the Oppressions of the Present Day*, 1773

David Hume, *Dialogues Concerning Natural Religion*, 1779

John Newton, *Utterance of the Heart*, 1781

Hannah Adams, *View of Religious Opinions*, 1784

G.W.F. Hegel, *Early Theological Writings*, c. 1790

Immanuel Kant, *Religion within the Limits of Reason Alone*, 1793

Samuel Hopkins, *System of Doctrines*, 1793

William Wilberforce, *Real Christianity*, 1797

4.1

The Marrow of Theology (1623)
William Ames (1576–1633)

The life and works of William Ames[1]

On December 21, 1609, William Ames delivered a riveting, controversial sermon that took his life in a new direction. With the coming of the Christmas season at Christ's College, where Ames taught as a fellow, he knew that the school would allow students to engage in all kinds of, in his view, questionable activities, including gambling and card playing. So he decided to speak out against such licentious conduct and the partying that accompanied it. What motivated Ames was a desire to promote devotion to God in all areas of life.

In the wake of his sermon, Ames soon found himself before the new master of the school, Valentine Cary. To Cary, Ames's sermon identified him with radical Puritanism, the very movement opposed by King James I, who appointed Cary to his post. Because Ames's denunciation was a direct assault on the religious leaders of his day, the school's authorities suspended his degrees, leaving his future hanging in the balance. Ames decided it was time to leave his homeland and set sail for Holland, where a number of other English Puritans had already resettled.[2]

As the outcome of these events illustrates, Ames was not a man unacquainted with grief. His trials began as a child, when he lost both of his parents. Through the compassion and generosity of his uncle, Robert Snelling, young William received an education and was enabled to attend Cambridge University. There he was converted under the preaching of

William Perkins (1558–1602), whose *The Arte of Prophesying* (1592) became an influential Puritan text in the seventeenth century. Perkins exhibited the Puritan dissatisfaction with the progress of reform in Queen Elizabeth's (r. 1558–1603) Church of England.

Ames imbibed Puritanism from Perkins and others at Cambridge during its formative years, graduating with his bachelor of arts in 1598 and his master of arts in 1601, just two years before the queen died. The ascendency of King James I (r. 1603–1625) brought the delicate balance between High Church Anglicans and Puritans during Elizabeth's reign to an end, as evidenced by the university politics that closed the doors to Ames's promising academic career at Christ's College following his 1609 Christmas sermon.

After fleeing to Holland, Ames engaged the pressing theological issues of his day, particularly through his involvement with the Synod of Dort (1618–1619).[3] This synod responded to the Remonstrants, a group following the teachings of Jacobus Arminius (1560–1609) and protesting what they believed were Calvinistic extremes, especially the doctrine of God's unconditional election of only some to salvation. Ames served as a consultant, not an official delegate (since he was not Dutch), helping to shape the response to the Remonstrants. That response became a defining theological standard, laying out the basis for five points of Calvinism commonly known by the acronym TULIP (total depravity, unconditional election, limited atonement, irresistible grace, and the perseverance of the saints). While Ames fully affirmed this Calvinistic theology, he was nonetheless "the most sensitive to the criticisms advanced by the opposition party," something visible in the way he developed his Calvinistic theology, discussed below.[4]

After the synod, Ames supported his family through tutoring and lecturing at his private "house college" for three years before settling as a professor of theology at Franeker University, where he taught from 1622 to 1632.[5] There he drafted a shorter, preliminary version of *The Marrow of Theology* (or *Medulla theologiae*) in 1623, drawn from a series of lectures given at his "house college," and then he finished his complete edition in 1627. He also wrote *Conscience with the Power and Cases Thereof* in 1630, essentially an outworking of Book Two of the *Marrow*. His *Philosophemata*, published posthumously in 1643, included six short treatises like his *Technometria* (1631) that summarized his thoughts on philosophy and the arts.[6]

Ames left Franeker largely because he felt a pull to go to the New World, where fellow Puritans had recently launched the Massachusetts Bay Colony (1630) to set up a model society for Mother England to follow. Ames moved to Rotterdam, Holland, in 1632 to co-minister to a congregation there until he could sail for America. But when a river flooded his home in October 1633, the exposure to the cold put him into a feverish state that took his life a few days afterward.

Ames died planning to go to America. While he never made it there in person, his ideas suffused the young colony. For most of the next century, Ames's influence would continue to be felt, especially through his most enduring work, *The Marrow of Theology*.

Augustinian, Calvinist, and . . . Ramist?

Readers can detect clear echoes of earlier theologians in Ames's *Marrow*. He wrote his *Marrow* within the contours of both an Augustinian tradition— following Augustine of Hippo (354–430)—and a Reformed-Puritan tradition—based on the theology of Reformed thinkers like John Calvin and sifted through the English context of Puritans at odds with the Church of England. While not a slave to either, he was indebted to both.[7]

Yet some scholars have charged that by not holding tightly enough to these traditions, Ames actually left the fold of Reformed orthodoxy. This charge especially appears in relation to his treatment of the will (see the next section). What should we say? Ames certainly gave his Calvinist theology a distinct flavor, but he did so as one working within a clearly Calvinist framework.[8]

What made Ames stand out was his aim for devoted, heartfelt Christianity. That's why he wrote *The Marrow of Theology* in plain-style language. Like his mentor Perkins, Ames wanted anyone to be able to read it, layperson and student alike. He purposed to write not a massive, rhetorically impressive treatment of theology but a shorter, straightforward, precise volume that was "better suited to instruct, to stir conviction."[9] Ames aimed for the soul.

Ames helped define Puritan style by developing Calvinism using the Ramist method, which made theology "both methodical and usable in daily life" and helped him pursue his focus on holiness.[10] What exactly is Ramism? Petrus Ramus (1515–1572), a French philosopher who embraced Calvinism, developed this philosophy to correct the errors of the Aristotelianism in his day, which he believed had artificially separated thought and life, theology and ethics. To bring these two realms together, Ramus employed a form of logic that dissected ideas into their various parts by divisions and subdivisions, progressing from the general to the particular.[11] Ames followed Ramus by organizing his entire treatise with a series of divisions that moved from the general to the particular, dividing theology into two parts (faith and obedience) and continuing with multiple subdivisions from there.[12]

Working within an Augustinian-Calvinist-Puritan framework, Ames used the Ramist method to emphasize practical theology and logic. As Sprunger aptly observes, "Puritanism infused Ames's theology with its intense piety and urgency; Ramism added precision to Puritanism's holy passion."[13]

Theology as living to God

Ramism contributed to Ames's overarching understanding of theology, which he defined as "the doctrine or teaching [*doctrina*] of living to God," an echo of Ramus's phrase to describe theology, *Deo vivere*, "to live to God," (77).[14] In this way, Ames stood in line with Calvin and Perkins, but he paved new ground by *beginning* his treatise not with knowing God, as Calvinists were wont to do, but with living to God.[15]

To establish this fundamental assertion, Ames described living as "the noblest work of all" and argued that "[s]ince the highest kind of life for a human being is that which approaches most closely the living and life-giving God," living to God is humanity's highest pursuit. In Ames's view, living to God meant that people live not primarily for their own happiness but "in accord with the will of God, to the glory of God, and with God working in them" (77).

To nurture this kind of theological living, Ames prioritized the will. He saw theology as concerned with not just the intellect, the will, or the affections but all three together in "the whole man" (78).[16] And yet, Ames placed a primacy on volition, differentiating his thought from the Reformed theological currents of the day, most of which placed intellect before volition.[17] As he stated, "the first and proper subject of theology is the will." (78).

However, Ames's emphasis on the will was not a complete departure from earlier Reformed theologians. The way Ames discussed the primacy of the will reflected "the soteriological emphasis of Calvin" that prioritized God's initiative, while it also moved toward "a more holistic understanding of faith." Still, by highlighting the will, Ames "cleared a new theological path" in the Calvinist tradition that framed theology as "a practical doctrine."[18] By highlighting the will, Ames sought to find the middle path between what he believed was the ethereal speculation of Aristotelianism and the works righteousness of Arminianism. From this angle, then, he argued that "the chief end of theology" is "stirring up pious motives" so that people exercise their will in accord with the will of God (188).

Book One: faith

As already noted, Ames divided his definition of theology, in Ramist fashion, into two parts: faith and observance. No other aspects of theology were necessary, in Ames's mind, because faith concerns the essence of theology while observance concerns its operation (79). In Book One he discussed faith, treating traditional theological themes such as the Trinity, creation, sin, and redemption, and he tied them in Book Two to questions of observance or action.

But what exactly is faith? Ames drew together practice and belief even in how he defined faith. While many generally associate faith with intellectual assent, Ames again centered on the will. Faith is "an act of choice, an act of the whole man—which is by no means a mere act of the intellect." Certainly, knowledge of God and the gospel is essential to saving faith, but it is not sufficient. Saving faith is "a single virtue" that includes both intellect and volition. In true faith, then, "we not only believe God or about God but in God." So rather than keeping faith in the realm of knowledge, Ames thrust it into the arena of action, connecting it with his definition of theology: "faith is the first act of our life whereby we live to God in Christ" (80, 82, 83).

By focusing on the will as "the center of faith,"[19] Ames boldly stated that we can only understand faith as it is joined to the will.[20] For Ames, faith—not the doctrines of God, creation, or Scripture—stood as the beginning point of theology. Even so, Ames connected this active view of faith with God's predestination and initiative in saving souls apart from any human works or merit. In this theological tension, Ames sought to affirm human inability while defining faith with biblical language: "To believe in God, therefore, is to cling to God by believing, to lean on God, to rest in God as our all-sufficient life and salvation" (82).

This view of faith set the stage for the rest of Book One. He moved next to the essence and subsistences (or persons) of God, exploring Trinitarianism via the Ramist method of division. Ames went on to discuss God's decrees and God's will and the way he worked out his will in creation and providence. The effect of human sin on God's creatures gave way to the solutions available through God's plan of restoration, secured by the redemption of Christ, and applied through the covenant of grace. This redemptive covenant unites the elect to Christ through predestination, calling, justification, adoption, sanctification, and glorification. The covenant of grace also concerns the church, its ministers and sacraments, and its varied application in the eras before Christ, between Christ and the end of the world, and at the end of the world.

This brief summary of Book One illustrates the way that Ames used Ramist logic and division to organize the major elements of Christian theology. In treating these topics, he framed knowledge in the context of the will, highlighting the human impulse to act in response to divinely bestowed faith, which leads us to Book Two.

Book Two: observance

As Ames defined it, "Observance [*observantia*] is the submissive performance of the will of God for the glory of God." A key term here is *submissive*. Many creatures perform God's will without knowing it or without meaning to. But observance entails the creature's *willful* and *submissive* performance of God's will. Again Ames emphasized the human *will*, for the "principal subject of observance is the will, as it is in living faith." Thus out of observance comes "a necessary conformity between the will of God and ours." That said, the creature can only willfully obey God because of sanctifying grace, "the very power by which we are lifted up to accommodate our will to the will of God." By faith, then, we passively depend upon God, which promotes his glory (219, 220, 222, 223).

Ames broke down observance into two parts: virtue (or a disposition "located in the will") and good works (or actions). Virtue functions as the foundation of action, which again ties faith and observance together. Said another way, Ames rejected those who separated theology and ethics, "as if ethics ... had nothing to do with inward affections, and theology did not teach outward as well as inward obedience." Instead, virtue stands as the foundation of action: "An act of virtue is one which flows from the disposition of virtue." Thus, "the goodness of an act depends first and chiefly upon the will" (224, 226, 232, 235). Again, the will looms large in Ames's understanding of observance, even while it is tied to the virtues nurtured only by the gracious work of God in human hearts.

For Ames, observance—as both virtue and action—manifests itself in two spheres, reflecting the two tables of the Ten Commandments: *religion*, the sphere of relating with God, and *justice*, the sphere of relating with people. The sphere of religion includes virtues (faith, hope, and love) and various acts, such as hearing the Word, prayer, oaths, lots, and testing God.[21] The human sphere of justice includes actions such as honoring others, attending to humanity, upholding chastity, telling the truth, and being content. This abbreviated account displays again Ames's use of logic and organization to dissect the nature of theology, even as he viewed it holistically under the umbrella of observance and tied that to the broad arena of faith, which together made up the *whole* of theology.

Covenant theology

A final theme that demands attention is covenant theology. For all of his discussion about the will and an active faith, Ames showed himself firmly committed to God's sovereignty and grace through his development of a theology based on God's covenants with humanity. As Beeke and van Vliet put it, the way Ames sought to find the balance between faith and practice, between right thinking and right living, was by "placing obedience within the covenant," demonstrating that "there is harmony, not contradiction, between grace and obedience."[22]

Ames did not invent covenant theology per se. Notably, the Heidelberg theologians Caspar Olevian (1536–1587) and Zacharias Ursinus (1534–1583) incorporated covenant principles into their theology, as did Calvin and some early Puritans.[23] Their work laid the foundation for the way seventeenth-century figures like Ames and, later, Johannes Cocceius (1603–1669) developed covenant theology. Even so, no one had given the covenant such a foundational role in his theology prior to Ames, who has been considered "the first to build an entire system of Reformed covenant theology."[24]

Within this system, Ames emphasized the covenant of grace (in contrast to the covenant of works) even more so than preceding and succeeding Reformed thinkers. This stress brought out his focus both on Christ and on God's initiative in salvation, which is why "the unconditional covenant of grace" was "perhaps the most important biblical teaching" in Ames's mind, providing the basis for all the actively volitional elements in his broader theology.[25]

To understand the covenant of grace, one must grasp the covenant of works. In this covenant, God gave the creature commands to obey, making the covenant depend entirely on the creature's moral deeds. Obedience brought a happy reward, while disobedience brought punishment. In the covenant of works, Adam stood as the public representative of all mankind, and "[h]is posterity were to derive all good and evil from him" (113). When Adam failed to obey God's commands, he passed the penalty for sin on to the whole human race. The fall created the need for another, different kind of covenant, the covenant of grace, which is where Ames focused his attention.

Ames described this new covenant as the "application" of Christ to the redeemed. It is coterminous with the gospel, the good news of salvation. By calling it a *covenant*, God signified that "it is a firm promise." To highlight the special nature of the new covenant, Ames laid out several contrasts between the new and the old: Rather than a bilateral covenant between two parties, the new covenant was unilateral, made solely by God. The old covenant could be established only by "the ability of man himself," but the new relied only on Christ Jesus. While the old promised life, the new promised "righteousness and all the means of life" through restoration. Unlike the old covenant, the new was "everlasting . . . for the grace of this covenant continues forever with those who are once truly in it" (149–152). These contrasts make clear why Ames focused his attention on the covenant of grace, which, in his estimation, constituted the only sure foundation for living to God.

For Ames, the theme of covenant gave him a basis for explaining divine sovereignty and human response. It offered a way to draw together the apparently opposed concepts of faith and observance. And it left a lasting impact on Puritan and Reformed theology for decades to come.

Legacy

Ames's *Marrow* became the standard treatment of the Puritan way for over a century.[26] His greatest influence lay not in his home country, England, but in Holland and America. In Holland, his ideas influenced Gisbertus Voetius (1589–1676), a leader of the Dutch Further Reformation; Johannes Cocceius (1603–1669), who further developed Ames's covenant theology; and Petrus van Mastricht (1630–1706), a leading Dutch theologian.[27]

In America, Ames's *Marrow of Theology* became required reading at Harvard for decades. In many ways, New Englanders embraced Calvinism less from John Calvin and more through Ames's interpretation of Calvinism in his *Marrow*. Jonathan Edwards (1703–1758) imbibed Ames, making copious notes in his personal copy of the *Marrow*, and he also drank deeply from van Mastricht, an Ames devotee.[28]

Thomas Goodwin (1600–1680) captured the thoughts of many in the Puritan tradition when he said that "next to the Bible, he esteemed Dr. Ames, his *Marrow of Divinity*, as the best book in the world."[29]

Conclusion

In reading Ames's *Marrow of Theology*, one finds a seminal theological text in the Puritan and Reformed traditions. Much of what followed in these traditions in the seventeenth and early eighteenth centuries was indebted to his work. Certainly the rise and reach of covenant theology owes much to the way that Ames used Ramist method and logic to develop the Augustinian-Calvinist tradition he received for Puritan and Reformed theology.

Ames's *Marrow* also reminds us of the need for both analysis of details and a holistic grasp of how those details fit together as a whole. His volume can serve as a sort of reference manual on theology, one that helpfully breaks down topics into their component parts and thus makes it easier to digest complex theological matters. Ames pursued this theological vision with an eye always on an engaged will, tracing the movement from principles to action, from faith to observance, and structuring his whole theological program ultimately as "living to God."

Notes

1. For the life of William Ames, we have relied on John Dykstra Eusden, "Introduction," in William Ames, *The Marrow of Theology*, ed. John Dykstra Eusden (Grand Rapids, MI: Baker, 1968), 1–66; Joel R. Beeke and Randall J. Pederson, *Meet the Puritans: With a Guide to Modern Reprints* (Grand Rapids, MI: Reformation Heritage, 2006), 39–51; Joel R. Beeke and Jan van Vliet, "*The Marrow of Theology* by William Ames (1576–1602)," in *The Devoted Life: An Invitation to the Puritan Classics*, eds. Kelly M. Kapic and Randall C. Gleason (Downers Grove, IL: InterVarsity, 2004), 53–56; Keith L. Sprunger, *The Learned Doctor William Ames: Dutch Backgrounds of English and American Puritanism* (Urbana, IL: University of Illinois Press, 1972).
2. Sprunger, *Learned Doctor*, 21–24.
3. For more on Ames's interaction with theologians and disputes of the Dutch Reformed church, see Jan Van Vliet, *The Rise of Reformed System: The Intellectual Heritage of William Ames*, Studies in Christian History and Thought (Eugene, OR: Wipf and Stock, 2013), 162–84.
4. Eusden, "Introduction," 7.
5. Beeke and van Vliet, "*Marrow*," 54.
6. Sprunger, *Learned Doctor*, 105–26.
7. Eusden, "Introduction," 12–36.

8. Beeke and van Vliet, "*Marrow*," 52; Eusden, "Introduction," 17. See, e.g., Ames, *Marrow*, 97–98

9. Ames, *Marrow*, 70. Hereafter, all further references to this work shall be noted employing in-text parenthetical citations.

10. Sprunger, *Learned Doctor*, 128–29. For more on Ramus's influence on Ames, see van Vliet, *Reformed System*, 71–75; Eusden, "Introduction," 37–47.

11. Sprunger, *Learned Doctor*, 134–35; Beeke and Pederson, *Meet the Puritans*, 43; Donald K. McKim, "Ramus, Peter (1515–1572)," in *Encyclopedia of the Reformed Faith*, ed. Donald K. McKim (Louisville, KY: Westminster/John Knox, 1992), 314.

12. Eusden, "Introduction," 37–47. See the chart showing the structure of the book in Ames, *Marrow*, 72–73.

13. Sprunger, *Learned Doctor*, 142.

14. Eusden, "Introduction," 38.

15. Eusden, "Introduction," 47.

16. See Beeke and van Vliet, "*Marrow*," 57.

17. Sprunger, *Learned Doctor*, 146; Beeke and van Vliet, "*Marrow*," 58.

18. Van Vliet, *Reformed System*, 70, 83. See also Beeke and van Vliet, "*Marrow*," 57; Sprunger, *Learned Doctor*, 144.

19. Beeke and van Vliet, "*Marrow*," 58.

20. Eusden, "Introduction," 48–49.

21. Ames warned of a sinful testing of God, which arises from doubt that God will do what he says or makes God's actions dependent on human will. Nonetheless, Ames also believed it appropriate to test God "as an act of faith" because in that way it leads us to obey God's commands "with the expectation of the fruit and blessing he has promised." *Marrow*, 277.

22. Beeke and van Vliet, "*Marrow*," 63, 64.

23. On Olevian and Ursinus, see Christoph Strohm and Jan Stievermann, eds., *The Heidelberg Catechism: Origins, Characteristics, and Influences: Essays in Reappraisal on the Occasion of Its 450th Anniversary* (Heidelberg: Gütersloher Verlagshaus, 2015).

24. Beeke and van Vliet, "*Marrow*," 53. See also van Vliet, *Reformed System*, 27–58, 103–104; Eusden, "Introduction," 55.

25. Eusden, "Introduction," 52–54. Quotation on 54.

26. For an extensive treatment of Ames's context and influence, see van Vliet, *Reformed System*. See also Sprunger, *Learned Doctor*, 127–28; Eusden, "Introduction," 1, 37, 64–65.

27. Eusden, "Introduction," 65. On Ames's influence on Mastricht, see van Vliet, *Reformed System*, 211–32.

28. Eusden, "Introduction," 2, 11, 64–65; Beeke and van Vliet, "*Marrow*," 62; van Vliet, *Reformed System*, 233–63. On Mastricht's influence on

Edwards, see Jonathan Edwards to the Reverend Joseph Bellamy, January 15, 1747, in *Works of Jonathan Edwards*, Vol. 16, *Letters and Personal Writings*, ed. George S. Claghorn (New Haven, CT: Yale University Press, 1998), 217. For a discussion of how Edwards appears to have developed the Reformed Amesian tradition, see Philip J. Fisk, "Divine Knowledge at Harvard and Yale: From William Ames to Jonathan Edwards," *Jonathan Edwards Studies* 4, no. 2 (2014): 151–78, http://jestudies.yale.edu/index.php/journal/article/view/160.

29. Quoted by Increase Mather in "To the Reader," in James Fitch, *The First Principles of the Doctrine of Christ* (Boston: John Foster, 1679), [v].

Select Bibliography

Primary sources

Ames, William. *Medulla Theologiae, ex sacris literis, earumque interpretibus extracta, & methodice disposita*. Amstelodami: Joannem Janssonium, 1627.
Ames, William. *The Marrow of Theology*. Edited and translated by John Dykstra Eusden. 3rd ed. 1629. Reprint, Grand Rapids, MI: Baker, 1968.
Ames, William. *Conscience with the Power and Cases Thereof*. 1639. Reprint, Norwood, NJ: Walter J. Johnson, 1975.
Ames, William. *Technometry*. Edited and introduced by Lee W. Gibbs. Philadelphia: University of Pennsylvania Press, 1979.

Secondary sources

Beeke, Joel R., and Jan van Vliet. "*The Marrow of Theology* by William Ames (1576–1602)." In *The Devoted Life: An Invitation to the Puritan Classics*, edited by Kelly M. Kapic and Randall C. Gleason, 52–65. Downers Grove, IL: InterVarsity, 2004.
Nethenus, Matthew, Hugo Visscher, and Karl Reuter. *William Ames*. Translated by Douglas Horton. Cambridge, MA: Harvard Divinity School Library, 1965.
Sprunger, Keith L. *The Learned Doctor William Ames: Dutch Backgrounds of English and American Puritanism*. Urbana, IL: University of Illinois Press, 1972.
Van Vliet, Jan. *The Rise of Reformed System: The Intellectual Heritage of William Ames*. Studies in Christian History and Thought. Eugene, OR: Wipf and Stock, 2013.

4.2

Pneumatology, or a Discourse Concerning the Holy Spirit (1674–1693)
John Owen (1616–1683)

The life and works of John Owen[1]

On January 30, 1649, the English people beheaded their king, Charles I. The very next day, John Owen preached a sermon to Parliament, calling for national reform. That sermon would redirect Owen's life, intertwining him with the volatile politics of seventeenth-century England.

But Owen was not first a politician. He was a theologian, and an influential one at that. That's why Carl Trueman says that he was "without doubt the most significant theological intellect in England in the third quarter of the seventeenth century."[2] Kelly Kapic similarly describes him as "*the* theological giant among the Puritans."[3] And J.I. Packer calls Owen "one of the greatest of English theologians," who, "[i]n an age of giants," "overtopped them all."[4]

Born to Henry Owen, a vicar in Stadhampton (near Oxford), John was raised in a home sympathetic to Puritan sentiments at a time when Puritans were often despised. In fact, his early years paralleled the rise of William Laud, a fierce anti-Puritan who became Archbishop of Canterbury in 1633. Owen studied at Queen's College, Oxford, which had a tradition of robust scholarship steeped in the Reformed faith, earning his BA and MA and beginning studies for his bachelor of divinity.[5] But as Laud's power grew and his anti-Puritan policies spread, Owen grew uneasy and in 1637 decided to leave Oxford.

Figure 4.1 Portrait of John Owen

In 1642 Owen moved to London, a haven for Puritans, where he had a conversion of sorts upon hearing the sermon of an unnamed country preacher. His piercing message led Owen to find assurance that he had been truly reborn by the Holy Spirit. Peter Toon argues that this experience "cannot really be over-rated" because it settled his commitment to experiential piety and planted a seed that resulted thirty years later in his "monumental study of the Holy Spirit."[6]

In the 1640s, Owen's reputation as a theologian grew with the publication of his first work, *A Display of Arminianism* (1642), and other works like *The*

Death of Death in the Death of Christ (1647). Political tensions also increased as those loyal to King Charles I waged war against the Parliamentarians, which eventually led to Charles I's execution. When his son Charles II fled England in 1651, the civil wars ended, and Parliamentary rule was established. Eventually, the leader of the Parliamentarian army, Oliver Cromwell, came to rise as the Lord Protectorate of the new British government.

Cromwell cinched Owen's involvement in politics. The sermon Owen preached the day after Charles I was beheaded was well received in Parliament, so they invited him to preach again on April 19, 1649. That day, Cromwell heard his sermon and then happened to run into Owen the day after. Impressed with his preaching, Cromwell recruited Owen, hesitant though he was, to minister as his chaplain on his upcoming expedition to Ireland.[7] That meeting with Cromwell began a friendship that opened doors for Owen to serve as dean of Christ Church and vice-chancellor at the University of Oxford (1651–1657), where he raised the bar of learning, promoted spiritual disciplines, and attempted to influence politics.[8] Together, Owen and Cromwell joined forces to help guide the nation.

But when Cromwell considered having himself crowned king, a move Owen opposed, they parted ways. Cromwell died a year later in 1658, and Parliamentary rule slowly fell apart, giving way to the restoration of Charles II to the throne in 1660. The new king soon issued the Act of Uniformity, which required all clergy to conform to High-Church Anglican worship by August 24, 1662, St. Bartholomew's Day, or else lose their parishes. At that point, Owen and nearly two thousand other Puritan clergy were ejected from the Church of England.

In the remaining years of his life, Owen was a leader in the nonconformist movement, comprising those who refused to conform to Charles II's religious demands. During that time, Owen wrote *Pneumatology* (1674–1693), his massive commentary on the epistle to the Hebrews (1668–1684), and *Meditations and Discourses on the Glory of Christ* (1684). Other important works include *The Mortification of Sin* (1656) and *Communion with God* (1657). Owen breathed his last twenty-one years to the day after the Great Ejection of Puritans from the Church of England on St. Bartholomew's Day, August 24, 1683.

Pneumatology

John Eusden argues that one characteristic that uniquely marked English Puritanism was "a stress on the work of the Holy Spirit in religious experience."[9] While others such as John Calvin (1509–1564) and William Ames (1576–1633) helped to define this emphasis,[10] no one provided as extensive a treatment of the Holy Spirit as John Owen.

Owen did not produce his massive *Pneumatology* in one full swing. Volumes appeared piecemeal in 1674, 1677, 1678, and 1682, and posthumously in 1693. We will focus our time on the first and largest of these volumes, *Pneumatologia, or, A Discourse concerning the Holy Spirit*. The other four volumes deal with the Spirit's work in illuminating Scripture, helping believers pray, comforting the church, and authoring spiritual gifts.[11]

Owen's theological context sheds light on his treatment of the Spirit. He wrote in part to answer those who opposed traditional ways of understanding the Spirit's nature and work, particularly Socinians and those like them who rejected the Spirit's deity or the supernatural and redemptive nature of grace.[12] Owen sought to define the truly gracious work of the Spirit in an individual by avoiding the extremism of mystics on the one hand and moralists on the other.[13] Yet he also addressed those who denied an orthodox doctrine of the Spirit not with their mouths but with their lives, highlighting a practical aim in his work (9).[14]

All the false teachings about the Spirit demanded that a full exposition of the person and work of the Holy Spirit be set forth. So Owen set himself to the task, seeking to be faithful to Scripture and to historic orthodoxy. Nothing less than God's glory, the truth of the gospel, and the "everlasting welfare of . . . souls" were at stake (7, 37, 44, quotation on 44).

The Spirit as a divine person

We first consider the Spirit's nature. Owen devoted much time to discussing the Spirit's works, but even more important than his works is his nature, for "[t]he nature and being of God is the foundation of all true religion and holy religious worship in the world" (64). Said another way, God has created us to worship him, but everything about our worship of God hinges on us getting his nature right.

Owen argued that the Spirit is "a distinct, living, powerful, intelligent, divine person." He defended this claim because many in his day attacked the Spirit either by denying his deity (e.g., casting him as a created spirit heading up the angels) or by denying his personhood (as if he were a mere force) (67–68).[15]

Owen's defense of a traditional understanding of the Spirit was far from simplistic.[16] His core response was to appeal to how Scripture presents the

Holy Spirit. The Bible describes the Spirit as having understanding, a will, and power to act—all properties we ascribe to *persons*, not mere forces. He also defended the Spirit's divinity, noting that the Scripture "expressly" calls the Spirit "God" in numerous passages and assigns "*divine properties*"—such as eternity, ubiquity, and omnipotence—to the Spirit (64–92, quotations on 89, 91). He thus pursued the balance of "acknowledg[ing] the continued active work of the Spirit without embracing seventeenth-century extremes of enthusiasm."[17] Given the way Scripture presents the Spirit, Owen concluded, "To suppose now that this Holy Ghost is not a divine person is for men to dream whilst they seem to be awake" (89).

The Spirit within the Trinity

In Owen's view, a discussion of the Holy Spirit required a treatment of the Spirit in relation to the other members of the Godhead. For example, in the Trinity's united action in redemption, the three persons have distinct operations. All that God gives to us—his love, grace, wisdom, and so on—are "originally *the Father's things*"; they become the Son's things because he is the mediator through whom the Father gives them to humanity; yet these things are "*actually communicated* unto us by the Holy Spirit." While every divine work is "inseparably and undividedly" the work of God, the Holy Spirit has a specific role, "the *concluding, completing, perfecting acts,*" for "without him no part of any work of God is perfect or complete" (199, 94). This Trinitarian framework casts the Spirit as essential to our redemption.

One of the unique ways that Owen discussed the Spirit from a Trinitarian viewpoint was in describing his work in the human nature of Christ. The Spirit was responsible for preparing a body for Christ in the Virgin Mary, for sanctifying the human nature of Christ, for raising his dead body to life, and for glorifying his human nature. The Spirit's work in Christ's human nature formed the basis for his work in Christ's mystical body, the church. Thus "he who prepared, sanctified, and glorified the human nature, the natural body of Jesus Christ, the head of the church, hath undertaken to prepare, sanctify, and glorify his mystical body, or all the elect given unto him of the Father" (162–183, 188–206, quotation on 189).

Trueman notes that Owen's extensive treatment of the Spirit's work in the human nature of Christ underscores "the profoundly Trinitarian way in which he understands Christology."[18] And this in turn informs how we become holy, for the only way we can live in holiness is through Christ, and yet "by [the Holy Spirit] alone is the grace of Christ communicated unto us and wrought in us" (27, cf. 188). Owen's treatment of the Spirit within the Trinity thus forms both an essential component of his pneumatology and a foundation for our hope of redemption in Christ.

The Spirit as giver and gift

In emphasizing that the Spirit communicates Christ to the believer, Owen used the metaphor of *giving*, and as Kapic points out, this concept illuminates our understanding of Owen's *Pneumatology*. Owen differentiated between the Spirit as a divine person (divine presence) and the graces that flow from the Spirit (divine action), which allowed him to describe the Spirit both as a person with the freedom to give and as a gift given through Trinitarian action. Thus, Owen viewed the Trinity "along the lines of God as the Giver, Given, and Gift."[19] The Spirit was a gift of God given freely by God.

Yet the Spirit was also the giver of gifts and graces. On the one hand, we receive the Spirit himself in full measure; on the other hand, we receive different spiritual gifts from the Spirit in various "kinds and degrees," which in no way divides the Spirit but merely expresses the variation of gifts that he gives. By distributing these gifts, the Spirit establishes his work among believers. Thus Owen concluded that "the principal respect that we have unto him ... is as he is the author of these various gifts and graces" (123–124).

The Spirit's work in sanctification (discussed below) further reflects this concept of *gift*, for Owen describes "the entire Christian life as the outworking of this Gift." All this is viewed through the lens of Trinitarianism, as Kapic explains: "As God's Gift, the Spirit brings new life, knowledge, and sanctification. Sent from the Father and the Son, the Spirit freely comes to accomplish the will of the Father through the mediation of the Son."[20] We experience God through the gift of the Spirit. In Owen's words, "Good things are given unto us from Christ by the Spirit" (197).

The Spirit's work in regeneration

As a giver, the Spirit actively works in creation. Indeed, God does not "bestow any good thing on us but by his Spirit." The only way for us to receive "any spiritual or *saving good* from first to last" is by the Holy Spirit (155, 27, cf. 157). The Spirit communicates good things to believers especially through his two great works of regeneration and sanctification, to which Owen devoted significant time in his treatise.

Again, Owen wrote extensively about regeneration in response to those like the Socinians who argued that regeneration was essentially the process of a person reforming his or her morals. To counter such proposals, Owen emphasized the depth of human sin, highlighting how people could not reform themselves on their own. They needed something more. They needed a whole new start. They needed to be reborn. Since humans are by nature "*spiritually dead*," they cannot perform moral deeds in their own power; they require "*an internal, powerful, effectual work of the Holy Ghost ... to deliver them out of this state and condition by regeneration*" (242–297, quotation on 282).

What, then, is regeneration? Put succinctly, regeneration refers to the Spirit's "effectual communication of a new principle of spiritual life unto the souls of God's elect." Owen repeats this language of "principle" frequently in his discussion of regeneration. It is not simply new actions; it goes deeper to a person's disposition. That "*new, real, spiritual* principle ... of spiritual life, light, holiness, and righteousness" destroys and replaces the "contrary, inbred, habitual principle of sin and enmity against God." This new principle highlights that regeneration is a supernatural work of the Spirit. Said another way, regeneration is not "*a reformation of life* ... in the exercise of moral virtue" but rather "a *secret, mysterious* work of the Spirit of God in and upon the souls of men" (207, 219, 211).

That's not to say that morals have nothing to do with regeneration. But one must properly understand the relationship between the Spirit's work and the morals that work produces. Holiness necessarily *follows* regeneration, but it cannot precede it. Instead, regeneration causes "renewed faculties, with *new dispositions, power,* or *ability*," out of which flow moral acts (221).

We might summarize the high points of Owen's discussion of regeneration as follows: it is accomplished fully by the Holy Spirit, who replaces a dead, sinful principle in believers with a living, holy principle. Regeneration is "an inward spiritual work," by which the Spirit instills "*a principle of obedience and love*" into a soul reborn. This regeneration is "the head, fountain, or beginning of our sanctification" (320, 328, 299). Thus, after an extensive discussion of how the Spirit works in regeneration, Owen tied it directly to his next major topic, the Spirit's work in sanctification.

The Spirit as sanctifier

One of the primary works of the *Holy* Spirit is to make believers *holy*—that is, to sanctify them. Why must believers be made holy? In short, humans desperately need a cure for their wickedness because God's holy nature demands that they be holy to dwell with him (658–691, 641–651, cf. 591–641). Without holiness, no one will see God (Heb. 12:14).

Sanctification differs from regeneration. While regeneration is "*instantaneous*" and complete, sanctification is "*progressive*, and admits of degrees." Still, the two works of the Spirit share similarities. Just as we are unable to regenerate ourselves, so "[t]here is not any thing done in us or by us that is *holy and acceptable unto God*, but it is an effect of the Holy Spirit" (387, 27). In other words, we can be holy *only* if the Holy Spirit works in us.

How does this take place? While the Holy Spirit is the "*principal efficient cause*" of our sanctification, the "effective cause" is the blood of Christ, which "*immediately purgeth* us from our sins." Only by the sacrificial and mediatorial work of Christ can we have grounds for forgiveness. But how do we partake of the blood of Christ? Here again, Owen underscores the Spirit's role. The Spirit reveals the "*pollution of sin*" in us, presents to us "the only *true remedy*," works faith in us, and then "*actually communicates* the cleansing, purifying virtue of the blood of Christ unto our souls." We can have no part of Christ without the Spirit, for it is the Spirit who unites us to Christ and communicates the grace of Christ directly to us through that union. Owen thus drives home his point that we need the Spirit's divinely personal work: "[n]o person ... whatever, who hath not been made partaker of the washing of regeneration and the renovation of the Holy Ghost, can possibly have any union with Christ" (436, 438, 442–445, 464, cf. 368, 516–523, 533). In fact, a theme that "undergirds Owen's entire treatise on the Holy Spirit," Kapic argues, is that "the application and actualization of redemption are only possible by the work of the Holy Spirit."[21]

If we could summarize Owen's expansive discussion on the Spirit's positive work of sanctifying believers into two points, we might say (1) that the Spirit preserves, nurtures, and increases the new principle of living to God in the heart of the believer, and (2) that the Spirit's work effectively results in "our *actual obedience* unto God." No act of true holiness occurs apart from a preceding "habit of holiness" or supernatural principle infused into the person performing the act by the Spirit (469, 474). Thus, we see how sanctification flows directly out of regeneration: "that power which we have and do exercise in the progress of this work, in sanctification and holiness, proceeds from the *infused principle* which we receive in our regeneration" (336–337).

Owen succinctly describes the doctrine of sanctification in a definition that highlights the Spirit's work within the Trinity to transform sinful human beings so they might dwell with God: sanctification is "the universal renovation of our natures by the Holy Spirit into the image of God, through Jesus Christ" (386).

Legacy

Peter Toon argues that Owen's work on the Spirit is "the most exhaustive exposition of the doctrine of the Holy Spirit in the English language."[22] His treatise was well received in his day, but Owen was a victim of his time. Having associated with Parliamentary rule, which many had come to regret and scorn, Owen was soon viewed as a bygone. His forms of thinking also increasingly clashed with the emerging empirical learning of the day.[23] So Owen fell out of favor largely because of forces outside his control.[24]

Despite his towering reputation in the seventeenth century, Owen receives less attention today perhaps mainly because many view his writings as inaccessible. Admittedly, Owen's work is thick—layered with long sentences, meandering digressions, and scholastic verbiage—which not a few would find intimidating.[25] Still, others such as Packer argue that those who read Owen with an engaged mind often find his "expansiveness suggestive and his fulsomeness fertilising."[26]

As Trueman notes, John Owen is an ideal person to study if one wants to understand seventeenth-century Reformed theology and nonconformists in Restoration England.[27] Yet Owen's treatment of the Holy Spirit also offers more than a historical text; it provides a thoughtful entrée into the nature and work of the Spirit and how that affects believers in their daily Christian life.

Conclusion

It is sometimes charged that for many Protestants, the Holy Spirit is the neglected member of the Trinity. Such cannot be said of John Owen. For those wanting to understand a Reformed view of the person and work of the Holy Spirit, perhaps there is no better place to turn than to Owen's

Pneumatology. His tome thoroughly explores the divine and personal nature of the Holy Spirit within the triune God, and it challenges readers to recognize the Spirit's essential role in regenerating and sanctifying believers and in equipping them to use their gifts to be a gift to others, as he is a gift to the church.

Notes

1. For Owen's life, we have relied especially on Robert W. Oliver, "John Owen—His Life and Times," in *John Owen—The Man and His Theology*, ed. Robert W. Oliver, Papers Read at the Conference of the John Owen Centre for Theological Study, September 2000 (Phillipsburg, NJ: P&R, 2002), 9–40; Peter Toon, *God's Statesman: The Life and Work of John Owen* (Exeter: Paternoster, 1971); Carl R. Trueman, *John Owen: Reformed Catholic, Renaissance Man*, Great Theologians Series (Burlington, VT: Ashgate, 2007), 1–5. See also Andrew Thomson, "Life of Dr. Owen," in vol. 1 of *The Works of John Owen*, ed. William H. Goold (1850–1853; repr., Edinburgh: Banner of Truth, 1965), xix–cxxii.
2. Trueman, *John Owen*, 1.
3. Kelly M. Kapic, "*Communion with God* by John Owen (1616–1683)," in *The Devoted Life: An Invitation to the Puritan Classics*, ed. Kelly M. Kapic and Randall C. Gleason (Downers Grove, IL: InterVarsity Press, 2004), 167.
4. J.I. Packer, *A Quest for Godliness: The Puritan Vision of the Christian Life* (Wheaton, IL: Crossway, 1990), 191.
5. Sebastian Rehnman, "John Owen: A Reformed Scholastic at Oxford," in *Reformation and Scholasticism: An Ecumenical Enterprise*, eds Willem J. van Asselt and Eef Dekker, Texts and Studies in Reformation and Post-Reformation Thought (Grand Rapids, MI: Baker Academic, 2001), 182–83. On the streams of thought influencing Owen, see Rehnman, "John Owen," 181–203.
6. Toon, *God's Statesman*, 13.
7. See especially Toon, *God's Statesman*, 33–37.
8. Trueman, *John Owen*, 4.
9. John Dykstra Eusden, "Introduction," in William Ames, *The Marrow of Theology*, ed. John Dykstra Eusden (Grand Rapids, MI: Baker, 1968), 21. See also Packer, *A Quest for Godliness*, 179; Geoffrey F. Nuttall, *The Holy Spirit in Puritan Faith and Experience* (Oxford: Blackwell, 1946).
10. Sinclair B. Ferguson, "John Owen and the Doctrine of the Holy Spirit," in *John Owen—The Man and His Theology*, ed. Robert W. Oliver, 103–4; Eusden, "Introduction," 36.

11. See Toon, *God's Statesman*, 166; Carl R. Trueman, *The Claims of Truth: John Owen's Trinitarian Theology* (Carlisle, UK: Paternoster, 1988), 75–90; Packer, *A Quest for Godliness*, 219–30.

12. John Owen, *Pneumatologia*, vol. 3 of *The Works of John Owen*, ed. Goold, 8. Hereafter, all further references to this work shall be noted by employing in-text parenthetical citations. On the difficulty of defining Socinianism, see Kelly M. Kapic, "The Spirit as Gift: Explorations in John Owen's Pneumatology," in *The Ashgate Research Companion to John Owen's Theology*, eds Kelly M. Kapic and Mark Jones (Burlington, VT: Ashgate, 2012), 115–16.

13. "Prefatory Note," in Owen, *Pneumatology*, 2–3; Kapic, "The Spirit as Gift," 114–20; Toon, *God's Statesman*, 167; Ferguson, "John Owen," 105–6.

14. Toon, *God's Statesman*, 167.

15. Trueman, *John Owen*, 53–56. For a similar defense of the Spirit's deity and personhood in *Communion with God*, see Kelly M. Kapic, *Communion with God: The Divine and Human in the Theology of John Owen* (Grand Rapids, MI: Baker Academic, 2007), 194–204.

16. Trueman, *John Owen*, 56.

17. Kapic, *Communion with God*, 202.

18. Trueman, *John Owen*, 92–98. Quotation on 98. See also Ferguson, "John Owen," 107–26.

19. Kapic, "The Spirit as Gift," 113–14, 120–25, 139–40. Quotation on 125.

20. Kapic, "The Spirit as Gift," 137, 139. See also Ferguson, "John Owen," 116–17.

21. Kapic, *Communion with God*, 61.

22. Toon, *God's Statesman*, 167.

23. Owen alludes to this epistemological shift in *Pneumatology*, 274, 498.

24. Trueman, *John Owen*, 1–2. See Owen's discussion about reason in *Pneumatology*, 11–14.

25. See Toon's similar assessment in *God's Statesman*, 177.

26. Packer, *A Quest for Godliness*, 194.

27. Trueman, *John Owen*, 2.

Select Bibliography

Primary source

Owen, John. *The Works of John Owen*. Edited by William H. Goold. 24 vols. 1850–1853. Reprint, Edinburgh: Banner of Truth, 1965. Volumes 3–4 contain Owen's five volumes that make up his treatise on the Holy Spirit.

Secondary sources

Kapic, Kelly M. "The Spirit as Gift: Explorations in John Owen's Pneumatology."
    In *The Ashgate Research Companion to John Owen's Theology*, edited by Kelly
    M. Kapic and Mark Jones, 113–40. Burlington, VT: Ashgate, 2012.
Kapic, Kelly M., and Mark Jones, eds. *The Ashgate Research Companion to John
    Owen's Theology*. Burlington, VT: Ashgate, 2012.
Toon, Peter. *God's Statesman: The Life and Work of John Owen*. Exeter:
    Paternoster, 1971.
Trueman, Carl R. *John Owen: Reformed Catholic, Renaissance Man*. Great
    Theologians Series. Burlington, VT: Ashgate, 2007.

4.3

Pia Desideria[1] (1675)
Philip Jacob Spener
(1635–1705)

The life and work of
Philip Jacob Spener

On an August day in 1670, Philip Jacob Spener did something unusual—even radical, in the eyes of most of his fellow ministers. He invited several parishioners into his home to sit and talk about spiritual matters. Even laymen (though not women) were welcome to speak openly in the pastor's presence as they asked questions and discussed sermons, devotional literature, and eventually the Bible itself. Thus began a lifelong journey of promoting vibrant religion through an emphasis on the laity—a journey that would transform Christianity in Lutheran Germany and around the world.[2]

While many criticized him, Spener believed that gathering laypeople together to talk about spiritual matters would revive the hearts of God's people. In fact, he saw himself as simply continuing the goals of Martin Luther and the Reformers. While they had introduced vital change into the church, especially by correcting false doctrines, they had not finished the work. Spener sought to complete the Reformation.

Spener was born on January 13, 1635, in Rappoltsweiler, a village in Alsace (modern-day France). His early voracious reading nurtured his learned mind, and next to the Bible, his favorite book was *True Christianity* (1605–1610), by Johann Arndt, a Lutheran mystic who sought to elevate moral living over theological precision. Although steeped in Lutheranism, Spener also imbibed the devotional literature of Puritans such as Lewis Bayly

(1565–1631) and Richard Baxter (1615–1691), who called for holiness without Arndt's mysticism.[3]

At age sixteen, Spener entered the University of Strasbourg, where he earned his master's degree in 1653. In his further studies, he fell under the influence of John Conrad Dannhauer (1603–1666), who guided him to Martin Luther's theology and planted some of the seeds for his later reform program. Spener subsequently spent time in Tübingen, Basel, and Geneva, which exposed him to Reformed ways of life and theology. In Geneva the French Reformed preacher-mystic Jean de Labadie (1610–1674) again echoed the call for prioritizing piety.[4]

After his travels, Spener married and received his doctor of theology degree—on the same day. He would eventually have eleven children with his wife, Susanna Ehrhardt. Spener planned on a life of teaching, but as happened with many theologians in church history—one thinks of Augustine and John Calvin—his plans were derailed with a call to serve in ministry.[5]

He accepted the invitation and moved to Frankfurt am Main in 1666. As senior clergyman, Spener oversaw eleven clergy and their congregations and quickly immersed himself in his duties. There he experimented with ideas for renewing lay religion. Many of these practices formed the outline of his recommendations in *Pia Desideria*, but they also elicited criticism.[6]

Embroiled in controversies, Spener left Frankfurt in 1686 and became chaplain to Elector John George III of Saxony in Dresden. His relationship with the elector was fraught with tension, due largely to John George's excessive drinking, but in Dresden Spener became friends with an important figure, August Herman Francke (1663–1727), who would later take up his mantle and create institutions to spread Pietist ideas.[7]

Five years after moving to Dresden, Spener was invited to serve as the dean of the Lutheran clergy and pastor of St. Nicholas Church in Berlin—a welcome relief from Dresden but also a demotion. There he spent the rest of his life and devoted much of his time to defending the Pietist movement against critics and their charges of heresy, radicalism, and fanaticism. His collection of more than one thousand letters shaped the nature of early Pietism and earned him the title, "the spiritual counselor of all Germany."[8] He died peacefully in Berlin on February 5, 1705.[9]

In addition to *Pia Desideria* (1675), Spener's major works include *The Spiritual Priesthood* (1677), a defense of his *collegia pietatis* (pious groups for laypeople); *Use and Abuse of Complaints about Christianity* (1684), a gentle rebuke to the *collegia* separating from the church; and *Theologische Bedencken*

[*Theological Thoughts*] (1700–1702), the first major collection of his letters and articles.[10]

Pia Desideria

Spener grew up in the midst of the Thirty Years War (1618–1648), initially sparked by religious differences between Catholics and Protestants, though involving a complex variety of social and political factors. The Peace of Westphalia in 1648 ushered in a new era of peace in Europe, but Pietists worried that the church structure it introduced, specifically by making ministers state officials, eroded spiritual vitality. In their perception, the peace agreement contributed to lay nominalism and exacerbated a growing culture of bitter theological polemics.

Facing religious indifference and intellectualism, Spener devoted himself to finding effective ways to renew the church. His book *Pia Desideria*, or *Heartfelt Desire for a God-pleasing Reform of the True Evangelical Churches*, captures the spirit of Pietism, a movement that transformed Christianity in Lutheran Germany and helped spark the movement that became known as evangelicalism.

Pia Desideria, Spener's earliest published and most important work, had an unusual debut. It began as a preface to a series of sermons by Johann Arndt (1555–1621), author of the frequently republished multivolume work, *True Christianity*. A half-century after Arndt's death, Lutherans were still reprinting his sermons.[11] But in 1675, Spener's preface to Arndt's sermons quickly eclipsed the main work.

Soon republished as a standalone work, *Pia Desideria* achieved a state of influence its author had not anticipated. It has been called the "*Programmschrift*," or manifesto, of Pietism and "an epoch-making document," and its importance has been compared to Martin Luther's "Ninety-Five Theses."[12] Spener's influence through *Pia Desideria* earned him the title, "the father of Pietism," though we stand on safer ground to call him "the popularizer of Pietism," since he synthesized ideas from others such as Arndt, Bayly, and Labadie.[13] What made *Pia Desideria* stand out from other programs was that Spener both resisted separatism and offered "clear reform proposals rather than mere gripes."[14]

Three major themes arise in Spener's *Pia Desideria* that mirror the threefold structure of the volume: problems in the church, prospects of the church, and proposals for the church. These capture well the thrust of the work, and we will treat each in turn.

Problems in the church

Spener believed that the Reformation was "God's blessing" to the church. In fact, he saw himself as working in the train of Martin Luther, whom he held in high regard and referenced frequently in *Pia Desideria*—once describing him as "our sainted Luther." But in the decades following Luther's life and the Reformation, things had gone awry. Spener grew deeply concerned for the health of the church, specifically the Lutheran church. While he valued Luther's defense of justification by faith alone, Spener also believed his era demanded a greater focus on works (39–40, 73, 91).[15]

His anxieties arose directly from his pastoral ministry as he "labored in [God's] vineyard," and he decided to address in this book the issues that had, in his words, "again and again sorely distressed me." He viewed the "wretched conditions" of the church as a "sickness" that needed a suitable "cure" (31–32). What exactly was ailing the church in Spener's day?

Spener identified two broad problems. First, the church suffered from persecutions coming from Roman Catholics, who had won back formerly Lutheran territories. Because God used persecutions to purify the church, God's allowance of such persecutions in Spener's day signified that "our church as a whole is not in the condition in which it should be, that there is very much gold that glitters from the outside but does not meet the test when it is smelted" (31–32, 42).

The second broad problem, the "principal reason for the lament," was disappointment everywhere in the church (42). Spener specifically probed at the defects in the civil authorities, the clergy, and the common people.

In the wake of the Thirty Years War, church and state grew tightly intertwined, with the state exercising a fair amount of control over the church. Spener worried that the civil authorities abused their powers and that "their apparent zeal for our religion stems from a factious spirit or a design to further some political interest rather than from a love of truth!" (43).

Still, Spener had far more words for the clergy than the magistrates and even implicated himself in the rebuke. He described the "ecclesiastical estate" as "thoroughly corrupt." Too many pastors failed to "understand and practice true Christianity," living lives "marked by carnal pleasure, lust of the eye, and arrogant behavior." In fact, Spener even posited that many "do not actually possess the true marks of a new birth"—a charge against clergy that evangelical preachers would echo in the eighteenth century (44–46). The visible moral failures of the clergy exposed their hypocrisy.

Relatedly, Spener censured his fellow clergy for their obsession with doctrinal disputes. Instead of devoting sufficient time to nurturing Christian virtues, they eagerly bogged themselves down in theological controversies. In an era of Protestant scholasticism, theologians frequently debated the finer points of theology, but while Spener appreciated orthodoxy, he called them to tone down the polemics. Thus, he criticized writings of "showy human erudition, of artificial posturing, and of presumptuous subtleties" (52). Such disputing only drew Christians away from moral action.

These negative examples in the civil authorities and clergy only led the common people into a spiritual quagmire. Topping Spener's list of concerns stood their failure to love in actions. "If we judge by this mark," he noted, "how difficult it will be to find even a small number of real and true disciples of Christ among the great mass of nominal Christians!" (57). This foundational deficit resulted in other disconcerting developments: drunkenness, bitter lawsuits, greediness, licentious living, ritualism, and insincere confession of sins. In Spener's view, the average churchgoer had missed how God's grace leads to a living faith. And the church as a whole was in a lamentable, worsening condition.

Prospects of the church

Spener's description of the church's tragic state raised a fundamental question about the prospects of the church. Can it even improve? Spener answered unequivocally: "If we consult the Holy Scriptures we can have no doubt that God promised his church here on earth a better state than this" (76). While Spener devoted less time to this section than to the other two sections in the book, it undergirded everything that followed (98).

His positive view of the future of the church on earth represented one of his unique theological emphases and foreshadowed the doctrine that would later come to be known as postmillennialism.[16] Specifically, Spener pointed to prophecies in the Bible that the Jews would be largely converted (Hos 3:4–5; Rom 11:25–26) and that papal Rome would fall (Revelation 18–19). He believed that such prophecies promised a gradual improvement of conditions in the church.

In thinking about the prospects of the church, Spener also promoted the notion of Christian perfection, an idea that John Wesley (1703–1791) would later popularize. Countering claims that Christians should not expect perfection until eternity, Spener argued, "we are not forbidden to seek perfection, but we are urged on toward it" (80). Thus he implored people to pursue perfection.

Nonetheless, he conceded that perfection was an "illusion." Just as a student several years into her studies understands how little she knows far better than the beginning student, so "the farther a godly Christian advances, the more he will see that he lacks." In trying to hold a balance between pursuing perfection and perceiving flaws, Spener said that all Christians are "under obligation to achieve *some degree* of perfection" (80, italics added).

The remarkable moral purity and fidelity of early Christians put "our hot-and-cold condition to shame," Spener noted, yet also demonstrated that the pursuit of perfection "is not impossible." Since the same Holy Spirit at work in the early church is "neither less able nor less active today," we can and ought to improve the condition of the church (84, 85). Setting the doctrine of perfection in this chapter on the church's prospects, Spener envisioned not only individuals but the corporate body of Christ progressing toward perfection.[17]

Proposals for the church

In the third section of his book, Spener laid out six practical proposals of reform, both to address the problems of the church and to pursue the prospect of perfection he had described. The first of these was for a "more extensive use of the Word of God among us." This priority on Scripture clearly connected him with the Reformation principle of *sola scriptura*. In Spener's view, like that of the Reformers, God's Word is "the powerful means" for transformation, and "the diligent use of the Word of God" is "the chief means for reforming" (87, 91).

To elevate Scripture practically, Spener proposed the implementation of *collegia pietatis*. Christian ministers or knowledgeable lay leaders were to meet with the laity in small groups to share insights into God's Word, allowing people to ask questions and discuss the material, rather than simply listen passively to sermons.

Spener anticipated that this innovative idea would attract criticism, but he saw innumerable benefits. Not only would ministers get to know their parishioners, but laypeople would attain a clearer understanding of God's Word and would be better equipped to teach their own families. Spener acknowledged that this small group setting for discussing the Bible could lead to theological chaos, but he thought churches could avoid such a scene by authorizing ministers to "tactfully cut off" any "meddlesomeness, quarrelsomeness, self-seeking, or something else of this sort" (90). In his view, the benefits far outweighed the dangers, and in fact, the entire practice stood fully in line with Luther's own sentiments about the priority of the Scriptures for all people.[18]

In our day when many churches subsist on small group ministries, it is hard to see how this proposal sounded so threatening, but it did. Police even began checking in on these lay groups as early as 1677 in Spener's Frankfurt.[19] What unsettled church leaders was the threat to church authority and the potential for heresy and separatism. For Spener, despite the controversy and the possibility of groups separating from the church, the *collegia pietatis* offered a concrete activity for bringing the Word of God to the people of God. He thus defended their function as little churches within the church (*ecclesiolae in ecclesia*), not separate churches unto themselves.[20]

In addition to elevating Scripture, Spener called secondly for "the establishment and diligent exercise of the spiritual priesthood." He denied that the spiritual priesthood of all believers would damage the minister's station. Instead, precisely because the minister was limited, he needed others to help in serving the needs of the people. By opening "all spiritual functions ... to all Christians without exception," the church could radically improve its lowly state (92, 93).

Spener's third proposal was to emphasize that Christianity consists not merely in knowledge, but in practice. While the Reformation had drawn the church back to right doctrine, the church had since become so focused on orthodoxy that it grew lax in practice. Spener sought to join the two together, emphasizing what the church needed most at the time—action.

Related to this concern, theological debates in that time often degenerated into hostile arguments, and thus Spener proposed as his fourth recommendation that "*[w]e must beware how we conduct ourselves in religious controversies* with unbelievers and heretics." While embracing the need to oppose heresy, Spener worried that Christians' bitter attacks were driving away the unconverted. Rather than our criticisms, he said, they need our prayers, our gentle though firm presentations of the truth, and our "heartfelt love" (97, 99). In his own debates with opponents—and he had many—Spener modeled this very form of irenic engagement.[21]

Fifth, Spener called for reform in the schools where pastors received their education in preparation for the ministry. In fact, he devoted more time to this proposal than any of the other five. Professors and students, he argued, should grow not only in learning but also in holiness. Fostering spiritual devotion is, for the theology student, "not merely an ornament but a very necessary work." As he memorably stated, "a young man who fervently loves God, although adorned with limited gifts, will be more useful to the church of God with his meager talent and academic achievement than a vain and worldly fool with double doctor's degrees who is very clever but has not been taught by God" (107, 108).

Here readers get a glimpse of the Pietist emphasis on heart religion— sometimes to the slighting of religious knowledge. When people today express fears that education may actually harm budding pastors or argue that pastors are better off *without* a degree, they are reflecting Pietist impulses, impulses originally intended to cultivate both spiritually vibrant *and* educated ministers, but sometimes resulting in a backlash against theological knowledge.

Finally, Spener proposed that students should learn always to preach with the goal of edification. God saved people through the preaching of God's Word, he argued, and thus pastors should preach so that their average congregants would understand. Spener hoped to inspire pastors "to preach the heart of Christianity ... with simplicity and power" and stir "the inner man"—another reminder that Pietism centered on *heart religion* (117, 122).

Legacy

How did people respond to Spener's *Pia Desideria*? Many feared the implications of his work. Unleashing the laity could lead to an explosion of heretical views. Worse, the emphasis on the believer's *subjective* experience of redemption seemed to cloud the more important element of God's *objective* act of salvation in history, an emphasis Luther himself highlighted. In essence, Spener's focus on experience sounded to some like salvation by works, replacing saving grace with morality. Furthermore, his proposal to use small groups smelled of separatism, and some small groups did actually break from the Lutheran church.[22]

Still, the vast majority responded positively to Spener's work, which sparked the rise of the Pietist movement throughout Germany, particularly at the University of Halle under the direction of August Hermann Francke (1663–1727) and at Herrnhut under the guidance of Nicholas Ludwig von Zinzendorf (1700–1760). Pietism radically changed German Lutheranism, unseating the old orthodoxy and giving Lutheran piety a facelift.[23]

Its influence reached even beyond Lutheranism, as the Pietist Moravians from Herrnhut led the way in the modern missions movement. It also contributed to the rise of evangelicalism as Pietists like Spener contributed key ideas of heart religion, Bible reading, and lay activity to the evangelical movement that coalesced in the eighteenth century. Its direct impact can be traced from Spener's *Pia Desideria* to Nicholas von Zinzendorf and the Moravians to the evangelical leaders John Wesley and George Whitefield (1714–1770).[24]

Conclusion

Spener's approach to theological questions about the church, the Christian experience of salvation, and faithful living influenced Protestants for decades to come, which is why some, like biographer K. James Stein, have called him "the most important leader, after Martin Luther, in the history of German Protestantism."[25] Reading Spener's work offers a taste of how one influential theologian responded to the frequent failure of Christian leaders to join head and heart for the laity and also reveals the Pietistic impulse toward heart religion and spiritual experience.

In short, *Pia Desideria* offers a relatively brief and focused volume from a spiritually vibrant pastor-theologian who shared a vision for overcoming religious nominalism. It captures the spirit of a man dedicated to the laity who outlined a practical program for renewing the church. That program transformed the Lutheran church and helped launch the evangelical movement that continues to shape Christians with its message of heart religion down to today.

Notes

1. Translated as "Heartfelt Desire for a God-pleasing Reform of the True Evangelical Churches."
2. K. James Stein, *Philipp Jakob Spener: Pietist Patriarch* (Chicago: Covenant, 1986), 85–86.
3. Theodore G. Tappert, "Introduction: The Times, the Man, and the Book," in *Pia Desideria*, by Philip Jacob Spener (Philadelphia: Fortress, 1964), 8–10. Hereafter, all further references to this work shall be quoted by employing in-text citations.
4. Stein, *Philipp Jakob Spener: Pietist Patriarch*, 60–61.
5. Stein, *Philipp Jakob Spener: Pietist Patriarch*, 67–75.
6. K. James Stein, "Philipp Jakob Spener (1635–1705)," in *The Pietist Theologians: An Introduction to Theology in the Seventeenth and Eighteenth*

Centuries, ed. Carter Lindberg (Malden, MA: Blackwell, 2005), 84; Stein, *Philipp Jakob Spener: Pietist Patriarch*, 73–106; Tappert, "Introduction," 13.

7. Stein, "Philipp Jakob Spener," 85; Stein, *Philipp Jakob Spener: Pietist Patriarch*, 107–126; Tappert, "Introduction," 21–22.

8. Kohl, "Spener's *Pia Desideria*," 61.

9. Stein, "Philipp Jakob Spener," 85; Stein, *Philipp Jakob Spener: Pietist Patriarch*, 127–45; Reginald W. Ward, *Early Evangelicalism: A Global Intellectual History, 1670–1789* (Cambridge, UK: Cambridge University Press, 2006), 25–26.

10. Kohl, "Spener's *Pia Desideria*," 69–70; Stein, *Philipp Jakob Spener: Pietist Patriarch*, 93; F. Ernest Stoeffler, *The Rise of Evangelical Pietism* (Leiden: Brill, 1965), 244.

11. Mark A. Noll, *The Rise of Evangelicalism: The Age of Edwards, Whitefield and the Wesleys*, Vol. 1 in *A History of Evangelicalism: People, Movements and Ideas in the English-Speaking World* (Downers Grove, IL: InterVarsity, 2003), 60–61.

12. Manfred W. Kohl, "Spener's *Pia Desideria*: The Programmschrift of Pietism," in *Contemporary Perspectives on Pietism: A Symposium*, co-sponsored by North Park Theological Seminary and the Pietism Section of the American Academy of Religion (Chicago: Covenant, 1976), 61, 69. See also Theodore G. Tappert, trans., "Philipp Jacob Spener," in *Seventeenth-Century German Prose*, ed. Lynne Tatlock (New York: Continuum, 1993), 93; Frederick Herzog, *European Pietism Reviewed* (San Jose, CA: Pickwick, 2003), 16.

13. Stoeffler, *The Rise of Evangelical Pietism*, 230–32. On the question of Spener's originality in *Pia Desideria*, see Kohl, "Spener's *Pia Desideria*," 62–63.

14. Herzog, *European Pietism Reviewed*, 16. See similar observations in Kohl, "Spener's *Pia Desideria*," 69; Stein, *Philipp Jakob Spener: Pietist Patriarch*, 102; Stoeffler, *The Rise of Evangelical Pietism*, 235; Ward, *Early Evangelicalism*, 24.

15. Stein, "Philipp Jakob Spener," 85; Stoeffler, *The Rise of Evangelical Pietism*, 238–39.

16. Stein, "Philipp Jakob Spener," 94–96; Ward, *Early Evangelicalism*, 32.

17. Kohl, "Spener's *Pia Desideria*," 67.

18. On the similarity between Spener's and Luther's approaches to Scripture, see Stein, "Philipp Jakob Spener," 87–89.

19. Herzog, *European Pietism Reviewed*, 19.

20. Stein, *Philipp Jakob Spener: Pietist Patriarch*, 90–92; Ward, *Early Evangelicalism*, 29.

21. Stein, *Philipp Jakob Spener: Pietist Patriarch*, 100–1.

22. Noll, *The Rise of Evangelicalism*, 62; Stein, "Philipp Jakob Spener," 86. For an analysis of Spener's achievements in *Pia Desideria* and valid and invalid

criticisms of his theological arguments, see Allen C. Deeter, "An Historical and Theological Introduction to Philipp Jakob Spener's *Pia Desideria*: A Study of Early German Pietism" (Ph.D. diss., Princeton University, 1963).
23. Stein, *Philipp Jakob Spener: Pietist Patriarch*, 102; Stoeffler, *The Rise of Evangelical Pietism*, 246.
24. Noll, *The Rise of Evangelicalism*, 17–18, 60–65. On Spener as a precursor of evangelicalism, see Stoeffler, *The Rise of Evangelical Pietism*, 228–46; Ward, *Early Evangelicalism*, 24–39.
25. Stein, "Philipp Jakob Spener," 96.

Select Bibliography

Primary sources

Erb, Peter C., ed. *Pietists: Selected Writings*. Classics of Western Spirituality. New York: Paulist, 1983.
Spener, Philipp Jakob. *Pia Desideria*. Translated and edited with an introduction by Theodore G. Tappert. Philadelphia: Fortress, 1964.
Spener, Philipp Jakob. *Pia desideria: Umkehr in die Zukunft: Reformprogramm des Pietismus*. Brunnen: Brunnen-Verlag Gießen, 1995.

Secondary sources

Stein, K. James. "Philipp Jakob Spener (1635–1705)." In *The Pietist Theologians: An Introduction to Theology in the Seventeenth and Eighteenth Centuries*, edited by Carter Lindberg, 84–99. Malden, MA: Blackwell, 2005.
Stein, K. James. *Philipp Jakob Spener: Pietist Patriarch*. Chicago: Covenant, 1986.
Stoeffler, F. Ernest. *The Rise of Evangelical Pietism*. Leiden: Brill, 1965.
Ward, Reginald W. *Early Evangelicalism: A Global Intellectual History, 1670–1789*. Cambridge, UK: Cambridge University Press, 2006.

4.4

A Treatise Concerning Religious Affections (1746)

Jonathan Edwards (1703–1758)

Figure 4.2 Portrait of Jonathan Edwards

The life and work of Jonathan Edwards

Shrieks and cries echoed inside the church sanctuary. "Oh, I am going to hell!" moaned one. "What must I do to be saved?" called another. The groans grew so loud that the preacher was forced to stop. Jonathan Edwards stepped down from the pulpit and joined the other ministers present at the event. Together they spoke with individuals in the congregation, offering spiritual counsel for the salvation of souls.[1]

Edwards is best remembered for his sermon *Sinners in the Hands of an Angry God*, which he preached at Enfield, Massachusetts (now Connecticut), on July 8, 1741. A fiery message that centers on the moment right before a person slips into eternity, *Sinners* stands out as a literary piece because Edwards used several searing metaphors to awaken the unregenerate from their spiritual slumber. His most memorable metaphor compared the sinner to a spider dangling by a thread above flames ready to singe the lifeline and plunge the sinner into hell.

Not surprisingly, selected portions of *Sinners* have often been used in literature anthologies to illustrate the hellfire preaching of the American Puritans, what many today consider an outdated culture of horror. But just as there is more to *Sinners* than what one might find in an anthology of American literature, so there is more to Edwards than what one finds in *Sinners*.

Born on October 5, 1703, in East Windsor, Connecticut, Edwards was the only son among Timothy Edwards and Esther Stoddard Edwards' eleven children. (Timothy sometimes spoke of his sixty feet of daughters.) As the sole son of pastor Edwards and a grandson of Solomon Stoddard, the most influential pastor in the Connecticut River valley, Jonathan was on a path for ministry from day one. He received early training from his father in Latin, Greek, and Hebrew and enrolled in Yale College at age twelve.

A spiritually sensitive boy, Edwards led prayer meetings in the woods at age nine. Yet these experiences lacked the staying power that Edwards believed comes with true salvation. Instead, he traced his conversion to spring 1721, when at age seventeen he finally experienced the lasting sweetness of God that could only be explained by supernatural grace. He recalled that "there came into my soul . . . a sense of the glory of the divine being," which would often "kindle up a sweet burning in my heart."[2]

At Yale, Edwards studied traditional works like William Ames' *The Marrow of Theology* (1627), but he also drank at the well of Enlightenment-era thinkers like John Locke and John Tillotson. He graduated at age sixteen with his bachelor's and stayed to study for his master's degree. After two short pastoral posts and a tutorship at Yale, he joined his grandfather, Stoddard, in Northampton. Ordained in 1727, Edwards spent the next twenty-three years of his life serving in this Congregational church, taking full responsibility after Stoddard died in 1729.

Early on, Edwards felt a pastoral concern for his flock due to their backsliding. After preaching a sermon series on justification by faith, he was delighted to see a spiritual awakening in Northampton (1734–1735). He captured the tenor of that revival in his *Faithful Narrative of the Surprising Work of God* (1737), which became the model for promoting revival on both sides of the Atlantic in the ensuing decades.

When the revival fires cooled, Edwards stirred for renewed spiritual heat and became a leading proponent of the Great Awakening. In the midst of those transatlantic revivals, he preached *Sinners* and wrote a number of works in support of the awakenings, including *Distinguishing Marks of a Work of the Spirit of God* (1741), *Some Thoughts Concerning the Present Revival of Religion in New England* (1743), and *A Treatise Concerning Religious Affections* (1746). Edwards' best-selling work was his *Life of David Brainerd* (1749), whom he portrayed as a model individual transformed by the revivals.

A series of events in the 1740s raised tensions between Edwards and his Northampton congregation, and in 1750 the church fired the renowned pastor. Despite other offers, Edwards opted to move to Stockbridge and minister to the Indians because he believed missions formed a central component of God's plan of redemption. During his years there (1751–1757), he wrote several major theological works (two of which were published posthumously): *Misrepresentations Corrected, and Truth Vindicated* (1752; a response to the Communion controversy that led to his dismissal, written partly in Stockbridge), *Freedom of the Will* (1754), *Original Sin* (1758), and *Two Dissertations: I. Concerning the End for Which God Created the World. II. The Nature of True Virtue* (1765).

In late 1757, the trustees of the pro-revival College of New Jersey (later Princeton) invited Edwards to become the new president. He reluctantly accepted the call. Soon after his arrival, he sought to make an example to the students by getting a smallpox inoculation, but complications led to his death on March 22, 1758. America's greatest theologian had passed from the scene, but his life and works would continue to influence Christians for generations.

Religious Affections

Edwards' *Treatise Concerning Religious Affections* stands as a classic treatment of religious experience in the Christian tradition. Its recognized value arises in large part from the context in which he wrote it: The Great Awakening.[3]

Edwards published an account of the religious awakenings in his own congregation, publicly spoke out in support of the revivals, and wrote to defend them in the face of criticism. He promoted the awakenings because he wanted his people to be saved from sin and hell and to live eternally with the God of glory. He was a pastor concerned for the souls of his flock, and he believed the spread of the gospel would hasten the coming millennium.

However, not all professing Christians in colonial America responded positively to the awakenings. Many worried that they produced nothing but wild enthusiasm—complete with people shrieking, shaking, and fainting—and would leave no lasting impact on society except the undermining of traditional social and hierarchical values. One opponent, a Congregational pastor named Charles Chauncy, bitterly attacked Edwards and the revivals for promoting an unfettered spiritual frenzy.

As revival fervor rose and fell in New England and across the Atlantic, Edwards was forced to take stock of the fruit of these awakenings. Unlike Chauncy, he saw definite, lasting value in them. But he agreed with Chauncy that some had taken them too far and that some of the fruit was simply fading emotionalism. Edwards thus, over time, staked out a moderate position on the revivals. Chauncy's criticisms even induced Edwards to fine-tune his position, which resulted in the more carefully nuanced *Religious Affections*.[4] Out of the revival context came Edwards' classic and most mature work on the nature of Christian religious experience.

Affections

In *Religious Affections*, Edwards pursued a twofold aim: (1) to define the nature of true religion, and (2) to discern between true and false signs of God's work of grace in a person's soul. Central to these purposes was the concept of "affections."

So what exactly did Edwards mean by "affections"? In recent years, many have erred by identifying affections with human emotions. However, it is not quite that simple. Edwards used the term "affections" in a particular sense, and to understand his work, one must grasp his meaning: "the affections are no other, than the more vigorous and sensible exercises of the inclination and will of the soul."[5]

This definition requires some unpacking. In Edwards' view, God created the soul with two faculties or innate powers: the understanding and the inclination. With the faculty of understanding, a human perceives things in the world; that is, he "discerns and views and judges of things." With the faculty of inclination—sometimes referred to as the heart, mind, or will— the individual looks upon the things perceived with a certain proclivity, "liking or disliking, pleased or displeased, approving or rejecting" (96).

Viewing the person as a unified being, Edwards held that the understanding guides humans in making decisions. As he stated in more detail in *Freedom of the Will*, "the will always follows the last dictate of the understanding." People make choices based on their final perception of the options. That perception may or may not be accurate, but the will chooses whatever "appears most agreeable and pleasing, all things considered." That is, based on what one understands, one opts for "the greatest apparent good."[6]

Each human, then, exercises his or her will in everyday choices. These exercises refer to the faculty of inclination as it interacts with the faculty of understanding. We do what we want based on what we see. The "affections," then, are a *subset* of the exercises of the will. They refer to those exercises that reflect a stronger degree of love or aversion—thus they are the more "vigorous" exercises of the inclination. Because they often cause some bodily sensation, they are the more "sensible" exercises.

This description of "affections" was central to how Edwards defined the nature of religion: "true religion, in great part, consists in holy affections." What kind of religion does God accept? Certainly not a "weak, dull and lifeless" religion, a state of spiritual indifference. Rather, Edwards appealed to Scripture—pointing to passages such as Deut 6:4–5; 10:12; Luke 24:32; Rom 12:11; and 2 Tim 1:7—to argue that "God, in his Word, greatly insists upon it, that we be in good earnest, fervent in spirit, and our hearts vigorously engaged in religion" (95, 99).

He went on to discuss several reasons to support the claim that holy affections constitute a key element of true religion. Because God links true Christianity to practice and because human actions spring from affections, true religion must consist in affections. People act when they are affected in their heart. And as Scripture points to love as the sum of religion (Matt 22:37–40), it follows that the affections are part of the warp and woof of true religion. The example of biblical saints and Christ himself reinforces the centrality of affections to authentic spirituality.

To be sure, Edwards denied that true religion could be distilled to religious affections. It must include "something else besides affection," yet "there can be no true religion without them." Edwards embraced head and heart, light and heat. For "where there is heat without light, there can be nothing divine or heavenly in that heart," and "where there is a kind of light without heat, a head stored with notions and speculations, with a cold and unaffected heart, there can be nothing divine in that light" (120).

With his focus on religious affections, Edwards chose to center his whole treatise around 1 Peter 1:8, "Whom having not seen, ye love; in whom, though now ye see him not, yet believing, ye rejoice with joy unspeakable, and full of glory."[7] As Edwards explained, this passage links

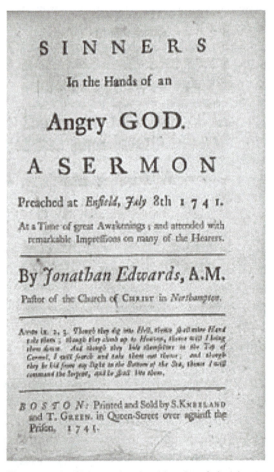

Figure 4.3 *Sinners in the Hands of An Angry God* by Jonathan Edwards

true faith in Christ inextricably with "love to Christ" and "joy in Christ" (93–95).

What is true religion? For Edwards, entailed with the doctrines that define authentic Christianity are holy affections of love to God and people, and this includes vigorous and sensible exercises of one's inclination. This portrayal of religious affections reflects the theme of "heart religion" that drove a whole band of Protestants in the eighteenth century to promote the preaching of the gospel in revivals. These became known as the first generation of evangelicals. In many ways, their emphasis on heart religion, as captured in Edwards' discussion of affections, has constituted the core of evangelicalism down to the twenty-first century.

Discerning signs of God's grace

Edwards could not take for granted that his readers would agree with him about the importance of the affections. The chaos of the revivals had so disturbed some—like Chauncy—that many rejected a role for affections altogether. Even Edwards eventually shunned some of the more radical elements of the revivals. But he also believed they made a mistake who "despise and cry down all religious affections" (121).

Instead of tossing out the whole package, he called people to sift through affections to distinguish between true and false, "approving some, and rejecting others; separating between the wheat and the chaff, the gold and the dross, the precious and the vile" (121). And he devoted the vast bulk of his treatise to discerning the validity of various affections.

In Edwards' view, humans in their fallen state cannot rightly love and desire God and all his divine goodness. Instead, original sin has disoriented their affections. Their inclination is averse to God and his ways. They love sin and self. To make matters worse, humans cannot produce holy affections on their own. Only the Holy Spirit can reorient affections to love what is good. Thus, authentic affections are a sign of God's grace. If people want to know if they are truly regenerated, they should look for evidence of God's gracious influence. They should look for true religious affections.

This impulse to seek "evidence" reflected the Enlightenment emphasis on empirical proof. In the eighteenth century, epistemological shifts caused many to place greater authority in that which can be verified by the five senses, moving away from the authority of the church or even Scripture. Human experience formed an important piece of evidence.[8]

In *Religious Affections*, Edwards sought to help people identify reliable evidence of God's gracious influences in their experience. While the interest in signs of God's work is as old as the human race, the eighteenth century saw an increased pursuit of such signs in a modern framework that aimed to base conclusions on observable evidence.

To distinguish between true and false signs, Edwards first described what he called "negative" signs. This terminology can be confusing. By "negative" signs Edwards did *not* mean signs that disprove God's gracious activity. Rather, he meant signs that may or may not indicate God's gracious influences (e.g., bodily effects or intensive feelings). When people experienced these signs, they could not conclude that God had saved their soul—thus Edwards pushed back against radical revivalists. At the same time, they could not conclude that such experiences were from the devil—here Edwards rejected anti-revivalist sentiment.

Edwards outlined twelve negative signs. He argued that high and heated affections did not indicate God's influence one way or another. Great effects on the body, even if involuntary, were unreliable signs. People might talk fervently about religious things or might spend inordinate amounts of time in worship. They might have many kinds of affections. Even godly people may be convinced of the authenticity of their experiences. But such things did not necessarily point to the Holy Spirit's gracious influences.

Edwards then turned to describe twelve "positive" signs, indicators that God had done a supernatural work in an individual's life. He began with a sign that was, in some ways, not properly a sign at all: "Affections that are truly spiritual and gracious, do arise from those influences and operations on the heart, which are *spiritual, supernatural* and *divine*." By beginning here, Edwards established the source of holy affections by differentiating between the natural man and the regenerated man. The natural man cannot delight in spiritual things like the regenerated man because he lacks the Holy Spirit. On the other hand, the regenerated man has the Holy Spirit dwelling in him, and the Spirit gives him "new principles of nature," or, as Edwards famously put it, a "new spiritual sense" (197, 206). Michael McClymond and Gerald McDermott note that Edwards' "new sense of the heart" has been called "the most original idea in all of his theology."[9]

To illustrate this new sense, Edwards used the metaphor of honey. A man without the sense of taste might enjoy honey for its texture or color, but could never delight in its flavor. But a man with the sense of taste could delight fully in the taste of honey. So it is with divine things. The Holy Spirit gives the regenerated soul a new spiritual sense to delight in the things of God. He gives him authentic holy affections (208–209).

From this foundation, Edwards described observable signs of truly gracious affections. One who has been regenerated appreciates divine things as excellent in and of themselves without any thought of the benefits available to himself. He loves moral excellency simply for its beauty. The Holy Spirit enlightens his mind to understand divine things, and he experiences a change in nature, not a fickle excitement for a time but an abiding alteration. His life is marked by humility, a tenderness of spirit, and "the lamblike, dovelike spirit and temper of Jesus Christ" (344). This sampling of signs illustrates how Edwards perceived the Holy Spirit's influence on an individual, resulting in a new sense that delighted in divine things.

Yet Edwards saved the chief sign for last: "Gracious and holy affections have their exercise and fruit in Christian practice." If the Holy Spirit had truly indwelled an individual, she would persevere in Christian practice in every part of her life and would continue in holiness until she died. Thus Edwards described Christian practice as "the sign of signs," "the most proper evidence" of God's grace (383, 444). So while Edwards fully affirmed that the Holy Spirit regenerates souls apart from works, he also strenuously rejected antinomianism and pointed to holy Christian practice as the supreme sign of the Holy Spirit's gracious influences.

Legacy

In *Religious Affections*, Edwards carved out a moderate response to the revivals, rejecting the radical revivalists on the one side and the anti-revivalists on the other. But successors have not always embraced Edwards' nuanced position in *Religious Affections*. Even in his day, those on the popular level generally failed to heed his careful distinctions, and *Religious Affections* made little immediate impact.[10]

However, his work became influential especially in nascent evangelicalism, a movement that has celebrated and promoted heart religion. Edwards offered a theology for thinking about heart religion, and *Religious Affections* soon won a readership in Britain and continental Europe, influencing Independents like Isaac Watts, Baptists like William Carey, evangelicals like William Wilberforce, and even the Dutch Reformed network through the Scotsman John Erskine.[11] His handling of spirituality in *Religious Affections* justified evangelicals' preaching tactics and revivals, and his theological successors, known as the New Divinity, embraced his moderate approach to revivals during the Second Great Awakening in the United States.[12]

And so, in keeping with the evangelical impulse of interdenominational activism, a wide-ranging group of people have claimed Edwards as their own. Thus, for example, both charismatics and non-charismatics appeal to Edwards for their particular approach to revivalism. Despite their differences, both are heirs of the evangelical heart religion that Edwards promoted in *Religious Affections*, a treatise that became one of his most important, enduring works.

Conclusion

Why pick up *Religious Affections*? Edwards argues in the preface to his work that "[t]here is no question whatsoever, that is of greater importance to mankind ... than this, what are the distinguishing qualifications of those that are in favor with God, and entitled to his eternal rewards?" (84). In Edwards' view, every single individual should prioritize an assessment of the state of his or her soul. Until that question is settled, everything else pales in comparison.

Edwards offers guidance in addressing that question. With an ear attuned to Scripture and an eye that observed the experiences of many people in one of the most renowned religious movements in church history, Edwards stands at a unique vantage point. His collective work on revivalism represents the most important work in Christian theology on discerning an authentic work of the Holy Spirit.[13] And his "project of spiritual discernment" was, according to McClymond and McDermott, "among the most penetrating and subtle in Christian history."[14] In short, *Religious Affections* gives readers a systematic exploration of the nature of heart religion.

Edwards' *Religious Affections* affords readers an opportunity to consider the signs of God's gracious influences in their own lives. It also offers clarity on the nature of true religion in an era when Christians differ sharply over what constitutes authentic spirituality. And this volume introduces some of the key ideas driving the theology and ministry of the early evangelicals, giving insight into the nature of the evangelical movement that has expanded around the globe today.

Notes

1.   Stephen Williams, "Stephen Williams' Eyewitness Account of the Preaching of *Sinners*," in *Jonathan Edwards's Sinners in the Hands of an Angry God*:

A Casebook, eds Wilson H. Kimnach, Caleb J.D. Maskell, and Kenneth P. Minkema (New Haven, CT: Yale University Press, 2010), 122–25.

2. Jonathan Edwards, "Personal Narrative," in *Letters and Personal Writings*, ed. George S. Claghorn, vol. 16 of *The Works of Jonathan Edwards* (New Haven, CT: Yale University Press, 1998), 792–93.

3. For more on the eighteenth-century revivals, see Thomas S. Kidd, *The Great Awakening: The Roots of Evangelical Christianity in Colonial America* (New Haven, CT: Yale University Press, 2007).

4. Robert Davis Smart, *Jonathan Edwards's Apologetic for the Great Awakening, with Particular Attention to Charles Chauncy's Criticisms* (Grand Rapids, MI: Reformation Heritage Books, 2011), 313.

5. Jonathan Edwards, *Religious Affections*, ed. John E. Smith, Vol. 2 of *The Works of Jonathan Edwards* (New Haven, CT: Yale University Press, 1959), 96. Hereafter, all further references to this work shall be noted by employing in-text parenthetical citations. On the distinction between affections and emotions and the unity of head and heart in Edwards' thought, see Michael J. McClymond and Gerald R. McDermott, *The Theology of Jonathan Edwards* (New York: Oxford University Press, 2012), 311–15; and John E. Smith, "Religious Affections and the 'Sense of the Heart,'" in *The Princeton Companion to Jonathan Edwards*, ed. Sang Hyun Lee (Princeton, NJ: Princeton University Press, 2005), 103–14.

6. Jonathan Edwards, *Freedom of the Will*, ed. Paul Ramsey, Vol. 1 of *The Works of Jonathan Edwards* (New Haven, CT: Yale University Press, 1957), 147–48.

7. We are using the King James Version, the English translation Edwards used in *Religious Affections* and preferred in his preaching ministry.

8. On experience as evidence and the evangelical interest in evidential reasoning in the eighteenth century, see Catherine A. Brekus, *Sarah Osborn's World: The Rise of Evangelical Christianity in Early America* (Yale University Press, 2013), especially 1–12, 93–118, 133, 137–51.

9. McClymond and McDermott, *The Theology of Jonathan Edwards*, 316.

10. Brekus, *Sarah Osborn's World*, 102; Smart, *Jonathan Edwards's Apologetic*, 287–88.

11. Michael J. McClymond, "'A German Professor Dropped into the American Forests': British, French, and German Views of Jonathan Edwards, 1758–1957," in *After Jonathan Edwards: The Courses of the New England Theology*, eds Oliver D. Crisp and Douglas A. Sweeney (New York: Oxford University Press, 2012), 208; Smart, *Jonathan Edwards's Apologetic*, 289–90.

12. David W. Kling, "Edwards in the Second Great Awakening: The New Divinity Contributions of Edward Dorr Griffin and Asahel Nettleton," in *After Jonathan Edwards: The Courses of the New England Theology*, eds Oliver D. Crisp and Douglas A. Sweeney (New York: Oxford University Press, 2012), 139.

13. Douglas A. Sweeney, *Jonathan Edwards and the Ministry of the Word: A Model of Faith and Thought* (Downers Grove, IL: IVP Academic, 2009), 120.
14. McClymond and McDermott, *The Theology of Jonathan Edwards*, 320.

Select Bibliography

Primary sources

Edwards, Jonathan. *The Works of Jonathan Edwards*. 26 vols. Edited by Perry Miller, John E. Smith, and Harry S. Stout. New Haven, CT: Yale University Press, 1957–2008.

Edwards, Jonathan. *Religious Affections*. Edited by John E. Smith. Vol. 2 of *The Works of Jonathan Edwards*. New Haven, CT: Yale University Press, 1959.

Edwards, Jonathan. *The Works of Jonathan Edwards Online*. 73 vols. Jonathan Edwards Center at Yale University, 2008. http://edwards.yale.edu/.

Secondary sources

Marsden, George M. *Jonathan Edwards: A Life*. New Haven, CT: Yale University Press, 2003.

McClymond, Michael J. and Gerald R. McDermott. *The Theology of Jonathan Edwards*. New York: Oxford University Press, 2012.

Smart, Robert Davis. *Jonathan Edwards's Apologetic for the Great Awakening, with Particular Attention to Charles Chauncy's Criticisms*. Grand Rapids, MI: Reformation Heritage Books, 2011.

Sweeney, Douglas A. *Jonathan Edwards and the Ministry of the Word: A Model of Faith and Thought*. Downers Grove, IL: IVP Academic, 2009.

4·5

The Tenth Muse Lately sprung up in America. Or Several Poems . . . By a Gentlewoman in those parts (1650); Several Poems . . . By a Gentlewoman in New England (rev. ed., 1678)

Anne Bradstreet (1612–1672)

The life and work of Anne Bradstreet

At age nineteen, Anne Bradstreet suffered an illness that she feared would take her life. Two years earlier, in 1630, she had traveled on the famed *Arbella* to play her part in establishing the new Massachusetts Bay Colony. But like many women in early colonial America, it appeared that her role would be short-lived. In those circumstances, she penned these words:

> Twice ten years old, not fully told
> Since nature gave me breath.
> My race is run, my thread is spun,

lo here is fatal Death.
All men must dye, and so must I
   this cannot be revok'd
For Adams sake, this word God spake,
   when he so high provok'd.
Yet live I shall, this life's but small,
   in place of highest bliss,
Where I shall have all I can crave,
   no life is like to this.
For what's this life, but care and strife?
   since first we came from womb,
Our strength doth waste, our time doth hast,
   and then we go to th' Tomb ...
The race is run, the field is won,
   the victory's mine I see,
For ever know, thou envious foe,
   the foyle belongs to thee.[1]

This excerpt comes from Bradstreet's earliest surviving poem, which foreshadows some of the core themes in her corpus—the uncertainty and suffering of this world, God's sovereign will, and the hope of eternal life. Despite this early illness, Bradstreet would live four more decades to become one of the most celebrated women of colonial New England. In her poetry we not only get a glimpse of seventeenth-century colonial America, but we also find a housewife whose poetic theological reflections captivated the minds of many in the transatlantic world.

How did this woman in a patriarchal world achieve such heights?[2] Aside from her natural giftedness, her privileged training in youth prepared her for later poetic endeavors. Anne was born in Northampton, England, in 1612 or 1613 to Thomas Dudley (1576–1653) and Dorothy Yorke (1582–1643). In 1619, Dudley became steward to the Earl of Lincoln, and on the Earl's estate, young Anne enjoyed a decade of access to his well-endowed library, where she read Latin and Greek classics, Sir Walter Raleigh's (1554–1618) *History of the World* (1614), possibly William Shakespeare (1564–1616), and especially the Geneva Bible (1560, 1599).[3]

Anne's contributions were not simply poetic but deeply religious. Raised by Puritan parents, she felt early on a sensitivity to God's requirement of holiness. Even at age six or seven, her conscience convicted her for lying and disobedience, and in her early teenage years, she was ashamed for falling into "the follyes of youth," noting, "I found my heart more carnall."[4]

At age sixteen, though, a severe bout of smallpox finally led her to convert. That same year, she married Simon Bradstreet (1603–1697), the son of a nonconformist minister whom Anne's father had hired to work for the Earl of Lincoln in 1622. Anne was fully immersed in the world of Puritanism, both through her parents' rearing and her union with Simon.[5]

But Puritans faced increasing persecution in England after Charles I (1600–1649) ascended the throne in 1625. Weighing their options, several Puritans explored the possibility of emigrating to America to set up a Puritan outpost. As John Winthrop (1587–1649) so memorably captured in his sermon, "A Model of Christian Charity," on the *Arbella*, the Puritans who set out to launch the Massachusetts Bay Colony aimed to create a "city on a hill," an example to Mother England. Among those on the *Arbella* were Anne Bradstreet and her husband and parents.

When the *Arbella* landed in Massachusetts in the summer of 1630, Bradstreet wrote that she "found a new world and new manners, at which my heart rose," meaning that her heart was filled with anxiety.[6] Indeed, life in the new world presented many challenges, yet both the harsh environment and her personal struggles would provide fodder for her poetic musings. And soon the transatlantic world would read the poetry of Anne Bradstreet, the first British colonial woman to publish a book and the first British colonist— male or female—to publish a book of poetry.

Several Poems

Bradstreet's poetry first saw the light of publication without her involvement or awareness. A small group of friends circulated her poems, which led her brother-in-law and pastor in North Andover, Massachusetts, John Woodbridge, to get his hands on a copy. When he left in 1647 to aid the Puritan cause in England, he took her poems with him and published them as *The Tenth Muse Lately sprung up in America. Or Several Poems . . . By a Gentlewoman in those parts* (1650).[7]

Over the ensuing decades, Bradstreet revised several poems in the volume and wrote new ones. After her death (1672), family and friends compiled them and published her work in 1678 under the more modest title, *Several Poems . . . By a Gentlewoman in New England*. Her poetry depicts a uniquely American experience, yet one that cannot be understood apart from her faith.

The earthly family and a heavenly home

Bradstreet constantly exhibited a tension between the temporal, material world and the eternal, spiritual world, and her discussion of her family illustrates this tension well. She lived fully in this world and had great love and appreciation for her family, but, at the same time, she had to keep reminding herself that ultimately only God could satisfy her inner yearnings.

In several places, Bradstreet displayed her deep love for her husband. But because Simon, who served for a time as governor of the colony, regularly traveled on colonial business, Anne had to make do by herself on several occasions. In one poem lamenting his absence, she called him "the man more lov'd then life" and described herself as "his widdowed wife" to show how much she longed for his presence.[8]

At times this love competed with her love for God. While Bradstreet extolled her husband as her "chiefest comforter on Earth," his absence led her to seek sustenance from God: "my God, who never failed me, was not absent, but helped me, and gratiously manifested his Love to me." She reminded herself that she should trust in God, "the only Portion of his Servants."[9]

Elsewhere she related how her heart longed for her beloved in this world, but she recalled "a more beloved one":

Tho: husband dear bee from me gone,
   Whom I doe love so well;
I have a more beloved one
   Whose comforts far excell.
O stay my heart on thee, my God,
   Uphold my fainting Soul!
And, when I know not what to doe,
   I'll on thy mercyes roll.[10]

Bradstreet often worried about the loss of her husband and children and wrote poems of thanksgiving to God for restoring them to her. Even in these instances, though, she prioritized the spiritual state of her family. When her grown daughter Hannah suffered from "a dangerous feaver," Bradstreet thanked God for delivering her, but added,

Graunt shee remember what thou'st done,
   And celebrate thy Praise;

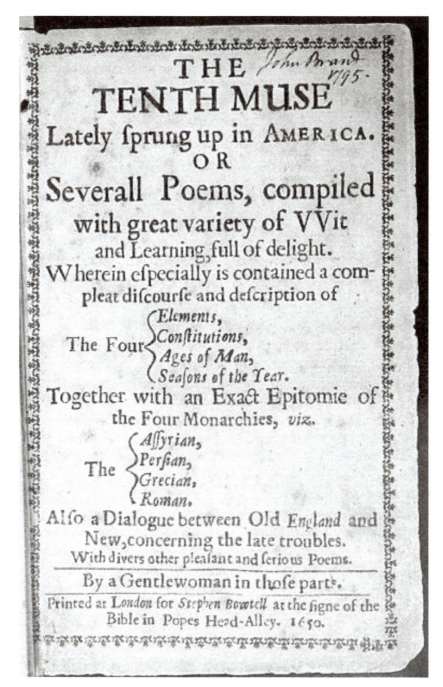

Figure 4.4 *The Tenth Muse* by Anne Bradstreet

And let her Conversation say,
    Shee loves thee all thy Dayes.[11]

Ultimately, everything ought to point her and others to the joy found in God alone:

Tho: children thou hast given me,
    And freinds I have also:
Yet, if I see Thee not thro: them,
    They are no Joy, but woe.[12]

Family and friends offered wondrous joy in this life, but the knowledge of the soul's eternal existence and of a heavenly home placed this world—and even one's family—in proper perspective.

Divine providence and sovereignty

The temporality of family joys called for an explanation, and as a Puritan, Bradstreet naturally gravitated toward the Calvinist doctrine of God's sovereignty to provide one. As she observed the world and considered the ordering and suffering of life, she found comfort and clarity in affirming God's providence and sovereign control.

For example, Bradstreet explained the vast diversity of people on the earth by pointing to God's sovereign and good will. We see "some set in the highest dignity that mortality is capable off; and some so base, that they are viler then the earth; … some exceeding beautyfull; and some extreamly deformed." How does one account for such differences? "[N]o other reason can be given of all this," she explained, "but so it pleased him, whose will is the perfect rule of righteousnesse." In the same way, God even so ordered the world "by his providence" that no country has everything it needs, but that all rely on each other, "so there may be a mutuall Commerce through the world."[13]

Arguably, the doctrine of God's providence stands behind Bradstreet's longer quaternions: "The Four Elements," "The Four Humours in Man's Constitution," "The Four Ages of Man," and "The Four Seasons." In these poems, each element, humor, age, and season argues for its superiority. The collective impact of reading their arguments, though, is the sense that each of the four (in each category), while necessary, excels and falters in ways its sisters do not. Ultimately, God in his providence established balance in the elements of the earth and the body, in the changing of the seasons, and in the stages of human life.[14]

God's gracious providence, however, did not mean that human life would escape suffering. On the contrary, in a world steeped in sin due to Adam's fall, God used and even redeemed suffering to accomplish his sovereign purposes.

Thus, when Bradstreet endured a "sore sicknes" that lasted several weeks in the spring of 1657, she sought to have "a contented, thankfull heart under my affliction and weaknes, seeing it is the will of God it should bee thus" for her spiritual advantage. After another bout of "weaknes and fainting," Bradstreet desired "not only willingly, but thankfully, to submit to him, for I trust it is out of his abundant Love to my straying Soul which in prosperity is too much in love with the world."[15]

She also looked to God to accomplish his will with her family. When her eldest son, Samuel, sailed for England on November 6, 1657, she appealed to God's power for his safety but resigned herself to his sovereign will, leaving his future—and hers—in God's hands while prioritizing her son's eternal destiny above earthly desires:

> If otherwise I goe to Rest,
> Thy Will bee done, for that is best;
> Perswade my heart I shall him see
> For ever happefy'd with Thee.[16]

Though Samuel returned home safely nearly four years later, Bradstreet did not always receive the answers to prayer that she desired. In those moments, she sought comfort in God's will. After three grandchildren died in young age, she attributed their deaths to God's sovereign hand while still affirming his goodness:

> Three flours, two scarcely blown, the last i'th' bud,
> Cropt up by th' Almighties hand; yet is he good,
> With dreadful awe before him let's be mute,
> Such was his will, but why, let's not dispute,
> With humble hearts and mouths put in the dust,
> Let's say he's merciful, as well as just.[17]

Bradstreet believed Christians should "adore the Soverainty of God, who will not be tyed to time nor place, nor yet to persons, but takes and chuses when and where and whom he pleases." These realities gave her comfort in an uncertain world, which she hoped would cause others "to admire the justice and mercy of God, and say, how unsearchable are his ways."[18]

Transience and mortality

Of all the theological themes in Bradstreet's writings, her treatment of transience and mortality stands out most poignantly. Her world was filled with suffering, the threat of illness and death always lingering on the horizon, and Bradstreet processed these difficulties by casting them in light of not only God's sovereignty but also God's redemptive purposes in them. With that focus, she kept an eye constantly on eternity.

Bradstreet framed her world of suffering within the biblical story of humanity's fall into sin.[19] In her longer poem, "The Four Ages of Man," Bradstreet showed that humans begin with sin and enter a world of sorrow:

> Ah me! conceiv'd in sin and born with sorrow,
> A nothing, here to day and gone to morrow . . .
> Stained from birth with *Adams* sinfull fact,
> Thence I began to sin as soon as act . . .
> As many are my sins, so dangers too;
> For sin brings sorrow, sickness death and woe.[20]

After sowing "wild oates" in youth and reaping the results in middle age, people find little hope in old age as mind and flesh lose their vitality. Yet people could reassure themselves of hope in a final redemption:

> And when this flesh shall rot and be consum'd,
> This body by this Soul shall be assum'd:
> And I shall see with these same very eyes,
> My strong Redeemer coming in the Skies.
> Triumph I shall o're sin, o're death, o're Hell,
> And in that hope I bid you all farewel.[21]

This poem captures the thrust of much of Bradstreet's understanding of human life. Stained by original sin, people stumble through the world and often fail to make much progress on their own, even with the knowledge of inevitable death. Yet despite these difficulties, Christians can find hope in their blessed Redeemer, Jesus Christ, a hope that will ultimately overcome sin, death, and hell.

That hope included God's remedial intentions in the suffering of this world. In Bradstreet's view, suffering, illness, and pain were instruments in God's hand for the good of his children. Reflecting on one bout of sickness, she noted that "he doth it for my Advantage," and "if he knowes that weaknes and a frail body is the best to make me a vessell fitt for his use, why should I not bare it, not only willingly but joyfully?" In fact, she believed illness and loss were "the times of my greatest Getting and Advantage, yea I have found them the Times when the Lord hath manifested the most Love to me."[22]

As part of her remedial view of earthly sufferings, Bradstreet repeatedly placed the temporal in eternal perspective. In one poem Bradstreet personified "Flesh" and "Spirit" as two quarreling sisters, reflecting the battle between the flesh and the spirit in Gal 5:16–24. While Flesh lauded the benefits of this world—"take thy fill / Earth hath enough of what you will"—Spirit set everything in the context of spiritual eternity:

> My garments are not silk nor gold,
> Nor such like trash which Earth doth hold,
> But Royal Robes I shall have on,
> More glorious then the glistring Sun.[23]

In "The Vanity of all worldly things," Bradstreet sought similarly to expose the lie that the treasures and pleasures of the earthly world will satisfy; rather, only the eternal world will last. Ultimately, she kept her eye on the hope of "Joy unto Eternity." Thus, when earthly joys were squelched, as when Bradstreet's house burned down, she hoped instead in an imperishable house:

> Thou hast an house on high erect
> Fram'd by that mighty Architect . . .
> The world no longer let me Love,
> My hope and Treasure lyes Above.[24]

The loss of her house drove her to look for a permanent dwelling in heaven. In the same way, she observed, "If we had no winter the spring would not be so pleasant: if we did not sometimes tast of adversity, prosperity would not be so welcome."[25]

Bradstreet used the image of the *pilgrim*—a common metaphor for Puritans—to capture this focus on the eternal world while living in the temporal world. Echoing the vision of the faithful in Hebrews 11, who desired "a better country, that is, a heavenly one" (Heb 11:16), Bradstreet believed all Christians should identify themselves as pilgrims: "a Christian is sailing through this world unto his heavenly country . . . We must, therfore, be heer as strangers and pilgrims, that we may plainly declare that we seek a citty above, and wait all the dayes of our appointed time till our chang shall came."[26]

Near the end of her life, Bradstreet described herself as a "weary pilgrim" hoping ultimately in that anticipated "chang," the resurrection:

And when a few yeares shall be gone
   this mortall shall be cloth'd upon
A Corrupt Carcasse downe it lyes
   a glorious body it shall rise
In weaknes and dishonour sowne
   in power 'tis rais'd by Christ alone
Then soule and body shall unite
   and of their maker have the sight
Such lasting joyes shall there behold
   as eare ne'r heard nor tongue e'er told
Lord make me ready for that day
   then Come deare bridgrome Come away.[27]

Anne Bradstreet lived fully in this world, but knew well the earthly realm's transience. As a Puritan who reflected often on the vicissitudes of life, she believed God used temporal struggles to wean imperfect creatures' affections off this world in preparation for final redemption in eternity. That divinely instituted path to redemption, as Robert Daly observes, required travelers to "steer a middle course" between loving the creature too little, which is breaking God's commandments, and loving the creature too much, which is idolatry. Bradstreet's poems, Daly argues, "were records of that middle course; they were prayers, religious acts," and were "essentially about and part of her pilgrimage to heaven."[28]

Legacy

Both Old England and New warmly received Bradstreet's poetry. In 1658 bookseller William London included *The Tenth Muse* in his *Catalogue of the Most Vendible Books in England*. Her influence lasted longer in New England, where, for example, her volume was the only book of poetry to appear in the library of Edward Taylor, a renowned poet of the next generation. In his 1702 *Magnalia Christi Americana*, the eminent theologian Cotton Mather also praised her writing, calling her poems "a Monument for her Memory beyond the Stateliest *Marbles*." Bradstreet's poetry had a continuing appeal through the mid-nineteenth century in America.[29]

While her work fell out of favor in the late-nineteenth century, the mid-twentieth century witnessed a revival of attention to her poetry, often winning the interest more of those in the secular academy—particularly in literature departments—than of Christians.[30] Yet while many have lauded her as a modern woman before her time, readers should not overlook the ways in which her Puritan religious commitments saturated and drove her poetry.

Conclusion

Bradstreet's poems offer readers an uncommon glimpse of theology forged in lived experience, seen through the eyes of a regular housewife and set in engaging verse. Her poetic musings illustrate how theology informs the way people interpret life's experiences, whether placing their bonds of affection for family members on earth in the perspective of eternity or reorienting their temporal desires around God's sovereign will.

Perhaps more than anything, Bradstreet's work forces readers to consider the uncertainty of life. She offers wisdom for wrestling with the reality of living in a transient world marked by unavoidable death. While many Westerners in the twenty-first century often evade such reflection, Bradstreet offers an example of one Christian who found great benefit in considering our inescapable mortality in light of God's sovereign purposes for suffering in a fallen world.

Notes

1. Anne Bradstreet, "Upon a Fit of Sickness," in *Several Poems*, 2nd ed. (Boston: John Foster, 1678), 237–38. In quoting both the 1678 edition of Bradstreet's poems and the 1867 version edited by John Harvard Ellis, we have retained the original spelling and punctuation, but have modernized lettering styles. When referring to poems from Bradstreet's corpus, we cite the 1678 edition as *Several Poems* and Ellis's 1867 edition as *Works*; hereafter,

2. For Bradstreet's life, we have relied on Anne Bradstreet, "To My Dear Children," in *The Works of Anne Bradstreet in Prose and Verse*, ed. John Harvard Ellis (Charlestown, MA: Abram E. Cutter, 1867), 3–10; John Harvard Ellis, "Introduction," in *Works*, xi–vxxi; Charles E. Hambrick-Stowe, ed., *Early New England Meditative Poetry: Anne Bradstreet and Edward Taylor*, Sources of American Spirituality series (New York: Paulist, 1988), 7–38; Jeannine Hensley, ed., *The Works of Anne Bradstreet* (Cambridge, MA: Belknap, 2010); Mark A. Noll, "The Poetry of Anne

Bradstreet (1612–1672) and Edward Taylor (1642–1729)," in *The Devoted Life: An Invitation to the Puritan Classics*, ed. Kelly M. Kapic and Randall C. Gleason (Downers Grove, IL: InterVarsity Press, 2004), 251–69; and Elizabeth Wade White, *Anne Bradstreet: The Tenth Muse* (New York: Oxford University Press, 1971).

3. Noll, "Poetry of Anne Bradstreet," 254; Hambrick-Stowe, ed., *Early New England Meditative Poetry*, 15, 22; Jeffrey A. Hammond, *Sinful Self, Saintly Self: The Puritan Experience of Poetry* (Athens: The University of Georgia Press, 1993), 104–5.

4. Bradstreet, "To My Dear Children," 4.

5. Bradstreet, "To My Dear Children," 5.

6. Bradstreet, "To My Dear Children," 5.

7. White, *Anne Bradstreet: The Tenth Muse*, 254–57; Noll, "Poetry of Anne Bradstreet," 257.

8. Bradstreet, "Another," in *Several Poems*, 241.

9. Bradstreet, "Submission and Reliance on God," in *Works*, 17.

10. Bradstreet, "In her solitary hours in her Husband's absence," in *Works*, 35.

11. Bradstreet, "Upon her daughter, Hannah Wiggin's recovery from a Fever," in *Works*, 28. See also Bradstreet, "Meditations, Divine and Moral," in *Works*, 47.

12. Bradstreet, "In her solitary hours in her Husband's absence," 36.

13. Bradstreet, "Meditations, Divine and Moral," 59–60, 73.

14. Bradstreet, *Several Poems*, 5–68.

15. Bradstreet, "After Sickness and Weakness," in *Works*, 21; Bradstreet, "Submission to Chastisement from God," in *Works*, 23.

16. Bradstreet, "Poem upon her son Samuel's going to England," in *Works*, 25. See also her similar sentiment regarding her husband's travels to England in "On her Husband's going to England," in *Works*, 33.

17. Bradstreet, "On my dear Grand-child Simon Bradstreet, Who dyed on 16. Novemb. 1669," in *Several Poems*, 250. See also Bradstreet, "To the memory of my dear Daughter in Law, Mrs. Mercy Bradstreet, who deceased Sept. 6. 1669," in *Several Poems*, 250–51; Bradstreet, "Verses upon the burning of her house," in *Works*, 40.

18. Bradstreet, "Meditations, Divine and Moral," 68.

19. Bradstreet, "Contemplations," in *Several Poems*, 224, 228.

20. Bradstreet, "The Four Ages of Man," in *Several Poems*, 45, 47.

21. Bradstreet, "The Four Ages of Man," 51, 58.

22. Bradstreet, "To My Dear Children," 6; Bradstreet, "After much Sickness," 20. See her similar reflections on God's remedial use of suffering in "Meditations, Divine and Moral," 70; "Meditations on Spiritual Consolations," in *Works*, 16.

23. Bradstreet, "The Flesh and the Spirit," in *Several Poems*, 230, 232.

24. Bradstreet, "The Vanity of all worldly things," in *Several Poems*, 235;

Bradstreet, "Verses: Joy in God," in *Works*, 19; Bradstreet, "Verses upon the burning of her house," 41–42.

25. Bradstreet, "Meditations, Divine and Moral," 69.

26. Bradstreet, "Meditations, Divine and Moral," 62.

27. Bradstreet, "Verses: Longing for Heaven," in *Works*, 42–44.

28. Hammond, *Sinful Self, Saintly Self*, 83–87, 103–24, 140–41; ed., Hambrick-Stowe, *Early New England Meditative Poetry*, 21–22; Robert Daly, *God's Altar: The World and the Flesh in Puritan Poetry* (Berkeley: University of California Press, 1978), 126–27.

29. Pattie Cowell, "The Early Distribution of Anne Bradstreet's Poems," in *Critical Essays on Anne Bradstreet*, ed. Pattie Cowell and Ann Stanford (Boston, MA: G. K. Hall & Co., 1983), 270–79; Cotton Mather, quoted in *Critical Essays on Anne Bradstreet*, 10. For examples of eighteenth- and nineteenth-century appreciation of Bradstreet's work, see the early essays in Cowell and Stanford, eds., *Critical Essays on Anne Bradstreet*, 1–40.

30. Robert Hutchinson, "Introduction," in *Poems of Anne Bradstreet*, ed. Robert Hutchinson (New York: Dover, 1969), 30–33; Ann Stanford, *Anne Bradstreet: The Worldly Puritan: An Introduction to Her Poetry* (New York: Burt Franklin & Co., 1974), 122–24.

Select Bibliography

Primary sources

Bradstreet, Anne. *Several Poems . . . By a Gentlewoman in New England*. 2nd ed. Boston: John Foster, 1678.

Ellis, John Harvard, ed. *The Works of Anne Bradstreet in Prose and Verse*. Charlestown, MA: Abram E. Cutter, 1867.

Hambrick-Stowe, Charles E., ed. *Early New England Meditative Poetry: Anne Bradstreet and Edward Taylor*. Sources of American Spirituality series. New York: Paulist, 1988.

Secondary sources

Cowell, Pattie, and Ann Stanford, eds. *Critical Essays on Anne Bradstreet*. Boston, MA: G. K. Hall & Co., 1983.

Daly, Robert. *God's Altar: The World and the Flesh in Puritan Poetry*. Berkeley: University of California Press, 1978.

White, Elizabeth Wade. *Anne Bradstreet: The Tenth Muse*. New York: Oxford University Press, 1971.

4.6

Sermons
George Whitefield
(1714–1770)

The life and work of George Whitefield

[I]n the morning about 8 or 9 of the Clock there came a messenger and said Mr Whit[e]field ... is to preach at Middletown this morning at ten of the Clock, I was in my field at Work, I dropt my tool that I had in my hand and ran home to my wife telling her to make ready quickly to go and hear Mr Whit[e]field preach at Middletown, then run to my pasture for my horse with all my might; fearing that I should be too late ...

When I saw Mr Whit[e]field come upon the Scaffold he Lookt almost angelical; a young, Slim, slender, youth before some thousands of people with a bold undaunted Countenance.... And my hearing him preach, gave me a heart wound; By Gods blessing: my old Foundation was broken up, and I saw that my righteousness would not save me.... My heart was broken; my burden was fallen of[f] my mind; I was set free.[1]

Such was the experience of Nathan Cole, a Connecticut farmer whose life was radically changed in 1740 the day that he scrambled to hear George Whitefield preach. Thousands shared Cole's eagerness to hear the itinerant speak, flocking to see this international "celebrity."[2]

George Whitefield began his life in humble origins, the son of innkeepers. His father died when he was two, and before he turned eight, his mother began an unhappy marriage that only made the boy's life harder. He feared he would be stuck as an innkeeper but managed to attend Oxford's Pembroke College.[3]

There, after a series of fits and starts, his spiritual wrestling began in earnest, in part through meeting John and Charles Wesley, whose pursuit of holiness helped lead him to conversion. It took months of fasting, losing sleep, and pleading with God for Whitefield to wage his "titanic spiritual struggle" against the devil. Gradually, he realized he could not do it on his own, and finally in 1735, he experienced deliverance. Whitefield was born again—and he would take that message to thousands.[4]

Ordained as a deacon in the Church of England on June 20, 1736, Whitefield started preaching the following week. Then, after John Wesley suggested that he minister in the new colony of Georgia, Whitefield set sail on January 6, 1738, beginning a life of transatlantic travel and preaching. Whitefield would eventually cross the Atlantic thirteen times.[5]

Though he was ordained as an Anglican priest in 1739, Whitefield did not bind himself to a local congregation.[6] Rather, he led a mobile ministry that earned him the title the "Grand Itinerant."[7] His popularity—and the controversy surrounding him—surged when he started preaching outdoors, inspired by the contemporary Welsh revivalist Howell Harris.[8] When he sailed to the American colonies for the second time, he returned as a known entity, and that preaching tour helped spark the transatlantic Great Awakening.[9]

Whitefield continued to hold a busy schedule of preaching the new birth both in England and the American colonies, so busy that it ran down his health. In September 1769, Whitefield embarked one last time for America. He continued to preach relentlessly. After giving his final sermon on September 29, 1770, his health finally gave way, and he died early the next day. He was buried at Newburyport, Massachusetts.[10]

The life of Whitefield's sermons

Biographer Harry Stout argues that Whitefield's "most distinctive contribution to his times" was his preaching: through his "extemporaneous, open-air preaching to mass audiences, he transformed the traditional sermon," showing that "preaching could be both edifying and entertaining."[11] His printed sermons capture much of that ethos and extended his influence beyond his public preaching and even his lifetime.[12]

Whitefield's friends and supporters began encouraging him to publish his sermons in 1737, only a year after he began preaching.[13] And so Whitefield launched his "preach and print" strategy that allowed him to reach more people with the gospel through his printed sermons.[14]

One early volume of sermons went through three editions by 1738. Supporters even subsidized the printing of his messages to make it possible for people to give copies away, and newspapers, like Benjamin Franklin's *Pennsylvania Gazette*, also covered Whitefield's speaking tours and published his sermons.[15] He promoted his message through new media forms in this way, using the emerging consumer revolution to establish and extend his ministry—something later evangelicals would heartily embrace in their evangelistic strategies.[16] And for many, reading Whitefield's sermons had just as significant an impact on them as hearing him preach.[17]

An incomparable delivery

In discussing Whitefield's sermons, we could highlight several theological themes. Whitefield preached on family worship, the priority of prayer, the duty of charity, how best to observe Christmas, the sin of drunkenness, and even political matters.[18] With our limited space, we will focus on his unique delivery and three major sermonic themes.

First, what drew so many large crowds to his preaching? Whitefield was a master of dramatization. He had immersed himself in school plays as a youngster, and although he later condemned the theater with its worldly trappings, he never quite renounced the theatrical.[19] Instead, as Harry Stout notes, he was "[a]t heart" "an actor-preacher."[20] For example, in preaching on Abraham offering up his son Isaac, Whitefield envisioned what might have happened: "Methinks I see the good old man walking with his dear child in his hand and now and then looking upon him, loving him and then turning aside to weep."[21] This dramatization created emotional ties with his listeners, who themselves began to weep.[22]

Whitefield also connected with individuals through personal application. In one instance, he interrupted his recounting of blind Bartimeus's narrative to note that as Bartimeus begged Jesus unashamedly, so ought we to put away our pride and willingly beg for what we need from Jesus.[23] Whitefield elsewhere explained, "I must question you as I go along, because I intend, by the Divine help, to preach not only to your heads but your hearts."[24] Indeed,

Whitefield sought "to reach their hearts" by "cloth[ing his] ideas in such plain language" that the lowliest listener would understand him.[25]

Finally, Whitefield's passion shone through his sermons with such intensity that many could not help but be moved. In one sermon, he exclaimed, "This is a part of the discourse which I long to come to, it being my heart's desire and earnest prayer to God, that your souls may be saved."[26] He often spoke of his "heart's desire," namely the salvation of his hearers.[27] In one case, he said, "Precious souls, for God's sake think what will become of you when ye die, if you die without being converted. . . . Behold then I show you a way of escape—Jesus is the way."[28] Whitefield was passionate about drawing people to Christ, and he used his dramatic gifts to spread gospel truths.

The *Solas*

This passion for proclaiming the gospel explains the theological emphases in Whitefield's sermons. Lee Gatiss observes that Whitefield's "main subject" in his preaching was "the gospel of God's grace towards justly condemned sinners," a theme that incorporated the basic gospel elements of human sin, warnings of judgment, and the *solas* of the Reformation—that salvation comes by grace alone (*sola gratia*) through faith alone (*sola fide*) in Christ alone (*solo Christo*).[29]

When Whitefield preached on Genesis 3:15—one of his "oft-repeated sermon[s]"—he dramatized the biblical story of the fall to magnify the free grace of God offered to humanity in the gospel.[30] The fall left Adam and Eve "naked" (Gen. 3:7)—"[n]aked of God, naked of everything that was holy and good and destitute of the divine image." Once they became aware of their nakedness, they futilely sewed fig leaves together to try to cover themselves. In the same way, Whitefield noted, "[w]e labour to cover our nakedness with the fig-leaves of our own righteousness." This biblical account, Whitefield believed, magnified God's "free grace" and "plainly shows us, that salvation cometh only from the Lord." While the first Adam failed us, we look to Jesus, "the second Adam," who extends the hope of redemption: "they can now do nothing of or for themselves and should therefore come to God, beseeching him to give them faith, by which they shall be enabled to lay hold on the righteousness of Christ."[31] Sin's devastation, Christ's righteousness, free grace, the instrument of faith—by weaving together these elements, Whitefield preached the gospel through the lens of Reformation theology.

Looming large in all these discussions was the Reformation doctrine of justification by faith alone, which Whitefield defined as meaning that "you have your sins forgiven and are looked upon by God as though you never had offended him at all." He called this doctrine the "great and fundamental article of our faith," because it establishes that salvation is God's free gift and that we are saved only by the imputed righteousness of Christ.[32]

In his sermon on Isaiah 44:5, which became a "staple of Whitefield's preaching," he again highlighted the *solas* of Reformed Christianity.[33] While the law reveals your sinful nature, it also prepares you to receive the "free unmerited grace" of God, who "hunted thee out of the trees of the garden of thy performances" and made you "willing to embrace him, as freely offered to thee in the everlasting gospel."[34] This sermon exhibited how Whitefield sought to woo people to Christ: He did preach the dangers of a literal hell.[35] But he also preached the bliss of being joined to Jesus. To effectively draw people to Christ, he believed he had to proclaim the basic foundation of the gospel as expounded by the *solas* of the Reformation.[36]

The new birth

While his preaching of the *solas* highlights his continuity with the Reformation era, his emphasis on the doctrine of regeneration underscores his unique way of promoting the gospel message. That is not to say that the Reformers shunned regeneration. However, the eighteenth century saw an explosive interest in this topic, especially among revivalists like George Whitefield. In fact, he became marked for his incessant preaching of the new birth.

He feared that while so many people "have a Christ in their heads, they have no Christ in their hearts."[37] The New Testament made it blatantly clear that "unless a man be born again, he cannot enter into the kingdom of God" (John 3:3), and Whitefield believed that meant that people needed to be changed, to "become as little children" (Matt. 18:3 KJV). Transformation was the key evidence that one had been born again: "there must be some great, some notable and amazing change pass upon our souls."[38]

Whitefield touched on this theme frequently in his sermons.[39] He expounded it most clearly in his sermon on 2 Corinthians 5:17, "On Regeneration" (also titled "The Nature and Necessity of Our New Birth in Christ Jesus"), which Thomas Kidd describes as one of Whitefield's "signature exhortations" and which Timothy Smith calls "one of the most influential sermons ever published in Christendom."[40]

Whitefield taught that regeneration stands as "one of the most fundamental doctrines of our holy religion." He pointed out that to be "in Christ" (2 Cor. 5:17) must mean something more than nominal association with Christ through baptism or church membership. Rather, it means something that occurs only "by an inward change and purity of heart and cohabitation of his Holy Spirit," making someone a new creature. Being "a new creature" (2 Cor. 5:17) points to the inexplicable work of the Holy Spirit, whose exercises in our hearts make our souls "so purged, purified, and cleansed from their natural dross, filth, and leprosy . . . that they may be properly said to be made anew." In defining the nature of regeneration, Whitefield emphasized inner, individual transformation, calling each person to know "experimentally"— that is, through the tests of experience—whether the Holy Spirit has given him or her a new heart.[41]

As Whitefield's treatment of regeneration reveals, he devoted significant time to the person and work of the Holy Spirit—so much that he departed from many earlier theologians.[42] He boldly stated that "the Holy Spirit is the common privilege of all believers" and that we all "must receive the Holy Ghost, before we can be truly called the children of God."[43] The only way for people to experience the new birth was if the Holy Spirit caused them to be spiritually reborn.[44] Fully convinced of the Holy Spirit's inward working in the new birth, Whitefield argued that if you never felt an "experimental sense of your own unworthiness and sinfulness every way . . . the Comforter [Holy Spirit] never yet effectually came into your souls, you are out of Christ."[45]

Whitefield's preaching on the new birth unsettled listeners and readers because it took away their security in externals. Because many weren't sure they "felt" the internal moving of the Spirit as Whitefield described it, they accused him of emotional fanaticism. This ridicule reveals how Whitefield's emphasis on "true, vital, internal piety" marked a shift in Christian theology.[46] Some earlier theologians did promote a religion of the heart, such as seventeenth-century Pietists like Philip Jacob Spener and Puritans like Joseph Alleine. But Whitefield increasingly emphasized feeling as an evidence of God's supernatural work, in many ways mirroring the empirical thrusts of the Enlightenment era. Whereas earlier Protestants tended to focus on the objective work of Christ, Whitefield and others like him increasingly highlighted the subjective work of the Spirit, setting the tone for new emphases on the new birth, inner spirituality, and the Holy Spirit that would characterize the broad evangelical movement in later centuries.

Line drawing

Whitefield sought to keep the boundaries of evangelical Christianity as broad as possible. In appealing to people of different denominations, he admonished his hearers to "love the brethren," and by "brethren" he meant those "of whatever denomination."[47] He lamented divisions in the church: "There is nothing grieves me more than the differences amongst God's people."[48] He sought to elevate only the "essential truths" necessary for "eternal salvation."[49]

At the same time, Whitefield also aimed to draw clear lines that opposed "the great currents of heresy in his day," especially "Arminianism" (a catchall term that he used for any teaching downplaying salvation by grace alone) and antinomianism (or opposition to using the observance of the law as a barometer of genuine Christian piety).[50] Whitefield saw these as "two bad extremes": while Arminianism implied to Calvinist preachers like Whitefield that people were saved in part by their own good works, antinomianism suggested to them that free grace obviates the duty of personal righteousness.[51]

Whitefield was not surprised that people are "so fond of Arminian principles" because "[w]e all naturally are legalists, thinking to be justified by the works of the law."[52] In response, he strongly defended the doctrine of original sin, which he argued was written in "legible characters in the word of God" and was "the very foundation of the Christian religion."[53] He affirmed that humans "are conceived and born in sin," which is "plain from the whole tenor of the book of God."[54] While it was "no uncommon thing" in his day to "deny the doctrine of original sin," Whitefield believed human pride had elevated mere morality and thus undermined the pure gospel of salvation by grace alone.[55]

On the other extreme, many criticized Whitefield for preaching antinomianism, a lawlessness that encouraged people to sin. In response, he said that he proclaimed "not a faith of the head only but a faith of the heart," where the Holy Spirit instills "a living principle in the soul," "exciting him, out of a principle of love and gratitude, to show forth that faith."[56] Whitefield regularly sought to undermine the charge of antinomianism by calling for devoted lives of obedience.[57] He believed that, in connection with justification by faith alone, "good works have their proper place. They justify our faith, though not our persons. They follow it and evidence our justification."[58]

Legacy

Whitefield left a mixed legacy. For example, he owned slaves and even played a role in legalizing slavery in Georgia.[59] Nonetheless, he was remembered as a friend of slaves. Upon his death, the young slave girl and soon-to-be renowned poet Phillis Wheatley wrote her first published poem, an elegy to Whitefield. In it she captured his evangelistic zeal for all:

> Thou didst, in Strains of Eloquence refin'd,
> Inflame the Soul, and captivate the Mind. . . .
>
> He pray'd that Grace in every Heart might dwell:
> He long'd to see *America* excel; . . .
>
> Take HIM, ye *Africans*, he longs for you;
> Impartial Saviour, is his Title due.[60]

The minister Ebenezer Pemberton similarly praised him, noting that "[h]is zealous, incessant and successful Labours, in Europe and America, are without a Parallel."[61]

Whitefield's printed sermons continued to influence readers beyond his death. In part, his impact is visible in the development of evangelicalism. As Kidd notes, he "indelibly marked the character of evangelical Christianity," particularly with his use of media, emphasis on preaching, and devotion to the Bible.[62] His sermons gave others a model for evangelistic preaching, and in his train stand several evangelists such as D.L. Moody and Billy Graham who worked across denominational lines to spread the gospel.

The accolades Whitefield received from later figures show how his sermons have inspired many. Bishop J.C. Ryle remarked of him, "No Englishman, I believe, dead or alive, has ever equalled him" as a preacher.[63] And D. Martyn Lloyd-Jones claimed that Whitefield was "beyond any question, the greatest English preacher who ever lived."[64]

Conclusion

During the course of his life, George Whitefield preached upwards of thirty thousand formal sermons and informal religious talks.[65] He had a grand vision for transforming the world, stating, "the whole world is now my parish."[66] Kidd concludes that "[p]erhaps [Whitefield] was the greatest evangelical preacher the world has ever seen."[67]

In reading Whitefield, you will encounter a passionate evangelist devoted to the gospel doctrines of the Reformation and to heart transformation, which only comes through Christ's atoning work and the supernatural grace of the Holy Spirit. Though he desired unity across denominational lines, he nonetheless proclaimed a message that entered into the controversies of his day, seeking a balance between works righteousness and cheap grace. His sermons also help us understand the emphasis on preaching for conversion and the interdenominational efforts that mark evangelicalism to our own time. Whitefield devoted himself to dramatizing Scripture and preaching theologically thoughtful sermons because he longed for people to experience the matchless grace of Jesus Christ.

Notes

1. Nathan Cole, "A Farmer Hears Whitefield Preach," in *The Great Awakening: A Brief History with Documents*, ed. Thomas S. Kidd (Boston: Bedford/St. Martin's, 2008), 61–63.
2. Harry S. Stout, *The Divine Dramatist: George Whitefield and the Rise of Modern Evangelicalism* (Grand Rapids, MI: Eerdmans, 1991), xvi.
3. Thomas S. Kidd, *George Whitefield: America's Spiritual Founding Father* (New Haven, CT: Yale University Press, 2014), 5–12, 15–19.
4. Kidd, *Whitefield*, 20–21, 26, 32.
5. Kidd, *Whitefield*, 36–39, 41–54.
6. Kidd, *Whitefield*, 63.
7. Stout, *Divine Dramatist*, xiii.
8. Kidd, *Whitefield*, 61–68.
9. See Thomas S. Kidd, *The Great Awakening: The Roots of Evangelical Christianity in Colonial America* (New Haven, CT: Yale University Press, 2007).
10. Kidd, *Whitefield*, 249–51; Stout, *Divine Dramatist*, 276–280.
11. Stout, *Divine Dramatist*, xvi.
12. All of Whitefield's sermons cited in this essay come from *The Sermons of George Whitefield*, ed. Lee Gatiss, 2 vols. (Wheaton: IL: Crossway, 2012), a standard collection of his sermonic output.
13. Kidd, *Whitefield*, 47.
14. Ian J. Maddock, *Men of One Book: A Comparison of Two Methodist Preachers, John Wesley and George Whitefield* (Eugene, OR: Pickwick, 2011), 34–35, 103–116.
15. Kidd, *Whitefield*, 48–49, 84–85.

16. Frank Lambert, *"Pedlar in Divinity": George Whitefield and the Transatlantic Revivals, 1737–1770* (Princeton, NJ: Princeton University Press, 1994), 8. See also Stout, *Divine Dramatist*, xvi–xxiv.

17. Kidd, *Whitefield*, 154, 166, 191–92.

18. Whitefield, "The Great Duty of Family-Religion" (Joshua 24:15), 1:96–108; "Intercession Every Christian's Duty" (1 Thessalonians 5:25), 2:336–346; "The Great Duty of Charity Recommended" (1 Corinthians 13:8), 2:250–61; "The True Way of Keeping Christmas" (Matthew 1:21), 1:297–306; "The Heinous Sin of Drunkenness" (Ephesians 5:18), 2:314–325; "Britain's Mercies and Britain's Duty" (Psalm 105:45), 1:123–38.

19. Kidd, *Whitefield*, 12–15; Stout, *Divine Dramatist*, xviii–xxiv.

20. Stout, *Divine Dramatist*, xviii–xix.

21. Whitefield, "Abraham's Offering Up His Son Isaac" (Genesis 22:12), 1:88.

22. Whitefield, "Abraham's Offering," 1:91. See also Whitefield, "Christ the Believer's Husband" (Isaiah 44:5), 1:234.

23. Whitefield, "Blind Bartimeus" (Mark 10:52), 1:456–57.

24. Whitefield, "The Holy Spirit Convincing the World of Sin, Righteousness and Judgment" (John 16:8), 2:156. See also Whitefield, "Abraham's Offering," 1:83, 86.

25. Whitefield, "Christ the Believer's Husband," 1:218. See also Whitefield, "Marks of a True Conversion" (Matt. 18:3), 1:395.

26. Whitefield, "Christ the Believer's Husband," 1:237.

27. Whitefield, "Marks of a True Conversion," 1:384; "What Think Ye of Christ?" (Matthew 22:42), 1:420.

28. Whitefield, "Marks of a True Conversion," 1:401. See also Whitefield, "Blind Bartimeus," 1:465; "Holy Spirit Convincing," 2:165; "The Indwelling of the Spirit, the Common Privilege of All Believers" (John 7:37–39), 2:128; "Walking with God" (Genesis 5:24), 1:81; "What Think Ye?," 1:408, 418.

29. Lee Gatiss, "Introduction," in *The Sermons of George Whitefield*, ed. Lee Gatiss, 2 vols. (Wheaton: IL: Crossway, 2012), 20.

30. Kidd, *Whitefield*, 128.

31. Whitefield, "The Seed of the Woman and the Seed of the Serpent" (Genesis 3:15), 1:51, 52, 55–56, 58.

32. Whitefield, "Of Justification by Christ" (1 Corinthians 6:11), 2:241, 239. See also 2:241–49; "Abraham's Offering," 1:93; "Holy Spirit Convincing," 2:162.

33. Kidd, *Whitefield*, 165.

34. Whitefield, "Christ the Believer's Husband," 1:227, 225.

35. Whitefield, "The Eternity of Hell Torments" (Matthew 25:46), 1:443.

36. See also Whitefield, "The Method of Grace" (Jeremiah 6:14), 1:423–40; "Christ the Best Husband" (Psalm 45:10–11), 1:109–22.

37. Whitefield, "Marks of a True Conversion" 1:385.
38. Whitefield, "Marks of a True Conversion" 1:385.
39. See, e.g., Whitefield, "Christ the Best Husband," 1:113–14; "What Think Ye?," 1:417; "Marks of Having Received the Holy Ghost" (Acts 19:2), 2:190.
40. Kidd, *Whitefield*, 47; Timothy L. Smith. *Whitefield and Wesley on the New Birth* (Grand Rapids, MI: Francis Asbury, 1986), 63.
41. Whitefield, "On Regeneration" (2 Corinthians 5:17), 2:275, 277, 278, 285–286.
42. Kidd, *Whitefield*, 36.
43. Whitefield, "Indwelling of the Spirit," 2:116.
44. Whitefield, "What Think Ye?," 1:417.
45. Whitefield, "Holy Spirit Convincing," 2:158. For more on Whitefield's teaching about the Holy Spirit, see "Indwelling of the Spirit," 2:115–28; "Holy Spirit Convincing," 2:153–68; "Marks of Having Received," 2:187–99.
46. Whitefield, "Christ the Believer's Husband," 1:218. See also Whitefield, "Holy Spirit Convincing," 2:155; "Indwelling of the Spirit," 2:121; "Christ the Believer's Husband," 1:218; Kidd, *Whitefield*, 47, 64, 95.
47. Whitefield, "Christ the Believer's Husband," 1:232.
48. Whitefield, "Marks of a True Conversion," 1:400.
49. Whitefield, "What Think Ye?," 1:404.
50. Gatiss, "Introduction," 21.
51. Whitefield, "Seed of the Woman," 1:58.
52. Whitefield, "Christ the Believer's Husband," 1:219; Whitefield, "Holy Spirit Convincing," 2:157.
53. Whitefield, "Of Justification by Christ," 2:242; "Marks of a True Conversion," 1:388.
54. Whitefield, "Marks of a True Conversion," 1:388.
55. Whitefield, "Indwelling of the Spirit," 2:122. See Whitefield, "What Think Ye?," 1:405, 407; "Of Justification by Christ," 2:239, 245.
56. Whitefield, "What Think Ye?," 1:411–12.
57. See, e.g., Whitefield, "Walking with God," 1:64–81; "Abraham's Offering," 1:94; "Christ the Believer's Husband," 1:232.
58. Whitefield, "Abraham's Offering," 1:94.
59. Kidd, *Whitefield*, 209.
60. Phillis Wheatley, "An Elegiac Poem on the Death of . . . Mr George Whitefield," appended to Ebenezer Pemberton, *Heaven the Residence of Saints* (Boston: Dilly, 1771), 29–30.
61. Ebenezer Pemberton, *Heaven the Residence of Saints* (Boston: Dilly, 1771), 17.
62. Kidd, *Whitefield*, 260.
63. J.C. Ryle, *Christian Leaders of the Eighteenth Century*, 4th ed. (1866–1867; repr., London: Thynne and Jarvis, n.d.), 44, 50.

64. D. Martyn Lloyd-Jones, "John Calvin and George Whitefield," in *The Puritans: Their Origins and Successors* (Edinburgh: Banner of Truth, 1987), 104.
65. Gatiss, "Introduction," 15.
66. Quoted in Maddock, *Men of One Book*, 41.
67. Kidd, *Whitefield*, 263.

Select Bibliography

Primary sources

Whitefield, George. *George Whitefield's Journals*. Carlisle, PA: Banner of Truth Trust, 1960.
Whitefield, George. *The Sermons of George Whitefield*. Edited by Lee Gatiss. Wheaton, IL: Crossway, 2012.

Secondary sources

Dallimore, Arnold A. *George Whitefield: The Life and Times of the Great Evangelist of the Eighteenth Century*. 2 vols. Carlisle, PA: Banner of Truth Trust, 1970, 1980.
Kidd, Thomas S. *George Whitefield: America's Spiritual Founding Father*. New Haven, CT: Yale University Press, 2014.
Stout, Harry S. *The Divine Dramatist: George Whitefield and the Rise of Modern Evangelicalism*. Library of Religious Biography. Grand Rapids, MI: Eerdmans, 1991.

4·7

The Declaration of Sentiments (1608)

Jacobus (James) Arminius (1559–1609)

Background

> There lived in Holland a man
> whom they who did not know
> could not sufficiently esteem,
> whom they who did not esteem
> had never sufficiently known.

These words were uttered near the end of Arminius' funeral oration by his good friend Peter Bertius. They were carved in Arminius' gravestone in the Pieterskerk at Leiden in 1934 at the 300th anniversary of the founding of the Remonstrant Seminary in Amsterdam.[1] A freshly hewn gravestone with the same epitaph was placed on the Pieterskerk grave at the 1960 commemoration of Arminius' birth.[2] It is appropriate to begin this essay with the nostalgic words from his funeral oration, because a good case can be made that James Arminius is one of the most misunderstood Protestant theologians in church history.

His *Declaration* has three distinct parts. Part One is an overview of a multiplicity of accusations against Arminius, namely that he steadfastly refused to come clean about what he really believed about divine election and predestination, especially in connection with the primary doctrinal

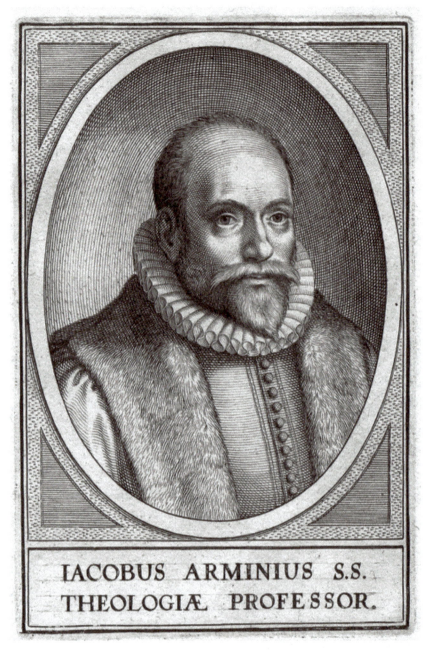

Figure 4.5 Jacobus Arminius

affirmations of his day (i.e., The Heidelberg Catechism and the Belgic Confession). As if this were not enough, Arminius was also accused of being less than transparent with his ministerial colleagues when they personally asked him to clarify his positions. Added to this were differences of opinion about whether he should be held accountable by regional ecclesial authorities (The Synod) or whether, as a university professor, he was actually only accountable to university officials. The mistrust actually begins during Arminius' tenure as pastor in Amsterdam.

Arminius the pastor

After beginning his theological studies in Leiden, the city fathers of Amsterdam sponsored Arminius' theological education in Geneva, the bastion of Calvinism, upon the condition that he return to Amsterdam as pastor. Arminius returned in 1587 after completing his studies in Switzerland, and he remained as pastor until 1603, when he was named professor of theology at his alma mater, Leiden. At the time of his appointment as pastor in Amsterdam, it was not yet readily apparent that there was something of a theological divide among the more tolerant city fathers, who stood squarely with Arminius on most issues, and the more conservative ("less tolerant") ministers of the local clergy council (diocese). Here an important difference between their context and our current context must be noted, as there was a very different understanding of the relationship between clergy and the laity in connection with the appointment and retention of a pastor. In the Netherlands at this time, there was no formal separation of church and state. The Dutch form of governance—Erastianism—provided that the right of final approval for the appointment and retention of a minister was held by the city council. The local clergy council and the laity of the congregation had input, but the final authority was held by the mayor and city governors. This crucial distinction must be kept in mind when reading the *Declaration*.

When Arminius began as a *proponent* (ministerial candidate on trial) in the Old Church of Amsterdam on February 7, 1588, his duties were to lead in prayers and to preach. On July 21, the local consistory unanimously voted to forward his name to the city council for approval. The city fathers granted their approval on July 28, and Arminius was confirmed as pastor on August 11 of that same year. He was ordained on Saturday night, August 27, and celebrated his first service of Holy Communion on Sunday, August 28, 1588. There were five other ministers serving in the Amsterdam area at the time of his ordination. Among them there were four who would be counted as "moderate," but there was one that definitely should be counted among the less tolerant "strict Calvinists," Rev. Peter Plancius. Indeed, Plancius was a thorn in the side of Arminius throughout his tenure in Amsterdam, and Plancius continued to spread doubt about Arminius' orthodoxy even after he went to Leiden as professor of theology. When Arminius mentions his accusers, we may be sure that Plancius was always among them.

By all accounts, and reflected also in the attendance at worship, Arminius was a popular preacher. This notwithstanding, Arminius found himself in tenuous circumstances rather early in his Amsterdam tenure. At this point, the tension was not related to the content of his preaching but rather in connection with a formal request that he defend Genevan orthodoxy on the issue of predestination. Having studied at Geneva under the tutelage of John Calvin's immediate and chosen successor to head the theological academy, Theodore Beza, it seems to have been assumed that Arminius would know well and totally identify with the form of predestinarian theology developed and taught by Beza. Unlike Calvin, who was more careful to stay with biblical language and metaphors for this doctrine, Beza developed a logical schema that entailed a strict supralapsarianism—that God had chosen before the foundation of all creation specifically who would be saved and who would be damned. Furthermore, it was also decreed by God, according to Beza, that divine provision was made for the damned to commit sin so that their damnation would be deserved.[3]

It seems that Arminius was requested, both by his consistory in Amsterdam and then subsequently by Professor Martinus Lydius, to write an apologetic defending Beza's teachings on predestination. By all accounts, Arminius was open to setting out his own thoughts on the issue, even if he did not intend simply to defend Beza's supralapsarianism. Even in Arminius' own lifetime his actual intentions seem to have been misinterpreted. In his "Funeral Oration," Peter Bertius asserts an interpretation for which there is no written evidence in any of Arminius' writings:

> But while he was contriving a proper refutation, and had begun accurately to weigh the arguments on both sides, and to compare different passages of scripture together ... he was conquered by the force of truth, and, at first, became a convert to the very opinions which he had been requested to combat and refute. But he afterward disapproved of them ... because he did not think the doctrine contained in them [infralapsarianism][4] to be correct according to the scriptures ... [and finally] he turned towards those opinions which he finally embraced, and which to the close of his life he constantly maintained.[5]

These assertions by Bertius were taken over uncritically by James Nichols in the English translation of the *Works*, and Nichols even embellishes the process by which Arminius changed his mind: "When further light from heaven was communicated to him, he abandoned without regret the sublapsarian scheme which he has recently embraced, and [he] entrenched himself within the stronghold of General Redemption."[6] Then Nichols goes even further to certify the magnitude of this supposed change of mind:

> Arminius departed from the supralapsarian doctrines, which he had imbibed in his very boyhood, and which were afterwards confirmed and fixed in him by the authority and persuasive eloquence of the venerable Beza, who had magnified them into such importance as to make the recognition of them and of all their eventful consequences a *sine qua non* [indispensable element] to salvation.[7]

This all sounds quite logical; however, it is a marvelous example of how a story twice-told eventually bears little resemblance to the events themselves. There is not a shred of textual evidence to support these claims about Arminius changing his mind on election and predestination. Furthermore, the latter assertion by Nicholson is unfair to Beza, who, although quite strong in his opinions on the subject, made generous allowance for differences of opinion on predestination. It is simply not the case that Beza made it the *sine qua non* of Reformed Protestant identity. Arminius' theological opponents in Amsterdam (Peter Plancius) and at Leiden (Franciscus Gomarus) were quite willing to do so, and this accounts to a large extent why Arminius found himself defending serial accusations in both places.

The modern reader can hardly be surprised that there is some confusion about what Arminius actually taught and believed, since he was misunderstood and misrepresented from the very beginning by those who held him in highest esteem. This misunderstanding is compounded by the fact that his own student, Simon Episcopius, made subtle shifts in Arminian theology when he was the chief spokesperson for the Arminians (Remonstrants) at the Synod of Dort, 1618–1619. The shifts by Episcopius are not so much contradictions of Arminius as they are slight changes that shift the trajectory of Arminian theology on the doctrines of soteriology— sin and salvation.[8] Arminius was essentially a follower of Saint Augustine on the doctrine of sin. Here Arminius would agree with Martin Luther with regard to the "bondage of the will" because of the effects of human depravity. In harmony with this, Arminius would never speak of a "free will" (except with the first Adam at creation prior to the Fall), but always rather of a *freed* will—the human will set free by the intervention of divine grace. Episcopius, on the other hand, spoke of free will as a human capacity, without making the point that divine intervention is required for human freedom to be actuated in connection with salvation. Arminius taught that God's prevenient grace reaches out to all of humanity; but because some do not believe, we are left with the mystery of salvation as to why this is so. The slight step taken by Episcopius with regard to freedom ultimately leads to subsequent generations of Arminians conceiving human freedom as a divine spark intrinsic to the status of being human. In so doing, the doctrines of sin and depravity are shoved to the margins. As we shall note in our discussion of his *Sentiments*, this is a step that Arminius would never take.

A brief history of the document

James Arminius' *Verklaring* ("Declaration of Sentiments") was delivered orally before the States of Holland in The Hague, October 30, 1608. His Dutch manuscript was first published in 1610 at Leiden, with the original full title fairly translated as *The Declaration of Jacobus Arminius, of Blessed Memory.* This document was published in Latin shortly thereafter, *Declaratio sententiae de predestinatione*, but Arminius himself would have had no part in its production. He died the year before, and he was quite ill with tuberculosis throughout his final days. It was the Latin text, taken up as a permanent part of Arminius' *Opera*, that served as the basis for English translations until very recently.[9] The first English text of the declaration appeared in 1657,[10] and this was followed two centuries later by the first full English edition of his works, based also on Latin versions.[11] In 2012, a fresh translation into English from the original Dutch was done for the first time; it is this edition of Arminius' *Declaration* that serves as the basis for this essay.[12]

When one reads the events that finally culminated in Arminius' giving his oral declaration before the States of Holland, we discover that Arminius only had a few days advance notice to prepare his formal statement. While this time line is accurate, the reader must remember that part of his teaching responsibility at Leiden was to prepare and supervise (with his students) what were called "public" and "private" disputations—theological debate forums. We add to this the considerable time and energy that Arminius devoted to sorting out his theological opinions while he was a pastor at Amsterdam. He preached an extended series of exegetical sermons on

Romans, and he also wrote a long rebuttal exposition to the Cambridge theologian, William Perkins, on predestination. In addition, we also know that even while a pastor, Arminius was writing what we might call a systematic theology, his "Synopsis of Common Places in Divinity." Regarding this doctrinal piece, Arminius writes: "I have determined to re-read all the ancient and modern divines which are at hand and which can be obtained . . . I am making a beginning with the Doctrine of God . . ." (163). While it is true that he only had a couple of days to prepare his oral statement in 1608, he had actually been in preparation for this moment for two decades. His adversaries had for many years been attempting to hold an ecclesial trial to judge Arminius' opinions, so it was a shrewd political move on his part to request that this be done in the forum of public domain before the governors of the land, The States of Holland.[13]

An overview of *The Declaration of Sentiments*

Section One

Arminius begins with some comments about his previous appearance before the States of Holland, and then he proceeds to a detailed account of the disputes over doctrine. He recounts the continued efforts of the various ecclesial representatives and synods to hold him accountable. He admits openly that he has refused to yield to their demands, citing the following as justifications for his refusal: (1) As a university professor, he is under the jurisdiction of the university curators. (2) It would be unfair to be held accountable by a synod because there would be a lack of equity. The way that members would be appointed to such a synod would assure that Arminius and those of his sentiment would not be equally represented. (3) To make his case for this second point, he draws attention to how spurious rumors against him had been spread maliciously. He had been forced to point out time and again that these rumors had no basis in fact, but once the rumor was spread, the damage in public opinion could not be reversed (98–99).

Section Two

With this as an overarching frame of reference as to why this public forum was needed, Arminius proceeds to his doctrinal analysis. First, he deals with predestination. He describes the doctrine under nine headings (103–107), which he then reduces to four foundational points with which he disagrees. This is evidently for purposes of symmetry, as he will also describe his position under four headings. Regarding predestination:

1 God has decreed to save and damn certain particular persons. This occurred in the mind of God prior to all creation.

2 In order to carry out that divine decree, God decided to create Adam and all of humanity, and humanity was created in an original state of righteousness, blameless before God. God also ordained that Adam would commit sin and thereby be deprived of his original righteousness. By this culpable act, humanity would no longer be blameless before God.

3 God decreed not only the salvation of the elect but the means to it so that they could do no other than believe, persevere in the faith, and be finally be saved.

4 God decreed also to deny these salvific means to the reprobate, the damned (107).

In all of Arminius' previous dispositions, he has been content to assert that charity should prevail with regard to differences of opinion on these points. That charity is not in place here. He now asserts that teaching such a doctrine is intolerable, and he gave twenty reasons why this is so (108–130). Both history of doctrine and theological logic are called upon to make his case, since he believed such a doctrine of predestination is not the foundation for Christianity. The logic of scriptural salvation is this:

They who believe shall be saved;
I believe;
Therefore, I shall be saved.

Arminius is of the opinion that his logic is biblical, and he protests that supralapsarian logic does not work in harmony with scriptural logic. Supralapsarian logic contains neither the first nor the second proposition of his syllogism. He asserts that his logic is not only scriptural; it is the logic that has informed the greater part of early orthodox Christianity, indeed, Christianity through the ages. It was never admitted, decreed or approved in any council, either general or specific, for the first six hundred years after Christ. After surveying all the early councils, he moves to the Reformation era. This predestination theory is not in the First Helvetic (Swiss) Confession, and the confessions of Basel and Saxony mention it only briefly, in three words. The Augsburg Confession speaks of it in such a manner that the Genevan editors found it necessary to make a warning annotation. The Second Helvetic Confession has to be "stretched" to accommodate the teaching (111). And these points bring Arminius to the formal doctrinal statements most pertinent to his context: the Belgic Confession and the Heidelberg Catechism.

He quotes Article 14 of the Belgic Confession, that humanity "willfully subjected himself to sin ... giving heed to the words of the devil." He asserts: "I conclude that humanity did not sin on account of necessity due to a preceding decree of predestination ..." (112). He makes this same point with regard to Article 16 of the Belgic Confession, and then he proceeds to the Heidelberg Catechism, Question 20: "Will all men, then, be saved through Christ as they became lost through Adam? No. Only those who, by true faith, are incorporated into him and accept all his benefits." Arminius then makes his oft-repeated assertion: "From this sentence I infer that God has not absolutely predestined anyone to salvation, but that in predestining them, he views them as believers in Christ" (112). He gives similar treatment to Question 54 in the Heidelberg Catechism.

Arminius is operating within a large anthropological and theological frame. He strongly believes that the supralapsarian doctrine is contrary to the nature of God, especially divine wisdom, justice, and goodness. It is contrary to the nature of humanity, created in the image of God with freedom and an aptitude for eternal life. It is opposed to the essential goodness of creation. Furthermore, it is inconsistent with the nature of sin as the disobedience that is the meritorious cause of damnation. Problematically, supralapsarianism makes sin a means by which God executes the decree of damnation. Consequently, such teaching is contrary to the nature of divine grace, to the glory of God, to Jesus Christ our Savior, and to the salvation of humanity. Such a perverse doctrine, he argued, is in open hostility to the ministry of the gospel; it subverts the foundation of the Christian religion; and it has therefore been rejected by the greater part of Christians both in the past and in the present day.

Arminius then turns to a positive affirmation of his own teachings on these crucial points (135). Whereas the rebuttal of his opponents is quite extensive, the exposition of his own theology is concise and to the point. He affirms predestination and divine decree, but in quite a different fashion from his adversaries: God has decreed to appoint his Son as the Savior, to receive into divine favor those sinners who by grace repent and believe in Christ. Through Christ, God administers the means that are sufficient and efficacious for this faith. God further decrees the salvation and damnation of particular persons on the basis of divine foreknowledge of their faith, belief, and perseverance in the faith; or in the case of those who are eternally lost, their lack of faith and belief. He then engages in a twenty-point argument defending his position (136–138). He asserts that his theology reflects the sum and total of the gospel as taught in scripture and that his position was never contravened by the early church. It also is in comprehensive harmony, he asserts, with the Dutch Confession and the Heidelberg Catechism. Nothing he argues, he believes, does violence to the nature of God, the dignity of humanity, or the goodness of creation. Instead, it contributes to the glory of God and honor of Jesus Christ as savior. Approved throughout history by the majority of Christians, it contributes to the potential salvation of all of humanity and renders intelligible the preaching of this same gospel.

On the crucial issue of divine and human initiative, Arminius is explicit. God both wills and performs good acts, but God only freely allows those that are evil. God is in no way, form, or fashion the author of sin or of sinful acts. Humanity after the first Adam, lost in sin, is unable to exercise freedom to do any good at all in relation to salvation unless divinely regenerated and continually aided by grace. This grace of God is a gratuitous affection, an infusion of the gifts of the Spirit, and a perpetual assistance that constitutes the beginning, the continuance, and the consummation of anything that is good. It is not, however, an irresistible force. Divine grace may be resisted, but to those who by grace receive and participate in God's salvific design, the Spirit witnesses to the believer that they have been favorably received by God.

Arminius goes into some detail on the topic that has occupied Arminians in the Wesleyan tradition, namely, the doctrine of holiness. Is there a perfection of believers in this life? Here Arminius turns again to Augustine and agrees with him. He answers this question with a qualified "yes," but hastens to add that such a perfecting love is *only* possible by continually abiding in grace. By grace, it is "possible not to sin" (143–144). Typical of his argumentation, he quotes scripture: "Apart from me you can do nothing" (John 15:15).

Section Three

The *Declaration* concludes with an extended discussion regarding whether he is advocating that the Dutch Confession ought to be revised. His conclusion is that only the scriptures themselves are not open for revision.

All our other documents are human documents that should be analyzed in the light of the only final authority, the bible. He makes the point that other Protestant creeds have been reviewed (and changed!) from time to time when they were found wanting in the light of scripture.

Conclusion

Clearly, Arminius thought that his teachings were scriptural and that they conformed to the foundational assumptions of both the Belgic Confession and the Heidelberg Catechism. In his *Declaration of Sentiments*, we encounter Arminius' last official theological formulation. It is also his most concise statement on soteriology. Arminian disciples and anti-Arminian detractors would do well to read it carefully. In so doing, Arminius' detractors will likely discover that they have horribly caricatured his theology, and his "friends" will likely discover that they too have done him no favors: *There lived in Holland a man whom they who did not know could not sufficiently esteem, whom they who did not esteem had never sufficiently known.*

Notes

1. The word "Remonstrant" refers to the first adherents to Arminian theology who remonstrated ("spoke out against") the hyper-Calvinist doctrine of predestination advocated by Arminius' adversaries.
2. We are now very confident that Arminius was born in 1559. Cf. Carl Bangs, *ARMINIUS. A Study in the Dutch Reformation* (Nashville: Abingdon Press, 1971), 26.
3. W. Stephen Gunter, *Arminius and "Declaration of Sentiments." An Annotated Translation with Introduction and Theological Commentary* (Waco: Baylor University Press, 2012), 33. Hereafter, all references to this work shall be noted by employing in-text citations.
4. These terms require definition for the modern reader. It is perhaps helpful to be aware that the Latin word *lapsare*, "to fall," is the root word. In the compound words, *supra* means "above," "before," or "prior to," and *sub* means "under" or "within." (1) Supralapsarianism: God decreed with individual specificity *before* all creation who would be saved and who would be damned; moreover, God made provision that the damned would commit damnable sin, but that those predestined to be saved would persevere in the faith. A slight variation on this is that God graciously

chooses to save some, while simply passing others by—leaving them in their state of sinfulness to receive their just reward, damnation. (2) Infralapsarianism/sublapsarianism: God's decision to save and to damn is not made prior to all creation, but within the context of human sinfulness. Those who championed infralapsarianism were attempting to avoid the charge that God was the author of sin in order to accomplish divine election and predestination. Arminius saw no real difference between the two definitions, as the practical result was the same.

5.   Arminius, *Works*, "Funeral Oration," I:30.
6.   Ibid., I:63. General redemption is a synonym for universal redemption. This is not the same as universalism, that all will be saved, but rather that all that respond positively to God's saving initiative *may* be saved.
7.   Ibid., I:65.
8.   Cf. my essay, "From Arminius (d.1609) to the Synod of Dort (1618–1619)," in *Perfecting Perfection: A Festschrift in Honor of Henry D. Rack* (Eugene, Oregon: Pickwick, 2015), 8–28.
9.   Arminius, Jacobus. *Jacobi Arminii opera theologica* (Leiden: G. Basson, 1629).
10. *The Just Man's Defence; or, The Declaration of the Judgement of James Arminius before the States of Holland . . . to the Regulators of the University of Leyden with Their Solution*. Translated by Tobias Conyers (London: Henry Eversden, 1657).
11. *The Works of James Arminius: The London Edition. Translated by J. Nichols and W. Nichols*. Introduction by Carl Bangs, 3 vols. (Kansas City: Beacon Hill, 1986). First edition, London, 1825–1875.
12. W. Stephen Gunter. *Arminius and "Declaration of Sentiments." An Annotated Translation with Introduction and Theological Commentary* (Waco: Baylor University Press, 2012).
13. In modern parlance a reference to Holland is understood as a synonym for The Netherlands. Strictly speaking, that is not accurate. There are the provinces of North and South Holland, which are part of the country as a whole. In the period under consideration, "States of Holland" was a term that referred to the assembly of those elected to represent the united provinces.

Select Bibliography

Primary sources

Arminius, James. *The Works of James Arminius: The London Edition. Translated by J. Nichols and W. Nichols*. Introduction by Carl Bangs. 3 vols. Kansas City: Beacon Hill, 1986. First edition, London, 1825–1875.

Arminius, James. *The Declaration of Sentiments* in W. Stephen Gunter, *Arminius and His "Declaration of Sentiments." An Annotated Translation with Introduction and Theological Commentary*. Waco: Baylor University Press, 2012.

Secondary sources

Bangs, Carl. *ARMINIUS. A Study in the Dutch Reformation*. Nashville: Abingdon Press, 1971.

Boer, William den. *God's Two-fold Love*. Translated by Albert Gootjes. Göttingen: Vandenhoek & Ruprecht, 2010.

Gunter, W. Stephen. "John Wesley. A Faithful Representative of Jacobus Arminus," in *Wesleyan Theological Journal*. 42:2 (Fall, 2007), 65–83.

Gunter, W. Stephen. "The Loss of Arminius in Wesleyan-Arminian Theology," pp. 71–90 in Keith D. Stanglin, Mark G. Bilby, and Mark H. Mann, eds., *Reconsidering Arminius. Beyond the Reformed and Wesleyan Divide* (Nashville: Kingswood Books, 2014).

Gunter, W. Stephen. "From Arminius (d. 1609) to The Synod of Dort (1618–19)," pp. 8–28 in Robert Webster, ed., *Perfecting Perfection: Essays in Honor of Henry D. Rack* (Eugene, OR: Pickwick Publications, 2015).

Stanglin, Keith D. *Arminius and the Assurance of Salvation: The Context, Roots, and Shape of the Leiden Debate, 1603–1609*. Leiden: Brill, 2007.

Stanglin, Keith D. and Thomas H. McCall. *Jacob Arminius: Theologian of Grace*. Oxford: Oxford University Press, 2012.

4.8

The Appeals to Men of Reason and Religion (1743–1745)
John Wesley (1703–1791)

Figure 4.6 John Wesley preaching

Background

John Wesley was an English clergyman who, with his poet brother Charles, is credited with founding the movement known as Methodism. This evangelical movement includes the theological underpinnings of modern Pentecostalism as well as the Holiness Movement—denominations like the

Church of the Nazarene, Free Methodist Church, and Wesleyan Church. Historians have recognized that the growth of Methodist evangelicalism in England was transformational in English society, and was perhaps even instrumental in preventing England from getting caught in the civil turmoil that produced a revolution in France. In North America, the growth and influence of Methodism was phenomenal, and by the 1850s Methodism was the single largest denomination in North America.

John and Charles were born into the home of Rev. Samuel and Susanna Annesley Wesley. Susanna's father had been a dissenting minister (i.e., a protestant who refused to conform to Anglicanism), and Susanna herself proved to be something of a Nonconformist, which was reflected in her decision to leave her father's dissenting tradition as a young teenager to become an Anglican. We gain here an important insight into John Wesley's design to always follow the dictates of his religious conscience regardless of the consequences. John followed in the footsteps of his father in studying at Oxford, entering Christ Church [College] in 1720. He earned his Bachelor of Arts in 1724 and immediately matriculated to pursue a Master of Arts. He was ordained a deacon in September 1725—the order of deacon being a probationary ordination on the way to becoming an Anglican priest. This also opened the door for him to become a fellow and tutor at Oxford, a post he later took at Lincoln College, Oxford (March 1726). Receiving this post provided a room for him at college as well as a regular income. From the very beginning, then, John Wesley was both scholar and priest.

The founding of Methodism was quite by accident, as Wesley remained for his entire life an Anglican priest, as did his brother Charles. Methodism began as a renewal movement within the Church of England, and it was not until after his death in 1791 that Methodism was formed as a separate Protestant denomination in England—although it had formed as a separate entity in North America in 1784. Notwithstanding the fact that it was a renewal movement, distinctive Methodist teachings emerged in Wesley's lifetime, thus necessitating the formulation of theological treatises to clarify and sustain the vitality of the revival movement. *The Appeals to Men of Reason and Religion* is among the most important of these writings, and was published in four sequential tracts[1]:

An Earnest Appeal to Men of Reason and Religion (1743)
A Farther Appeal to Men of Reason and Religion, Part I (1744)[2]
A Farther Appeal to Men of Reason and Religion, Part II (1745)
A Farther Appeal to Men of Reason and Religion, Part III (1745)

Wesley's case for a "reasonable" Methodism

Although the *Appeals* were published in three segments under two titles, after the publication of the initial tracts, Wesley's apologetic for Methodism was subsequently always viewed as a single treatise. They appeared as a whole in the first and every subsequent edition of his *Works*. The *Earnest Appeal* comprises 101 sections, a compact 51 pages. The *Farther Appeal*, published in two segments in the following years, is a more meandering document—222 pages in total length. In the first apologetic the reader encounters the heart of Wesley's theological method, and in the second longer document, we encounter detailed arguments and rebuttals to Methodism's accusers. They were legion, and many were from the highest courts of Anglicanism—the bishops of the church. In some ways the early Methodists were akin to modern Pentecostalism in its appeal to the masses that were not being reached by the established church. This reality seems to have been lost on the Anglican bishops. It was not lost on them in the sense that tens of thousands were reached with the gospel and were filling Methodist class meetings and accountability groups, but it does seem to have been lost on them in the sense that they underappreciated the level of religious fervor exhibited among the margins and social underbelly of society. The less sophisticated and uneducated segments of society that comprised most of early Methodism felt no constraints about the propriety of expressing their feelings openly when they got converted. Under the preaching of Wesley and his (mostly) lay itinerant preachers, the converts were swept up in a religious fervor quite unheard of in the more staid Anglican services rooted as they were in sacramental demonstration and ecclesial office.

When the first Methodist Conference (all lay preachers and a few ordained clergy) gathered in June 1744, Wesley's associates urged him to "write a farther appeal," the *Earnest Appeal* having been published the year before. Wesley agreed, and Part I of *A Farther Appeal* appeared in December 1744. The second and third parts were published a year later. Once again, Wesley's aim was apologetic. He set out to meet objections that "partly relate to the *doctrines* I teach, partly to my *manner* of teaching them, and partly to the effects which are supposed to follow from teaching these doctrines in this manner."[3] He proceeds to set out precisely the presenting issues: "Now all I teach respects either the nature and condition of justification, the nature and condition of salvation, the nature of justifying and saving faith, or the Author of faith and salvation."[4]

Bringing reason, emotions, and experience together

Misunderstanding surrounding the assumptions undergirding the revival movement was one factor that led to *The Appeals* and many other Wesleyan tracts. The original Methodists were to a large extent "enthusiasts," a term loosely equivalent to the modern phrase "religious fanatic." Literally, the word enthusiast (*en* + *theos* = "in God") implies persons who assert that they talk to and hear from God. In the early stages of Enlightenment thought, this was clearly not accepted as a reasonable assertion. Over time Wesley's prolific writing carried the day, and when he died on March 2, 1791, in his eighty-eighth year, time had brought remarkable changes. From being initially characterized as a religious fanatic, Wesley had won a recognized, even respected place in public life. "It seems," he wrote in 1777, "after being scandalous near fifty years, I am at length growing into an honourable man."[5] To be sure, many of his contemporaries (Anglican and Dissenter alike) still disagreed with certain of his views. Others were more distressed by his practices of field preaching and extemporaneous prayers, but even his critics came to concede that he had profoundly affected the lives of multitudes. In the end, they made allowances for his eccentricities, and wherever he went he was treated with respect. Part of this was due to his popular influence, but part of it was also due to his ability to make the case theologically for Methodism. Wesley was steadfast in his affirmation of experience as fundamental to vital Christianity. On his father's deathbed, Samuel Wesley had said to John, "The witness of the Spirit son. Above all, you must have the witness of the Spirit." This echo of Roman 8:16 remained with Wesley all his life. In every assertion that experience is essential to vital Christianity, Wesley underscored that this was a reasonable assertion. Indeed, to fail to affirm this scriptural teaching was most unreasonable for a Christian.[6]

Wesley's *Appeals* are in some ways a curious amalgam of early church foundations, English Protestant nonconformity, and Puritanism. Both of Wesley's grandfathers were Puritan ministers ejected from the Anglican Church in 1662, so both his parents had Puritan assumptions at work even as they were both Anglicans by the time John was born. Reading the theological writings of John Wesley and to read the Puritans like John Flavel and Richard Baxter, one encounters a startling similarity in content and emphasis. With regard to the doctrines of sin and depravity, St. Augustine and Wesley are on the same page. Both assert total depravity and the absolute impossibility of salvation apart from gracious divine intervention. From the Eastern fathers and mothers, Wesley borrowed his assumptions about sanctification—that true believers enter into an experience of *participatio dei* ("participation in God") that leads increasingly into Christlikeness. But Wesley did not have to go back to the Cappodocians to learn this, as it was also a fundamental tenet of the "Holy Living Divines" of Anglicanism. Similar assertions may be made for the influence of the German Moravians, especially with regard to interior piety. These German Pietists were intensely missionary in their setting up *collegia pietatis* (small spiritual accountability groups) throughout England, which Wesley first encountered when serving as a curate near Epworth. These Pietists influenced both Anglicanism as well as Nonconformist Puritans. In the final analysis, however, Wesley was neither Puritan nor Moravian. When we say that he remained an Anglican, it must simultaneously be asserted that he was an Anglican of a very particular sort. In his conjunction of piety, sacrament, experience, and reason—with scripture always his final touchstone—he was a Methodist. With scripture always as his final authority, he consistently appealed to both reason and experience.

Even though eighteenth-century thinkers were comprehensively suspicious of emotions, Wesley reasoned that emotions were an indispensable part of vital religion because they were constitutive of what it means to be human. So, in his *Appeals*, Wesley makes the case for religious experience as a constitutive part of the Christian faith. At the same time, he argued, "When you despise or depreciate reason, you must not imagine that you are doing God [a] service; least of all are you promoting the cause of God when you are endeavouring to exclude reason out of religion."[7] In his *Appeals* we discern that Wesley steadfastly refused to separate faith from reason. He had been converted in a Moravian meeting while listening to the Preface of a Luther commentary being read, but he was horrified when he discovered that Luther was dismissive of reason insofar as he was willing to "decry reason, right or wrong, as an irreconcilable enemy to the Gospel of Christ."[8] Wesley presupposed revelation on the part of God as well as the human appropriation of that revelation by the mind. He maintained that the mind is subordinate to revelation, but that a reasoning mind is required to receive and appropriate divine revelation: "We therefore not only allow, but earnestly exhort all who seek after true religion to use all the reason which God hath given them in seeking out the things of God."[9]

Sin and salvation

Modern Methodism in almost all its expressions has left behind one of Wesley's key theological assumptions, that humanity is fundamentally sinful and lost. Without the intervention of divine grace, humanity is doomed to perdition. This assumption underscores why Wesley is continually preoccupied with soteriology (the doctrine of salvation) and practices of effective evangelism. The entire corpus of Wesley's sermons is an extended set of treatises on the absolute necessity of salvation, so we are not surprised when we see that this is the foundational set of assumptions with which he opens his *Earnest Appeal*.[10] Wesley is not making the case for academic theology, but he does develop here an extensive apologetic for a transformational "practical divinity."

Salvation, for Wesley, is a divine therapeutic that entails more than forgiveness of sins and being declared right with God. It is a comprehensive salvation rooted in an optimism of grace that he described with the biblical word sanctification, paraphrased as "being perfected in love." For Wesley, sanctification involved the ethical transformation of the believer. To most Anglicans this smacked either of pride or of religious self-delusion. To Calvinists it implied some form of works-righteousness. When one reads the tracts to which his *Appeals* are a response, it is easily discernible that he is answering his critics. Wesley repudiates the imputations of both the Calvinists and the Anglicans, but he did not find it easy to reduce his teaching to consistently intelligible terms. He clearly interpreted "perfection" in more relative terms than most of his critics assumed, but he never backed away from his assertion that God's grace is capable of working this transformation, and that God's design is that this can be so in this present life.[11]

If the teachings on perfection themselves did not actually entail enthusiasm, then Wesley was accused that his religious practices were dangerous. This was evidenced in multiple examples of his being excluded from Anglican pulpits, as for example at St. Mary Arches at Exeter, when he was told that he would not be preaching at Evensong, having preached there that morning at Matins: "Not," noted the rector, "that you preach any false doctrine. I allow all that you have said is true; and it is the doctrine of the Church of England. But it is not guarded. It is dangerous. It might lead people into enthusiasm or despair."[12]

There is a famous painting of Wesley preaching atop his father's tomb adjacent to St. Andrews, Epworth. The reason Wesley was denied access to the pulpit his father had occupied was most certainly because he was regarded as an enthusiast. When we see just how pervasive was the fear about religious enthusiasm, it makes it the more understandable that Wesley would write his extended appeals to reason in an attempt to demonstrate that his Methodism was quite thoroughly reasoned. It was not rationalism, to be sure, but it was thoroughly reasonable. Wesley was forced time and again to describe the difference between enthusiasm and enthusiasm "properly so called."[13]

Properly grounding the Christian religion

What we encounter in the four theological *Appeals* is not so much a set of doctrinal expositions as a widely framed apologetic for the nature of the Christian religion itself. It is for this reason that the issue of enthusiasm is an important part of the framing assumptions. If religion is pure reason, then rationalism is the answer. Wesley was convinced that rationalism was itself inadequate to the task of defining religion. An adequate grasp of the Christian religion was founded in scripture, but it also required reasoning rooted in tradition and experience. Here Wesley is purposely adding "lived experience" to the Anglican triad of scripture, tradition, and reason.

Volume eleven of Wesley's *Works* contains not only his *Appeals* but also multiple other long letters and tracts, and for good reason. They are responses to his primary critics, mainly Anglican bishops and leading lights who found his teachings dangerous to the wellbeing of the Church. Wesley had all these persons in view when he wrote the *Appeals*, and the student who wishes to get the full picture will be instructed by reading them as well. Although they appeared initially as three publications with four distinct parts, Wesley (and his theological heirs) always refer to them as a single entity. This being the case, it is clear that Wesley assigned the *Appeals* a distinctive and important place among his writings. In his mind, they are a telling defense of his teachings and of the Methodist movement as a whole. He referred to them repeatedly in his *Letters* as well as in his *Journal*.[14] Indeed, he is not reticent to assert that, taken as a whole, his *Appeals* constitute an apologetic *tour de force*: "I have again and again communicated my thoughts on most heads to all mankind; [and] I believe intelligibly, particularly in the *Appeals to Men of Reason and Religion*."[15]

The *Earnest Appeal* is more compact than *A Farther Appeal*, more closely reasoned and tightly knit rhetorically. As a result, it is also the more telling in apologetic force. All of the assumptions that get unpacked in his *Farther Appeal* are in place in the first treatise. His aim is to persuade "either men of no religion at all or men of a lifeless, formal religion" that "there is a better religion to be attained."[16] Wesley is certain that most of his conversation partners are "men of reason," self-assured because of their superior intelligence, feeling no need of true religion, though they were clearly ignorant both of its nature and of its power. The presenting problem for his rationalist brethren is that the "men of religion" were too often lulled into a false sense of security by the formal propriety of the faith they professed.

Wesley never depreciated the importance of correct belief (orthodoxy), but that was not his fundamental concern. His concern was to establish the primacy of love for God and love for neighbor. When our love for God responds to God's love for us, then we are able to love our neighbor adequately and properly. We discover that this love is "the fountain of all the good we have received and of all we ever hope to enjoy."[17] Wesley was convinced, and he was determined to convince all who would listen to him or read his tracts and sermons, that a proper definition of the Christian faith was always and indissolubly connected to lived-out patterns of life. It was a matter of both the head and the heart. "Faith," he asserted, "is that divine evidence whereby the spiritual man discerneth God, and the things of God. It is with regard to the spiritual world what the [five] sense[s] are with regard to the natural order. It is the spiritual sensation of every soul that is born of God."[18] For Wesley this included the full range of spiritual sensibilities, and among these he included not only feelings and emotions, but also sight, hearing, and taste as well. He conceived the human being as a fully interconnected creature among all of these faculties, and he takes considerable care in his *Appeals* to develop a theology that accounts for the wholeness of humanity.

The essential argument of *The Appeals*

Due to the increasing volume of polemic against him and the revival leaders, Wesley was well aware that in many quarters his theology was regarded as novel and dangerous. With some care he defined exactly what he meant by the technical terms he used, and then he proceeded to "prove" that in every instance his interpretation coincided exactly with that of the official pronouncement of the Church of England. By voluminous quotation he showed that the Book of Common Prayer, the Thirty-nine Articles, and the Anglican *Homilies* all supported his teachings. Then in a brief summary, he epitomized his argument thus far:

> The doctrine of the Church of England appears to be this: (1). That no good work, properly so called, can go before justification. (2). That no degree of true sanctification can be previous to it. (3). That as the meritorious cause of justification is the life and death of Christ, so the condition of it is faith, faith alone. And, (4). That both inward and outward holiness are consequent on this faith, and are the ordinary stated condition of final justification.[19]

Time and again we read from Wesley that Methodism was in fact no more than the retrieval of authentic Anglicanism, lost in a cloud of English moralism that substituted being polite and publicly moral for the transformational power of the gospel. Indeed, Wesley maintained that this constituted a recovery of orthodox Christianity from the first centuries of the church, what he termed "primitive Christianity." To read Wesley's *Appeals* is to discover that the first Methodists were characterized by a love for scripture, a deep personal piety, a commitment to the historic Christian faith, and a comprehensive conviction that divine saving grace was available to all—a saving grace sufficient to fully transform from sinner to saint.

Notes

1. *The Appeals to Men of Reason and Religion and Certain Related Open Letters*, Ed. Gerald R. Cragg. *The Bicentennial Edition of the Works of John Wesley,* XI (Oxford: The Clarendon Press, 1975), 37–325.
2. *A Farther Appeal* consists of three parts and was published in two stages; however, it is intended to be viewed as a single work. At least, Wesley usually referred to it as such. No fewer than ten editions of the *Appeals* appeared in Wesley's lifetime, and they were always published together as a single work in four parts.
3. *A Farther Appeal*, Pt. I, initial paragraph.
4. Ibid.
5. *Journal*, Jan. 26, 1777.
6. Modern Methodists have proposed the "Wesleyan Quadrilateral" to account for Wesley's addition of experience to the Anglican triad of scripture, tradition, and reason; however, this expression was never used by Wesley.

Since Wesley never used the word quadrilateral, it is anachronistic to use it or discuss the modern convention in relation to an eighteenth-century document. Cf. W. Stephen Gunter, ed., *Wesley and the Quadrilateral. Renewing the Conversation* (Nashville: Kingswood Books, 1989).

7. *Sermons*, "The Case of Reason Impartially Considered," II.10.
8. *Journal*, June 15, 1741. Wesley had been reading Luther's Commentary on Galatians.
9. *An Earnest Appeal,* §31. See also, §§ 20–28.
10. Ibid., §§2–12.
11. Ibid., §§ 55–56. See also *Sermons*, "Christian Perfection;" "A Plain Account of Christian Perfection;" and, "Brief Thoughts on Christian Perfection."
12. *Journal*, Nov. 24, 1739.
13. *A Farther Appeal*, Pt. I, I.27, and Pt. III, II. 10, and III.I. Wesley's most comprehensive apologetic for his brand of enthusiasm is his sermon, "The Nature of Enthusiasm." His sermons on the "Witness of the Spirit" are also instructive.
14. *Journal*, Jan. 28, 1745; Jan. 8, 1746; Jan. 6, 1748; Sept. 20, 1748; Apr. 26, 1756.
15. *Journal*, Jan 5, 1761.
16. *An Earnest Appeal*, §2.
17. Ibid., §§ 2,3.
18. Ibid., §6.
19. Ibid. Pt. I, II.8. In the 1772 edition of his works, Wesley took care to indicate the supreme importance he attached to this passage of the *Farther Appeal*.

Select Bibliography

Primary sources

Wesley, John. *The Works of John Wesley*. 14 vols. Edited by Thomas Jackson. Reprint of 1872 Wesleyan Conference Edition. Kansas City: Beacon Hill Press, 1958.

Wesley, John. *The Appeals to Men of Reason and Religion and Certain Related Open Letters*, Ed. Gerald R. Cragg. *The Bicentennial Edition of the Works of John Wesley,* XI (Oxford: The Clarendon Press, 1975).

Wesley, John. *The Bicentennial Edition of the Works of John Wesley*. Editors: Frank Baker, Richard P. Heitzenrater, and Randy Maddox. Oxford: Clarendon Press and Nashville: Abingdon Press, 1975. To date twenty-one volumes of this critical edition have been published.

Wesley, John. *Sermons*. 4 vols. Edited by Albert C. Outler. *The Bicentennial Edition of the Works of John Wesley*. Nashville: Abingdon Press, 1984–87.

Secondary sources

Collins, Kenneth J. *The Theology of John Wesley: Holy Love and the Shape of Grace*. Nashville: Abingdon Press, 2007.

Gunter, W. Stephen Gunter. *The Limits of "Love Divine" John Wesley's Response to Antinomianism and Enthusiasm*. Nashville: Kingswood Books, 1989.

Ibid. Editor. *Wesley and the Quadrilateral: Renewing the Conversation*. Nashville: Abingdon Press, 1997.

Heitzenrater, Richard P. *Wesley and the People Called Methodists*. Nashville: Abingdon Press, 1995.

Maddox, Randy L. *Responsible Grace. John Wesley's Practical Theology*. Nashville: Kingswood Books, 1994.

Rack, Henry. *Reasonable Enthusiast. John Wesley and the Rise of Methodism*. Nashville: Abingdon Press, 1992.

The Pilgrim's Progress (Part 1, 1678; Part 2, 1684)

John Bunyan (1628–1688)

Figure 4.7 John Bunyan

The life and works of John Bunyan[1]

When John Bunyan arrived at the village of Lower Samsell in November 1660 to preach to a house congregation, a friend warned him to turn back home. Justice Francis Wingate was hoping to arrest him there. Bunyan wrestled with whether or not he should go but finally determined that he must set an example of strength for his congregation. So on November 12, 1660, Bunyan began the service in a small house but made it no further than the opening prayer. The constable immediately arrested him for preaching without a license.[2]

While Bunyan was on his way to jail, two friends secured a promise that he would be freed if he simply agreed to stop preaching. Bunyan was a tinker (a metal-utensil repairman), and the authorities wanted him to keep to his profession. They believed the state should regulate who should preach—only trained, licensed pastors—and where—only established Church of England parishes, not unauthorized gatherings in homes. All Bunyan had to do was promise to stop preaching. But he refused. Bunyan repudiated the notion of no longer proclaiming the gospel. And because he would not go against his conscience, he remained in prison—for twelve years! But those twelve years provided the environment out of which would emerge one of the most celebrated works in all history, *The Pilgrim's Progress*.[3]

Born in 1628 in the village of Elstow, near Bedford, England, John Bunyan grew up in the midst of tensions between King Charles I (r. 1625–1649) and the mostly Puritan English Parliament. At age sixteen, Bunyan was pressed into military service for Parliament in Oliver Cromwell's (1599–1658) New Model Army.[4] Eventually Charles I lost the war (and his head), and Parliament began to rule, establishing a degree of religious tolerance for groups like the separatists, who significantly influenced Bunyan's spiritual development.

In the early 1650s, Bunyan suffered a "period of despair" that mirrored his later fictionalized Slough of Despond. Through the preaching of separatist Baptist preacher John Gifford, Bunyan came to a crisis of faith, first despairing of salvation and then finding assurance. This religious experience served as the basis for his description of the pilgrim in *The Pilgrim's Progress*.[5]

About a year after Gifford died in 1655, Bunyan himself began to preach and was well received. However, by 1660 King Charles II (r. 1660–1685) was restored to the throne, ending Parliamentary rule and its limited religious toleration.[6] That was the same year that Bunyan's unlicensed preaching landed him in prison, where he remained for twelve years (1660–1672). While his imprisonment cut him off from his people, it gave him focused time to write a number of religious works, including his spiritual autobiography, *Grace Abounding to the Chief of Sinners* (1666),[7] and much of Part 1 of *The Pilgrim's Progress* (c. 1668–1671).[8]

As soon as Bunyan was released in 1672, he began preaching and showed no slowed pace in writing. When a renewed persecution of separatists and nonconformists broke out in 1675, Bunyan was imprisoned again, and during that six-month period in jail, he likely completed Part 1 of *The Pilgrim's Progress*. Theologian and nonconformist leader John Owen (1616–1683)[9] seems to have intervened on Bunyan's behalf, securing his release as well as a publisher for *The Pilgrim's Progress*, Part 1 of which was published in 1678, followed by Part 2 in 1684.[10] In his last twelve years, Bunyan avoided further imprisonment while he continued preaching. Yet preaching meant traveling, and exposure to ill weather led to Bunyan's death on August 31, 1688.[11]

Bunyan's most important work by far is *The Pilgrim's Progress*. He also penned follow-up volumes to this allegory, *The Life and Death of Mr. Badman* (1680) and *The Holy War* (1682).[12] Besides his five fictional books and seven poetry collections, he wrote mostly nonfictional works, forty-six of which have survived, including sermons, a catechism, children's books,[13] pamphlets on theological controversies, and works of practical theology.[14]

Allegory

John Bunyan's *The Pilgrim's Progress* is theology in the form of a story—more specifically, the form of an allegory. That classification should not leave one with the idea that the story is mere fantasy. To the contrary, the characters, places, and journey all represent something larger about real life, illuminating the *types* of people who live in this world and travel to the next.[15]

Bunyan's "Dream"[16] recounts the tale of the pilgrim "Christian" as he runs for his life from his home town, the City of Destruction. On his voyage, he faces challenge after challenge—the Slough of Despond, the Valley of Death, Vanity Fair, Doubting Castle, and many other trials that portray the very real challenges presented to Christians. He also has many moments of joy and relief. Part 1 ends with Christian and his companion Hopeful crossing the River Death and entering the Celestial City. Part 2 of *The Pilgrim's Progress* tells the journey of Christian's wife, Christiana, and their four boys. While they originally refused to follow Christian, they change their minds and set off on their own pilgrimage. Ultimately, they make it through many trials, largely by traveling with the brave, reliable Great-heart.

While seventeenth-century Protestants harbored suspicions of interpreting the Bible allegorically, they had never lost their appreciation for typological interpretation, which helps explain the success of *The Pilgrim's Progress*. Bunyan defended his use of metaphors and figures by arguing that the Bible employs them too. He appealed to Hosea 12:10, where God says, "I have ... used similitudes" (KJV). He believed that through "dark words" rays of truth "shine" through (1, 5). As Batson puts it, Bunyan viewed allegory as "a persuasive way of making important matters known through figurative expression."[17] Allegory illuminates the reader's world and his or her experience in it.

Scripture

W.R. Owens says that the significant role of the Bible on Bunyan's thought "cannot be overemphasized."[18] The Bible dominated English culture in the seventeenth century, and it was Bunyan's most important source in his writings.[19] It spilled out in the very language of *The Pilgrim's Progress*—a nod to the fruit of the Reformation watchword *sola scriptura*.

The Bible appears in the first picture we get of Christian. Bunyan says, "I saw a man cloathed with Raggs ... a Book in his hand, and a great burden upon his back. I looked, and saw him open the Book ... and as he Read, he wept and trembled ... saying, *what shall I do?*" (10). From the very beginning, this "Book" drives Christian's journey. In it he sees his dire situation in the City of Destruction and finds the guidance he needs to leave in pursuit of life.

It naturally follows that the rest of the narrative—not to mention the marginalia—is saturated with biblical language and references. Christian returns to "the Book" as his source for truth time and again. He and his companions Faithful and Hopeful often quote Scripture to those opposed to their journey and also encourage each other with it (e.g., 14–15, 39, 80, 102–103, 148). The Bible is completely reliable because, as Christian's son Matthew affirms, it is "the Holy Word of God" (213). With such a high view of Scripture, it is no surprise that Bunyan took his overarching metaphor of the pilgrim from the Bible (see Heb. 11:13–16).[20]

Calvinism

The metaphor of pilgrimage highlights the human experience, as we will see below. Yet Gordon Campbell argues that Bunyan's almost exclusive focus on human experience "results in the suppression of one of his central beliefs—election to salvation and reprobation."[21] Campbell's argument goes too far. Roger Pooley brings out Bunyan's Calvinism clearly when he notes that "the journey [Christian] takes is not that of an Everyman figure, but of an elect Christian."[22] As Richard Greaves observes, someone can only enter the Celestial City if he or she first walks through the Wicket-gate, "which can only be opened by Christ"—a clear allusion to the doctrine of election.[23]

The doctrine of predestination underscores the belief that salvation comes only by God's grace, not by human works. So Christian goes on pilgrimage because "the Light of Light was given him," a reference to God's gracious initiative. God's initiating grace is comforting because God is powerful enough to overcome barriers that humans cannot. So if the Sun of Righteousness determines to "arise upon" a "Man in a Mountain of Ice," that man's "frozen Heart shall feel a Thaw." As Bunyan observes in a marginal note, "There is no perswasion will do, if God openeth not the eyes" (169, 232, 39).

A discussion of Bunyan's Calvinism, however, requires some nuance. As a separatist, he agreed on the basic tenets of Calvinist theology yet differed from strict Calvinists in certain respects (e.g., baptism, church government). Bunyan's thought also had a "hybrid character," drawing together Luther's writings, his Calvinist theology, and Independent Baptists beliefs, thus leading Greaves to caution against attaching any single label to Bunyan.[24]

Perhaps this mixed theological pedigree helps explain the tension in Bunyan's theology of election as presented in *The Pilgrim's Progress*, which Batson highlights clearly: "Even though one is among the elect and election is final and unchangeable, the 'elected' individual must still go through the various stages on the way from the City of Destruction to the Celestial City."[25] Bunyan held firmly to a Calvinist view of election, yet he wrote from the viewpoint of the human pilgrim.

Pilgrimage

On the book's title page, Bunyan describes the story as showing the pilgrim's progress "from This World, to That which is to come." Christian is on pilgrimage to "a better Countrey; that is, an Heavenly." His is a "desperate Journey," one that looks like foolishness to the world but is the only sensible option to those who trust in the King of the land. Thus, in one of the most poignant—and controversial—images in the book, Christian sticks his

Figure 4.8 John Bunyan in *The Pilgrim's Progress*

fingers in his ears to block out the cries of his family calling him to return. How could he leave his kin for such a perilous path? We find out in the words he shouts as he runs: "Life, Life, Eternal Life" (1, 50, 68, 13). This scene illustrates several issues connected with pilgrimage. We will highlight five particulars.

First, Christian faces several challenges on his way to the Celestial City. *The Pilgrim's Progress* shows well that the journey of faith leading to heavenly bliss is no walk in the park. It demands perseverance through trials. As the Visitor says to Christiana, "The bitter is before the sweet: Thou must through Troubles ... enter this Celestial City." Evangelist sums it up by saying that the only way to enter the kingdom of heaven is "through many tribulations" (171, 85; cf. 256).

Second, Christian runs into numerous people with erroneous views who threaten to lead him astray. His wife and children represent such figures in the beginning, but the number and variety of misguided people only increases. The figure Mr. By-ends embodies a life of seeking to be friends with all while having convictions about nothing. Ignorance believes that pilgrims can arrive at the Celestial City by any number of paths, as if all religious roads lead to heaven (98, 120). These and other characters represent enticing yet false views about the journey to God.

Third, while Christian gets many things right, he also gets many things wrong. Evangelist reprimands him for listening to Mr. Worldly-Wiseman. Christian berates himself for falling asleep on the hill called Difficulty and losing his sealed roll. Hopeful and Christian even break into an argument (20–23, 44, 123–125). Christian addresses his flaws by appealing to his repentance from sin and to God's forgiveness, finding comfort in God's presence (59, 63).

Fourth, God's presence is perhaps most palpable in human companionship. Christian cannot go it alone. An invaluable aspect of such companionship is conversation with other pilgrims, leading Mullett to note that "the book is a dialogue at least as much as it is a travelogue"[26] (131, 253). Part 2 especially underscores that the road is best traveled in the company of others. With so many more travelers, Part 2 also illustrates a diversity of people who make it to the Celestial City—not only Faithful and Hopeful but also Fearing, Feeblemind, Despondencie, and Much-a-fraid (164–65, 286–88). Because of God's grace, people from all walks of life and of all temperaments can enjoy the bliss of the Celestial City.

Finally, we see that the journey is completely worth every trial, even the temporal loss of kin. Bunyan illustrated this in the celebration of Christian and the other pilgrims arriving at the Celestial City. Yet Bunyan devoted far less time to portraying the Celestial City than the journey to get there, and so Owens argues that "the central, enduring quality of his book lies in its portrayal of the pilgrims' lives in the world."[27] On the one hand, he is right: the book *is* about the pilgrimage. And yet the Celestial City remains the linchpin of that pilgrimage. Without it, the whole program falls to pieces. With it, pilgrims can endure various trials and find freedom from every failure, encouraging each other on the way.

Grace

It is significant that the name Christian is given to him after he begins his journey. Previously he was known as Graceless (47). This transformation shows how central grace is to Bunyan's plot. He who is Graceless can only become a Christian by receiving the good grace of God.

Grace highlights the inability of humans to meet God's standard and God's gift to undeserving humans of freedom from sin and entrance into bliss. The freedom from sin comes to Christian when he approaches the cross, where suddenly "his burden loosed from off his Shoulders, and fell from off his back" and rolled away until he "saw it no more." In response to his burden tumbling away, Christian rejoices that God has "given me rest, by his sorrow; and life, by his death" (37). By emphasizing that Christian receives this gift by mere sight of the cross, Bunyan showed that freedom from sin is indeed "given" by God, not merited by sinners.

Perhaps the clearest statement on grace comes from Christian's conversation with Ignorance. Ignorance believes he will be justified through God's "gracious acceptance of [his] obedience to his Law." Christian shows that this thinking is erroneous because it "maketh not Christ a Justifier of thy person, but of thy actions; and of thy person for thy actions sake." On the contrary, Christian argues, grace is not God justifying our actions but God justifying us because we flee to Christ, whose righteousness is imputed to us. Ignorance's response is telling: "What! would you have us trust to what Christ in his own person has done without us?"[28] This discussion echoes the longstanding disagreement between Protestants and Catholics over the nature of justifying faith.

Justifying faith, however, does imply more than a mere assent to the gospel, as Talkative's counterfeit faith illustrates. Talkative rightly acknowledges that "a man can receive nothing except it be given him from Heaven; all is of Grace, not of works." But while Talkative understands that grace is a gift, he only talks about it without ever placing his faith in Christ. Yet only the "knowledge that is accompanied with the grace of faith and love … puts a man upon doing even the will of God from the heart" (76, 80).

Such an argument seems to constitute a denial of the Reformation doctrine of justification by faith alone. But in the larger context of the book, we see that Bunyan is bringing out a tension between God's grace and the Christian's struggle. Christian's dialogue with Ignorance makes this clear. As Mullett explains, "Bunyan does not so much contradict his own acceptance of the Protestant doctrine of justification by faith, as strive for a balance between the antinomian error of faith (or talk without good works) and

Pelagian over-confidence in personal virtue."[29] Said another way, the free grace Bunyan celebrated in his book still assumed that recipients of such grace would change, for no one believes that "a man can be a living Monument of Grace, that is a Slave to his own Corruptions" (247; cf. 81–83). This tension shows how, in writing this work, Bunyan aimed "to entice people to embrace the gospel," yet at the same time also sought to "edify and support those who had already embarked on the pilgrimage."[30]

Legacy

The Pilgrim's Progress ranks as one of the most beloved books from the modern era. Later literature has made countless allusions to this story, and it has been translated into more than two hundred languages.[31] Even in his own day, Bunyan's masterpiece was a blockbuster, becoming "the most popular work of prose fiction in the seventeenth century."[32] At the same time, those in the upper echelons of society and even some of his own friends looked down on it as a vulgar work for the populace—"satire, laughter and popular fiction."[33]

That assessment continued to hold some sway in eighteenth-century high society, but in the nineteenth century, Bunyan's fame soared as the Victorians rediscovered and celebrated *The Pilgrim's Progress*.[34] It influenced such writers as Charlotte Brontë, George Eliot, and Charles Dickens, and it appealed to all classes, being printed in countless editions—expensive for the wealthy, cheap for the poor, and heavily illustrated for the illiterate.[35] The exploding missionary enterprise of the nineteenth century also took the book around the world.[36]

Themes from *The Pilgrim's Progress* echoed into the twentieth century.[37] While the allegory has gradually lost its eminent position,[38] *The Pilgrim's Progress* has seen continued interest in the twenty-first century among not only committed Christians but also literary scholars. Thus, Anne Dunan-Page concludes that *The Pilgrim's Progress* is "arguably the finest allegory in the English language"[39]—a fitting assessment for a book with such wide-reaching influence.

Conclusion

For all the interest English departments have shown it, *The Pilgrim's Progress* was written by a man ultimately interested less in literary accolades than in altered lives. For that reason, Gerald Bray rightly describes Bunyan as "a spiritual giant" who "left an indelible mark on the spirituality of the church ever since," especially in the evangelical movement that sprang up in the eighteenth century and spread apart from the institutional church.[40] This movement mirrored Bunyan's own separatist sympathies and his emphasis on the individual experience so palpable in *The Pilgrim's Progress*.

Bunyan explained that he wrote of one pilgrim so that he might "make a Travailer" of the reader, that the reader might find "Truth within a Fable." Ultimately, though the narrative seemed like a "Novelty," he held that it contained "Nothing but sound and honest Gospel-strains," which might help the traveler find "the everlasting Prize" (8). He aimed to inspire and encourage all to enter through the Wicket-gate and walk the arduous path to the Celestial City. While our end rests in the hands of a sovereign God, Bunyan believed that should give us hope, for we are unable to make it there on our own. Only God provides life-giving grace, thus making it possible for people to be transformed and to overcome the inevitable challenges of this world. Read *The Pilgrim's Progress* to better understand yourself, to grasp the contours of the dangerous journey of the Christian life, and to find hope that you—whether a Hopeful, a Great-heart, a Christiana, or a Feeblemind—might also arrive, by God's grace, at the Celestial City.

Notes

1. For Bunyan's life, I have relied especially on Richard L. Greaves, *John Bunyan*, Courtenay Studies in Reformation Theology 2 (Grand Rapids, MI: Eerdmans, 1969), 15–26; Lynn Veach Sadler, *John Bunyan*, Twayne English Authors 260 (Boston: Twayne, 1979), 13–31. For an extensive treatment of Bunyan's life, see Richard L. Greaves, *Glimpses of Glory: John Bunyan and English Dissent* (Stanford, CA: Stanford University Press, 2002). For more on Bunyan's historical context, see Anne Laurence, W.R. Owens, and Stuart Sim, eds., *John Bunyan and His England, 1628–88* (London: Hambledon, 1990).
2. Greaves, *Glimpses of Glory*, 1–2, 131–32; Sadler, *John Bunyan*, 20–21.
3. Greaves, *Glimpses of Glory*, 1–2, 127–45; Sadler, *John Bunyan*, 21–25.
4. Greaves, *John Bunyan*, 16.
5. Greaves, *John Bunyan*, 16–19; Sadler, *John Bunyan*, 14–15.
6. Greaves, *John Bunyan*, 21; W.R. Owens, "Introduction," in John Bunyan, *The Pilgrim's Progress*, ed. W.R. Owens, Oxford World's Classics (New York:

Oxford University Press, 2003), xv–xvi. On Bunyan's promotion of religious toleration in *The Pilgrim's Progress*, see Greaves, *Glimpses of Glory*, 222–27.

7. See Michael Davies, "*Grace Abounding to the Chief of Sinners*: John Bunyan and Spiritual Autobiography," in *The Cambridge Companion to Bunyan*, ed. Anne Dunan-Page (Cambridge, UK: Cambridge University Press, 2010), 67–79.

8. Greaves, *Glimpses of Glory*, 218.

9. See the chapter on Owen in this volume (Chapter 4.2).

10. Sadler, *John Bunyan*, 26–27; Anne Dunan-Page, ed., *The Cambridge Companion to Bunyan* (Cambridge, UK: Cambridge University Press, 2010), xvii.

11. Sadler, *John Bunyan*, 29.

12. See Stuart Sim, "Bunyan and the Early Novel: *The Life and Death of Mr. Badman*," in Dunan-Page, *The Cambridge Companion to Bunyan*, 95–106; David Walker, "Militant Religion and Politics in *The Holy War*," in Dunan-Page, *The Cambridge Companion to Bunyan*, 107–19.

13. See Shannon Murray, "*A Book for Boys and Girls: Or, Country Rhimes for Children*: Bunyan and Literature for Children," in Dunan-Page, *The Cambridge Companion to Bunyan*, 120–34.

14. Anne Dunan-Page, "Introduction," in Dunan-Page, *The Cambridge Companion to Bunyan*, 5.

15. On possible contemporary identities for Bunyan's characters, see Roger Pooley, "*The Pilgrim's Progress* and the Line of Allegory," in Dunan-Page, *The Cambridge Companion to Bunyan*, 85–88; Sadler, *John Bunyan*, 54–55.

16. John Bunyan, *The Pilgrim's Progress*, ed. W.R. Owens, Oxford World's Classics (New York: Oxford University Press, 2003), 10. In quotations of *The Pilgrim's Progress*, I have changed dialogue originally set in italics (when used for differentiating speakers) to roman type. Hereafter, all further references to this work shall be noted by employing in-text parenthetical citations.

17. E. Beatrice Batson, *John Bunyan: Allegory and Imagination* (Totowa, NJ: Barnes & Noble, 1984), 30–31. For more on *The Pilgrim's Progress* as an allegory, see Batson, *John Bunyan*, 28–55; Owens, "Introduction," xix–xxiv.

18. Owens, "Introduction," xxiv. See also Owens, "John Bunyan and the Bible," 47–48; Sadler, *John Bunyan*, 108; Michael Mullett, *John Bunyan in Context*, Studies in Protestant Nonconformity (Keele, Staffordshire: Keele University Press, 1996), 206.

19. W.R. Owens, "John Bunyan and the Bible," in Dunan-Page, *The Cambridge Companion to Bunyan*, 39–50. On Bunyan's sources for *The Pilgrim's Progress*, see Greaves, *Glimpses of Glory*, 229–43.

20. Owens, "Introduction," xxvi.

21. Gordon Campbell, "The Theology of *The Pilgrim's Progress*," in *The Pilgrim's Progress: Critical and Historical Views*, ed. Vincent Newey (Totowa, NJ: Barnes & Noble, 1980), 256.

22. Pooley, "Line of Allegory," 86. See also Dunan-Page, "Introduction," 6; Sharrock, "Life and Story," 62.

23. Greaves, *Glimpses of Glory*, 261; Batson, *John Bunyan*, 41. For more on Bunyan's understanding of election, see Greaves, *John Bunyan*, 49–67.

24. Greaves, *John Bunyan*, 23–25, 159. Quotation on 25.

25. Batson, *John Bunyan*, 41. Christopher Hill makes a similar argument in "Bunyan's Contemporary Reputation," in Laurence, Owens, and Sim, *John Bunyan and His England, 1628–88*, 13.

26. Mullett, *John Bunyan in Context*, 194; Bunyan, *The Pilgrim's Progress*, 131, 253.

27. Owens, "Introduction," xxxviii.

28. Bunyan, *The Pilgrim's Progress*, 140. In contrast, see Christian and Hopeful's gratitude for grace at 23, 28, 133–34.

29. Mullett, *John Bunyan in Context*, 201.

30. Greaves, *Glimpses of Glory*, 221, 222.

31. Owens, "Introduction," xiii; Dunan-Page, "Introduction," 3.

32. Richard L. Greaves, "Bunyan through the Centuries: Some Reflections," *English Studies* 64 (1983): 113. See also N.H. Keeble, "John Bunyan's Literary Life," in Dunan-Page, *The Cambridge Companion to Bunyan*, 22–23.

33. Mullett, *John Bunyan in Context*, 202. See also Keeble, "Literary Life," 22; Anne Dunan-Page, "Posthumous Bunyan: Early Lives and the Development of the Canon," in Dunan-Page, *The Cambridge Companion to Bunyan*, 138; Greaves, *Glimpses of Glory*, 219–20.

34. Greaves, "Bunyan through the Centuries," 113–17; Emma Mason, "The Victorians and Bunyan's Legacy," in *The Cambridge Companion to Bunyan*, 150–61; Dunan-Page, "Introduction," 3; Hill, "Bunyan's Contemporary Reputation," 15.

35. Mason, "Victorians," 153–59.

36. Owens, "Introduction," xxxviii.

37. Greaves, "Bunyan through the Centuries," 117–21; Dunan-Page, "Introduction," 3; Isabel Hofmeyr, "Bunyan: Colonial, Postcolonial," in Dunan-Page, *The Cambridge Companion to Bunyan*, 162–76.

38. Roger Sharrock, "Life and Story in *The Pilgrim's Progress*," in Newey, *The Pilgrim's Progress: Critical and Historical Views*, 49; Greaves, "Bunyan through the Centuries," 117–18.

39. Dunan-Page, "Introduction," 7. See the similar assessments by Pooley, "Line of Allegory," 92; Mullett, *John Bunyan in Context*, 206.

40. Gerald Bray, *God Has Spoken: A History of Christian Theology* (Wheaton, IL: Crossway, 2014), 725.

Select Bibliography

Primary sources

Bunyan, John. *The Works of John Bunyan*. Edited by George Offor. 3 vols. Glasgow: Blackie and Son, 1853.

Bunyan, John. *The Pilgrim's Progress*. Edited by W.R. Owens. Oxford World's Classics. New York: Oxford University Press, 2003.

Secondary sources

Dunan-Page, Anne, ed. *The Cambridge Companion to Bunyan*. Cambridge, UK: Cambridge University Press, 2010.

Greaves, Richard L. *John Bunyan*. Courtenay Studies in Reformation Theology 2. Grand Rapids, MI: Eerdmans, 1969.

Mullett, Michael. *John Bunyan in Context*. Studies in Protestant Nonconformity. Keele, Staffordshire: Keele University Press, 1996.

Sadler, Lynn Veach. *John Bunyan*. Twayne English Authors 260. Boston: Twayne, 1979.

4.10

The Westminster Standards (1643–1647)

The story of the Westminster Standards[1]

Many believe that the Westminster Standards represent the apex of Reformed theology in the early modern period.[2] They certainly culminated more than a century of theological reflection. These documents, though drafted in a few short years, drew on decades of doctrinal debates within the Reformed tradition and even on centuries of Christian dialogue. And yet, had it not been for political tensions on the British Isles, the Westminster Standards may never have been written.

Standing in the background of those political tensions was a longstanding struggle between Roman Catholicism and Protestantism. Though a Roman Catholic at heart, King Henry VIII (r. 1509–1547) introduced a quasi-Protestantism into England largely because of his complicated relations with women and pursuit of a male heir. His children dealt with the fallout. Edward VI (r. 1547–1553) took England sharply toward Protestantism, but his half-sister Mary (r. 1553–1558) swung the pendulum back to Catholicism, producing several martyrs along the way. When their half-sister Elizabeth (r. 1558–1603) became queen, she sought to establish a middle way that kept England mostly Protestant but retained some Catholic liturgical elements.

Elizabeth's settlement set the stage for the seventeenth-century battles, as many wanted to purify the Church of England of those Catholic elements—these purists became known as Puritans. James I (r. 1603–1625) disappointed English Puritans by rejecting their reforms. When Charles I (r. 1625–1649) ascended the throne, he tried to impose the English Book of Common

Prayer on the Church of Scotland along with rituals that they deemed Catholic, reigniting English–Scottish tensions. Things got bad enough in 1640 that the king, who had been ruling without Parliament for eleven years, was forced to call Parliament into session to get their approval of funds for war. Parliament distrusted King Charles I in part because many perceived him to be a crypto-Catholic undermining all the Protestant progress in the foregoing century. Together these developments led not only to war with Scotland but also to civil war within England and eventually to war with Ireland.

With Parliament back in session, the House of Commons organized their list of religious grievances, which they gave to Charles I in December 1641— and which he ignored. Finally, in June 1643 Parliament disregarded him and called for a synod to address these matters. That summer the Westminster Assembly began meeting.

They started by revising the Church of England's Thirty-Nine Articles (1571), a statement of religious belief that codified the Elizabethan settlement. Puritans finally had a chance to rid it of any Roman Catholic elements. But the Assembly never completed the task because on September 25, 1643, the English Parliament made a treaty with Scotland against their king. Parliament had wanted Scotland as a military ally, but Scotland demanded religious solidarity as well. As Scottish minister Robert Baillie (1602–1662) put it, "The English were for a civill Leage, we for a religious Covenant."[3] So to ensure Scottish military aid, England signed the Solemn League and Covenant, committing themselves to join Scotland in reforming religion, and this agreement redirected the whole course of the Assembly. From that point, they broadened their goals, seeking to establish an entirely new form of church government, worship, and belief.

In April 1645 the Assembly turned their attention to a new confession of faith. Working in part from the Irish Articles of Religion (1615), a committee wrote the article on Scripture first and presented it to the full Assembly for debate, which was then refined by another committee before the Assembly approved the final form. The Westminster divines completed this painstaking process for all thirty-three articles on November 26, 1646. Since Parliament had appointed them merely as an advisory body, the Assembly had to present their work to Parliament for ratification, rejection, or redaction, which they did in December 1646. At the behest of Parliament, they added Scripture proof texts to the Confession, submitting the final version to Parliament in April 1647. The two catechisms followed, the Larger in October 1647 and the Shorter that November.

The Scottish Parliament ratified the Confession in 1649, and the English Rump Parliament adopted a slightly modified version in 1660. However, with the Restoration of the monarchy in 1660, the Confession was doomed to die an early death in the Church of England, which soon reinstated the Book of Common Prayer and the Thirty-Nine Articles. Nonetheless, the legacy of the Westminster Standards lived on in dissenting English churches and especially in Scottish Presbyterianism.

Roots and fruit

The authors[4] of the Westminster Standards drew on and synthesized several streams of thought, including patristic theology, sixteenth- and seventeenth-century Reformed theology, Lutheran theology, and other confessional documents (such as the Synod of Dort and the Irish Articles).[5] These multiple roots show that the Westminster divines were "not one-dimensional Calvinists."[6] In fact, the Westminster Assembly intentionally sought to build some theological latitude into the Standards, making room for a broad swath of Calvinists who agreed on much but debated some finer points of theology.[7] The Standards, then, display a significant degree of continuity with the sixteenth-century Reformers,[8] even as they reflect broader aims in a changed context.[9]

The Westminster Assembly produced a number of guiding documents, including the Directory for the Public Worship of God,[10] the Directory for Family Worship, *The Summe of Saving Knowledge*, and the Form of Presbyterial Church-Government. Much could be said about each of these documents, but we will focus on the Confession and two Catechisms, which have borne the longest-lasting influence. In treating the Westminster Standards, we could discuss all kinds of themes—they do, after all, outline an entire system of theology. But we will limit ourselves to four: glorifying and enjoying God, the Bible, God's sovereignty, and the Christian life. Recognizing that the text of the Westminster Standards has changed in some places over the years,[11] I quote from a 1647 edition of the Confession and a 1651 edition of the Catechisms.[12]

Glorifying and enjoying God

Perhaps the best-known language from the Westminster Standards comes from the opening question in the Shorter Catechism: "What is the chief end of man?" (WSC 1). In beginning with this question, the Catechism exposes perhaps the most burning questions for every human: Why am I here? What is my purpose?

The Shorter Catechism's answer is pithy and memorable: "Mans chief end is to glorifie God, and to enjoy him for ever" (WSC 1; cf. WLC 1). From the view of Westminster, every aspect of life is to be cast in the light of glorifying God. Immediately this statement redirects our focus from ourselves to God, inviting us to take in a grand vision of the Creator and find a greater purpose for life. Thus, in B.B. Warfield's view, the Westminster Shorter Catechism achieves what perhaps no other catechism has achieved, beginning not with the human condition or other "lower things" but "under the illumination of the vision of God in His glory."[13]

This emphasis on God's glory undergirds the whole theological program of Westminster. God has all glory within himself and derives none from his creatures (WC 2.2; cf. WLC 7; 9; WSC 6). Indeed, all that he does is for the purpose of his glory (WC 2.1), whether creation (WC 4.1), providence (WC 5.1; WLC 18; 19), the fall (WC 6.1), justification (WC 11.3), Christ's kingship (WLC 45), the appointment of civil magistrates (WC 23.1), or the final judgment (WC 33.2; WLC 56). Even God's eternal decrees—whether God's free electing grace or ordaining wrath—are for "the manifestation of his glory" (WC 3.3; cf. WSC 7; WLC 12; 13). God's aim for redeemed humanity is that they too might live for God's glory, might be glorified like Christ, and might dwell in God's glory (WC 3.6; 8.1; 9.5; 16.5; 18.1; 26.1; 32.1, 3; WSC 37; 38; WLC 65; 74; 82; 83; 85–87; 90).

The result of living a life that glorifies God is true enjoyment. Only when one lives in such a way that God's name is praised does one find the freedom to enjoy life, for one can only enjoy life if one is enjoying the Giver of life. So in discussing the similarly stated first question of the Larger Catechism, Johannes Geerhardus Vos argues that glorifying God contrasts starkly with man seeking first his own happiness because that places the purpose of life ultimately "within man himself," whereas "man's real happiness results from his recognizing and seeking his true end, namely, to glorify and enjoy God his Creator."[14]

The Bible

The Shorter Catechism moves directly from humanity's purpose of glorifying and enjoying God to the Scriptures as "the onely rule to direct us how we may glorifie and enjoy him" (WSC 2; cf. WLC 3). The Standards principally teach "what man is to believe concerning God, and what duty God requires of man" (WSC 3; cf. WLC 3).

The Standards' clearest statement on Scripture comes from the first article of the Confession: "Of the holy Scriptures." Its foremost position and its content echo the Reformation watchword *sola scriptura*. The Bible permeates the Standards; the margins of the Confession and Catechisms are literally filled with notes of Scripture proofs. The elevation of Scripture is, as J. V. Fesko puts it, "the pulse that throbs through the Westminster Standards."[15]

The opening paragraph argues for the *necessity* of Scripture. God has revealed much in creation, but "the Light of Nature" is "not sufficient" for the knowledge "necessary unto salvation," so God spoke in various ways to the prophets and apostles and then preserved his word in writing, which makes the Scripture "most necessary" (WC 1.1). Scripture is also *sufficient*, especially for salvation; God in his Word has given "all things necessary for … mans salvation, Faith and Life" (WC 1.6; cf. WC 1.1).

The Confession goes on to assert the *authority* of Scripture, an authority that rests not on humans or human institutions, such as the church, but on God alone. Because God "is Truth it self" and "the Author" of Scripture, "it is to be received" as "the Word of God" (WC 1.4). The authority of Scripture is supported by the *nature* of Scripture as inspired by God (WC 1.2). Two centuries later, theologians debated whether this meant that the Confession affirmed the inerrancy of Scripture.[16] But while the late nineteenth-century context raised questions not discussed in the seventeenth-century and while the Confession did not use the term *inerrancy*, the Assembly nonetheless assumed the full reliability of the Bible. Thus they described it as having "incomparable Excellencies," noted "the intire perfection thereof," and affirmed their "full perswausion and assurance of the infallible truth, and Divine authority thereof" (WC 1.5).

This first article sets the tone for the rest of the Confession, defining both the sources of theology and the method for developing doctrine[17]— particularly the principle that Scripture is the best interpreter of Scripture (WC 1.9). The Westminster divines elevated Scripture as the supreme guide in their theological program.

God's sovereignty

The Assembly's confidence in Scripture arose in part from their belief in God's sovereignty. As the fully sovereign Creator of all existence (WC

4.1–2), God is able to reveal and preserve his Word. And he equally exercises his providential control over all existence (WC 5.1–7). This emphasis on God's sovereignty constituted a defining mark of the Westminster Standards.

The Westminster divines weaved the doctrine of God's sovereignty throughout the Standards. From creation to redemption to consummation, the triune God is the agent of action. Highlighting his sovereign power, the Confession states that God is "almighty, most wise, most holy, most free" (WC 2.1). Because God "alone" is "all-sufficient," he "hath most Soveraign Dominion over [his creatures], to do by them, for them, or upon them whatsoever himself pleaseth" (WC 2.2). But he is not capricious; rather, his action is confined by his holiness. Thus the Confession portrays God as both "most loving, gracious, merciful" and "most just, and terrible in his judgments" (WC 2.1). This juxtaposition sets up the Confession for its controversial discussion of God's decrees.

In the opening of the third chapter, "Of Gods eternall Decree," we find what Fesko claims "is arguably one of the most cherished and at the same time vilified statements in the history of theology."[18] The chapter begins, "God from all eternity did, by the most wise and holy counsell of his own Will, freely, and unchangeably ordain whatsoever comes to pass" (WC 3.1). Some balk at this statement for its apparent fatalism. Yet the authors nuanced their understanding of God's sovereignty.[19] In their view, this assertion laid no blame at God's feet for sin because God's ordaining of future history did no "violence" to human free will (WC 3.1); thus the creatures are to blame for the fall into sin, which in turn curtailed their freedom by making them slaves to sin (WC 6.1–6; cf. WC 5.4). Furthermore, God works through "second Causes" to accomplish his foreordained decrees (WC 3.1; cf. WC 5.2).

The Confession fleshes out God's sovereignty by asserting that God predestined to eternal life a particular, unchangeable number whom he elected not based on foresight of anything they would do—in contrast with the teachings of Jacob Arminius (1560–1609)[20]—but by "his meer free grace and love" (WC 3.3; cf. WC 3.2, 5). In affirming this doctrine, the Westminster divines sought to expunge any glory for humans and instead exalt the glory of God's grace.

The natural corollary of God electing some to eternal life is God foreordaining others to eternal death (WC 3.3). Thus "God was pleased," the Confession states, "to pass by" the rest of mankind and "to ordain them to dishonour and wrath for their sin," magnifying God's "glorious justice" (WC 3.7). The doctrine of double predestination is distasteful to many, but one should not miss that the Westminster divines described it as a "high Mystery" beyond human understanding that must be "handled with speciall prudence and care," one that is meant to provide assurance and "consolation" to believers (WC 3.8).

The Christian life

With the Westminster Confession's emphases on God's glory and sovereignty and with its penchant for theological precision, some have criticized it as dry, intellectual, and detached. On the contrary, the members of the Assembly themselves were deeply committed to Christ and to nurturing warm-hearted spiritual experiences.[21] And they devoted a full two-thirds of the Confession to analytically describing the Christian life.[22]

One of the ways the Westminster divines attended to the Christian life was by adopting covenant theology, which moderated the abstract divine decrees by focusing on how God worked them out in history and thus on how God and humanity engaged with each other.[23] In many ways William Ames's (1576–1633) covenantal approach to theology—in which he sought to unpack the practical outworking of theology—paved the way for the moral theology of the Westminster Standards.[24]

This connection between theology and practice is visible in the structure of the Standards, which reflects the conviction that transformed living follows transformed thinking. Moving from God's sovereignty to redemptive history, the Confession then highlights five stages of the Christian experience: effectual calling, justification, adoption, sanctification, and glorification. By far the most time is spent on the sanctification stage, addressing practical matters from good works and Sabbath keeping to oaths, marriage, and divorce. It devotes significant space to how Christians should conduct themselves in worship and in community.

The Catechisms follow the same general structure. The Larger Catechism is particularly known for its extensive treatment of the Ten Commandments. The law is universally useful in that it teaches people God's holy nature, their duty to God, and their inability to keep it, thus driving them to Christ for mercy (WLC 95). But it is also "of special use" for the regenerate, "to provoke them to more thankfulness" and to encourage them to take "greater care to conform themselves" to God's standards (WLC 97). By exploring each commandment in detail, the Larger Catechism synthesizes the moral teaching of the Bible and applies it to the believer's daily life.[25] Far from an abstract treatment of obscure doctrines, the Standards deal with the application of that theology in the Christian life.

Legacy

The Westminster Standards have remained influential among Reformed churches to our day. They became the theological touchstone for Presbyterians and also set the doctrinal tone for Congregational churches in their 1658 Savoy Confession and Baptist churches in their 1689 London Baptist Confession of Faith (written in 1677), both slightly modified versions of the Westminster Confession.[26] Their modifications highlight areas of debate among Reformed Christians, specifically one's view of church government (Savoy) and of baptism (London).

In subsequent centuries, the Westminster Confession wielded significant influence in English-speaking Presbyterian circles, though it was also the subject of disputes.[27] Thus, while the Assembly sought to provide latitude for differing viewpoints, some remained dissatisfied. For example, in the wake of the United States' War for Independence, American Presbyterians revised the Confession's statements on church and state.[28] The nineteenth century saw questions become more acute, even as many responded to proposed difficulties while trying to maintain fidelity to the Confession.[29]

In the early twentieth century, ideological battles continued as theological liberals gradually undermined the authority of both the Bible and the Westminster Standards in some circles. So in 1924 the Auburn Affirmation reinterpreted Westminster doctrines as theories that ministers no longer had to affirm.[30] Thus, the Westminster Confession lost its hold in many American Presbyterian churches, leading to splits and the formation of new Presbyterian denominations (such as the Orthodox Presbyterian Church) that upheld the Westminster Confession.

Despite debates over the enduring value of the Westminster Standards,[31] they continued to play a formative role in many Reformed circles throughout the twentieth and into the twenty-first centuries—especially the Confession and Shorter Catechism.[32] The Standards even influenced Presbyterianism in non-Western countries, particularly Korea, where the Westminster Shorter Catechism led most Presbyterian churches to adopt the Confession and Larger Catechism.[33]

Conclusion

Not all have smiled upon the theology of the Westminster Standards. To be sure, the Arminian theological tradition has found its treatment of human free will dissatisfactory, and the history of efforts to revise the Confession shows how people have continued to wrestle with its formulations.

Yet while some have quibbled with aspects of the Westminster Standards, others have embraced their broad Calvinism as a mature systematization of the theology begun with the likes of Martin Luther and John Calvin. They have certainly proved to be some of the most influential confessional documents produced in the aftermath of the Reformation—surprising results of political upheaval. What one finds in the Westminster Standards is a theological system prioritizing Scripture and modeling doctrinal precision, one that frames all reality within God's sovereign power and initiative and emphasizes the heavenly heights of God's glory without neglecting life in the terrestrial realm.

Notes

1. For the history of the Westminster Standards, I have relied especially on J.V. Fesko, *The Theology of the Westminster Standards: Historical Context and Theological Insights* (Wheaton, IL: Crossway, 2014), 33–63; John H. Leith, *Assembly at Westminster: Reformed Theology in the Making* (Richmond, VA: John Knox, 1973); Carl R. Trueman, *The Creedal Imperative* (Wheaton, IL: Crossway, 2012), 125–27; and James S. McEwen, "How the Confession Came to Be Written," in *The Westminster Confession in the Church Today: Papers Prepared for the Church of Scotland Panel on Doctrine*, ed. Alasdair I.C. Heron (Edinburgh: Saint Andrews Press, 1982), 6–16.
2. E.g., Fesko, *Theology*, 23; Leith, *Assembly*, 11–12.
3. Quoted in Fesko, *Theology*, 53.
4. On the men who made up the Westminster Assembly, see Leith, *Assembly*, 45–55; James Reid, *Memoirs of the Lives and Writings of Those Eminent Divines Who Convened in the Famous Assembly at Westminster in the Seventeenth Century*, 2 vols. (Paisley: Stephen and Andrew Young, 1811, 1815).
5. Fesko, *Theology*, 58–63; Leith, *Assembly*, 37–43.
6. Fesko, *Theology*, 33.
7. Fesko, *Theology*, 167; Leith, *Assembly*, 38.
8. Scholars debate this point, but Fesko persuasively argues for continuity in *The Theology of the Westminster Standards*.
9. Leith, *Assembly*, 31–36, 65–74.
10. For more on the Directory for the Public Worship of God, see Richard A. Muller and Rowland S. Ward, *Scripture and Worship: Biblical Interpretation*

and the Directory for Public Worship, The Westminster Assembly and the Reformed Faith (Phillipsburg, NJ: P&R, 2007).

11. Fesko, Theology, 29–30.

12. The Humble Advice of the Assembly of Divines . . . Concerning A Confession of Faith . . . (London and Edinburgh: Evan Tyler, 1647); The Confession of Faith and the Larger and Shorter Catechisme . . . (London: Company of Stationers, 1651). Both were retrieved from the Post-Reformation Digital Library, www.prdl.org. I refer parenthetically to the Westminster Confession as WC, the Westminster Larger Catechism as WLC, and the Westminster Shorter Catechism as WSC. I have updated the swash s but have retained original spellings.

13. Benjamin Breckinridge Warfield, "The First Question of the Westminster Shorter Catechism," in The Westminster Assembly and Its Work (New York: Oxford University Press, 1931), 379.

14. Johannes G. Vos, The Westminster Larger Catechism: A Commentary, ed. G.I. Williamson (Phillipsburg, NJ: P&R, 2002), 4.

15. Fesko, Theology, 66. See also Sinclair B. Ferguson, "The Teaching of the Confession," in Heron, Westminster Confession in the Church Today, 35; Benjamin Breckinridge Warfield, "The Westminster Doctrine of Holy Scripture," chap. 3 of The Westminster Assembly and Its Work.

16. Leith, Assembly, 76–77. See, e.g., Benjamin Breckinridge Warfield, "The Doctrine of Inspiration of the Westminster Divines," chap. 4 in The Westminster Assembly and Its Work.

17. Leith, Assembly, 76.

18. Fesko, Theology, 96. On the debate over the placement of this chapter so early in the ordo salutis ("order of salvation"), see Fesko, Theology, 95–124; Walter W. Bryden, The Significance of the Westminster Confession of Faith (Toronto: University of Toronto Press, 1943), 28–29; Leith, Assembly, 89; James B. Torrance, "Strengths and Weaknesses of the Westminster Theology," in Heron, Westminster Confession in the Church Today, 45–48.

19. Fesko, Theology, 123.

20. Fesko, Theology, 111–16.

21. David W. Hall, "Westminster Spirituality," in The Westminster Confession into the 21st Century: Essays in Remembrance of the 350th Anniversary of the Westminster Assembly, ed. J. Ligon Duncan (Fearn, Scotland: Mentor, 2004), 2:117–54.

22. Leith, Assembly, 101.

23. Leith, Assembly, 93.

24. Jan Van Vliet, The Rise of Reformed System: The Intellectual Heritage of William Ames, Studies in Christian History and Thought (Eugene, OR: Wipf and Stock, 2013), 105–28, esp. 127–28. For more on Ames's treatment of covenant theology, see the chapter on William Ames in this volume. For

the history and roots of covenant theology, see Fesko, *Theology*, 127–37; R. Scott Clark and Joel Beeke, "Ursinus, Oxford and the Westminster Divines," in Duncan, *Westminster Confession into the 21st Century*, 2:1–32.

25. Fesko, *Theology*, 272–76.
26. Trueman, *The Creedal Imperative*, 129–30.
27. See the following essays from Heron, *Westminster Confession in the Church Today*: Alexander C. Cheyne, "The Place of the Confession through Three Centuries" (in Scotland), 17–27; John M. Ross, "The Westminster Confession in the Presbyterian Church of England," 84–89; John Thompson, "The Westminster Confession in the Presbyterian Church in Ireland," 90–94; John H. Leith, "The Westminster Confession in American Presbyterianism," 95–100; George S.S. Yule, "The Westminster Confession in Australia," 101–3; Ian Breward, "The Westminster Confession in New Zealand," 104–6.
28. "American Revisions to the Westminster Confession of Faith as Adopted (for example) by the OPC," Center for Reformed Theology and Apologetics, accessed September 15, 2015, www.reformed.org/documents/index.html?mainframe=www.reformed.org/documents/wcforiginal.html.
29. David B. Calhoun, "Old Princeton Seminary and the Westminster Standards," in Duncan, *Westminster Confession into the 21st Century*, 2:33–61.
30. Calhoun, "Old Princeton Seminary," 2:51–61.
31. See, e.g., Bryden, *Significance*; G.I. Williamson, *The Westminster Confession of Faith for Study Classes* (Philadelphia, PA: Presbyterian and Reformed, 1964), vi, 266; Alasdair I.C. Heron, "Introduction," in Heron, *Westminster Confession in the Church Today*, 1–5.
32. W. Robert Godfrey, "An Introduction to the Westminster Larger Catechism," in Johannes G. Vos, *The Westminster Larger Catechism: A Commentary*, ed. G.I. Williamson (Phillipsburg, NJ: P&R, 2002), ix.
33. Chi Mo Hong, "The Influence of the Westminster Confession on the Korean Presbyterian Church," in Duncan, *Westminster Confession into the 21st Century*, 2:381–407.

Select Bibliography

Secondary sources

Bower, John, ed. *The Larger Catechism: A Critical Text and Introduction*. Grand Rapids, MI: Reformation Heritage, 2010.

Dennison, James T., ed. *Reformed Confessions of the 16th and 17th Centuries in English Translation*. Vol. 4, *1600–1693*. Grand Rapids, MI: Reformation Heritage, 2014.

Duncan, J. Ligon, ed. *The Westminster Confession into the 21st Century: Essays in Remembrance of the 350th Anniversary of the Westminster Assembly.* 3 vols. Fearn, Scotland: Mentor, 2003–2009.

Fesko, J.V. *The Theology of the Westminster Standards: Historical Context and Theological Insights.* Wheaton, IL: Crossway, 2014.

Leith, John H. *Assembly at Westminster: Reformed Theology in the Making.* Richmond, VA: John Knox, 1973.

Muller, Richard A., and Rowland S. Ward. *Scripture and Worship: Biblical Interpretation and the Directory for Public Worship.* The Westminster Assembly and the Reformed Faith. Phillipsburg, NJ: P&R, 2007.

Van Dixhoorn, Chad, ed. *The Minutes and Papers of the Westminster Assembly 1643–62.* 5 vols. New York: Oxford University Press, 2012.

4.11

A Short and Easy Method of Prayer (1685)

Madame Guyon[1]

(1648–1717)

For the modern reader, Madame Guyon's *Short and Easy Method of Prayer* is neither short nor easy by today's standards. A prolific writer of some fame both during her life as well as after her demise, her complete writings come to forty volumes and include a commentary on the entire Bible. Our focus is her essay on prayer, which has a rather prolific publishing history in the English language.[2] There are dozens of English translations of her autobiography, her spiritual letters, and especially her essay on prayer—many of which are still readily available in print as well as the ubiquitous online versions. It is not an exaggeration to say that Guyon has had more influence within the spirituality of the twenty-first century than during her day, as she spent the years 1698–1703 in the Bastille and saw her mystical writings condemned by the Catholic hierarchy. The contemporary reader may find this curious, since she was an ardent advocate and embodiment of saintliness, however, we must remember that she was also an ardent supporter of Quietism—emphasizing the abandonment of the self to God, annihilation of the will in union, pure love, and an intense life of inner prayer.

As an interpreter of Scripture and a teacher to her many followers, she asserted that this mysticism did not require any ecclesial hierarchy or priesthood. It was open to all, so in this sense she was curiously modern. She not only undermined ecclesial hierarchy, she contravened the intellectual methods of Jesuit (Society of Jesus) spirituality rooted in Thomas Aquinas. It is doubtful that she was fully aware of the political significance of her writings, but her democratization of spirituality coincided with intellectual and religious currents beyond France. She became immensely popular among German Pietists, Swiss and Dutch Protestants, Quakers, and Methodists. John Wesley included an extract of her autobiography in his fifty-volume *Christian Library* as required reading for early Methodist itinerant preachers. Madame Guyon's *Short and Easy Method of Prayer* was widely read among holiness and Pentecostal leaders well into the early twentieth century. Publication and wide dissemination of the booklet indicate that there is a resurgence of interest in her work in the twenty-first century.

A biographical vignette

Madame Guyon was a leader in the Quietist movement in France. Quietism was characterized essentially by the teaching that one must be quiet and patient in seeking an encounter with the divine. Waiting quietly was deemed to be spiritually superior to actively seeking. The foundation of her Quietism was laid in her study of St. Francis de Sales, Madame de Chantal, and Thomas à Kempis.

Guyon was the daughter of Claude Bouvier, a procurator of the tribunal of Montargis. He was a man of position and some wealth, and he was deeply pious—having come from a family among whom many were considered saintly. Guyon's childhood was spent mostly between the convent and home, but due to her frail health she does not seem to have received the superlative education that her family's social and economic status would have allowed. Indeed, there was not much stability in her early life, as her well-to-do family moved almost every year in her early childhood.

Due to her station in life, she received many marriage proposals, and at the age of sixteen she married Jacques Guyon (age thirty-eight), a wealthy man of weak health. In part due to their difference in age, but more likely due to a tyrannical mother-in-law, theirs was an unhappy marriage. To be sure, her misery was compounded by the death of her half-sister, followed by the demise of her mother, her beloved son, her daughter, and her father—all within a very brief span of time. The combination of these drove her into increased solitude, where she became increasingly convinced that even such grief was part of God's greater providence in her life—a perfect plan. She became convinced that she would be blessed in her suffering, and she bore another son and a daughter shortly before her husband's death in 1676. At the time of his death, she was twenty-eight. From this point on, we might say that Madame Guyon became an evangelist for Quietism. Deeply influential at this point was her reading of *The Spiritual Guide* by Miguel de Molinos.

Perhaps the most famous of her Quietist disciples was François Fenelon, whose influence spread her Quietism among the higher echelons of French aristocracy. The practical result of this was that she became a woman of some notoriety, but fame is a fickle beast. In 1694, under the influence of the Archbishop of Paris, her writings were condemned as heretical. Guyon went into hiding, but she was arrested on December 24, 1695, and was ultimately incarcerated in the Bastille in Paris until March 21, 1703. After her release, she went to live with her son in the Diocese of Blois, where she passed some fifteen years in silence and isolation. She penned an immense volume of pious poetry during those years.

An overview

Insights into the life and thought of Guyon provide a helpful way to introduce her tract on prayer; indeed, her autobiography is part of the same literary genre as her instructions on prayer: "Prayer is the key of perfection and of sovereign happiness. It is the efficacious means of getting rid of all vices and of acquiring all virtues; for the way to become perfect is to live in the presence of God . . . Prayer alone can bring you into His presence, and keep you there continually."[3] As she wrote in one of her poems:

> There was a period when I chose
>   A time and place for prayer
> But now I seek that constant prayer
>   In Inward Stillness known[4]

In accordance with Roman Catholic practice in her day, Madame Guyon, as a devout aristocratic woman, had a priest assigned to her as spiritual director. She took matters of conscience and spiritual concern to him with the expectation that he would provide advice and guidance. Her *Autobiography*, from which our biographical information is drawn,[5] was written originally for her spiritual director as part of his program of guidance. Guyon penned it in 1688 during her first Bastille imprisonment, but later added to and revised it in 1709. It is likely that she sensed that it would be published to a wider audience. It was first published in Cologne, Germany in 1720, less than three years after her death.

From the very first lines, we begin to sense the deep spiritual humility so typical of the French mystical writers:

GOD ALONE.—Since you wish me to write a life so worthless and so extraordinary as mine, I wish to do what you desire of me; although the labor appears to me a little severe in the state I am in, which does not allow me to reflect much. I should extremely wish to make you understand the goodness of God to me, and the excess of my ingratitude; but it would be impossible for me to do it, as well because you do not wish me to write my sins in detail, as because I have lost the memory of many things.[6]

The trait of extreme humility is common to every reflection written by the mystics, as well as a pervasive sense of divine providence in even the smallest details of life. For Guyon this sense of providence commences with her birth. She was born at least a month premature, and in those days babies born at less than full term seldom survived: "They carried me to a nurse, and I was no sooner there than they came to inform my father I was dead." Her father immediately summoned a priest to perform last rites. She notes, "It is true they could not observe in me any sign of life. The priest went away, and my father also, in extreme desolation." Her reflections on this traumatic set of events reveals a disposition toward divine providence that we see throughout her life: "These alternations of life and death at the commencement of my life were fateful auguries of what was to happen to me one day; now dying by sin, and now living by grace." Remember, she is in prison for publicly declaring her faith when she writes these lines. She continues, "Oh, if it was permitted to me to have that confidence, and I would believe at last that life will be forever victorious over death! Doubtless it will be so if you alone live in me, O my God, who seem to be at present my only life, and my only love."[7]

By her own account, Guyon was severely treated and neglected by her mother, who showed a clear preference for her brother. The negative disposition of her mother toward her continued throughout her life, and it left an indelible mark on the girl. She expresses deep gratitude that her father rescued her (at least temporarily) from an unloving mother when he sent her at the age of seven to live with the Ursulines—a Roman Catholic order of Sisters founded in 1535 specifically for the care and education of girls. Here she discerns both the providence of a heavenly as well as an earthly father: "You, O my God, who continually watched over a child who incessantly forgot you, permitted that my father came home and saw me. As he loved me very tenderly, he was so vexed that, without saying a word to any one, he took me straight away to the Ursulines."[8] She was seven years old, but in her recounting, she discerns already a willful disposition reflective of sin as she describes herself as, "A child who incessantly forgot you." She deemed it providential that among the Ursulines she was placed under the care of her biological sister whom Guyon describes as, "One of the most capable and the most spiritual persons of her time, and most fit to form young girls."[9]

The theme of sinfulness and willful neglect remains a theme throughout her life, and it is foundational to the assumptions that inform her instructions on prayer. We may let a single remembrance from her youth suffice. Her father was of such influence that the Queen of England visited their home when she was about eight years of age. The monarch was so taken by this precocious girl that she proposed to take her into the royal court as maid of honor. Her father did not deem this wise, and Guyon's response was: "Oh my God, it was you who permitted the resistance of my father, and thereby turned aside the stroke on which, perhaps, depended my salvation. For being as weak [spiritually] as I was, what could I have done at Court but destroy myself?"[10]

Biography and prayer life

There is a deep and pervasive poignancy to the life of Guyon, and this is perhaps the best way to gain perspective on her *Short and Easy Method of Prayer*. Herein we discern the essence of the Quietist pursuit. The soul must be "quietened" in order for God to have His full way with the believer. The "self" has to be completely abandoned, and in so doing the spiritual seeker loses herself in God. This is an "other worldly" frame of reference for the modern reader whose life is consumed with activities and activism of every sort, right down to multi-tasking during every waking hour. If we look at her method of praying through the lens of specific events in her life, then we can perhaps get around the strange otherworldliness of her admonitions. Her teachings are rooted in what happened to her in the course of her life.[11]

There are twenty-four short chapters in her *Method of Prayer*. I would give these the following descriptive titles:

1 The Universal Call to Prayer
2 The Method of Prayer
3 The First Degree of Prayer
4 The Second Degree of Prayer
5 Of Spiritual Aridity
6 Of Self-Surrender
7 Of Sufferings

When we interface excerpts from her autobiography with her *Method of Prayer* we get a sense of this spiritual woman and we also get insights into her mystical ways of prayer and spirituality. In her biography she records:

> On taking up the pen, I did not know the first word of what I was about to write. I set myself to write without knowing how, and I found it came with a strange impetuosity. What surprised me most was that it flowed from my central depth, and did not pass through my head ... Before writing I did not know what I was going to write. When it was written, I thought of it no more. (*Bio.*, 200)

We encounter this same simplicity in the early pages when she writes on prayer. I simply must "persuade [others] to the love of God and to His service of perfect liberty," and to do so in a "simple and easy manner" (*Prayer*, x). Throughout these writings we encounter the juxtaposition of ease and difficulty. When Guyon says that prayer is easy, she does not mean that it is not difficult. Intimate communication with God does not happen as long as we remain the most important subject. God must become the only subject, and that is hard for us to do:

> I could not succeed in it [prayer], as it then appeared to me, because I could not imagine anything, and I was persuaded that without forming to ones' self distinctions and much reasoning one could not pray. This difficulty for a long

time caused me much trouble. I was, however, very assiduous at it, and I earnestly begged God to give me the gift of prayer. (*Bio.,* 17)

When the seeker is divinely enabled to get out of the way and make God the supreme subject, she is on the way to divine union, perfection. The goal of such prayer is to "live in God Himself" (*Prayer,* 18), because "prayer is the application of the heart to God, and the internal exercise of love" (15). It is the "key to perfection and the sovereign good; it is the means of delivering us through the blood of Christ (I Jn. 1:7) from every vice, and effecting in us every virtue (II Peter 1:3–9), for the one great way to become perfect is to walk in the presence of God" (17). Indeed, the essence of genuine prayer is to "live in God Himself" (18).

Guyon is explicit in her admonitions about how the hard work must be done if one is to ever truly pray in the Spirit and gain union with God. Sustained meditation and patient reading and waiting are prerequisites: "Those who read fast reap no more advantage than a bee would by only skimming over the surface of a flower, instead of waiting to penetrate into it and extract its sweets." This is not reading over something to gain some quick information. The quest is for divine truth: "To receive real profit from spiritual books, we must . . . become gradually habituated to and more fully disposed for prayer" (*Prayer,* 21).

> When, by an act of lively faith, you are placed in the presence of God, recollect some truth wherein there is substance and food; pause gently and patiently thereon, not to employ the reason, but merely to calm and fix the mind; for you must observe, that your particular exercise should ever be the presence of God; your subject, therefore, should rather serve to stay the mind, than exercise the understanding (21–22). The right way to penetrate every divine truth, to enjoy its full relish, and to imprint it on the heart, is dwelling on it while its savor continues (24).

The "first degree" of prayer begins with adoration and abasement before God and proceeds through meditating on the Divine Presence, repeating the Lord's Prayer in one's native tongue and meditating upon the meaning of the words, remaining a few moments in silence before God, and intermittent times of supplication, silence, and repetition of the Lord's Prayer. The "second degree of prayer" requires a slight change in the sense that it is characterized by utter simplicity (29). This simplicity focuses on cherishing the "sense of the Divine Presence" (30). If the spiritual pilgrim naively believes that such prayer and meditation will invariably be characterized by a rich sense of Divine Presence, they will be quite wrong. "Aridity" will happen in the prayer life of even the most faithful. In her autobiography Guyon notes, "Meditation in which state I then was did not give me true peace in the midst of such great troubles" (*Bio.*, 35); however, she faithfully maintains, "My dear souls ... with patient love, with self-abasement and humiliation, with the reiterated breathings of an ardent but peaceful affection, and with silence full of the most profound veneration, you must wait the return of the Beloved" (*Prayer*, 33). Indeed, Guyon depicts a seven-year period of spiritual aridity in her own life and notes: "This heart, which was occupied only with its God, found itself no longer occupied but with the creature" (*Bio.*, 99). In other words, her spiritual dryness was rooted in her being preoccupied with herself rather than being invested totally in ascertaining and living into the Divine Presence. "Abandonment is a matter of greatest importance in our spiritual growth ... Abandonment is the casting off of all selfish care, that we may be altogether at the Divine disposal" (*Prayer*, 34–35). "Surrender yourselves, then, to be led and disposed of just as God pleaseth, with respect both to your outward and inward state" (36). Guyon consistently connects this self-abandonment to the Cross and cross-bearing: "It is impossible to love God without loving the cross; and a heart that favors the cross, finds the bitterest things to be sweet" (38).

The process of self-renunciation through prayer leads to the cultivation of virtue as one moves into deeper communion with God, who is the "fountain and principle of virtue." Here the modern reader would perhaps expect an extended discussion of the source and character of the virtues, but that would be the work of a scholastic theologian. Guyon is a mystic, and accordingly she offers a short panegyric (a hymn of praise) to love, which she characterizes as the chief of all virtues. Her goal in prayer is to become one with God, who is himself love, and who loved so supremely that he took up residence among us. When we learn to love God supremely, to the exclusion of all other loves, then we may become one with God. Indeed, in the mind of Guyon, we may be said to be perfected in love.

Conclusion

The spiritual world of the mystics may sound distant and strange to folks in the twenty-first century. In many ways, reading Guyon's *Short and Easy Method of Prayer* may feel like traveling through time to a distant country. Indeed, there is much about the subject of prayer and about Guyon's style of writing that is alien to us. Nonetheless, Madam Guyon's *Short and Easy*

Method of Prayer has proven to be an excellent guide into the inner regions of prayer for readers across centuries. If the reader keeps in mind the principles we have set out, then one may find in her short work a key that opens the door into a shared mystical reality. Here, one might even encounter the Divine.

Notes

1. Her full name is Jeanne-Marie Bouvier de la Motte (Mothe) Guyon.
2. For a comprehensive overview of Guyon's publications in English, see Patricia A. Ward, "Madame Guyon in America: An Annotated Bibliography," *Bulletin of Bibliography* 52.2 (June 1995): 107–11.
3. This paraphrase is based on A *Short and Easy Method of Prayer*, trans. Thomas Digby Brooke (London: Hatchard & Co., 1867), 17.
4. "Constant Prayer," in *Poems of Madame Guyon*, trans. William Cowper (New York: Day, 1834), 112.
5. *The Autobiography of Madame Guyon*, trans. Thomas Taylor Allen (New Canaan, Connecticut: Keats Publishing, 1980).
6. Ibid., 3.
7. Ibid., 6–7.
8. Ibid., 9.
9. Ibid., 10.
10. Ibid., 11.
11. In the following citations, *Bio* references *The Autobiography of Madame Guyon*, trans. Thomas Taylor Allen (New Canaan, CT: Keats Publishing, 1980), and *Prayer* references *A Short and Easy Method of Prayer*, trans. Thomas Digby Moore (London: Hatchard & Co., 1867).

Select Bibliography

Primary source

Guyon, Madame. *A Short and Easy Method of Prayer*. Translated by Thomas Digby Brooke. London: Hatchard & Co., 1867.

Guyon, Madame. *Poems: Translated from the French of Madame De La Mothe Guion*, by the late William Cowper. New York: Mahlon Day, 1834.

Guyon, Madame. *The Autobiography of Madame Guyon*. Translated by Thomas Taylor Allen. Edited by Warner A. Hutchinson. New Canaan, CT: Keats Publishing, 1980.

Secondary sources

Bruneau, Marie-Florine. *Women Mystics Confront the Modern World*. Albany: State University of New York Press, 1998.

Forbes, Cheryl. *Women of Devotion through the Centuries*. Grand Rapids: Baker, 2001.

Ward, Patricia A. "Madame Guyon in America: An Annotated Bibliography," *Bulletin of Bibliography* 52.2 (June 1995): 107–11.

Ward, Patricia A. "Madame Guyon and Experiential theology in America," *Church History* 67 (1998): 484–98.

Ward, Patricia A. "The Legacy of Madame Guyon from 1850 to 2000." Pages 189–206 in *Experimental Theology in America: Madame Guyon, Fénelon, and their readers*. Waco, TX: Baylor University Press, 2009.

Ward, Patricia A. "The Reputation of Madame Guyon." Pages 11–40 in *Experimental Theology in America: Madame Guyon, Fénelon, and their readers*. Waco, TX: Baylor University Press, 2009.

4.12

Natural Theology (1802)
William Paley (1743–1805)

Figure 4.9 William Paley

The life and works of William Paley[1]

The first time he went to Christ's College, Cambridge, William Paley (1743–1805) was fifteen years old, riding on a pony behind his father. He was such a poor horseman—and would remain so throughout his life—that he fell off seven times that journey. When William would fall, his father would simply say, "Get up, and take care of thy money, lad." Perhaps that practical reminder seemed all too fitting for Paley, a tall, clumsy boy who often wandered around musing to himself, gaining the reputation of being "a bit crazed."[2] Yet Paley made up for his awkwardness with his intellect, something his father recognized in him from an early age.

Paley was born in Peterborough, Cambridgeshire, in 1743, and grew up, from age two onward, in Giggleswick. Though he enrolled in Christ's College in 1758, young Paley did not enter residency there until 1759, at age sixteen. Well-liked with a happy disposition and a sharp wit, he spent his first two years mainly enjoying social gatherings. When the third year brought his first exams, though, he established a new regimen of disciplined study, which yielded impressive results. Paley took up mathematics, natural philosophy, logic, metaphysics, and moral philosophy, and he excelled, earning the Bunting scholarship, the highest Cambridge prize for mathematics, in 1761; being recognized as "senior wrangler," or first in his class, in 1763; and receiving the Members' Prize for the best Latin prose essay by a Cambridge graduate in 1765.[3]

Yet for all his promise in mathematics and philosophy, Paley also desired to serve in the church. After teaching for three years in a private academy in Greenwich, he came of the age when he could join the priesthood; he thus began working in the curacy of Greenwich and was ordained an Anglican priest in 1767. That same year, Paley was also elected a fellow of Cambridge, where he would hold various posts through 1776, teaching moral philosophy, metaphysics, and Greek.

However, Paley knew he would not remain in academia forever. He believed dangers accompanied a life cooped up in the ivory tower, and as a Cambridge don, he was also obliged to remain celibate. So in 1776 he accepted a parish in Westmorland from Bishop Edmund Law (1703–1787), the father of his friend and Cambridge colleague, John Law (1745–1810). That same year, Paley married Jane Hewitt, with whom he had eight children who survived infancy. He would go on to hold a number of benefices in the church, and though he never received a bishopric, as many thought he deserved, he did manage to land the archdeaconry of Carlisle.

Paley first made a name for himself with *The Principles of Moral and Political Philosophy* (1785), drawn from his lectures at Cambridge. Matthew Eddy and David Knight observe that "Paley was not an original thinker . . . but he was a wonderfully clear, fresh writer and guide to conduct," which led to the book's success.[4] In 1794 he published his *Evidences of Christianity*, in which he sought to defend the historical truth claims of Christianity; the book soon became a required text at Cambridge. His final work, *Natural Theology* (1802), moved beyond his focus in *Evidences* on the special revelation of Scripture to the general revelation of nature. In his dedicatory letter in *Natural Theology*, he summarized his contributions in this trilogy—in reverse order—as "the evidences of natural religion, the evidences of revealed religion, and an account of the duties that result from both."[5]

Paley lived a largely comfortable, happy, and "eminently undramatic" life.[6] He was a clergyman who loved fishing and engaged the weighty intellectual questions of his day. In 1800 severe stomach pains forced him to halt his church office duties but also freed him up to complete his *Natural Theology*.[7] He died on May 15, 1805, at the age of 62.

Design

William Paley's *Natural Theology* is best known for its opening chapter in which he describes an extended analogy of someone finding a watch in a field. Upon discovering and examining such a mechanism, one would naturally conclude that the watch had a designer. The analogy of the watch encapsulates Paley's argument that the evidence of design in nature points to the existence of God.

If a person found such a watch, Paley suggested, he would "hardly think" that "the watch might have always been there," because "its several parts are framed and put together for a purpose ... to point out the hour of the day." The various parts of the watch bear testimony to the designer's careful construction, from its steel spring for elasticity to its glass face for displaying the hour. The "inference," Paley argued, "is inevitable": "there must have existed, at some time and at some place or other, an artificer or artificers who formed it for the purpose which we find it actually to answer."[8]

Such a conclusion raised other questions, Paley acknowledged, yet he held that those questions in no way undermined this deduction. A person may not know an artisan capable of crafting a watch, and the watch may sometimes go wrong, but that would not invalidate the implication that the watch's complexity necessitated a designer. Even if a person discovered that the watch could reproduce another one of its kind, such knowledge would only increase one's awe for the designer.[9] Paley concluded,

> There cannot be design without a designer; contrivance without a contriver; order without choice; arrangement, without any thing capable of arranging; subserviency and relation to a purpose, without that which could intend a

purpose; means suitable to an end, and executing their office in accomplishing that end, without the end ever having been contemplated, or the means accommodated to it. Arrangement, disposition of parts, subserviency of means to an end, relation of instruments to an use, imply the presence of intelligence and mind.[10]

The watch analogy shows that Paley was very much a man of his time; choosing a mechanism like a watch resonated with readers living through the Industrial Revolution (c. 1750–1830), who increasingly came in contact with mechanical contraptions.[11] So Paley naturally explored other mechanical metaphors as well, such as comparing the eye with a telescope. Both were designed with a purpose: "the eye was made for vision," and "the telescope was made for assisting it." Paley marveled at the mechanical complexity of the eye, which could control the rays of light so as to form an image on the retina: "Can any thing be more decisive of contrivance than this is? The most secret laws of optics must have been known to the author of a structure endowed with such a capacity of change."[12]

Here we find a key term that Paley used frequently in his book: *contrivance*. By *contrivance*, Paley meant the use of skill to bring about something to serve a particular purpose. It implied both "*design* and *construction*" in the biological world.[13] By endowing nature with mechanical complexity, God testified to his existence, agency, and wisdom through "the display of contrivance," which is "the scale by which we ascend to all the knowledge of our Creator which we possess."[14]

Throughout the book, Paley described various natural mechanisms in close detail, spending the most time on human and animal bodies. In the human frame, for example, the spine is "a chain of joints of very wonderful construction"—"firm, yet flexible" and something humans themselves cannot reproduce.[15] Paley also talked about teeth and talons; different animal secretions such as blood, sweat, and tears, each with its unique function; the number and arrangement of muscles; and the intestinal network that draws nourishment from the food that enters at the mouth and delivers nutrients throughout the body via the blood.[16] The list and the accompanying details of each structure could go on and on. Paley found that reflecting on the intricacies of animal bodies left one astounded at the intention and beauty they displayed.

Paley also explored other areas of nature, including insects, plants, the elements, and astronomy.[17] Taken together, all these examples demonstrated the need for some great designer. Paley rejected other notions, such as the idea that everything can be explained by "a *principle of order*" in nature," for such a concept boiled design down to "a mere substitution of words for reasons," for "what is meant by a principle of order, as different from an intelligent Creator"?[18] In Paley's view, anyone who took a close look at nature would find the kind of evidence that necessitated an intelligent designer.

Argumentation

Paley explored aspects of nature systematically in close detail to show how the complexity of the natural world screams for a designer. In essence, Paley's argument from design was a teleological argument for the existence of God, one that finds the natural world's evidence of purpose to be sufficient grounds for the existence of a Creator being. The argument predated Paley by centuries, but his version became, in LeMahieu's words, "the most consistent and searching statement of the teleological argument in the English language."[19]

In making his claim, Paley mirrored the values of his day by emphasizing empirical evidence, appealing to "experience and observation" as giving reliable indicators about reality.[20] His myriad examples of human and animal bodies reflect his interest in what could be touched, seen, and examined.

While empirical evidence loomed large in his presentation, Paley also employed an argument from probability, which held increasing epistemological weight in the late eighteenth century. He did not seek to make a "knock-down" argument from deductive reasoning based on a string of axioms.[21] Rather, as Paley explained, he made an "argument cumulative." By this he meant that each of his countless examples could stand on its own, independently proving the necessity of a designer, yet that he strengthened his central thesis by layering several independent proofs upon each other. Thus, objecting to a single piece of evidence could not doom the argument as a whole. As Paley put it, "For the purpose of addressing different understandings and different apprehensions, for the purpose of sentiment, for the purpose of exciting admiration of the Creator's works, we diversify our views, we multiply examples; but, for the purpose of strict argument, one clear instance is sufficient."[22]

This multifaceted approach to argumentation shows Paley both to be standing in a long tradition of philosophical arguments for God's existence and to be reshaping that tradition in new ways that resonated with the thinking of his time. Thus, he sought not only to reassure Enlightenment-era Christians that religion was compatible with new scientific findings but also to respond to arguments by skeptics like David Hume (1711–1776).[23] One of the most distinctive aspects of Paley's argument from design was his discussion of the designer's nature.

The nature of the Deity

The big challenge facing the argument from design was the evil in the world. If nature necessitated a designer and yet nature so often went wrong, what should one say about that designer? Rather than turning to the Christian doctrine of humanity's fall into sin, Paley kept himself within the realm of natural theology to answer that question, arguing that nature gave proof of a personal, infinite, single, and good God as the ultimate Creator. After describing in intricate detail the various mechanics in nature, Paley drew the reader to his very specific goal: to prove from the natural world not only the existence but also the nature of the deity.

First, Paley showed that the Creator is a person, not a mere force. He argued that contrivance proves "the *personality* of the Deity, as distinguished from what is sometimes called nature," because a contriver exhibits the capacities of a person, especially a mind, perception, and volition. While the contriver may use many second causes, nonetheless "there must be intelligence somewhere." Paley concluded, "The marks of *design* are too strong to be got over. Design must have had a designer. That designer must have been a person. That person is God."[24]

Second, the natural attributes of an intelligent designer, Paley argued, must be "adequate to the magnitude, extent, and multiplicity of his operations," which from the human vantage point means that they must be "infinite, because they are unlimited on all sides." Paley believed that "natural religion" pointed to several aspects of God, including his "omnipotence, omniscience, omnipresence, eternity, self-existence, necessary existence, spirituality."[25]

Third, Paley argued that "the *uniformity* of plan observable in the universe" proves "the unity of the Deity."[26] Throughout the world we see the same laws of nature at play, providing a consistency that points to one Creator who set in place the laws of nature that provide regularity and order.

Paley's fourth point—and by far his longest—was that nature proves the goodness of the deity. It was also the one that has drawn the greatest criticism.[27] Paley based this point on two propositions: (1) that the design of contrivance is in a plethora of cases beneficial, and (2) that animal sensations enjoy "superadded *pleasure*" far beyond what is necessary. With regard to the first proposition, Paley sought to put things in perspective by noting that God could have made "every thing we tasted bitter; every thing we saw loathsome; every thing we touched a sting; every smell a stench; and every sound a discord." Instead, at every point of contrivance—in contrast to some human designs—we see that the natural world is "directed to beneficial purposes." In the second proposition, Paley argued that nature's provision of superadded pleasures shows a further design than mere existence. As Paley put it, "Why should the juice of a peach applied to the palate, affect the part so differently from what it does when rubbed upon the palm of the hand? This is a constitution, which, so far as appears to me, can be resolved into nothing but the pure benevolence of the Creator." While evil admittedly existed within human engagement, Paley tried to resolve the appearance of natural evil by showing that the Creator's design spread happiness throughout nature, from a bee among flowers in spring to a fish leaping out of water. He concluded, "It is a happy world after all."[28]

However, not all found this world to be a happy place, and thus not all found this aspect of Paley's argument compelling. For Paley, however, the notion that mechanism in nature necessitates a personal, infinite, single, and good designer was also meant to motivate people to live ethical lives and spread such happiness. He intended *Natural Theology* to lead to *The Principles of Moral and Political Philosophy*. Thus Paley concluded that "the world from thenceforth becomes a temple, and life itself one continued act of adoration. The change is no less than this, that, whereas formerly God was seldom in our thoughts, we can now scarcely look upon any thing without perceiving its relation to him."[29]

Natural theology

One final issue demands discussion, and that is the question of how Paley's *Natural Theology* fits into the larger tradition of natural theology.[30] Clarke defines *natural theology* as "theology as it can be deduced from the world of nature."[31] Paley clearly sought to limit himself to the natural world in his final work (though, importantly, not in previous works), and yet his particular approach to natural theology differentiated him from both preceding and subsequent natural theologians.

The practice of natural theology and the design argument can be traced back to the ancient world, as early as Socrates and perhaps most classically

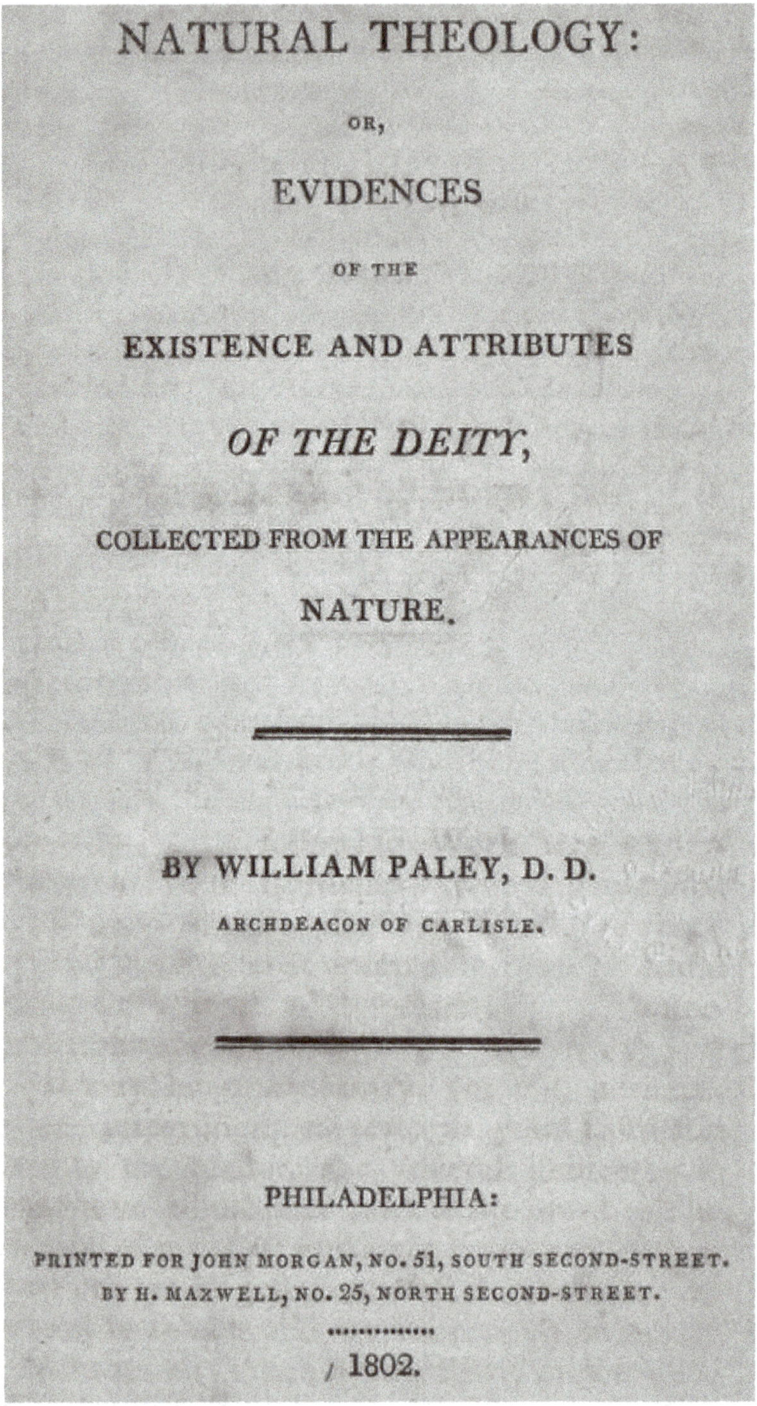

NATURAL THEOLOGY:

OR,

EVIDENCES

OF THE

EXISTENCE AND ATTRIBUTES

OF THE DEITY,

COLLECTED FROM THE APPEARANCES OF

NATURE.

―――――

BY WILLIAM PALEY, D. D.

ARCHDEACON OF CARLISLE.

―――――

PHILADELPHIA:

PRINTED FOR JOHN MORGAN, NO. 51, SOUTH SECOND-STREET.
BY H. MAXWELL, NO. 25, NORTH SECOND-STREET.

•••••••••••••

/ 1802.

Figure 4.10 *Natural Theology* by William Paley

expressed by Cicero in *De Natura Deorum* (or, *On the Nature of the Gods*). Paley, in fact, modeled much of his argumentation on Cicero's rhetoric.[32] Theologians such as Thomas Aquinas (1225–1274) and John Calvin (1509–1564) also found value in nature, but they saw strict limits as to what it could accomplish.[33] In the seventeenth century, natural theology attracted increasing interest and took new forms in response to scientists like Robert Boyle (1627–1691) and Isaac Newton (1642/3–1727), who emphasized mechanism in nature.[34]

Natural theology met several detractors in the eighteenth century, such as David Hume, who pilloried it in his *Dialogues Concerning Natural Religion* (1776), arguing that nature fails to prove that the deity is either good or a unity.[35] These arguments over natural theology led to new controversies over the relationship between religion and science, though for the most part, the question was not *whether* natural theology had a role to play but rather how *extensive* that role might be.[36]

Paley believed it had a large role to play, and his *Natural Theology* distinguished him from earlier natural theologies in the degree to which he believed nature could reveal specific truths about the Creator. As we saw earlier, he claimed that nature proved the deity to be personal, infinite, single, and good. He went so far as to argue that proving the existence of an intelligent Creator from nature lays "the foundation of every thing which is religious" and "facilitates the belief of the fundamental articles of *Revelation*."[37]

It is at this point that Paley has received the sharpest criticism. In fact, the only early criticisms came from evangelicals like William Wilberforce (1759–1833), who appreciated his work but disliked the way it presented an argument for God apart from revealed religion (Scripture).[38] Evangelicals viewed natural theology as inadequate because it failed to teach humanity the "central aspects of evangelical faith: atonement and salvation."[39] Similarly, later theologians like John Henry Newman (1801–1890) found that Paley's approach to natural theology could be useful in showing that Christianity could make sense of the natural order but that it failed miserably in saying anything about Christianity.[40]

At the same time, Graham Cole notes that, when properly limited, natural theology could still have a place alongside special revelation: "Natural theology shows both the probability of God's existence and of a future state. Revealed theology shows their certainty."[41] Thus, reflecting such reasoning, evangelicals like Thomas Chalmers (1780–1847) "warmly embraced distinctively evangelical forms of natural theology" in the decades following the publication of *Natural Theology*.[42]

Still, Paley gave natural theology a foundational role that troubled many. Brooke notes that while natural theology sought to prove the existence of God, it ironically contributed to the increase of doubt about the existence of God. And so Paley represented a significant shift in natural theology by trying to burden the teleological argument with far more than it had traditionally carried.[43]

Legacy

Brooke calls Paley's *Natural Theology* "one of the most popular works of philosophical theology in the English language."[44] Paley's arguments were "generally accepted during the next fifty years or so,"[45] though they did eventually meet with criticism from groups as diverse as evangelicals, Tractarians, and theological liberals.[46] Various writers also built on Paley's arguments to develop natural theology beyond Paley, often in response to new scientific discoveries.[47]

The biggest development, of course, was Charles Darwin's evolutionary theory as presented in *The Origin of Species* (1859). A young Darwin actually found himself "charmed and convinced by the long line of argumentation" in *Natural Theology*, yet in time he also came to very different conclusions than Paley about what nature tells us concerning God and design.[48] Evangelicals responded to Paley and then to Darwin in varied ways, though in general nineteenth-century evangelicals believed science and revelation would somehow harmonize.[49]

Debates over the relationship between science and religion continued into the twentieth century, with *Natural Theology* again drawing more interest in the late twentieth century. In criticizing Paley, atheist Richard Dawkins (1941–) argued that the "only watchmaker in nature is the blind forces of physics."[50] Christian theologian Alister McGrath (1953–) was harsher toward Paley than Dawkins, calling his work "decidedly second-rate" scholarship[51]—though Cole finds McGrath's characterization to be anachronistic.[52] While many have criticized Paley's *Natural Theology*, it continues to appeal to scientific thinkers today, particularly those in the Intelligent Design movement.[53]

Conclusion

William Paley's *Natural Theology* gives readers a good sense of how an eighteenth-century Anglican clergyman drew from the latest scientific knowledge about anatomy and nature to shape the classic teleological argument for God's existence in his day. This work set the stage for much of the debate over science and religion in the two centuries since it was published. Paley had a contagious wonder of the natural world, and he interpreted nature through the lens of Christianity, seeing the handiwork of God everywhere he turned. He believed God left his fingerprints particularly on the mechanisms visible in creation, which should lead his creatures to look for a Creator. Reading *Natural Theology* takes one into the intricacy of created things, particularly into the remarkable structure of the human body. Paley's descriptive examinations of the world can lead one toward awe of nature. Yet Paley never wanted it to stop there. Rather, he hoped it would mark the beginning of a journey that led first to awe for the Creator, then to the study of his historically reliable revelation in Scripture, and finally to a life of moral principles.

Notes

1. For Paley's life, I have relied especially on M.L. Clarke, *Paley: Evidences for the Man* (Toronto: University of Toronto Press, 1974), 1–56; D.L. LeMahieu, *The Mind of William Paley: A Philosopher and His Age* (Lincoln, NE: University of Nebraska Press, 1976), 1–28; Matthew D. Eddy and David Knight, "Introduction," in William Paley, *Natural Theology, or Evidence of the Existence and Attributes of the Deity, collected from the appearances of nature*, Oxford World's Classics (New York: Oxford University Press, 2006), xiii–xvii, xxxvi–xxxvii.
2. Clarke, *Paley*, 3.
3. Eddy and Knight, "Introduction," xiii, xxxvi.
4. Eddy and Knight, "Introduction," xiv. Several writers note Paley's skill with writing, including LeMahieu, *Paley*, 79. Paley himself sought to find a balance between being "altogether abstruse and recondite" and being "merely popular." William Paley, *Natural Theology, or Evidence of the Existence and Attributes of the Deity, collected from the appearances of nature*, Oxford World's Classics (New York: Oxford University Press, 2006), 278. For more on his *Moral and Political Philosophy*, see Clarke, *Paley*, 57–88; LeMahieu, *Paley*, 115–52.
5. Paley, *Natural Theology*, 4.
6. LeMahieu, *Paley*, 2.
7. Paley, *Natural Theology*, 3–4.
8. Paley, *Natural Theology*, 7, 8.
9. Paley, *Natural Theology*, 8–12.

10. Paley, *Natural Theology*, 12.
11. Alister E. McGrath, *Darwinism and the Divine: Evolutionary Thought and Natural Theology* (Oxford: Wiley-Blackwell, 2011), 91–92.
12. Paley, *Natural Theology*, 16, 20.
13. Alister E. McGrath, *Dawkins' God: Genes, Memes, and the Meaning of Life* (Malden, MA: Blackwell, 2005), 101. Italics original. See also McGrath, *Darwinism and the Divine*, 92–95.
14. Paley, *Natural Theology*, 27.
15. Paley, *Natural Theology*, 56.
16. Paley, *Natural Theology*, 40–42, 50–53, 71, 93.
17. Paley, *Natural Theology*, 170–212.
18. Paley, *Natural Theology*, 42. Italics original.
19. LeMahieu, *Paley*, 58. Graham A. Cole gives a similar assessment. "William Paley's *Natural Theology*: An Anglican Classic?" *Journal of Anglican Studies* 5, no. 2 (2007): 223. See also Alvin C. Plantinga, *God, Freedom, and Evil* (Grand Rapids, MI: Eerdmans, 1974), 81.
20. Paley, *Natural Theology*, 17.
21. Eddy and Knight, "Introduction," xix–xxi. Quotation on xxi.
22. Paley, *Natural Theology*, 45–46, 64.
23. LeMahieu, *Paley*, 67, 89; Clarke, *Paley*, 94.
24. Paley, *Natural Theology*, 213, 218, 229.
25. Paley, *Natural Theology*, 230, 231.
26. Paley, *Natural Theology*, 234.
27. Eddy and Knight, eds., *Natural Theology*, 336. E.g., Francisco José Ayala, "From Paley to Darwin: Design to Natural Selection," *Back to Darwin: A Richer Account of Evolution*, ed. John B. Cobb Jr. (Grand Rapids, MI: Eerdmans, 2008), 62–67.
28. Paley, *Natural Theology*, 237, 242, 243–50, 251, 238–39, 238.
29. Paley, *Natural Theology*, 278–79.
30. On the history and tenets of natural theology—in its various expressions—see John Hedley Brooke, *Science and Religion: Some Historical Perspectives* (Cambridge: Cambridge University Press, 1991), 192–225; McGrath, *Darwinism and the Divine*; Charles E. Raven, *Natural Religion and Christian Theology*, 2 vols. (New York: Cambridge University Press, 1953).
31. Clarke, *Paley*, 89.
32. M.D. Eddy, "The Science and Rhetoric of Paley's Natural Theology," *Literature and Theology* 18 (2004): 6–8; Clarke, *Paley*, 89–90.
33. Brooke, *Science and Religion*, 194–96.
34. Eddy and Knight, "Introduction," x–xi.
35. Clarke, *Paley*, 91.
36. Brooke, *Science and Religion*, 193–94, 197–98.

37. Paley, *Natural Theology*, 278, 280.
38. Aileen Fyfe, "The Reception of William Paley's 'Natural Theology' in the University of Cambridge," *British Journal for the History of Science* 30 (1997): 323–24.
39. Aileen Fyfe, *Science and Salvation: Evangelical Popular Science Publishing in Victorian Britain* (Chicago: University of Chicago Press, 2004), 8. See also Jonathan R. Topham, "Science, Natural Theology, and Evangelicalism in Early Nineteenth-Century Scotland: Thomas Chalmers and the Evidence Controversy," in *Evangelicals and Science in Historical Perspective*, ed. David N. Livingstone, D.G. Hart, and Mark A. Noll, Religion in America (New York: Oxford University Press, 1999), 148.
40. McGrath, *Darwinism and the Divine*, 129; McGrath, *Dawkins' God*, 98, 103–4. See similar remarks as Newman's in Plantinga, *God, Freedom, and Evil*, 83; Cole, "Paley's *Natural Theology*," 220–23.
41. Graham A. Cole, "Paley and the Myth of 'Classical Anglicanism,'" *The Reformed Theological Review* 54, no. 3 (1995): 108.
42. Topham, "Science, Natural Theology, and Evangelicalism," 143.
43. Brooke, *Science and Religion*, 194–96.
44. Brooke, *Science and Religion*, 192.
45. Clarke, *Paley*, 97.
46. Clarke, *Paley*, 131–34; Fyfe, *Science and Salvation*, 111–12.
47. Brooke, *Science and Religion*, 219–25; McGrath, *Darwinism and the Divine*, 108–26. See also Jonathan R. Topham, "Science and Popular Education in the 1830s: The Role of the *Bridgewater Treatises*," *British Journal for the History of Science* 25 (1992): 397–430; Topham, "Science, Natural Theology, and Evangelicalism," 143–74; LeMahieu, *Paley*, 153–55, 168–81.
48. Quoted in McGrath, *Darwinism and the Divine*, 104. On Paley's influence on Darwin, see Eddy and Knight, "Introduction," xxviii; Ayala, "From Paley to Darwin," 72–73.
49. David W. Bebbington, "Science and Evangelical Theology in Britain from Wesley to Orr," in Livingstone, Hart, and Noll, *Evangelicals and Science in Historical Perspective*, 120–35; Mark A. Noll, "Science, Theology, and Society: From Cotton Mather to William Jennings Bryan," in Livingstone, Hart, and Noll, *Evangelicals and Science in Historical Perspective*, 99–119; Fyfe, *Science and Salvation*, esp. 1–15; Topham, "Science, Natural Theology, and Evangelicalism," 143–74.
50. Richard Dawkins, *The Blind Watchmaker: Why the Evidence of Evolution Reveals a Universe without Design*, 3rd ed. (New York: Norton, 2006), 9.
51. McGrath, *Dawkins' God*, 85–107. Quotation on 102. See also Alister McGrath and Joanna Collicutt McGrath, *The Dawkins Delusion? Atheist Fundamentalism and the Denial of the Divine* (Downers Grove, IL: InterVarsity Press, 2007), 24–25.

52. Cole, "Paley's *Natural Theology*," 218–19.
53. Cole, "Paley's *Natural Theology*," 210, 220–24. But see William A. Dembski, *The Design Revolution: Answering the Toughest Questions about Intelligent Design* (Downers Grove, IL: InterVarsity Press, 2004), 64: "Paley's business was natural theology. Intelligent design's business is much more modest: it seeks to identify signs of intelligence to generate scientific insights. Thus, instead of looking to signs of intelligence to obtain theological mileage, as Paley did, intelligent design treats signs of intelligence as strictly part of science."

Select Bibliography

Primary sources

Paley, William. *The Works of William Paley*. Seven vols. London: Rivington et al., 1825.

Paley, William. *Natural Theology, or Evidence of the Existence and Attributes of the Deity, collected from the appearances of nature*. Oxford World's Classics. New York: Oxford University Press, 2006.

Secondary sources

Clarke, M.L. *Paley: Evidences for the Man*. Toronto: University of Toronto Press, 1974.

Cole, Graham A. "William Paley's *Natural Theology*: An Anglican Classic?" *Journal of Anglican Studies* 5.2 (2007): 209–26.

LeMahieu, D.L. *The Mind of William Paley: A Philosopher and His Age*. Lincoln, NE: University of Nebraska Press, 1976.

Part V

The Nineteenth and Twentieth Centuries

Introduction to the Nineteenth and Twentieth Centuries

Kelly M. Kapic

During the nineteenth and twentieth centuries, early modern tendencies that developed in the seventeenth and eighteenth centuries were affirmed by some but passionately questioned by others. Many remained confident in the role of reason in their quest to affirm a respectable religion, while others (e.g., Romanticists) began to argue that following the Enlightenment path of rationalism led not to the Divine but instead to a dehumanized religion. While early modernity assumed that the "universal" and "rational" were proper goals, presupposing an underlying uniform reality, new doubts about the possibility of such goals emerged by the end of the twentieth century: scholars grew convinced that concepts like "nature" and "objectivity" were far more culturally and experientially shaped than had been earlier imagined. Here we ask how Protestant Christian thinkers fit into this discussion.

The Enlightenment habit of questioning authority and tradition led many nineteenth-century biblical scholars to investigate the biblical texts as scientifically as possible, as if putting together an ancient puzzle (e.g., JEDP theory). They were looking for evolutionary patterns in the ancient faith(s) of Judaism and Christianity, often focusing on the developments and differences that arose (e.g., history of religions school). During this period, scholars and even church leaders grew more comfortable with apparent tensions and assumed inconsistencies within those texts. More and more these sacred writings were treated as either simply historically interesting or possibly of abiding ethical value: but assuming that they contained *revelation* from the Divine became a ditch too vast for many to jump across. How could knowledge of the transcendent be discovered within the realm of history? Maybe what Christianity taught us was more about ourselves than God?

Some thinkers reacted against Rationalism and its cold objectivity by investigating the function of the individual believer's subjectivity. This turn toward the subjective both grew out of rationalism and eventually exposed the Enlightenment's reliance upon the supposed neutrality of reason. Friedrich Schleiermacher, for example, addressed some of his work to the "cultured despisers of religion," encouraging them to see that God was discovered in that feeling (*Gefühl*) of absolute dependence, which was one's consciousness of the divine. While Schleiermacher could speak of God in a way that other Romantics of the period resonated with, his critics asked if he was losing Christianity in the process. *The Christian Faith* was an attempt to answer questions like this. Despite that effort, however, we must ask whether—to paraphrase Barth's later memorable critique—his attempts to speak about God were no more than speaking in a loud voice about humans? Or did Schleiermacher see something more profound, creatively articulating the Christian faith in a way that moved beyond the ancient grammar of Nicaea and Chalcedon, but that still pointed to the same divine reality?

Hegel joked (unfairly!) that if Schleiermacher's religious ideal of absolute dependence was correct, then a dog was the most faithful example to follow. By way of contrast, Hegel spoke with massive, even cosmic, confidence, believing that God's revelation is found in history, process, and development. By observing the dynamics of historical processes, we will discover not merely historical events, but nothing less than the Divine disclosing itself through events happening in a pattern of thesis, antithesis, and synthesis. But again we must ask whether, amid this stunning creativity and genius, was the uniqueness of Jesus at risk of being lost?

Other theologians attempted to remain tied to the orthodoxy of previous centuries while playing by as many Enlightenment rules as possible. They believed in miracles and they affirmed the incarnation and resurrection, but they organized and communicated their theology in a very "scientific" manner. Such orthodox approaches to theology are worth recognizing because in books like the present volume we tend to highlight only what is new or different, rather than what seeks to affirm the received tradition. But for Protestant theology in the nineteenth–twentieth centuries, it would be an incomplete story if we only observed those who called into question the orthodox theology they received. For example, at Princeton Seminary Charles Hodge used his powerful intellect to defend what he saw as historical orthodox Protestant Christianity. In this work he was not simply repeating the past, but trying to sing this inherited theology to a slightly modernist tune. His conservative *Systematic Theology* made intentional links between the past and the currents of his own day.

Danish philosopher Søren Kierkegaard, in his context, worried that the Christianity of the nineteenth century was no longer true Christianity. While there was much religion around him, he did not hear the living, demanding, personal God of Abraham, Isaac, and Jesus proclaimed by the institutional churches of Denmark. In response, he called for people to recognize the paradox of Christ and the demands of God's call, to take a leap of faith by submitting to a crucified Messiah. While not hugely influential in his day, Kierkegaard would become a major voice in the twentieth century, influencing many theologians, and even non-Christian existentialists in the early part of the twentieth century.

Familiar with the realities of poverty, depression, and disenfranchisement, Walter Rauschenbusch also pushed hard against the status quo and Christian complacency. He wanted his Christian audience to rediscover that Jesus was a King who sought to bring restoration by healing the sick and feeding the hungry. Here was a political Savior who was certainly occupied with earthy practical concerns rather than abstract academic debates. His Church, therefore, best exhibits faithfulness not by doctrinal precision but by going to the margins, demonstrating concern for the needy and seeking to meet the social crises of the day.

Karl Barth began his career having been soaked in the dominant theological Liberalism passed down from the Ritschlian school. The Great War, however, revealed the dependence of this liberalism on the failed cultures of Europe—especially as he saw his respected theological professors supporting the German war effort. Preaching through Romans he rediscovered the demands of the God of the apostles and prophets, who was not distant, who was not bourgeois, but a present and confrontational God, breaking in and making demands, the very demands that God himself, and he alone through his Son, could fulfill. Moving from *destruction*—showing the weaknesses of Liberal theology—to *construction*—positing a theology for the Church—was not an easy venture. Nevertheless, Barth attempted to rediscover and represent orthodoxy to his age.

Paul Tillich went the opposite direction of Barth, doing everything he could to contextualize Christianity to the modern world. The goal was not to affirm ancient beliefs and practices, but to take the abiding truths behind Christianity and make sense of them for his own twentieth-century readers.

Faith was not about affirming the eternal Son of God who became fully human, bringing redemption through his historic death and bodily resurrection; instead, the faith of Christianity meant having the courage to discover real existence: God is called the "ground of being" in Tillich's attempt to make his Protestant faith relevant to mid-twentieth century listeners.

The optimism and ethics of the nineteenth century quickly receded after the two World Wars. As the power of Modernity began to fade—or, as others convincingly argue, as Modernity fully blossomed—confidence in objective reason and universal norms became increasingly suspect. Was this "Post"-Modernity? When examined closely, too many "norms" turned out not to express underlying universal truths but to be expressions of power and manipulation; furthermore, the face giving voice to those "truths" was almost always a white educated male.

A new appreciation for the global nature of the Christian faith and the diversity of believers began to find voice in various new leaders. For example, James Cone did not simply raise consciousness about hidden "white" presuppositions, but also argued for the value of "black" perspectives on this ancient faith. José Miguel Bonino worried that observing the status quo meant that the Church had too often sided with those in power rather than with the poor and oppressed, and he wondered if the Gospel was lost in the process: *Doing Theology in a Revolutionary Situation* called for fresh thinking and action that had too often been neglected. Japanese author Kosuke Koyama highlighted the place of humility by seeking to focus on the local rather than the universal, learning more from people on the ground than from German university professors. And Sally McFague asked uncomfortable questions about inherited Christian conceptions of God, taking seriously what had been missed as a result of the silencing of women through the ages. These concerns were not merely about how one lives, but also about who one imagines God to be and how people might relate to that God.

George Lindbeck represents a mediating postliberal approach, offering a cultural-linguistic model of theology. He begins by incorporating the insights of those who emphasized embodied Christian communities as legitimately providing and shaping beliefs. Next, he recognizes that these were not merely tribal imaginations, but practices shaped around the narrative of the biblical texts. Thus, even amid differences through the ages and cultures, one could enter into this living faith that rightly centers on Jesus the Christ with his continuing authority found in the community shaped by this distinctive narrative.

We conclude by again recognizing that Protestantism is no uniform movement, but rather a vibrant ever-changing phenomenon. Tracing its roots back to the ancient Church and then in reaction to certain perceived abuses from the late medieval period, this expression of the Christian faith has now developed its own tradition(s). While Presbyterians, Pentecostals, Lutherans, and Methodists are all considered "Protestant," each expression of faith has developed its own instincts and practices, and normally even within these traditions there is wide latitude between those who claim the label (e.g., among Baptists). Some Protestants advocate that the way forward is by looking back to the wisdom of the early Church. Others argue that survival of this faith comes only by taking more seriously the pressures and apparent insights of the twenty-first century. While one group pushes for renewed commitment to sacred texts, others demand greater appreciation of the reality that biblical texts are not ahistorical nor are their contemporary readers: greater attention is needed not merely to the ancient context, but also to our own. And so, the conversation continues. It is into this conversation that we invite you.

List of Classic Works of the Nineteenth and Twentieth Centuries

Georg Wilhelm Friedrich Hegel, *Phenomenology of Spirit*, 1807

Francis Asbury, *Journal of Francis Asbury*, 1821

Friedrich Schleiermacher, *The Christian Faith*, 1821

Johann Adam Mohler, *Symbolism*, 1832

Ludwig Feuerbach, *Essence of Christianity*, 1841

Phoebe Palmer, *Way of Holiness*, 1843

Søren Kierkegaard, *Christian Discourses*, 1848

Ernest Renan, *The Life of Jesus*, 1863

Charles Spurgeon, *John Ploughman's Talks*, 1869

Hannah Whitall Smith, *The Christian's Secret of a Happy Life*, 1875

Fyodor Dostoevsky, *The Brothers Karamazov*, 1880

Leo Tolstoy, *What I Believe*, 1882

Hugh Price Hughes, *Social Christianity?*, 1889

Pope Leo XIII, *Rerum Novarum*, 1891

Adolf von Harnack, *What Is Christianity*, 1900

Albert Schweitzer, *The Quest of the Historical Jesus*, 1906

G.K. Chesterton, *Orthodoxy*, 1908

Rudolf Otto, *Idea of the Holy*, 1917

Franz Pieper, *Christian Dogmatics*, 1917–24/1950–53

Benjamin B. Warfield, *The Plan of Salvation*, 1918

Karl Barth, *The Epistle to the Romans*, 1919

John Gresham Machen, *Christianity and Liberalism*, 1923

Anders Nygren, *Agape and Eros*, 1930–36

Abraham Kuyper, *Lectures on Calvinism*, 1931

Emil Brunner, *Divine Imperative*, 1932

Karl Barth, *Church Dogmatics*, 1932–67

Charles Harold Dodd, *Parables of the Kingdom*, 1935

Dietrich Bonhoeffer, *The Cost of Discipleship*, 1937

T.S. Eliot, *Idea of a Christian Society*, 1939

Rudolf Bultmann, *The New Testament and Mythology*, 1941

Dorothy L. Sayers, *The Mind of the Maker*, 1941

C.S. Lewis, *The Screwtape Letters*, 1942

Kwesi A. Dickson, *Theology in Africa*, 1942

Dietrich von Hildebrand, *Transformation in Christ*, 1948

H. Richard Niebuhr, *Christ and Culture*, 1951

Martin Luther King Jr., *Strength to Love*, 1964

Dorothee Sölle, *Christ the Representative*, 1967

Wolfhart Pannenberg, *Jesus: God and Man*, 1968

John Mbiti, *African Religions and Philosophy*, 1969

John Howard Yoder, *The Politics of Jesus*, 1972

Gustavo Gutiérrez, *A Theology of Liberation*, 1973/88

Jürgen Moltmann, *The Crucified God*, 1973

T.F. Torrance, *Divine and Contingent Order*, 1981

Gerhard Forde, *Justification by Faith*, 1982

Elisabeth Schüssler Fiorenza, *In Memory of Her*, 1983

Desmond Tutu, *Hope and Suffering: Sermons and Speeches*, 1983

Thomas C. Oden, *The Living God*, 1987/92

Elizabeth Johnson, *She Who Is*, 1991

Rosemary Radford Ruether, *Sexism and God-Talk*, 1983

John Piper, *Desiring God*, 1986

Carl Braaten, *No Other Gospel!*, 1992

Stanley Hauerwas, *God, Medicine, and Suffering*, 1994

Miroslav Volf, *Exclusion and Embrace*, 1996

N.T. Wright, *Jesus and the Victory of God*, 1996

Mercy Oduyoye, *Introducing African Women's Theology*, 2001

Marva Dawn, *Powers, Weakness, and the Tabernacling of God*, 2001

Marcella Althaus-Reid, *Indecent Theology*, 2002

Lamin Sanneh, *The Changing Face of Christianity*, 2003

Marilyn McCord Adams, *Christ and Horrors*, 2006

James H. Cone, *The Cross and the Lynching Tree*, 2011

Sarah Coakley, *God, Sexuality and the Self*, 2013

Katherine Sonderegger, *Systematic Theology: Doctrine of God*, 2015

5.1

The Christian Faith[1] (1821; revised 1830)

Friedrich Daniel Ernst Schleiermacher (1768–1834)

Figure 5.1 Portrait of Friedrich Schleiermacher

Schleiermacher: the father of modern theology?

In the preface to the second edition of *The Christian Faith*, Friedrich Schleiermacher protested those who described him as the founder of a new theological school of thought. Nevertheless, to this day he is widely referred to as "the father of modern theology," due in large part to his monumental reshaping of theological method and Protestant theology in *The Christian Faith*. Does Schleiermacher deserve this title, and if so, how does *The Christian Faith* lay a foundation for modern Protestant theology? To address these questions, we must begin with understanding Schleiermacher in his context.

Friedrich Schleiermacher was born in 1768 in Breslau, Prussia (present-day Wroclaw, Poland) to parents firmly situated within the Reformed tradition. His father, Gottlieb Schleiermacher, was a Reformed pastor, a chaplain in the Prussian army, and himself the son of a Reformed pastor. Having experienced religious renewal through contact with the Moravian Brethren, Friedrich's parents decided to send him to the Moravian boarding school in Niesky in 1783. During these and subsequent years at the Moravian Seminary in Barby, Schleiermacher imbibed a deep piety that would influence the rest of his life, although he would eventually classify himself as a "Moravian of a higher order." During his stint at Barby, this budding Pietist was plagued with doubts about traditional methods and forms of expressing the Christian faith. These doubts motivated him to transfer to the University of Halle in 1787, where he immersed himself in the works of leading thinkers of his day, most notably the philosopher Immanuel Kant. After finishing his studies at Halle, Schleiermacher began the process of becoming a minister of the Reformed Church and worked as a tutor for the aristocratic Dohnas family (1790–1794). Once he completed the ordination process, Schleiermacher served as an assistant pastor of a Reformed church in Landsberg (1794–1796) and then as chaplain to Charité Hospital in Berlin (1796–1802).

Moving to Berlin was a significant event in Schleiermacher's life, as it placed him in contact with the leading intellectuals of his day, including defenders of Rationalism and Romanticism. Exacerbated by these intellectuals' dismissal of religion, Schleiermacher wrote *On Religion: Speeches to Its Cultured Despisers* (1799) in hopes of confronting their "enlightened" slumber. This work wielded an enormous impact, leading eventually to Schleiermacher's appointment as a professor and university preacher at the University of Halle in 1804. Napoleon's invasion of Halle in

1806 and its detachment from Prussia, however, motivated Schleiermacher to move to Berlin. There he married Henriette von Willich (1809), served as a minister of Trinity Church (1809 until his death), and became involved in the formation of the University of Berlin, which opened in 1810 with Schleiermacher as a professor and dean of the theological faculty.

During his twenty-four years as a professor at the University of Berlin, Schleiermacher lectured on an array of topics, including hermeneutics, psychology, pedagogy, aesthetics, ethics, dialectics, and politics. He approached his lectures on theology with the same rigor devoted to these other topics and with an overarching concern for knowledge advancement and practical instruction. His *Brief Outline on the Study of Theology* (1811) divides theology into three categories—philosophical, historical, and practical—with historical theology including exegetical theology, church history, and dogmatic theology. Dogmatic theology is further subdivided into Christian doctrine (the science of faith, or *Glaubenslehre*) and Christian ethics (the science of morality, or *Sittlichkeit*). This explains why in *The Christian Faith*, which Schleiermacher referred to as his *Glaubenslehre*, he defines dogmatic theology as "the science which systematizes the doctrine prevalent in a Christian Church at a given time" (§19). In short, this is theology done within a socio-historical framework rather than deduced from philosophical principles.

The purpose of *The Christian Faith*, therefore, is to present a system of doctrine that arises out of the particular faith experience of the church Schleiermacher called home most of his adult life and where he preached, namely, Trinity Church (*Dreifaltigheitskirche*) in Berlin. Originally a Reformed Church, Schleiermacher urged the congregation to join the Evangelical Church of the Old Prussian Union in 1817 (*Evangelische Kirche der altpreußischen Union*), a union of the Lutheran and Reformed traditions. *The Christian Faith* shares this unifying objective, while at the same time presenting a way forward for Protestant theology in the wake of rationalism and skepticism. The first German edition appeared in 1821–1822 entitled *Der christliche Glaube nach den Grudsätzen der evangelischen Kirche im Zusammenhange dargestellt* (*The Christian Faith Presented as a Coherent Whole According to the Fundamental Principles of the Evangelical Church*), but was significantly revised in 1830–1831 to reflect Schleiermacher's ongoing struggle and desire to match doctrinal expression with his experience of faith. Despite its widespread impact, *The Christian Faith* was not translated into English until 1928, but it had already influenced a whole new generation of theologians seeking to articulate Christian belief in the shadow of the Enlightenment.

Religion within the limits of feeling

In the Introduction to *The Christian Faith* Schleiermacher explains that, at its core, religion is a matter of feeling. This perspective was particularly at odds with the rationalists in nineteenth-century Europe who, following Kant, believed that religion was primarily a product of reason. In referring to "feeling," Schleiermacher does not merely mean emotions, but a more basic level of feeling he calls "immediate self-consciousness" (§3). Having self-consciousness entails being aware of the capacity to act but also the reality of being acted upon. In other words, self-consciousness involves the feeling of freedom and the feeling of dependence on everything outside the self. It is a sense of active spontaneity and passive receptivity. Since it is impossible to be absolutely spontaneous and absolutely receptive at the same time, receptivity or dependence is ultimately determinative. For Schleiermacher, this "feeling of absolute dependence" is the same as being conscious of God. In fact, "God" is the term he uses to describe the feeling of absolute dependence, which is the core of all religions.

Just as Schleiermacher views "God" as a description of the feeling of absolute dependence, he similarly explains all doctrines as religious feelings expressed in language (§15). For example, the doctrines of divine attributes— God's eternity, omnipresence, etc.—do not represent something special in God, but are simply different ways of describing the feeling of absolute dependence (§50). In addition, to say that God is Creator or Sustainer of the universe is not to articulate the truth of God's historical action in the world, but rather it is an appropriate way of expressing the entire world's dependence on God (§36).

If doctrines are ways of describing the feeling of absolute dependence, it is easy to see how some doctrines may be particularly useful and others may be considered superfluous. As Schleiermacher progresses through the traditional topics of Christian theology, he devotes attention to delineating doctrines related to the feeling of absolute dependence—such as absolute divine causality (§51)—but hurries quickly over other doctrines he deems irrelevant. For instance, since the existence of angels has no impact on or relevance to religious experience, they have no dogmatic importance (§43). Similarly, a historical account of creation is not necessary because it would not clarify the feeling of absolute dependence (§40.2). Furthermore, a doctrine such as the virgin birth of Jesus is superfluous because all that is really necessary is the divine power to enable a supernatural conception ensuring the perfection of a Redeemer (§97.2). One final example is the doctrine of last things or eschatology to which Schleiermacher assigns lesser value because these doctrines do not arise from the inner life; rather, they are the "efforts of an insufficiently equipped faculty of premonition" (§159.2, 706).

By grounding doctrine in feeling, Schleiermacher not only gives rationale for dividing useful from superfluous doctrine, but he also provides a defense of doctrinal change and adaptation. Perhaps the most well-known example in *The Christian Faith* in this regard is Schleiermacher's resistance to two-nature formulations of Christology and his alternative proposal. In his opinion, the language of Christ having a divine nature and human nature, indivisibly yet distinctly united in one person, is unnecessarily confusing and only leads to inevitable errors. If the confluence of divinity and humanity in the person of Christ is understood in terms of Christ's perfect God-consciousness, argues Schleiermacher, not only does this make more sense, but it also directly relates to our feeling of fellowship with God (§96). Schleiermacher's Christology will be explored further below, but at this point it is instructive to observe how constructing doctrine from the foundation of feeling influences his perspective at every juncture.

It might be tempting to assume that if religion and doctrine function within the limits of feeling, Schleiermacher has little concern for Scripture. The opposite is actually the case, and he boldly confesses the sufficiency of the Holy Spirit working through Scripture. In typical Reformed fashion, he affirms the efficacy of the Scriptures: "So that if one day there should exist in the Church a complete reflection of Christ's living knowledge of God, we may with perfect justice regard this as the fruit of Scripture, without any addition of foreign elements having had to come in" (§131.2, 606). Schleiermacher's reasons for affirming the authority of Scripture, however, differ from the defense of *sola scriptura* during the Protestant Reformation. Essentially, he affirms the normativity of scripture because it is the expression of original Christian consciousness into language. Because this Christian consciousness only arose after Jesus, it is possible to see why, although Schleiermacher views Scripture as a norm, the Old Testament is not nearly as relevant or normative as the New Testament. Earlier in *The Christian Faith*, he all but dismisses the Old Testament as completely superfluous (§27.3). In a later section, however, Schleiermacher clarifies that the Old Testament is useful to the extent that it illuminates the New (§132). Overall, it is faith in Christ, as present among the early church, which grounds the authority of Scripture, not Scripture which grounds faith in Christ.

Just as Schleiermacher both affirms and revises the doctrine of Scripture within the limits of feeling or consciousness, the same is true with his understanding of faith itself. It is significant to note that the title page of the German original contains two quotes from Anselm: "Nor do I seek to understand in order that I may believe, but I have faith in order that I may understand" and "For he who does not believe does not experience, and he who does not experience, does not understand." By placing these two quotes together, Schleiermacher is making two important points. First, faith is primarily about experience, or more specifically, it is an inward "certainty concerning the feeling of absolute dependence" (§14.1, 68). Second, faith is the ground of knowledge and understanding, which brings us back to the centrality of feeling in Schleiermacher's entire project. Feeling is the foundation on which everything rests, and it leads him to a unique explanation of Christianity as a religion of redemption.

Christianity as a religion of redemption

Christianity is unique among religions, according to Schleiermacher, because it relates everything to the redemption accomplished by Jesus of Nazareth (§11). Before discussing the place of Jesus and Christology in *The Christian Faith*, however, it is helpful to grasp how Schleiermacher articulates the need for and nature of redemption. He begins by showing how the feeling of absolute dependence always includes both a feeling of turning away from God and a feeling of drawing near to God (§62, 261). This feeling of alienation from God is the essence of sin, stemming from our own lack of God-consciousness. The feeling of fellowship with God is something that comes from God himself, and this is what Schleiermacher calls grace (§63). The whole second part of *The Christian Faith*, which is by far the largest part, is structured by exploring this antithesis of sin and grace, which are present at every moment of the Christian life.

Schleiermacher insists that any feeling of fellowship is a Redeemer-communicated grace (§91), whereas any feeling of alienation, any feeling not oriented toward consciousness of God, is a self-originating sin (§66). Much of what Schleiermacher says about sin matches traditional Reformed and Lutheran perspectives, such as the existence of original sin, the inevitability of actual sin, and the hopelessness of achieving redemption apart from the gracious work of the Redeemer. The biggest difference, of course, is that he takes this traditional presentation and translates it as lack of

God-consciousness. Thus, original sin is the lack of God-consciousness that exists in every individual and makes apparent the universal need for redemption (§70–71). Similarly, actual sin is every human person's active suppression of or lack of desire for a perfect God-consciousness, flowing from our natural incapacity for fellowship with God. While traditional perspectives link original sin with Adam and Eve's first sin, Schleiermacher identifies original sin as an inherent incapacity for good, which, along with the inherent capacity for God-consciousness, constitute universal human nature (§72). Consequently, there is no imputation of the first parents' sin to the rest of humanity, which would make sin—and, by implication, the work of redemption—something external rather than an internal reality (§72.4, 300–01).

As such, Schleiermacher views redemption as an inward process of being drawn toward greater and greater consciousness of God. More precisely, it is the process of being drawn into the power of the Redeemer's own perfect consciousness of God that we could never achieve with our own power. Only through receptivity to the Redeemer can humans experience living fellowship with God. In this way, fellowship with God is the same as fellowship with the Redeemer. Schleiermacher repeatedly emphasizes that this redemption never occurs in isolation, but always involves being assumed into reconciled fellowship with others who are experiencing the Redeemer's blessings (§101). As a result, Schleiermacher's view of redemption is inherently relational, and at the hub of all these relationships is the Redeemer himself. This leads us to consider at greater length the significance of Jesus and the extent to which *The Christian Faith* can be considered a Christ-centered work of theology.

The uniqueness of Christ the Redeemer

One of Schleiermacher's most influential students, David Friedrich Strauss (1808–1874), once commented that *The Christian Faith* really has a single dogma: the person of Christ.[2] This can already be seen by the fact that Schleiermacher believed that every element of Christianity is related to the Redeemer's person and work. What makes the Redeemer unique, and the crux of Schleiermacher's Christology, is "the constant potency of His God-consciousness, which was a veritable existence of God in Him" (§94). In other words, Christ is unique and can be distinguished as the Redeemer because he perfectly experienced the feeling of dependence on and fellowship with God, so much so that this is how we should understand Christ's divinity.

Schleiermacher is uncomfortable with the traditional language of Christ having two natures—divine and human—in one person. He thinks this language is misplaced because it confuses and distracts us from what really makes Christ unique, namely, "the innermost fundamental power within Him, from which every activity proceeds and which holds every element together" (§96.3, 397). Therefore, he deems it legitimate to speak of Christ as "the Word become flesh" or "the image of the invisible God" because Christ's constantly perfect God-consciousness is the very meaning of God becoming incarnate.

The power of God in Christ—Christ's perfect feeling of fellowship with God—is what makes redemption possible for the rest of humanity. In articulating the details of how Christ assumes people into his perfect fellowship with God, Schleiermacher critiques the Protestant notion of vicarious satisfaction, preferring to speak of Christ as a "satisfying representative" (§104.4, 461). Christ does not make satisfaction for our lack of God-consciousness to the extent that we no longer have any responsibility to pursue fellowship with God. Rather, Christ represents "the perfecting of human nature" (§104.4, 461) and by his free surrender to death frees people from their inability—with its accompanying guilt—to eradicate the feeling of alienation.

The Redeemer assumes believers into his perfect fellowship with God through an ongoing and comprehensive process, but Schleiermacher does pinpoint some particular moments. He recognizes a turning point—regeneration—at which the Redeemer's God-consciousness begins to influence others, although this turning point cannot be isolated from the overall process of experiencing the blessedness of the Redeemer (§106.1, 476–77). Likewise, Schleiermacher explains conversion as the moment when a passive consciousness is transformed into an active consciousness. Attempting to identify the particular time and place of conversion, however, is an "arbitrary and presumptuous restriction of divine grace," since the activation of God-consciousness can take many different forms (§108.3, 487f). Justification is interdependent with conversion as God's act of changing our relation to him, but embedded within this relational reorientation is the ongoing influence of Christ's power on our consciousness (§109.3, 502–03). Justification and sanctification are therefore part of the same process of growing in Christlike fellowship with God, although sanctification stresses the progressive nature of this growth (§110).

It is important to stress that Schleiermacher views all these elements and moments of redemption as happening not just within individuals, but within the common life of believers. All those who are experiencing the process of sanctification have a mutual influence on one another, so much so that Schleiermacher identifies the mutuality that develops among the fellowship of believers as the communication of the Holy Spirit (§121). In other words, the Holy Spirit is none other than the common Spirit present among those who experience living fellowship with the Redeemer (§123–24). By describing the Spirit in this way, Schleiermacher places pneumatology in a symbiotic relationship with ecclesiology, which naturally raises the question: what implication does this have for Schleiermacher's understanding of the Trinity?

Schleiermacher places his short discussion of the Trinity at the very end of *The Christian Faith*, primarily because it does not express anything immediately arising from the feeling of absolute dependence. Instead, it is a doctrine that culminates from the articulation of other doctrines, such as Christology and ecclesiology (§170). The Trinity is not a foundational doctrine on which all other doctrines rest, but the "coping-stone" or capstone of Christian doctrine (§170.1, 739). Many theologians have critiqued Schleiermacher for relegating a full discussion of the Trinity to a short conclusion in a massive work of dogmatic theology, but Schleiermacher did not make this decision because he thought this doctrine to be unimportant. On the contrary, take away the Trinity as three Persons equal to each other and the divine essence, he claims, and "everything most important in Christianity would be changed" (§171.1, 742–43). Schleiermacher was hoping for a transformation of trinitarian theology, and subsequent theologians have taken up his challenge, both those who share his fundamental principles and those who categorically disagree, such as Karl Barth.

Mention of Karl Barth brings us back to Schleiermacher's Christology, for despite the vast differences between these two seminal theologians, both have been described as placing Christ at the center of their theological projects. An important difference, however, is that Schleiermacher does not begin with Christ; as we have seen, his starting point is the feeling of absolute dependence and the consciousness of a Creator God. Accordingly, Christ is the measure of true humanity, the one who possesses perfect God-consciousness and through whom all humanity can experience a new life of receptivity to God. As such, Richard Niebuhr identified Schleiermacher's theology as "Christo-morphic" rather than Christo-centric, since his system does not resemble "the artificial simplicity of a circle."[3] Therefore, whereas it might not be accurate to agree with Strauss that Christology is the one single dogma of *The Christian Faith*, it is possible to conclude that the overarching purpose of this work is to present the possibility and indeed the necessity of living fellowship with Christ the Redeemer.

Protestant theology after Schleiermacher

Whether or not Schleiermacher intended to found a new theological movement, *The Christian Faith* charted a new way of doing theology in the modern world. Rather than reacting with skepticism to the limits of human knowledge, Schleiermacher showed how it is possible to ground theology in religious experience and to connect doctrine intrinsically to the life of faith. He inspired the main proponents of what would eventually be considered liberal Protestant theology in Germany and beyond, as represented by Albrecht Ritschl (1822–1889) and later Rudolf Bultmann (1884–1976) and Paul Tillich (1886–1965). But even more than that, he influenced new trends in the social sciences and arts more broadly, as evident in the work of Wilhelm Dilthey (1833–1911).

The fact that even some of Schleiermacher's strongest critics in the twentieth century—such as Karl Barth (1886–1968) and Emil Brunner (1889–1966)—were committed to understanding and lecturing on *The Christian Faith* shows its enduring significance. Despite his radical opposition to Schleiermacher's methodology, Barth confessed the genius of Schleiermacher: "All the so-to-speak official impulses and movements of the centuries since the Reformation find a center of unity in him: orthodoxy, pietism, the Enlightenment."[4] Indeed, *The Christian Faith* shows how Pietism could survive in the shadow of the Enlightenment, although the extent to which Schleiermacher preserved orthodoxy has been an ongoing debate between his ardent appreciators and disgruntled detractors.

What is not subject to debate, however, is the fact that *The Christian Faith* arose out of and fed back into the life of the church. From the beginning to the end of his career, Schleiermacher was committed to the local church, dedicated to ecumenical efforts in uniting Lutheran and Reformed traditions, and devoted to preaching in a way that connected with the affections and intellects of his congregations. In his *Brief Outline on the Study of Theology*, he posited that someone who combined religious and scientific sensibilities and who was capable of serving both theoretical and practical purposes deserves the title "prince of the church."[5] It is thus fitting that one contemporary admirer has applied this title to Schleiermacher himself, as *The Christian Faith* certainly wielded both wide-ranging theoretical and practical influence.[6]

In light of this vast influence, it is also appropriate to consider Schleiermacher a "father of modern theology," although most scholars will agree that this title must be applied equally to G.W.F. Hegel (1770–1831).

What sets these two thinkers apart is their unprecedented use of a material norm to organize and evaluate every detail in a theological system.[7] As we have seen, for Schleiermacher this material norm is the feeling of absolute dependence. This feeling is the foundation of all religion and the source of all doctrine, and ultimately it is this feeling that leads people to experience redemption through Christ the Redeemer.

Notes

1. Translated from *Der christliche Glaube nach den Grudsätzen der evangelischen Kirche im Zusammenhange dargestellt*; all references to this work (Friedrich Schliermacher, *The Christian Faith* [eds MacKintosh, H.R.; Stewart, J.S.; London/New York: T&T Clark, 1999]) shall be noted by employing in-text parenthetical citations.
2. David Friedrich Strauss, *The Christ of Faith and the Jesus of History: A Critique of Schleiermacher's Life of Jesus*, trans. Leander E. Keck (Philadelphia: Fortress Press, 1977), 4.
3. Richard R. Niebuhr, *Schleiermacher on Christ and Religion* (London: SCM Press, 1964), 212.
4. Karl Barth, *The Theology of Schleiermacher: Lectures at Göttingen, Winter Semester of 1923–24*, ed. Dietrich Ritschl, trans. Geoffrey W. Bromiley (Grand Rapids: Eerdmans, 1982), xv.
5. Friedrich Schleiermacher, *Brief Outline on the Study of Theology*, trans. Terrence N. Tice (Richmond: John Knox Press, 1970), 21.
6. Brian A. Gerrish, *A Prince of the Church* (London: SCM Press, 1984).
7. For an excellent introduction to this definition of modern theology, see Bruce L. McCormack, "Introduction: On 'Modernity' as a Theological Concept" in *Mapping Modern Theology: A Thematic and Historical Introduction*, eds. Kelly M. Kapic and Bruce L. McCormack (Baker, 2012), 7–9.

Select Bibliography

Primary sources

MacKintosh, H.R. and Stewart, J.S., eds. *The Christian Faith*. London/New York: T&T Clark, 1999.

Schafer, Rolf, ed. *Der christliche Glaube nach den Grudsätzen der evangelischen Kirche im Zusammenhange dargestellt*, 2nd ed. Berlin: Walter de Gruyter, 2008.

Secondary sources

Kelsey, Catherine L. *Thinking about Christ with Schleiermacher*. Louisville: Westminster John Knox Press, 2003.

Mariña, Jacqueline. *The Cambridge Companion to Friedrich Schleiermacher*. Cambridge: Cambridge University Press, 2005.

Niebuhr, Richard R. *Schleiermacher on Christ and Religion*. Eugene: Wipf and Stock, 2009 [reprint].

Redeker, Martin. *Schleiermacher: Life and Thought*. Philadelphia: Fortress Press, 1973.

Tice, Terrence N. *Schleiermacher*. Abingdon Pillars of Theology. Nashville: Abingdon Press, 2006.

5.2

Systematic Theology (1871–1872)

Charles Hodge (1797–1878)

Figure 5.2 Charles Hodge

Old School headmaster

Recent biographers of Charles Hodge coined three memorable monikers to portray his vast influence as a theologian, educator, and churchman: *pride of Princeton, guardian of American orthodoxy,* and *pope of Presbyterianism.*[1] If

Hodge deserves the third title, it is only as preeminent spokesperson for Old School Presbyterianism, not the New School variety. As a result, the extent to which one views Hodge as the custodian of orthodoxy depends on which side of the Presbyterian fence one prefers. What cannot be contested, however, is the enormous impact Hodge wielded on generations of theology students at Princeton and on the defense and propagation of confessional Reformed theology in America and around the world.

In 1797, Charles Hodge was born into a distinguished merchant family in Philadelphia. Tragically, when Charles was only six months old, his father died of yellow fever. His mother was more than capable of raising him, and Hodge was well prepared at age fifteen to enter the classical academy in Somerville, New Jersey. He continued on to study at the College of New Jersey (later Princeton University) and then the newly formed Princeton Seminary. During this time, Hodge experienced a conversion that he described as a culmination of Christian nurture, and he eagerly received the tutelage of Archibald Alexander, a prominent professor of theology at Princeton Seminary.

As Princeton grew, an urgent need arose for a professor to teach biblical languages, and Alexander asked Hodge to fill this role, only after his roommate and best friend, John Johns, declined the invitation. Hodge readily accepted after a brief stint in Philadelphia caring for his mother and preaching in local churches, and quickly discovered his love for teaching. In 1822, after two years of teaching and his ordination in the Presbyterian Church, he received an official appointment at Princeton Seminary as professor of oriental and biblical literature. In the same year, he married Sarah Bache, the great granddaughter of Benjamin Franklin, with whom he would enjoy the blessing of eight children.

Despite his love for teaching, Hodge became painfully aware of his inadequacies in languages and burgeoning biblical scholarship. As a result, he requested a study leave to Europe in order to gain proficiency in French and German as well as contemporary European scholarship. His two years in Paris, Halle, and Berlin (1826–1828) proved enormously formative, both in terms of academic learning and the friendships he formed that would enable him to maintain connections with European centers of learning. His encounter with Schleiermacher was one among many critical encounters that solidified his distress over the "German mind," making him increasingly resolute to articulate an alternative theological vision.

His main avenue for doing so was *The Biblical Repertory and Princeton Review*, a journal Hodge started just before departing for Europe. Upon returning to Princeton, he assumed the role of editor and began a lifetime of prolific publication, the bulk of which appeared in this journal. Poor health plagued him in the 1830s and would remain with him the rest of his life, but he still managed to persist in teaching duties and wield leadership within the Presbyterian Church. Hodge was not squeamish about debates, and his resolute positions gained him notoriety as a defender of Old School Presbyterianism, typically siding with order over ardor and confessionalism over pietism. Hodge did not oppose piety and religious experience, but insisted on their congruence with doctrinal orthodoxy and church order. His *Commentary on Romans* (1835) demarcated his views from Albert Barnes, Nathaniel Taylor, and other New School Presbyterians, precipitating the Old School/New School schism in 1837.

In 1840, Hodge was appointed professor of exegetical and didactic theology at Princeton Seminary. Throughout his fifty-plus years of teaching, he trained more students than any other American professor in the nineteenth century. At his fiftieth anniversary as professor in 1872, thousands of people gathered to celebrate his accomplishments, including the first two volumes of his *Systematic Theology* (vols. 1–2, 1871; vol. 3, 1872), which had already replaced Francis Turretin's *Elenctic Theology* (1679–1685) as the core theology textbook at Princeton. While sharing Turretin's concern to systematize and preserve confessional Reformed theology, Hodge's *Systematic Theology* engaged extensively with contemporary scholarship and is recognized by some as inaugurating a new era of comprehensive theological study.[2] Hodge distilled decades of theology lectures and hundreds of articles addressing contemporary figures and debates into these thick volumes. As such, Mark Noll rightly concludes that the *Systematic Theology* "is not so much the capstone of his life as the caboose at the end of a very long train."[3] That train reached the end of the line on June 19, 1878, but the legacy of Charles Hodge laid long tracks for the journey of Princeton Seminary and confessional Reformed theology in North America.

Just the biblical facts

The *Systematic Theology* spans four broad topics in the space of three volumes: theology proper or doctrine of God, anthropology, soteriology, and eschatology. In terms of general structure and several heading titles, it matches the layout of the *Westminster Confession of Faith* (1646), the confessional standard for the Presbyterian Church. A major difference, however, is that the *Systematic Theology* does not include a section on ecclesiology. Hodge did lecture extensively on the church, however, and these lectures were published soon after his death.[4] Although Hodge had intended to revise this material for his *Systematic Theology*, as it stands there is more than enough substance to understand the methodology and main themes of his theology.[5]

In the Introduction, Hodge defends an inductive theological method versus a speculative, mystical, or Roman Catholic method. The essence of this method is that the Bible contains all the facts necessary for theology, and the task of systematic theology is to gather all of these facts, show their relationship, and formulate principles based on them. Undergirding this method are several key presuppositions. First, Hodge presupposes that theology is a science, and just as good science begins with facts and builds a scientific theory or system based on observation, so theology moves from the facts of Scripture to a theological system. In short, "the Bible is to the theologian what nature is to the man of science."[6] No fact of Scripture should be ignored. For example, the Bible contains facts about Christ knowing all things, but it also includes instances where Christ displays ignorance. The doctrinal conclusion of these disparate facts, according to Hodge, is that Christ has both a divine and human nature in one unified personality (1:12).

Second, Hodge privileges the facts of Scripture because he believes the Bible to be the inspired revelation of God containing every truth necessary for theological knowledge and personal salvation. Biblical revelation will be consistent with the facts discerned through reason and experience, because all truth comes from God. Only Scripture, however, can be the ultimate ground and guide for theology and life. Hodge recognizes a dynamic interplay between religious experience and biblical doctrine, for whereas the facts of Scripture must authenticate spiritual experience, the inward teaching of the Spirit must also interpret biblical doctrine. In fact, a "theology of the heart" as expressed in prayers and hymns was so important for Hodge that he confessed his theology would be nothing if "not sustained by the devotional writings of true Christians of every denomination" (1:17).

A third presupposition of Hodge's inductive method is the trustworthiness of our senses, mental operations, and self-evident truths. These same assumptions guide natural scientists, and when adopted by theologians, they provide guidelines for realistic doctrinal discovery. Many scholars have rightly highlighted the influence of Scottish Common Sense Realism on Hodge's theology, although this claim should be qualified. There is no doubt that since its founding by Scot-American John Witherspoon, Princeton had been a hotbed for philosophical realism in the tradition of Thomas Reid. According to this tradition, certain truths, such as the distinction between right and wrong or self-existence, should be received by common sense and not submitted to scathing skepticism. Hodge affirms the existence of these truths (1:10), but in no way asserts that they are a test for doctrine or diminish the need for supernatural revelation. When philosophers in this tradition, such as William Hamilton, began to deny the possibility of knowing a personal God, Hodge and other Princetonians readily rejected this philosophy (1:346–65).[7]

In other words, Hodge remained committed to an inductive method of moving from biblical facts to doctrinal system, in contrast to a speculative method of moving from philosophical principles to doctrinal system. The supernatural revelation of Scripture needs to prove every truth of reason, and therefore Scripture is the ultimate source for theology. In general, Hodge targets Deism and Transcendentalism as theological systems that fall prey to rationalism and a speculative method (1:34–60). As his treatment of various doctrines unfolds, Hodge repeatedly remarks on speculative distortions of these doctrines. Regarding the doctrine of sin, for example, he critiques the speculative habit of identifying an external philosophical principle—sin as limitation of being, privation, sensuousness, or selfishness, etc.—that lacks congruence with biblical facts (2:132–49). He contrasts these philosophical perversions with doctrines as attested by the early church, Protestant confessions, and ultimately the Bible.

Mysticism is another erroneous method Hodge critiques, which moves from feelings to doctrinal system. Like the speculative method, mysticism displaces the authority of Scripture by recognizing feelings or experience as the ultimate source. Hodge recognizes a dangerous mystical strain running through every era of Christian tradition, but focuses on Quietism and heterodox Quakerism as particular expressions. In his critique of the latter, Hodge distinguishes between orthodox Quakers who rightly emphasize the illumination of the Spirit and heterodox Quakers who espouse Deism, limit Christ's work to its subjective effects, and elevate the "inner light" to an authority equal to or greater than Scripture (1:92–97). Throughout the *Systematic Theology*, Schleiermacher bears the brunt of Hodge's critique as a modern mystic, particularly since Hodge sees him as representing many of the ills plaguing the modern German mind.

A third method Hodge contrasts with his inductive scheme is the Roman Catholic approach, which moves from Scripture and tradition to doctrinal system. Although tradition plays a major role in the *Systematic Theology*,

Hodge opposes this method because it treats tradition as another form of revelation, and thus a standard for faith. Protestants affirm the consent of the universal church, but only on essential matters of faith and those doctrines plainly revealed in Scripture (1:115–16). Once again, everything for Hodge goes back to the facts of Scripture, and if these are not the starting point for theology, the whole system is doomed to distort God's revelation.

The threat of anti-theism

Hodge begins his "Theology Proper" by showing how it is possible to approach the Bible with confidence that God can actually be known, albeit not comprehensively. He defines theism as "the doctrine of an extramundane, personal God, the creator, preserver, and governor of the world" (1:204). Atheism, therefore, is not merely the denial of God's existence; it includes anti-theism, the denial of an extramundane, personal God (1:241). As varieties of anti-theism, Hodge deals with polytheism, hylozoism, materialism, and pantheism, but gives by far the most attention to the latter two.

Materialism is a system that reduces everything to physical forces, denying the existence of a mind or spirit. Hodge locates the seed of materialism in the philosophy of Epicurus, which germinated through Hobbes, Locke and others, and flowered through the positivism of Auguste Comte (1798–1857). According to positivism, knowledge is restricted to physical phenomena and their observable relations. Consequently, any discipline purporting to deal with metaphysical or supernatural reality is rejected or completely revised in positivist fashion. Hodge has no patience for this worldview, arguing that it contradicts the facts of consciousness, reason, and experience (1:276–83). Whereas some forms of materialism do not explicitly deny the existence of God, Hodge claims that all forms are atheistic since their fundamental principles undermine theistic belief.

Pantheism is far more beguiling than materialism, for it often goes under the guise of Christian theology while denying fundamental truths. Most basically, it denies the distinction between God and the world, thus renouncing the unique personality of God and the finite individuality of human beings. Hodge spares no punches for pantheism, claiming that it destroys human freedom, the distinction between good and evil, and rational religion itself. In short, it is the worst form of atheism (1:333). He demonstrates its tragic rise in popularity through the work of Spinoza, Fichte, Schelling, Hegel, Schleiermacher, and others. The haste with which Hodge lumps thinkers into anti-theistic camps, however, has caused some scholars to doubt his grasp of proper distinctions. Brian Gerrish, for example, wonders whether Hodge adequately distinguished between Schleiermacher and Hegel, mistakenly viewing them both as pantheists and instances of the "modern German mind."[8]

Of these two German thinkers, Hodge extends much more effort in critiquing Schleiermacher, possibly because Hodge regarded him "as the most interesting as well as the most influential theologian of modern times" (2:440). While judging his theology a contradictory mess, Hodge held great respect for Schleiermacher's piety, conjecturing in a famous footnote that since Schleiermacher sang praises to Christ on earth, it is most likely he will be praising Christ his Savior in heaven (2:440, n. 1). Despite this underlying respect and charitable hope, Hodge was ruthless in his critique. He accuses Schleiermacher of being unbiblical, speculative, pantheistic, anti-trinitarian, and at odds with orthodox forms of anthropology, Christology, and soteriology (2:442–54). Regarding his Christology, Hodge links every problem to Schleiermacher's propensity to collapse the God–world distinction. Since anything Schleiermacher says of God is simply an expression of self-consciousness, it is impossible for him to affirm the existence of an extra-mundane, personal God and his incarnation as the person of Christ.

In contrast to these anti-theistic threats, Hodge articulates his doctrine of God, the Trinity, and Christ using traditional terms and meanings as articulated in the early church and Reformed confessions. The danger of pantheistic portrayals, he claims, is that they retain traditional terms (Redeemer, Mediator, Incarnation, Spirit, etc.) while changing their meaning. Such a shift in meaning is a result of pantheists embracing a principle external to Scripture rather than submitting to the facts and authority of Scripture. For example, Hodge accuses many of his contemporaries for opposing the doctrine of regeneration, which claims that God brings alive those who were spiritually dead according to his will and power. Hodge argues that such opposition is based on a variety of prejudiced philosophical principles, with no regard to clear statements in Scripture to the contrary (3:37–40). On this issue, Hodge submits everyone outside the Reformed tradition to the criticism that their theological priorities displace Scripture as the ultimate authority, including his New School Presbyterian interlocutors: Nathanael Emmons, Charles Finney and Nathaniel Taylor (3:7–14).

Given Hodge's persistent emphasis on biblical induction, it is curious to note that some sections of the *Systematic Theology* do not include any treatment of biblical material, and those that do are sometimes organized in piecemeal fashion. For instance, while the section on regeneration just discussed contains substantial quotes from John Calvin, John Owen, Turretin, the Canons of Dordt, and the Westminster Standards, only one page in this lengthy portion contains scant quotes from Scripture (3:34). Other sections include deep biblical investigation, such as his defense of the divinity of Christ (1:483–521), but the objection nevertheless remains that sometimes Hodge fails to show how his doctrinal system arises from the biblical facts. Furthermore, there are instances where Hodge's interpretation and application of these biblical facts could be contested. To pick one example, in commenting on the sixth commandment, he resolutely defends the necessity of capital punishment for murderers (3:363–64) and pronounces that those who commit suicide will lose their soul (3:367). In earlier writings, he also articulated a troubling position on slavery, arguing that while abusive slaveholding is wrong, the institution of slavery should only be phased out gradually rather than hastening emancipation.[9] Underdeveloped elements of the *Systematic Theology*, therefore, include an awareness of how social and cultural location impact interpretation of biblical facts and a more thorough defense of why these facts should be viewed through Reformed theological lenses. Without paying attention to this process, a bad habit may emerge of staring at the lenses and ignoring the facts themselves or taking them for granted.

Reading the facts with Reformed lenses

Hodge roots his Reformed reading of Scripture in Augustinianism. In fact, he uses "Reformed" and "Augustinian" interchangeably to distinguish his anthropology and soteriology from competing views, whether Pelagianism or semi-Pelagianism, Roman Catholicism, Remonstrant theology, Arminianism, or later varieties of Lutheranism. What sets the Augustinian-Reformed perspective apart from these other systems is a commitment to God's control over the plan of salvation and his determination of who will be saved (2:330). Hodge insists that all other systems give humans a determinative role, although they lie on a spectrum from heretical Pelagianism to the more minor errors of later Lutheranism and Wesleyan Arminianism. Whereas the former denies the corruption of human nature and affirms a natural capacity to do good works, the latter groups affirm the comprehensive depravity of human nature and deny any natural ability to cooperate with God's grace. Hodge places the Roman Catholic and Remonstrant positions in the middle of this spectrum, but to varying degrees he accuses all these systems of promoting a synergistic account of salvation. In other words, at some point they make human ability or obedience determinative of salvation, rather than ascribing every portion of this process to God alone. Hodge insists that one's entire theological system depends on whether one chooses synergism or monergism, so it is no surprise that he utilizes this distinction throughout the *Systematic Theology* to delineate his positions.

For instance, Hodge maintains a monergistic account of faith and justification in contrast to synergistic versions. This is one point where Hodge finds agreement between Reformed and Lutheran perspectives: justification is the work of God alone accomplished by grace alone through faith alone. Justification is dependent on nothing else except the righteousness of Christ graciously imputed to those who believe, which itself is a gift of God. By contrast, Hodge criticizes the Remonstrants and Arminians for making obedient faith a condition of justification. Furthermore, Romanists make a muddle of justification by believing that works done after regeneration gain merit for final justification (3:135–37). Hodge celebrates the extent to which these theological systems preserve the central truths of the Gospel—doctrines articulated in the first ecumenical creeds—but he laments the ways in which human works displace Christ as the ultimate ground of justification.

Once the human element has been introduced, Hodge observes, it begins to crop up at every point in the drama of salvation. Rather than maintaining the high standards of God's law and humanity's helpless need for God's empowering grace, Hodge argues that these synergistic systems introduce the dangerous possibility of perfection by lowering the law's demands and overemphasizing human ability. He sees the dangers of Pelagianism resurfacing among Arminians at Oberlin University, such as Charles Finney, who limit sin to voluntary actions and deny any inherent moral corruption. Less extreme but equally erroneous, Romanists and Wesleyan Arminians view perfection as attainable, but only because they think believers are bound to a milder version of the law (3:250–58). In response to these views, Hodge resolutely articulates the impossibility of perfection and launches into a lengthy exposition of the law (3:259–465). He does this to show that no amount of external obedience can fulfill God's demands, and the only possible perfection is the righteousness obtained in Christ by the Spirit.

At each point in his soteriology, Hodge distinguishes his Reformed, monergistic account of salvation with synergistic systems. This pattern continues as he deals with the sacraments and no doubt would have continued if he had managed to complete a fourth volume on ecclesiology. The result is arguably the most cogent and comprehensive summary of Reformed theology ever produced in North America. In the midst of the dizzying profusion of theological trends and centers of learning during the latter half of the nineteenth century, Hodge provided a solid foundation for those seeking to maintain their confessional, Reformed heritage.

Hodge's heritage

Hodge's *Systematic Theology* accomplished more than preserving and propagating Reformed theology among nineteenth-century Presbyterians. It modeled a way of doing theology that brings a Protestant confessional tradition into conversation with modern thought and culture for the sake of the church. His awareness of religious thought and culture at home, attentiveness to leading scholarship abroad, and insatiable interest in every area of knowledge is evident in the *Systematic Theology*, but it is best captured by his voluminous contributions to *The Biblical Repertory and Princeton Review*.

"Old School Headmaster" is an appropriate title for Hodge given his leadership position among Old School Presbyterians, but it also communicates his commitment to address theological debates of his day with the old answers of orthodoxy. At the end of volume two of the *Systematic Theology*, he acknowledges the great number of theological debates that surfaced in the nineteenth century, but he argues that "into these debates no new questions have entered." The form of these questions may be new, but "the principles involved in these controversies are the same as those involved in the earlier conflicts in the church" (2:732). The same rationale undergirds Hodge's controversial statement that nothing new ever originated out of Princeton Seminary. His intention in saying this, of course, was to affirm that there is nothing new under the sun, and the best answers to seemingly new controversies are the old, tried and true ones. This passion for countering contemporary scholarship with orthodoxy as expressed in the Reformed tradition is the heritage Hodge passed on to several generations of theologians and leaders at Princeton Seminary. It was a legacy upheld by his son, A.A. Hodge, and later by B.B. Warfield and J. Gresham Machen. When Machen left Princeton Seminary in 1929 to found Westminster Seminary, Hodge's heritage lived on through the fundamentalist battle against modernism.

Despite Hodge's vehement critique of modern theological approaches that supplant biblical authority with philosophical principles, it is possible to argue that Hodge shared one fundamental characteristic with these theologians. Like other modern theologians, Hodge used an overarching norm to structure and evaluate every detail in his theological system. As articulated above, that norm is that God is sovereign and he alone determines who is saved. This may be a theological rather than philosophical principle, but it functions in a similar way by providing a framework to interpret all the facts of revelation and experience. The extent to which this principle derives from Scripture itself has been a persistent debate in Protestant theology. Furthermore, it seems that the focus Hodge placed on this norm led him to misinterpret aspects of the biblical material by not taking into consideration other relevant sources for theology, such as the experience of slaves. It is now commonly recognized that every theologian inevitably uses lenses to interpret reality and revelation. Some are embedded in our vision by virtue of upbringing and cultural context, while others are intentional prescriptions that differ according to theological tradition. Reading Hodge's *Systematic Theology* provides a valuable reminder to discern the extent to which these lenses clarify or obscure reality and revelation.

Notes

1. The former is from Andrew W. Hoffecker, *Charles Hodge: The Pride of Princeton*, (Phillipsburg, NJ: P&R Publishing, 2012). The latter two are from Paul C. Gutjahr, *Charles Hodge: Guardian of American Orthodoxy* (Oxford/New York: Oxford University Press, 2011).
2. Gutjahr, *Charles Hodge*, 352.
3. Mark Noll, "Charles Hodge as Expositor of the Spiritual Life," in *Charles Hodge Revisited: A Critical Appraisal of His Life and Work*, edited by John W. Stewart and James H. Moorhead (Grand Rapids: Eerdmans, 2002), 208.
4. Charles Hodge, *The Church and Its Polity* (New York: Thomas Nelson and Sons, 1879). Forgotten Books published a reprint of this book in 2012, and Logos Bible Software released *The Collected Works of Charles Hodge* (29 vols.), which includes this volume.
5. In the foreword to *The Church and Its Polity*, A.A. Hodge indicates that his father desired to write a fourth volume on ecclesiology for his systematics, but waning health prevented him from doing so. We also know this was

      Charles's intention because his outline of theological "departments" in the *Systematic Theology* ends with ecclesiology (32).

6.   Charles Hodge, *Systematic Theology* (3 vols., Peabody, MA: Hendrickson, 1999), 1:10. Hereafter, all further references to this work shall be noted by employing in-text parenthetical citations.

7.   For a thorough explanation, see Peter Hicks, *The Philosophy of Charles Hodge: A Nineteenth-Century Evangelical Approach to Reason, Knowledge and Truth* (Lewiston/Queenston/Lampeter: The Edwin Mellen Press, 1997), 7–22. Despite his critiques of Hamilton, Hodge still held high respect for his philosophy and recommended his works for further reading (see 1:365, n. 1).

8.   B.A. Gerrish, "Charles Hodge and the Europeans," in *Charles Hodge Revisited*, 157.

9.   Hodge deals most directly with slavery in a review article published in the *Biblical Repertory* in 1836. For an analysis of his perspective, see Allen C. Guelzo, "Charles Hodge's Antislavery Movement," in *Charlges Hodge Revisited*, 299–326.

Select Bibliography

Primary sources

Hodge, Charles. *Systematic Theology*. 3 vols. New York: Charles Scribner and Co., 1871 [vols. 1 and 2]; New York: Scribner, Armstrong, and Co., 1872 [vol. 3].

Hodge, Charles. *Systematic Theology*. 3 vols. Peabody, MA: Hendrickson, 1999.

Secondary sources

Gutjahr, Paul C. *Charles Hodge: Guardian of American Orthodoxy*. Oxford/New York: Oxford University Press, 2011.

Hicks, Peter. *The Philosophy of Charles Hodge: A Nineteenth-Century Evangelical Approach to Reason, Knowledge and Truth*. Studies in American Religion, vol. 65. Lewiston/Queenston/Lampeter: The Edwin Mellen Press, 1997.

Hoffecker, W. Andrew. *Charles Hodge: The Pride of Princeton*. Phillipsburg, NJ: P&R Publishing, 2012.

Stewart, John W. and James H. Moorhead, eds. *Charles Hodge Revisited: A Critical Appraisal of His Life and Work*. Grand Rapids: Eerdmans, 2002.

5.3

Lectures on the Philosophy of Religion[1] (1821; 1824; 1827; 1831)

Georg Wilhelm Friedrich Hegel (1770–1831)

Figure 5.3 Portrait of G.W.F. Hegel

Theologian of the Spirit

Hegel is not usually considered the father of modern theology—a title more commonly applied to Schleiermacher—largely because many view him as a philosopher rather than a theologian. For Hegel, however, both philosophy and theology are oriented toward the same object: God as absolute truth and Spirit (*Geist*). Not only that, but both philosophy and religion are ways of serving God, although they do so in different ways. A more accurate portrait of Hegel, therefore, will present him as a philosopher-theologian, someone passionately concerned to know God as God knows and manifests himself as Spirit. Consequently, as a "theologian of the Spirit" who launched a theological trajectory in a radically different direction than Schleiermacher, Hegel stands next to his colleague and challenger at the University of Berlin as another father of modern theology.[2]

Born on August 27, 1770, in Stuttgart, Hegel was a bookworm from an early age, and by the time he matriculated at the Protestant Seminary (*Stift*) at Tübingen in 1788, he acquired the nickname "the old man" for his scholarly habits. Hegel had received the best of Enlightenment learning at the *Gymnasium Illustre* in Stuttgart, which eventually set him at odds with theological traditionalism and ministerial expectations at the Seminary. Along with his friends Friedrich Hölderlin and Friedrich Schelling, Hegel became enamored with classical Greek and Roman ideals and devoted his life to the pursuit of freedom, beauty, and philosophical grandeur.

During his seven years as a private tutor, first in Bern (1793–1796) and then in Frankfurt (1797–1800), Hegel had space to articulate some of his ideals in writing. In these early writings, we observe Hegel the philosopher-theologian searching for the essence of religion, which leads him to critique "The Positivity of the Christian Religion."[3] By "positivity," Hegel actually means something quite negative: the eclipse of reason and freedom under the authoritarian control of institutional, dogmatic, and irrational religion. At its heart, however, Christianity is a religion of love. In his essay "The Spirit of Christianity and Its Fate," Hegel identifies love as the core of God's kingdom: the beautiful communion of humanity in God. These themes continue to pervade even Hegel's most philosophical work as he explores the dynamic relation between the finite world and an infinite God.

Hegel turned his attention more directly to philosophy after obtaining a lectureship in Jena (1801–1807). During this time, he founded the *Critical Journal of Philosophy* with Schelling and wrote what would become his most famous work, *The Phenomenology of Spirit* (*Die Phenomenologie des Geistes*, 1807). In this work, Hegel articulates his vision of God not as a transcendent, unknowable Being, but as the absolute Spirit constantly revealed through finite reality, human community, and the historical process. He also planted seeds for his dialectical understanding of religion, which came into full bloom in his *Lectures on the Philosophy of Religion*. Hegel did not lecture specifically on religion until several years after he filled the chair of philosophy previously occupied by Johann Gottlieb Fichte at the University of Berlin (1818). As rector of a Gymnasium in Nuremburg (1808–1816), he was preoccupied with his three-volume *Science of Logic*, and as a professor in Heidelberg (1816–1817), he focused on the *Encyclopedia of the Philosophical Sciences in Outline*.

In all these works and many more, religion remained at the heart of Hegel's system of thought. If Hegel is thus viewed as a philosopher-theologian, then the *Lectures on the Philosophy of Religion* represent his *summa theologica*.[4] First presented in 1821, Hegel repeated these lectures three more times—1824, 1827 and 1831—each time adapting his material in response to new criticisms and to clarify previous conclusions. For example, in 1824 Hegel responded in particular to Schleiermacher's recently published and popular *The Christian Faith*, whereas in 1827 he turned attention to August Tholuck and others charging him with pantheism and atheism.

When Hegel died suddenly in 1831 during a cholera outbreak, just a year after becoming Rector of the University of Berlin, his lectures on the philosophy of religion had not yet been published. This was quickly remedied, with an edition appearing in 1832 based on Hegel's manuscript and several student transcripts. The history of subsequent editions is complex, but in the 1980s a team of scholars produced a new edition and translation (published concurrently in German, English, and Spanish) based on careful attention to all available sources.[5] In doing so, they kept lecture material from each year separate in order to show the development and differences between the lectures. Soon after the publication of this three-volume collection, an abridged version became available based solely on the 1827 lectures, providing a more accessible entry point to this dense material.[6] Because of this accessibility and the more mature thought represented by the 1827 lectures, our review will rely on this one-volume edition (LPR1) while drawing attention to the complete three-volume edition (LPR3) when necessary. Before exploring the particular content of these lectures, however, it is important to grasp a few key concepts undergirding Hegel's philosophy of religion.

Holistic perspective and dialectic process

Like every philosopher and theologian of his day, Hegel stood in the shadow of Immanuel Kant (1724–1804). While appreciating Kant's emphasis on mental categories that filter the sensory data of reality, Hegel felt stifled by his agnosticism toward knowing the essence of things, including the nature and being of God. Hegel bemoaned this blinding prejudice, resolving to step out from behind Kant's shadow to explore the continuity between thought and reality by the light of reason. If we deny the possibility of knowing God, Hegel explains, then philosophy of religion is restricted to our perceived relation to an unknowable God (LPR1, 89). This approach is content merely to mess about in a finite cave, rather than encountering and knowing the beauty of the infinite. As such, Barth astutely concludes that Hegel handled Kant as "a manikin loyally improvising his resources, however sadly limited by the cave in which he plies his handiwork."[7]

In other words, Hegel desires to replace cramped bifurcations with a spacious, holistic perspective. Faith and knowledge, objectivity and subjectivity, God and the world, transcendence and immanence: these are deadly divisions that detract from the dynamic unity of all things. At the heart of this unity is Hegel's understanding of God as the dynamic, unifying principle of reality. In contrast to more traditional, metaphysical theology, Hegel presents God not just as the infinite substance or object, but also as the infinite Spirit or subject who exists in a constant state of manifestation in the world (LPR1, 118–19). The reality of God, therefore, includes his infinite Being, his manifestation in everything finite, and the reconciliation of that Being and otherness throughout history. In short, all of world history, including the history of religions, can be described as the movement of God's revelation and self-knowledge through the process of humanity knowing and relating to God.

As Hegel's holistic perspective became more popular in Berlin and beyond, some of his contemporaries accused him of promoting pantheism and even atheism.[8] In the 1827 *Lectures on the Philosophy of Religion*, Hegel denies these accusations and attempts to clarify his position. Strictly speaking, pantheism maintains that everything is God, whether a sheet of paper or the flux of history. Rather than promoting this kind of static or abstract unity, however, Hegel asserts that particular things may *participate* in the being of God, but that does not mean they *are* God. Everything is united in God but it is still possible to maintain a distinction between God and the rest of reality (LPR1, 122–28). Other scholars have applied the label *panentheism* to Hegel's position, which acknowledges the difference as well as the inseparable unity between God and the world.[9]

For Hegel, the deep structure of reality as the unfolding of absolute Spirit (Being, non-being, becoming) is reflected in the structure of thought itself (thesis; antithesis; synthesis or sublation). Intrinsically linked with the dialectical movement of Spirit, rationality is the process of a universal idea being differentiated by a particular modification of this idea and then moving to a new level of truth through what Hegel calls "sublation." This dialectical pattern structures every part of Hegel's system, including his philosophy of religion. The dialectic of religion thus exists in three moments: the concept of religion, particular determinations of religion throughout history, and the consummation of religion, which Hegel identifies with Christianity. Within this holistic perspective and dialectic process, the movement of religion is the very movement of Spirit, which exists as pure concept, determines itself in history, and returns to itself in perfect reconciliation (LPR1, 100–03).

Religion and knowledge of God

At its most basic level, Hegel defines religion as consciousness of God (LPR1, 104). It involves an immediate knowledge or certainty (*Gewißheit*) that God exists (LPR1, 133). This is part of what it means to have faith in God, but faith also includes feeling (*Gefühl*) in which this general consciousness of God becomes personal (LPR1, 138). Hegel expands on what he means by "feeling" in the 1824 lectures, where he distinguishes his position from Schleiermacher's definition of religion as "the feeling of absolute dependence." He faults Schleiermacher for several reasons: first, when we relegate religion exclusively to the realm of feeling, we lose any objective and common ground to develop knowledge of God. Second, both animals and humans possess feeling, so focusing here keeps the conversation at a base level. Third, we should view feeling as the lowest form of religion, compared to the highest form—thought—because "God *is* essentially in thought" (LPR3, 1:273).

Although Hegel misrepresented Schleiermacher's perspective on the nature of religion by aligning feeling with animal passion, his critique does highlight a critical difference between these two fathers of modern theology. As articulated above, Hegel desired to move out from under the shadow of Kant by seeking objective knowledge of God and its representation in images, narratives, and doctrine. Schleiermacher, who accepted Kant's epistemological limits, viewed doctrine merely as religious feelings fixed in language with no objective referent. To Schleiermacher, therefore, Hegel's approach was riddled with intellectual hubris; to Hegel, Schleiermacher's system was spineless and irrational.

As religion seeks its objective content, it takes the form of representation (*Vorstellung*). By this Hegel means biblical and theological language, including images, stories, and traditional doctrines. For example, when we represent God as a Father who begets a Son, we are using images or metaphors to express our consciousness and feeling of God in a way that actually corresponds to divine reality (LPR1, 146). Even more directly, doctrinal language that articulates God's attributes or actions is a form of representation. For instance, to say that God created the world represents the concept of God differentiating himself, so in order to understand what this means, we need to transform these representations into thought (*Denken*). Similarly, saying God is all-wise, wholly good, and righteous represents something true about God, but it is still not wholly objective knowledge because it needs to deal with the concepts that undergird this statement, such as identity and difference (LPR1, 148–51, 152–54). The highest form of knowledge is conceptual or speculative knowledge, which reaches beyond the imagistic and mythological language of theology to grasp the rationality of reality.

Within this theoretical movement of religion, there is also a practical element, which Hegel calls worship or cultus (*Kultus*). This element involves all the ways, both implicit and explicit, that humans participate in the process of reconciliation with God (LPR1, 191). Whether expressed internally (prayer) or externally (sacraments), cultus is critical for true knowledge of God because it requires getting involved personally in this process. Cultus is not limited to what might be identified as "religious life," but includes an entire life of service to God, which Hegel calls "the most genuine cultus" (LPR1, 194). In this selfless performance of life, knowledge of God becomes real as humanity is elevated into relation with God.

Determinate and consummate religion

Having defined the concept of religion, Part Two of the lectures addresses the particular determinations of this concept in the history of religions. Hegel organized this material differently for each delivery, but what stays constant is his overarching belief that determinate religions are "necessary conditions for the emergence of true religion, for the authentic consciousness of spirit" (LPR1, 205). In the 1827 lectures, these religions are divided in three categories: immediate religion, spiritual religion, and purposive religion. In immediate or nature religion, Hegel identifies a unity of the spiritual and natural realms. This kind of religion is not nature worship, but an approach toward the spiritual element of humanity as the most natural element (LPR1, 219). Hegel deals with many religions under this category, including African traditional religions, Chinese Taoism, Buddhism, Lamaism, Hinduism, and the religions of ancient Persia and Egypt. Contemporary readers will not be satisfied by Hegel's treatment of these religions at certain points, but neither was Hegel, who continued to rearrange and adapt the material in his 1831 lectures.

The next stage includes those religions that elevate the spiritual element above the natural element by highlighting concrete individuality (Greek religion) and thought (Jewish religion). Though Hegel places Judaism at the apex of the determinate religions, in his interpretation it still does not achieve the reconciliation of divinity and humanity because of its external adherence to divine commands (LPR1, 374). Before arriving at the consummate religion, Hegel briefly discusses the purposive or Roman religion, which combines elements of Greek beauty and Jewish sublimity, but only in an expedient and external manner. Only Christianity internalizes all these particular determinations and unites them in a religion that does not look elsewhere for fulfillment but contains fulfillment within itself (LPR1, 391–93).[10]

As the consummate religion, Hegel also calls Christianity the revealed religion, because here the infinite God completely reveals and gives himself to what is finite: God becomes incarnate. This religion may come in external forms, such as the Bible and church doctrines, but its content must always be received spiritually. For example, even though the Bible contains Christian doctrines, it must always be subjectively appropriated "with one's innermost being, one's spirit, one's thought, one's reason, being touched by them and assenting to them" (LPR1, 399). Hegel does not believe that holding exclusively to the Bible as the source of truth is a truly scientific approach, as Charles Hodge would argue several decades later. Rather, everything represented in the Bible and in dogmatic theology needs to be transformed into conceptual, speculative form, and Hegel seeks to achieve such transformation as he explores the content of the consummate religion.

Speculative Christianity

The three elements of consummate religion are three modes of God's being and vitality as Spirit: God existing for himself, God creating everything finite, and God reconciling all things in community. The entire religion, therefore, has a trinitarian structure, as does the very fabric of reality. God in and for himself—the first element of Christianity—corresponds with what traditional theologians would call the immanent Trinity, or God's eternal being. This stands in contrast to the economic Trinity, or God's triune revelation and action in history. In Hegel's perspective, however, this language, as well as describing Father, Son, and Spirit as three co-equal and co-eternal persons, is merely representational rather than conceptual. He describes God's trinitarian being as a speculative idea, for this is the only way to transcend the mystery of understanding (LPR1, 422). Other scholars have chosen different terms to refer to Hegel's speculative trinitarianism, such as inclusive and holistic Trinity, but even these terms fall short of the concepts he has in mind.[11]

Likewise, the doctrine of creation represents a speculative idea about God differentiating himself so that the world is "released as something free and independent" (LPR1, 434). The world is therefore other than God, but it is still included within God's being and actuality, just as the Son is distinct yet one with the Father. As a part of creation, humanity is by nature both good and evil, which creates an estrangement within each person and a longing for this rift to be reconciled. Hegel insists we should not mistake the story of the fall for something that actually happened; rather, like the story of creation, it signifies the rational process by which humanity obtains consciousness (knowledge of good and evil) and experiences a rupture in their relationship with God and the world. In this sense, the fall is still a tragedy, but it is a necessary tragedy that creates the possibility of reconciliation.

God himself is an eternal process of reconciliation, but this reconciliation appears concretely through the life, death and resurrection of one human being: Jesus the Christ, the God-man. Hegel admits this is a "monstrous compound," one that contradicts understanding but nevertheless points to the concept of infinity fused with finitude, the unity of divinity and humanity (LPR1, 457). Humanly speaking, Christ dies as a criminal; but religiously speaking he dies as God in order to achieve a new relationship with God, a consciousness and certainty of God's presence and love (LPR1, 464). The resurrection and ascension of Christ are not physical realities that point to the continuing humanity of Christ; they are spiritual realities making way for the outpouring of Spirit within the community.

Hegel thus transitions to the third element of consummate religion: the Spirit-community. It is appropriate to hyphenate these terms because in

Hegel's scheme, community *is* Spirit: "God existing as community" (LPR1, 473). Community exists as a moment in the existence of the triune God, who determines himself through creation, reconciles himself through incarnation, and becomes present to himself through community. In this final section, Hegel explains how individuals are initiated and sustained in community through baptism, faith, doctrine, repentance, and the sacrament of communion. On the surface, it may seem as if Hegel aligns himself with traditional doctrines, such as the Lutheran position on mystical communion (LPR1, 480–91). Yet to grasp what Hegel is trying to accomplish, it is always important to recognize that such doctrines only represent speculative truth. In the end, Hegel hopes for Spirit-community to be realized in ethical forms of life (LPR1, 483–84). Scholars have interpreted this hope in multiple and sometimes contradictory ways, either as promoting religion's eventual resolution or complex dissonance with the modern world. The fact that Hegel's ideas have spawned opposing positions, however, reflects uncanny fittingness to the dialectical movement of his thought.

Hegelianism in manifold hues

Even among Hegel's immediate successors, there was no such thing as pure and simple Hegelianism. Only a few years after his death, a spectrum of scholarship had already emerged that ranged from those seeking to harmonize Hegel's thought with Protestant theology (right or old Hegelians) to those desiring to discard the theological elements and enlist Hegel's system to build humanistic agendas (left or young Hegelians). Most notable within the latter group are Ludwig Feuerbach (1804–1872), who viewed theology as a mere projection of human imagination and experience, and Karl Marx (1818–1883), who approached religion as a tool used by ruling elites to control society. These left Hegelians, therefore, while sharing Hegel's interest in the dialectical movement of history, purged this process of objective religious content and wielded it for more overtly political purposes. Situated in the middle of the left–right Hegelian spectrum are a myriad of theologians, philosophers, and biblical scholars who pursued a more balanced mediation between Christianity and modern science and society. Some of these "mediating theologians," such as Richard Rothe (1799–1867) and Isaak Dorner (1809–1884), drew on Hegel's conceptual framework to a certain extent but were also significantly influenced by Schleiermacher and his emphasis on religious experience.

Outside Germany in the nineteenth century, the impact of Hegel's thought was most clearly seen in British idealism and American transcendentalism. British idealists such as Thomas Hill Green (1836–1882) and Francis Herbert Bradley (1846–1924) applied Hegel's insights in a more strictly philosophical direction as an alternative to empiricism and utilitarianism. Transcendentalism, by contrast, was a more holistic literary, political, and cultural movement, and a figure such as Ralph Waldo Emerson (1803–1882), sometimes called "America's Hegel," exerted enormous sway over the rise of individualism and mystical spirituality within American Protestantism.

Although few Protestant theologians in the nineteenth and twentieth centuries adopted Hegel's system of thought wholesale, his influence can be most clearly traced through various forms of immanentism: philosophical and theological approaches that closely identify God and the world. Process theologians, for example, do not *equate* God and the world (and thus disavow pantheism as Hegel did), but place God and the world in such *dynamic interplay* that one cannot be conceived without the other. Other prominent Protestant theologians of the twentieth century, such as Wolfhart Pannenberg (1928–2014) and Jürgen Moltmann (b. 1936), have leveled critiques against process theology or panentheism. Nevertheless, their theology continues to emphasize the immanence of God within history while seeking to maintain God's future-originated transcendence. Another sign of Hegel's influence can be seen in Protestant theology that seeks harmonious integration of philosophy, culture, and religion. One prime example is Paul Tillich (1886–1965), who also espoused a variation of Hegel's immanentism as filtered through his fondness for existentialism. More recently, and especially since the new edition of the *Lectures on the Philosophy of Religion*, an increasing number of Protestant theologians have engaged with Hegel's thought directly and in a favorable light, viewing it as a fruitful attempt to articulate God's being and action in an anti-theological milieu.[12]

Another group of Protestant theologians, beginning with Søren Kierkegaard (1813–1855), have maintained the opposite perspective by seeking to demonstrate Hegel's inherent failure to maintain God's transcendence, and by implication, the essence of Christianity. Karl Barth surmises that Hegel might have become the Thomas Aquinas of Protestant theology, but he failed by making God dependent on his creation, thus erroneously turning theology into an anthropological enterprise.[13] Similarly, Charles Taylor bemoans that Hegel's heterodox conflation of God and the world completely jettisons the gifting relationship between God and humanity.[14] Whether one sides with these scathing critiques or with those who see Hegel as a fruitful conversation partner for theology, there is no doubt that he stands alongside Schleiermacher as a father of modern theology.

Notes

1. Translated from *Vorlesungen über die Philosophie der Religion*; hereafter, all references to this work are taken from the English translation by Peter C. Hodgson (see notes 5 and 6 below for detailed bibliography).
2. Peter Hodgson popularized the title "theologian of the Spirit" in *G. W. F. Hegel: Theologian of the Spirit* (Minneapolist: Fortress, 1997).
3. G.W.F. Hegel, *Early Theological Writings*, trans. T. M. Knox (Chicago: University of Chicago Press, 1948).
4. See Hans Küng, *The Incarnation of God: An Introduction to Hegel's Theological Thought as Prolegomena to a Future Christology*, translated by J.R. Stephenson (Edinburgh: T&T Clark, 1987), 348–49.
5. Peter C. Hodgson, ed., *Lectures on the Philosophy of Religion*, vols. 1–3, translated by R.F. Brown, P.C. Hodgson, and J.M. Stewart (Berkeley/Los Angeles: University of California Press, 1984–87). A reprint edition is available from Oxford University Press, published in 2006. Hereafter quoted as LPR3, followed by volume and page number.
6. Peter C. Hodgson, ed., *Lectures on the Philosophy of Religion: One-Volume Edition, Lectures of 1827*, translated by R.F. Brown, P.C. Hodgson, and J.M. Stewart (Berkeley/Los Angeles: University of California Press, 1988). A reprint edition is available from Oxford University Press, published in 2006. Hereafter quoted as LPR1, followed by page number.
7. Karl Barth, *Protestant Theology in the Nineteenth Century* (London: SCM Press, 1972), 380.
8. The accusations of pantheism began to emerge in the mid–1820s, particularly in F.A.G. Tholuck, *Die Lehre von der Sünde und vom Versöhner*, 2nd edition (Hamburg, 1825), 231; Cf. Anonymous [Hülsemann], *Ueber die Hegelsche Lehre, oder: Absolutes Wissen und moderner Pantheismus* (Leipzig, 1829). Charges of atheism were often linked to associating Hegel's thought with Spinozism, which German philosopher Friedrich Jacobi had interpreted as atheism (*Briefe uber die Lehre Spinozas*, 1785). By contrast, Hegel interpreted Spinoza's thought as acosmism, in which everything finite is a limitation or negation of the One (LPR1, 124–25).
9. See Peter C. Hodgson, *Hegel and Christian Theology* (New York: Oxford University Press, 2005), 68; James C. Livingston, *Modern Christian*

Thought: The Enlightenment and the Nineteenth Century, 2nd edition
(Minneapolis: Fortress Press, 2006), 138.

10. The best summary of the movement from the concept of religion to
    particular determinations of religion and finally to consummate religion is
    found toward the beginning of Part Three (LPR1, 404–10).
11. Hodgson, *Hegel and Christian Theology*, 113.
12. A good example is Peter Hodgson's *Hegel and Christian Theology*, and the
    last chapter of this book provides a helpful summary of those who see
    either promise or failure in Hegel's theology.
13. Barth, *Protestant Theology in the Nineteenth Century*, 370.
14. Charles Taylor, *Hegel* (Cambridge: Cambridge University Press, 1975), 493.
    Another recent example of exposing Hegel's heterodoxy is William
    Desmond, *Hegel's God: A Counterfeit Double?* (Aldershot: Ashgate, 2003).

Select Bibliography

Primary sources

Hodgson, Peter C., ed. *Lectures on the Philosophy of Religion: One-Volume
    Edition, The Lectures of 1827*. Oxford: Oxford University Press, 2006.
Jaeschke, Walter, ed. *Vorlesungen über die Philosophie der Religion*, vols. 1–3.
    Hamburg: Meiner, 1983–85.

Secondary sources

De Nys, Martin J. *Hegel and Theology*. London/New York: T&T Clark, 2009.
Hodgson, Peter. *Hegel and Christian Theology: A Reading of the Lectures on the
    Philosophy of Religion*. New York: Oxford University Press, 2005.
Küng, Hans. *The Incarnation of God: An Introduction to Hegel's Theological
    Thought as Prolegomena to a Future Christology*. Translated by
    J.R. Stephenson. Edinburgh: T&T Clark, 1987.
Pinkard, Terry. *Hegel: A Biography*. New York: Cambridge University Press,
    2000.
Yerkes, James. *The Christology of Hegel*. Albany: State University of New York
    Press, 1983.

5·4

Practice in Christianity[1] (1850)
Søren Aabye Kierkegaard (1813–1855)

Becoming a Christian

Many people know and appreciate Kierkegaard for his philosophy, and some even consider him the father of existentialism. In his own perspective, however, Kierkegaard was first and foremost a religious writer and theologian. In the posthumously published *The Point of View for My Work as an Author*, he makes this point clear: "... my whole authorship pertains to Christianity, to the issue: becoming a Christian, with direct and indirect polemical aim at that enormous illusion, Christendom."[2] Kierkegaard desired above all to present a vision for what it really means to become a Christian. He sought to do so by unmasking the illusion of Christendom that, in nineteenth-century Denmark, led to the blasphemous assumption that everyone was Christian.[3] His goal of waking the established church out of its nominal slumber may not have succeeded in his lifetime, but his writings have provided enduring inspiration for subsequent generations of theologians and pastors who found themselves in similar battles against the established order.

Søren Aabye Kierkegaard was born on May 5, 1813, in Copenhagen, the center of Danish government, religion, and culture. His father, Michael Pederson Kierkegaard, was a trader in the clothing business and a faithful member of the established Lutheran Church, although he was also deeply influenced by Moravian piety. Michael Kierkegaard suffered from debilitating depression, which may have influenced his decision to retire at an early age. One beneficial result of his retirement is the time he devoted to entertaining

Figure 5.4 Unfinished portrait of Søren Aabye Kierkegaard

friends for dinner and having lengthy discussions about philosophy and theology, which no doubt had a lasting impact on young Søren.

Following his father's wish, Søren began his studies in theology at Copenhagen University in 1830 at the age of seventeen, and he remained there until his graduation in 1840. As he began university, Kierkegaard encountered both rationalism and romanticism, and he was initially inspired by aesthetic and speculative ideals. Eventually, however, he became dissatisfied with the speculative disconnection between theory and life, which was particularly manifest in Hegelianism. As a result, he began to search for a better way to integrate the pursuit of truth with subjective experience. In 1835, Kierkegaard experienced a turning point where he realized his passion to discover a truth that actually makes a difference, "to find the idea for which I am willing to live and die."[4] Kierkegaard pursued this aim as an independent scholar and religious writer until his sudden death twenty years later at the age of forty-two.

At the outset of his writing career, Kierkegaard's books offered a critique of speculative idealism represented by Hegel and his followers. For example,

Either/Or (1843) places paradox at the heart of reality as opposed to Hegel's both/and unification of the finite and infinite. Similarly, *Philosophical Fragments* (1844) contains in its title an intentional contrast with philosophy as a totalizing system. *Smulen* is the Danish word usually translated as *fragments*, and it literally means just a few bits and scraps. According to Kierkegaard, offering these mere scraps was far better than constructing a philosophical or theological system, for these systems far too easily anesthetize readers to the urgency of action and the appropriation of truth within personal existence. Kierkegaard also used pseudonymous authorship to bring readers to points of personal, decisive action rather than detached understanding. By writing under different pseudonyms, Kierkegaard was able to portray rival worldviews and modes of existence, creating a dialectical knot that readers are required to untie.[5] For example, *Philosophical Fragments* and *Concluding Unscientific Postscript to Philosophical Fragments* (1846) are written by Johannes Climacus, a pseudonym named after the sixth-century monk and author of *The Ladder of Divine Ascent*. The views of Johannes Climacus do not correspond with Kierkegaard's own perspectives; rather, they represent someone who has yet to climb the ladder of ascent to God.

Kierkegaard identifies *Concluding Unscientific Postscript* as a turning point from his first period of authorship (1836–1846) to a second and more thoroughly religious period (1846–1855).[6] In this book, Climacus insists that true Christianity is not just a doctrine to understand, but an "existence-communication," a truth to be grasped with passionate inwardness and rigorously lived out.[7] In later books, particularly those written under the pseudonym Anti-Climacus, this passionate existence is articulated with uncompromising clarity, particularly in contrast with the contortion of Christianity within Christendom. Anti-Climacus does not represent the opposite of Climacus, but rather an extraordinarily devout Christian in contrast to someone who is barely a Christian.[8] Kierkegaard included his name as editor on every book authored by these two pseudonyms, which indicates his own placement somewhere in the middle of these dialectic poles, both of which are necessary to discover what it means to become a genuine Christian.[9]

The first work by Anti-Climacus, *The Sickness Unto Death* (written in 1848, published in 1849), presents the problem to which his second book, *Practice in Christianity* (written in 1848, published in 1850), provides the solution. In fact, Kierkegaard originally considered titling this book *The Radical Cure* as a reflection on the relationship with Christ that brings healing from the sickness of sin.[10] He also contemplated giving it a descriptive subtitle: "A Contribution to the Introduction of Christianity into Christendom."[11] In addition to presenting a vision of true Christianity, therefore, *Practice in Christianity* also proposes how to keep the established Church from abolishing Christianity (36). Originally, Kierkegaard did not intend for this book to constitute an outright attack on the established Church, but rather to provide a basis for its existence.[12] Particularly disheartening, however, was the flat response from Jacob Peter Mynster, Kierkegaard's childhood pastor and Primate of the Danish Church since 1834. Kierkegaard had expected either repentance or stiff opposition from Mynster, but when they met after the book was published, Mynster made a few comments, but otherwise "the conversation was just as usual."[13] This was only one disappointment in an unfortunate series of events motivating Kierkegaard to critique the established Church more vehemently as he reached the end of his life. In 1855, a year after Mynster's death and a few months before his own, Kierkegaard prefaced the second edition of *Practice in Christianity* by asserting that Christendom was indeed indefensible.[14] Although this book did not have the impact he had hoped, Kierkegaard still considered 1848 his most fruitful year as an author and *Practice in Christianity* "the most perfect and truest thing" he had ever written. Although Kierkegaard claims authorship in his journals, this essay will continue to refer to the author of *Practice in Christianity* as Anti-Climacus, given the distinction between this pseudonym and Kierkegaard's own position.[15]

Christianity vs. Christendom

Between the authorship of *Practice in Christianity* in 1848 and its publication in 1850, great social and political changes had swept through Denmark and the rest of Europe. Following the revolution of 1848, Denmark emerged with a representative government and adopted a new constitution. Like the government, the Church now belonged to the people instead of the ruling aristocrats, having been renamed The People's Church (*Folkekirke*). It maintained strong links to the state, however, and for all practical purposes it remained the established Church. In light of these changes, Kierkegaard recognized this as the opportune time to call the Danish people and church leaders to embrace true Christianity and to dispel the charade of Christendom.[16]

The major calamity of Christendom, according to Anti-Climacus in *Practice in Christianity*, is that becoming a Christian is too easy, like putting on socks instead of carrying a cross (35). Becoming a Christian was no longer associated with pursuing a different way of life—a life of suffering—

so people could become Christian without even noticing. With no outward manifestation of true faith, the visible distinction between Christians and non-Christians evaporates, producing a "slack universalism" (112). Anti-Climacus argues that if becoming a Christian has anything to do with Christ, then Christians should expect to come into conflict with the established order, just like Christ came into conflict with the scribes and Pharisees (85–86). Christianity without conflict is Christianity without Christ, and in the end, it is no better than paganism (107).

Another way Anti-Climacus highlights the difference between Christianity and Christendom is by contrasting the militant Church and the triumphant Church. The triumphant Church believes that all is settled because Christ reigns in his glory. The struggle is over because the victory has been won in Christ. While containing a partial truth, the triumphant Church fails to recognize that until we are lifted up in glory like Christ, we are called to follow him in his lowliness. Ultimately, therefore, the triumphant Church is a complete illusion (209). By contrast, the militant Church embraces the radical call to confess and follow Christ. Rather than being content with knowing about Christ and making observations about his life, members of the militant Church grasp the truth of Christ as a way of life (205–07). The militant Church embraces the struggle and rigorousness of following Christ no matter how foolish this may appear to comfortable members of the establishment (228–30).

Christendom may bear the name of Christ, but in reality, it is "the secularization of everything" (91). By aligning Christianity with the established order, one's relationship with God no longer has priority over everything else, purged of its capacity to judge every other commitment and activity. Connected with this criticism is the danger Anti-Climacus perceives in viewing Christianity as the inevitable progression of world history and development of the human race. The problem with this Hegelian perspective is that it links God so closely to history and humanity that the infinite difference between God and everything he has created disappears, along with the paradox of the God-man (221–22). The ultimate antidote to the disease of Christendom is to encounter Christ: not the historical Jesus, but the contemporary Christ who is received by faith.

Contemporaneity with Christ

Anti-Climacus insists that we cannot know anything about Christ through history, precisely because we "cannot *know* anything at all about *Christ*; he is the paradox, the object of faith, exists only for faith" (25). When historians and philosophers pursue knowledge of Christ, what they fail to grasp is that there is no contact point between God and humanity that enables us to know Christ as the God-man. There is an "infinite qualitative difference" between humanity and divinity, which means that in Christ, humanity and divinity are united in a paradox that cannot be the object of historical inquiry (28–29). Anti-Climacus likewise makes the case that Christ's divinity cannot be "demonstrated," which is blasphemy, but can only be received by faith (26). For example, whereas some may claim that Christ's miracles "prove" his divinity, this would in effect make faith unnecessary. Neither miracles nor anything else can prove the paradox of Christ; instead, they lead us either to take offense or to have faith (97).

Faith is therefore the opposite of knowing historical facts about Christ. Faith is belief in the truth of Christ *for me* (64). Rather than a *historical* trust in Christ, faith is a *contemporary* trust in Christ (9). In other words, "a believer must be just as contemporary with Christ's presence as his contemporaries were" (9). We must receive Jesus's words of invitation just as his disciples who walked with him during his ministry. Christ declared and demonstrated the way of salvation in the first century, but equally he declares and demonstrates this way to us today. Faith is the process of responding to and imitating Christ in the urgency of the present moment. Thus, becoming a Christian is becoming contemporary with Christ (63). Because of this radical contrast between faith and historical knowledge, some popular works have explained the kind of faith advocated in *Practice in Christianity* and the whole Kierkegaardian corpus as a subjective leap in the dark.[17] Most scholars try to tread more carefully, however, showing how contemporaneity is not so much a leap lacking all understanding, but rather it is a leap into action from a position of personal understanding and passionate allegiance to Christ.[18] That being said, subsequent philosophers and theologians have rightly challenged Anti-Climacus's claim, which Kierkegaard also makes elsewhere, that Christ can only be believed rather than known by offering a broader concept of knowledge inclusive of its personal and relational modes.[19]

Coming into contemporaneity with Christ means encountering him in the paradox of his loftiness and lowliness. Both of these aspects of the God-man have the potential to offend, whether a human being claiming to be God (loftiness) or God claiming to be human and suffering the consequences (lowliness). Anti-Climacus traces both forms of offense as witnessed in the

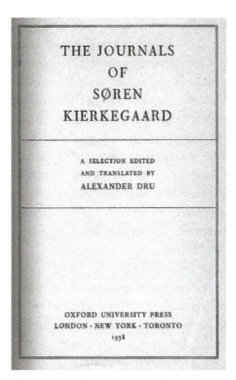

THE JOURNALS
OF
SØREN
KIERKEGAARD

A SELECTION EDITED
AND TRANSLATED BY
ALEXANDER DRU

OXFORD UNIVERSITY PRESS
LONDON · NEW YORK · TORONTO
1938

Figure 5.5 The cover of the first English edition of *The Journals* by Søren Aabye Kierkegaard

Gospels, and presents both as options for contemporary offense. This offense does not arise when we learn a doctrine about Christ, but when we encounter Christ himself in his loftiness and lowliness (106). Members of Christendom do not approach Christ in contemporaneity, and therefore they destroy the possibility of both offense and faith. They are too comfortable to entertain the radical implication of God revealing himself through the suffering of an individual human being. This implication, of course, is that the only way to become a Christian is to imitate the suffering of Christ, converting the offense into active faith.

From admiration to imitation

The paradox of Christ's lofty lowliness also serves as the paradigm or prototype for Christian existence. To become a Christian, it is not enough to admire the paradox of Christ; we must imitate him as a personal paradigm. To illustrate this point, Anti-Climacus refers to the tendency of young people to imagine the ideal Christian existence. This is a promising starting point, but it is not complete until that young person begins to actively will that ideal into existence. We must not just imagine the ideal; we must become the ideal (220). Living solely in the world of imagination and admiration is an adolescent error, and Anti-Climacus associated this error with many of the pastors and preachers in Denmark. They love to admire Christ and make profound observations about his life, but their own lives bear no resemblance to the beautiful form of Christ's ideal (239). True admiration does not remain at a distance from its object, but seeks to move closer and closer, eventually becoming what it admires. Likewise, true admiration of Christ involves active imitation of Christ (241).

Like a theatre audience, admirers of Christ are content to remain detached from the play and make appropriate comments in hushed tones (244). But this is no mere metaphor. Anti-Climacus uses this opportunity to condemn Christian artists in general, because they create illusions of reality and do so with indifference to the subject matter (254). Despite this critical attitude toward Christian art, one way of understanding what Anti-Climacus is commending here is to take the theatre metaphor one step further. In this case, the true spectator is the one who gets up off the seat and joins the other actors and Christ himself on the stage, casting off all illusions and participating in the play for real.[20] But too many people fear what would happen if they embraced the idea of this play with passionate inwardness and moved from admiration to imitation of the main character.

The essence of imitating Christ is suffering, and it begins by leaving the audience and participating in the action. Suffering is inevitable for believers because they are contemporary with Christ in his abasement. This is the "danger of actuality" that puzzled Nicodemus when he came to question Jesus at night (Jn 3:1–15). It also caused the rich young ruler to despair, for the challenge was too great (Lk 18:18–23). Both are examples of men who could not grasp the "infinite difference between an admirer and an imitator" (249). Similarly, the triumphant, established Church is full of admirers who refuse to be imitators, and this is the tragedy of Christendom. The challenge to move from admiration to imitation goes out to each individual, and the only way to make an appropriate response is to appropriate the truth of Christ with unconditional inwardness. For Anti-Climacus, this means focusing so intensely on Christ and being so turned inward in contemporaneity with Christ "that one is quite literally alone in the whole world, alone before God, alone with Holy Scripture as a guide, alone with the prototype before one's eyes" (225). Passages like this have led some to accuse Kierkegaard of subjectivism and individualism. While there is certainly some credence to this critique, it is important to keep Kierkegaard in his context and remember the forces and trends to which he was reacting, particularly speculative philosophy and the established Church. In addition, a continuing difficulty in interpreting Kierkegaard is determining the proper relationship between his self-authored and pseudonymous works. Scholars often mention, for example, that his self-authored *Works of Love* (1847), written just a year before *Practice in Christianity*, counterbalances the individualistic strain appearing in other works. Needless to say, this debate highlights the fact that interpreting Kierkegaard is an ongoing task, and his legacy is by no means monolithic.

Kierkegaard's diverse kin

Kierkegaard's works did not reach a wider audience until after World War I, partly because of delayed translation and partly because speculative approaches were still the norm for Western theology. Upon wider circulation, his work was often met with mixed reactions, although the cultural milieu after the War was more amenable to Kierkegaard's call for personal engagement and suffering witness. Overall, his influence on Protestant theology can be seen among theologians seeking to move away from rationalist speculation and toward personal engagement with Christ and radical response to his challenges. Just as Kierkegaard's perspective brought him into conflict with the established order, the same is often true of theologians who appreciated his radical perspective, particularly in his later years. No doubt one of the most prominent examples is Dietrich Bonhoeffer (1906–1945), who leveled a similar critique against those who were contorting Christianity by aligning themselves with the Nazi regime. His commitment to the costly grace of Christ led him into a life of suffering and abasement, a prime example of Kierkegaard's admonition to move from admiration to imitation of Christ. For both Kierkegaard and Bonhoeffer, Christianity is a way of life focused on the concrete person and work of Christ, not detached adherence to abstract principles.

The influence of Kierkegaard on twentieth-century theology is also evident among those who emphasize the "infinite qualitative difference" between God and humanity. For example, Scottish theologian P.T. Forsyth (1848–1921) demurred from Protestant liberalism by emphasizing the problem of guilt and sin and its resolution in the atonement of Christ. Forsyth blazed the trail for Karl Barth (1886–1968), whose work represents an explosive attack against German liberalism in an effort to rehabilitate God's infinite freedom and transcendence. Despite this point of resonance with Kierkegaard, Barth later accused Kierkegaard of promoting works righteousness because of his staunch challenges in *Practice in Christianity* and other works. Many others have defended Kierkegaard against this accusation, however, hailing him as a prophet calling Christians to authentic repentance and a life of personal obedience to Christ.

Paul Tillich (1886–1965) is yet another prominent theologian influenced by Kierkegaard's dialectical method, emphasis on the infinite distinction between God and humanity, and critique of the establishment. As Tillich's theology developed, however, he placed greater emphasis than Kierkegaard would have sanctioned on correlating the Gospel with contemporary culture and expressing these truths in abstract terms. A similar pattern of influence yet divergence is evident in the work of Reinhold Niebuhr (1892–1971), who drew heavily on Kierkegaard's theological anthropology and whose critique of secular and religious liberalism in America contains obvious resonance with Kierkegaard's quarrel with Christendom.

Many additional strains of Kierkegaard's influence might be explored within both theology and philosophy, but even this short survey shows his enduring impact on Protestant theology. One would be remiss, however, to seek Kierkegaard's legacy within the halls of academia alone. The most direct progeny of the vision articulated in *Practice in Christianity* are those Christians who hear Christ's invitation and actively respond by imitating him in his abasement and suffering. In sum, Kierkegaard's closest kin are those who personally confess Christ and embrace Christianity as a way of life, no matter the cost.

Notes

1. Translated from *Indøvelse i Christendom*; hereafter, all references to this work (*Practice in Christianity*, Vol. 20, *Kierkegaard's Writings* [Eds and trans. Howard V. Hong and Edna H. Hong, Princeton: Princeton University Press, 1991]) shall be noted by employing in-text parenthetical citations.

2. Søren Kierkegaard, *The Point of View for My Work as an Author*, in *The Point of View*, edited and translated by Howard V. Hong and Edna H. Hong (Princeton: Princeton University Press, 1998), 23.

3. Ibid., 88, 90.

4. Søren Kierkegaard, *Papers and Journals: A Selection*, edited and translated by Alastair Hannay (London: Penguin Books, 1996), 32.

5. Kierkegaard hints at the purpose of pseudonymity in several places, but the language of "dialectical knot" comes from *Practice in Christianity*, edited and translated by Howard V. Hong and Edna H. Hong (Princeton: Princeton University Press, 1991), 133. Hereafter, references to this book will be included parenthetically in the text.

6. Kierkegaard, *Point of View*, 31, 94.

7. Søren Kierkegaard, *Concluding Unscientific Postscript*, vol. 1, edited and translated by Howard V. Hong and Edna H. Hong (Princeton: Princeton University Press, 1992), 379–80.

8. Kierkegaard, "Selected Entries from Kierkegaard's Journals and Papers Pertaining to *Practice in Christianity*," in *Practice in Christianity*, 279–80. Kierkegaard's Journals and Papers are available in six separate volumes, but for ease of reference, I will be referencing the supplement provided for *Practice in Christianity*, hereafter cited as *Supplement*.

9. *Supplement*, 283.

10. Ibid., 273.

11. Ibid., 307–8.

12. Kierkegaard, *Point of View*, 18.

13. *Supplement*, 357.

14. Quoted in Howard V. Hong and Edna H. Hong, "Historical Introduction," in *Practice in Christianity*, xvi–xvii.

15. *Supplement*, 287.

16. Bruce H. Kirmmse, *Kierkegaard in Golden Age Denmark* (Bloomington/Indianapolis: Indiana University Press, 1990), 381. This book offers an excellent introduction to the social and political context of *Practice in Christianity* and all of Kierkegaard's works after 1846.

17. Sam Harris, *The End of Faith: Religion, Terror, and the Future of Reason*, reprint edition (New York: W. W. Norton, 2005), 62–65.

18. Murray Rae, *Kierkegaard and Theology* (London/New York: T&T Clark International, 2010), 55–57. See *Practice in Christianity*, 158.

19. For example, see Karl Barth, "Faith as Knowledge," in *Dogmatics in Outline*, translated by G. T. Thomson (London: SCM Press, 1949), 22–27.

20. In *Concluding Unscientific Postscript*, Climacus makes a similar observation that if a person considers himself a spectator in The Drama of Dramas, "he is simply forgetting that he himself is supposed to be the actor" (158).

Select Bibliography

Primary sources

Kierkegaard, Søren. *Practice in Christianity*. Vol. 20. *Kierkegaard's Writings*. Edited and translated by Howard V. Hong and Edna H. Hong. Princeton: Princeton University Press, 1991.

Kierkegaard, Søren. *Indøvelse i Christendom, En opbyggelig Tale og To Taler ved Altergangen om Fredagen*. Vol. 12. *Søren Kierkegaards Skrifter*. Edited by Niels Jørgen Cappelørn, Joakim Garff, Anne Mette Hansen and Johnny Kondrup. Copenhagen: Søren Kierkegaard Research Center and GEC Gad Publishers, 2008.

Secondary sources

Kirmmse, Bruce H. *Kierkegaard in Golden Age Denmark*. Bloomington/ Indianapolis: Indiana University Press, 1990.

Pattison, George. *Kierkegaard and the Theology of the Nineteenth Century*. Cambridge: Cambridge University Press, 2012.

Rae, Murray. *Kierkegaard and Theology*. London/New York: T&T Clark International, 2010.

Walsh, Sylvia. *Kierkegaard: Thinking Christianly in an Existential Mode*. Oxford: Oxford University Press, 2009.

5.5

Christianity and the Social Crisis (1907)

Walter Rauschenbusch (1861–1918)

Doing theology in Hell's Kitchen

Before moving to the northern border of Hell's Kitchen, a working-class and poverty-stricken neighborhood in New York City, Walter Rauschenbusch had not realized the serious social crisis "beneath the glitter" of booming American cities.[1] Eleven years of pastoral ministry in this environment, however, transformed Rauschenbusch into a champion for the social gospel. Rauschenbusch steadily rose as a leader within the social gospel movement, but the stunning success of *Christianity and the Social Crisis* in 1907 launched him into the limelight. Rauschenbusch developed into the preeminent spokesperson for the social gospel, and *Christianity and the Social Crisis* was the movement's *magnum opus*.[2]

His father, August Rauschenbusch, was educated at Berlin University and served as a Lutheran pastor in Altena. In 1846, not long after beginning this pastoral ministry, August sensed a calling to missionary service to America, where he first worked as the director of the American Tract Society's program for German immigrants. After becoming a Baptist in 1850, he ministered as a church planter and pastor to German Baptist communities until his appointment as a professor at Rochester Theological Seminary in 1858.

Walter Rauschenbusch was born in Rochester, New York, in 1861. When he was three years old, however, the whole Rauschenbusch family moved back to Germany for four years, reinforcing his bicultural and bilingual upbringing. He later returned to Germany to attend Evangelische Gymnasium zu Gütersloh (1879–1883), acquiring the equivalent of an American university education. After coming back to Rochester in 1883, he enrolled in Rochester Theological Seminary while finishing some courses at Rochester University. During his three years at seminary, Rauschenbusch became familiar with the nascent social gospel movement as represented by Washington Gladden (1836–1918), Richard Ely (1854–1943), and Josiah Strong (1847–1916). He also began to question some traditional Baptist doctrines, such as substitutionary atonement, with ideas he had first encountered in Germany. While appreciating many elements of his Baptist heritage, Rauschenbusch increasingly diverged from theological positions generally espoused at the seminary and among conservative Baptists.[3] This caused some inevitable tension, one consequence being the denial of his application for foreign missionary service in India on the basis of a cautionary reference from an Old Testament professor.

Rather than going to India in 1886, Rauschenbusch accepted a call as pastor of Second German Baptist Church in New York City in an area known as Hell's Kitchen. Immediately confronted by the dire living conditions in the neighborhood, Rauschenbusch started forming friendships with others interested in addressing the plight of the poor in New York City. One such friend was Leighton Williams, with whom he launched *For the Right* in 1889, a small monthly newspaper seeking to reach and give a voice to the working class. This venture folded a few years later, but it had led Rauschenbusch into frequent personal encounters with the multi-dimensional social crisis of his day.

Plagued by partial deafness since an illness in 1888, Rauschenbusch was growing increasingly doubtful about his ability to continue pastoral ministry. As a result, in 1891 his church encouraged him to take a sabbatical to Germany. There, he studied more thoroughly the theology of Albrecht Ritschl (1822–1889) and was impressed by Adolf von Harnack (1851–1930), who only a few years prior had been appointed professor of church history at the University of Berlin. Rauschenbusch also began writing a book called *Revolutionary Christianity*, which was never published but would eventually form the basis for *Christianity and the Social Crisis*. He returned to New York with renewed vigor, forming a progressive caucus within the Baptist Congress called the Brotherhood of the Kingdom. The growing interest among Protestant leaders in tackling social maladies, as well as his marriage to Pauline Rother in 1893, gave Rauschenbusch an extra boost for his final years of ministry in New York City.

In 1897, Rauschenbusch became a professor in the German department at Rochester Theological Seminary, following in his father's footsteps. This was the same year that Charles Sheldon published *In His Steps*, a popular novel exploring what it means to follow in Jesus's footsteps in personally confronting issues of poverty and social deprivation. While Rauschenbusch appreciated the theme of imitating Christ, he later would critique Sheldon's work for its individualism and not demanding the transformation of social institutions.[4] In 1902, Rauschenbusch was appointed professor of church history in the English department at Rochester Seminary. His years teaching church history provided him the opportunity to explore the historical roots of Christianity's social vision and why this vision had failed to bloom. This historical inquiry is the burden of *Christianity and the Social Crisis* (1907), with *Christianizing the Social Order* (1912) outlining a more positive way forward.

Christianity and the Social Crisis brought Rauschenbusch widespread recognition, not because he was attempting something entirely new, but because of its sparkling prose and the unique combination of historical, theological, political, and social perspectives. It sold 50,000 copies in the first three years, making it the best-selling religious book besides the Bible.[5] Throughout the next ten years, Rauschenbusch wrote several other books, including a collection of prayers entitled *For God and the People* (1910). Such efforts demonstrate Rauschenbusch's desire to fuse personal spirituality and social action, which is also evident in the short book *Dare We Be Christians?* (1914). Most of his books have a historical orientation, but in *Theology for the Social Gospel* (1917) Rauschenbusch recognizes that "We have a social gospel. We need a systematic theology large enough to match it and vital enough to back it."[6] In this book, his overarching optimism is balanced by a new emphasis on "the kingdom of evil" and a social conception of sin, no doubt influenced by the atrocities of World War I. Tragically, Rauschenbusch never lived to see the end of the War, but died of colon cancer on July 25, 1918. Nevertheless, his kingdom vision had inspired many Christians to pursue a new social order.

Kingdom vision

For Rauschenbusch, the purpose of Christianity is "to transform human society into the kingdom of God by regenerating all human relations and reconstituting them in accordance with the will of God."[7] The first three chapters of *Christianity and the Social Crisis* explain how this purpose arose from the Hebrew prophets, Jesus, and the early Church. The following four chapters unveil the various forces that distracted from and derailed this purpose, provide an overview of the contemporary social crisis, and suggest how the Church might realign itself with its original vision and purpose.

The Hebrew prophets addressed the major problem that has plagued God's people throughout the centuries: the eclipse of public morality by personal piety. The prophets had no patience for this, breaking down the divide between private and public religion and calling God's people to faithfulness in every sphere of life (6–8). They chided a people who had forgotten the importance of seeking justice for the oppressed and were instead "consumed in weaving the tinsel fringes for the garment of religion" (5). In calling God's people to embrace kingdom morality, the prophets were resolutely on the side of the poor, an orientation already embedded at the heart of Old Testament law (8–16). False prophets emerged who were mere purveyors of popular opinion, propagating deceptive optimism rather than the authentic realism of God's true prophets (28–29). Rauschenbusch claims that with Israel's national destruction came the demise of its social morality. In later prophets like Jeremiah, we see a turn toward personal piety, although hope remained for national restoration (19–26). Based on this prophetic heritage, Rauschenbusch argues that the burden of proof is on those who think Christianity is ritualistic, sacramental, personal, and on the side of the rich (31). It is an impressive case, despite his tenuous genealogy of Hebrew religion (natural to prophetic to personal) and his limited exploration of the Old Testament canon (similar themes permeate the Psalms and wisdom literature). He had nevertheless set a solid stage on which to explore the social aims of Jesus as a continuation of the prophetic tradition.

Jesus was a prophet in unique communion with the Father, not just a social reformer or a teacher of timeless truths (42–44). His purpose was to fulfill the prophetic hopes and usher in a kingdom even greater than they imagined. Jesus's kingdom involved the transformation of every social relation, but this would not be achieved by violence, ushered in instantaneously from heaven, or limited to the Jewish people. Jesus's kingdom is inherently peaceable and realized through organic growth of just human relationships (53–54). At the heart of this kingdom is love, which Rauschenbusch describes as a "society-making quality," since love creates and keeps people in fellowship, resisting coercion, exploitation, and inequality (55). By contrast, wealth is a divisive force that makes it difficult to sustain a society of love, service, and equality. The rich young man who encountered Jesus (Mark 10:17–31) was not so much unfit for heaven because of his greedy spirit, but unfit for the earthly kingdom of God (61–62). Throughout his explanation of Jesus's social aims, Rauschenbusch reflects themes and interests common within the burgeoning quest for the historical Jesus.[8] His central concern is not to demonstrate the metaphysical union of divinity and humanity in Jesus's incarnation, but to show the union of religious and social life that would provide the ultimate model for social life and existence.[9] Jesus embodied a "revolutionary consciousness" and a counter-cultural reversal of values, and those who call themselves Christians should be and do likewise (68–72).

The early Church (or "primitive Christianity") sought to embody a similar spirit, although there was some measure of inevitable "leakage, evaporation, and adulteration" of Jesus's kingdom vision (82). Despite persecution, they maintained hope that Jesus would soon return to consummate his kingdom, a hope that included personal victory over sin but was predominantly hope for humanity's perfect social life (90–91). Sustained by this hope, early Christians organized into "fraternal communities" that cut across lines of social division and exhibited a radical way of sharing possessions and their entire lives together. According to Rauschenbusch, these first "churches" were primarily social communities rather than worshipping communities, which is perhaps one instance where Rauschenbusch is not as careful to avoid false dichotomies (99). Overall, the early Church gives a glimpse at what the kingdom of God should look like, but tragically, the Church was not able to sustain this vision and effectively work toward social transformation.

The roots and reality of social crisis

In chapter four, Rauschenbusch asks the question: why has Christianity never undertaken the work of social reconstruction? He lists a litany of reasons, beginning with the particular limitations of the early Church. These include pervasive persecution, belief in the imminent return of Christ, general hostility toward the Roman Empire, and the gradual diminishment of an earthly, kingdom vision together with the rise of an otherworldly emphasis on eternal life. Instead of focusing on a social ideal, therefore, the imagination of the Church was increasingly captured by an ascetic ideal and a longing for liberation from worldly, embodied existence. As Christianity transitioned from its marginal status to the established religion of the Empire, additional impediments to social engagement emerged. Ritual "numbed ... ethical passion" (148) and dogma acted "as a narcotic on the intellect of the people" (149). As the Church rose in power and prominence, the distinct goal of Christ-likeness was eclipsed by "churchly correctness" (150) and the "all-absorbing and all-dominating ecclesiastical organization" (154). Not only that, but the Church's subservience to the State deformed socially active, fraternal communities into an institution inundated by "bureaucratic despotism" (158). The picture of church history Rauschenbusch paints is grim. He claims, though, that his point is not so much to condemn the Church as simply to highlight its shortcomings (164). The Reformation was one high point in this history, but Rauschenbusch sees the modern socialist movement as the fulcrum in the kingdom drama. In a phrase reminiscent of Kierkegaard, he holds out hope that "Christianity itself is being converted to Christ" (171).[10] If this conversion is to occur, however, the Church must collectively confront the comprehensive social crisis.

Rauschenbusch is writing in the midst of the Industrial Revolution. At the center of his critique is the power of the machine. Machines created the promise of modern cities, but within this promise lies a tragic paradox: "The instrument by which all humanity could rise from want and the fear of want actually submerged a large part of the people in perpetual want and fear" (181). Rauschenbusch wrestles with many aspects of this tragedy, but most prominent is the gaping divide between wealthy employers and poor wage earners. With profit as the bottom line, workers become a means to an end, diminishing proper concern for their morale, physical health, living conditions, and family life. He identifies rampant diseases such as tuberculosis and alcoholism as inherently social diseases, rooted in the unjust chasm between rich and poor (198–99). Rauschenbusch likens unequal wealth distribution to manure: if it's spread evenly over the soil it will enrich the land, but if left in heaps most of the land will be impoverished while suffocating vegetation under the heaps (227). Since those with the wealth control both the industrial and political machines, political democracy crumbles when economic equality does (207–14). What will the Church do in the face of such a crisis? Will it simply stand by and watch civilization fall? Or will it hear the "Spirit of the First Century" (177–78) and rise to the challenge by standing for justice and love? In short, Rauschenbusch calls the Church to choose between "a revival of social religion or the deluge" (230).

Social reconstruction and the Church

Although the bulk of *Christianity and the Social Crisis* charts the crisis, the final two chapters hint at some solutions that Rauschenbusch develops more fully in *Christianizing the Social Order*. Before offering particular suggestions, however, Rauschenbusch explains why the Church has a critical stake in the social movement. While some may argue that the Church should simply deal with healing wounds caused by the social crisis, much like the Good Samaritan cares for the injured man, Rauschenbusch takes this parable one step further. Of course, the Samaritan should not go after the robbers with a shotgun, but if other Samaritans continued to find injured people along the road, it would be their responsibility to figure out the cause and source of their woundedness (248). In other words, the Church should not abandon relief work and caring for individuals, but it should be equally committed to addressing systemic injustice. If the Church does not confront unjust systems, these systems will conquer the Church. For instance, Rauschenbusch remarks: "If the Church cannot Christianize commerce, commerce will commercialize the Church" (255). Although some church leaders disagreed with this optimistic proposal for "Christianization," his prophetic diatribe spurred many to action. For many in the social gospel movement, another persuasive element in Rauschenbusch's warning was that, if society decays and disintegrates, so will the Church (274). The very survival of the Church is wrapped up in effectively addressing the social crisis. But what can be done?

To begin, Rauschenbusch deals with what the Church should *not* do. The Church should not revert to older stages of economic development, base its social action on outdated biblical models, retreat into communistic colonies, or tackle the process of social transformation on its own. The first thing the Church *should* do is repent and believe the gospel. Rauschenbusch's overt emphasis on repentance and faith reflects his goal to fuse personal religion with social action. He was adamant that the greatest contribution to social transformation is a "regenerated personality" (287). It is also critical to observe, however, that when Rauschenbusch refers to repentance and faith, he primarily means repentance of *social* sins and faith in the possibility of *social* transformation (287). His conception of salvation is similarly social: the transformation of all human relations and the redemption of everyday life (288–91). Preaching can play a critical role in this social evangelization, and it should do so by displaying the mind rather than being a platform for political lobbying (295). Ministers will be most effective in addressing the social crisis if they mingle with both rich and poor, thereby understanding both worlds and mediating between them. In all its ministries and activities, Rauschenbusch views the Church's task as opposing "materialism and mammonism" by living out a theology that puts God before self and by supporting a political economy that puts the human person before wealth (300–301).

Ultimately, this means the Church and State should work together toward the same goal: to "transform humanity into the kingdom of God" (308). Rauschenbusch uses the word "communism" to describe this goal, but for him, this word was synonymous with "communalism" or "socialism" and did not have any associations with totalitarian regimes. Specifically, he identifies the home, school, Church, and State as all "communistic institutions," simply because they exist to serve the common good (314–17). The Church shares the same goal as these other institutions to the extent that it supports social solidarity more than individualism and its concomitant selfishness (320). In other words, Rauschenbusch envisions the transformation of society through the influence of Christian socialism. This socialism is based on "the brotherhood of men and solidarity of interests" (322), and it shares with the modern labor movement a commitment to the upward mobility of the working class (322–30). Rauschenbusch insists that this dream is not a "utopian delusion," but a realistic hope that a new social order can emerge from the wreckage of the social crisis (237). There is no such thing as a perfect social order, but the possibility remains for achieving a close approximation. In his famous words, "the kingdom is always but coming" (338). Although the past is riddled with roadblocks to the kingdom's emergence, Rauschenbusch interprets the present as the opportune time to resist the forces of evil and to participate in social transformation.

Rauschenbusch and the rise of social theology

Many rose to Rauschenbusch's challenge. The peak of the social gospel movement is often associated with the period from 1907—the year *Christianity and the Social Crisis* was published—to 1914 and the beginning of World War I. Although the movement inspired by Rauschenbusch lost some of its resilience and optimism after the War, it is possible to trace the influence of his kingdom vision on subsequent champions of social and political liberation. For example, Martin Luther King, Jr. (1929–1968) praised Rauschenbusch for "insisting that the gospel deals with the whole man" rather than restricting the gospel to spiritual matters. He continues: "It has been my conviction ever since reading Rauschenbusch that any religion which professes to be concerned about the souls of men and is not concerned about the social and economic conditions that scar the soul, is a spiritually moribund religion only waiting for the day to be buried."[11] Rauschenbusch's involvement with women's liberation, however, was ambiguous. While he addressed the particular cruelty shown to women within the industrial economic system (223–5), his support of women's suffrage was tepid, causing some to criticize his "Anglo-Saxonist chauvinism."[12]

Rauschenbusch's influence was also felt as his vision for the social gospel united theologians and church leaders from various traditions, both within and beyond Protestantism. In 1882 Rauschenbusch and Leighton Williams founded the Brotherhood of the Kingdom, which initially showed the potential for ecumenical collaboration among social gospel advocates. The most prominent example, however, was the Federal Council of Churches (FCC), which Rauschenbusch helped launch in 1908. In fact, most of the key leaders in the FCC were also leaders of the social gospel movement, which found its way into the Council's constitution. Its fourth point proposed "to secure a larger combined influence for the churches of Christ in all matters affecting the moral and social condition of the people, so as to promote the application of the law of Christ in every relation of human life." This was a lofty goal, and prominent among those theologians who doubted its optimism was Reinhold Niebuhr (1892–1971). In Niebuhr's preface to the 1956 edition of *An Interpretation of Christian Ethics*, delivered as the Rauschenbusch Memorial Lectures at Colgate-Rochester Divinity School in 1934, he hailed Rauschenbusch as "the most celebrated exponent" of the social gospel and placed himself within this movement. Nevertheless, he was critical of its conflation of justice and love, a problem stemming from a denial of original sin and obliviousness to individual and collective self-regard.[13] Niebuhr's ethical realism became one major alternative to the theological and social optimism of Rauschenbusch's legacy.

Even though, as Gary Dorrien notes, the biblical exegesis, cultural conservatism, and optimism of Rauschenbusch are dated and have been challenged by convincing alternatives, his enduring legacy is the recognition that theology must not be done in a vacuum and the Church cannot ignore the social and political dimensions of existence.[14] Liberation theology, black theology, feminist theology, political theology, and many other forms of social theology all have links to *Christianity and the Social Crisis*. Although primarily a pastor and a church historian, the work of Walter Rauschenbusch was pivotal in placing Protestant theology on a trajectory toward greater social awareness and engagement.

Notes

1. "Beneath the Glitter" is an article Rauschenbusch published in the *Christian Inquirer* on August 2, 1886, two years after moving to New York as a pastor. The article narrates the economic and personal misery beneath the façade of New York's wealth and success.
2. As described in Christopher H. Evans, *The Kingdom is Always But Coming: A Life of Walter Rauschenbusch* (Grand Rapids: Eerdmans, 2004), xviii.
3. The theology prevalent at Rochester Seminary in the late-nineteenth century is best represented by Augustus Strong's *Systematic Theology* (1886), published the same year Rauschenbusch graduated. Strong left an indelible mark on the Seminary through his long stint as President from 1872 to 1912.
4. Walter Rauschenbusch, *Christianizing the Social Order* (New York: Macmillan, 1912), 46.
5. As observed by Paul Brandeis Rauschenbusch, "Foreword," in *Christianity and the Social Crisis in the 21st Century* (New York: HarperOne, 2007), xi.
6. Walter Rauschenbusch, *A Theology for the Social Gospel* (New York: Macmillan, 1917), 1.
7. Walter Rauschenbusch, *Christianity and the Social Crisis in the 21st Century*, edited by Paul Rauschenbusch (New York, HarperOne, 2007), xxi. This is a reprint edition of *Christianity and the Social Crisis* with reflections from contemporary theologians after each chapter. Because this is the cheapest and most widely available edition currently in print, parenthetical page numbers throughout this essay refer to this text.
8. Two books Rauschenbusch mentions with particular favor within this field of study are Francis Peabody's *Jesus Christ and the Social Question* (1900) and Shailer Matthews's *The Social Teaching of Jesus* (1897).
9. In *A Theology for the Social Gospel*, he is more explicit about these aims: "The speculative problem of christological dogma was how the divine and human natures united in the one person of Christ; the problem of the social gospel is how the divine life of Christ can get control of human society. The social gospel is concerned about a progressive social incarnation of God" (148).

10. A similar appeal later in the book to "re-Christianize the Church" (271) sounds similar to Kierkegaard's concern, particularly evident in *Practice in Christianity* (1850), to introduce Christianity into Christendom. The major difference, of course, is while Kierkegaard's ideal was the militant Church suffering within society, Rauschenbusch's ideal was closer to what Kierkegaard called the triumphant Church in which Christianity and society become synonymous.

11. Martin Luther King, Jr., *Stride Toward Freedom* (New York: Harper & Row, 1958), 91.

12. Gary Dorrien, *The Making of American Liberal Theology: Idealism, Realism, and Modernity, 1900–1950* (Louisville: Westminster John Knox, 2003), 154.

13. Reinhold Niebuhr, *An Interpretation of Christian Ethics*, Library of Theological Ethics (Louisville: Westminster John Knox Press, 2013), xxxi.

14. Gary J. Dorrien, *Reconstructing the Common Good: Theology and the Social Order* (Maryknoll: Orbis Books, 1990), 47.

Select Bibliography

Primary sources

Rauschenbusch, Walter. *Christianity and the Social Crisis*. New York: Macmillan, 1907.

Rauschenbusch, Walter. *Christianity and the Social Crisis*. Library of Theological Ethics (Louisville: Westminster John Knox Press, 1992).

Rauschenbusch, Walter. *Christianity and the Social Crisis in the 21st Century*. Edited by Paul Rauschenbusch. New York: HarperOne, 2007.

Secondary sources

Dorrien, Gary. "Thy Kingdom Come: Walter Rauschenbusch, Vida Scudder, and the Social(ist) Gospel" in *The Making of American Liberal Theology: Idealism, Realism, and Modernity, 1900–1950*. Louisville: Westminster John Knox, 2003.

Evans, Christopher H. *The Kingdom is Always But Coming: A Life of Walter Rauschenbusch*. Grand Rapids: Eerdmans, 2004.

Handy, Robert T., ed. *The Social Gospel in America, 1870–1920*. New York: Oxford University Press, 1966.

Smucker, Donovan E. *The Origins of Walter Rauschenbusch's Social Ethics* (Montreal/Kingston: McGill-Queen's University Press, 1994).

5.6

Dynamics of Faith (1957)
Paul Tillich (1886–1965)

Figure 5.6 Paul Tillich

Boundary theologian

Paul Tillich was a theologian who lived on the boundary between many different worlds. In an autobiographical work written a few years after his move to America, Tillich identified several dimensions of his boundary existence. Partly because of circumstance and partly out of choice, Tillich found himself living between personal temperaments, city and country, social classes, reality and imagination, theory and practice, heteronomy and autonomy, church and society, religion and culture, Lutheranism and socialism, idealism and Marxism, native and alien land, and philosophy and theology.[1] Tillich's correlations between religion and culture and between philosophy and theology are perhaps most well known, but each facet of his boundary existence shaped his identity and method as a theologian. Wherever he taught and lectured, Tillich encountered both gushing praise and goring opposition, which confirms both the originality and difficulty of his passion to mediate between different disciplines and worlds.

Paul Tillich was born on August 20, 1886, in the town of Starzeddel, just outside of Berlin. His father, Johannes Tillich, was a Lutheran pastor, and so naturally Paul was confirmed in the Lutheran Church in 1902. In fact, despite his eventual departure from Lutheran orthodoxy, Tillich always considered himself a Lutheran theologian. He studied theology in Berlin, Tübingen, and Halle, identifying with the analysis of human existence offered by Karl Barth in opposition to liberal theology, while also adopting the historical-critical approach of Rudolf Bultmann and Ernst Troeltsch. He was also a voracious reader of philosophy from an early age and developed a particular appreciation for Friedrich Schelling, who was the subject of his Doctor of Philosophy awarded in 1911. In 1912, Tillich completed his theology degree and was ordained in the Lutheran Church, becoming an Assistant Minister in Moabit, the workers section of Berlin. He married Margarethe "Grethi" Wever in September 1914. Four days later, however, Tillich volunteered for military service and served as a chaplain in the German army until January 1919.

The war had a deep and lasting impact on Tillich, not least because of the emotional and physical anguish experienced on the front lines. Tillich also returned to a wife who had been unfaithful, and they were eventually divorced in 1921. He was remarried to the artist Hannah Werner in 1924, but this was a notoriously unconventional and often strained marriage, which Hannah documented in her own autobiography.[2] These tragedies led Tillich to believe that theology and philosophy must somehow do justice to the abyss in our lives.[3] Upon returning from the war, Tillich started teaching theology at the University of Berlin (1919–1924) and then for three semesters at Marburg (1924–1925), where he was meant to replace Rudolf Otto. At Marburg, Tillich encountered "the strong but tight-fitting armor of Barthian supranaturalism," which he believed led to an anti-humanistic attitude.[4] Because of this, he gladly accepted an offer as Professor of Religious Studies at the Dresden Institute of Technology, which at that time did not have a theology department.

In Dresden, Tillich began to find his own unique style, both in life and in scholarship. He adopted a Bohemian lifestyle, pursuing his love for expressionism and modern dance and often using his home as a place to practice and reflect on the arts. His voracious interest in culture was expressed in *The Religious Situation* (1925), which also articulated his perspective of "belief-ful realism" in contrast to pessimistic realism and utopian idealism. From 1929 to 1933, Tillich was Professor of Philosophy at the University of Frankfurt, where he lectured and wrote widely on social ethics and political philosophy. He also put his beliefs into action, joining the Social Democratic Party and writing *The Socialist Decision* (1932). Because of his outspoken position and critique of the Nazis, Tillich was dismissed from his university position in 1933, and on the invitation of Reinhold Niebuhr he came to America as Visiting Professor of Religion and Systematic Theology at Union Theological Seminary in New York. While also lecturing in philosophy at Columbia University, Tillich struggled to find his niche at Union, not only because of cultural and linguistic barriers, but also because of his unique blend of philosophy and theology. Nevertheless, he stayed at Union for a total of twenty-two years, becoming Assistant Professor of Philosophical Theology (1937–1945) and then full Professor (1940–1955).

The much-anticipated first volume of Tillich's *Systematic Theology* was published in 1951, which outlined his theological form (apologetic), method (correlation), and norm (New Being in Jesus as the Christ). In contrast to the kerygmatic theology of Barth and others, Tillich insisted that the message of Christianity is always inherently related to the questions arising out of cultural situations. As such, theology is always apologetic theology or "answering theology," implying a common ground with culture that Barth denied.[5] Tillich's method, therefore, involved correlating "questions and answers, situation and message, human existence and divine manifestation."[6] Tillich invokes the opening sentence of John Calvin's *Institutes of the Christian Religion* in support of his position that existential questions and theological answers are interdependent.[7] This method departed from Calvin and Protestant orthodoxy, however, by asserting a plethora of sources for theology, rather than privileging historical and biblical revelation.[8]

Just a year after Tillich launched his *Systematic Theology*, he also published *Courage to Be* (1952), which together with *Dynamics of Faith* (1957) would be his most popular books. The goal and appeal of these slim volumes was their revision of traditional religious language in a way that was informed by and connected to contemporary culture. In particular, Tillich was keen to build a connection with experiences of doubt and despair as represented by existentialism.[9] *Dynamics of Faith* appeared the same year as the second volume of Tillich's *Systematic Theology*, while he was University Professor at

Harvard (1955–1962). Tillich finished his career as Professor of Theology at University of Chicago Divinity School (1962–1965), where he released his third volume of the *Systematic Theology* (1963). In these last years, he also wrote and lectured extensively on morality and world religions. His illustrious career was cut short, however, after he suffered a heart attack, dying several days later on October 22, 1965.

Reinterpreting faith

The premise of *Dynamics of Faith* is that the concept of faith has been distorted, and it needs reinterpretation, reinvention, and healing (xxi).[10] Rather than being a term that divides and confuses people, faith should be an idea that empowers unified, clarified existence. Tillich defines faith as "ultimate concern." By this, he means giving total surrender to what one considers ultimate in hope of experiencing total fulfillment (1). As ultimate concern, faith includes both an objective referent (the Ultimate) and subjective involvement (concern). It is a passionately human act oriented toward an ultimate reality (9–14).[11] In Hebrew religion, that ultimate reality is Yahweh and his justice; in Christianity, it is New Being in Jesus as the Christ. But faith is not a "sacred" phenomenon divorced from the "secular" world. Everyone has faith because everyone has an object of ultimate concern, whether that is God, the nation, or economic success (2–4). The problem with these "faiths" just mentioned, according to Tillich, is that they contain "false ultimacy" by deeming a finite object (e.g., the nation) as something ultimate (13). Only an infinite or absolute object is worthy of our ultimate concern; everything else is idolatry.

Another distortion of faith is identifying it with only one aspect of human personality. True faith, on the contrary, is an act of "total personality," involving our minds, wills, emotions, and bodies. It is conscious and unconscious, rational and nonrational. As such, faith is an act of integration, a "centered act" that keeps each aspect of personality in dynamic interplay (4–9). Tillich addresses three particular distortions of faith that focus on merely one aspect of personality. The intellectual distortion defines faith as belief, a cognitive assent to the Bible or some kind of authority (35–41). The voluntaristic distortion defines faith as action, which is manifest either as the Catholic "will to believe" or the Protestant "obedience of faith" (41–44). The emotional distortion sees feelings as the source of faith, a position represented by Schleiermacher. Tillich objects to this approach because it avoids orienting ultimate concern toward truth and ignores the brokenness of human experience (46).[12] When the act of faith involves every element of personality, however, it possesses an integrative, healing power. Yet this healing can never be complete, as disintegration is always present (125–27).

Part of this inevitable disintegration is the presence of doubt. Since faith is a matter of finite being relating to the infinite, it always involves a measure of uncertainty (18). In a phrase reminiscent of Kierkegaard, Tillich claims the only absolute certainty is our complete inability "to bridge the infinite distance between the infinite and the finite from the side of the finite" (122). Doubt is not an enemy of faith; it is faith's necessary companion. In this sense, doubt is the dialectical opposite of faith as ultimate concern. The way to deal with this doubt is not to deny it, but to accept the risk of faith and respond to it with courage (115–22). The "courage to be" is to persevere in faith in the midst of despair and in the face of inevitable idolatry.[13] Every human being—let alone every theologian—is simultaneously a person of faith and a doubter.[14]

Comprehending faith

If faith is ultimate concern, then to what extent is this concern reasonable? How is the truth of faith comprehended and how does it relate to scientific, historical, and philosophical truth? First, it is important to remember that Tillich views faith as an act of total personality, so the mind is inevitably

Figure 5.7 Bust of Paul Tillich

involved. If faith and reason were at odds, then faith would be a dehumanizing act. There is a degree of conflict between faith and reason, however, because we experience estrangement from our true nature as integrated beings.[15] Yet Tillich affirms the inseparable relationship between faith and reason (85–91). In sum, "reason is the presupposition of faith, and faith is the fulfillment of reason" (88).[16]

No inherent tension exists, therefore, between science and faith (92–98). Conflict arises only when science becomes the object of ultimate concern, thus becoming faith rather than science. Tillich observes this problem with the theory of evolution and with naturalism more generally, both of which exemplify going beyond the limits of scientific analysis and thus coming into conflict with the truth of faith. When the boundaries between faith and science remain intact, however, then faith has nothing to fear or gain from science.

Tillich maintains a similar distinction between the truth of faith and historical truth (98–102). He presupposes that we have no access to the historical events on which the biblical accounts are based. Something has happened that transformed history, but finding out exactly what happened is not the responsibility of faith. It is the task of historical research to determine what parts of the Bible are historically verifiable. This is separate from the task of faith, which is simply to utilize biblical stories as symbols for ultimate concern. For example, the Fall of Adam and Eve may not be a historical event, but it can be interpreted as a symbol for humanity's estrangement. Jesus of Nazareth may not have risen from the dead in actual history, but the biblical testimony to Jesus as the risen Christ is a powerful symbol for New Being. In this way, the truth of faith and historical truth remain independent, liberating both to pursue their separate tasks.

Of all the different spheres of truth, Tillich recognizes the greatest degree of overlap between the truth of faith and philosophical truth, although there are important distinctions (104–09). Both faith and philosophy are oriented toward ultimate reality, but philosophy articulates this reality in concepts, whereas faith articulates it in symbols. As an intellectual discipline, philosophy is detached from its object of contemplation, but faith is inherently participatory. At the same time, genuine philosophy is carried out with passionate faith, and faith naturally leads one to ask philosophical questions. Tillich observes no conflict between faith and philosophy, but neither does he seek a synthesis.[17]

If scientific, historical, and philosophical truths do not constitute criteria for judging the truth of faith, then what does? For Tillich, faith contains truth to the extent that "it adequately expresses an ultimate concern" (110).

By "adequate," Tillich means an expression of ultimate concern that creates an active response within a community, whether in the form of morality, ritual, art, or other modes. These modes of expression change throughout time, however, so we cannot make them absolute. Every affirmation of truth must be accompanied by a negation, which is why Tillich considers Christ the most powerful symbol, since affirming this symbol also means accepting its negation: Christ crucified (112).

Expressing faith

As we have already observed, Tillich views the truth of faith as something expressed in symbols. Since the ultimate cannot be expressed directly, it must be expressed symbolically. Tillich explains several functions of a symbol, including signifying a reality beyond itself, participating in this reality, opening up new levels of reality, and unlocking new dimensions of the soul (47–50). God is the most fundamental symbol, since this symbol is always present within our ultimate concern. Tillich anticipates the criticism that this makes God *merely* a symbol by reminding his readers that symbols participate in the reality they signify. Tillich cryptically remarks: "God is a symbol for God" (53).[18]

Faith is expressed in symbols, and symbols are organized into stories. This is what Tillich refers to as myth: "symbols of faith combined in stories about divine-human encounter" (56). On the one hand, Tillich is adamantly opposed to demythologizing myths by giving them scientific interpretations because the power of myths is precisely their existence as myths. But on the other hand, Tillich warns against the error of literalism, which links symbols with historical or scientific truth. In Tillich's perspective, the danger of literalism is its fixation on temporary and conditional expressions of truth, rather than focusing on the eternal truth signified by concrete symbols. For example, he asserts that viewing the Messiah's virgin birth as a literal, biological event robs faith of its ultimacy by chaining it to the finite (59–60). Christianity is an expression of ultimate concern, says Tillich, and therefore it is and must remain a myth.

Faith is expressed through symbols and myths, but it is also expressed through forms of life. In this regard, Tillich identifies two main types of faith: ontological and moral. The ontological type seeks to experience the holiness of being itself, whereas the moral type responds to the holiness of being by seeking what ought to be (64–65). For the former, Tillich addresses sacramental, mystical, and humanist faith (66–74). For the latter, he discusses juristic (Talmudic Judaism and Islam), conventional (Confucianism), and ethical (Jewish prophets) faith (74–80). While distinguishing between different types of faith, Tillich also recognizes their underlying unity. The cause of conflict between types of faith is not divergent beliefs, but the extent to which they express ultimate concern most adequately (76). Dialogue between faiths should entail neither "tolerance without criteria" nor "intolerance without self-criticism" (143). Tillich believes that Protestantism has the potential to unify the types of faith and express ultimate concern most adequately (at least better than Catholicism or fundamentalism), but he claims it must first deal with its aversion to the sacramental (83, cf. 140). Ultimately, he points to the New Testament— and Paul's Spirit-centered faith in particular—as a unification of the sacramental and mystical elements of faith with the moral and rational elements (82–83).

When Tillich discusses the expression of faith, he clarifies that this is not merely an individual expression, but takes places within the community. On a fundamental level, this is because faith is dependent on language, and language arises within community (27). It is the community of faith that provides the content for ultimate concern, although this content—such as the creeds or liturgies—should never be the object of ultimate concern. In Tillich's opinion, this would violate the precious "Protestant principle"—that criticism and doubt are embedded within the act of faith—and so annihilate the risk of faith (33). In addition to providing the language of faith, the community is also the context for the active expression of faith as it works itself out in love. Tillich defines love as the desire to be united with the object of ultimate concern (130). Faith implies love, and love determines action. In several respects, therefore, Tillich insists that "the state of ultimate concern is actual only within a community of action" (136).[19] Even more profoundly, where there is no community of faith, true community does not exist, because faith is the force that truly binds people together (137–38).

Tillich and the correlationists

Paul Tillich made a massive contribution to twentieth-century Protestant theology, but his legacy pertains more to his unique method and mood of doing theology rather than the content of his theological claims. Tillich was responsible for popularizing a correlationist theological method and a mood of "self-transcending realism." His correlationist method explored the dynamic interplay between cultural questions and biblical-theological answers, while his self-transcending realism grew out of his concern to cultivate a kind of realism infused with faith-driven idealism.[20] Several other theologians before and during Tillich's career leveled realistic critiques against the social gospel and idealistic liberalism, including Karl Barth in Germany and H. Richard Niebuhr and Reinhold Niebuhr in America. But in contrast with Barth in particular, Tillich responded by finding a new way to engage culture, while Barth responded by forging a new way to engage with the Word of God. In fact, Reinhold Niebuhr observed that if Barth was the Tertullian of his day, then Tillich was the Origen of his day, at least in terms of relating the Gospel to culture.[21]

Indeed, Barth and Tillich are often linked with two distinct ways of doing Protestant theology today, a distinction represented by Yale-school theologians in contrast to Chicago-school theologians. Generally speaking, Yale-school or postliberal theologians promote post-foundational theology performed in and for the church, whereas Chicago-school or correlationist theologians advance public theology that correlates revelation with human reason and experience.[22] Although he only taught at the University of Chicago for three years, Tillich's theology had notable influence on several Chicago-school theologians, including Langdon Brown Gilkey (1919–2004) and David Tracy (1939–). Gilkey, who studied under Tillich at Union, developed a similar dialogue to Tillich's between philosophy and theology, addressing in particular the "death of God" movement and its impact on religious language.[23] David Tracy shares Tillich's commitment to orient theology toward the human situation, but he critiques Tillich for not listening to the cultural answers together with the cultural questions, thus offering his own method of "critical correlation."[24]

The influence of Tillich's theology and method of correlation, of course, extends beyond theologians who have taught at the University of Chicago, including prominent Protestant theologians John Macquarrie (1919–2001) and Gordon Kaufmann (1925–2011), Catholic theologians Karl Rahner (1904–1984) and Bernard Lonergan (1904–1984), and many liberation and feminist theologians. One example of the latter is Mary Daly (1928–2010), who attended Tillich's lectures at Harvard. Daly explains how Tillich's *Courage to Be* was particularly motivating for her feminist agenda as the courage to be liberated from patriarchy.[25] She also criticized Tillich, however, for his own personal and theoretical blindness to patriarchal oppression, which she saw as stemming from his abstract symbolization of the cross.[26]

In addition to these wide-ranging influences, Tillich's theological engagement with science, politics, psychology, literature, painting, and many other areas of culture impacted the rise of interdisciplinary dialogue between theology and non-theological disciplines. Tillich's voracious interest in culture corresponded with his passion for theology and religion, for he believed that "as religion is the substance of culture, so culture is the form of religion."[27] Although it is difficult to categorize Tillich given his existence on the boundary, "cultural theologian" is perhaps the most fitting description and a theology of culture his most lasting legacy.

Notes

1. These are the chapter titles of Paul Tillich, *On the Boundary* (New York: Charles Scribner's Sons, 1966). "On the Boundary" was originally Part One of Tillich's *The Interpretation of History* (New York: Charles Scribner's Sons, 1936).
2. Hannah Tillich, *From Time to Time* (New York: Stein and Day, 1973).
3. Tillich, *On the Boundary*, 52.
4. Ibid., 41.
5. Paul Tillich, *Systematic Theology*, vol. 1 (London: SCM Press, 1978), 6.
6. Ibid., 8.
7. Ibid., 63.
8. More specifically, Tillich contrasted his correlationist method with supranaturalism (theology derived from revealed truths), naturalism (theology derived from human truths), and dualism (a supranatural structure on a natural basis). Ibid., 64–66.
9. This was also Tillich's goal in his *Systematic Theology*, although in more academic fashion. The terms he uses throughout his corpus, however, remain the same: sin is *estrangement*, grace is *reunion*, God is the *ground and aim of Being*, faith is *ultimate concern*, Holy Spirit is *Spiritual Presence*, and Christ is *New Being*.
10. Page numbers are taken from the reprint edition: Paul Tillich, *Dynamics of Faith* (New York: HarperCollins, 2009).
11. Cf. Tillich, *Systematic Theology*, vol. 1, 12–14, 214–15.
12. In the *Systematic Theology*, Tillich explains that experience is the medium rather than the source of theology (ibid., 42).
13. Tillich addresses the concept of courage in *The Courage to Be* (New Haven: Yale University Press, 1951).
14. As this applies to theologians, see Tillich, *Systematic Theology*, vol. 1, 10.
15. For an extensive discussion of the estrangement of existence, see Tillich, *Systematic Theology*, vol. 2, 44–75.

16. Elsewhere, Tillich unpacks the semantic, logical, and methodological rationality of faith. See Tillich, *Systematic Theology*, vol. 1, 54–59.
17. For more on the relationship between philosophy and theology, see ibid., 18–28.
18. For more on the meaning of "God," see ibid., 211–18.
19. For Tillich's full explanation of the Spiritual Community as a community of faith and love, see Tillich, *Systematic Theology*, vol. 3, 172–82.
20. For more on the phrase "self-transcending realism," see Tillich, *The Protestant Era* (Chicago: Chicago University Press, 1948), 75f.
21. Reinhold Niebuhr, "Biblical Thought and Ontological Speculation in Tillich's Theology," in *The Theology of Paul Tillich*, edited by Charles W. Kegley (New York: The Pilgrim Press, 1982), 216–27.
22. These are broad generalizations, especially given the fact that the Chicago school is technically much older, beginning with the founding of the University of Chicago Divinity School in 1890. The Yale school did not emerge until the 1970s with the work of Hans Frei and George Lindbeck. In the 1960s, roughly corresponding to the time when Tillich was professor of theology at the University of Chicago, a new phase of the Chicago school emerged that could be appropriately called correlationist or revisionist in contrast with the more modernist, scientific liberalism of the previous phases.
23. Langdon Brown Gilkey, *Naming the Whirlwind: The Renewal of God-Language* (Indianapolis: Bobbs-Merrill, 1969). See also *Gilkey on Tillich* (New York: Crossroad, 1990).
24. David Tracy, *Blessed Rage for Order* (New York: Seabury Press, 1975), 46.
25. Mary Daly, *Beyond God the Father: Toward a Philosophy of Women's Liberation* (Boston: Beacon Press, 1973), 23.
26. Mary Daly, *Gyn/Ecology: The Metaethics of Radical Feminism* (Boston: Beacon Press, 1978), 94f.
27. Paul Tillich, *On the Boundary*, 69–70.

Select Bibliography

Primary source

Tillich, Paul. *Dynamics of Faith*. New York: Harper & Row, 1957.

Secondary sources

Kegley, Charles W., ed. *The Theology of Paul Tillich*, revised and updated edition. New York: The Pilgrim Press, 1982.

Manning, Russell Re. *The Cambridge Companion to Paul Tillich*. Cambridge: Cambridge University Press, 2009.

O'Neill, Andrews. *Tillich: A Guide for the Perplexed*. London: T&T Clark, 2008.

Pauck, Wilhelm and Marion Pauck. *Paul Tillich: His Life and Thought*, vol. 1: *Life*. New York: Harper & Row, 1976.

5·7

Church Dogmatics[1] (1932–1967)
Karl Barth (1886–1968)

Barth's theological bombshell

Karl Barth is often hailed as one of the greatest theologians of the twentieth century. Whatever judgment one makes on Barth's theological proposals, it is difficult to contest this acclaim, especially when considering his voluminous *Church Dogmatics*. More than a decade before he began this vast work, however, Barth had dropped "a bombshell onto the playground of the theologians."[2] The bombshell was his Romans commentary, and the playground was the liberal establishment in which Barth received his education. In subsequent years, Barth was called a theologian of crisis, a dialectical theologian, and the founder of neo-orthodoxy, but none of these labels adequately describe the breadth of Barth's theological endeavors and achievements.

Born in Basel, Switzerland on May 10, 1886, Karl was the oldest son of Fritz and Anna Barth. Three years after his birth, his father was appointed Lecturer of New Testament and Early Church History at the University of Bern, eventually succeeding Adolf Schlatter as full professor. Karl received an excellent education in Bern, which is also where he began his theological studies before moving on to Berlin, Tübingen, and Marburg. In Berlin, Barth attended lectures by Adolf von Harnack and was thoroughly impressed. Even more impressive for Barth, however, was Wilhelm Hermann, with whom he studied in Marburg. Hermann was an avid appreciator of Schleiermacher, and Barth admits that he "absorbed Hermann [and by implication Schleiermacher] through every pore."[3]

When Barth finished his theological education at Marburg, he served as a part-time pastor in Geneva from 1909 to 1911. There he devoted his time to preaching and studying John Calvin's *Institutes of the Christian Religion*. After this short stint, he became a pastor of a Reformed church in the agricultural and industrial parish of Safenwil in Aargau, Switzerland. Here Barth encountered the plight of industrial workers while beginning to wrestle with the predicament of religion conceived as a human project. These years were a mix of happiness and sadness, as he married Nelly Hoffman in 1913 yet experienced the outbreak of World War I in 1914. Barth became increasingly distressed by support for Kaiser Wilhelm's war policy among his former teachers, most notably Adolf von Harnack. This distress, combined with his study of Romans, brought Barth to point of a *krisis*, a term that includes the meaning of English transliteration "crisis" while carrying overtones of judgment, trial, and separation. In the second edition of his Romans commentary (1922), Barth identified the core of this *krisis* as submission to what Kierkegaard called the "infinite qualitative distinction" between time and eternity or between God and humanity.[4]

This perspective gained Barth an audience, and when he became Professor of Dogmatic Theology in Göttingen in 1921, a movement called "dialectical theology" was gaining momentum around him. Together with theologians such as Rudolf Bultmann, Friedrich Gogarten, and Emil Brunner, Barth started to chart an alternative to the popular liberal theology of Schleiermacher, Harnack, and Ritschl. Dialectical theology began with divine revelation rather than religious experience or philosophy, and it emphasized the dialectical movement between the "Yes" and "No" of God, or between God's revelation and hiddenness. While in Göttingen, Barth co-founded a new journal, *Between the Times*, and lectured extensively on Reformed confessions and theologians, various portions of Scripture, and dogmatic theology (1924–1925, eventually published as *Göttingen Dogmatics*). In 1925, he transferred to Münster, where he also lectured on dogmatics (*Die christliche Dogmatik im Entwurf*, 1927). Barth later considered this a failed attempt to begin his dogmatics, although some of this material is reworked and expanded in his definitive *Church Dogmatics*.

By the time Barth became a professor of theology at Bonn in 1930, he had charted his own theological path and parted ways with Bultmann, Brunner, and other early enthusiasts of dialectical theology.[5] Barth identified his study of Anselm of Canterbury as a critical stage in his development and a catalyst for his *Church Dogmatics*. He resolved to build his dogmatic theology on Jesus Christ, rather than on "the eggshells of a philosophical system."[6] He called this a "Christological concentration" of theological tradition, particularly Reformed theology.[7] In 1932, Barth published the first volume of the *Church Dogmatics*, which he so titled because dogmatics finds its life and structure within the church (I/1, xiii). Furthermore, Barth distinguishes dogmatics from systematic theology, since the former bears progressive witness to the truth rather than codifying truth into a closed system.

Barth labored over the *Church Dogmatics* for the rest of his life, the result being four "volumes"—Doctrine of the Word of God, Doctrine of God, Doctrine of Creation, and Doctrine of Reconciliation—each containing several books. The last volume was never finished, and the planned fifth volume on the Doctrine of Redemption or eschatology remains unwritten. Debates persist regarding the unity and development of thought within these volumes, with many identifying a shift between the two books in the Doctrine of God (II/1 and II/2) because of Barth's Christological revision of election. Barth maintained, however, that "no important breaks or contradictions [exist] in the presentation" (IV/2, xi), so it is important not to overplay this supposed shift. Reading through these volumes is an enormous yet rewarding task, and Barth tried to assist readers by keeping his main argument in normal print while setting apart biblical exegesis and historical theology in small print. Barth admits that "at a pinch," the main text can be understood without the small print, but certainly not *vice versa* (I/1, xii).[8]

While in Bonn, Barth wrote the Barmen Declaration (1934) as a spokesman of the Confessing Church, opposing Hitler and the Third Reich by asserting the lordship of Jesus Christ and the separation of church and state. Because of this position, Barth lost his chair in Bonn and was deported to Basel, Switzerland in 1936, where he remained until his death in 1968. During these years, he worked tirelessly on the *Church Dogmatics* and other writings, supported ecumenical efforts, and lectured throughout Europe and around the world. Before he retired from his teaching post in 1962, Barth gave his "swan song" lectures on the topic of evangelical theology, which he also delivered throughout the United States. In his foreword to the American edition of *Evangelical Theology*, Barth affirmed that his *Church Dogmatics* is in no way a conclusion, but rather the initiation of a new theological conversation centered on the God of freedom revealed in Jesus Christ.[9]

Symphonic theology

George Hunsinger compares the experience of reading the *Church Dogmatics* to entering a magnificent cathedral: once one's eyes are adjusted to the light, the spectacle is awe-inspiring and unparalleled.[10] This is an apt aesthetic metaphor, except for the fact that Barth objected to viewing the *Church Dogmatics* as a house to enter, since houses are static. He preferred to see this work as an introduction to a dynamic way of life.[11] Better, therefore, is Hans Urs von Balthasar's suggestion to read Barth's *magnum opus* as one would listen to a Mozart symphony.[12] This is especially fitting given Barth's love for Mozart, whose music he enjoyed every morning before beginning his work. Barth even wrote a book on Mozart, appreciating most of all how Mozart broke free from the "snail shell of his own subjectivity" into the "free objectivity" of the aural universe.[13] Barth viewed the purpose of theology in similar terms, and so admired Mozart that he resolved to seek him out first upon arrival in heaven.[14]

Other features of the *Church Dogmatics* lend themselves to a musical, even symphonic, description. First, Barth's perspective on any given topic cannot be summarized in a single statement but, as John Webster notes, "only in the interplay of a range of articulations of a theme."[15] Like a symphony, the *Church Dogmatics* contains four "movements," which are connected not by a neat, linear argument but by a complex intermingling of melodies and countermelodies. Consequently, Barth's logic follows a sonata form—exposition, development, recapitulation—more than a syllogistic one.[16] Most of the time this musical logic is not stated overtly, but at one point Barth does describe how the polyphony of creation is harmonized in the symphony of the covenant (IV/3.1, 159).

Second, Barth's admiration for the beautiful, objective form of Mozart's music matches his preference for theological objectivism instead of expressivism or emotivism. Theology is not merely anthropological projection, but exists as a response to the authoritative voice of Jesus Christ. As such, faith and knowledge are not inherent human capabilities, but depend entirely on hearing Jesus in the present moment (I/1, 41). The Church is inherently a hearing Church before it is a teaching Church (I/2, 797). Symphonic theology is only an echo of the objective music of revelation. Third, identifying the *Church Dogmatics* as symphonic theology is appropriate given the overall tone of triumph and joy rather than despair, the same tone of resolution that Barth appreciated in Mozart.[17] In Barth's understanding, evil has no real existence; it is nothingness, much like the pauses in music (III/3, 163). Although dissonance does exist in Barth's theology, it is a dialectical dissonance that enters into darkness for the sake of hearing God's "Yes" in Christ even more clearly. Fourth and finally, Barth's symphonic theology, which focuses on the beauty of Christ, is a fitting contrast to what

Figure 5.8 Karl Barth

he calls the "utterly unmusical" form of natural theology (II/1, 666). According to Barth, while natural theology embarks on the joyless and futile task of seeking truth apart from the Word of God, dogmatic theology is a "particularly beautiful science" that bears witness to the glory of God in Christ (II/1, 662).

Encountering the Word of God

Church Dogmatics commences with the doctrine of the Word of God, but this doctrine also permeates every volume, leading T.F. Torrance to call Barth a "theologian of the Word."[18] For Barth, the Word of God exists in threefold form as the Word of God preached, written, and revealed (I/1, §4). The former two manifestations—church proclamation and the Bible—are only indirectly the Word of God, since the only direct form of God's Word is God himself. In his act of revelation, God always remains a mystery, infinitely free and beyond human grasp (I/1, 321). If God's Word could be identified with something static, like words on a page, then God could be domesticated and controlled. Consequently, the Bible itself is not revelation, but a *witness* to revelation (I/1, 111) that becomes God's Word as God addresses us through the biblical words (I/2, 109).

The Word of God is the free speech and action of God addressed to humanity; it is God as he reveals himself for us and for our salvation. Since God speaks and acts as Father, Son, and Spirit, God's revelation is inherently triune. "God reveals himself. He reveals Himself *through* Himself. He reveals *Himself*" (I/1, 296). In other words, the triune God is Revealer (Father), Revealed (Son), and Revealedness (Spirit). Consequently, through the prism of revelation, it is possible to see how God exists in a threefold mode of being (I/1, 299), with each mode dynamically participating in the other modes (I/1, 370). In contrast with Schleiermacher, therefore, Barth demonstrates how the Trinity prefaces, structures, and controls the entire project of Christian theology, rather than being tacked on at the end (I/1, 301).

The triune God does not reveal himself generally, but does so particularly and concretely in the person and work of Jesus Christ. In fact, Barth contends that the revealed Word is identical with Jesus Christ, and as such, any theology that seeks to take its bearing from divine revelation is "fundamentally Christology" (I/2, 123).[19] This insight leads to what are perhaps the most radical reformulations of Reformed theology throughout the *Church Dogmatics*, whether in connection with doctrines of creation, election, anthropology, ethics, or reconciliation. Some have labeled these reformulations, usually with critical intent, Barth's "Christomonism," although Barth abhorred this "unlovely term" (IV/3, 713). In keeping with his Reformational heritage, Barth desires to take the *solus Christus* (in Christ alone) principle seriously, but he never endorses Christomonism in the sense that Christ's history obliterates responsible human action (IV/4, 23).

Humans are responsible actors in the drama of redemption, yet God's Word and action in Christ by the Spirit always takes primacy in this drama. In fact, Barth believes that divine revelation is a drama rather than mere data, because revelation is always an act, a personal event involving particular people at particular times. Because the "being, activity, and speech of Jesus Christ" is a particular history unfolding through particular events, Christology is essentially "the unfolding of a drama" rather than an "obscure metaphysics" (IV/3, 137). We are not just spectators of the dramatic revelation of Christ, however, because this drama is also our drama (I/2, 498). We do not watch the drama of Christ unfold from a distance; we encounter Christ as fellow-performers who must respond to this event (III/1, 387). In sum, Christ is the principal performer of this drama, and the Church exists as a real yet completely dependent participant in the theater of the Word (I/2, 690; III/3, 332).

Receiving the grace of God

For Barth, humanity's complete dependence on God is rooted in our natural antagonism toward God and our incapacity to know and relate to him (I/1, 168). Consequently, any receptivity to the Word of God and active participation in the drama of salvation is an act of grace. Faith itself is created by the Word and received as a gift of the Holy Spirit (I/1, 244). This is the crux of Barth's objection to liberal theology and the notion of "religion" in general, arguing that it represents a futile attempt to achieve self-salvation rather than relying entirely on the grace of God (I/2, §17). God's grace is his free decision to be for us rather than against us. It is the overflowing of God's love, which is the very being of God. As such, it is unconstrained and unconditional (II/2, 9–10).

The grace of God is not limited to his loving and covenantal interaction with humanity, but includes the acts of creation and providence. The Creator God is the same God who freely gives himself in Christ by the Spirit, so Barth views the doctrine of creation through the lens of Christology. Both creation and providence, therefore, are bound up with the gracious acts of the triune God for us and for our salvation (III/1, 42). To return to Barth's dramatic metaphor—which he draws in large part from John Calvin—creation is a theater or a stage for the drama of the covenant of grace (III/1, 44). The relationship between creation and covenant is not one of nature and grace, since everything is under the grace revealed in Jesus Christ. The doctrine of creation, therefore, is a statement of faith not accessible in a *natural* way (III/1, 3). This helps explain why Barth was so vehemently opposed to the natural theology promoted by Brunner and several of his contemporaries.[20]

At the heart of God's free decision to be gracious is his election (II/2, 121). Barth is even so bold as to say that divine election is the whole of the Gospel (II/2, 13). What he means by election, however, is very different than normally articulated within theological tradition. In short, God elects himself in Jesus Christ, the one who is both reprobate and elect for the sake of humanity. In other words, Jesus is "the original and all-inclusive election" (II/2, 117). Because the electing God is also the Elect one, Barth places the doctrine of election within the doctrine of God. He critiques those theologians who discuss the eternal decree or will of God in an abstract or static manner, arguing that this decree is dynamically and concretely revealed in Jesus Christ. In talking about the election of individuals, Barth distinguishes between the elect who are witnesses to the truth and the rejected as those who choose godlessness and who isolate themselves from God. As the Elect one, however, Christ represents both classes of people, and as such embodies the "Yes" of God's mercy and the "No" of God's judgment for all humanity. This unique position on election has led some theologians to accuse him of universalism.[21] In reality, Barth claims that we cannot make the salvation of all people either inevitable or impossible, since God is free to accomplish whatever he chooses (II/2, 417–18). All is dependent on the mysterious grace of God.

This emphasis on the free and boundless grace of God permeates the *Church Dogmatics*. As we have already seen, *general* grace is already present within the doctrine of creation, and redemptive or *special* grace is a ubiquitous theme in the doctrine of reconciliation (III/1, §58.1). At every turn, Barth reminds his readers that the Christian life—and even all creaturely life—is an existence of grace. Some scholars have objected that grace "triumphs" so resolutely in Barth's theology that it blunts the reality of evil and undercuts the necessity of human action.[22] Yet Barth demurred, asserting that if anything is central in his theology, it is the freedom of Jesus Christ, the very freedom that liberates the responsibility of human persons.[23]

Responding to the command of God

According to Barth, human action in the drama of redemption serves to give an account of God's grace as we respond to the existence of Jesus Christ (II/2, 576). Because human action takes place as a response to God's action, Barth places ethics within the doctrine of God (II/2, §36–39). Encountering God means encountering his demands, which God gives us the grace to fulfill (II/2, 512). Barth also views ethics as a critical component that concludes every volume of the *Church Dogmatics* (I/2, §22.3; III/4, §52–57; *The Christian Life*, §74–78).[24] Ethics is dogmatics and dogmatics is ethics, held together by the command of God in Jesus Christ. Jesus is the answer to the question "what is good?" (II/2, 516), and our actions witness to the rightness of his action (II/2, 543).

In addition to linking ethics to Christology, Barth also connects ethics to anthropology (III/2, §45). To be a created human being is to exist in relational and responsive encounter with God and other people. In short, response-ability is inherent to personhood. Because of God's grace, we relate to him not merely as creatures but as covenant partners through the mediation of Christ. We are not on equal footing in this partnership, since God is infinitely distinct from his covenant partners. It is, however, a real partnership in which we encounter God, hear his command, and respond within our creaturely limits (III/4, §56).[25]

When Barth writes of the command of God, he means God's direct command to us in the present, not the commands recorded in Scripture. Like God's revelation, his command is always an event: concrete and personal (II/2, 548). By implication, ethics is concrete or "special," given the concrete responses of the Christian community to the concrete Word of God (III/4, §52.1). Just like Barth's aversion to natural theology, he opposes philosophical ethics in favor of theological ethics that takes its bearing from a responsive relationship to Jesus Christ (II/2, 543–44).

Barth's new melody

Although Barth's early Romans commentary was considered an explosive bombshell, this violent metaphor is not the most appropriate way to describe Barth's theology. It seems more fitting to describe the *Church Dogmatics* as a mature work of symphonic theology that introduced a new theological melody into what Barth perceived as the cacophony of anthropological projection in Protestant theology. Other theological melodies emerged in reaction to Protestant liberalism in the twentieth century that improvised off Barth's and provided countermelodies with varying levels of consonance and dissonance. A theologian like Reinhold Niebuhr, for example, resonated with Barth's themes of human inability and divine grace in constructing his political theology, but his approach clashed with Barth's in other ways, both theologically and politically.[26] Another example is postliberal theology, also called the Yale School, which shares Barth's conception of the task of theology and his critique of correlationist theological method (Paul Tillich). George Lindbeck, for example, resonates with Barth's emphasis on biblical narrative and the community of faith.[27] What he does not share, however, is the rational, reality-referential nature of Barth's theology and his placement of Scripture as an authority over tradition.[28] Dissonance also exists among those who enlist Barth for the construction of non-foundational, postmodern theology.[29] Most notably, these theologians fail to appreciate the particularity of Barth's doctrine of revelation, both in its objective reality and its absolute claims.[30]

If some theologians think Barth is too biblical and theologically traditional, others think he is not enough so. The latter is often the case with evangelical theologians, who have experienced a conflicted relationship with Barth's theology. Some, like Cornelius Van Til, condemned "Barthianism" as unorthodox, while others, such as Bernard Ramm, saw Barth's theology as a means for moving beyond fundamentalism.[31] Overall, Barth continues to receive this mixed reaction among evangelicals, who appreciate his emphasis on salvation by grace alone through faith alone in Christ alone, while often critiquing Barth's views on revelation, Scripture, and election.[32] Of course, "evangelical" is a slippery term with a usage further complicated by its diverse meanings throughout history and within different cultures. Many Reformed theologians who are students and lifelong appreciators of Barth would identify with this label to varying extents, which is a fitting move to the extent that Barth understood himself as a theologian committed to the Gospel (*euangelion*) of Jesus Christ. It is no doubt testimony to the significance and sheer scope of Barth's theological melody that it has been replayed and reworked by such a diverse range of theologians and ethicists.[33] Given his resounding influence, it is appropriate to speak of Protestant theology before and after Karl Barth.

Notes

1. Translated from *Die Kirchliche Dogmatik;* hereafter, all references to this work (Karl Barth, *Church Dogmatics* [13 vols.; eds G.W. Bromiley and T.F. Torrance; trans. G.W. Bromiley, et al.; Edinburgh: T&T Clark, 1936–1969]) shall be noted by employing in-text citations.
2. Karl Adam, "Theologie der Krisis," *Das Hochland* 23 (1926): 276–77.
3. In the autobiographical sketch *Fakultätsalbum der Evangelisch-theologischen Fakultät Münster* (1927), quoted in Eberhard Busch, *Karl Barth: His Life from Letters and Autobiographical Texts,* trans. by John Bowden (London: SCM Press, 1976), 45.
4. Karl Barth, *Epistle to the Romans,* trans. Edwyn C. Hoskyns (London: Oxford University Press, 1933), 10.
5. Barth resisted himself identifying with any theological school or movement, including the label "dialectical theology" (*CD* I/1, xv).
6. Karl Barth, *How I Changed My Mind* (Edinburgh: Saint Andrew Press, 1969), 43.
7. Ibid.
8. Another accessible way into the Church Dogmatics is to pick up a reader that selects key sections, such as R. Michael Allen, *Karl Barth's Church Dogmatics: An Introduction and Reader* (London: T&T Clark, 2012).
9. Karl Barth, *Evangelical Theology: An Introduction* (Grand Rapids: Eerdmans, 1963), xi–xii.
10. George Hunsinger, *How to Read Karl Barth: The Shape of His Theology* (New York: Oxford University Press, 1991), 27–28.
11. A conversation with youth chaplains of the Rhineland in 1963, quoted in Eberhard Busch, *Karl Barth: His Life from Letters and Autobiographical Texts,* trans. John Bowden (London: SCM Press, 1976), 375.
12. Hans Urs von Balthasar, *The Theology of Karl Barth: Exposition and Interpretation,* trans. Edward T. Oakes (San Francisco: Ignatius Press, 1992), 28–29.
13. Karl Barth, *Wolfgang Amadeus Mozart,* trans. Clarence K. Pott (Grand Rapids, MI: Eerdmans, 1986), 49–51.
14. Ibid., 16.
15. John Webster, "Introducing Barth," *Cambridge Companion to Karl Barth,* ed. John Webster (Cambridge: Cambridge University Press, 2000), 9.
16. Theodore A. Gill, "Barth and Mozart," *Theology Today* 43 (1986): 409.
17. Barth, *Mozart,* 34.
18. Thomas F. Torrance, *Karl Barth: Biblical and Evangelical Theologian* (Edinburgh: T&T Clark, 1990), chapter 3.
19. Elsewhere Barth likewise affirms that Christology "is the touchstone of all knowledge of God in the Christian sense, the touchstone of all theology."

Dogmatics in Outline, trans. G.T. Thomson (New York: Harper & Row, 1959), 66. This short book is another way of getting a sense for the themes and perspectives of the *Church Dogmatics*, but it should not be considered a substitute.

20. Brunner's pamphlet on natural theology was published as *Natur und Gnade: Zum Gespräch mit Karl Barth* (Tübingen: J. C. B. Mohr, 1934). Barth's response was *Nein! Antwort an Emil Brunner* (Munich: Chr. Kaiser Verlag, 1934). They were combined in an English translation by Peter Fraenkel under the title *Natural Theology* (London: Centenary Press, 1946). Some scholars have pointed out how this disagreement was based on some critical misunderstandings. See Trevor Hart, "The Capacity for Ambiguity: Revisiting the Barth-Brunner Debate," in *Regarding Karl Barth: Essays Toward the Reading of His Theology* (Carlisle: Paternoster Press, 1999), 139–72.

21. One of the first and most scathing critiques in this regard came from Emil Brunner in *Dogmatics, Vol. 1: The Christian Doctrine of God*, trans. Olive Wyon (London: Lutterworth Press, 1949), 349. For an excellent summary of Barth's position, see Hunsinger, *How to Read Karl Barth*, 128–35.

22. Most famously, see G.C. Berkouwer, *The Triumph of Grace in the Theology of Karl Barth*, trans. Hans R. Boer (London: Paternoster, 1956).

23. See Barth's letter to Berkouwer on December 30, 1954, in which he suggests replacing "freedom" for "triumph" and "Jesus Christ" for "grace." Quoted in Busch, *Karl Barth*, 381.

24. *The Christian Life* is the "ethics of reconciliation" with which Barth intended to conclude volume 4 of the *Church Dogmatics*. He was only able to complete the section on baptism before his death, however, so this volume is a posthumously published collection of Barth's lecture manuscripts. *The Christian Life: Church Dogmatics* IV/4: *Lecture Fragment*, trans. Geoffrey W. Bromiley (Grand Rapids: Eerdmans, 1981).

25. For an excellent exploration of the nature of human responsibility in Barth's theology, see John Webster, *Barth's Moral Theology: Human Action in Barth's Thought* (Edinburgh: T&T Clark, 1998).

26. See the fascinating and fictional conversation between Barth, Niebuhr, a feminist, and a liberationist in Daniel L. Migliore, *Faith Seeking Understanding: An Introduction to Christian Theology*, 2nd ed. (Grand Rapids: Eerdmans, 2004), 384–401.

27. George Lindbeck, *The Nature of Doctrine: Religion and Theology in a Postliberal Age* (Louisville: Westminster John Knox, 1984).

28. See George Hunsinger, "Truth as Self-Involving: Barth and Lindbeck," in *Disruptive Grace: Studies in the Theology of Karl Barth* (Grand Rapids: Eerdmans, 2000), 305–18.

29. For example, see Walter Lowe, *Theology and Difference: The World of Reason* (Bloomington: Indiana University Press, 1993); Graham Ward, *Barth, Derrida, and the Language of Theology* (Cambridge: Cambridge University Press, 1995); William Stacy Johnson, *The Mystery of God: Karl Barth and the Postmodern Foundations of Theology* (Louisville: Westminster John Knox Press, 1997).

30. For a similar assessment, see Bruce L. McCormack, *Orthodox and Modern: Studies in the Theology of Karl Barth* (Grand Rapids: Baker, 2008), 113–37.

31. Cornelius Van Til, *Christianity and Barthianism* (Philadelphia: Presbyterian and Reformed Publishing, 1962); Bernard Ramm, *After Fundamentalism: The Future of Evangelical Theology* (San Franscisco: Harper & Row, 1983).

32. For a range of reactions, see Bruce L. McCormack and Clifford B. Anderson, eds, *Karl Barth and American Evangelicalism* (Grand Rapids: Eerdmans, 2011); Sung Wook Chung, ed., *Karl Barth and Evangelical Theology: Convergences and Divergences* (Grand Rapids: Baker, 2008); and David Gibson and Daniel Strange, eds., *Engaging with Barth: Contemporary Evangelical Critiques* (New York: T&T Clark, 2009).

33. Space does not allow us to trace out Barth's unique impact on theological ethics, but those who stand in his trajectory yet critique him at various points include Stanley Hauerwas, John Howard Yoder, Oliver O'Donovan, and Nigal Biggar.

Select Bibliography

Primary sources

Barth, Karl. *Church Dogmatics*. 13 vols. Edited by G.W. Bromiley and T.F. Torrance. Translated by G.W. Bromiley, et al. Edinburgh: T&T Clark, 1936–1969.

Barth, Karl. *Die Kirchliche Dogmatik*. Munich: Christian Kaiser Verlag, 1932 (I/1). Zurich: Evanglischer Verlag, 1938–67 (I/2–IV/4).

Secondary sources

Bromiley, Geoffrey W. *Introduction to the Theology of Karl Barth*. Edinburgh: T&T Clark, 1979.

Busch, Eberhard. *Karl Barth: His Life from Letters and Autobiographical Texts*. Translated by John Bowden. London: SCM Press, 1976.

Hart, Trevor A. *Regarding Karl Barth: Essays Toward a Reading of His Theology*
   Carlisle: Paternoster Press, 1991.
Hunsinger, George. *How to Read Karl Barth: The Shape of His Theology*. New
   York: Oxford University Press, 1991.
Webster, John, ed. *Cambridge Companion to Karl Barth*. Cambridge:
   Cambridge University Press, 2000.

5.8

Black Theology and Black Power (1969)

James Hal Cone (b. 1938)

Embracing blackness

In the 1960s, the United States was a cauldron of social struggle and protest. At the heart of this struggle was the Civil Rights movement, seeking equal rights and opportunities for African Americans. As this movement progressed, however, some African Americans became increasingly critical of desegregation, celebrated distinctly black culture, and began to rally under the banner of "black power." All of this was happening as James Cone finished his Ph.D. in theology and began his teaching career. Despite all of his education, the Civil Rights and Black Power movements awakened Cone from his theological slumber.[1] Driven by a desire to relate theology to the struggle of black people, Cone's first writing project was *Black Theology and Black Power*. Nothing like it had ever been written, and it set Cone on a trajectory to be the father of black liberation theology.

James Cone was born in 1939 during the age of Jim Crow. In his hometown of Bearden, Arkansas, segregation was a daily reality, whether at schools, water fountains, movie theaters, or churches. In his own church—the Macedonia African Methodist Church—Cone had a real and lasting encounter with Jesus, but he also encountered an uncritical faith embedded in an otherworldly mentality. This mentality was incapable of dealing with the harsh realities of life, which led to a divide between "churchpeople" and

Figure 5.9 James Cone at the 174th Convocation of Union Theological Seminary in the City of New York

"bluespeople," the latter finding "the Sunday religion of Jesus inadequate for coping with their personal problems and the social contradictions they experienced during the week."[2] Needless to say, Cone was not content with the anti-intellectual and socially evasive culture of his upbringing.

While attending Shorter College (1954–1956) and Phillander Smith College (1957–1058), Cone was involved in leading several small churches, and his desire to be well grounded theologically compelled him to enroll in the Master of Divinity program at Garrett Theological Seminary. At Garrett he discovered his love for theology, and instead of pursuing a permanent church ministry position, Cone chose postgraduate study at

Northwestern University. He completed his Ph.D. in systematic theology in 1965, writing his dissertation on the anthropology of Karl Barth. During brief stints teaching theology and religion at Philander Smith College and then Adrian College, he realized that the Western theology he had come to love—exemplified by Bultmann, Barth, and Tillich—was not adequate to address the situation of black oppression. Inspired by the March Against Fear in 1966, Stokely Carmichael's articulation of black power, the Newark and Detroit riots of 1967, and finally by the assassination of Martin Luther King, Jr. in 1968, Cone was convinced that theology must embrace blackness, and he devoted himself to writing *Black Theology and Black Power*.

Cone identifies his "turn to blackness" as an even deeper conversion experience than his turn to Jesus.[3] Because of this conversion, he now saw himself as a *black* theologian addressing *black* existence. In his Preface to the 1989 edition of *Black Theology and Black Power*, Cone explains how this book was his first attempt to fuse the visions of Martin Luther King, Jr. and Malcolm X.[4] On the one hand, Martin stood up against injustice while calling blacks to love their enemies nonviolently. On the other hand, Malcolm asserted that blacks must first and foremost love themselves—love blackness—and then must defend blackness by any means necessary. In bringing together Martin and Malcolm as "the yin and yang in the black attack on racism,"[5] Cone was the first theologian to articulate "liberation as the heart of the gospel and blackness as the primary mode of God's presence" (vii).

Black Theology and Black Power unleashed a torrent of responses, both energetically supportive and indignantly critical. To address these responses and to flesh out his original thesis, Cone wrote *A Black Theology of Liberation* (1970), which confirmed his status as a leading liberation theologian. In the same year, he became the first black systematic theologian at Union Theological Seminary in New York City, where he continues to teach today. One of the common critiques of Cone's early work was his propensity to rely on white theological concepts rather than black experience. However accurate this critique, in subsequent works—such as *The Spirituals and the Blues* (1972) and *God of the Oppressed* (1975)—Cone expanded his sources and drew more consistently on black concepts and culture. In these books and his subsequent work, including his latest *The Cross and the Lynching Tree* (2011), Cone clearly articulates the preeminence of blackness in his personal experience and theological reflection: "I am *black* first—and everything else comes after that."[6]

Blackness and the gospel

Because of his commitment to being black before everything else, Cone begins *Black Theology and Black Power* by addressing what it means to be black in the United States. Given the history of white oppression, Cone recognizes that being black should inevitably lead to a commitment to black power. He defines black power as the "complete emancipation of black people from white oppression by whatever means black people deem necessary" (6). In blunter terms, Cone concurs with Stokely Carmichael that black power means "taking care of business" the black way, not the white way.[7]

Cone compares the concerns of black power to existential themes arising in Tillich's theology and the philosophy of Camus. Riffing off Tillich's *The Courage to Be*, he views black power as the way forward because it enables black people to affirm their being and humanity (6–7). Black people say "yes" to their being by rebelling and fighting back, rather than wallowing in despair or plodding forward in weak neutrality. Black power is essentially a complete and consistent "affirmation of the humanity of black people in the face of white racism" (16).

Integration into a white system is not an option, because this ignores the root problem, giving the appearance of victory while hiding ongoing oppression. In radical language taken from *The Rebel* by Albert Camus, Cone asserts that it would be better to die than to capitulate to white oppression, because life without freedom is worse than death. This marks the absurdity of the black situation, which only black power can adequately address. To stand up against white oppression is not a form of racism; it is humanity-affirming rebellion. In fact, Cone maintains that the problem of race in America is a white problem, and merely lending black people a helping hand cannot remove this guilt (22). White and black people are simply deluded if they fail to realize that an extreme, oppressive situation requires extreme, revolutionary action. As Cone presents it, this is a matter of life and death; everyone must be willing to die in order to secure life for all.

If the task of theology is to show how God's revelation applies to particular situations, then in Cone's perspective, most theologians have failed to do good theology, because they have been silent regarding the oppression of black people (31). Black theology, by contrast, not only speaks out against this oppression; it aligns God and his gospel with this struggle. According to Cone, the gospel must be emancipated from its "whiteness" and should be identified with black liberation from white oppression (32). Black power *is* the gospel, because it is the contemporary expression of Jesus's liberating mission. Echoing the words of Kierkegaard, Cone claims that Jesus is our contemporary, and that he is present in the ghetto and in the black rebellion against white oppression (37–38).

To be a Christian is to embrace the liberating work of Christ that leads to true freedom. In one sense, Christ won the battle against oppression on the cross, but bringing God's freedom and justice to bear in the present is a continual campaign (40). Drawing on insights from Jürgen Moltmann and Karl Barth, Cone emphasizes that justification by faith inevitably leads to political responsibility. Justified by God, we are liberated to fight for justice, joining with the work of God in history (47).

At this point, Cone addresses a major objection against identifying Christianity with black power, namely, that it contradicts Jesus's command to love our enemies. For Cone, this supposed contradiction dissolves when we recognize, as Tillich did, the inseparability of love, power, and justice.[8] When these are intertwined, love resists sentimentality and justice transcends legalism (51). True love does not just accept the current situation, but it instead works to destroy anything that opposes love. In other words, love is truncated if limited to random acts of kindness, but it flourishes by "working for political, social, and economic justice, which always means a redistribution of power" (55). Moreover, Cone explains that love may require violence if it is necessary to achieve lasting justice (55–56). In sum, for Cone, embracing the gospel means nothing less than embracing black power. If people are filled with the Holy Spirit, they will be committed to justice for oppressed black people (58). Similarly, a mark of the true church is caring for and identifying with the poor and needy, which means identifying with Christ. Cone argues therefore that the church that opposes black power opposes Christ himself.

Blackness and the Church

Putting his discussion in the context of the biblical narrative, Cone defines the church as God's suffering people, "that people called into being by the power and love of God to share in his revolutionary activity for the liberation of man" (63). The church is no doubt a people committed to God's Word, to service, and to fellowship, but the church only exists where it identifies with and fights for the liberation of the oppressed. The white church has actively oppressed black people rather than fighting for their liberation, and therefore it cannot be the true church. Cone minces no words for describing the failure of the white church, identifying its accommodation to "sick, middle class egos" (80) and "chaplaincy to the forces of oppression" (90). The white racist church is no more orthodox than the portion of the church that supported Arius and his denial of Christ's incarnation in the fourth century. Like the Arians, the white church denies the Incarnation because it refuses to see Christ among black people (73).[9]

In contrast to this heresy, Cone articulates a new kind of orthodoxy: "*Christ is black baby*, with all of the features which are so detestable to white society" (68). The affirmation that Christ is black, Cone contends, is just as important in the twentieth century as understanding him as Jewish in the first century (69).[10] Christ is black because he always identifies with the oppressed, and the church will be black to the extent that it does the same. Unless the white church converts and embraces liberating action, it will continue to be the anti-Christ. In short, Cone calls the white church to repent and believe the gospel. What this means practically is "a radical reorientation of their style in the world toward blacks," not claiming "lofty neutrality," but "tasting the sting of oppression themselves" (81).

Cone's critique of the white church is unflinchingly harsh, but the black church hardly fares any better. Because the black church was born out of slavery and protest, it initially grasped the gospel and its liberating hope and power. Although some in the black church capitulated to the worldview of white slave owners, a vision of an oppression-free future inspired protest against slavery in the present, as expressed in the best of black preaching and spirituals. After the Civil War, however, the black church started losing its resolve to pursue comprehensive liberation, capitulating to Jim Crow laws and the agenda of white churches. In this way, black ministers began perpetuating white oppression, which was only partly caused by their fear of opposing segregation and discrimination (106–107). This is why Martin Luther King, Jr. stood out: he refused to accept the current state of existence for black people. He rekindled the dream for an authentically black church (108).

King's dream was cut short, but he paved the way for the emergence of black power, which Cone recognizes as "the only hope of the black church in America" (109). Black power is not only the sole hope for the black church, but for organized Christianity as a whole. If the essence of Christianity is liberating the oppressed and defending the needy, then black power shows the way forward. The church is the body of Christ in the world, "and in twentieth-century America, *Christ means Black Power!*" (112). Cone thus challenges both the white church and the black church: will we join the revolution, or will we retreat into comfortable havens? Cone recognizes no neutral or easy option for renewal; the church will choose either "costly obedience" or "confirmed apostasy." And costly obedience will be fueled by a thoroughly worldly theology.

Blackness and theology

By worldly theology, Cone means theology that refuses abstractions and addresses concrete realities of oppression. This is the kind of theology that will lead to words and deeds that are "harmonious with Jesus Christ" (84). Understood in this way, theology is not primarily an intellectual exercise but a risky, creative, and prophetic response to life and society. This response is genuinely Christian when it flows from identification with the disinherited. Cone commends Barth as a prime proponent of this kind of theology, given his stance against Nazi oppression of the Jews (86–88).

Black theology is a prime example of worldly theology. Its task is "to analyze the black man's condition in light of God's revelation in Jesus Christ with the purpose of creating a new understanding of black dignity among black people, and providing the necessary soul in that people to destroy white racism" (117). The point of departure for black theology, therefore, is the predicament of black people and the problem of oppression. Since black people only know Christ through oppression, says Cone, this reality and the struggle for freedom is the only binding authority for black theology (120). Every Christian doctrine should therefore relate to and support blackness and emancipation for black people. Despite Cone's criticism of theoretical modern theology, his vision for black theology places him firmly within the trajectory of modern theology, given its characteristic use of a material norm to organize and evaluate doctrines.[11]

One example of how Cone reconstructs doctrine from the perspective of the black predicament is his approach to eschatology. He bluntly observes how an otherworldly ethos is a "white lie" that has corrupted many black churches (122). Hope in Jesus, in this sense, is merely a ploy to avoid the harsh realities of injustice. By contrast, black theology maintains an earthly focus, more concerned with overturning white oppression in the present than adjudicating between different views of the end times. Drawing on Moltmann, Cone maintains that eschatology is more about this world being transformed than the hope of a distant, heavenly reward. "Our future expectations must be turned into present realities": justice and black self-determination (126).

It is perhaps even more evident that Cone uses the black predicament as his point of departure and binding authority when it comes to his understanding of reconciliation. First, reconciliation with God "means that white people are prepared to deny themselves (whiteness), take up the cross (blackness) and follow Christ (black ghetto)" (150). Justification happens by becoming black, not literally, but figuratively, by aligning one's heart, soul, mind, and body with the dispossessed (151). Unless white people become "black," reconciliation will not be possible. In fact, reconciliation cannot happen until black people have experienced emancipation, because otherwise the white oppressors will determine the terms of reconciliation. Until then, violence may be the means necessary for black people to obtain freedom. Cone is clear that unless white racists repent and overturn their systemic violence against black people, a violent revolution may be necessary to make blackness beautiful once again (138–43).

According to Cone, black theology is not just one way among many to think and live as a Christian. Black theology makes Christianity "*really* Christian" and exists "to destroy heretical white American Christianity" (130–31). Cone ends his book with an invitation and a challenge. Anyone— black or white—can take up the mission of black theology. What matters is not black skin but a black heart, which is evident through a resolute stance with oppressed blacks and against white oppressors. Everything rests on how one answers and lives out the questions, "Where is your identity? Where is your being?" (152)

Cone and the birth of black theology

Most scholars identify the 1966 statement by the National Committee of Negro Churchmen as the first expression of black theology in conjunction with black power. Cone's *Black Theology and Black Power*, however, represents the first book-length exposition of these themes and the first extended effort to locate liberation of oppressed blacks at the heart of the gospel. Soon after its publication in 1969, others added their voices to the growing chorus of black theologians, including Vincent Harding, Jacquelyn Grant, Gayraud Wilmore, Albert Cleage, William R. Jones, Charles Long, C. Eric Lincoln, J. Deotis Roberts, Joseph Washington, and Preston Williams. This first generation of black theologians labored to legitimize their theological interpretation of the black situation as they continued to battle against marginalization and discrimination.

In the Preface to the 1989 edition of *Black Theology and Black Power*, Cone rearticulates why black theology was necessary in the 1960s, but he also admits to several shortcomings in his inaugural attempt. First, he acknowledges his blindness to sexism. In reviewing his book twenty years later, Cone is "embarrassed by its sexist language and patriarchal perspective" (x). Instead of changing this language in the revised edition, however, he decided to leave the original "as a reminder of how sexist I once was and also that I might be encouraged never to forget it" (x). He insists on remembering his insensitivity to the oppression of women, because "amnesia is the enemy of justice" (xi). As such, Cone expresses gratitude for how his sexism was challenged by the rise of womanist theology, led by theologians like Jacquelyn Grant, Katie Cannon, and Delores Williams. These theologians exposed the inconsistency of black liberation theology that remained blind and silent to the oppression of black women, revealing vast theological and practical consequences of ingrained misogyny. For example, Delores Williams, who was a student of Cone's and later his colleague at Union Theological Seminary, criticizes Cone for using the Exodus as a paradigm for liberation, when this liberation did not apply to non-Hebrew female slaves.[12] As it developed in the 1990s, womanist theology thoroughly revised Christian theology through the lens of the black female experience, including traditional theories of the atonement.[13]

The second shortcoming Cone identifies in his first book is the failure to link the black struggle for liberation with parallel experiences in the Majority World. He recognizes that both Martin Luther King, Jr., and Malcolm X maintained a global perspective, which was necessary for understanding oppression at home. Cone links his blindness to non-Western oppression to his overreliance on Western theology, particularly his dependence on Karl Barth.[14] Cone still appreciates the centrality of Christ championed by Barth, but he views Barth's aversion to natural theology as a hindrance to black theology. Finally, and directly related to the second shortcoming, Cone laments how *Black Theology and Black Power* disregards classism. He recognizes how greater awareness of global economic realities would have enabled him to view the black struggle as more than a racial one, and how class privilege is pervasive in both white and black communities in the United States.

Beginning in the early 1980s, a second generation of theologians joined Cone in his passionate pursuit of black theology. In general, these theologians worked on "strengthening ties between scholarship, ministry, and social activism."[15] Dwight Hopkins and Cornel West are two notable theologians in this second generation, although they pursue divergent methodologies. Dwight Hopkins follows in Cone's footsteps by advancing the "black hermeneutic school," which remains committed to Christian faith as expressed within black communities and affirms the blackness of Jesus. Cornel West, by contrast, participates in the "black philosophical school," which pursues "humanocentric theism" allied with philosophical investigation.[16] Despite their different norms, methods, and goals, both of these approaches are indebted to Cone's vanguard expression of black theology. Cone was not only the father of black theology in all its contemporary forms, but remains an influential voice shaping social, contextual, and political theology in the Protestant tradition.

Notes

1. James H. Cone, "Looking Back, Going Forward: Black Theology as Public Theology," in *Black Faith and Public Talk: Critical Essays on James H. Cone's Black Theology and Black Power*, edited by Dwight N. Hopkins (MaryKnoll, NY: Orbis Books), 250.
2. Ibid., 247.
3. Ibid., 251.
4. James H. Cone, *Black Theology and Black Power* (Maryknoll, NY: Orbis Books, 1997), viii. Hereafter, all references to this work shall be noted by employing in-text parenthetical citations.
5. Cone, "Looking Back, Going Forward," 256.
6. James H. Cone, *God of the Oppressed*, revised edition (Maryknoll, NY: Orbis Books, 1997), xi.
7. Similar to the terms "black" and "blackness," Cone intends both a literal and figurative-theological meaning for the terms "white" and "whiteness." Whiteness is being on the side of oppressors—whether intentionally or through supposed neutrality—and blackness is being on the side of the oppressed. According to Cone, these groups can be generally distinguished by skin color, although both white and black come in different shades.
8. Paul Tillich, *Love, Power, and Justice* (New York: Oxford University Press, 1960).
9. See discussion of Arianism in the earlier chapter on Athanasius' *On the Incarnation* by George Kalantzis and Amy Hughes in the current volume, *Reading Christian Theology in the Protestant Tradition*.

10. Elsewhere, Cone explains that the literal color of Jesus's skin is irrelevant, just as "blackness" comes in different shades. Christ is black simply because he was against oppression and for liberation as the incarnate suffering servant. Nevertheless, Cone also points out that Christ was not *white* "in any sense of the word, literally or theologically." James H. Cone, *A Black Theology of Liberation* (New York: J. B. Lippincott Company, 1970), 218.

11. For a nuanced conception of how "modern" might best be understood in a distinctly theological context, see Bruce L. McCormack, "Introduction: On 'Modernity' as a Theological Concept" in *Mapping Modern Theology: A Thematic and Historical Introduction*, eds Kelly M. Kapic and Bruce L. McCormack (Baker, 2012), 1–20.

12. Delores Williams, *Sisters in the Wilderness: The Challenges of Womanist God-Talk* (Maryknoll, NY: Orbis Books, 1993), 147.

13. Not all womanist theologians are equally critical of traditional Protestant theology, as represented by the fascinating essays in *Feminist and Womanist Essays in Reformed Dogmatics* (Louisville: Westminster John Knox Press, 2006), edited by Amy Plantinga Pauw and Serene Jones. While in his 1997 preface to *God of the Oppressed* Cone voices agreement with womanist rejection of patriarchal doctrines and acknowledges that their insights have been personally transformative, he still maintains that the cross of Christ can be a source of liberation and empowerment. Cone, *God of the Oppressed*, xv–xviii.

14. Cone, *God of the Oppressed*, xi–xiii.

15. Frederick L. Ware, "Black Theology," in *Global Dictionary of Theology*, edited by William A. Dryness and Veli-Matti Kärkkäinen (Downers Grove: IVP Academic, 2008), 113.

16. Frederick Ware delineates these categories in his article on black theology in *Global Dictionary of Theology*, but more fully in *Methodologies of Black Theology* (Cascade: Wipf & Stock, 2008). In addition to the hermeneutic and philosophical school, he also identifies a human sciences school of black theology.

Select Bibliography

Primary source

Cone, James. *Black Theology and Black Power*. New York: Harper & Row, 1969.

Cone, James. *Black Theology and Black Power*. Maryknoll, NY: Orbis Books, 1997.

Secondary sources

Burrow, Rufus, Jr. *James H. Cone and Black Liberation Theology*. Jefferson, NC: McFarland & Company, 1994.

Hopkins, Dwight N., ed. *Black Faith and Public Talk: Critical Essays on James H. Cone's* Black Theology and Black Power. Maryknoll, NY: Orbis Books, 1999.

Hopkins, Dwight N. and Edward P. Antonio. *The Cambridge Companion to Black Theology*. Cambridge: Cambridge University Press, 2012.

Ware, Frederick L. "Black Theology." In *Global Dictionary of Theology*, edited by William A. Dryness and Veli-Matti Kärkkäinen, 112–18. Downers Grove: IVP Academic, 2008.

5·9

Doing Theology in a Revolutionary Situation (1975)
José Míguez Bonino
(1924–2012)

Theologian seeking effectiveness

José Míguez Bonino was a pioneer of Protestant liberation theology in Latin America. Born in 1924 in Santa Fe, Argentina, Bonino's parents were Italian immigrants and active participants in the Methodist Church. After two years of medical school, Bonino completed an undergraduate degree in theology at the Evangelical School of Theology in Buenos Aires, graduating in 1948. Following graduation, he served churches in Bolivia and Argentina before pursuing a Masters in Theology at Chandler School of Theology in Atlanta. Bonino came back to Argentina to teach Dogmatic Theology, but then returned to the United States to complete a Ph.D. in ecumenism at Union Theological Seminary.

These formative years of ministry and education equipped Bonino for his role, beginning in 1961, as director of the Evangelical School of Theology (later the Evangelical Institute of Theological Studies, or ISEDET) in Buenos Aires. Meanwhile, he continued serving as a Methodist pastor and launched a lifelong involvement with the World Council of Churches (WCC). At first, he participated in the WCC's Commission on Faith and Doctrine (1961–1975), but he eventually served as the Council's President (1975–1983). In addition to this ecumenical leadership, Bonino was the only Latin American Protestant invited to observe the Second Vatican Council, and he also attended the 1968 Conference of Latin American Bishops in Medellín, Colombia.

Although Bonino engaged widely in ecumenical efforts and taught at several international seminaries as a visiting professor, he remained rooted in Argentina and committed to the Latin American context. Bonino's first major publication in English was *Doing Theology in a Revolutionary Situation* (1975). Later, he translated this book into his native Spanish as *Fe en Busca de Eficacia* (1977), or *Faith Seeking Effectiveness*. In doing so, Bonino proposed a way of doing Protestant theology that diverged from European theology influenced by Saint Anselm's methodology of "faith seeking understanding." In Bonino's perspective, theology arises out of and is oriented toward effective—even revolutionary— action. Following this original manifesto on liberation theology, Bonino continued his account of faith in action in *Christians and Marxists: The Mutual Challenge to Revolution* (1976) and *Toward a Christian Political Ethics* (1983).

Through his publications, pastoral ministry, theological education, and leadership within the WCC, Bonino emerged as a widely respected leader, not just of liberation theology, but also of Protestantism in Latin America. In 1993, Bonino was invited to deliver the Carnahan Lectures, which were published as *Faces of Latin American Protestantism* (1997). In these lectures, he traced the four main faces of Latin American Protestantism: mainline, evangelical, Pentecostal, and immigrant. Bonino believed that the revolutionary situation that arose in mid-twentieth century Latin America created potential for a common goal among Protestants, if indeed each "face" would open its eyes to see and respond to their common reality.

Bonino confesses that when he looks at the Latin American situation, he does so as an "*evangélico*," someone who "belongs to the grace of God."[1] This dependence on grace motivated and strengthened Bonino's resolute commitment to the kind of theology that constantly moves toward practical and political effectiveness. The revolutionary theologian, just like any Christian, has nothing to fear, because "a Christian can offer his praxis to the fire of criticism totally and unreservedly on the trust of free grace just as he can offer his body totally and unreservedly in the hope of resurrection." This freedom is "the very center of the gospel," and the foundation of revolutionary action.[2]

Emergence of a revolutionary situation

To understand the revolutionary situation, Bonino begins *Doing Theology in a Revolutionary Situation* by urging his readers to grapple with the colonial legacy in Latin America (5–7). Intertwined with the economic and political purposes of the sixteenth-century European colonization of Latin America was a theological mission: Christianizing the known world. In contrast to this utopian dream, however, colonizers constructed a social and political order that legitimized genocide, class stratification, and subservience of church to state. Consequently, rather than transforming the new world into the kingdom of God, conquest and colonization merely made this world an extension of European empire. With the exception of a few lone figures, the church did not question this colonial project, but rather baptized the social and economic order as God's eternal order. The lasting legacy of colonization is the dependence of the working class on a dominating ruling class.

As political structures began to change at the turn of the nineteenth century, Latin America experienced an era of disorganization and chaos, which set the stage for a new project of modernization beginning in 1870. Development was the mantra of modernization, but Bonino argues that this "development" simply represented a new form of dependence. Instead of depending on the dominant class in their own country, the Latin American people simply shifted their dependence to those who controlled the free market system, whether in their country or abroad (10–13). Modernization was linked with Protestantism from the beginning, since both share a commitment to freedom and democracy. In reality, however, Protestantism promoted and supported the rise of neo-colonialism, which also gained Catholic support after Vatican II.

Neo-colonialism continues the pattern of dependence and domination, with northern countries benefitting from Latin American dependence and underdevelopment. In this new era, "Latin America has discovered the basic fact of its dependence," along with the "hoax of democracy" (15). If dependent nations refuse to be used as factories for northern development, northern countries train and fund repressive police states to protect production. Ruling elites in Latin America become more dependent on foreign interests and less interested in the plight of their own people. This whole system, claims Bonino, is perpetuated by mass media, which coaxes everyone to consume and encourages escapism from the harsh realities created by this very consumption (30–31).

This neo-colonial system—domination and dependence, capitalist production and consumption, northern development conjoined with southern underdevelopment—created the revolutionary situation with its post-colonial possibilities. As dreams of development deteriorated, the response of churches and Christian leaders covered a wide spectrum, from traditional to progressive to revolutionary. The most faithful response, according to Bonino, is to move away from development and to join with the socialist project of liberation. Bonino identifies various methods and allegiances among those promoting a project of liberation in Latin America. Nevertheless, he highlights seven common elements: rejecting developmentalism, promoting social revolution, viewing the political dimension of life as determinate, working toward a strong centralized state, encouraging citizen participation, supporting an authentically Latin American brand of socialism, and pursuing holistic transformation (38–39).

It should come as no surprise, Bonino notes, that Christians are among the most ardent participants in the project of liberation, since its global, historical, and human dimensions are inherently theological. The struggle for liberation is not a bandwagon Christians jumped on in order to be culturally relevant; liberation is inherently Christian. As Camilo Torres Restrepo, the Columbian priest and prominent forerunner of liberation theology, once stated: "I am a revolutionary because I am a priest" (43). Latin American Christians began to develop a theology of liberation because, as human beings and as Latin Americans, they were inextricably involved in the struggle for liberation. While the church as a whole was slow to take a stance—whether for its desire to protect church unity or because of its implicit fear of revolution (57)—several Christian leaders forged ahead in practicing and understanding revolutionary action.

Bonino highlights five theologians committed to this new way of doing theology in Latin America. Juan Segundo, a Uruguayan Jesuit, maintained deep connections with European theology (particularly Rahner's anthropology and Chardin's eschatology), but was also deeply committed to contextual socio-historical analysis that fosters fitting action (62–65).[3] Following the Second Vatican Council, Argentinean priest Lucio Gera emerged as a leader of the Movement of Priests for the Third World, championing the mission of the church among the poor (65–68).[4] Dominican priest Gustavo Gutiérrez was the first to popularize the language of liberation in his widely acclaimed *A Theology of Liberation* (1971), which asserts that sociopolitical struggle, human development, and reconciliation with God are a unified reality (69–71).[5] Hugo Assmann, a Brazilian priest, demonstrated how theology is action and action is theology, seeking to unmask the ideology of praxis (72–73).[6] Finally, Brazilian Protestant theologian Rubem Alves courageously took European theology to task, criticizing Barth's transcendentalism, Bultmann's existentialism, and Moltmann's futurism alike for failing to embrace "messianic humanism," which entails real political action on behalf of the oppressed (74–77).[7]

Reflection in the revolutionary situation

Liberation theology in Latin America—whether Protestant or Catholic—shares a shift in theological method from metaphysical speculation to anthropological reflection, from the inner-personal realm to the public-historical, and from abstract concepts to political and historical concreteness (78). Bonino claims that some European and American theologians—most notably Jürgen Moltmann, Johann Baptist Metz, and Harvey Cox—align with the first two shifts but have not embraced the third.

In particular, Bonino has a bone to pick with Moltmann, specifically his discussion of political liberation in *The Crucified God*.[8] Bonino appreciates the fact that the German theologian identifies "demonic circles of death" (poverty, violence, racial and cultural deprivation, industrial destruction of nature, meaninglessness), but laments that he does not delve into their socio-analytic roots. What dismays Bonino even more is that Moltmann describes the crucified God as the God of the poor while claiming this God is classless and without country.[9] "But," Bonino retorts, "the poor, the oppressed, the humiliated *are a class* and *live in countries*" (148, emphasis original). To be for the poor, argues Bonino, is to be for them in their concrete, historical situations, which means refusing to remain ideologically neutral. If you claim to remain neutral, as Moltmann does, you just end up aligning with the "liberal, social-democratic project" in opposition to socialism (150).

Moltmann took Bonino's criticism seriously, writing what has been deemed the first significant response to liberation theology from a prominent Western and Protestant theologian.[10] He is disturbed by Bonino's position while also being "deeply moved" by his passion for liberation, celebrating that both European political theology and Latin American liberation theology share a turn toward real people in real situations. The major difference, Moltmann explains, is their divergent assessments of the situation. Whereas Bonino sees the need for revolution, Moltmann believes liberation can be achieved through a democratic process. He concludes: "However we analyze our situation, hope is faithfulness to the resurrection and therefore perseverance in the cross."[11]

Moltmann represents the most common response to liberation theology among the critical crowd, namely, accusing it of ideologization. But is there an alternative, wonders Bonino, for those who suffer oppression and live in such a reality? According to Bonino, there is no other option in this situation than for theology to be political and partisan. The task of theology is not to formulate abstract concepts and then apply them to particular situations. Rather, theology is reflection in the midst of action (89–90). Truth and action are fused to the extent that understanding arises out of doing, and doing informs understanding. This radical synthesis of thought and practice, explains Bonino, is the new way of doing theology in Latin America, in which orthopraxy takes precedence over orthodoxy.

In other words, the task of theology is to understand and live faithfully within history, rather than seeking to understand and then apply metaphysical concepts. The latter approach is not possible, since we have "no direct access from words and meaning to a theological reality outside time and history" (81). As such, theology's main tools are socio-analytic rather than philosophical. Bonino explains that Marxism is theologically helpful to the extent that it is used as a historical tool rather than a philosophical one. Received in this way, Marxism is "the best instrument available for an effective and rational realization of human possibilities in historical life" (97).[12] Theologians who fail to see Marxism as a profitable instrument do so as a result of a historical dualism: dividing world history from salvation history. Bonino believes, "with due reserve," that this dualism can be traced back to Augustine's *City of God*, where the city of man, or world history, is a "mere stage" for the city of God, or salvation history (136). By contrast, faith does not introduce "a different history, but a dynamic, a motivation, and in its eschatological horizon, a transforming invitation" (138). In other words, while the kingdom of God is not completely coterminous with history as its natural development, it does grow and come to fruition within real history.

If Marxism structures Christian obedience, then how is Christian obedience distinct from Marxist action? How are the actions of God and Jesus determinate in understanding history and forming Christian obedience? Bonino responds to these questions by identifying the death and resurrection of Jesus as "intrinsic tests" for Christian obedience (100). In other words, these are real events that occurred in real history, and therefore—contrary to the existentializing perspective of Rudolf Bultmann— they have a tangible bearing on our history. Of course, the death and resurrection of Jesus are inevitably approached from a subjective perspective, but Bonino still asserts their objective historicity, bolstered by his belief that the Bible faithfully witnesses to these events. There is a "hermeneutical circulation," rather than a circle, between these germinal events and Christian interpretation and obedience in the present context (102). Because these historical events and actions of God provide the ultimate framework for

Christian obedience, it moves Christian praxis away from mere feeling and toward relevant, and, if necessary, revolutionary action. This is a dangerous path, but then, "obedience is always a risk" (104).

Acting in a revolutionary situation

Christian obedience is a risk because it involves forging solidarity with the poor and resisting the oppressor. True solidarity involves recognizing that poverty robs people of their humanity because it takes away the dignity, creativity, and joy of work. Bonino appreciates Marxism for its understanding of human beings as workers, and he insists that if Christian theology ignores this dimension of life, it will "falsify both the gospel and man's most authentic experience." If that happens, Christian talk of redemption becomes "a parody lived out in the realm of ideas (doctrine) or of subjectivity (intention or feeling) instead of the real world of creation," thus becoming, as Marx claimed, the "opiate of the people" (110). Christians must therefore confront the alienated nature of work and the inevitability of class struggle, while recognizing this alienation is deeper than the capitalist system. The poor need to break free from the dominating class, but they also need to break free from their bondage to sin, which requires trusting in God's promises.

What does practical Christian action look like, then, in a revolutionary situation? Is it legitimate to battle the oppressors with violent action, and to do so from a Christian perspective? Bonino resists any discussion of violence and peace that begins from an abstract starting point. Only the concrete situation should be the starting point. For example, the biblical narrative records several concrete situations where God and his people violently break out of oppressive and dehumanizing situations. If we start with the concrete, it is difficult to deny that there were times in history when violence was appropriate (117–18). But how do we deal with the concrete example of Jesus and his submission to violence for the sake of redemption? Doesn't that provide a different paradigm for revolutionary struggle? It does, but Bonino first unmasks an understanding of love as "tolerance, compromise, or acceptance" and shows how Jesus's demonstration of love involves a willingness to condemn, criticize, resist, and reject. In this way, Jesus took the side of the oppressed and joined their struggle, but he also refused to lead an armed revolt and chose instead to give up his power (123). Because of this, Christians should not be abstractly and categorically opposed to any and all violence, but nonetheless *nonviolent* action is the most appropriate way to work out Christian obedience in a revolutionary situation (126–27). Whatever the case, Christians should not and cannot remain neutral. Love is never neutral. It moves us to act in concrete situations; it moves us to take sides. What makes Christian faith distinct from a revolutionary mindset, however, is the ultimate hope that motivates present action. For the Marxist, the ultimate goal is socialist revolution, but for the Christian Marxist, revolution may be an immediate goal, but the ultimate hope is the Second Coming of Christ and the consummation of the kingdom of God (130).

In this revolutionary situation, where Christians are joining the revolutionary struggle driven by hope in Christ's return, what is the nature and role of the Church? Bonino maintains that the foundation of the Church is not any static identity—whether doctrine, structures, or norms—but its concrete, historical task of being a "Church-for-others" (156). Moving away from more static "marks of the church" is fitting in an era of greater ecclesial fluidity, where charismatic, revolutionary, and evangelical identities cut across more traditional lines. In Latin America, this creates an opportunity for churches, regardless of confessional or denominational affiliation, to crystallize their identity around praxis and becoming a Church for the poor. For Bonino, this is an urgent task, for "only in the struggle for the liberation of the poor will the Church become the one true Church of Jesus Christ" (162). In the midst of this struggle, however, the Church must not be equated with social and political revolution, for then "either the Church and Jesus Christ are made redundant or the political and social revolution is clothed in a sacred or semi-sacred gown" (163).

Bonino's ecclesiological vision arises from his commitment to the unity of human history and the germinal significance of Jesus's death and resurrection. In his perspective, a more adequate ecclesiology will fuse the creational and soteriological dimensions of human existence. Bonino draws on the language of Reformed theology to relate the "covenant of creation"— which originally placed humanity in relational responsibility to God, each other, and the rest of creation—to the "covenant of redemption," which seeks to restore these relationships and fulfill their purpose in Christ (165). In this view, salvation is a completion of creation, not a departure from it. The redemption accomplished by Christ enables humanity to fulfill their historical and creational vocation to love God, each other, and the rest of creation. Within this Reformed theological framework, Bonino defines the Church as "the fellowship of those who embrace a historical task in the freedom of God's forgiveness and sanctification" (169). That historical task is the liberation of humanity to experience the fullness of life and freedom intended by God for his entire creation. This is why the Church never exists statically, but dynamically becomes the Church wherever Christians confess, celebrate, and enact their commitment to liberation for oppressed humanity. This is the Church that witnesses to the already-present-yet-still-coming kingdom of God, the Church that performs faithful action in a revolutionary situation.

Bonino, Protestant theology, and the mission of liberation

In *Doing Theology in a Revolutionary Situation*, Bonino laid the groundwork for a distinctly Latin American Protestant theology. Bonino would later build on that foundation in *Toward a Christian Political Ethics*, and then attempt a more comprehensive and descriptive account in *Faces of Latin American Protestantism*. In this later work, Bonino doubts whether Western attempts to pinpoint a material principle for Protestantism are adequate, especially for Latin American theology. He argues that doctrines such as justification by faith or the Reformational *solas—sola fide, sola gratia, sola scriptura, soli deo gloria, solus Christus*—usually serve a polemical rather than constructive purpose, and therefore are inadequate for making sense of the struggle for liberation.[13] Bonino admires Paul Tillich for attempting to get to the heart of Protestantism by interpreting justification by faith as an "anti-idolatrous principle" signaling a protest against any absolute claim.[14] But he also agrees with Rubem Alves, who believes Protestantism abandoned that principle in Latin America by absolutizing "the Protestantism of right doctrine" and conservatism.[15] Latin American Protestants have consistently upheld traditional Protestant doctrines, but these doctrines do not actually describe the theological core that unifies and provides a common experience for liberal, evangelical, Pentecostal, and immigrant Protestants in Latin America.

Instead of identifying a particular doctrine as this unifying core, Bonino argues that if there is a material principle for Latin American Protestantism, it is mission. To be clear, Bonino is not claiming that any particular *theology* of mission is the material principle, but the practice of mission itself, which is "an ethos that permeates the speech, worship, and life of Protestant communities, a self-understanding manifested in all attitudes, conflicts, and priorities."[16] To relate this back to *Doing Theology in a Revolutionary*

Situation, Bonino is asserting that Latin American Protestantism will be true to itself to the extent that it effectively enacts its mission within particular contexts, revolutionary or otherwise. In *Faces of Latin American Protestantism*, Bonino more overtly articulates the Trinitarian dimensions of this mission, describing it as "the invitation to participate in faith in the very life of the triune God and hence in the totality of what God has done, is doing, and will do to fulfill God's purpose of being 'all in all.'"[17] In doing so, Christians are "actors or coactors in the divine mission" as we seek to embody justice, mercy, and peace in every area of life and society.[18]

Throughout his entire body of work, Bonino expressed a distinctly Protestant approach to liberation theology in Latin America and beyond.[19] Rebecca Chopp notes how Bonino's perspective on liberation and solidarity with the poor diverges in notable ways from Gustavo Gutiérrez, whom many consider the father of liberation theology. Whereas Gutiérrez embraces solidarity with the poor because the poor manifest God's presence, Bonino embraces solidarity with the poor out of obedience to God's living and incarnate Word to whom the Bible bears witness.[20] This approach reveals Bonino's Protestant, Barthian, and distinctly Latin American way of doing theology, which leads him to interpret and engage with concrete situations in light of the Word.[21] Bonino's distinctive contribution to Protestant liberation theology is his additional commitment to hear and interpret the Word in light of mission and the praxis of liberation.

Notes

1. José Míguez Bonino, *Faces of Latin American Protestantism*, translated by Eugene L. Stockwell (Grand Rapids: Eerdmans, 1997), viii.
2. José Míguez Bonino, *Doing Theology in a Revolutionary Situation* (Philadelphia: Fortress Press, 1975), 100. Hereafter, all references to this work shall be noted by employing in-text parenthetical citations.
3. Bonino references several of Segundo's books, most notably *Teología Abierta para el Laico Adulto*, 5 vols (Buenos Aires: Ediciones Carlos Lohlé, 1968–72). A reprint of the English translation is still available as *A Theology for Artisans of a New Humanity*, 5 vols. (Eugene: Wipf & Stock, 2011).
4. Bonino notes how "Gera's theological production consists mostly of unpublished theological documents, frequently of great depth and scholarship, related to the concrete problems faced by the Church in the Argentine situation" (*Doing Theology in a Revolutionary Situation*, 65 n. 3).

5. Gustavo Gutiérrez, *A Theology of Liberation* (Maryknoll, New York: Orbis Books, 1973). Original Spanish: *Teología de la Liberación* (Lima: Editorial Universitaria, 1971).

6. Assmann's most notable early work was *Teología desde la praxis de liberación* (Salamanca: Sígeueme, 1973), translated into English as *Theology for a Nomad Church* (Maryknoll: Orbis Books, 1975).

7. Rubem Alves completed his Ph.D. at Princeton Theological Seminary in 1968, and his thesis was published in English as *A Theology of Human Hope* (Washington, DC: Corpus Books, 1969).

8. Jürgen Moltmann, *The Crucified God* (London: SCM Press, 1974). Original German: *Der gekreuzigte Gott* (Munich: Christian Kaiser Verlag, 1972).

9. Ibid., 305.

10. Jürgen Moltmann, "An Open Letter to José Míguez Bonino," *Christianity and Crisis* 36.5 (March 29, 1976): 57–63.

11. Ibid., 63.

12. For more on how Bonino relates Christianity and Marxism, see his *Christians and Marxists: The Mutual Challenge to Revolution* (Grand Rapids: Eerdmans, 1976).

13. Bonino, *Faces of Latin American Protestantism*, 129.

14. Paul Tillich, *The Protestant Era* (Chicago: University of Chicago Press, 1957), 163. Quoted in Bonino, *Faces of Latin American Protestantism*, 130.

15. Rubem Alves, *Protestantism and Repression: A Brazilian Case Study* (Maryknoll, N.Y.: Orbis, 1984). Quoted in Bonino, *Faces of Latin American Protestantism*, 130.

16. Bonino, *Faces of Latin American Protestantism*, 131.

17. Ibid., 144.

18. Ibid., 142.

19. Leonardo and Clodovis Boff locate Bonino in the foundational stage of liberation theology's development, along with Protestants Emilio Castro and Rubem Alves and Catholics Gustavo Gutiérrez, Juan Segundo, Hugo Assmann, and Lucio Gera, an almost identical list to the primary figures Bonino interacts with in *Doing Theology in a Revolutionary Situation*. Leonardo Boff and Clodovis Boff, *Introducing Liberation Theology*, translated by Paul Burns (Maryknoll, NY: Orbis, 1987), 70.

20. Rebecca S. Chopp, *The Praxis of Suffering: An Interpretation of Liberation and Political Theologies* (Eugene, OR: Wipf and Stock, 2007), 167, n. 43.

21. In 1986, Bonino wrote an introduction to the Spanish translation of Karl Barth's *Evangelical Theology*, revealing his indebtedness to Barth, whose theology provided fertile ground for his own development of liberation theology.

Select Bibliography

Primary source

Bonino, José Míguez. *Doing Theology in a Revolutionary Situation*. Philadelphia: Fortress Press, 1975.

Bonino, José Míguez. *La Fe en Busca de Eficacia: Una Interpretación de la Reflexion Teológica Latinoamericana de Liberación*. Salamanca, España: Ediciones Sígueme, 1977.

Secondary sources

Boff, Leonardo and Clodovis Boff. *Introducing Liberation Theology*. Translated by Paul Burns. Maryknoll, NY: Orbis, 1987.

Bonino, José Míguez. *Faces of Latin American Protestantism*. Translated by Eugene L. Stockwell. Grand Rapids: Eerdmans, 1997.

Chopp, Rebecca S. "José Míguez Bonino: The Conversion to the World," In *The Praxis of Suffering: An Interpretation of Liberation and Political Theologies*, 82–100. Eugene, OR: Wipf and Stock, 2007.

Moltmann, Jürgen. "An Open Letter to José Míguez Bonino," *Christianity and Crisis* 36.5 (March 29, 1976): 57–63.

5.10

Water Buffalo Theology (1974)
Kosuke Koyama (1929–2009)

Figure 5.10 Wild buffalo

Stammering about God with a crucified mind

Kosuke Koyama grew up in war-torn Tokyo. He received Christian baptism in 1942, the same year American planes began raiding Japanese cities. As the bombs intensified, Koyama hunkered down with John Bunyan's *Pilgrim's Progress*. The experience of reading Bunyan while enduring the bombing of

Tokyo was pivotal for Koyama's initial growth as a Christian and his later formation as a theologian. He realized the journey of a Christian toward God is riddled with danger, most notably the reality of violence and the peril of idolatry.[1] The Christian resists idolatry and endures violence by cultivating a crucified mind and rejecting a crusading mind. The crucified mind is the mind of the crucified Christ, which desires to serve others in all their complexity. By contrast, the crusading mind "bulldozes people and history without appreciation of their complexities" (159).

Koyama's training as a theologian began in 1946 with a preparatory course at Tokyo Union Theological Seminary, where he graduated in 1952 with a thesis on Francis of Assisi. From there, he studied in the United States for the rest of his twenties, earning a BA at Drew University and a Ph.D. from Princeton Theological Seminary on Martin Luther's interpretation of the Psalms. Thirty years old and a newly minted Ph.D., the United Church of Christ in Japan commissioned Koyama, now with a young family, as a missionary to Thailand. He dove headlong into studying the Thai language, which he described as "my second spiritual baptism, a baptism into the unfamiliar sounds and symbols of a different culture and religion" (173).

Despite his rudimentary grasp of the Thai language, in 1961 Koyama began lecturing at Thailand Theological Seminary in Chiengmai. As he worked out how to do theology with and for the Thai people, Koyama wrestled with the influence of his Japanese upbringing and American theological training. He realized he needed to start with the local culture and context, but this required a "triple accommodation process with Tokyo, New Jersey, and Chengmai" (174). His pioneering effort to construct a local, inter-cultural, and ecumenical theology led to an invitation, in 1968, to join South East Asia Graduate School of Theology in Singapore as their dean. In 1974, after six years in Singapore, he became Senior Lecturer in Religious Studies at the University of Otago in New Zealand.

That same year, a collection of Koyama's essays was published as *Water Buffalo Theology*, which was recognized as a groundbreaking work in local or contextual theology. Some of the essays express theology firmly grounded in the Thai context, while others are oriented to the broader Asian context. Koyama wrote several other books in English while in New Zealand, including *Fifty Meditations* (1975), *No Handle on the Cross: An Asian Meditation on the Crucified Mind* (1976), and *Three Mile an Hour God* (1979). In 1980, Koyama joined the faculty of Union Theological Seminary in New York City as professor of ecumenics and world Christianity, where he taught until his retirement in 1996. While in New York, Koyama deepened his inter-cultural and ecumenical approach to theology through dialogue with Judaism and other world religions. In addition, he became increasingly interested in the topic of violence, which was a major theme in *Mount Fiji and Mount Sinai: A Critique of Idols* (1984). According to Koyama, the ultimate test of Christian theology and mission is the removal of violence. Overall, Koyama wrote thirteen books, many of which have not been translated from his native Japanese, including a three-volume study on the Christian life. Of all Koyama's books, *Water Buffalo Theology* is perhaps his most poetic and raw. There is no thesis or argument that builds neatly from beginning to end, but each essay is riveting, insightful, and often surprising. Koyama reveals his desire to keep his contextual methodology open for that very reason: so that doing theology can be "a journey full of surprises" (xi). If he adopted any methodology while doing theology in Thailand, it was "to see the face of God in the faces of people" (x). In that sense, it was a "theology from below," with the audience guiding the theological process. For *Water Buffalo Theology*, that audience was Thai farmers, the ones familiar with water buffaloes roaming in the rice fields. Koyama gave these farmers priority instead of any particular theologian or theological system. Koyama claimed that as a missionary in Thailand, true understanding of great works such as Thomas Aquinas's *Summa Theologiae* or Karl Barth's *Church Dogmatics* occurs only out of relating them to the lives of Thai farmers (xv–xvi).

As a theology that arises out of and orients itself toward a particular place, *Water Buffalo Theology* takes steps toward ecological theology, but does so more experientially than substantively (xiii). Nevertheless, Koyama demonstrated that local theology inevitably incorporates and addresses the ecological dimension of life. The main concern and focus of *Water Buffalo Theology*, however, is people. For Koyama, theology is the process of engaging with local people in their local language in order to offer a "stammering description" of God whose historical action culminates in a local crucifixion and resurrection (135). That stammering comes from a crucified mind, which Koyama characterizes elsewhere as a mind theologically inspired, honest and careful, weak yet strong, and foolish yet wise, but not a sickly, mutilated, paternalistic mind.[2] It is a shaken mind, "which has decided to live by the power of the crucified Lord."[3]

Local people

Koyama views theology and life as the collision of particular people with a particular God. Theology is "neighborology" and neighborology is theology

(64–67). God's reality must be viewed in light of the reality of our real neighbors and *vice versa*. If this does not happen, we misjudge the reality of both. In short, Christological exegesis and neighborly exegesis are inextricable. This is the heart of what Koyama identifies as missionary existence: a life lodged between the real Christ and real neighbors (65). He advocates a form of correlationism, but not in the vein of Paul Tillich who saw philosophy and culture providing the questions and theology the answers.[4] Rather, it is neighbors who ask the questions and Christ that we seek for answers. For Koyama, this brings theology to the ground where it belongs. "Philosophy neither sweats nor hungers nor feeds water buffaloes. But his neighbor does! Theology can become a religious crossword puzzle. But his Christ cannot be reduced to a game" (66).

If theologians have sometimes been guilty of reducing theology to a game, missionaries have been guilty of using Christianity as a gun. To the extent that the missionary enterprise was linked with militaristic colonialism, it was a gun (wounding) together with ointment (healing). As the West brought modernization to the East, it was a similar mix of gun and ointment, or ointment with a sting. Since the missionary story is linked with the modernization story, Koyama admits the lamentable "entanglements between mission ointment and the conquest-expansion gun" (42). If missionary existence is to bring more ointment than gun, it needs to be oriented toward real neighbors and the real Christ. Moreover, missionaries must recognize the inherent ointments within Asian culture while bringing the healing message of Christ. Identifying these indigenous ointments requires paying attention to real people, to neighbors that bear the image of God.

Paying attention to these particular people takes precedence over understanding their system of belief. That means interacting with Buddh*ists* before trying to understand Buddh*ism*. Christian theology and mission misses the mark to the extent that it pays more attentions to "isms" (ideas) than it does to "ists" (people). Koyama admits that when he moved to Thailand, he held a negative impression of Theravada Buddhism. He witnessed other missionaries writing off Buddhism as demonic, and this influenced his initial cautionary—even fearful—approach. But the more he got to know actual Buddhists, the more he was intrigued and humbled by their way of life. He began to see their mutual human faults and desires, and realized his need to live the doctrine of the *imago dei*. Through this experience, Koyama saw more clearly the dangerous "tyranny of doctrines," where *ism* matters more than *ist* (95). The most critical interaction and dialogue happens between Christians and Buddhists, not between Christianity and Buddhism.

Koyama discusses this with brutal honesty. He regrets his seminary education that drove him to understand ideas more than people. "They did not teach me that it is more interesting to know a Hindu than to know Hinduism; it is more rewarding to know a Buddhist than Buddhism, a Marxist than Marxism, a revolutionary than revolution, a missionary than missiology, a wife than the "marriage and the family" course, Jesus Christ than Christology" (150). Giving priority to interactions with living persons makes life and theology far more satisfying but also more complex. A person is irreducibly complex; consequently, interacting with a Buddhist produces much greater nuance and creativity than interacting with Buddhism. "Library-Buddhism" can provide a framework for relationships with "street-Buddhists," but it's the relationships that matter (151). Only when real relationships take precedence is genuine communication of the gospel possible. In encounters between particular people, "communication" is not merely the delivery of a message, but the sharing of a life. In a word, it is incarnational. Mission is to participate in "God's concrete drama of dead-alive—lost-found" while interacting with concrete neighbors (157). It is to adopt the crucified mind and to decrease before Christ and our neighbors so that their stories can increase. When missionaries decrease, "the local people increase," in hope that they might encounter Christ and let him increase. The pattern of decrease-increase is "the wave of salvation-history, the beginning and end of which is Jesus Christ" (159).

Local language

If local theology seeks attentiveness to local people, it must know and use their language. Koyama recounts how many Thai Buddhists have rejected Christianity simply because the language seems strange, because Western terms invoke "cultural resistance, psychological antipathy, and emotional reaction" (59). To do theology in Thailand, one has to ask: How should I talk about Christ in a Thai kitchen? What language would really connect with Thai people? Koyama uses the kitchen analogy to propose that local theology should also be "kitchen theology." In the case of theology in Thailand, this kitchen theology should be seasoned with a variety of spices, both "Aristotelian pepper and Buddhist salt" (56–63). There is no such thing as unseasoned theology, theology that has not taken on the language and flavors of a particular place and culture. Consequently, "imagining an unseasoned and raw Christ is as absurd and impossible as a de-Hebraized Yahweh" (63). Cultural and linguistic seasoning should be used sparingly, however, since not every spice complements the fragrance of Christ. Likewise, theology in Thailand should not throw out all the Aristotelian pepper from the West, but the theology will lack flavor to the locals if it is not seasoned with some local Buddhist salt.

Koyama practices what he preaches, for *Water Buffalo Theology* is thoroughly sprinkled with Buddhist concepts and language. For example, in the chapter "Cool *Arhat* and Hot God," Koyama shows how *dukkha*, *anicca*, *anatta*, and *arhat* can spice up the story of Israel to Thai taste while also revealing the distinct ingredients of a Hebrew worldview. Within Buddhism, *dukkha* is existence in all its unsatisfactoriness, suffering, and stress. The goal is to escape *dukkha* and move along *sotas* (the stream of emancipation) toward *nirvana* and the transcendence over *dukkha*. Moving along *sotas* involves embracing *annica* (impermanence) and *anatta* (self-elimination) in order to reach the final state of *arhat*, or complete detachment.

When these terms are used to describe the story of Israel, they are historicized and brought into covenantal perspective. In this story, it is Israel—and indeed, all of humanity—who is *dukkha*, *annica*, and *anatta*, not just inwardly but in relation to the covenant God. *Dukkha*, *annica*, and *anatta* are marks of covenant unfaithfulness, and the solution is not further detachment, but greater covenant attachment between God and his people. Instead of moving toward "cool *arhat*," the biblical story is about a "hot God" attaching himself to an unsatisfactory, impermanent, self-destructive people (114–15).[5] In Christ, God embodied the opposite of *arhat*, embracing *dukkha*, *annica*, and *anatta* not for the sake of eliminating the self, but for the resurrection of self: new creation.

This is Koyama at his best: adding Buddhist salt and Hebrew pepper into a fragrant theological pot. He calls this particular attempt to "kitchenize theology" a process of "Hebraization" or "covenantization," which injects "the covenant concept into the Thai indigenous spiritual and religious concepts" (115). The result is a theological dish that Thai people will actually eat and maybe even enjoy and decide to integrate into their lives. Koyama insists that this method is not syncretistic; rather, it is the way to engage with local people in their local language so that they can taste the goodness of a hot God in a culture of cool tranquility. According to Koyama, some parts of the Bible are already poised to do this effectively in the Thai context. He identifies the letter of James, for example, as a book that connects with a "cool" mindset while introducing "hot" elements of covenantal existence (118–24). Several aspects of James radiate coolness—the transience of life, the trap of evil desires, the virtue of patience—and yet its hotness is undeniable. It draws the audience into more involvement with neighbors and attachment to history, not less. What is true religion? It is precisely to pursue greater attachment to needy and marginal people, to embrace suffering with joy, and to do the Word. It is through these "hot" attachments that the Christian way of life offers detachment, "a detachment not from the world, but from the corrupting influence of the world" (124).

Engaging with local people in their local language is something Koyama had to learn to do by trial and error, but he acknowledges that Japanese theologian Kazoh Kitamori provided a compelling model in his *Theology of the Pain of God*.[6] In this book, Kitamori fused two Japanese words—*tsutsumu* (to embrace what is good and bad) and *tsurasa* (to suffer so others can live)—to express the heart of the gospel within Japanese culture. Kitamori shows how both *tsutsumu* and *tsurasa* are present in the action of Christ, and this insight was pivotal for "re-rooting" the gospel in post-war Japan. By theological re-rooting, Koyama means "a thoughtful attempt to translate the inner meaning of the message of Jesus Christ from one culture milieu and root it in another" (86). Re-rooting is a hermeneutical task, since both the message of Jesus Christ and the cultural milieu need to be interpreted. Within this interpretive process of re-rooting, Koyama contends, the gospel is actually discovered in its radiant fullness (87). Thus, the gospel permeates a culture, but also the culture and its language illuminate the gospel in new ways. Engaging with local people in their local language, in other words, enables us to stammer a bit more poetically about the local God.

Local God

Koyama never specifically refers to God as "local," but his method of contextualization is overtly grounded in the person of Christ, who "indigenized the message of God through his life of suffering" (17). The God of Israel and the Church is a historical God, and while his action is global and even universal, it is also always local. The Creator interacts at the level of his creation. The once-for-all, beyond-nature God engages with the many-times world of monsoons, mosquitoes, and the people that get wet and bitten. Yet, Koyama hopes the question of chapter two is rhetorical: Will the monsoon rain make God wet? Of course not, because "God is the Lord of the monsoon rain" (31). Yet God is involved in the cycles of nature just as he is involved in the linear progression of history toward its goal of new creation. Doing theology in Thailand means combining the biblical, linear view of history with the cycles of nature into a unified "history-and-nature" (20): an ascending spiral over which the Lord God gets locally involved.

Because God is involved in history, he is inherently passionate, both in promoting righteousness and opposing unrighteousness. With Lactantius, the early Christian apologist, and Martin Luther, the Protestant reformer, Koyama rejects the *apatheia* of God and affirms the capacity for God to be "perturbed" (68). In Thai culture, largely influenced by Buddhism, tranquility and detachment are the epitome of virtue, and the notion of a perturbed God causes confusion and offense. Nevertheless, Koyama insists that God is moved to wrath and joy because he is involved in history, and therefore Christian theology must wrestle with the "strange work of God" (73). This is one example where the Buddhist salt should not be added to the theological pot, since anti-historical, perturbance-averse Buddhism is fundamentally at odds with the impassioned God of history. For the Thai people, the greatest stumbling block, as well as the reality most capable of transforming hearts and lives, is the historical incarnation of God in the person of Jesus. In the ultimate act of involvement, this God-man experienced every aspect of *dukkha* in order to provide not just salvation from *dukkha*, but salvation for new life within *dukkha*.

God's local, historical action also challenges the technological mindset spreading across the globe. Koyama is not against technology and technological efficiency, but he does believe it presents greater challenges for hearing God's Word and appreciating the way God works. God's primary mode of operation is love, and love is supremely inefficient and inconvenient (46). One of the aggravating and awe-inspiring aspects of the biblical story is how long things take. Forty years in the wilderness? "Wasn't there a more efficient way?" In the Internet age, we expect things to move at the speed of light, but God moves at the speed of love.[7] The action of God, therefore, has its own efficiency; is the efficiency of the Crucified One (48–49). What could be less efficient than being nailed down? And yet what could be more efficient in revealing God and the depth of his love? Those who bear the name of the Crucified and Risen One will have a distinct mode of presence in our increasingly technological world: a stumbling, discomforted, unfree presence (163–70). It is in this "strange mode of life" that Christians are able to participate in "God's *pathos* toward all scattered things which are held together in the *glory* of the *crucified* Lord" (170).

Locally ecumenical theology

In the preface to the twenty-fifth anniversary edition of *Water Buffalo Theology*, Koyama describes his work as "distinctively local and openly ecumenical," in that it was rooted in northern Thailand while aware of its "global webbedness" and connection to the universal church (x). In the first chapter Koyama outlines the "raw situations" in several Asian countries ripe for theological engagement. Doing theology in these various contexts should look different because the situations are unique, but each calls for a similar cultivation of a crucified mind. According to Koyama, theology—whether theology in Asia, America, or anywhere else—should be a theology of the cross. This is the core of his ecumenical theology.

As the church and its theology develop in particular places, they inevitably take on local color. While it is appropriate to speak of the church in Thailand or any other locality, Koyama maintains that the local church is first and foremost the "church of Christ." There is only one church: the church of Christ in various localities (142). Likewise, although it is appropriate to speak of Thai theology, the underlying continuity between this and other local theologies is Christ and him crucified. Therefore, while Koyama believes denominations and confessions contain much value, he contends they must never morph into a "dominating theological insight." In fact, theological domination is the very definition of denominationalism, which Koyama describes as deadly and demonic, for it "monopolizes Christ theologically" (145). Christians who identify with a denomination are called to great humility and must identify preeminently with Christ himself. In Koyama's perspective, being a Methodist, Baptist, Lutheran, or Presbyterian is helpful only to the extent that it helps you make much of Christ and adopt his form of life: self-denial. Lamentably, denominational identification and promotion is often shot through with pride, which divides Christ. Denominations and their theological contributions will remain fruitful if they are willing to be "mocked, spat upon, scourged, killed, and cast out," just like Christ (149).

To relate this back to "kitchen theology," each local theological dish will have different flavors, but each one should emit the fragrance of the crucified Christ. Subsequent attempts to trace out a methodology for local theology have drawn upon Koyama's culinary metaphor,[8] but few have communicated with equal force that any theological dish that cares about Christ will be a "spat-upon" dish.[9] In doing so, Koyama was both a pioneer of local theology and a champion of ecumenical theology centered on the cross. Although

Koyama never traced out a detailed methodology for doing local theology, others have helpfully plotted his work among the rapidly increasing body of local, indigenous, inculturated, and contextual theologies.[10] Within Asian contextual theology, Moonjang Lee suggests three primary strands. The first strand engages with the social, political and economic reality in Asia, such as Minjung theology, the Korean version of liberation theology. The second strand interacts with the cultural reality of Asia. The third strand focuses on inter-religious or inter-faith dialogue.[11] Although Lee places Koyama within the second strand of Asian contextual theology, Koyama's writing actually combines elements of all three strands. Overall, Koyama's theology does not fit neatly into any "strand," and is simultaneously local, inter-cultural, and ecumenical.

In the Afterword to a collection of essays commemorating Koyama's retirement from Union Theological Seminary in 1996, former president Donald Shriver not only remarks on Koyama's groundbreaking work in contextual theology, but ranks him among the twentieth century's greatest biblical theologians.[12] Of course, Koyama did not pursue biblical studies according to the strictures of the Western academic guild. According to Shriver, however, that is precisely what makes him so great. He had the courage to take his neighbors seriously, bringing the world of the Bible to bear on their concrete lives. As a result, he made that strange world come alive, not just for those neighbors, but also for everyone who has the pleasure of sitting in Koyama's theological kitchen.

Notes

1. Kosuke Koyama, *Water Buffalo Theology*, 25th anniversary ed. (Maryknoll, NY: Orbis Books, 1999), 171–72. All parenthetical page numbers refer to this revised anniversary edition. Koyama's book *Mount Fuji and Mount Sinai* (1985) is an extended critique of idolatry within a Japanese context.
2. Kosuke Koyama, *No Handle on the Cross: An Asian Mediation on the Crucified Mind* (Eugene, OR: Wipf and Stock, 2011), 12.
3. Ibid., 8.
4. Paul Tillich, *Systematic Theology*, vol. 1 (London: SCM Press, 1978), 63.
5. When Koyama uses the adjectives "hot" to describe God, therefore, he's referring to God's passionate, covenantal involvement with his people, which is scandalous in a culture that prizes "cool" detachment.
6. Kazoh Kitamori, *Theology of the Pain of God* (Eugene, OR: Wipf and Stock, 2005). Originally published in Japanese in 1946.

7. Koyama unpacks this metaphor in *Three Mile an Hour God* (London: SCM Press, 1979), 7.

8. For example, see Clemens Sedmak, *Doing Local Theology: A Guide for Artisans of a New Humanity* (Maryknoll, NY: Orbis Books, 2002), 17–20.

9. This is a common theme throughout Koyama's writing, and in *No Handle on the Cross*, he writes that the reality of a spat-upon Jesus requires "spat-upon theology" and "spat-upon churches" (93).

10. Robert Schreiter explains how these terms are generally interchangeable, although "contextual theology" and "contextualization" have become the standard terms in Protestant circles. Robert Schreiter, "Local Theologies," in *Global Dictionary of Theology*, edited by William A. Dyrness and Veli-Matti Kärkkäinen (Downers Grove: IVP Academic, 2008), 500.

11. Moonjang Lee, "Asian Theology," in ibid., 74–77.

12. Donald W. Shriver, Jr., "An Afterword," in *The Agitated Mind of God: The Theology of Kosuke Koyama*, edited by Dale T. Irvin and Akintunde E. Akinade (Maryknoll, NY: Orbis Books, 1996), 228.

Select Bibliography

Primary source

Koyama, Kosuke. *Water Buffalo Theology*. Maryknoll, NY: Orbis Books, 1974.
Koyama, Kosuke. *Water Buffalo Theology*. Maryknoll, NY: Orbis Books, 1999.

Secondary sources

Irvin, Dale T. and Akinade, Akintunde E, eds. *The Agitated Mind of God: The Theology of Kosuke Koyama*. Maryknoll, NY: Orbis Books, 1996.

Lee, Moonjang. "Asian Theology." In *Global Dictionary of Theology*, edited by William A. Dyrness and Veli-Matti Kärkkäinen, 74–77. Downers Grove: IVP Academic, 2008.

Sedmak, Clemens. *Doing Local Theology: A Guide for Artisans of a New Humanity*. Maryknoll, NY: Orbis Books, 2002.

Sugirtharajah, R.S., ed. *Asian Faces of Jesus*. Maryknoll, NY: Orbis Books, 1993.

5.11

The Nature of Doctrine: Religion and Theology in a Postliberal Age (1984)
George Lindbeck (1923–)

The making of a postliberal theologian

George Lindbeck never expected *The Nature of Doctrine* to make such a splash. Originally intended as the prolegomenon to a comparative Christian dogmatics, this slim volume demonstrated a new way of doing theology that was neither traditional nor liberal. Building on the work of Hans Frei, Lindbeck proposed a "postliberal" paradigm for understanding religion and Christian doctrine. Although Lindbeck later insisted that postliberalism is primarily a research program rather than a school of theology, his groundbreaking work revealed new possibilities for theologians sharing his dissatisfaction with bifurcated theological methods and a desire for ecumenical collaboration.[1]

As a child, Lindbeck was steeped in both Lutheranism and Chinese culture. Born to Swedish-American missionaries in Loyang, China, illness kept young George from going off to boarding school in Korea until just before his teenage years, which provided more opportunity for him to experience life in Loyang. Immersion within a foreign culture and the confessional fortitude of his parents were two early influences on Lindbeck's personal and theological formation.

Lindbeck's educational journey began at Gustavus Adolphus College in Minnesota, where he graduated with a BA in 1943. Subsequently, he continued his studies for three years at Yale (BD, 1946), one year at the Pontifical Institute of Medieval Studies in Toronto with Étienne Gilson, and two years at the École Pratique des Hautes Études in Paris with Paul Vignaux. During these years, Lindbeck found "unappealing" the work of Descartes, Hegel, Nietzsche, Heidegger, Sartre, and Bultmann, but was increasingly drawn to medieval theologians such as Thomas Aquinas, the Reformers and their neo-orthodox progeny, the twentieth-century Jesuit theologians Karl Rahner and Hans Urs von Balthasar, and both Brevard Childs and Hans Frei at Yale with their narrative-canonical approach.[2] In terms of non-theological disciplines, Lindbeck was strongly influenced by the philosophy of Thomas Kuhn and Ludwig Wittgenstein, the sociology of Peter Berger, and the anthropology of Clifford Geertz.[3]

After his stint in France, Lindbeck landed back at Yale, completing a Ph.D. (1955) on late medieval theologian Duns Scotus while teaching courses on medieval philosophy and seminars on Augustine and Calvin. This work launched him into his official teaching career, and although his initial teaching load revolved mostly around philosophy, he enjoyed interaction with theologians Hans Frei, Paul Holmer, and David Kelsey. From 1962 to 1965, Lindbeck received the honor of representing the Lutheran World Federation at the Second Vatican Council, and later served for two decades on the Joint Commission between the Vatican and the Lutheran World Federation (1968–1987).

These experiences nourished the ecumenical roots of *The Nature of Doctrine* (1984), in which Lindbeck delineated a form of Protestant theology that avoided the conservative-liberal conundrum of modern Protestantism. Lindbeck hoped this approach would be better poised to create constructive dialogue with other Christian traditions and non-Christian religions. Later, Lindbeck reflected that the starting point of *The Nature of Doctrine* is "neither biblicist nor experientialist, and certainly not individualistic, but dogmatic: it commences with the historic Christian communal confession of faith in Christ."[4] That said, he also described the book later as "an utter mess" because of how it claims the priority of Christian confession while borrowing copiously from modern terms and concepts.[5]

Whether it's methodologically "messy" or "neat" is a matter of ongoing debate, but *The Nature of Doctrine* no doubt struck a chord with those seeking an ecumenical alternative to conservative and liberal forms of Protestantism, one that respects tradition while fully engaging with contemporary thought. Despite the widespread popularity of this book, Lindbeck has not published another monograph, although he has been prolific in writing reviews, essays for edited volumes, and numerous articles, several of which James Buckley edited together as *The Church in a Postliberal Age* (2003). Although many wish Lindbeck had completed the comparative dogmatics to which *The Nature of Doctrine* was intended to serve as an introduction, it remains a paradigmatic work in twentieth-century theology. In the introduction to the twenty-fifth anniversary edition, Bruce Marshall observes: "In the fragmented, even chaotic, world of contemporary Anglophone theology, *The Nature of Doctrine* is one of the few books that practically everybody thinks they need to know something about."[6]

Religious theories and the promise of postliberalism

At the outset, Lindbeck identifies three theories for making sense of religion and doctrine. First, cognitive-propositionalism emphasizes the way doctrines make truth claims and how religion is organized according to propositional statements about objective realities. This is the common approach of traditional orthodoxy, and can be classified as a preliberal religious theory, which still holds sway among theologians of a conservative stripe. Second, experiential-expressivism emphasizes the "inner feelings, attitudes, or existential orientations" represented by religious doctrines and symbols (2). Lindbeck traces this approach back to the seminal work of Friedrich Schleiermacher, the father of theological liberalism. A third theory combines the two approaches, as attempted by Roman Catholic theologians Karl Rahner and Bernard Lonergan. Although Lindbeck communicates respect for these theologians, he still considers this a struggling two-dimensional approach in search of a truly three-dimensional alternative.

Of the three theories, Lindbeck recognizes that experiential-expressivism represents a uniquely modern "turn to the subject," engendering habits of thought that "are ingrained in the soul of the modern West, perhaps particularly in the souls of theologians" (7). Given the modern proclivity toward individualism and self-expression, the cognitive-propositional approach was bound to lose ground as the plausibility of objectivity eroded. Despite the prominence of the experiential outlook, Lindbeck laments the way in which this paradigm begins to blend religions together as symbolizations of the same human experiences. Given his interest in genuine ecumenical dialogue, Lindbeck is not satisfied with any theory that assumes the basic unity of all religions, since this erodes genuine differences in doctrine and practice.

As an alternative, therefore, Lindbeck proposes a cultural-linguistic theory of religion and doctrine. In this theory, doctrines are neither objective propositions nor descriptions of subjective religious experience, but languages that regulate certain forms of life. Rather than an internal idea or feeling, religion is an external phenomenon that shapes internal thoughts and feelings. Just as language enables us to structure our existence, so religion is a comprehensive scheme that brings order and meaning to what we experience. According to Lindbeck, one of the greatest benefits of the cultural-linguistic theory is its symbiosis with non-theological approaches to religion. Since anthropologists, sociologists, historians, and philosophers have, by and large, jettisoned an experiential-expressive theory of religion, the cultural-linguistic theory makes dialogue possible between theology and non-theological disciplines (11).

From a cultural-linguistic perspective, religion is not primarily beliefs or experiences, but the living framework that makes meaningful beliefs and experiences possible. In this way, the cultural-linguistic theory of religion reverses the experiential-expressive theory by showing how an external story or scheme shapes internal experience, not the other way around. As such, it shares some characteristics with the external grounding of the cognitive-propositional theory while avoiding intellectualism. Lindbeck writes: "A comprehensive scheme or story used to structure all dimensions of existence is not primarily a set of propositions to be believed, but is rather the medium in which one moves, a set of skills that one employs in living one's life" (21).

In other words, Lindbeck sees religion as embodied participation in a dramatic narrative that in turn shapes beliefs and experiences. When the situation and context changes, a living religion finds new concepts and symbols to deal with any gaps or anomalies in everyday experience. As an example, Lindbeck claims that Martin Luther's "tower experience" did not lead him to embrace the doctrine of justification by faith alone. Rather, Luther discovered the doctrine of justification in the biblical narrative, and this set the stage for his tower experience. In sum, "First come the objectivities of the religion, its language, doctrines, liturgies, and modes of action, and it is through these that passions are shaped into various kinds of what is called religious experience" (25). If religion produces experiences, not *vice versa*, then the field is wide open to compare religions as genuinely different cultural-linguistic schemes. In contrast to liberalism, therefore, the goal of studying religions is not to boil them down to common human experiences. Instead, the goal is to encounter diverse forms of life that generate different and sometimes conflicting experiences. This leads to both the challenge and the promise of ecumenical dialogue from a postliberal perspective.

Religious claims and the promise of ecumenism

Lindbeck identifies three primary "interreligious problems—unsurpassability, dialogue, and the salvation of 'other-believers'" (33). When it comes to comparing religions and searching for an unsurpassable one, the cognitive-propositional approach examines the truth or falsity of doctrines as propositional statements. The religion with the greatest number of propositions that correspond to the truth is the one true religion. Within experiential-expressivism, religions are more or less "true" by virtue of how effectively they symbolize human feelings. Since proponents of this approach trace these symbols back to common human experiences, however, Lindbeck evaluates this form of comparing religious claims as relatively weak.

From a cultural-linguistic perspective, religions should be compared on the basis of categorical adequacy rather than propositional truth or symbolic efficacy. In other words, religions should be compared based on the extent to which their structural categories adequately point to ultimate reality and shape life accordingly. Lindbeck writes: "The categorically and unsurpassably true religion is capable of being rightly utilized, guiding thought, passions, and action in a way that corresponds to ultimate reality" (38). Stated otherwise, an unsurpassable religion is the language that best aligns thought and life with ultimate reality. Or to use an additional metaphor Lindbeck introduces at this point, the preeminent religion is the map that best charts reality and leads the map user to the desired destination.

While comparison of religions is a critical part of ecumenical dialogue, Lindbeck underscores another important goal. The purpose of this dialogue is not just conversion to the unsurpassable religion, but moving adherents of each religion to be better speakers of their own language and better performers of their own drama. If this is the focus of interreligious exchange, then it is possible for each participant to benefit: Christians can become better Christians, Jews can become better Jews, Buddhists can become better Buddhists, and so on (40). This result is most likely when attention shifts from either propositional truths or a common experiential core to the different forms of life and the languages that describe them. Again, in reaction to the pervading liberal environment of much ecumenical dialogue in the 1980s, Lindbeck insists that the cultural-linguistic approach is stronger than the experiential-expressive one. Dialogue partners who embrace the former method "can regard themselves as simply different and can proceed to explore their agreements and disagreements without necessarily engaging in the invidious comparisons that the assumption of a common experiential core make so tempting" (41). In short, if religious differences don't extend down to the core, then interreligious dialogue remains shallower than it should be.

When it comes to the possibility of salvation outside the Christian religion, Lindbeck treads lightly yet persistently. He expresses dissatisfaction with the "anonymous Christian" proposal of Rahner and Lonergan, but he does so for a different reason than traditional propositionalists. According to Rahner and Lonergan, people can have an inarticulate experience of the divine as a nascent form of Christ's saving grace. For the propositionalist, this is inadequate because faith requires assent to certain essential, propositional truths. For Lindbeck, the anonymous Christian proposal is inadequate because it assumes a common experiential core and minimizes the necessity of encountering an external word (*fides ex auditu*). You need to know enough of the Christian language before you can decide whether to embrace it or reject it. This can get blurry, however, because whether a person stutters the Christian language or speaks it fluently, they're still speaking the same language. In fact, Lindbeck insists that when it comes to speaking about God, "all human beings are toddlers" and we never achieve mastery of the language (46–47). The cultural-linguistic perspective on this issue preserves the significance of evangelism, albeit with an emphasis on sharing the Christian story and its distinct language. Lindbeck explains: "The communication of the gospel is not a form of psychotherapy, but rather the offer and the act of sharing one's beloved language—the language that speaks of Jesus Christ—with all those who are interested, in the full awareness that God does not call all to be part of the witnessing people" (47).

Religious doctrines and the promise of pragmatism

After all this talk about religion, what about doctrine itself? Although some traditionalists argue that doctrine plays a diminished role within a cultural-linguistic framework, Lindbeck contends that this theory displays doctrine's usefulness within a culture largely antipathetic to norms of any kind, let alone theological ones (63). Lindbeck is especially concerned to explore how doctrines can stand the test of time while also changing with the times when necessary. He proposes that a cultural-linguistic framework has an easier time accounting for this flexibility because doctrines do not function as first-order propositions, but as second-order rules. In other words, doctrines do not refer directly and unequivocally to the nature of God and reality; instead, they are rules for correctly reading the story of God revealed in the Bible. That story—which culminates in the person and work of Jesus—does not change, but many of the doctrines that help us talk about the story do. Determining which doctrines change and which ones do not is the tricky part, so Lindbeck delineates three different types of doctrine and devotes an entire chapter to test these types with practical examples.

First, doctrines can be "unconditionally necessary" (71). This type of doctrine—like the law of loving God and neighbor—applies in every culture and situation. In other words, there are no conditions that would instigate doctrinal change. Second, some doctrines are "conditionally essential." These doctrines—like pacifism—arose because of particular historical or individual circumstances, and may or may not be reversible. For example, a conditional doctrine like slavery is reversible because historical developments paved the way. Third, doctrines may be merely accidental but nevertheless permanent because of how habitual or normative they have become. The date of Christmas, for example, is accidental, but it would be virtually impossible to change it.

Which doctrinal type fits the Trinitarian doctrines that form the backbone of the ecumenical creeds of Nicea and Chalcedon? In making his case, Lindbeck distinguishes between the content and form of Trinitarian doctrine. While the form or precise terminology of the creeds is conditional, Lindbeck argues for the unconditional necessity of the content, because it expresses essential rules for reading the biblical story accurately. Lindbeck identifies at least three "regulative principles" at work in the creeds: monotheism, the historical specificity of Jesus, and Christological maximalism or Christ as the key to understanding God (80). If these rules were abandoned, it would erode the Christian faith. By contrast, Lindbeck comes to a different conclusion regarding Marian dogma such as Mary's sinlessness. Lindbeck classifies this doctrine as "conditionally essential," albeit reversibly so, given its formulation in a cultural milieu with very different perspectives on sin (83). As a more complex example, Lindbeck tackles the doctrine of infallibility, which is the rule that distinguishes who or what has authority over doctrinal formulation and change. While Lindbeck prefers to locate the power of infallibility in the whole church that speaks the Christian language, he realizes that this has more affinity with Orthodoxy and is currently irreconcilable with the biblical infallibility of Protestants and the magisterial infallibility of Roman Catholics (84–90).

Yet if one buys into the cultural-linguistic theory of religion, Lindbeck proposes the pressure is off to figure out which tradition is ontologically correct when it comes to doctrines like infallibility. The issue is not whether the doctrine corresponds to ontological truth but whether it coheres with the biblical narrative and generates faithful forms of life and worship. As Lindbeck clearly states: "Which theory is theologically best depends on how well it organizes the data of Scripture and tradition with a view to their use in Christian worship and life" (92). In other words, doctrines should be judged based on how well they describe the biblical drama and enable the church to perform their role within it. In fact, it is through performing the biblical drama in worship and everyday life that the church learns the biblical story.[7] All of this has an "intratextual" logic: the biblical world is the lens through which the church understands and lives in the world, yet the church's doctrines and practices are true to the extent that they accurately represent the biblical story.

What Lindbeck calls "intratextuality" others have deemed circular, irrational, relativistic, or fideistic. Lindbeck anticipated these objections, and claims that all of them cling too tenaciously to some form of foundationalism. For Lindbeck, there is no foundation independent of the biblical narrative and its presentation of God's revelation in Jesus Christ.[8] To try to find some independent foundation in reason or universal human experience would be to diminish the biblical narrative itself as the source of truth. Therefore, Lindbeck argues for a different kind of reasonableness and intellectual standard that requires a kind of aesthetic skill to discern. "In short, intelligibility comes from skill, not theory, and credibility comes from good performance, not adherence to independently formulated criteria" (117).

Showing someone the reasonableness of Christianity, therefore, is more a matter of performing the story beautifully than trying to win an argument. Or to return to Lindbeck's overarching linguistic metaphor, the best way to engage in Christian mission is to speak the Christian language beautifully and learn how to live in ways congruent with the poetry. If the church is faithful in this mission, the hope is that others will want to speak the language. As they do, they too will experience "the ancient practice of absorbing the universe into the biblical world" (121).

Postliberal theology after Lindbeck

As one might anticipate, Lindbeck's postliberal proposal stirred up mixed reactions among both theological traditionalists and liberals. The first substantial response among conservative evangelicals came from Carl Henry, whose concerns with the ahistorical, anti-propositional nature of narrative theology interacted more with Hans Frei, but nevertheless applied equally to Lindbeck's project.[9] Several additional evangelical and postliberal interlocutors were invited to the Wheaton Theology conference in 1995, where it became evident that while some evangelicals resisted postliberalism for a variety of reasons,[10] a growing number of evangelicals were interested in utilizing Lindbeck's insights to move in a "postconservative" direction.[11] These latter evangelical theologians share a concern to appropriately adapt their way of doing theology to a postmodern milieu. For example, Stanley Grenz and John Franke interact appreciatively with Lindbeck as they chart a way to move theology beyond foundationalism.[12] Kevin Vanhoozer counters Lindbeck's proposal by suggesting a "canonical-linguistic" approach to Christian theology, preserving Lindbeck's connection between doctrine and church practice while ensuring that Scripture generates and norms both. With a nod to Lindbeck, Vanhoozer describes his canonical-linguistic approach as postpropositional, postconservative, and postfoundational.[13] Finally, Roger Olson, although interacting less with Lindbeck, shows how postconservative evangelical theology emerged and provides an evangelical alternative to postliberalism.[14]

From a liberal perspective, Lindbeck's postliberal proposal was merely a repackaging of traditional confessionalism. For example, in reflecting on *The Nature of Doctrine*, David Tracy remarks that "the hands may be Wittgenstein and Geertz, but the voice is the voice of Karl Barth."[15] Gordon Kaufman agrees, lamenting that Lindbeck's proposal merely revamps conservative theology and keeps it cloistered within Christian communities.[16] Several other prominent theologians demurred, maintaining that postliberalism is a viable alternative for transcending the traditional-liberal divide. Although this postliberal tribe is often called the "Yale school," a label used to distinguish them from "Chicago school" liberals, George Hunsinger calls this a misnomer.[17] Nevertheless, many who taught and studied at Yale with Frei and Lindbeck identify with the postliberal project. For instance, William Placher followed Lindbeck's lead by modeling an "unapologetic" mode of doing Christian theology, which is "less like a philosophically inclined apologist and more like a sensitive anthropologist."[18] Stanley Hauerwas, although indifferent to the "postliberal" label, shares Lindbeck's conviction that theology and ethics are ecclesial disciplines, since the role of the church is to speak and perform the biblical story.[19] Kathryn Tanner shares the "cultural turn" of postliberal theology, but she takes umbrage with Lindbeck's desire to find certain rules that show the unsurpassability of the Christian religion.[20] Dozens of additional theologians could be mentioned, and although they have varied appreciation of Lindbeck's version of postliberalism, they share his desire "to recover the significance for Christian theology of Christian specificity."[21] As Jeffrey Stout mused, it may be "too soon to tell" if postliberal theology is a "*cul de sac* or the harbinger of a new theological age," but there is no doubt that Lindbeck was instrumental in stimulating a way of doing theology that moved Protestant theology beyond the tired binaries of modernity.[22]

Notes

1. Timothy R. Phillips and Dennis L. Okholm, eds., *The Nature of Confession: Evangelicals and Postliberal in Conversation* (Downers Grove: InterVarsity Press, 1996), 247.

2. George Lindbeck, *The Church in a Postliberal Age*, edited by James Buckley (Grand Rapids: Eerdmans, 2003), 3.

3. One could argue that Wittgenstein has the strongest influence of all, even when compared to the theologians. James K.A. Smith observes: "Trying to read Lindbeck without understanding Wittgenstein is like trying to read Derrida without understanding Husserl, or trying to read John Calvin without knowing anything of St. Augustine." *Who's Afraid of Relativism: Community, Contingency, and Creaturehood* (Grand Rapids: Baker Academic, 2014), 152.

4. Lindbeck, *Church in a Postliberal Age*, 5.

5.   John Wright, ed., *Postliberal Theology and the Church Catholic: Conversations with George Lindbeck, David Burrell, and Stanley Hauerwas* (Grand Rapids: Baker Academic, 2012), 71.

6.   Bruce Marshall, "Introduction," in George Lindbeck, *The Nature of Doctrine: Religion and Theology in a Postliberal Age* (Louisville: Westminster John Knox Press, 2009), vii. All subsequent references will be to this edition, using in-text parenthetical citations.

7.   This has led C.C. Pecknold to observe the following: "If it can be agreed that 'scripture' might be the first word to come from the lips of a postliberal theologian, a second word might be 'practices', or arguably better still, 'pragmatism', the study of practical consequences." C.C. Pecknold, *Transforming Postliberal Theology: George Lindbeck, Pragmatism, and Scripture* (London: Bloomsbury T&T Clark, 1995), 11.

8.   It's at this point that Lindbeck acknowledges his debt to Karl Barth.

9.   Carl Henry, "Narrative Theology: An Evangelical Appraisal," *Trinity Journal* 9 (Spring 1987): 3–19.

10. For example, see Alister McGrath, *The Genesis of Doctrine: A Study in the Foundation of Doctrinal Criticism* (Grand Rapids: Eerdmans, 1996). McGrath's title is an obvious riff on *The Nature of Doctrine*, but he criticizes Lindbeck for being reductionistic and argues that doctrine does more things than Lindbeck allows.

11. The papers from the 1995 Wheaton Theology were published in Timothy R. Phillips and Dennis L. Okholm, eds., *The Nature of Confession: Evangelicals and Postliberals in Conversation* (Downers Grove: InterVarsity Press, 1996).

12. Stanley J. Grenz and John R. Franke, *Beyond Foundationalism: Shaping Theology in a Postmodern Context* (Louisville: Westminster John Knox Press, 2000).

13. Kevin Vanhoozer, *The Drama of Doctrine: A Canonical-Linguistic Approach to Christian Theology* (Louisville: Westminster John Knox Press, 2005), 265–305. Vanhoozer also shows how Lindbeck's critique of cognitive-propositionalism and experiential-expressivism fits with Hans Urs von Balthasar's critique of "epic" and "lyric" approaches to theology. Then, taking his cue from Balthasar, Vanhoozer shows how a "dramatic" theory of doctrine can take the performative goal of doctrine identified by Lindbeck and integrate it with "catholic-evangelical orthodoxy."

14. Roger Olson, *Reformed and Always Reforming: The Postconservative Approach to Evangelical Theology* (Grand Rapids: Baker Academic, 2007). Olson also shows how some evangelical theologians were setting the course for postconservativism even before Lindbeck, most notably

Bernard Ramm in *After Fundamentalism: The Future of Evangelical Theology* (San Francisco: Harper & Row, 1983).

15. David Tracy, "Lindbeck's New Program for Theology: A Reflection," *The Thomist* 49 (1985): 465.

16. Gordon Kaufman, "Review of 'The Nature of Doctrine: Religion and Theology in a Postliberal Age,' by George Lindbeck," *Theology Today* 42 (1985): 240–41.

17. George Hunsinger, "Postliberal Theology," in *The Cambridge Companion to Postmodern Theology*, edited by Kevin Vanhoozer (Cambridge: Cambridge University Press, 2003), 42–57. Hunsinger also argues that Lindbeck is more revisionist than many postliberals are comfortable with, particularly those who claim close affinity with Barth. He proposes how postliberalism can build on Barth's theology more carefully than Lindbeck does in "Beyond Literalism and Expressivism: Karl Barth's Hermeneutical Realism," in *Disruptive Grace: Studies in the Theology of Karl Barth* (Grand Rapids: Eerdmans, 2000), 210–25.

18. William C. Placher, *Unapologetic Christianity: A Christian Voice in a Pluralistic Conversation* (Louisville: Westminster John Knox Press, 1989), 36. For a more recent work by Placher, see *The Triune God: An Essay in Postliberal Theology* (Louisville: Westminster John Knox Press, 2007).

19. Stanley Hauerwas, *Performing the Faith: Bonhoeffer and the Practice of Nonviolence* (Grand Rapids: Baker Academic, 2004); *Working with Words: On Learning to Speak Christian* (Eugene, OR: Cascade Books, 2011).

20. Kathryn Tanner, *Theories of Culture: A New Agenda for Theology* (Minneapolis: Fortress Press, 1997).

21. John Webster, "Theology After Liberalism?" in *Theology After Liberalism: A Reader*, edited by John Webster and George P. Schner (Oxford: Blackwell, 2000), 57.

22. Jeffrey Stout, *Ethics After Babel: The Languages of Morals and Their Discontents* (Princeton: Princeton University Press, 2001), 301.

Select Bibliography

Primary source

Lindbeck, George. *The Nature of Doctrine: Religion and Theology in a Postliberal Age*. Louisville: Westminster John Knox Press, 1984.

Lindbeck, George. *The Nature of Doctrine: Religion and Theology in a Postliberal Age*. Louisville: Westminster John Knox Press, 2009.

Secondary sources

Lindbeck, George. *The Church in a Postliberal Age*. Edited by James Buckley. Grand Rapids: Eerdmans, 2003.

Michener, Ronald T. *Postliberal Theology: A Guide for the Perplexed*. London/New York: Bloomsbury T&T Clark, 2013.

Webster, John and Schner, George P. *Theology After Liberalism: A Reader*. Oxford: Blackwell, 2000.

Wright, John, ed. *Postliberal Theology and the Church Catholic: Conversations with George Lindbeck, David Burrell, and Stanley Hauerwas*. Grand Rapids: Baker Academic, 2012.

5.12

Models of God: Theology for an Ecological, Nuclear Age (1987)
Sallie McFague (1933–)

Falling in love with the world

For Sallie McFague, Christian theology and discipleship are concerned with loving God by loving the world. It took several "conversions" and decades of teaching and writing, however, for McFague to settle into her cosmological, ecological approach to theology and Christian living.[1] Nevertheless, this journey established McFague as a leading voice not only in ecological theology but also in metaphorical and feminist theology. Those who encounter her teaching and writing come away with new perspectives on why and how theology matters, not just within our human lives but also to the entire created world.

McFague describes her first conversion as becoming aware of her own existence and the reality of God. She was seven years old at the time, attending school in her hometown of Quincy, Massachusetts, and from that point on, her experience of God continued to grow and expand. From 1951–1955, she studied literature at Smith College, during which she experienced her second conversion. She was reading Karl Barth's *Commentary on Romans* and was suddenly struck by the transcendence or radical otherness of God.[2] She had an overwhelming sense of the "Godness" of God, which she later identified with the "radical monotheism" promoted by H. Richard Niebuhr and the "Protestant principle" espoused by Paul Tillich. McFague does not interpret this experience entirely in positive terms, however, since it kept her from appreciating the immanence and presence of God in the world.

After graduating from Smith College, McFague earned several graduate degrees from Yale Divinity School and University, completing her Ph.D. in 1964 on the topic of Christianity and literature.[3] This launched McFague into her long and illustrious teaching career, the bulk of which she spent as a professor of theology at Vanderbilt Divinity School in Nashville (1970–2000). While at Vanderbilt, McFague went through her third conversion, this one inspired by Gordon Kaufman's *Theology for a Nuclear Age*.[4] Impressed by the relevance of Kaufman's approach, McFague decided from that point on to do theology through an ecological lens, shifting from an anthropological to a cosmological paradigm. This was a theological and vocational shift for McFague, requiring just as much ecological literacy as theological acumen.

Shortly after this third conversion, McFague wrote *Models of God: Theology for an Ecological, Nuclear Age*, which won the American Academy of Religion Award for Excellence in 1988. This book combines her earlier work in literature and metaphor with her new concern for ecological attentiveness.[5] Following this work, all of McFague's publications have been permeated by an ecological focus, whether reimagining the contours of traditional theology, as in *The Body of God: An Ecological Theology* (1993), or focusing more specifically on ecological themes, as she did in *Super, Natural Christians: How We Should Love Nature* (1997).

Toward the end of her time at Vanderbilt, McFague experienced her fourth conversion, which she describes in a personal and contemporaneous way: "After years of teaching *about* God . . . I am becoming acquainted *with* God."[6] She describes entering into new rhythms of spiritual direction, meditation, and nature appreciation, all of which began to open up an alternative view on the "abundant life." In 2000, McFague wrote *Life Abundant* and left Vanderbilt to become Distinguished Theologian in Residence at Vancouver School of Theology, where she still resides. Her most recent work has specifically addressed the issue of climate change while reflecting on the dynamic interplay between contemplation and action, divine transcendence and immanence, and love for God and love for the world.[7] McFague's theological and personal journey began with an encounter with God and intensified by falling in love with the world, but the biggest stage in that journey was her realization that these are one and the same.

The need for new theological models

The underlying premise in *Models of God* is that traditional theological models—Father, King, Lord, etc.—are no longer relevant and adequate for life in a late-twentieth-century context. McFague argues that these models actually work against the cultivation and preservation of life in an "ecological, nuclear age." They are patriarchal, hierarchical, and triumphalistic models that perpetuate habits of domination and submission rather than encouraging habits of nurture and interdependence. As such, the most important thing for McFague is to find theological models that carry the most contextual relevance, leaving behind a concern for whether or not these models are true in some absolute sense.

To find the most adequate models, therefore, one must accurately understand the cultural context. For McFague, the "new sensibility" that requires new models of God involves the holistic interdependence of all things. We no longer live in an age of the isolated individual or dualistic universe. We live in an "ecological age," which among other things means that every singular thing plays a critical role in the interdependent web of life. That web of life is beautiful but fragile, easily disturbed and destroyed by power that ignores or denies this interdependence. The greatest threat to this ecological balance, according to McFague, is nuclear extinction. McFague wrote *Models of God* during the height of the Cold War, when the threat of nuclear attack was causing widespread anxiety. In the midst of that cultural climate, McFague was asking: what kind of theological models represent the opposite of nuclear domination and destruction?

McFague answers that question by pointing to "evolutionary, ecological, mutualistic" models.[8] In other words, the only models adequate for a nuclear age will be cosmological rather than anthropological, organic rather than mechanistic. These models will emphasize the interdependence of all things, including God, rather than perpetuating a sense of hierarchy and dualism. The models of God as king, ruler, lord, and master may have been fitting for a different age and culture, but a new age calls for new models. In fact, McFague suggests, this is the primary task of theology: to deconstruct old models and reconstruct new models that are fitting to the perspectives and responsibilities of a particular time and place.

The nature of theological models

According to McFague, all theology is metaphorical theology. In other words, the task of theology involves finding images and metaphors of the God-world relation that fit a particular cultural climate. The criterion for choosing these metaphors is not whether they are true in some ultimate sense, but whether they are imaginatively credible and ethically productive. As a result, metaphorical theology is inherently exploratory, experimental, and provisional. Some metaphors will stick and others will not, which means that searching for adequate metaphors is an ongoing process. If a metaphor proves to have "staying power," it becomes a theological model: "a metaphor that has gained sufficient stability and scope so as to present a pattern for relatively comprehensive and coherent explanation" (34).[9] The goal of metaphorical theology, therefore, is to discover effective theological models. As a whole, McFague defines metaphorical theology as "a kind of heuristic construction that in focusing on the imaginative construal of the God-world relationship, attempts to remythologize Christian faith through metaphors and models appropriate for an ecological, nuclear age" (40).

Within this approach, the process of theological construction involves an ongoing work of interpretation. The theologian needs to interpret both the cultural situation and the Christian tradition in order to generate fodder for imaginative construction. The place of Scripture in this process is not to supply authoritative metaphors and models of God, but rather to provide a paradigm for how metaphorical theology should be done. McFague views Scripture as a "case study, classic, or prototype" of Christian experience and theological expression (43).[10] When theologians experiment with new theological models, McFague argues, they are simply following the trajectory of Scripture itself, which contains a diversity of theological models constructed for a variety of cultural milieus.

The story of Jesus provides the interpretive clues necessary for deconstructing outdated theology and reconstructing relevant metaphorical theology. The way McFague reads the story of Jesus is similar to the interpretive patterns of liberation theology. What the diverse strands of liberation theology have in common, McFague maintains, is the destabilization of conventional divisions and dualisms, the inclusion of outsiders and outcasts, and the deconstruction of traditional hierarchies (47–48). These themes continue to point back to the paradigmatic story of Jesus, since Jesus destabilizes expectations through his parables, includes outsiders in his table fellowship, and made salvation available to all through his radical identification demonstrated on the cross. In the story of Jesus, therefore, we find "a destabilizing, inclusive, nonhierarchical vision of fulfillment for all of creation" (49).

Inspired by this paradigm, McFague launches into her search for new theological models that will enable us to reimagine God's relationship with the world. In doing so, she again emphasizes the inadequacy of traditional models, paying particular attention to the model of God as king. According to McFague, this model suggests a God who wields distant control of his realm, rules over his human subjects to the exclusion of nonhuman reality, and exercises his rule through militant domination or passive benevolence (66–68). As one replacement for this model, McFague suggests imagining the world as God's body rather than God's realm (69–78). She does not intend for this model to be perfect or permanent, but she does suggest it might have more resonance with the current age than some traditional models. To accentuate this pragmatism and provisionality, she admits to "experimenting with a bit of nonsense to see if it can make a claim to truth" (69). From her perspective, the greatest benefit of imagining the world as God's body is that sin is now inextricably linked to ignoring and breaking ecological harmony. If the earth suffers, God suffers. Protecting and caring for the earth takes on new meaning as a way to love God's body. McFague returns to this model throughout the book, but at this point it functions as a precursor to the primary models McFague explores: God as mother, lover, and friend.

God as mother, lover, and friend

In choosing which models to explore, McFague agrees with Gordon Kaufman that these models should resonate with the new ecological sensibility.[11] She disagrees with Kaufman, however, regarding his willingness to jettison personal models (80). For McFague, it would be a travesty to exclude personal models because they are often the most imaginatively potent. Not only do we relate most readily to personal models, but these metaphors also support a view of a God who is "radically relational, immanental, interdependent, and noninterventionist" (83). McFague chooses to imagine God through the lens of three of the most basic personal relationships: mother, lover, and friend. She traces out how each metaphor presents a different portrait of God's love, God's activity, and God's ethic.

As the basis for imagining God as mother, McFague wonders: if God created both men and women in God's own image, then why should we not use both sexes as models to talk about God? God is neither male nor female, so why should we privilege one sex over another in imagining God? In fact, McFague maintains that since God is beyond gender, it is actually idolatrous to restrict theology to male metaphors. In exploring female metaphors, however, McFague is careful to keep outdated notions of femininity from sneaking in and spoiling the creative exercise. When imagining God as mother, she deals with general characteristics of mothering rather than any particular cultural forms or expectations. For instance, she highlights the impartial, giving, nurturing kind of love that mothers express. In classical terms, this is a way of understanding God's *agape* love. God as mother exhibits generative and sacrificial love, connected as intimately to creation as a mother is to her own child. This model accentuates God's creative activity, but from a particular angle. As one who creates by birthing, God is neither totally distinct from nor totally distant from that creation. To return to her earlier metaphor, if creation is God's child, it remains in one sense God's body. This model also impacts how we view God's interaction with the world. How might God's judgment as mother be different from God's judgment as artist-creator? While an artist might be able to maintain critical distance from her work, a mother never has that kind of distance from her child. Indeed, within this model, God's purpose as mother is not to deliver final condemnation or pardon like a judge, but to reorder the cosmic household to ensure that everyone flourishes. In other words, "God as the mother-judge is the one who establishes justice, not the one who hands out sentences" (118). To join in God's mothering work, therefore, is to participate in the cause for justice. We are God's children, but we also share in God's parenthood of the world. McFague calls this "universal parenthood," which involves treating every part of the world, no matter how seemingly insignificant or weak, as a critical member of the cosmic family. Overall, to participate in God's ethic as mother is to be a preserver: "those who pass life along and who care for all forms of life so they may prosper" (122).

The second personal model McFague explores is God as lover, which highlights God's love as *eros*. As with the model of God as mother, McFague defends this exploration not just because the metaphor of God as lover appears in Scripture, but because this is one of our most fundamental relationships. If God is love, then the world is the beloved, and this creates a unique perspective from which to imagine God's salvific activity. The greatest tragedy for lovers is to be separated, which means that God's greatest desire when it comes to his beloved world is presence and union. The model implies "that the world is valuable, that God needs it, and that salvation is the reunification of the beloved world with its lover, God" (131). In testing the value of this model, McFague emphasizes once again that constructing new models is not a matter of establishing dogmatic truth. Rather, it is an imaginative process of examining how plausible, illuminating, and timely the model can be within an ecological age. One of the strongest elements of the model, in McFague's view, is its emphasis on reciprocity or interdependence. God needs the world just as the world needs God, and both are involved in the reunification process. In fact, sin is the very refusal of relationship in preference for isolation. Sin is a rejection of interdependence and the need for mutual love (139). By implication, salvation is willing participation in a mutual relationship of love and healing. Salvation is not just done for us; we are a part of it. Jesus provides a paradigmatic example of salvation, but he is not the only savior. McFague explains: "if the one thing needed is reunification of the shattered, divided world, there must be many saviors" (150). Within the model of God as lover, the line between salvation and ethics is blurred, because to be involved in the process of healing divisions in the world is to contribute to the process of salvation. Anyone who exhibits radical, inclusive love—especially to people and parts of the world that suffer—is playing the part of lover-liberator.

The last model McFague investigates is God as friend, which focuses on God's *philia* love. In tracing out the possibilities of this model, McFague surfaces three "paradoxes" of friendship that present new ways to imagine God's friendship with the world. First, while friendship is a free relationship between two people, it also involves a voluntary bond of trust and commitment. Likewise, the relationship between God and human beings is free, but it is also a side-by-side commitment with the same goal, namely, "the well being of the world" (163). Second, friendship is a relationship between two particular people, and yet it has an inclusive dynamic, bringing others of similar vision into its fold. In a similar way, God's friendship maintains particularity while remaining open to everyone who shares the desire for reunification and healing (164). Third, while friendship is most natural for children, it requires the adult characteristics of mutuality, reciprocity, and shared responsibility. Consequently, to be God's friend is to be invited into a relationship of childlike trust and mature responsibility (165). God shares with his friends and companions the responsibility to sustain and guide all forms of life. In traditional theology, this sustaining work is linked to God as Spirit, but McFague suggests that the model of God as friend has greater power because it is more personal and less "ethereal, shapeless, [and] vacant" (170). Imagining friendship with God gives us a picture of sitting down to a shared meal as companions (literally: together at bread) while showing hospitality to strangers. The stability of friendship with God gives us a place from which we can be open and receptive to whatever is different, unexpected, and strange. To be God's companions gives us the fortitude to be the world's companion and to fight boldly for justice. McFague concludes: "as friends of the Friend of the world, we do not belong to ourselves nor are we left to ourselves," defying despair while at the same time denying possession (179).

In her conclusion, McFague addresses whether or not these personal models of God—mother, love, and friend—are meant to be a replacement Trinity. While acknowledging some similarities to the tripartite division of God's activity as the creating Father, saving Son, and sustaining Spirit, McFague clearly states that her three models are not meant to establish a "new Trinity." Rather, her purpose is simply to reimagine the relationship between God and the world in a useful, accessible, and illuminating way (182–84). Three models are able to do this better than two, because they avoid any potential dualism and provide ample complementarity. McFague emphasizes that while these may be adequate models of God for an ecological, nuclear age, they are still imaginative fictions that may live for a time only to give way to fresher, more relevant models.

McFague and postmodern theology

Models of God is a prime example of constructive postmodern theology. Like other works of postmodern theology, *Models of God* shares a certain "condition" that accentuates the perspectival, provisional, and pragmatic nature of theological knowledge.[12] Given her background in literature and the study of metaphor, McFague's work corresponds with the constructive, imagination-oriented methodology of Gordon Kaufman,[13] which sets them apart from postmodern theology with a more deconstructive bent.[14] While McFague has some interest in dismantling outdated and oppressive theological models, she puts more energy into constructing models that she hopes will resonate with contemporary sensibilities without making claims to absolute truth or trans-cultural permanence. As such, McFague shares much in common with the cultural-linguistic approach of postliberal theologian George Lindbeck, although Lindbeck ascribes greater authority to the biblical narrative in the process of theological construction.[15]

Given her interest in ecological matters, McFague is widely recognized as one of the mothers of ecotheology and ecofeminism, along with notable Catholic theologians such as Rosemary Radford Ruether.[16] Like other ecofeminists, McFague links patriarchal domination and ecological destruction as different forms of the same drive for oppressive power. In the Preface to *Models of God*, McFague explains how this book is "not a feminist theology in the sense that its guiding principle is the liberation of women," but her perspective as a woman provides "sufficient disorientation from middle-class, mainstream Christianity both to question it and to risk alternative formulations of Christian faith" (xiv). Her subsequent work follows this trajectory, with the ecological focus taking center stage while the feminist agenda mostly remains backstage but informs much of the way she packages and performs her theology.

The themes and concerns Sallie McFague wrestled with in *Models of God* continue to occupy her attention in her present work. In one of her most recent essays, she reflects that in the seventy years since her first conversion to the reality of God and his presence in the world, she has learned many things. But the primary thing she has learned is that loving the world is the same as loving God, because the world is God's body: "The world lives within, for, from, and toward God every minute of every day. Hence, we do not live now on earth away from God, but always, whether in life or death, we all live within God."[17] Sallie McFague is widely recognized for her pioneering work in metaphorical theology and ecotheology, but perhaps her greatest legacy will be the fusion—in both her professional and personal life—of love for God and love for the world.

Notes

1. All references to McFague's "conversions" are drawn from her autobiographical sketch in *Life Abundant: Rethinking Theology and Economy for a Planet in Peril* (Minneapolis: Augsburg Fortress Press, 2001), 3–14.
2. The second edition of the commentary was translated into English in 1933, the year Sallie McFague was born. Karl Barth, *Epistle to the Romans*, trans. Edwyn C. Hoskyns (London: Oxford University Press, 1933).
3. This was McFague's first published monograph, appearing as *Literature and the Christian Life* (New Haven: Yale University Press, 1966).
4. Gordon Kaufman, *Theology for a Nuclear Age* (Louisville: Westminster John Knox Press, 1985).

5. Her earlier works include *Speaking in Parables: A Study in Metaphor and Theology* (Minneapolis: Fortress Press, 1975) and *Metaphorical Theology: Models of God in Religion and Language* (Minneapolis: Fortress Press, 1982).

6. McFague, *Life Abundant*, 8.

7. *A New Climate for Theology: God, the World, and Global Warming* (Minneapolis: Fortress Press, 2008); *Blessed Are the Consumers: Climate Change and the Practice of Restraint* (Minneapolis: Fortress Press, 2013).

8. Sallie McFague, *Models of God: Theology for an Ecological, Nuclear Age* (Philadelphia: Fortress Press, 1987), 12. Hereafter, all references to this work shall be noted by employing in-text parenthetical citations.

9. McFague unpacks in more detail the relationship between theological metaphors and models in her *Metaphorical Theology*.

10. McFague acknowledges similarities between her view of Scripture and that of theologian David Tracy. See his *Analogical Imagination: Christian Theology and the Culture of Pluralism* (Spring Valley, NY: Crossroad, 1981).

11. Kaufman, *Theology for the Nuclear Age.*

12. In 1979, Jean François Lyotard was the first to delineate this "postmodern condition" and the shift away from modernity in his book *La Condition postmoderne*. This was first translated into English as Jean François Lyotard, *The Postmodern Condition: A Report on Knowledge*, trans. Geoff Bennington and Brian Massumi (Minneapolis: University of Minnesota Press, 1984).

13. Gordon Kaufman, *The Theological Imagination: Constructing the Concept of God* (Louisville: Westminster John Knox Press, 1981). Kaufman is one of McFague's most sympathetic critics, but he challenges her, as others do, to explore how her metaphorical theology could be translated into and perhaps even refine conceptual theology. See Kaufman's review of *Models of God* in *Theology Today*, 45.1 (April 1988): 95–101.

14. Excellent introductions to the constructive and deconstructive approaches to postmodern theology, in addition to other approaches, can be found in Kevin Vanhoozer, ed., *The Cambridge Companion to Postmodern Theology* (Cambridge: Cambridge University Press, 2003).

15. For two fascinating articles that compare and contrast the theological method of Lindbeck and McFague, see Terrence Reynolds, "Walking Apart, Together: Lindbeck and McFague on Theological Method," *The Journal of Religion* 77.1 (January 1997): 44–67; Terrence Reynolds, "Parting Company at Last: Lindbeck and McFague in Substantive Theological Dialogue," *Concordia Theological Quarterly* 63.2 (April 1999): 97–118.

16. See Rosemary Radford Ruether, *Gaia and God: An Ecofeminist Theology of Earth Healing* (New York: HarperCollins, 1992).

17. Sallie McFague, "Falling in Love with God and the World: Some Reflections on the Doctrine of God," in *Sallie McFague: Collected Readings*, edited by David Lott, 264 (Minneapolis: Fortress Press, 2013).

Select Bibliography

Primary source

McFague, Sallie. *Models of God: Theology for an Ecological, Nuclear Age*. Philadelphia: Fortress Press, 1987.

Secondary sources

Armour, Ellen T. "Sallie McFague." In *A New Handbook of Christian Theologians*, edited by Donald W. Musser, 279–86. Nashville: Abingdon Press, 1996.

Kaufman, Gordon. Review of *Models of God* by Sallie McFague. *Theology Today*, 45.1 (April 1988): 95–101.

Malone, Nancy H, ed. "A Discussion of Sallie McFague's *Models of God*." *Religion and the Intellectual Life* 5.3 (Spring 1988): 9–44.

McFague, Sallie. "A Brief Credo." In *Life Abundant: Rethinking Theology and Economy for a Planet in Peril*, 3–24. Minneapolis: Augsburg Fortress Press, 2001.

Reynolds, Terrence. "Two McFagues: Meaning, Truth, and Justification in *Models of God*." *Modern Theology* 11.3 (July 1995): 289–313.

Essay Abstracts

The early church period

The Didache—Dating back as early as the mid-first century, the Didache is the oldest extant Christian manuscript on church worship and piety. Intended for immediate application, the brief but useful text gives Christians today a glimpse into the life and worship of the earliest Christian communities. *Key words: early church; worship; community; apostles; baptism; teaching.*

Select Epistles—**Ignatius of Antioch**—On the road to his execution, Ignatius of Antioch penned seven letters to several influential churches during the second century, as well as to his fellow bishop Polycarp. Amid a trying time in his life, he exhorts these churches to truly be Christians and to live by faith in the suffering servant, Jesus Christ. *Key words: martyrdom; person of Christ; Eucharist; unity of the church.*

Dialogue with Trypho—**Justin the Martyr**—One of the earliest and most significant works in Christian apologetics, particularly aimed at Jews and Gentile pagans, the *Dialogue with Trypho* demonstrates how the divine Logos is assumed in the man Jesus of Nazareth. Through the Logos, creation exists and redemption is accomplished. *Key words: apologetics; early church; Logos; Greek philosophy; Scripture.*

Against the Heresies—**Irenaeus of Lyons**—*Against the Heresies* is a polemical work against the most significant heresies in the Christian faith with descriptions of how to refute such arguments. Intended for a Christian audience, the work aims to arm believers with tools to defend the faith while also encouraging Christians with the truth that Christ alone redeems all things. *Key words: Heresies; recapitulation; creation; Rule of Truth; Gnosticism; Marcion; Mary.*

On First Principles—**Origen of Alexandria**—Functioning as a sort of early systematic theology, Origen's *On First Principles* outlines an early Christian understanding of the doctrines of God, Christ, the Holy Spirit, rational beings, the material world, and redemption. In an attempt to illustrate the narrative of God's redemptive acts in the world, Origen continually returns to Christ as the quintessence of redemption. *Key words: theology; God; Holy Spirit; material world; rationality; persecution; cycles.*

Against Praxeas—**Tertullian**—Often referred to as the father of Latin theology, Tertullian defends the doctrines of the Trinity and Christ's divinity in this classic work against monarchianism. The distinctive understanding of God as triune, according to Tertullian, is what separates Christianity from Judaism. *Key words: Monarchianism; Trinity; Rule of Faith; substance; economy.*

On the Unity of the Catholic Church—**Cyprian**—Cyprian's *On the Unity of the Catholic Church*, while often billed as an apologetic for Catholic ecclesial structure, is a work focused on maintaining unity within the church, the body and bride of Christ. Written as a response to schismatic groups within the Carthaginian church following a third-century wave of persecution, Cyprian lays out a practical argument for how to handle and reconcile with apostates who desire to return to the church, while also arguing against those who would attempt to fracture the body of Christ. *Key words: ecclesiology; rigorist; laxist; Church unity; schism; Novatian.*

On the Incarnation—**Athanasius**—Arguably one of the most significant contributions to the doctrine of the person of Christ, *On the Incarnation* is a treatise defending the twofold nature of Christ as both fully God and fully man against the heresies of Athanasius' contemporary, Arius. This work likely follows the highly influential Council of Nicea, in which the church confesses that Jesus is fully divine. *Key words: Incarnation; homoousios; Arius; Nicea; Logos.*

To Ablabius: On Not Three Gods—**Gregory of Nyssa** and *Five Theological Orations*—**Gregory of Nazianzus**—These two Cappadocian Fathers address issues concerning the Christological controversy that dominated the church's discussion and worship during the middle of the fourth century. Writing post-Nicea, both of these premier and influential theologians discuss topics concerning the church's worship of Jesus as *homoousios* with the Father. *Key words: homoousios; Trinity; ad intra; ad extra; Arianism; Pneumatology.*

On Wealth and Poverty—**John Chrysostom**—In a series of seven sermons that make up *On Wealth and Poverty*, John Chrysostom, the "golden-mouthed" bishop of Constantinople, expounds upon Christ's parable of Lazarus and the rich man found in Luke 16:14–31. Chrysostom's late fourth-century sermons examine the responsibility of the rich to the poor, especially within the Church of Jesus Christ, urging the rich to freely give of their wealth so as to avoid becoming attached to the passions of this world. *Key Words: rich and poor; Lazarus; wealth and poverty; stewardship.*

Letter to Cyril—**Nestorius** and *On the Unity of Christ*—**Cyril of Alexandria**—Centered around early fifth-century debates over the relationship between Christ's divine and human natures, Nestorius' *Letter to Cyril* and Cyril of Alexandria's *On the Unity of Christ* provide rich discussion of how Christ's dual natures relate in the Incarnation. In response to Nestorius' inability to philosophically reconcile how Christ's divine and human natures could achieve ontological unity, Cyril argues that the unity between Christ's natures is a mysterious paradox that is, nonetheless, to be understood as the reality of the person of Christ. *Key words: Incarnation; natures of Christ; hypostasis; paradox; Nestorianism; communication of idioms.*

Confessions—**Augustine**—One of the most influential books in the history of the church, Augustine's *Confessions* documents his journey to faith, as well as acts as a philosophical exercise, a theological treatise, a defense, and a meditation on Scripture, among other things. Perhaps the simplest way to describe this work is Augustine's love letter and prayer to God as he meditates in God's presence, and has served the church for over a millennium. *Key words: Manichaeism; confession; Incarnation; Neoplatonism; rhetoric; Trinity.*

The medieval period

Pastoral Care—**Gregory the Great**—A classic in pastoral theology, Gregory's *Pastoral Care* examines several important aspects of the life of the bishop. The book deals primarily with the qualifications for a bishop, including their lifestyle, preaching, and an exhortation to remain humble in the midst of carrying out ministry. *Key words: pastoral theology; care of souls; homiletics; holiness.*

Ecclesiastical History of the English People—Bede—This influential work in the history of Christian chronology documents the origin of the English people, specifically their conversion to Christianity. With depth and surprising precision, Bede covers much of the evangelization of the English, providing the church with a timeless work. *Key words: English; evangelization; spiritual warfare; Easter; Cuthbert.*

The Orthodox Faith—John of Damascus—Designed to be an exposition of the Christian faith, *The Orthodox Faith* covers the most essential components of Christianity, including the Trinity, creation, the means of salvation, and eschatology. This sort of systematic theology became widely influential during the Middle Ages, and has served the church for centuries by helping define what it means to be Christian. *Key words: Trinity; Peter Lombard; creation; consummation; salvation; systematic theology; Reason.*

Why did God Become Man?—Anselm of Canterbury—Perhaps the most significant treatise on the relationship between incarnation and atonement in the history of the church, *Cur Deus Homo* defends the person and work of Christ through a satisfaction theory of the atonement, in which Christ satisfies God's wrath against sin through his death. Written as an imagined dialogue between Anselm and one of his disciples, the work also establishes faith and reason as cooperative faculties of man given by God. *Key words: incarnation; atonement; satisfaction; reconciliation; honor.*

The Song of Songs—Bernard of Clairvaux—Bernard's eighty-six sermons on the Song of Songs only covers the first half of the book. Here he argues that the Song of Songs can be read as an allegory of divine love, a description of the believer's experience of Christ, a relationship between the bride and the bridegroom, and overall a way of describing union with Christ, among other things. Although his hermeneutical methods have been treated more cautiously since the Reformation, his reflections, including his focus on union with Christ, continue to stimulate the imagination and faith of many Christians. *Key words: allegory; union with Christ; spiritual warfare; bridegroom; Christian life.*

Sentences—Peter Lombard—Similar to John of Damascus' *The Orthodox Faith*, from which the Lombard drew some of his structure, the *Sentences* cover the main theological questions concerning the Trinity, creation, and redemption, as well as a fourth section on "the signs of God's grace," where he addresses issues in the Western church. Lombard's work became the quintessential theological manual for centuries to come, right up to the Protestant Reformation, presumed as authoritative throughout much theological education. *Key words: Trinity; Holy Spirit; Christology; attributes of God; Western church; sacraments; resurrection of the dead.*

The Trinity—**Richard of St. Victor**—This treatise provides an understanding of the Trinity that reflects Chalcedonian orthodoxy. Richard spends considerable time unpacking God's communicable and incommunicable attributes, as well as writing about each individual person of the Trinity, Father, Son, and Spirit. *Key words: Trinity; divine attributes; substance; persons; self-existence.*

Summa Theologica—**Thomas Aquinas**—In one of the most ambitious endeavors ever taken by a Christian theologian, Thomas attempts systematically to cover the theological curriculum by addressing questions in a way that blends Scripture, tradition, and reason. Although ultimately unfinished, Thomas' *Summa* provides philosophical and theological reflection on the central doctrines of the faith, and it stands as one of the most influential theological works ever written. *Key words: Trinity; creation; human nature; virtue; justice; sacraments; Christology.*

The Defender of the Peace—**Marsilius of Padua**—Marsilius' work calls into question the legitimacy of the power of the pope in civil matters, and ultimately calls for a separation of church and state for the purpose of civil peace. His work was at one time condemned by the Roman Catholic Church, but later served as a catalyst for the thinking and convictions behind the Reformers of the sixteenth century concerning the distinction between papal and biblical authority. *Key words: civil society; peace; ruler; papacy; secular.*

Predestination, God's Foreknowledge and Future Contingents—**William of Ockham**—William of Ockham's treatise examines predestination and the difficulties that surround this controversial doctrine. Rejecting determinism while also upholding human freedom and God's sovereignty, Ockham's argument provided the basis for the Reformers' own explorations into the doctrine of predestination. *Key words: predestination; reprobate; contingents; foreknowledge.*

On the Truth of Holy Scripture—**John Wycliffe**—John Wycliffe's dissertation upholds the truth and authority of the Bible as the foundation of Christian belief. While providing commentary on hermeneutical approaches and a theology of scripture, *On the Truth of Holy Scripture* also takes clear aim at church teachings in Wycliffe's day that he deemed unbiblical, which would inform the later Reformers' doctrine of scripture. *Key words: authority of scripture; sola scriptura; Lollards; biblical interpretation.*

The Imitation of Christ—**Thomas à Kempis**—Perhaps the most widely read Christian book of the Middle Ages, Thomas à Kempis' *The Imitation of Christ* is a devotional centered around the spiritual life of the Christian. Thomas' emphasis on imitating the life of Christ as the heart of discipleship has resonated with Christians across the ages, and it was a crucial component in the spiritual renewal that anticipated the Protestant Reformation. *Key words: Christian spirituality; devotion; imitatio Christi; self-discipline; devotio moderna.*

The Reformation period

The Handbook of the Christian Soldier—**Desiderius Erasmus**—Erasmus' *The Handbook of the Christian Soldier* is a practical guide that demonstrates how theology impacts all areas of life for the Christian. This work by the sixteenth century's premier scholar calls Christians to live in light of Christ's victory on the cross and to follow Scripture as the means to internal transformation, which he hoped would bring about internal reform throughout the church of Jesus Christ. *Key words: philosophia Christi; Christian living; piety; virtue.*

The Freedom of a Christian—**Martin Luther**—In *The Freedom of a Christian*, Martin Luther expounds upon his vision of the Christian life that he famously hammered out in his *Ninety-Five Theses*. With energy and tenacity, Luther explains the freedom from condemnation Christians receive in Christ by grace through faith, which enables them to freely act and work in love before the face of God. *Key words: coram deo; coram homnibus; justification; simul iustus et peccator; theodidacti.*

The Large Catechism—**Martin Luther**—In an effort to provide Scriptural instruction for men and women from across the social spectrum, Martin

Luther wrote *The Large Catechism*. In the work, Luther touches on the relevance of the Ten Commandments, provides a creed of belief in Christ, expounds upon the importance of prayer, details a Protestant view of the sacraments and their role in the life of the Christian, and examines confession and repentance. At the heart of this "Lay Bible" is Luther's desire to see the people of God live in the freedom of God's grace as they live out the gospel in their daily lives. *Key words: commandments; law and gospel; sacraments; confession; catechism.*

The Institutes of the Christian Religion—**John Calvin**—John Calvin's famous *Institutes of the Christian Religion* is the defining work of Calvin's illustrious career. Teeming with wisdom and insight, Calvin's tome provides an exhaustive theological overview that is built upon Calvin's belief that at the center of all things is a sovereign, all-powerful, all-knowing, and all-loving God who graciously desires for his beloved creatures to be in an everlasting, secure union with him through Christ. *Key words: sovereignty; union with Christ; sensus divinitatis; predestination; election; life in the Spirit.*

Foundation of Christian Doctrine—**Menno Simons**—Menno Simons' *Foundation of Christian Doctrine* is exactly what its title suggests. Simons' sixteenth-century work is a foundational piece in the Anabaptist tradition; however, Simons' deep concern for practical holiness within the church, his belief in the importance of repentance for Christian living, and his insistence upon Christ as the cornerstone of faith often resonates with Christians of other traditions. *Key words: Anabaptist; repentance; life of the church; sacraments; peace.*

Women Writers of the Sixteenth Century—Argula von Grumbach, Katharina Schütz Zell and Elisabeth Cruciger—An often-overlooked part of the Reformation is the theological legacy of its female figures. Although women were often unable to occupy positions outside of the household, some like Argula von Grumbach, Katharina Schütz Zell, and Elisabeth Cruciger carved out significant roles for themselves as they effectively provided profound biblical teaching and theological insight through their letters, poems, and hymns, which in turn helped shape and inform the life of the Protestant Reformation. *Key words: mothers of the church; matristics; role of women.*

Reformation Confessions: Schleitheim Confession—**Michael Sattler;** *Augsburg Confession*—**Philip Melanchthon;** *Heidelberg Catechism*—

Zacharias Ursinus—Of all the works of the Reformation era, the confessions that emerged from different Protestant groups were perhaps the most influential works in shaping the theological identities and doctrinal frameworks of the churches that adhered to them. The Anabaptist *Schleitheim Confession*, the Lutheran *Augsburg Confession*, and the Reformed *Heidelberg Catechism* are prime examples of Protestant confessions that have shaped and continue to shape the hearts and minds of those who would carry on their respective traditions. *Key words: confession; catechism; Anabaptist confession; Lutheran confession; Reformed confession.*

The Book of Common Prayer—**Thomas Cranmer**—Thomas Cranmer's *The Book of Common Prayer* is more than a simple book of liturgy intended for use in the Church of England. Rather, Cranmer's book helped create uniformity and unity of practice in the administration of the sacraments across the diversity of Protestant movements forming throughout England in the sixteenth century. Aside from its practical, ecclesiastical purposes, *The Book of Common Prayer* is a beautiful work that captures the essentials of the English Protestant faith and has been treated as a useful devotional tool for Christians across the centuries. *Key words: liturgy; sacraments; English Reformation; Queen Elizabeth's Prayer Book.*

"Friendly Exegesis"—**Huldrych Zwingli**—Perhaps no document is more important to understanding the memorialism view of the Lord's Supper than Huldrych Zwingli's "Friendly Exegesis." In contrast to Roman Catholicism's view of transubstantiation and the Lutheran view of consubstantiation, Zwingli's "Friendly Exegesis" provides a third way, arguing from Scripture that Christ is present at the Eucharist in a spiritual sense only, as his Incarnate body is seated eternally with the Father, which in no way diminishes his real and immanent presence with his people at the Sacramental table. *Key words: the Eucharist; memorialism; spiritual presence; alloiosis; ubiquity.*

The Spiritual Exercises—**Ignatius of Loyola**—*The Spiritual Exercises* by Ignatius of Loyola stands as part of a tradition of guides to Christian Spirituality. Written in the contentious age of Reformation and counter-Reformation, Ignatius' *Exercises* encourages Christians across different theological traditions to seek true spirituality by humbly imitating Christ in order that they might know him and his will. *Key words: habitus; imitatio Christi; retreatant; counter-Reformation.*

The seventeenth and eighteenth centuries

The Marrow of Theology—**William Ames**—A seminal work of seventeenth-century Puritan theology, William Ames' *The Marrow of Theology* provides a unique theological compendium within the Reformed tradition. Ames' *Marrow* is notable for its logical construction, its insistence upon faith as the starting point of a theology lived to God, its upholding of human free will along with God's sovereignty in salvation, and its commitment to covenant theology as the framework through which to understand the biblical narrative. *Key words: Puritan theology; Ramism; human will; covenant theology.*

Pneumatology—**John Owen**—While Reformed Protestants are oft cited for their failure to emphasize the Holy Spirit, John Owen's *Pneumatology* is evidence to the contrary. Owen's work is a classic of the seventeenth century that underscores the Holy Spirit's unique role in the life of Christ as well as in the Christian's regeneration and sanctification, which encourages the Christian to give as the Spirit so graciously gives of himself to Christ's Church. *Key words: work of the Holy Spirit; pneumatology; Puritan theology; regeneration; sanctification.*

Pia Desideria—**Philip Jacob Spener**—*Pia Desideria* by Philip Jacob Spener has been affectionately called the manifesto of Pietism. Originally written as a preface to another work, *Pia Desideria* became famous in its own right due to its emphasis on a Christian faith that impacts the hearts and not only the minds of God's people as well as Spener's argument for what would later become church small groups. *Key words: pietism; collegia pietatis; heart religion; laity.*

Religious Affections—**Jonathan Edwards**—Jonathan Edwards, who is perhaps the greatest American theologian, authored his *Treatise Concerning Religious Affections* during the midst of the Great Awakening as a nuanced response to both radical revivalists and those who would criticize the spiritual fervor that swept across the colonies. In *Religious Affections*, Edwards provides a discussion on how to identify the true work of the Holy Spirit in the lives of those who would earnestly seek after God, giving the reader the ability to use spiritual discernment in evaluating their own heart's affections. *Key words: heart religion; religious experiences; revivals; Great Awakening.*

Poems—**Anne Bradstreet**—Anne Bradstreet's *Poems* are the remarkable work of a laywoman who had a profound sense of God's presence and action in daily life. Through her daily work Bradstreet was inspired by God's providence in the midst of her everyday experiences and the hardships of life in New England to write beautiful poetry in anticipation of the resurrection life that she believed was yet to come. *Key words: Puritan New England; God's sovereignty; providence; theology of pilgrimage.*

Sermons—**George Whitefield**—George Whitefield is unquestionably considered to be one of the preeminent preachers of all time. His gospel-centered *Sermons* from the Great Awakening stand in the lasting tradition of the Protestant Reformation as they encourage his audiences, both old and new, to experience transformation in light of Divine grace discovered through Christ and experienced by the Holy Spirit. *Key words: the Great Awakening; homiletics; Revivalists; regeneration.*

The Declaration of Sentiments—**Jacobus Arminius**—Perhaps one of the most misunderstood theological figures of all time, Jacobus Arminius was dedicated to understanding and explaining God's word contained in the scriptures as best he could. Arminius' rejection of predestination based on his interpretation of what he believed scripture and church history taught has been misunderstood by his advocates and his opponents, and both would do well to examine his *Declaration of Sentiments* to understand Arminius and his theology. *Key words: Arminianism; supralapsarianism; Synod of Dort; remonstrant.*

The Appeals to Men of Reason and Religion—**John Wesley**—John Wesley's *The Appeals to Men of Reason and Religion* is a public defense of his immensely successful efforts at reform and revival within the confines of the Anglican Church during the eighteenth century. While hailed as the founder of Methodism, Wesley's efforts were always aimed at grounding the Anglican Church in Scripture, tradition, reason, and—of the utmost importance to him—religious experience, which he believed was not only fundamental to Christian faith but essential to humanness itself. *Key words: Methodism; enthusiasts; participatio dei; evangelism.*

The Pilgrim's Progress—**John Bunyan**—John Bunyan's *Pilgrim's Progress*, which was initially written during Bunyan's imprisonment for his theological nonconformity to the Church of England, is a much beloved allegory of the Christian life that has been widely read since its publication. While proving to be an engaging story, *Pilgrim's Progress* subtly yet powerfully communicates the theological distinctives of Bunyan's Reformed worldview, including the doctrine of election, the theology of pilgrimage, and the all-sufficient grace of Christ. *Key words: separatists; allegory; theology of pilgrimage.*

The Westminster Standards—Seen by many as the height of orthodox Reformed theology, the Westminster Standards, including its accompanying Larger and Shorter Catechisms, is a grand synthesis of Reformational and Calvinist thought. While dealing with a number of subjects—including the authority of Scripture, God's sovereignty, and the Christian life—at the center of the Standards is the notion that the chief end of all creation is to glorify and enjoy the eternally magnificent triune God. *Key words: Reformed confessions; sola scriptura; God's sovereignty; covenant theology.*

A Short and Easy Method of Prayer—**Madame Guyon**—Madame Guyon's *A Short and Easy Method of Prayer* provides a window into the powerful prayer life of a woman mystic. While acknowledging that prayer is not always easy, Guyon's *Short and Easy Method of Prayer* encourages its reader to carefully and thoughtfully engage an abundance of spiritual works, to meditate on the Divine Presence, and to surrender and abandon selfishness in order that they might powerfully experience the intimacy of union with the loving One, God himself. *Key words: Quietism; mysticism; providence; prayer.*

Natural Theology—**William Paley**—Written as a response to the empirical, antitheist skepticism of David Hume, William Paley's *Natural Theology* sets out a teleological argument for the existence of God. Paley's argument has been criticized by friend and foe alike, but his famous watchmaker analogy—which argues that just as a watch evidences a watchmaker, so does creation evidence the existence of a personal and good Creator—has endured as a classic example of this type of argumentation. Whether viewed favorably or unfavorably, this classic volume is a must read for one to understand the rising confidence in reason and observation, or for the curious reader seeking to discover historic attempts at offering proof of God's existence revealed in his created order. *Key words: natural theology; teleological argument; apologetics; argument from design.*

The nineteenth and twentieth centuries

The Christian Faith—**Friedrich Schleiermacher**—Hailed by many as the "father of modern theology," Friedrich Schleiermacher altered the landscape of theological study with his famous work *The Christian Faith*. In the wake of rationalism and skepticism, *The Christian Faith* presents an alternative doctrinal system that arises out of experience and feelings. He focuses on the feeling of absolute dependence as the paradigm for salvation and faith, Christianity as the religion of redemption, and most importantly a unique Christology that emphasizes Christ as the perfector of human nature. *Key words: God-consciousness; Christology; Christo-morphic, material norm.*

Systematic Theology—**Charles Hodge**—Charles Hodge, "the pride of Princeton," stands as a leading theologian and scholar of the nineteenth century. His *Systematic Theology* endures as the seminal work of not only his career but of conservative American Reformed theology in the nineteenth century. *Systematic Theology* is structured around the study of the doctrine of God, anthropology, soteriology, and eschatology. In contrast to other systems founded on mysticism, rationalism, or speculation—Hodge's work is built on an inductive method that centers on the belief that God has revealed truth though the Scriptures which provide the foundation for theology. *Key words: inductive theology; Scottish Common Sense Realism; Reformed theology; theology as a science.*

Lectures on the Philosophy of Religion—**George Wilhelm Friedrich Hegel**—In terms of legacy, George Wilhelm Friedrich Hegel certainly stands alongside Friedrich Schleiermacher as a "father of modern theology." Hegel's intellectual genius is on full display in his *Lectures on the Philosophy of Religion*: here he presents his belief that the unifying principle of not only religion but reality itself is God, whose Spirit moves the historical process by revealing himself to humanity, making them conscious of his existence while reconciling and extinguishing the rift between creation and the Creator. *Key words: Geist; theologian of the Spirit; absolute Spirit; dialectic; Spirit-community.*

Practice in Christianity—**Søren Kierkegaard**—While often appreciated as a philosopher and sometimes considered the father of the existentialist movement, Søren Kierkegaard saw himself primarily as a theologian. In this capacity he continues to resonate with contemporary Christian readers. Writing under the pseudonym "Anti-Climacus," Kierkegaard authored *Practice in Christianity* to expose his native Denmark's façade of "Christendom"—the assumption that everyone has Christian faith based on their culture or country of origin. Kierkegaard proposes that this façade should be replaced by an authentic Christian faith that requires a person to receive and submit to Christ by faith and not see him as a historical abstraction to be admired; furthermore, the Danish author called people to actively imitate Christ even unto suffering. *Key words: Christendom; imitatio Christi; contemporary faith; suffering.*

Christianity and the Social Crisis—**Walter Rauschenbusch**—At the beginning of the twentieth century, Walter Rauschenbusch emerged as a leader of the social gospel movement with the publication of *Christianity and the Social Crisis*. In his work, Rauschenbusch responds to the social injustice he encountered firsthand in his work as a pastor in New York City, and he calls the church back to what he believes is the purpose of Christianity: to see the kingdom of God advanced; this results in the transformation of society as individuals reject materialism and pursue justice for the poor and powerless. *Key words: social gospel; kingdom vision; the kingdom of God; Christianization.*

Dynamics of Faith—**Paul Tillich**—Due to his variegated life, Paul Tillich referred to his own life as one lived on the boundary. It is because of his existence as a "boundary theologian" that Tillich was able to promote a public theology that mediated between religion and culture and between philosophy and theology. In *Dynamics of Faith,* Tillich's correlationist theology is on full display as he argues—in contrast to rationalist post-foundationalist theologies—that everyone has faith, which he defines as concern for the ultimate, which is God. While the ultimate is incapable of being expressed directly, according to Tillich, it can be expressed through symbols and myths that bridge the gap between the infinite God and his finite creatures, providing the framework for Christian faith. *Key words: faith; ultimate concern; correlationist theology; Chicago school theology; religion as myth.*

Church Dogmatics—**Karl Barth**—While acquiring a number of titles throughout his career, including the title "father of neo-orthodoxy," none of these names does justice to Karl Barth's remarkable theological career. Without question, the defining work of his productive life was the monumental four-volume *Church Dogmatics*. Though he never finished it, Barth's *Church Dogmatics* is a stunning work dealing with the Doctrine of the Word of God, the Doctrine of God, the Doctrine of Creation, and the Doctrine of Reconciliation. In opposition to the predominant Liberal theology of German universities of his day, Barth argues for theological objectivism in response to the authoritative word, person, and work of Jesus Christ, the principal actor in the Triune God's self-directed drama of grace and reconciliation in whom the promises of God's word find their great and final "Yes." *Key words: neo-orthodoxy; dogmatics; theological objectivism; dialectical theology; Christomonism.*

Black Theology and Black Power—James Cone—James Cone's *Black Theology and Black Power* was written during the midst of the Civil Rights movement of the 1960s, and it exists as one of the earliest and foremost texts on black theology. Although controversial, Cone's work uniquely seeks to use theology to address the social situation of black Americans, arguing that for the Church to be the true Church it must align itself with the heart of the gospel and God's mission to bring justice for oppressed black people, which requires that Christians have a "black heart" that identifies with and endures suffering alongside black people in the hopes of achieving black power through the defeat of white racism. *Key words: Black power; black liberation theology; liberation theology; Civil Rights Movement; social justice.*

Doing Theology in a Revolutionary Situation—José Míguez Bonino—As a Latin American liberation theologian, José Bonino worked to present a distinctly Protestant approach to this theology. *Doing Theology in a Revolutionary Situation* encapsulated his effort. In his work, Bonino challenges the Church to seek to effectively achieve the liberation of the poor and needy from societal oppression—through revolutionary and potentially violent means if necessary—in order to live out the biblically mandated mission of God's people and the center of the gospel itself, which is freedom. *Key words: liberation theology; revolutionary theology; orthopraxy; Christian Marxism.*

Water Buffalo Theology—Kosuke Koyama—Baptized in the midst of war-torn 1940s Japan, Kosuke Koyama emerged from the chaos of World War II with a strong sense that the Christian life is one of humility lived in the face of danger and suffering; this was meant to be combined with a desire to self-sacrificially serve others where they are. With the humility of a crucified mind, Koyama's *Water Buffalo Theology* reflects Koyama's personal willingness to learn from local people and apply the gospel to their lives in a manner that fits, appreciates, and appropriates parts of the local cultural and linguistic contexts while remaining centered on the person and cross of an indigenous and incarnate Jesus Christ who acts in time-space history. *Key words: contextual theology; contextualization; ecumenicalism; theology from below.*

The Nature of Doctrine: Religion and Theology in a Postliberal Age— **George Lindbeck**—Finding a middle ground between the theological foundationalists and liberals of his day, George Lindbeck's *The Nature of Doctrine* established postliberal theology, offering a fresh approach to understanding Christian theology. In his work, Lindbeck argues for a cultural-linguistic theory of religion—which is the belief that religion is participation in a culture-shaping narrative expressed in language. Furthermore, he believed Christianity represents the unsurpassable religion because its practices best match its story as revealed in Scripture and Jesus Christ. *Key words: Postliberal theology; cultural-linguistic theology; the Yale school; ecumenicalism.*

*Models of God: Theology for an Ecological, Nuclear Age—*Sallie McFague— Sallie McFague's *Models of God: Theology for an Ecological, Nuclear Age* is a stunning theological work of the late twentieth century. She argues that the traditional theological models of God as father, king, and lord are outdated and need to be replaced by new models that fit the contemporary age. To replace these patriarchal, hierarchical, and triumphalistic models, McFague proposes new metaphors of God as mother, lover, and friend, reflecting the postmodern context and her concern for an ecological rather than anthropological understanding of God and *her*—as McFague contends we may rightly call God—relationship to the world. *Key words: ecological theology; postmodern theology; ecofeminism; feminist theology.*

Index